Intimate Relationships

Intimate Relationships

Wind Goodfriend

Buena Vista University

Los Angeles | London | New Delhi
Singapore | Washington DC | Melbourne

FOR INFORMATION:

SAGE Publications, Inc.
2455 Teller Road
Thousand Oaks, California 91320
E-mail: order@sagepub.com

SAGE Publications Ltd.
1 Oliver's Yard
55 City Road
London EC1Y 1SP
United Kingdom

SAGE Publications India Pvt. Ltd.
B 1/I 1 Mohan Cooperative
Industrial Area
Mathura Road, New Delhi 110 044
India

SAGE Publications Asia-Pacific Pte. Ltd.
18 Cross Street #10-10/11/12
China Square Central
Singapore 048423

Printed in Canada

ISBN: 9781506386164

This book is printed on acid-free paper.

MIX
Paper from responsible sources
FSC® C103567

Acquisitions Editor: Lara Parra
Content Development Editor: Jennifer Thomas
Editorial Assistant: Megan O'Heffernan
Production Editor: Bennie Clark Allen
Copy Editor: Christina West
Typesetter: Hurix Digital
Proofreader: Sarah J. Duffy
Indexer: Integra
Cover Designer: Candice Harman
Marketing Manager: Katherine Hepburn

20 21 22 23 24 10 9 8 7 6 5 4 3 2 1

• Brief Contents •

• Detailed Contents •

• Preface •

Is there anything more exciting and relevant to students' lives than intimate relationships? Teaching a class on relationships is extremely gratifying, as the material is inherently appealing. Every single person in the room cares about how to build and maintain happy, healthy interactions and connections with others.

The Book's Approach

What makes this book different—why should you read it? There are a few really excellent textbooks available from other authors, and each has strengths. In writing this book, I've tried to pull together all of the aspects of learning and teaching that my own students appreciate and love. Hopefully this has resulted in a book that offers unique features designed specifically to appeal to both students and professors who care about a comprehensive, modern approach to the science of relationships.

A Thoughtful Progression of Chapters. This book opens by explaining how the field of relationship science is an interdisciplinary one and why it matters. Then, research methods and open science are discussed. One of the unique aspects of this book, compared to others, is that it then emphasizes a theoretical foundation by outlining the three most common approaches to research (attachment theory, the evolutionary perspective, and interdependence). No other book gives all three theories equal weight or presents them first, as a structure on which to build research. Next, this book covers how relationships change over an individual's lifetime. The rest of the chapters have been laid out to follow a typical relationship's trajectory: friendship, sexuality, social cognition, conflict, and communication are all examined. The last two chapters frame how students can think about long-term implications of relationships. One focuses on sexual assault and relationship violence, perhaps more explicitly than other books. While these subjects are hard, it is essential to understand them in order to ameliorate them. Finally, the last chapter discusses two possible outcomes: breakup or lasting love.

A Modern Approach to Gender and Sex. The world has progressed beyond assumed heterosexuality and a gender or sexual binary. LGBTQ populations should be respected and included in the conversation. This includes explicit approaches like covering research results when available, but it also includes more implicit approaches such as using gender-neutral pronouns (i.e., "they" instead of "he or she"). As a member of the LGBTQ community myself, this was an important goal for me and something that I hope makes this book stand out compared to competitors.

Scaffolded Learning. The chapters are guided by "big questions" and learning objectives that help students see the major goals of each section. There's also a glossary of terms, which is missing from some other popular books on this topic. In addition, those sections are followed by "check your understanding" multiple-choice questions and critical thinking discussion questions. These questions can be used for class conversations, or instructors can assign them as homework problems. Either way, these features are unique to this book and are evidence that the book is designed to help students see their own progression toward mastery of the material.

Unique and Exciting Features. While most textbooks include boxed features of additional material, the features chosen for this book are intended to really engage students in exciting ways. The first feature should be appealing to modern students; "Relationships and Popular Culture" points out where important concepts from each chapter can be seen in movies, television shows, or songs. Next, "What's My Score?" presents students with a self-report measure in each chapter. In this way, students can be engaged with the material on a personal level as well as gain an understanding of how certain relationship variables are operationalized and measured in research. Finally, the "Research Deep Dive" feature emphasizes the procedural approach of a specific study in each chapter. In this way, students are consistently reminded of important research methods terms and realize the "behind the scenes" efforts that have gone into all the findings presented throughout the book. Highlighting the *science* of intimate relationships is important.

A Conversational Tone. The best textbook is one that students actually *want* to read. While some books have a formal, scholarly tone, this one is different. I've written it with a tone or voice that parallels how I explain things to my own students in class. My hope is that the book is fun, accessible, and approachable while still being thorough and accurate. Students will be excited by a book they truly understand and can relate to their own lives and scientific interests. It's a personal goal that students who read this book will honestly enjoy it.

Although I'm proud to have this book on my own bookshelf, I know it can only improve. Reviewer suggestions in earlier drafts were so helpful—and I welcome additional ideas for future editions. The world of relationship science is only going to grow and evolve, so the future is even more exciting than the past. I hope we can take that journey together.

• Acknowledgments •

To Shawn Stone, Gary Lewandowski, Tom Heinzen, Lara Parra, Jen Thompson, Suzy Dietz, Pamela Simcock, Chris Agnew, Ximena Arriaga, Amanda Diekman, Dixee Bartholomew-Feis, Josh Merchant, Brian Lenzmeier, and Sam Loerts.

The author and SAGE would like to thank the following reviewers for their feedback:

Jennifer Brougham, Arizona State University

Julie A. Brunson, The Pennsylvania State University

Lynn M. DeSpain, Regis University

Rachel Dinero, Cazenovia College

William Dragon, Cornell College

Brandie Fitch, Ivy Tech Community College

Phyllis E. Gillians, Bowie State University

Mo Therese Hannah, Siena College

Michael Langlais, University of Nebraska, Kearney

Christopher Leone, University of North Florida

Julie Verette Lindenbaum, Russell State College

Connie Meinholdt, Ferris State University

Kate Nicolai, Rockhurst University

Sylvia Niehuis, Texas Tech University

Christina Pedram, Arizona State University

Lysandra Perez-Strumolo, Ramapo College

Harry Reis, University of Rochester

Steve Seidel, Texas A&M University, Corpus Christi

Karen Riggs Skean, Rutgers University

Susan Sprecher, Illinois State University

Melissa Streeter, University of North Carolina Wilmington

T. Joel Wade, Bucknell University

Gregory D. Webster, University of Florida

• About the Author •

 **Wind Goodfriend** has been teaching psychology at Buena Vista University, a small midwestern liberal arts school, for 14 years. In that time, she has won the Faculty of the Year award three times. She also received the Wythe Award for Excellence in Teaching, one of the largest teaching awards in the country. She serves as the principal investigator for the Institute for the Prevention of Relationship Violence. Wind has authored three textbooks for SAGE, including *Social Psychology, Case Studies in Social Psychology,* and this book. Her primary research areas are gender and sexual prejudice, prevention of relationship violence, and psychology in popular culture. She has written 14 book chapters on this final topic, covering topics including *Game of Thrones, Wonder Woman, The Joker, Star Trek,* and more. Wind has developed and taught 16 different courses so far, including special topics classes such as Psychology of Colonialism, Human Sexuality, Psychology in Popular Film, and Relationship Violence. She received her B.A. from Buena Vista University and both her master's and Ph.D. in Social Psychology from Purdue University.

1

An Introduction to Relationship Science

Big Questions	Learning Objectives
1. Why study intimate relationships?	1.1 Explain how relationships are associated with human survival, physical health, and mental health.
2. What are different kinds of intimate relationships?	1.2 Analyze theories regarding different types of liking and loving in human relationships.
3. How is this book organized?	1.3 Describe the order of chapters and within-chapter features you'll see throughout the book.

Intimate relationships might be the most important and influential aspect of daily life.

Our social connections are a fundamental part of us, a core aspect of being human. They affect our daily lives in a wide variety of ways. Relationships are vitally important—but how can we understand them from a scientific perspective? This book is designed to take you through the exciting and complicated world of the scientific study of intimate relationships.

No single text can contain all the theories, research studies, and applications that have been explored, but the goal here is not to provide a comprehensive, encyclopedia-like list of ideas that you memorize. Instead, I hope that you think critically about each section, apply it to your own life when relevant, and analyze what should happen next in the scientific study of each concept. In order to continue learning about and understanding intimate relationships, we need the next generation of scholars to get involved. Maybe that's you.

Why Study Intimate Relationships?

As we each navigate our own intimate relationships, they can often be a frustrating mystery.

Why doesn't the person I like find me attractive? Why can't my partner understand my perspective? How can I know whether I should commit to this person for the rest of my life? Intimate relationships can be confusing and emotional. So how can they really be studied and understood using scientific experiments, equations, and theories dreamed up by a bunch of professors who, to be honest, might not have the best relationships themselves?

The scientific study of intimate relationships is a relatively new endeavor. One of the best things about this field of study is that it is truly an **interdisciplinary approach** that combines ideas, methods, and results from a variety of academic fields. These fields include communication, sociology, biology, psychology, human development and family studies, anthropology, and more. Recently, attention has shifted from "traditional," heterosexual, monogamous relationships to other forms such as same-sex couples, polyamorous relationships, hookups, and so on, so this book also includes studies that highlight the wide diversity of forms of love.

Let's get started by considering why scholars have recently increased their attention toward a scientific study of intimate relationships.

A Rise in Scientific Interest

Attraction, love, and commitment are ethereal topics. Some people balk at the very idea that "love" could ever be understood by science—it kind of saps the romance. Despite this skepticism, thousands of researchers all over the world are giving it their best effort, and the findings from these studies have offered both theoretical and pragmatic insights in contexts such as marital and family therapy.

In general, there are two motivations behind research on any topic—including relationships. **Basic research** is done when scientists explore research topics simply to understand a phenomenon more clearly, to advance theory, or to expand our base of knowledge on a given topic. For example, scientists might want to further understand what kinds of personality traits are often found in perpetrators of relationship abuse.

Basic research is the foundation for any academic field and is a necessary first step for the second motivation, **applied research**. Scientists doing applied research are extending theories and patterns from basic research in attempts to solve real-world problems, help people who are struggling, or proactively make our world a better place. Once personality traits associated with abuse are identified (in basic research), applied research might use that information to design different kinds of treatment programs to reduce abusive behaviors. Different programs could be linked to various personality traits so that treatments can be personalized for individual perpetrators. In this way, the applied research tries to make a real change, based on the understanding we gained from the basic research.

Scholarly attention toward the topic of intimate relationships—in both basic and applied forms—has blossomed in just the past few decades. One way to examine

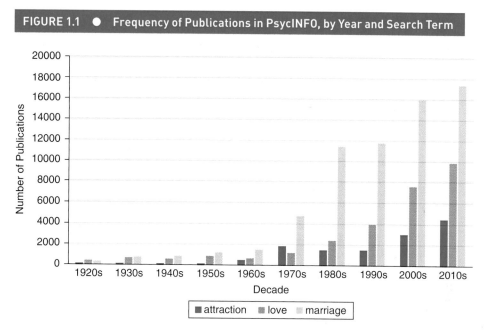

FIGURE 1.1 ● Frequency of Publications in PsycINFO, by Year and Search Term

Research on attraction, love, and marriage has greatly increased over time.

interest in the field is by simply counting the number of publications on relevant topics over the last 100 years. This can be done by searching for articles and book chapters in online archives and databases that list publications. For example, in psychology **PsycINFO** is a relatively comprehensive database of publications (it's available through most college and university libraries).

Figure 1.1 displays trends in publications listed in PsycINFO over the past 100 years. To create this chart, the search terms "love," "attraction," and "marriage" were entered by decade. Of course, different results would come if different search terms were tried, but this gives us a good idea of the general increase in publications from a **longitudinal** view, or one with repeated measurement over time and multiple sessions of data collection. It's clear that research using any of these terms has exploded in frequency, especially since the 1980s.

The Importance of Relationships in Our Lives

An increase in scientific scholarship regarding intimate relationships is great, but it doesn't answer the question of *why* interest has increased. In addition, a question that might be more interesting to you, personally, is why *you* should be studying the science of intimate relationships. Why are you reading this book? Healthy, happy relationships are the cornerstone of life for many individuals. Their premier importance can be seen in a variety of contexts.

Relationships and Human Survival

At least some interpersonal contact is needed for the survival of the human species.

Biologically speaking, reproduction usually means sexual bonding between a man and a woman (although with advances in technology, this isn't always true). Many studies are inspired by understanding how biological or evolutionary instincts apply to relationship and sexual behaviors. Thinking about relationships on the macrocosm level of the entire species is fascinating, and an entire future chapter of this book is devoted to an evolutionary perspective of human relationships.

For now, consider briefly that Charles Darwin (1859) suggested that humans (and other species) evolved over time largely through **natural selection**. In this process, certain traits help an individual survive and attract sexual partners—for example, intelligence or physical strength—and these traits are thus more likely to be passed on to the next generation. These traits, which provided **enhanced fitness** from a biological perspective, may also help the babies and children survive, and again those traits stay in the gene pool. What particular characteristics do you think are most useful to human survival and our potential to reproduce successfully? Chapter 4 will go into detail with several fascinating research studies on this topic.

However, the evolutionary approach to understanding relationships can be criticized and is somewhat limited (as all theories are, really). For example, not all relationships have a sexual motivation behind them; in fact, for the vast majority of people, the proportion of sexual relationships compared to *all* of the relationships they'll have over a lifetime is tiny. A second limitation of the evolutionary approach is that many relationships that *are* sexual are not heterosexual, and thus biological reproduction is not the driving force behind these relationships. Third, there are many heterosexual couples who choose not to have children. In fact, research has shown that heterosexual couples without children are statistically happier than couples with children—but that might be due to childless couples having more money and less stress (Wallace, 2016).

So relationships encompass more than simply thinking about sexual interactions and reproduction. Instinctively, we also care about relationships because forming groups or communities increases our survival. One of the major benefits to living in social groups and thus having the relationships of neighbors and friends is access to shared resources; we thus naturally form alliances and teams with people we think we can trust, even in abstract contexts like modern multi-player videogames (Belz, Pyritz, & Boos, 2013). In short, having friends and family around helps our survival, an instinct that's fundamental to our hopes and fears.

©iStock.com/kali9

Intimate relationships can affect our physical health, and vice versa.

Relationships and Physical Health

Relationships can also affect our physical health.

One popular area of research is the link between the presence of healthy relationships in someone's life and their ability to cope with challenges, failures, and stress. The general idea of these studies is that physical health will be associated with people's level of **social support**, or the number and quality of relationships they have on which they can rely in times of need (House, Landis, & Umberson, 1988). There are three specific types of social support (Wills, 1985):

- **Esteem support** occurs when other people in your life help you see yourself as a good person, worthy of love. They show you empathy and share your feelings.

- **Informational support** is offered by others when they provide facts or details that can help a stressful situation be understood or managed. They help you make decisions.

- **Instrumental support** comes from others when they offer physical aid, financial resources, or other pragmatic help. They provide tangible resources you need at the time.

For example, imagine a man whose wife of many years decides to divorce him. During this difficult and stressful time, his friends can offer all three types of social support. Esteem support may happen as they gather around to assure him that he's worthy of love and will eventually find another partner, if and when he wants a new relationship. Informational support might include helping him understand the state laws on divorce or providing recommendations for a good divorce lawyer. Finally, his friends might provide instrumental support if they loan him money, let him sleep in their guest room, or physically help him move his furniture into a new apartment.

How does social support translate into improved physical health? The first large-scale study to investigate this link was the Alameda County Study (Berkman & Syme, 1979). In 1965, researchers sent lengthy questionnaires to every single resident living in Alameda County, California, who was at least 20 years old; almost 7000 people completed and returned the surveys. One of the scales in the questionnaire asked about social support. It was measured by whether the respondents were married, how many friends and family members they had frequent contact with, and how many social groups they belonged to (such as church communities). The researchers then did follow-up checks with every participant over 9 years and tracked how many of them died.

Happily, death rates for people between 20 and 29 years old were very low, regardless of social support levels (so low they aren't even in Figure 1.2). As the trend in Figure 1.2 shows, for older participants, higher levels of social support were associated with lower death rates over the 9 years of the study. This trend was especially pronounced for men and was stronger as people got older. Overall, people with better social support were two to four times less likely to die. You can imagine how the three kinds of social support described earlier might contribute to healthier habits, more

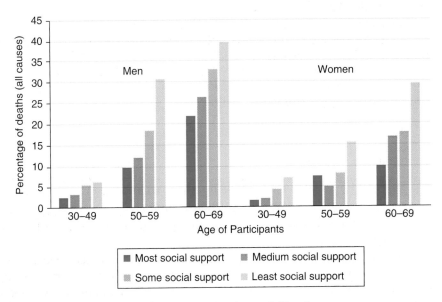

FIGURE 1.2 ● Connections Between Social Support and Mortality

The older we get, the more social support matters for mortality rates.

Source: Berkman and Syme (1979).

exercise, more visits to the doctor, and so on. People might have a friend with whom they go to the gym a few times a week, or someone's partner might remind them to take their pills or make doctor's appointments. In these ways, having better social support might lead to better physical health outcomes.

On the other hand, the other way around might also be true: People with worse health might be less likely to go out with friends, less likely to initiate romantic relationships, or even less likely to join social groups, so maybe worse health leads to lower social support. This is a good example of a phrase scientists like to use: *Correlation does not imply causation.* We know that physical health and social support are tied together, but we can't say for sure whether one *causes* change in the other without a different kind of research. We'll talk more about correlations and what they mean in Chapter 2.

The Alameda County Study is a famous example of research on the link between relationships and physical health. Over the past several decades, additional research has established more evidence that happy, healthy relationships are correlated with our physical health (for an entire book on this topic, see Agnew & South, 2014). For example, good relationships are associated with better resilience to heart disease (Coyne et al., 2001; Newman & Roberts, 2013), healthier neural and immune system responses (Loving & Keneski, 2014), better stress reactions at the hormonal level (Coan, Schaefer, & Davidson, 2006; Slatcher, 2014), and better management of chronic pain, especially for people in rural and relatively isolated locations (Tollefson, Usher,

& Foster, 2011). The flip side of the coin is also true: Unhealthy and abusive relationships are tied to worse physical health and may even be the cause of chronic illness in some cases (Jetter, 2013).

Relationships are also tied to the chemicals our bodies produce. Sexual contact with others—even cuddling!—can trigger the release of dopamine and oxytocin in the brain, two natural chemicals in the body associated with feelings of pleasure, relaxation, and recall of positive memories (Blaicher et al., 1999; Carmichael et al., 1987; Depue & Collins, 1999; Gonzaga, Turner, Keltner, Campos, & Altemus, 2006). Thus, the overlap between physical health and mental health matters.

Relationships and Mental Health

Of course, being surrounded by friends, family, and a loving partner would make anyone's life better. It should be no surprise that social support is also associated with better mental health across thousands of research studies. A term often used in this research is **well-being**, an overall or general summary of someone's happiness, mental health, and ability to cope with stress. In general, good intimate relationships are associated with better well-being.

In one simple exploration of the link between well-being and social support, 182 college students were given a survey that measured their anxiety, depression, hostility, and loneliness (Sarason, Sarason, Shearin, & Pierce, 1987). Social support was measured by asking each student these three questions:

- Who accepts you totally, including both your worst and your best points?

- Whom can you really count on to tell you, in a thoughtful manner, when you need to improve in some way?

- Whom do you feel truly loves you deeply?

Students who said both that they had *more* loving, supportive people in their lives (quantity) and that these relationships were satisfying (quality) said that they had lower anxiety, depression, hostility, and loneliness.

Across many studies, positive and secure intimate relationships are associated with better well-being (e.g., Birnbaum, Orr, Mikulincer, & Florian, 1997; Cooper, Shaver, & Collins, 1998; Karreman & Vingerhoets, 2012; Merz & Consedine, 2009). For example, college students in Israel with secure and supportive intimate relationships reported better coping to missile attacks during the Gulf War (Mikulincer, Florian, & Weller, 1993). Mothers with newborn infants suffering from congenital heart disease were better able to emotionally deal with the infants' special needs if they (the mothers) felt secure in their adult intimate relationships (Mikulincer & Florian, 1998). A wide variety of diagnosable mental illnesses are correlated with lower levels of social support, including personality disorders (Critchfield, Levy, Clarkin, & Kernberg, 2008), dissociative disorders (Ogawa, Sroufe, Weinfield, Carlson, & Egeland, 1997), eating disorders (Cole-Detke & Kobak, 1996), and schizophrenia (Fonagy et al., 1996). The list goes on and on, but it seems clear that intimate relationships can affect our mental health and happiness, and our mental health and happiness can affect our intimate relationships.

CHECK YOUR UNDERSTANDING

1.1 When understanding of any topic comes from combining theories, methods, and results from a variety of academic fields (such as psychology, biology, and anthropology), this approach is called:

a. Interdisciplinary
b. Cross-cultural
c. Longitudinal
d. Basic research

1.2 You are visiting a new city for the first time and find the subway system confusing. So, you call your friend who lives there and they explain what trains and stops you need. In this case, which type of social support is your friend providing?

a. Esteem support
b. Instrumental support
c. Egoistic support
d. Informational support

1.3 Which statement below is an accurate summary of the findings from the Alameda County Study?

a. Social support was not correlated with mortality rates in this study.
b. Surprisingly, more social support was associated with higher mortality rates.
c. More social support was associated with lower mortality rates, especially among older men.
d. Social support and mortality weren't correlated for people between the ages of 30 and 59, but they were correlated for people over 59 years of age.

APPLICATION ACTIVITY

Figure 1.1 displayed how the frequency of publications on intimate relationships has greatly increased over the last 100 years. However, this claim is based only on the three search terms used within PsycINFO ("attraction," "love," and "marriage"). Do you think different patterns would emerge if different search terms were used? Would certain terms have surges or declines in popularity in particular years or decades, based on events going on at the time? Are you curious about how common publications are on particular, specific topics such as gay or lesbian relationships, domestic violence, or interracial couples? What about in a database that lists articles in a field other than psychology? Choose three search terms and an online database of interest to you, personally, and create a graph similar to Figure 1.1. Then, analyze the patterns that appear to emerge.

CRITICAL THINKING

- This section introduced the idea of "basic" versus "applied" research. Which do you think is more valuable? Which do you, personally, find more interesting? Provide specific examples that support your opinion.

- Which of the three types of social support (esteem, informational, instrumental) do you value the most in your own life? What kinds of situations would change your answer, at least temporarily? Do different kinds of people value some types of support more, regardless of the situation? Choose one idea you have regarding these questions and formulate a specific hypothesis. How would you test this hypothesis?

- Can you identify a time in your own life when having a supportive friend, family member, or romantic partner improved your *physical* health? Describe the circumstances of this situation.

Answers to the Check Your Understanding Questions

1.1 a, 1.2 d, and 1.3 c.

What Are Different Kinds of Intimate Relationships?

On some levels the question "What are different kinds of intimate relationships?" is easy to answer. In your own life, you have relationships with your friends, your family members, your professors, your dating partner(s), and so on. Each relationship type could be considered a different relationship category. But what is "intimacy" in the first place? Are intimacy and love the same thing? Are you "intimate" with your friends? What about distant relatives you only see every few years?

It's important to know how researchers approach the definition and measurement of relationships. A **categorical approach** to relationships is one that groups types or forms of relationships into categories, like friends versus romantic partners. However, the question gets more interesting if you think about intimate relationships from a **continuous approach**, one that considers relationships on a sliding scale of intimacy. A continuous approach might, theoretically, look like what you see in Figure 1.3. Here, strong intimacy is one end of a possible range, with the other end being no connection at all.

Beyond whether relationships should be studied from a categorical or continuous approach, a difficulty in the scientific study of intimate relationships is how to define abstract ideas like "love." In academic fields, "love" is a **construct**, a theoretical, abstract, and invisible concept or idea. To study it in research, we have to **operationalize** it, which means defining it in very specific ways related to how we plan to measure it within a given study. As you can probably imagine, different researchers have operationalized or defined love in a wide variety of ways over the years. While some studies operationalize love using objective numbers such as length of a relationship in months or years, most researchers use subjective self-report scales to assess psychological feelings or thoughts regarding participants' experiences of love (Berscheid, Snyder, & Omoto, 1989; Knobloch, Solomon, & Cruz, 2001).

Defining and Measuring Love: Rubin's Scales

Over the years, many different researchers have defined love in many different ways. Everyday people also seem to have notions of different kinds of love, as heartbroken

FIGURE 1.3 ● A Continuous Approach to Types of Intimate Relationships

No feelings at all   Strong intimacy

Relationships could be conceptualized along a continuum, with strong intimacy on one end and no feelings at all on the other.

suitors often immediately understand the meaning of the sentence "I love you, but I'm not *in love* with you." Ouch.

Right around 50 years ago, one of the first scholars to operationalize "romantic love" was the social psychologist Zick Rubin (1970). His definition was this: "love between unmarried opposite-sex peers, of the sort which could possibly lead to marriage" (p. 266). Right away, you can probably see several problems with this definition:

- It assumes that most people in love are on a path toward marriage (while in fact many couples may not be interested in marriage at all).

- It assumes that romantic love exists only between "opposite-sex" peers, which means that only heterosexual, cisgender people feel love.

- It assumes that married people do not feel romantic love!

In spite of this severely limited (and, let's be honest, a tad offensive by today's standards) definition of romantic love, Rubin was still an important figure in the progression of research on intimate relationships because he was one of the first scholars to create a self-report measure of love that participants could complete in survey research. When he created his scale, he specifically made sure to include items that would distinguish "liking" from "loving" (a categorical approach), but scores on the scale also have a possible range to indicate strength of feeling (a continuous approach). The result is the scale shown in the "What's My Score?" feature. Try answering the questions yourself to see what your score is on each set of items.

When Rubin asked college students to complete his loving scale regarding their current partner back in 1970, he found that higher scores on the scale really were associated with their estimates of how likely they were to get married (as his original definition suggested). However, scores were not correlated with length of the relationship; it seems that some people fall in love quickly, while others take time (Rubin, 1970). Since 1970, many studies have found other interesting trends by including **Rubin's liking and loving scales**.

For example, one study (Kenrick, Gutierres, & Goldberg, 1989) showed participants nude centerfolds from either *Playboy/Penthouse* (male participants) or *Playgirl* (female participants). Results showed that men who looked at the images reported lower love scores for their partners afterward, but that the images didn't affect women's love scores. Note, however, that when researchers tried to replicate these findings, or confirm them by doing the study again, neither men nor women had lower love scores after looking at erotica across three different groups of participants (Balzarini, Dobson, Chin, & Campbell, 2017).

WHAT'S MY SCORE?

The Rubin Scales of Liking and Loving

Instructions: For the items below, you'll see an X in place of a person's name. When you think about the love scale, replace X with your current partner's name (if you don't have a current partner, try thinking about someone you *wish* you were dating). When you think about the like scale, replace X with your best friend's name. For each item, write your level of agreement using this scale:

1	2	3	4	5	6	7	8	9

Disagree
completely

Agree
completely

Love Scale

_____ If X were feeling badly, my first duty would be to cheer him or her up.

_____ I feel that I can confide in X about virtually everything.

_____ I find it easy to ignore X's faults.

_____ I would do almost anything for X.

_____ I feel very possessive toward X.

_____ If I could never be with X, I would feel miserable.

_____ If I were lonely, my first thought would be to seek X out.

_____ One of my primary concerns is X's welfare.

_____ I would forgive X for practically anything.

_____ I feel responsible for X's well-being.

_____ When I am with X, I spend a good deal of time just looking at him or her.

_____ I would greatly enjoy being confided in by X.

_____ It would be hard for me to get along without X.

Like Scale

_____ When I am with X, we are almost always in the same mood.

_____ I think that X is unusually well adjusted.

_____ I would highly recommend X for a responsible job.

_____ In my opinion, X is an exceptionally mature person.

_____ I have great confidence in X's good judgment.

_____ Most people would react very favorably to X after a brief acquaintance.

_____ I think that X and I are quite similar to each other.

_____ I would vote for X in a class or group election.

_____ I think that X is one of those people who quickly wins respect.

_____ I feel that X is an extremely intelligent person.

_____ X is one of the most likable people I know.

_____ X is the sort of person whom I myself would like to be.

_____ It seems to me that it is very easy for X to gain admiration.

Scoring: For each scale (love and like), add the items together to find your total score. The result should be a number between 13 and 117, with higher numbers indicating more loving or more liking.

(Continued)

(Continued)

When Rubin asked college students to take the scales back in 1970, the average scores were as follows:

- Men who took the love scale: 89.37
- Women who took the love scale: 89.46
- Men who took the like scale: 55.07

- Women who took the like scale: 65.27

Source: Rubin (1970).

Critical Thinking: Do you think that some of the items in this scale are out of date or would be interpreted differently by people of different genders or sexual orientations? If so, what questions could be updated or added?

Another study found that higher scores on Rubin's love scale were associated with more certainty and confidence about the status of people's relationships, as well as more confidence in their own feelings about their partner and in their partner's feelings (Knobloch et al., 2001). People report being more in love when their current partners match their ideal expectations in terms of trustworthiness, attractiveness, and status (Campbell, Simpson, Kashy, & Fletcher, 2001). When married couples filled out the Rubin love scale in another study, higher scores were correlated with better overall marital quality, more sexual satisfaction, and better communication (Perrone & Worthington, 2001). So, while Rubin's original definition of love may have been flawed, his ideas made him an early pioneer in inspiring research that continues today.

Sternberg's Triangular Theory of Love

Of course, Rubin is not the only person to develop a definition and measurement of love. One researcher (Fehr, 1988) even noted that many definitions exist because there might not *be* a single, comprehensive definition. In Fehr's research, people listed features they said were part of "love" but not part of "liking," such as gazing at each other, sexual passion, and feelings of euphoria. Other researchers have published typologies that make distinctions between styles of loving (Hendrick & Hendrick, 1986; Lee, 1977), love versus commitment (Kelley, 1983), and implicit models or styles of love and trust (Ainsworth, Blehar, Waters, & Wall, 1978; Bartholomew & Horowitz, 1991; Bowlby, 1958). The list could be longer—and many of these theories will be covered in later chapters—but you get the idea.

One of the most well-known theories attempting to define types of intimate relationship is the **Sternberg triangular theory of love** (Sternberg, 1986). It's called the "triangular" theory because Sternberg suggested that love is made up of three components, like ingredients in a recipe, and that the degree to which each of these components is present in any given relationship will determine its nature. In this way, Sternberg's triangular theory is both categorical (he suggests eight different types of relationship, as shown in Figure 1.4) and continuous, as levels of each component can range in degree or amount.

FIGURE 1.4 ● Eight Types of Love in Sternberg's Triangular Theory

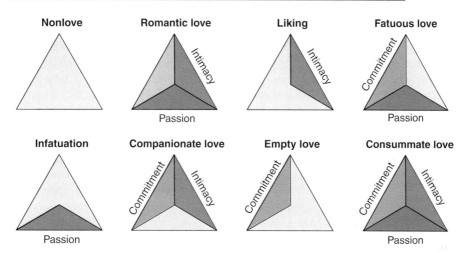

In this theory (Sternberg, 1986), there are eight kinds of love that vary based on whether they have intimacy, passion, and commitment.

Source: Sternberg, R. J. (1986). A triangular theory of love. *Psychological Review*, 93(2), 119-135, reprinted with permission.

Let's start with examining the three components that Sternberg (1986) said might be present in any given relationship:

- **Intimacy:** The emotional component, intimacy is feelings of closeness, connection, bonding, and warmth toward a partner. High intimacy is associated with the desire to protect a partner, with high regard for them, and with more self-disclosures such as revealing secrets or deeply personal information.

- **Passion:** The physical, motivational, or behavioral component; passion is sexual drive or attraction toward a partner, including physical arousal and other bodily changes (increased heart rate, release of brain chemicals, etc.). While passion for someone else is not necessarily in our control, we're usually aware of our physical attraction toward certain others.

- **Commitment:** The cognitive component, commitment is a thoughtful, reasoned decision to stay with a given partner and maintain the relationship, often exclusively. Sternberg (1986) notes, "Loving relationships almost inevitably have their ups and downs, and there may be times in such relationships when the decision/commitment component is all or almost all that keeps the relationship going" (p. 123).

If you think about these components as being simply present or absent, there are eight different types of relationship that are theoretically possible; these are shown in Figure 1.4.

If a relationship has none of the components, Sternberg calls it "nonlove"; these would be relationships with casual acquaintances, such as people in your class whom you don't know personally. Sternberg (1986) notes that "the large majority of our personal relationships" are nonlove (p. 123). The opposite would be "consummate love," or complete and perfect love. In Sternberg's theory, ideal romantic relationships have commitment, intimacy, and passion. If you have only one or two of these three essential components, you get one of the other six types of relationship. For example, "companionate love" is more like a deep friendship; it's missing sexual or physical attraction, but it has all the other aspects of being with a partner. The other forms are romantic, liking, fatuous, infatuation, and empty love, which you can see result from different combinations.

From a categorical perspective, you can probably think of people you know who represent these different types of relationship. Younger couples might be more driven by passion, for example, and thus be more likely to experience infatuation, while older couples more interested in an emotional connection might be considered closer to liking relationships. However, remember that while Sternberg categorized these eight different types of love based on whether each component was present or absent, he also approached relationships from a continuous approach. If passion, intimacy, and commitment can all range on a continuum, then a *single* relationship might change categories over time.

Take a look, for example, at Figure 1.5. Here we have a theoretical relationship between two people that ebbs and flows in its nature over the course of a relationship.

At the beginning of a new potential relationship, the two people involved barely know each other (nonlove); all three components are low. As time goes on, they quickly develop physical attraction toward each other; as their passion peaks and is the driving force behind spending time together, they are infatuated. This matches a finding (Walster, Aronson, Abrahams, & Rottman, 1966) that on first dates, physical attraction is the most important factor in how much people feel satisfied by the end. A bit later, if they become emotionally invested and decide to commit to each other, for a moment in time they achieve consummate love.

Consummate love is hard to maintain, though. Sternberg (1986) wrote, "Attaining consummate love can be analogous in at least one respect to meeting one's target in a weight-reduction program: Reaching the goal is often easier than maintaining it. The attainment of consummate love is no guarantee that it will last" (p. 124). In the theoretical relationship shown in Figure 1.5, the two couple members do slowly lose physical passion for each other, but their high levels of intimacy and commitment keep them together. This general pattern was mostly supported in a study (Sumter, Valkenburg, & Peter, 2013) that measured the three components in relationships of a wide range of ages (from 12 to 88 years); their results for participants currently in relationships are shown in Figure 1.6. In youth relationships (ages 12–17), all three components were relatively low, and all three peaked in young adult relationships (ages 18–29). In older couples (over 50), commitment stayed strong while intimacy and passion both declined.

While the vast majority of research studies inspired by Sternberg's (1986) theory have used the

FIGURE 1.5 ● Changing Components of Love in a Theoretical Relationship Over Time

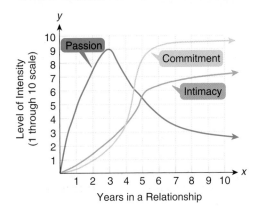

Commitment, intimacy, and passion can fluctuate up and down within a given relationship over time.

Source: Sternberg, Robert J., "A Triangular Theory of Love," *Psychological Review*, 93(2,) 119-135, reprinted with permission.

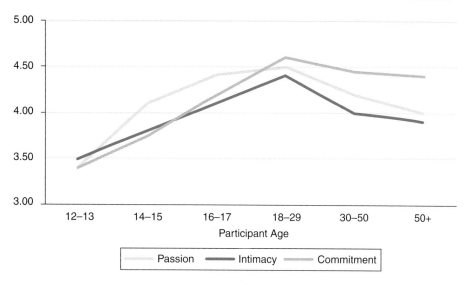

FIGURE 1.6 ● Changing Components of Love in Real Relationships Over Time

Research shows that the components of love tend to differ, depending on how old couple members are.

Source: Sumter et al. (2013).

WHAT'S MY SCORE?

Measuring Intimacy, Passion, and Commitment

Instructions: Think about your current partner. Next to each item below, write how much you agree using this scale:

1	2	3	4	5	6	7
Strongly disagree						Strongly agree

Intimacy

_____ My partner and I share personal information with one another.

_____ There is nothing I couldn't tell my partner.

_____ My partner and I self-disclose private thoughts and information to each other.

_____ There are things I could tell my partner that I can't tell anyone else.

(Continued)

(Continued)

_____ My partner understands my feelings.

_____ My partner and I are psychologically close to one another.

Passion

_____ I feel a powerful attraction for my partner.

_____ I am often aroused by my partner's presence.

_____ My partner and I are very passionate toward one another.

_____ My partner and I are very affectionate toward one another.

_____ My partner is sexually exciting.

_____ My partner and I have a very passionate relationship.

_____ Sex is an important part of our relationship.

Commitment

_____ I am committed to continuing our relationship.

_____ I think of our relationship as a permanent one.

_____ I am unlikely to pursue another relationship in the future.

_____ Commitment is an important part of our relationship.

_____ I think this relationship will last forever.

_____ I would rather be with my partner than anyone else.

Scoring: For each subscale, add the items together and then divide by the number of items to find the average (note that intimacy and commitment have six items, while passion has seven). Higher numbers indicate stronger or more extreme experiences of that component.

When Lemieux and Hale (1999) asked college students to complete the scales, the average scores were as follows:

- Men: 5.4 for intimacy, 5.6 for passion, and 4.5 for commitment

- Women: 5.9 for intimacy, 5.8 for passion, and 5.3 for commitment

Source: Lemieux and Hale (1999, 2000).

Critical Thinking: Does one of these factors matter more to you? Do you think one is more important for predicting a healthy, long-term relationship? Are monogamous, "forever" relationships realistic in today's world?

scale he created to measure the three components of love, others have pointed out that his scale may not be the most statistically reliable option. Therefore, an alternative scale that seems to stand up well to tests of reliability and internal structure has been validated for both college students (Lemieux & Hale, 1999) and married couples (with an average age of 38; Lemieux & Hale, 2000). That scale appears in the second "What's My Score?" feature.

CHECK YOUR UNDERSTANDING

1.4   What type of love would Sternberg say includes high levels of passion, intimacy, and commitment?

   a. Companionate
   b. Fatuous
   c. Consummate
   d. Romantic

1.5   According to research on Sternberg's triangular theory of love, which component below increases the most slowly, but also tends to stay relatively high after years of a couple being together?

   a. Intimacy
   b. Commitment
   c. Passion
   d. Liking

1.6   This section discussed the difference between "continuous" constructs and "categorical" constructs. Which of the constructs or variables below is categorical?

   a. Height
   b. Country in which you were born
   c. Number of sexual partners
   d. Scores on the Rubin "love" scale

APPLICATION ACTIVITY

Analyze two or three famous celebrity relationships you've seen in the news over the past several years. Do they seem to be driven by one, two, or all three of Sternberg's components in the triangular theory of love? Do these components seem to have changed over time? Do you think that the nature of celebrity lifestyles makes relationships play out differently, from the perspective of Sternberg's theory?

CRITICAL THINKING

- Most of the studies based on Sternberg's theory have been conducted with "Western" participants in countries like the United States or with similar cultures. Do you think the same three components exist in every culture? Do different cultures emphasize different components, at different times or with different types of people?

- Imagine that you knew you would be in only one, monogamous romantic relationship for the rest of your life—and that relationship could only have *one* of Sternberg's three components. Which one would you choose, and why?

- Do you prefer to think about intimate relationships in a continuous way or a categorical way? Why does this system appeal to you?

How Is This Book Organized?

Hopefully, you enjoy reading this book! But any textbook can seem overwhelming at first. Breaking down what to expect might help.

One way to anticipate what you'll read is to think about the order of chapters. There are really three major sections, although they aren't named or formalized. Chapters 1 and 2 are a basic introduction to how relationship scholars think about and study theory, from a scientific perspective. The next section of the book (Chapters 3, 4, and 5) is basically the "theoretical foundations" part. These chapters cover three of the most popular and broad-reaching theories used to understand relationship patterns. The theories attempt to explain why people act and think as they do in relationships, how that translates into different people's experiences, and how each theory can be applied in a wide variety of settings. This strong emphasis on a theoretical foundation can help you pull the theories through the rest of the book and, potentially, into your own thoughts or even research projects.

Finally, the second half of the book (Chapters 6 to 13) covers research regarding various forms of relationships and how relationships evolve over our individual lifetimes. The order of chapters is intentionally set up to take you through the beginnings of most relationships—friendship and attraction—through the next stages, like sexuality and commitment. Once a relationship is formed, how partners think about each other (social cognition), communicate, and resolve (or fail to resolve) conflict are covered. Finally, the last two chapters talk about the best and worst parts of intimate relationships. Chapter 12 discusses sexual assault and abuse, and the final chapter covers both breaking up (ending love) and research on how relationship partners can last the test of time (enduring love).

Within each chapter, you'll see "big questions" and learning objectives that guide it in the form of an outline, with two or three sections. Each chapter (starting with Chapter 2) includes three features. One is "What's My Score?" where you can take a self-report scale. Hopefully this will be a fun way to both see where you fall on an interesting variable and learn how that variable is operationalized in research studies. Next, "Relationships in Popular Culture" discusses how intimate relationships are featured in songs, television, or movies. Finally, the "Research Deep Dive" feature goes into detail about the method and results of a particular research study, reminding you of the scientific method behind all advances in the field of relationships.

Each section ends with some questions to make sure you understood the material, optional application activities, and critical thinking questions to consider or discuss with others. Finally, the end of each chapter provides a summary of the main ideas. The overall goal of the book is both to familiarize you with important research and applications of relationship science, and to get you to think about the relationships in your own life and social network. Relationships are all around us, an important part of our daily lives—so let's get started.

Chapter Summary

Why study intimate relationships?

The study of intimate relationships is interdisciplinary in that it combines research from several different fields of study (biology, anthropology, sociology, and so on). Scientific interest in the study of intimate relationships has grown quickly over the past 100 years, perhaps because relationships are important in so many different aspects of human life. Relationships are necessary for human survival and they affect our physical and mental health. One example of an important research study showing the link between social support and physical health is the famous Alameda County Study, which established links between levels of social support and mortality rates (meaning more social support was associated with lower probabilities of death); this association was especially strong as participants got older, and it was stronger for men than for women.

What are different kinds of intimate relationships?

How to define and measure "love" and related concepts has led to several theories regarding different types of intimate relationship. One of the first people to scientifically define romantic love was Zick Rubin, who distinguished between "liking" and "loving." The scales he created to measure each type of love are still used in research today and are an example of how defining love can be done with either a categorical approach (sorting types of relationship into groups or kinds of relationship) or a continuous approach (thinking about love on a range or continuum). Another popular early model of love is Sternberg's triangular theory of love, which suggests that love relationships are made up of three components: passion, intimacy, and commitment. Different levels of each component translate into different forms of love relationship. If all three components are present at high levels, a relationship is called "consummate" and is considered the ideal form of romantic love. Sternberg's components can also be considered as present or absent (a categorical approach) or as existing at different levels within any given relationship over time (a continuous approach).

How is this book organized?

The chapters in this book go from an introduction and research methods, to three major theoretical perspectives on relationships, to research on various aspects of a relationship as it evolves. Those later chapters follow along from friendship, attraction, sexuality, commitment, conflict, abuse, and both ending and enduring love. Each chapter has features to help readers understand and apply the material, such as self-report scales, application to popular culture, deep dives into research studies, and critical thinking questions.

List of Terms

Learning Objectives	Key Terms
1.1 Explain how relationships are associated with human survival, physical health, and mental health.	Interdisciplinary approach Basic research Applied research PsycINFO Longitudinal Natural selection Enhanced fitness Social support Esteem support Informational support Instrumental support Well-being
1.2 Analyze theories regarding different types of liking and loving in human relationships.	Categorical approach Continuous approach Construct Operationalize Rubin's liking and loving scales Sternberg triangular theory of love Intimacy Passion Commitment
1.3 Describe the order of chapters and within-chapter features you'll see throughout the book.	

Research Methods and Analysis

Big Questions	Learning Objectives
1. What research methods are used to study relationships?	2.1 Describe the scientific method, different types of research study, and ethical considerations.
2. How are results analyzed?	2.2 Compare and contrast the most common ways to analyze and interpret research results.
3. What is "open science"?	2.3 Analyze the "open science" movement and what it means for future research endeavors.

The scientific study of attraction, love, friendship, and everything else covered in this book is a hugely impressive feat.

We're talking about squishy, abstract concepts that even the people experiencing them can't explain. So anyone who decides to jump into the deep end of the science pool by trying to define, measure, and experiment on the world of intimate relationships is up for a challenge! And as you read about the theories and findings covered in this book, it's always important to ask *how* scientists arrived at these claims. Think of methods and statistics as the building blocks to finding answers, or a treasure map leading toward the riches of insight. A fundamental knowledge about different research approaches and how results are analyzed is essential to a true understanding of the science of relationships.

What Research Methods Are Used to Study Relationships?

As we've already started to discuss, the scientific study of love, attraction, friendship, sexuality, romance, and all the behaviors, thoughts, and emotions involved is a difficult task. Even the question of defining or operationalizing variables such as "love" is done in a widely different number of ways across different studies, as you read in Chapter 1. Let's start by considering how relationships researchers ask and answer questions from a scientific approach. Then, we'll review five different approaches to setting up a study. For an interesting link on how pioneering sex researchers have been portrayed in TV and movies, see the "Relationships and Popular Culture" feature as well.

The Scientific Method

Most academic disciplines that study intimate relationships approach the topic from the **scientific method**, a systematic and evidence-based approach to asking and answering questions. The general approach of the scientific method is displayed in Figure 2.1. Researchers will start by observing a pattern in the "real world" and will then generate a formal **hypothesis**, or a specific statement of what they believe will happen in a study designed to test the phenomenon of interest.

RELATIONSHIPS AND POPULAR CULTURE

Scientifically Studying Sex: Pioneers on the Screen

In the first half of the 1900s, studying human sexual behavior was quite controversial—even scandalous. One of the most controversial figures in the history of research on sex and intimate relationships was, unquestionably, Alfred Kinsey. One part of his legacy might even be the terms "sexology" and "sexologist," as he developed university courses on human sexuality and created one of the largest research efforts to understand the true nature of human sexual behaviors. Part of Kinsey's controversy were his views that women were capable of several different kinds of orgasm (e.g., from both vaginal and clitoral stimulation) and that everyone is at least a little bit bisexual. However, as shocking as those ideas might have been in the 1930s–1950s when he was a prominent professor, his research methodology itself was also controversial. Kinsey interviewed prostitutes, prisoners, abuse victims, and gay men—populations that had previously been ignored. He also crossed the boundaries between objective observer and participant as he engaged in sexual behaviors with his participants, graduate students, and colleagues on his research team. In 2004, Kinsey's fascinating life was made into a movie simply called *Kinsey*, starring Liam Neeson and Laura Linney (Coppola, Mutrux, & Condon, 2004).

Following in Kinsey's footsteps were the famous pair Masters and Johnson (specifically, William Masters and Virginia Johnson), who published research on human sexual behaviors over the entire second half of the twentieth century. They also studied phases of sexuality and tried to understand the female orgasm (which is apparently quite the mystery!), including how and why women are able to have multiple orgasms in a short period of time. Their lives and research have been fictionalized in the television series *Masters of Sex* that ran from 2013 to 2016 and starred Michael Sheen and Lizzy Caplan (Ashford, 2013–2016). As you can probably expect, both *Kinsey* and *Masters of Sex* are filled with content that might not be suitable for children to watch.

After operationalizing all the variables involved, making sure the study is ethical, and gathering data, researchers then interpret the results (often using statistical analysis). Once the pattern of results is known, the process can repeat again and again, each time providing a deeper or more detailed understanding of the topic. It's also important to think about standards of quality when designing a study.

There are several ways to analyze whether any given study is done well. First, a study should have solid **internal validity**. Internal validity relates to how well the study was constructed and whether any results can really be interpreted in the ways the researcher intends. For example, were all the variables operationalized and measured appropriately? If there are two groups being compared, are they identical in every way except for the main variable of interest, or are there other explanations at play? Internal validity can be compared to **external validity**, which is also important. While internal validity refers to the structure within the study and whether it was set up correctly, external validity relates to whether the study can be applied to other people or situations. Can the results generalize to people beyond those who actually participated? Does the study have any "real-world" implications?

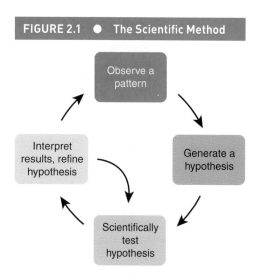

FIGURE 2.1 ● The Scientific Method

The scientific method starts by noticing interesting patterns and generating hypotheses regarding those patterns. Then, evidence is gathered that either supports or refutes the hypothesis. Those results help us refine hypotheses and keep testing them as we learn more.

Another concern that's receiving more and more attention is the ability to find a **replication** of any study's results. Replication means doing the same study again, with different people, and confirming the results by finding the same patterns over and over. If a study's results can never be found again, it calls into question whether the original study was really done properly. Replication—or lack of replication—can lead to controversy. A famous example occurred in the 1950s. A man named James Vicary claimed that when he hid subliminal messages of popcorn and Coke in film reels at movie theaters, there was a 58% increase in sales of popcorn and an 18% increase in sales of Coca-Cola (Pratkanis, 1992). After several years of scientists attempting to replicate similar behavioral effects of subliminal messages—and failing to do so—Vicary finally had to admit that he had made the entire study up!

This is an extreme example. Failure to replicate usually doesn't mean that the original study was bogus or that the findings aren't interesting and important. It does mean that we should ask questions, such as why other people can't seem to find the same results—and sometimes there are theoretically interesting answers that lead to additional hypotheses. Perhaps there was something special about the original participants, or there was something happening in the world that affected the results, or the sample of people in the study was too small, or the statistics were done incorrectly. . . . But if the researchers were, indeed, honest about their results (as the vast majority of scientists are), a lack of replication might actually lead to interesting developments in theory or practice.

Methodological Approaches

Imagine that you want to design a research study. For the purposes of the next few pages, let's use an example: You're interested in investigating whether introverts or extroverts are happier with the levels of intimacy within their social relationships. (By the way, both "extrovert" and "extravert" are acceptable spellings of the word.) Maybe extroverts (people who are more gregarious and social on most occasions) perceive that they have more close friends in terms of *quantity*, but introverts feel that their relationships are more intimate (e.g., better *quality*). You might make that your hypothesis. As we've already covered, you have to formally state your hypothesis and operationalize your variables (define them and decide how to measure them).

You also have a few other decisions to make, right off the bat. One is whether you will do a qualitative or a quantitative study. A **qualitative study** is one that gathers open-ended data, usually through surveys or interviews, in non-numerical form. You might set up interviews with 10 people who self-identify as introverts and 10 who self-identify as extroverts and ask them questions such as, "Tell me how you feel about the levels of intimacy in your relationships." This straightforward approach has the advantage of allowing the participants to be the experts in their own lives and provides an interesting level of detail and a personal touch in the results you gather.

A real example of a qualitative study is one by Rosen (1996). She interviewed 22 women who were survivors of abusive relationships. She asked the participants why they had initially been attracted to the person who later became their abuser and how they felt once the abuse started. Her interviews led to fascinating insights regarding the mindset of abuse victims (which are described for you in detail in Chapter 12). These women's stories, emotions, and insights might have been lost if they had only been asked questions in the form of numbers, like scales from 1 to 10.

However, you might prefer a **quantitative study**, in which the data you gather are in numerical form and thus better suited for most statistical analyses. Paralleling the theoretical example from before, you might ask the same 10 introverts and 10 extroverts to take surveys in which they answer a series of questions on a scale from 1 (strongly disagree) to 7 (strongly agree), then you average their answers. Quantitative data are useful for gaining an understanding of patterns of results across more people and have the advantage of additional statistical analyses, but they lose the personal feel of qualitative data.

An example of a real quantitative study is a survey used by Arnocky and Vaillancourt (2014). They asked participants to fill out several numerical scales regarding whether victims of relationship abuse were "responsible" for what happened to them (a form of victim blaming). Participants read different scenarios, and the results showed that participants blamed victims more (scores on the quantitative scale were higher) when the scenarios described a male victim, compared to a female victim. In other words, victim blaming appeared to be worse for male victims in this study, a finding based on numerical results that might have been harder to understand if participants only described their feelings.

Another decision to make is whether the study should be cross-sectional or longitudinal. A **cross-sectional study** occurs at a single time, whereas a longitudinal study takes place over two or more time periods or data-collection sessions.

"Cross-sectional" studies are called that because the general idea is that you can compare results across multiple groups at a single time. In contrast, remember the Alameda County Study from Chapter 1 (Berkman & Syme, 1979), which was longitudinal because it followed the participants over many years. Longitudinal studies have the advantage of seeing how patterns change over time. This is especially interesting in a relationships context, to see how friends or couple members change and adapt as their relationship grows in intimacy (or ends!). The disadvantages of longitudinal studies are the time, expense, and effort that they take, plus the fact that many of the participants might drop out of the study before it's done. Because of these disadvantages, cross-sectional studies are more common.

When recruiting participants for a study, it's important to get as many people as possible. In addition, ideally the participants have enough diversity that they represent a wide variety of cultures, sexualities, ages, religions, experiences, and so on. This ideal type of sample is called a **representative sample**, meaning the participants in your study serve as examples of a typical person in the larger population, and that the participants are diverse enough to cover many different perspectives. The best strategy to get a representative sample is to use **random sampling** of the larger population, meaning that everyone in the larger group has an equal chance of participating. That way, your study isn't biased toward only one type of person.

The ideal situation is for theories and hypotheses to be tested many times, with many different participants, in many settings. We can be more and more confident of claims when we replicate studies that have strong internal and external validity. Multiple methods, such as both quantitative and qualitative data, also help. So there are many different ways to test a hypothesis. Most studies used for this book fall into one of five basic structures or types of research methodology; each one is covered next.

Option 1: Archival Research

Archival data are stored pieces of information that were originally created for some other purpose. Newspapers, census data, Facebook posts, and even popular culture are all examples of archival data. To explore our study regarding introvert and extrovert differences in relationship intimacy, you could examine Facebook posts and profiles to see how many "friends" people have, how many times other people post to their page and vice versa, how many "likes" their posts get, how many times the owner of the profile self-discloses intimate information on their page, and so on.

Archival research has led to important insights in the world of intimate relationships. One interesting example is an understanding of abusive marriages. For years, some researchers believed that abusive relationships almost always had male perpetrators and female victims and that violent incidents were fairly severe. This perspective came from looking at archival data collected through police reports and profiles of victims in emergency shelters. However, researchers who were doing studies on abusive marriages through anonymous surveys found very different patterns, including female-to-male violence and many couples in which physically aggressive behavior was mutual (see Johnson, 1995, 2007). This debate is discussed further in Chapter 12, but for now the point is that the source of archival data is important in how it shapes our understanding.

Option 2: Naturalistic Observation

Another approach is **naturalistic observation**, or scientific surveillance of people in their natural environments—in other words, where the behaviors would be occurring anyway, even if you weren't there watching it happen. You might decide to go to a local bar to watch people interact with their friends or flirt with strangers and make notes of the patterns you see play out.

You might be thinking, "If some scientist came to the bar and started writing down everything I did, then I probably wouldn't react very naturally." You're right, and this is a potential challenge to good observational research. When people change their behavior due to awareness that they're being observed, it's called **reactivity**. One creative solution is a technique called **participant observation**, in which scientists disguise themselves as people who belong in that environment. It's kind of like going undercover. You pretend you're not doing research at all and hope to fade into the background—and still find some discreet way to record your observations. In our example, perhaps you pretend to simply be an innocent bar patron, or you act as the bartender so you have an excuse to talk with people about their thoughts.

Participant observation may create some ethical problems, so be careful. After all, you are deceiving people about why you are there. And it may be an ethical violation to observe people when they don't know they are being observed. The advantage of this technique—or any form of naturalistic observation—is that hopefully we get to see authentic social behaviors.

Option 3: Self-Report Surveys

Perhaps the most popular research method in studying intimate relationships is **self-report surveys**, in which people are directly asked to write down their own thoughts, feelings, and behaviors. The types of measures used in self-report surveys are scales like the Rubin liking and loving scales or the scale measuring Sternberg's love components that you saw in Chapter 1.

In the movie *21 Jump Street* (Moritz, Cannell, Lord, & Miller, 2012), two young police officers go undercover pretending to be high school students so they can bust a new drug that's hitting the community. In *Imperium* (Taufique, Lee, Ragussis, Walker, & Ragussis, 2016), Daniel Radcliffe's character works for the FBI and infiltrates a White supremacist group, pretending to be racist. If any of them had been social psychologists doing research with this "undercover" technique, it would have been called participant observation.

The main advantages to using self-report scales are that it's relatively inexpensive and fast to get a lot of data, lots of participants can take the survey (making the sample more diverse), and statistical techniques can analyze patterns of responses (if the surveys were quantitative). Self-report surveys are also often the only way to get access to people's intimate personal lives, such as their sexual fantasies, whether they want to cheat on their partner, or what they find sexually attractive.

Remember that one common problem with naturalistic observation is reactivity, or people changing their behaviors because they know they are being observed. Self-report surveys have their own concerns, and one of the big ones is dishonesty. People might not want to admit to cheating, abuse, and other behaviors generally not socially acceptable. The dishonesty problem is called **social desirability**, the idea that people shape their responses—exaggerate, manipulate, or just straight out lie—so that others will have positive impressions of them. (This problem is also sometimes known as impression management.)

WHAT'S MY SCORE?

Measuring Social Desirability

Instructions: Listed below are several statements concerning personal attitudes and traits. Please read each item and decide whether the statement is true or false as it pertains to you, personally. Circle T for true statements and F for false statements.

T F 1. Before voting I thoroughly investigate the qualifications of all the candidates.

T F 2. I never hesitate to go out of my way to help someone in trouble.

T F 3. I sometimes feel resentful when I don't get my way.

T F 4. I am always careful about my manner of dress.

T F 5. My table manners at home are as good as when I eat out in a restaurant.

T F 6. I like to gossip at times.

T F 7. I can remember "playing sick" to get out of something.

T F 8. There have been occasions when I took advantage of someone.

T F 9. I'm always willing to admit it when I make a mistake.

T F 10. There have been occasions when I felt like smashing things.

T F 11. I am always courteous, even to people who are disagreeable.

T F 12. At times I have really insisted on having things my own way.

Scoring: Give yourself 1 point each if you said TRUE for question 1, 2, 4, 5, 9, or 11. Then, give yourself 1 point each if you said FALSE for question 3, 6, 7, 8, 10, or 12. Then, add your points. Higher scores indicate great attempts to manage your impression on others, or a higher tendency toward socially desirable responding on self-report scales.

Source: Crowne and Marlowe (1960).

Critical Thinking: If a participant shows a high level of deception based on this scale, is the only option to ignore the rest of their data in any given research study? All you know is that they might not have been honest—you can't tell in what direction or to what degree they've been dishonest in the rest of their responses. So, what can you do with the rest of their data?

One creative way around this potential problem is to include a measure of social desirability in the survey, to see whether people admit to behaviors that almost everyone does. If someone denies something like gossiping or littering, for example, they're probably not being particularly honest just because pretty much everyone does these things at least occasionally. An example social desirability scale is shown in the "What's My Score?" feature.

Option 4: Quasi-Experiments

Many studies on intimate relationships are interested in comparing two or more groups of people to each other. For example, in our theoretical study, we want to compare introverts to extroverts. But we don't get to manipulate people's personality; we have no control over whether they are introverted or extroverted. When researchers gather data in which two or more *naturally occurring groups* are compared to each other, it's called a **quasi-experiment**. It's "quasi," meaning "half-formed" or "almost" because it's not a "true" experiment (those are explained in the next section).

Another example of a quasi-experiment would be to compare people who are in long-distance relationships to those who are not, to see if the quality of the two different types of relationship changes. When one of my students and I did this (Butler & Goodfriend, 2015), we found that relationship satisfaction levels were similar in each relationship type, but that people *believed* that satisfaction was lower in an "average" long-distance relationship. This belief might eventually lead to a self-fulfilling prophecy of lower satisfaction in long-distance couples—although we didn't test that possibility with longitudinal data. Quasi-experiments are very commonly done because researchers want to compare naturally occurring groups such as Republicans versus Democrats, married versus divorced people, heterosexual versus gay/lesbian relationships, people who grew up in abusive homes versus healthy homes, and so on. These are interesting and important questions, and quasi-experiments are the only way to find answers.

Option 5: Experiments

An **experiment** compares two or more groups of participants who have been formed through **random assignment**. Random assignment means that each participant is put in one of the groups by chance.

Imagine you wanted to know whether listening to love songs made people feel more positively toward their partner. So, you randomly assigned 50 people to listen to love songs (this would be called the **experimental group**) and randomly assigned 50 different people to hear no songs at all (if a "neutral" or comparison group exists in an experiment, it is called the **control group**). If it's true that the two groups really are equal in every way *except* for hearing love songs or not and then the two groups have different outcomes in terms of their feelings toward their partner, then it's fairly safe to conclude that the only possible explanation for their different feelings was the songs. You can say that the love songs caused an increase in feelings of love.

In an experiment, what makes the groups different, based on that random assignment, is called the **independent variable**. The independent variable is what the researchers set up to make Group 1 versus Group 2 (or Group 3, and so on). In the case of the theoretical experiment in the previous paragraph, the independent

TABLE 2.1 ● Examples of Studies, Independent Variables, and Dependent Variables		
Experiment Basics	**Independent Variable**	**Dependent Variable**
People listen to love songs or no songs and then rate how much they love their partner.	Presence or absence of love songs	Love ratings for partner
People list either positive or negative memories about their partner, then estimate their chances of being married in 10 years.	Memory type (positive or negative)	Estimates of marriage probability
Children play with either white-skinned or brown-skinned dolls, then answer questions about which magazine models they think are the prettiest.	Doll type (white-skinned or brown-skinned)	Perceptions of the models' attractiveness
Two strangers sit in a room together for 1 hour and are asked to get to know each other. The room is either well-lit (lights on) or dark (lights off). Researchers code how intimate their conversation becomes.	Lights on or off in the room	Level of intimacy in conversation

Experiments have independent variables, which separate participants into different groups. They also have dependent variables, or the outcome being measured.

variable is the presence or absence of love songs. There doesn't have to be a control or neutral group, but there always has to be some kind of comparison group. For example, this study could have compared people who listened to love songs with people who listened to jazz, country, or classical music. In a perfect study, the independent variable is the *only* difference between or among groups.

The outcome variable in an experiment is called the **dependent variable**. It's called "dependent" because if the hypothesis is correct, then scores or levels of this variable are "dependent" upon which group the participant was in. Here, the dependent variable is feelings toward a partner, and they're expected to be more positive after love songs are played. So love feelings are "dependent" on whether they heard the songs or not. In short, independent variables are the "cause" in an experiment, and dependent variables are the "effect" or outcome. For several more examples of independent and dependent variables in theoretical studies on intimate relationships, see Table 2.1.

Ethical Considerations Within Research Studies

Any research study done with living creatures needs to be done ethically. Investigations into people's personal, intimate lives is a context in which ethical considerations must be taken very seriously. Consider experiments in which researchers are actually trying to *manipulate* people's feelings, thoughts, or behaviors within their intimate relationships! Or surveys asking people about sexual abuse or domestic violence or secret affairs . . . just answering questions about these topics could lead to traumatic memories and emotions. Research on intimate relationships is challenging both for methodological reasons and for ethical and moral reasons.

There's a certain level of trust that happens when anyone shows up to participate in a research study. As researchers, we want to remember that we have a solemn responsibility to treat people with respect. Even when we use unobtrusive methodologies like naturalistic observation or archival studies, all people involved in the study of human social behavior should be valued. Researchers across all the sciences provide ethical and legal guidance about what it means to treat study participants with respect through **institutional review boards (IRBs)**, which are committees of people who consider the ethical implications of any study. Your local IRB committee is typically composed of representatives from different departments in a college, university, research institute, or corporation. The committees also often have a lawyer as a member, and sometimes they have a member with no background in research at all, to represent the "average person's" perspective.

Some of the participant rights required by most IRBs are the following:

- *Informed Consent:* Participants should be told what they will be asked to do and whether there are any potential dangers or risks involved in the study before it begins; this is called **informed consent**.

- *Deception:* Participants should be told the truth about the purpose and nature of the study as much as possible. **Deception**, or hiding the true nature of the study, is allowed only when it is necessary because knowing the truth would change how the participants respond.

- *Anonymity:* No participant's individual responses will be published in a way that identifies them publicly. Any identifying information (such as names or specific demographics) needs to be removed if individual responses are to be reported, such as answers during a qualitative interview.

- *Right to Withdraw:* Participants have the right to stop being in the study at any time, for any reason, or to skip questions on a survey if they are not comfortable answering them.

- *Debriefing:* After completing the study, all participants should be given additional details about the hypotheses of the study, allowed the opportunity to ask questions, and even see the results if they wish. This **debriefing** after the study is complete should definitely include an explanation of any deception that was involved (if deception occurred) so that participants have the opportunity to withdraw their data if they are upset about the deception.

CHECK YOUR UNDERSTANDING

2.1 Dr. X asks participants to complete a single survey in which they write essay responses to several questions. Everyone answers the same questions. This study is therefore an example of which type of research?

   a. Longitudinal
   b. Experimental
   c. Archival
   d. Qualitative

2.2 True experiments use random assignment to place each participant into one of the groups being studied. Random assignment helps ensure the groups are identical in every other way, which means that use of random assignment helps improve the study's:

   a. Ethics
   b. Replication
   c. External validity
   d. Internal validity

2.3 Dr. Z asks half of their participants to fill out Rubin's liking and loving scales in a very cold room and the other half to fill out the same scales in a very hot room. What is the dependent variable in this study?

   a. The number of participants Dr. Z has in the study
   b. Temperature of the room (hot or cold)
   c. Participants' answers to the Rubin scales
   d. Whether the participants are told Dr. Z's hypothesis

APPLICATION ACTIVITY

Choose a topic you think is very personal or controversial within the field of intimate relationships and search for a study done on that topic. Then, analyze the methodology that was used and discuss whether you think the participants were treated ethically. Were all of the typical IRB standards used, as far as you can tell? If not, do you think the study violated ethical guidelines for research studies? Could the study have been done differently, to improve ethical treatment?

CRITICAL THINKING

- If you wanted to study patterns of attraction or relationship behaviors within the students of your college or university, what kinds of archival data could you use? Consider public resources such as Facebook, library archives, the school newspaper, and so on.

- This section introduced you to a measure of social desirability that could be used to identify if participants are being honest in their responses. Imagine you did a survey study and 20 of 60 participants had high scores on this scale, indicating dishonesty. What do you do now with the rest of their survey answers? Do you throw them out completely? Why or why not? Do you need to collect more data, from other people, so you have more "honest" answers?

- Most people who are monitored during studies using naturalistic observation are never told that they are being watched or that their behavior might end up in a study (even if it is anonymous). Does this practice seem ethical to you? Why or why not?

Answers to the Check Your Understanding Questions

2.1 d, **2.2** d, and **2.3** c.

FIGURE 2.2 ● Comparing Two Groups of Participants: A *t*-Test

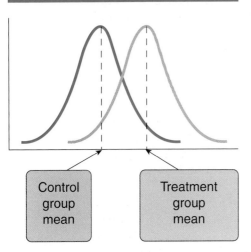

Control group mean

Treatment group mean

One way researchers look for patterns is by comparing average scores between different groups of participants. When we compare two groups, as here, we use a *t*-test. When we compare three or more groups, we do an analysis of variance, or ANOVA.

We have Guinness to thank for the statistic known as the *t*-test.

©iStock.com/MediaProduction

How Are Results Analyzed?

If you've chosen a quantitative design, you'll need to understand the results of your study using some basic statistical tests. Even if you, personally, never conduct a study, this book contains summaries of many other people's studies, so to understand them you need a foundational understanding of how scientists decide what their data really mean. Let's cover just the basics of two different sets of statistical approach that you'll see throughout this book: comparing groups to each other and doing correlations.

Comparing Groups: *t*-Tests and ANOVAs

In a survey, quasi-experiment, or true experiment, researchers often want to compare answers or behaviors across groups of participants. There are two basic statistical tests we use to do that. The first is called a ***t*-test**, which compares responses between two different groups. It might be men versus women, introverts versus extroverts, happy versus unhappy couples, people who listen to love songs or no songs, or any other two relevant groups of people.

You can remember that a *t*-test compares two groups by thinking that the "*t*" stands for "two." Just as you can see in Figure 2.2, a *t*-test will compare two things in each group: the average of each group and the variance or standard deviation (how widely distributed the scores are in each group) to see how much the two groups overlap. If they don't overlap very much, then the groups can be considered different from each other.

You might find it fun to know that we have beer (well, Irish dry stout to be exact) to thank for the invention of the *t*-test. William Sealy Gosset, a brewer at Dublin's Guinness Brewing Company, had to test the amount of stout in each batch of beer for quality control (Mankiewicz, 2004). It would have been impossible for him to sample from all of the thousands of casks produced every single day, so instead he took a random sample from the morning batches and a random sample from the afternoon batches and compared them to each other, to make sure they were the same. Gosset's invention of the math behind his comparison was published anonymously (under the fake name "Student") and is now used for much more than making sure our beer tastes great.

What if researchers want to compare three or more groups? For example, a study might be interested in analyzing relationships in each of the seven continents, to test for cultural differences. The principle for comparing multiple groups is the same as for comparing two groups.

For each group, we calculate the average score and the standard deviation, just like before, but when several groups are involved it's called an **analysis of variance**, or **ANOVA** for short. ANOVA tests will tell you whether at least one of the groups is different from the others, and additional follow-up analyses can tell you the details of which groups are different and how much they vary.

Patterns in a Single Group: Correlations

In Chapter 1, we talked about the difference between categorical and continuous variables. Variables that make different groups (Christians versus Muslims versus atheists, Canadians versus Brazilians versus Rwandans, people who listen to love songs versus a control group) are categorical and thus use *t*-tests and ANOVAs. The average scores and standard deviations of each group are compared to each other. However, many studies include a single group of participants and look for patterns of results among two or more continuous variables.

An example was covered in Chapter 1: the Alameda County Study (Berkman & Syme, 1979). There, social support was linked to mortality rates: People are less likely to die if they have a lot of social support. While *t*-tests and ANOVAs compare patterns of results in different groups, **correlations** look for patterns of results in a single group. Correlations test whether two different variables are systematically associated with each other, like social support and mortality were in Alameda County.

Correlations analyze the association between two continuous variables, meaning variables that have a range of scores that fall along a continuum. To test for a pattern, scores on each variable are gathered from as many people as possible and are then charted on a graph called a **scatterplot**. One variable is on the (horizontal) *x*-axis, and the other is on the (vertical) *y*-axis, and each dot on the scatterplot represents one person. Take a look at Figure 2.3 for an example (with theoretical data created for the purposes of this chapter—not from a real study).

The pattern shown in Figure 2.3 indicates that as people age through early adulthood, they are more likely to be in relationships with higher levels of commitment. The line summarizes the trend in the data. When a correlation is calculated, the number you get is called a **correlation coefficient**. It will always be a number between –1.00 and +1.00. How can you tell what the coefficient means? It's basically like a two-part code you can crack to understand what the pattern looks like on a scatterplot. There are two parts to the code: (1) the sign or direction (positive or negative) and (2) the number.

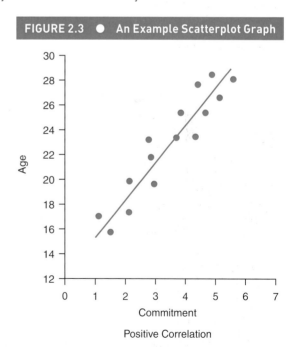

FIGURE 2.3 ● An Example Scatterplot Graph

Positive Correlation

In this fictional study, age and commitment go together: As people get older, their commitment also increases. That means there is a positive correlation between age and commitment.

First, the sign will always be either a positive or a negative (unless the correlation is exactly zero). A **positive correlation** (between 0.00 and +1.00) indicates that both variables move in the same direction. In other words, if scores or values on one of the variables go up, values on the other variable will also go up. If one goes down, the other will go down. The example in Figure 2.3 shows a positive correlation: As age goes up, so does relationship commitment. Positive correlations are shown in scatterplots when the pattern or summary line moves from the bottom left-hand corner to the upper right-hand corner.

In contrast, a **negative correlation** (between 0.00 and –1.00) indicates that the variables move in opposite directions. As one variable goes up, the other goes down. For example, in Alameda County, more social support was associated with lower mortality (death rates). As social support went up, likelihood of death went down. Negative correlations will be shown in scatterplots with a pattern that goes from the upper left-hand corner to the bottom right-hand corner.

The second part of a correlation coefficient is the number, which will always be between zero and one (either positive or negative). The number tells you how clear the pattern is on the scatterplot, or how well the different dots (which represent people) fall along the summary line. Basically, this number tells you how much variability there is in the data, or whether some people don't fit the pattern. In Figure 2.3 you can see that not all of the people fall exactly on the line. If the dots all fall *exactly* on the line, meaning the pattern is perfect, the number you get will be 1.00. As the number gets closer to zero, it means the pattern becomes slightly less clear.

Note that coefficients of +1.00 and –1.00 are *equally strong*—both indicate perfect patterns, with all of the dots exactly on the line. It's just that in one case the variables move in the same direction (+1.00), and in one case they move in opposite directions (–1.00). Figure 2.4 is a summary of how to understand correlations, showing a range of patterns that move from perfect and positive, through no correlation at all, to perfect and negative. A zero correlation coefficient means that the two variables have no relation to each other at all, such as relationship commitment and someone's height

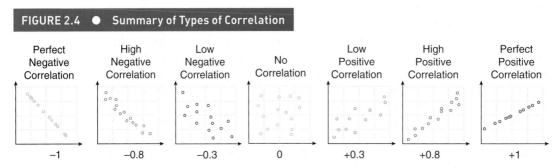

FIGURE 2.4 ● Summary of Types of Correlation

Correlations always range from –1.00 to +1.00. The sign (positive or negative) indicates whether the two variables move in the same direction or in opposite directions. The number (from 0.0 to 1.0) tells you how well each data point fits onto a general pattern. If a correlation is zero, it means there is no pattern or association between the two variables.

Source: Heinzen and Goodfriend, 2018.

or love of chocolate. These variables are not associated with each other at all, so the scatterplot would look like a bunch of random dots.

A final note, but a very important one, is that *correlation does not imply causation*. Being older doesn't *cause* someone to be more committed to relationships. It's possible that being older leads people to feel more prepared to make life plans, or being older leads to social expectations to marry and start a family. But without doing an experiment with random assignment to different conditions, causal inferences shouldn't be made.

An interesting example of this principle is, again, the Alameda County Study (Berkman & Syme, 1979). There, having more social support was negatively correlated with death rates. But does having more friends and family around lead to heathier behaviors? Or is it the other way around? Maybe being healthier leads to better quality relationships because people have more energy, participate in more activities, have more money to spend on luxurious gifts for their friends, and so on. A good understanding of the limitations within each research methodology and statistical analysis helps in knowing what conclusions should really be made within each study that's done.

Interpreting "Dyadic" Data

There's one more important point to consider regarding analyses of study results about relationships.

Most statistical tests work with the assumption that each participant's scores are independent from everyone else's in the study. In other words, the participants haven't influenced each other. However, if a study includes two or more people who are in a relationship with each other, that assumption goes right out the window. Clearly, the happiness, satisfaction, and so on of one person in a friendship or romantic couple is likely to be influenced by the other person. So if a study wants to include *both* people, the methods and statistics get much more complicated.

Methodologically, researchers will have to consider the pragmatics of holding study sessions when both people can be there. That automatically makes things complicated, with new considerations such as whether they'll need to find a babysitter, whether they both have the same work schedule, and more. If participants are being compensated with something like extra credit, what if one person is in the class offering compensation and the other isn't? How will the other person be compensated? And if the study is longitudinal, what happens to compensation if the couple breaks up halfway through the study, or one person wants to stop participating and the other wants to continue? Researchers will need to consider these additional aspects when couples or friends are supposed to participate together.

Statistically, the analyses will also become more complicated. Data will now have to be analyzed knowing that the results of one person are linked to another, using techniques called **dyadic analysis** (Kenny, Kashy, & Cook, 2006). Essentially each *couple* will be analyzed and then compared to the other couples, instead of comparing individual to individual—so slightly different formulas need to be used for these studies. Dyadic analysis is needed for parent to child, friend to friend, partner to partner, or any other method that includes people who influence each other. All of these considerations add another layer of challenge to people who want to make sure the science of intimate relationships is done well.

CHECK YOUR UNDERSTANDING

2.4   Dr. Y conducts a study in which they ask people over 50 years old how many sexual partners they have had in their lifetime. Dr. Y then compares the answers based on participants' socioeconomic status: lower class, middle class, or upper class. Which statistical analysis should Dr. Y do to understand their results?

   a. Analysis of variance
   b. *t*-test
   c. Scatterplot
   d. Correlation

2.5   Dr. Z asks half of their participants to run on a treadmill for 5 minutes, and the other half of the participants listen to calm, soothing music. All participants then rate how attracted they are to photographs. To analyze whether physiological arousal influenced perceived attraction in this study, what statistical analysis should Dr. Z do to understand their results?

   a. Analysis of variance
   b. *t*-test
   c. Scatterplot
   d. Correlation

2.6   Dr. X finds that the more introverted someone is, the more likely that person is to say they have a high self-esteem. What can be safely concluded from the results of this study?

   a. Introversion and self-esteem are positively correlated.
   b. Introversion and self-esteem are negatively correlated.
   c. Being introverted causes self-esteem to go up.
   d. Both a and c are correct.

APPLICATION ACTIVITY

Try to draw scatterplots that show the following results:

- A study of 10 people that resulted in a correlation of –1.00
- A study of 15 people that resulted in a correlation of exactly zero
- A study of 20 people that resulted in a correlation of +0.75

CRITICAL THINKING

- Consider correlation coefficients. A common mistake people make when they are first learning about correlations is that positive correlations are somehow "stronger" than negative correlations, even if the number is the same (e.g., +0.8 and –0.8). Why do people tend to make this mistake?

- "Correlation does not imply causation" is easy to say, maybe, but often hard for people to really follow as a rule. Try to identify three examples of real-life correlations in the world around you (e.g., "Calorie intake and body weight are positively correlated"). For each, identify whether you think there is a causal connection between the two variables where one causes the other, or whether both variables influence each other mutually, or whether there is a third variable that might be involved.

Answers to the Check Your Understanding Questions

2.4 a, 2.5 b, and 2.6 a.

What Is "Open Science"?

Ethics are always important.

We've already discussed some ethical considerations, such as avoiding deception in studies whenever possible, making sure we get informed consent before participants start in a research project, and so on. The ethics of science are even broader, though, when we start to think about how studies happen from start to finish. What if a researcher misrepresented their results, or they decided to form a hypotheses only after they had already done analyses? What if they refused to share their data with other people, who could confirm the findings?

Open science is a movement to make scientific research transparent, accessible, cooperative, reproducible, and honest. The aim of open science is to remove barriers for the creation of studies, sharing of data and results, and analysis of implications or conclusions. It's a way of saying to others, let's all do this together in an open, honest environment. One specific goal is to increase the number of studies focused on replication of previous work, so we can be confident in the conclusions we make and in the theories we teach in classes and textbooks (like this one!). Replication of results is the topic of this chapter's "Research Deep Dive" feature.

RESEARCH DEEP DIVE

Getting It Right: The Role of Replication in Relationship Science

As scientists we are obsessed with getting it right. This impulse is not entirely about us being right in the sense of seeing our predictions gain support (though that is nice), but more about getting the facts straight. Make no mistake, the stakes are high. Published research becomes the foundation for policies, college courses, textbooks, general audience books, and life decisions. In all cases, people put their faith in science to help improve their relationships.

Science is the gold standard for establishing facts because it requires that several key criteria be present for a finding to be considered authentic. For example, scientific information must be falsifiable, which means there has to be some way

to refute it or collect evidence that contradicts the alleged fact. Despite every scientist's best efforts, no study is 100% perfect. Thus there is always a chance a study's conclusions are wrong. Perhaps the most straightforward way to see if a statement of fact is false is to retest it. If someone else's research finds that a training program helps people find quality partners more easily, we need to be able to test that ourselves. That is, we need to check our work and test our theories.

A key way for relationship science (and all other scientific fields) to accomplish and demonstrate falsifiability is through replication, where scientists redo a study to determine if they get similar results each time. In fact, replication comes in a variety of forms, with each type along the continuum contributing to our knowledge base. The first type is a **direct replication** in which researchers

(Continued)

(Continued)

attempt to re-run the original study, sticking as closely as possible to the measures, manipulations, and/or procedures that other researchers used in the previous study. Direct replications help establish that a given finding exists. In other words, if two different research teams can obtain the exact same finding, then it gives us more confidence that the finding is real. Technically speaking, direct replications help falsify the null hypothesis (that there is no association between the variables in the study).

At the other end of the replication continuum is a **conceptual replication**, in which researchers study the exact same variables and test a similar association, but intentionally use different measures, manipulations, or procedures. Conceptual replications help establish the extent to which previously established associations between variables apply to other contexts. For example, if we find that being in love leads to higher relationship quality, is that true of each type of love? How about for other measures of relationship quality?

To make replication even easier, scientists are increasingly using more open science practices. It is important to realize that simply because replication in science in general is not perfect, it does not mean that it is not trustworthy. Even diamonds have their flaws. It simply means that you have to read scientific findings (as well as every piece of information you encounter) with a critical eye.

For more, read Lebel, P. E., Berger, Z. D., Campbell, L., & Loving, J. T. (2017). Falsifiability is not optional. *Journal of Personality and Social Psychology, 2,* 254–261.

There are several ways that open science encourages this kind of communication and exchange; a few are preregistration, results-blind peer review, and publication badges. We'll cover each idea below, but to learn more about this exciting trend in science, you can also go to the following websites:

- The Center for Open Science (https://cos.io/)

- The Open Science Framework (https://osf.io/)

- OpenScience (https://openscience.com/)

- ORION Open Science (https://www.orion-openscience.eu/)

- The FOSTER Portal (https://www.fosteropenscience.eu/)

Preregistration

Imagine that a scientist does a study in which they're not really sure what they're looking for or what the outcomes are expected to be. This is called exploratory research, and there's nothing wrong with it. But now imagine that after the results are analyzed, the scientist publishes the study and more or less pretends that they predicted the outcomes from the beginning. They look super smart! But it's not an honest approach.

Open science's solution is **preregistration**, a practice of specifying—in advance—your hypotheses, procedure, and statistical plan for analyses (see Nosek, Ebersole, DeHaven, & Mellor, 2017). This plan is made publicly available to anyone, so you are committing to everything in an open, transparent way. Several preregistration templates have been created to help people through this process, where researchers can post their plans on independent websites.

Preregistration is not without problems. For example, you might say that you're going to get 100 people for your study, but you can only get 75. Or you might assume that people will pay attention to instructions during your procedure, but some of them don't and they mess up what they are supposed to be doing. Or you might realize after you've collected data that you had a typo on your scale that changed what the question was asking. Scientists are certainly not perfect, and mistakes can be made. But all of these changes can simply be documented and explained. That way, readers of the research can understand exactly the process that occurred and why changes had to be made.

Typical questions you'll answer on a preregistration form are things like this:

- What are your hypotheses? If you're doing a quasi-experiment or experiment, what are the independent and dependent variables? If you're doing a correlation study, do you expect a positive or negative correlation?

- What exactly will the procedure be—what will participants do? What will be the order of procedural steps? How long will it take each person to do the study? How will you do random assignment (if relevant)?

- How will you recruit participants, and how many do you expect to find? Will anyone be excluded from data analysis—and if so, why?

- How will each of your variables be operationalized and calculated (if you're doing a quantitative study)? What statistical tests will you use to analyze the results?

Results-Blind Peer Review

Every academic field has professional journals, where researchers publish their results.

Most of these journals are what we call "peer-review" journals. That means that before any article is accepted for publication, it's sent out to other experts on that topic to see what they think. Those people, called reviewers, give the author(s) anonymous feedback about whether they think the article is worthy of being published.

Sometimes reviewers will make suggested changes that they want to see; if those changes are made, the journal will usually publish the article. Sometimes, however, the reviewers can simply say that they don't like the study and stop it from being published.

Until the open science movement, all of this reviewing happened after a study was completed and written up. That meant that the peer reviewers knew how the study

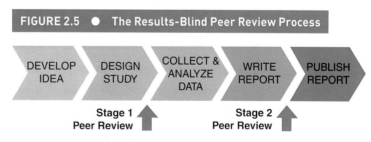

FIGURE 2.5 ● The Results-Blind Peer Review Process

When an article goes through the "results-blind peer review" process, outside experts give feedback about the quality and importance of an article before the data are actually collected. Then, they review a second time, focusing on whether the study followed the original design plan.

Source: Center for Open Science, used under Creative Commons Attribution 4.0 International license, https://creativecommons.org/licenses/by/4.0/.

turned out. The problem with this is that it can lead to biases in what is and isn't accepted for publication. Maybe the reviewers wouldn't like the results because they go against a theory they favor. A more common problem is that studies usually weren't published if their results didn't show statistically significant findings or results that matched their hypotheses.

These problems can largely be eliminated with a practice called **results-blind peer review**, which means that reviewers are asked about the importance of the study *before* they see the statistical outcomes, as shown in Figure 2.5. If they agree that the study has merit, they accept it for publication at this stage. Reviewers will also be asked for their feedback after the results are calculated—but now they comment on whether the study followed the preregistration plan and interpreted everything correctly. That way, even if the results surprise everyone, the study still gets published. Chris Chambers, the chair of a committee at the Center for Open Science, stated the benefits of this process like this: "The incentives for authors change from producing the most beautiful story to producing the most accurate one" (Center for Open Science, 2020b). Just like a relationship partner, science is even more beautiful when it's accurate and honest.

Publication Badges

Beyond the rewards of knowing you're doing good science, what incentives are there for people to engage in open science practices?

One reward is the use of **badges**, or visual icons that mark a study with signals that it has followed these procedures. You can see what the badges look like, at least for some journals, in Figure 2.6. If a study followed the requirements for each or all of the badges, the badges it earned will appear on the first page of the published article. For example, if they posted their original, raw data spreadsheets online, they get the "Open Materials" badge. Over 50 journals now use the badge system, and early trends show that they really do increase the number of scientists who share their data publicly (Kidwell et al., 2016; Rowhani-Farid, Allen, & Barnett, 2017). The open science movement is likely going to increase in usage and popularity over the next several years, as many people see it as the only way to make the scientific process truly objective and transparent.

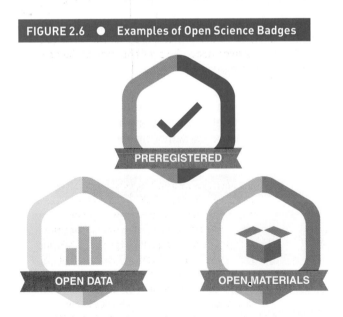

FIGURE 2.6 ● Examples of Open Science Badges

PREREGISTERED

OPEN DATA   OPEN MATERIALS

Professional journals are increasingly marking studies with these images, called "badges," when they follow open science guidelines. These examples are from the Center for Open Science.

CHECK YOUR UNDERSTANDING

2.7 The movement to make research more transparent, accessible, cooperative, and honest is called:

  a. Academic authenticity
  b. Public futurism
  c. Open science
  d. Methodological truth

2.8 Dr. X wants to replicate the idea behind someone else's study but to use new procedures and a different sample of people to see if the phenomenon holds up again under these new methods. What kind of replication would Dr. X's study be called?

  a. Abstract replication
  b. Conceptual replication
  c. Multiple replication
  d. Direct replication

2.9 Research on the use of "badges" by journals has shown that badges:

  a. Increase the number of scientists interested in publishing their work
  b. Decrease external validity in most studies
  c. Increase the number of scientists who publicly share their data
  d. Decrease the amount of deception used on participants in studies

APPLICATION ACTIVITY

While many people praise open science practices, they are not without drawbacks. One article that discusses some disadvantages can be found online by searching for the title "Open science isn't always open to all scientists" (Bahlai et al., 2019). Read this article and discuss or write your own opinion about the pros and cons of the open science movement.

CRITICAL THINKING

- Some professional journals charge for copies of their articles, or they require people to pay for subscriptions. Others offer their articles to readers for free, but they require that the scientists themselves pay to publish their work in the journal. What do you think is the best system for research to be available to other scientists or the general public, in terms of how it is funded? Should there be a new system, like a "science tax" that everyone pays but is used to make scientific progress available to everyone? Discuss how you think science should be funded, and why.

- The peer review process, even when done using the "results-blind" procedure, can be frustrating to people who want to publish their work. Sometimes, it seems unfair that anonymous people get to judge your work and decide whether it's "worthy." On the other hand, peer-reviewed articles are considered more credible because they have passed this hoop of acceptance. Do you think the peer-review system is good or bad, and why? If you don't like it, is there a better alternative?

- If you were a researcher, would badges make you more likely to engage in open science practices? Why or why not?

Answers to the Check Your Understanding Questions

2.7 c, 2.8 b, and 2.9 c.

Chapter Summary

Big Questions

1. What research methods are used to study relationships?

2. How are results analyzed?

3. What is "open science"?

What research methods are used to study relationships?

The scientific method consists of steps: observe a pattern, generate a hypothesis, test the hypothesis, and interpret the results. It then continues in a circular, repeatable cycle. Good research has high internal validity, external validity, and replicability. Researchers choose between a qualitative study, which gathers open-ended data through interviews or surveys, versus a quantitative study, which gathers data in numerical form (e.g., a scale that ranges from 1 to 7). In addition, several methods are used. These included archival research (or information originally gathered for another purpose), naturalistic observation (watching people in their natural environments), self-report surveys, quasi-experiments, and experiments. Each method has advantages and disadvantages. Finally, ethical treatment of participants includes practices such as obtaining informed consent, avoiding deception when possible, giving them the right to withdraw, and performing a thorough debriefing.

How are results analyzed?

When two groups are going to be compared to see if they are different from each other, the statistic used to analyze data is called a *t*-test. It compares the two groups' average scores and standard deviations, to see how much they overlap. The same principle is used to compare three or more groups, but then the statistical test is called an analysis of variance, or ANOVA for short. When a single sample is used in a study, but researchers want to test for associations between variables, correlation tests are used. Correlations can be positive (meaning both variables move in the same direction) or negative (the two variables move in opposite directions). The number for a correlation will always be between zero and one, with higher numbers meaning a stronger association between the two variables. Importantly, just because two variables are correlated with each other, it doesn't necessarily mean that movement of one causes movement in the other.

What is "open science"?

"Open science" is a movement to make research more transparent, cooperative, and honest. It involves practices like preregistration, where researchers specify their hypotheses, procedures, and statistical plan for analyses before any data are actually gathered. Another practice in open science is results-blind peer review, where other experts judge the value and quality of a study without knowing what the results were, so they can't be biased by the outcome of the study. Finally, many journals are now awarding "badges" for people who use open science. Badges are icons that appear on the first page of a published study that indicate the usage of various open science practices within a given study.

List of Terms

Learning Objectives	Key Terms
2.1 Describe the scientific method, different types of research study, and ethical considerations.	Scientific method Hypothesis Internal validity External validity Replication Qualitative study Quantitative study Cross-sectional study Representative sample Random sampling Archival data Naturalistic observation Reactivity Participant observation Self-report survey Social desirability Quasi-experiment Experiment Random assignment Experimental group Control group Independent variable Dependent variable Institutional review board (IRB) Informed consent Deception Debriefing
2.2 Compare and contrast the most common ways to analyze and interpret research results.	t-test Analysis of variance (ANOVA) Correlation Scatterplot Correlation coefficient Positive correlation Negative correlation Dyadic analysis
2.3 Analyze the "open science" movement and what it means for future research endeavors.	Open science Direct replication Conceptual replication Preregistration Results-blind peer review Badges

Attachment Theory

Big Questions	Learning Objectives
1. What is attachment theory, and how was it formed?	3.1 Explain the inspiration behind attachment theory and different attachment styles.
2. How is attachment theory measured and applied to adult relationships?	3.2 Apply attachment theory to adult relationships and analyze different ways to measure it.
3. What are important questions for and about attachment theory?	3.3 Analyze different contexts in which attachment theory is used to explain a variety of social behaviors.

Try to remember everything you can about the earliest relationship you had, as a baby. Your earliest relationship was likely with your parents or guardians.

Can you remember any specific incidents from your first 5 years of life? Maybe you remember a birthday party, a family trip somewhere, or maybe even a funeral. When you try to remember your earliest years, what feelings emerge? Are they feelings of comfort, trust, and security? Or do you feel lost, ignored, desperate, or angry? Now, when you try to reflect on the most important interpersonal relationships you have as an adult—with your friends, family members, or especially with a romantic partner—what kinds of feelings emerge? Are your relationships built on a fundamental understanding of trust and security? Do you think that your early relationships with parental figures are influencing your relationships now? The idea that our earliest relationships influence interpersonal dynamics for the rest of our life is the basis for the ideas discussed in this chapter.

Chapter 3, as well as Chapters 4 and 5, present the three most popular and well-researched theories regarding our behaviors, emotions, thoughts, and motivations within intimate relationships.

What Is Attachment Theory, and How Was It Formed?

The most emotionally charged relationships we have are usually with our parents, with our romantic partner(s), and eventually with our own children. When these relationships go well, we feel supported and loved. When we feel stress or anger due to work or school, we turn to these people for comfort. But if these relationships are rocky—if we don't feel sure that our parents or partners will be reliable sources of love and support—it can make things even more difficult.

John Bowlby, creator of attachment theory.

There are many theories that try to explain patterns and dynamics within social relationships, throughout the lifespan; you're learning about dozens of them by reading this book. This chapter focuses on what is probably the most famous and popular theory of them all. Just in the last 10 years, over 6500 studies have been published on the topic.

Attachment theory suggests that the relationship we have with our primary caregiver, as an infant, will influence the relationships we have with others for the rest of our lives, "from the cradle to the grave" (Bowlby, 1988, p. 82). In short, our very first relationship—usually with our mother or a similar figure—sets up an instinctive pattern or template for trust and love that we follow, sometimes without even realizing it. Before we get into more of the details within the theory, let's talk about the man behind the idea and the historical events that inspired it.

John Bowlby's Life and Inspiration

Attachment theory was created and developed by John Bowlby, who was born in England in 1907. The privilege of an upper-class family meant that his father and mother generally left him with his nanny most of the time. Bowlby had a loving and affectionate nanny until he was 1.5 years old. Then, she was replaced by a new nanny who was described by others as "cold, distant, and unaffectionate" (Bloom, 1999, p. 694). Perhaps on an unconscious level, this turbulence in his own early life led Bowlby to study how a child's interactions with caregivers during the first 2 years of life affect all of their later relationships.

After graduating from Cambridge in 1928, where he studied developmental psychology, Bowlby spent 6 months volunteering at a boarding school for emotionally disturbed children. While he was there, two children in particular had a deep influence on him (Ainsworth & Bowlby, 1991; Bretherton, 1992). The first was an isolated teenager who displayed no emotions and appeared to not want any friends or social connections. He had been expelled from another school and didn't appear to have any kind of loving mother figure. The second child was younger, age 7 or 8. This boy clung to Bowlby and followed him everywhere, seemingly desperate for attention. These two very different reactions to unstable families back home motivated Bowlby to study how early childhood experiences with parents can lead to relationship patterns later in life—the foundational idea within attachment theory.

Two Traumatic World Wars

Bowlby was still a young man when World War I hit Europe, and it was devastating for England. Around three-quarters of a million British men were killed, leaving behind an estimated 250,000 widows and 380,000 children without fathers (Newcombe & Lerner, 1982). When World War II hit, England was a pivotal location. Nazi Germany repeatedly bombed the city of London over a period of 8 months, killing around 43,000 civilians (BBC, 2018). This bombing campaign was known throughout the world as "The Blitz." To keep their children safe, many London parents sent their children out of the city, to family members in more protected locations, or even to strangers or orphanages in more rural areas. Over 1 million children were sent away from London and from their parents (Foster, Davies, & Steele, 2003).

Two studies were conducted at the time to see how these evacuations affected the children (Barnett House Study Group, 1947; Isaacs, Brown, & Thouless, 1941). Both concluded that the children displayed several negative effects, even after coming back home. Anna Freud, the famous daughter of Sigmund Freud, ran a residential war nursery called Hampstead and found that separation was hardest on children under the age of 5. Further, she found that sometimes when the children were reunited with their parents, they displayed anger and appeared to no longer feel emotionally attached to them (Burlingham & Freud, 1942).

A few years after the war, Bowlby was invited to work for the World Health Organization to write a comprehensive report on the mental health of children who were homeless or who had been separated from their families for extended periods of time (Bloom, 1999). This job meant that he became familiar with the research done on child evacuations during World War II, and that solidified his passion for understanding how our earliest childhood relationship experiences affect us.

An Ethological Approach to Attachment

Now that Bowlby wanted to study infant attachments to their primary caregivers, he needed a solid, scientific approach. He believed that attachment during infancy was of vital importance; he wrote, "If it goes well, there is joy and a sense of security. If it is threatened, there is jealousy, anxiety, and anger. If broken, there is grief and depression" (Bowlby, 1988, p. 4). He already had an idea that different kinds of bonds led to different outcomes. What was the best way to study this idea?

Bowlby started with an **ethological approach**, which is the study of human social behavior from a biological perspective; it compares humans to other animals to gain insights. He wrote:

The approach I regard as the most promising is again an ethological one. This assumes that in humans as well as in other species parenting behavior, like attachment behavior, is in some degree preprogrammed and therefore ready to develop along certain lines when conditions elicit it. (Bowlby, 1988, p. 83)

He preferred ethology over other approaches because at the time, psychology was still early in its history. One of the most popular theorists—especially in Europe—was Sigmund Freud. While Bowlby admired what Freud had accomplished, he had serious doubts about Freudian methodology and its emphasis on unconscious sexual desires between a child and their parent (Bowlby, 1988). Ethology was based on objective observations of animal behavior, which Bowlby thought was a more scientific approach.

To start, Bowlby read research on imprinting patterns in ducklings and goslings (baby geese). He noted that these baby birds instinctively attached themselves to a caregiver almost immediately. Importantly, however, in these species the babies *feed themselves*. Bowlby noted, then, that imprinting was not necessarily based on access to milk; the bond appeared to form for other, psychological reasons.

Bowlby then learned about Harlow's famous experiments with baby monkeys (this research is described thoroughly in Chapter 6). As a brief introduction for now, Harlow raised baby monkeys with two "false" mothers, one that was warm and soft and one that was hard but provided milk. When the babies were upset, they almost always ran to the warm, soft, comforting "mother." Again, Bowlby thought the evidence showed that attachment isn't just about access to food or survival. There appeared to be an emotional, psychological element to the bonding seen in a variety of animal species. He was ready to take the next step in his research, to explore how human infants bonded—and to do that, he needed to add someone else to his research team.

Mary Ainsworth and the Strange Situation

Mary Ainsworth started working with Bowlby right around 1950. One of their first research questions was to explore how infants respond to **maternal deprivation**, or temporary separation from a primary caregiver. Motivated by the boarding schools, orphanages, and evacuations during World War II, Bowlby and Ainsworth were interested in how babies would react when they were temporarily left alone, without their primary caregiver. They had observed that maternal deprivation often led children to develop a hardness or emotional anxiety that led to avoidance of attachment later (Bowlby, 1988). Note that during this time in history, the primary caregivers of infants were almost always their mothers—so the infant/mother bond was the focus of the research team.

Ainsworth created a famous laboratory procedure called the **strange situation**. In this case, "strange" simply means novel or unfamiliar (not weird). The situation was a clean, welcoming room set up with toys for an infant to play with. Mothers and infants were invited to the study for observation, one at a time. Over 20 minutes, Bowlby, Ainsworth, and other researchers observed both the mother and baby while eight steps occurred (see Table 3.1; Bretherton, 1992). Most importantly, the researchers watched what happened when the mother left the room for a few minutes, and again when she returned. How did the baby react? Were they upset, crying, and searching for her? Would they happily play with the toys? Once the mother returned, how did the baby react—and was the mother responsive to the baby's needs?

TABLE 3.1 ● Eight Steps in Ainsworth's "Strange Situation" Paradigm	
Step 1	Mother and baby are shown the room with toys; they are left alone to play together.
Step 2	A stranger enters and talks with the mother for a few minutes.
Step 3	The stranger begins to play with the baby.
Step 4	The mother leaves the room.
Step 5	The mother returns and the stranger leaves.
Step 6	The mother leaves again; this time the baby is alone (but observed constantly through a window, for safety).
Step 7	The stranger returns.
Step 8	The mother returns.

In Ainsworth's "strange situation," procedural steps are taken to see how an infant reacts to its mother leaving, then returning.

Source: Bretherton (1992).

Using this scientific procedure, the research team was able to observe how both the infants and their mothers responded to each step in the study. Interesting patterns started to emerge, and they seemed to align with patterns that Bowlby had seen in his earlier work before and during the war, when working with troubled children. The researchers identified three frequent patterns.

Three Attachment Styles

Using both the strange situation and, sometimes, observing the same children and mothers in their own homes, Bowlby and Ainsworth noticed that most infants displayed one of three patterns, which they eventually called **attachment styles**. A summary of the three styles and their different behaviors is shown in Table 3.2.

Secure Attachment

Most of the babies showed **secure attachment**. Secure babies explored their environment freely and happily, but with consistent checks to make sure that their mother was present, observant, and responsive. They were upset when she initially left the room but seemed to recover quickly, presumably because they knew she wouldn't be gone long. When their mother returned, they were greeted warmly (Bowlby, 1988). Later studies by Ainsworth showed that mothers of secure infants are more sensitive, more prompt, and more appropriately responsive to signals from their babies (Bell & Ainsworth, 1972; Blehar, Lieberman, & Ainsworth, 1977). More responsiveness from mothers led to babies with less crying and more behaviors that indicated confidence and self-esteem.

Importantly, Ainsworth believed that for a healthy and secure attachment style to develop, infants had to think of their mothers as a **secure base** (Ainsworth, 1967; Schaffer & Emerson, 1964). Think of "secure base" like home base in childhood games of tag, or even in baseball or softball. It's where you want to be, but you don't want

TABLE 3.2 ● Three Different Attachment Styles					
Attachment Style	Parents Were . . .	Level of Anxiety When Parent Leaves	Explore the Strange Situation Room?	Level of Adult Self-Esteem	Tendency to Be Jealous of Romantic Partners
Secure	Consistently good	Moderate	Yes	High	Low
Anxious/ ambivalent	Inconsistent	High	No	Low	High
Avoidant	Consistently bad	Low	Yes	Low	Low

Many researchers break attachment into three different types or styles.

to always stay there. Secure babies left their mothers to explore the world but knew that they would always have a supportive, welcoming place to return. Thus, a secure attachment style results in infants who feel sure enough about their mothers that they aren't overly clingy; they show independence and exploration, knowing they can always come back to their mothers if needed.

Insecure Attachment: Anxious–Ambivalent and Avoidant

Other, less happy patterns also emerged, which Bowlby and Ainsworth called **insecure attachment** styles. There are two kinds of insecure attachment in the original version of attachment theory.

The first is **anxious-ambivalent attachment**. Here, when their mother leaves the room, babies explore the environment little and are, instead, constantly worried about their mother's whereabouts (Bowlby, 1988). They cry excessively when their mother leaves, seeming desperate for her return—but when she does return, they are not sure how to reunite correctly. They appear to be both anxious about their mother's love and attention and ambivalent about how to get it, sometimes even hitting or kicking her away with anger (Bretherton, 1992).

Anxious-ambivalent attachments in babies are caused by parents who are inconsistent in their responsiveness. Sometimes they are attentive and loving—and at other times, they are distracted or even seem annoyed by their baby's needs. Bowlby (1988) summarized anxious-ambivalent children in this way:

> The individual is uncertain whether his [or her] parent will be available or responsive or helpful when called upon. Because of this uncertainty he or she is always prone to separation anxiety, tends to be clinging, and is anxious about exploring the world. This pattern, in which conflict is evident, is promoted by a parent being available and helpful on some occasions but not on others, and by separations and . . . by threats of abandonment used as a means of control. (p. 124)

The second type of insecure attachment is even more troubling: **avoidant attachment**. This time, babies display behaviors that imply they have more or less given up on having a bond with their mothers (Bowlby, 1988). These babies apparently have learned not only that their mothers are going to largely ignore them, but that any attempts for loving attention will be met with annoyance or anger. Over time, a baby with an unresponsive or even abusive primary caregiver "attempts to live his [or her] life without the love and support of others, [and] he or she tries to become emotionally self-sufficient" (Bowlby, 1988, p. 124). In the strange situation, avoidant babies won't appear to be upset when their mother leaves and won't seek her attention when she returns. These babies have learned to not even try.

Based on their many studies over the years, Bowlby, Ainsworth, and other members of their research team concluded that babies will form these attachment styles by the end of their first year of life (Bowlby, 1988). Remember, too, that Bowlby believed that once the pattern has been learned in this first relationship, it will affect all of one's future relationships, at least to some degree. He noted how important, then, a baby's first relationship is and the great responsibility that parents take on:

> For those who have children but fail to rear them to be healthy, happy, and self-reliant the penalties in anxiety, frustration, friction, and perhaps shame or guilt, may be severe. Engaging in parenthood therefore is playing for high stakes. (Bowlby, 1988, p. 1)

Attachment theory was not popular right off the bat. In fact, when Bowlby presented his emerging theory at the British Psychoanalytical Society, it was extremely controversial. One of his colleagues even published an attack on attachment theory and stated that it made "no contribution" to our understanding of human social relationships (see Bretherton, 1992, p. 763). Despite these early doubts, the field of psychology has almost completely changed its mind, with attachment theory being perhaps the most popular explanation of how early relationships affect later ones. Advances in the theory, approaches to measurement, and application of attachment theory to our understanding of adult romantic relationships are the topics for the remainder of this chapter.

How Is Attachment Theory Measured and Applied to Adult Relationships?

Remember that Bowlby (1988) believed that attachments were essential to life "from the cradle to the grave" (p. 82). A key principle in the theory is that our first relationship establishes an implicit or instinctive template. This template is our "attachment style," or the general foundation we use when interacting with others. Bowlby wrote that our attachment styles "tend to persist relatively unmodified at an unconscious level" (p. 82).

Do the effects of infancy really persist into adulthood? Do adults display different, reliable attachment styles that explain their behaviors? Does research support Bowlby's ideas? This section of the chapter reviews research on how attachment theory has been applied to adult relationships, as well as different approaches to measuring attachment styles in children and adults.

CHECK YOUR UNDERSTANDING

3.1   What historical event seems to have influenced and inspired John Bowlby's development of attachment theory?

    a. The assassination of Archduke Ferdinand

    b. The bombing of London during World War II

    c. The Spanish Civil War

    d. The kidnapping of Charles Lindbergh's son

3.2   Mary Ainsworth developed a scientific procedure in which infants and their mothers interact in a room with toys, then the baby is observed as the mother leaves and returns. What is the name for this procedure?

    a. The strange situation

    b. The play paradigm

    c. The experimental evacuation

    d. The parenting procedure

3.3   Josh is an 8-month-old baby. When Josh sees their mother leave the room, they start to scream and cry. When she returns, however, Josh turns away from her and starts to crawl away. Which attachment style most closely matches Josh's behavior?

    a. Anxious-ambivalent attachment

    b. Secure attachment

    c. Avoidant attachment

    d. Blitz attachment

APPLICATION ACTIVITY

Identify three fictional characters, from movies, TV, or books, who had troubled early childhoods involving parents who were abusive, who died, or who were separated from the main character for some reason. Analyze how these early childhood events seem to have affected the character's personality, outlook on life, and relationships later (as the character ages).

CRITICAL THINKING

- John Bowlby was inspired to develop attachment theory after witnessing how both World War I and II affected children. Can you think of at least two other theories from psychology that were influenced by world events? In addition, how do you think modern psychologists are influenced by what's happening in the world right now?

- When Bowlby first started speaking and publishing his ideas about attachment theory, many other psychologists responded with skepticism. It took years for the theory to become popular. What is your own opinion of attachment theory's basic ideas about how early relationships—even in infancy—affect us? Identify at least two things you like about attachment theory (or ways that you think it is useful) and at least two things you question or find troubling about attachment theory.

Attachment Styles in Adult Relationships

The main purpose of this book is to review scientific research that provides insight into adult intimate relationships. So, an important question is how well attachment theory and different attachment styles can help us understand people as they enter, maintain, and leave dating and long-term relationships with partners. In other words, studies have been done on **romantic attachment**, or our psychological bonds with intimate romantic partners in adolescence and adulthood.

Right away, you should know that research can easily classify most adults as fitting into one of the original attachment styles described earlier. About half of college students and other adults can be classified as fitting into a secure style, about a quarter (25%) are avoidant, and the remainder (19%) are anxious-ambivalent (Bartholomew, 1990). Similar percentages are found in most studies (e.g., Kobak & Sceery, 1988; Mikulincer, Florian, & Tolmacz, 1990; Pistole, 1989; van Ijzendoorn & Kroonenberg, 1988). Infants with these styles had different reactions to their caregivers leaving and returning. How do attachment styles lead to interesting patterns in adult relationships?

Attachment Outcomes

A long list of different kinds of outcomes have been studied in terms of attachment within adult relationships, including how different styles affect personality, well-being, gender differences, communication, conflict, relationship quality and stability, sexual satisfaction, and more (Feeney & Noller, 1996). Let's look at a few of these interesting studies.

Perhaps the two people who have done the most well-known research on adult romantic attachment are Cindy Hazan and Phillip Shaver. Their work goes back to 1987 (Hazan & Shaver, 1987), when they found several important differences based on attachment style. In their research, secure adults are most likely to be relaxed around other people and will usually describe their intimate relationships as happy and full of trust. Anxious-ambivalent adults report relationships full of emotional variation, going up and down all the time due to jealousy, sexual passion, obsessive distraction, distrust, and a desire to feel closer to their partners. Finally, avoidant people show just what we'd expect: They report a fear of closeness or feeling dependent on others, remember their parents as cold and distant, and generally seem cautious about bonding to anyone.

Do adults with different attachment styles really have different social interaction patterns? To answer this question, one study asked 125 people to complete daily "social interaction diaries" for a week (Tidwell, Reis, & Shaver, 1996). One-third of the participants were identified as having each of the major attachment styles (secure, avoidant, and anxious-ambivalent). Over the week of the study, each person filled out a form describing every important social interaction they had each day. The form asked questions about how intimate each interaction was, how supportive it felt to the participant, which person was more in control, and a range of possible feelings afterward, such as encouraged, appreciated, aroused, jealous, guilty, and distant (see Figure 3.1 for the full list of feelings).

The results showed three major patterns, all of which fit with what you might predict from attachment theory. First, secure people were most likely to have different patterns of answers on the form for interactions with their current partner compared to anyone else. This might mean that secure people treat their partners differently or that they choose to be with people who make them feel particularly good. Second, avoidant participants reported both lower levels of intimacy and positive emotions, and higher levels of negative emotions, after opposite-sex social interactions (compared to secure or anxious-ambivalent people). The authors thought this might mean that avoidant people engage in social situations in ways that minimize closeness with others. Finally, anxious-ambivalent people had the most variation in experiences from one interaction to the next. This type of up-and-down rollercoaster of emotions might have been predicted for anxious-ambivalent people, as they are predicted to be unsure of how to feel about themselves and others.

Another diary study was specifically interested in sexual interactions. Does attachment style predict better or worse sex? In this study (Birnbaum, Reis, Mikulincer, Gillath, & Orpaz, 2006), 500 people ranging in age from 17 to 48 years filled out a variety of self-report surveys measuring their sexual experiences. Items included various aspects of sex, including feelings of love, worry about disappointing the other

FIGURE 3.1 ● List of Potential Reactions From Social Interactions

During the interaction (or immediately after it), how much did you feel . . .

```
happy/encouraged.....................not at all  1  2  3  4  5  6  7  a great deal
sad/disappointed.....................not at all  1  2  3  4  5  6  7  a great deal
frustrated/irritated................not at all  1  2  3  4  5  6  7  a great deal
rejected/left out...................not at all  1  2  3  4  5  6  7  a great deal
comfortable/relaxed.................not at all  1  2  3  4  5  6  7  a great deal
needed/appreciated..................not at all  1  2  3  4  5  6  7  a great deal
bored/distant.......................not at all  1  2  3  4  5  6  7  a great deal
caring/warm.........................not at all  1  2  3  4  5  6  7  a great deal
hurt/treated badly..................not at all  1  2  3  4  5  6  7  a great deal
worried/anxious.....................not at all  1  2  3  4  5  6  7  a great deal
stimulated/invigorated..............not at all  1  2  3  4  5  6  7  a great deal
tense/ill at ease...................not at all  1  2  3  4  5  6  7  a great deal
successful/productive...............not at all  1  2  3  4  5  6  7  a great deal
sexually interested/aroused.........not at all  1  2  3  4  5  6  7  a great deal
envious/jealous.....................not at all  1  2  3  4  5  6  7  a great deal
accepted/like you belonged..........not at all  1  2  3  4  5  6  7  a great deal
embarrassed/self-conscious..........not at all  1  2  3  4  5  6  7  a great deal
disgusted/disapproving..............not at all  1  2  3  4  5  6  7  a great deal
ashamed/guilty......................not at all  1  2  3  4  5  6  7  a great deal
imposed upon/intruded upon..........not at all  1  2  3  4  5  6  7  a great deal
tired/low in energy.................not at all  1  2  3  4  5  6  7  a great deal
```

Source: Tidwell, M. C. O., Reis, H. T., & Shaver, P. R. (1996). Attachment, attractiveness, and social interaction: A diary study. *Journal of Personality and Social Psychology, 71*(4), 729-745, reprinted with permission.

person, and perceptions of physical "ecstasy" during sex. This time, attachment was measured using continuous self-report scales that resulted in separate scores for how much each person felt attachment anxiety or attachment avoidance (we'll talk more about measuring attachment in the next section). That meant that the results could be correlations. See Table 3.3 for some of the researchers' results.

The top four rows of Table 3.3 show that the more anxiety or avoidance people in this study felt, the more negative parts of their sexual experience were. Being insecure in either way was associated with estrangement, negative feelings, disappointment, and distraction. The bottom half of the table shows positive sexual experiences and highlights some interesting differences in anxious-ambivalent people compared to avoidant people. Avoidance was associated with significantly less love, lower feelings of sexual pleasure, and less focus on the other person's feelings. Being avoidant also meant that people didn't particularly care if their partner was sexually involved—although anxious-ambivalent people did care about this, very much. One summary of this study is that secure people seem to have the most satisfying sex because they're not distracted and they feel stronger bonds with their sexual partners.

What about conflict resolution? When couples fight, does attachment style predict different strategies? College students in one study (Pistole, 1989) completed a survey that measured three different approaches to conflict: (a) *compromising*, or trying to find a middle ground; (b) *obliging*, or just giving in to the other person's preferences; and (c) *integrating*, which is working together until a mutual solution is found. Compromising and integrating were the strategies most reported by secure people and least reported by avoidant people. As you probably would have guessed, anxious-ambivalent people were most likely to say that they simply gave in or obliged their

TABLE 3.3 ● Correlations Between Attachment Feelings and Sexual Experiences

	Anxiety	Avoidance
Sense of estrangement	.26	.32
Negative feelings	.32	.24
Disappointment	.30	.24
Distracting thoughts	.26	.28
Feel loved by partner	−.13	−.15
Feelings of pleasure	−.06	−.16
Focus on partner's feelings	.11	−.16
Love toward partner	−.07	−.27
Desire for partner involvement	.24	−.02

Shaded boxes indicate that the correlation is statistically significant at a level of $p < .01$.

partner's wishes during conflicts, probably because they are constantly worried about being loved and accepted.

Many other studies have found results that align with what attachment theory would likely predict, based on the three-style model originally suggested by Bowlby and Ainsworth. You might be particularly interested in studies done with college students. Here are just a few interesting findings about your peers in studies done within the last 10 years:

- Students with a secure style are more likely to send regular texts to a partner, whereas avoidant students are more likely to send "sext" messages (texts with sexual content or illicit photos; Drouin & Landgraff, 2012).

- Anxious-ambivalent students are more likely to jealously check on their partner's Facebook messages (Marshall, Bejanyan, Di Castro, & Lee, 2013).

- Secure people are less likely to accept violence or abuse in their relationships (McDermott & Lopez, 2013) and are more likely to display emotional sensitivity and social skills (Dereli & Karakuş, 2011).

- In gay couples, anxious-ambivalent men are less likely to require a partner to use a condom during anal sex (Starks, Castro, Castiblanco, & Millar, 2017).

For a fun side note on how attachment styles can be used to understand early love interests in the *Harry Potter* series, see the "Relationships and Popular Culture" feature. While the three-style model has guided hundreds of studies on child and adult attachment, a more modern approach suggests there might actually be *four* attachment styles. The next section explains this idea.

RELATIONSHIPS AND POPULAR CULTURE

Attachment Styles in Harry Potter

One of the best-selling book and movie franchises in history is the *Harry Potter* series, which follows the lives of several young wizards who fight evil (Rowling, 1997, 1998, 1999, 2000, 2003, 2005, 2007). Luckily for our purposes, the three main characters demonstrate the three major attachment styles first proposed by attachment theory (Bowlby, 1973, 1988).

Hermione Granger is a perfect example of the secure attachment style. Born of parents who are supportive without being suffocating, people with a secure attachment style are confident, feel free to express their emotions, and are happy to trust others. Although we don't see Hermione's parents much in the series, readers learn that they trust their daughter and are completely supportive, but they also show concern when she's in danger. Hermione thus projects this style onto her own teenage experiments in love. When Ron Weasley repeatedly shows that he's too scared to ask her out, she promptly moves on to someone else (Viktor Krum). She's jealous when Ron starts dating a fellow classmate, but Hermione waits patiently for him to realize that she's a better choice. In short, her self-esteem and her trust in both others and herself show that she's secure, which is considered the healthiest attachment style.

(Continued)

(Continued)

Her object of affection, Ron Weasley, is certainly not secure—he's what we call anxious-ambivalent. The hallmark of parents who produce anxious-ambivalent children is inconsistency. The Weasleys certainly love their seven children, but they are either screaming at them with magical messages or simply distracted and, thus, basically absent. This leads to children who are unsure of where they stand in relationships, always yearning for love but never confident that they'll actually get it. Ron shows this attachment style in his desire for Hermione and in his doubt that she'll return the interest. Instead, he dates "safe" girls who are less challenging. Ron's relationship personality becomes one of jealousy, clinginess, and, above all, insecurity.

Finally, Harry Potter displays what can be argued as the least healthy attachment style: avoidant. Harry's birth parents were certainly loving, but he never really knew them. His adoptive parents were cruel and abusive. This leads to Harry's avoidant style. He pushes everyone else away, never believing relationships will bring him any comfort. Harry prefers to do everything by himself, something he proves each and every time he has to face a challenge. In relationships, he avoids admitting that he likes anyone; when he can no longer deny it, his response is to do nothing. For both of his main love interests, Harry sits back and waits for them to make the first move. While the series has a happy ending for all of the main characters, their differences in social relationships make for an exciting story.

Attachment Updated: A Four-Category Model

Science evolves as we learn more and more about a given theory. While the three-category model of secure, anxious-ambivalent, and avoidant attachment is still popular, some researchers believe that a four-category model is even more useful. Secure attachment is consistent across both models; it's considered the healthiest attachment style. But what about insecure attachment?

The four-category model (Bartholomew, 1990; Bartholomew & Horowitz, 1991) splits insecure attachment into three groups instead of two. This split is based on what happens, psychologically, when people realize that their relationships aren't going well. When that happens, two different attributions could be made—someone could decide the problem is themselves (I'm not worthy of being loved) or the problem is other people (they're not reliable or trustworthy). Which attribution is made determines which type of insecurity people feel. This results in a matrix of four attachment styles, as shown in Figure 3.2. The four-category model includes secure attachment, **dismissing attachment**, **preoccupied attachment**, and **fearful attachment**.

As you can see, there are two major variables at play in this update to attachment theory: (1) your view of self (positive or negative) and (2) your view of others (positive or negative). A positive view of self is like high self-esteem; it means you feel worthy of being loved and believe you would make a good relationship partner. A positive view of others means that you find other people trustworthy in general and seek out healthy relationships. The combination of both views being positive is secure. If one or both views is negative, you get one of the three types of insecure attachment style.

When the researchers tested the updated attachment model with college students, they found the following patterns (Bartholomew & Horowitz, 1991):

- Secure people were most likely to have high levels of intimacy in both romantic relationships and friendships; they also showed self-confidence,

FIGURE 3.2 ● A Four-Category Model of Attachment		
	View of Self	
	Positive	Negative
View of Others Positive	**Secure** (comfortable with intimacy)	**Preoccupied** (anxious and jealous)
Negative	**Dismissing** (narcissistic, avoids long-term intimacy)	**Fearful** (avoids social connections in general)

In this model, attachment styles are split into four types based on positive versus negative views of the self and of other people.

warmth, and balance in their relationships. This style matches the one from the earlier model with only three styles.

- Dismissing people showed the highest levels of self-confidence, but they also showed very low levels of emotional expressiveness, empathy, and warmth toward others. They were less likely to rely on others in times of need and were less likely to share personal information with other people.

- Preoccupied people were the opposite of dismissing in almost every variable; they showed particularly low self-confidence but particularly high levels of personal self-disclosure, emotional expressiveness (such as frequent crying), and excessive caregiving behaviors.

- Finally, fearful people were very low on self-disclosures, intimacy, level of relationship involvement, reliance on others, and self-confidence. In general, they did not put much effort into relationships or expect others to do so.

Importantly for attachment theory, this study also showed moderate correlations between the participants' attachment both to family members and to peers. Bowlby originally hypothesized that attachment styles would be consistent across relationships—and these data (Bartholomew & Horowitz, 1991) support that hypothesis. Both the three-category and four-category models remain popular in research on attachment theory, but they are measured in slightly different ways.

Measuring Attachment Styles

You already know how attachment style is traditionally measured in infants: Observations are made in the "strange situation." Infants obviously can't fill out surveys or answer interview questions, so observational data are the only option. But there are many additional methods that people interested in the theory have developed. First we'll cover measurement approaches for children and adolescents, then we'll discuss how researchers measure attachment styles in adults.

In Children and Adolescents

Several variations of the strange situation have been developed over the years to measure attachment in children, but we won't spend a lot of time on those because you already know the basics of that method. We will cover two very different options so you can see some of the other potential procedures. These options were developed so that researchers could avoid the distress that is inevitably caused when a mother or father leaves a child alone in the lab setup (Target, Fonagy, & Shmueli-Goetz, 2003).

The first alternative to observing children in a strange situation (or in their own home) is to ask children questions they can easily understand. The **child attachment interview** (CAI) does this with questions specifically about attachment feelings and behaviors. The CAI was developed with British children between 7 and 12 years old. Children are asked the questions in Table 3.4, and their answers are coded by people trained in the system. Classification into different attachment styles is based on the children's expressed anger with each parent, emotional dismissal, apparent feelings of security, and so on.

Another approach is the use of various **projective tests**. A projective test is one that presents a participant with an ambiguous image or object that they interpret. The meaning, emotions, or conclusions made by the person about the vague, ambiguous image or object are thought to tell us something about the person's state of mind. The most famous projective test is the Rorschach inkblots.

TABLE 3.4 ● Questions in the Child Attachment Interview

1. Who is in your family? (lives with you in your house)
2. Tell me three words that describe yourself. (examples)
3. Can you tell me three words that describe what it's like to be with your mum? (examples)
4. What happens when mum gets upset with you?
5. Can you tell me three words that describe what it's like to be with your dad? (examples)
6. What happens when dad gets upset with you?
7. Can you tell me about a time when you were upset and wanted help?
8. What happens when you're ill?
9. What happens when you hurt yourself?
10. Has anyone close to you ever died?
11. Is there anyone that you cared about who isn't around anymore?
12. Have you ever been away from your parents for the night or for longer than a day?
13. Do your parents sometimes argue? Can you tell me about a time when that happened?
14. In what ways do you want/not want to be like your mum/dad?

The first projective test used specifically for attachment was created by Hansburg (1972) and modified by John Bowlby himself (Klagsbrun & Bowlby, 1976). They developed 12 photographs showing boys (six photos) or girls (six photos) in the following six situations:

- Parents going out for the evening, leaving their child at home

- Mother (or father) going away for the weekend, leaving child with aunt (or uncle)

- Child's first day of school as they part from the parent

- Parents going away for 2 weeks and giving the child an attractive toy

- Parents and child in a park; parents tell child to play alone so they can talk without the child

- Opposite-sex parent tucks child into bed and leaves the room

Girl participants are shown mostly photos of a girl and her mother, while boys are shown mostly photos of a boy and his father. Children are tested one at a time. They are shown each photo and told what is happening by the researcher. For each photo, the child is asked, "How does the little boy/girl in the picture feel?" and "What does the little boy/girl do?" The original photos used by Klagsbrun and Bowlby are shown in Table 3.5. Researchers record each child's responses and look for themes or patterns in the answers that indicate loneliness, sadness, rejection, withdrawal, fear, and other signs of insecure attachment.

Other people have developed additional projective approaches to measuring attachment styles in children. For example, one assessment asks children to play with dolls as they encounter preset stories, including parents leaving and a monster in their bedroom (Bretherton, Ridgeway, & Cassidy, 1990). What the children do with the dolls in each scenario is interpreted by researchers. Another idea is to ask children to draw pictures that can be interpreted later (Kaplan & Main, 1986). While these procedures are intriguing and creative, projective tests are generally somewhat unreliable. The researchers can be biased in how they interpret answers, and children may not be willing to express their inner doubts and fears. Fortunately, tests of attachment for adults are much more straightforward.

In Adults

In general, measuring attachment in adults is pretty simple: We just ask people to tell us about themselves and their relationship behaviors. The **adult attachment interview** (AAI; Main, Kaplan, & Cassidy, 1985; see Crowell, Fraley, & Shaver, 2008) is a semi-structured interview in which adults are asked about their childhood relationship experiences. Questions cover topics like experiences of loss through injury, separation, or conflict, as well as their parents' behaviors in these situations. Scoring is based on the participant's memories, language, and ability to analyze what happened in a meaningful way (for example, denial versus honest discussion).

TABLE 3.5 ● Projective Photographs Used to Measure Attachment

	Photos for Boys	Photos for Girls
Parents go out for the evening		
Child is left with aunt or uncle		
First day of school		

	Photos for Boys	Photos for Girls
Parents give toy before leaving		
Child and parents in park		
Opposite-sex parent tucks child into bed		

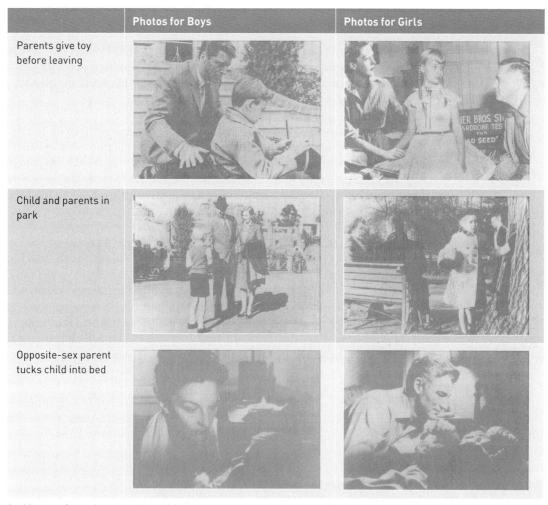

In this test of attachment style, children are asked to respond to photos of various situations.

Source: Klagsbrun, M., & Bowlby, J. (1976). Responses to separation from parents: A clinical test for young children. *British Journal of Projective Psychology & Personality Study, 21,* 7-27.

Probably the most common way to measure attachment style is through self-report surveys. You already know the advantages and disadvantages to self-report measures (see Chapter 2), so we won't go through that again now. Instead, it's good for you to be aware of different survey options. Some studies offer participants a *single* question that asks them to pick a description that sounds the most like themselves. For example, which of the paragraphs below most sounds like you?

- Option 1: I find it relatively easy to get close to others and am comfortable depending on them and having them depend on me. I don't often worry about being abandoned or about someone getting too close to me.

- Option 2: I am somewhat uncomfortable being close to others; I find it difficult to trust them completely, difficult to allow myself to depend on them. I am nervous when anyone gets too close, and often, love partners want me to be more intimate than I feel comfortable being.

- Option 3: I find that others are reluctant to get as close as I would like. I often worry that my partner doesn't really love me or won't want to stay with me. I want to merge completely with another person, and this desire sometimes scares people away.

By now you should be able to tell which attachment style goes with which description. As you probably already figured out, option 1 is secure, option 2 is avoidant, and option 3 is anxious-ambivalent (Hazan & Shaver, 1987). A similar single-item question has been developed for people who want to use the four-category model of attachment instead (see Table 3.6). This type of item is easy and quick, and it has been found to be a pretty good way to measure attachment styles if you want to put people into different categories.

But you might also remember a discussion we had in Chapter 1 about how we can measure variables in either "categorical" ways or "continuous" ways. Recall from our discussion of Sternberg's theory that the three components to love in his model could be thought of as present/absent (categorical) or as varying along *degrees* of amount (more or less of each component). Many researchers favor the continuous approach to measuring variables because it allows for more flexibility and nuance. For example, what if someone is *mostly* secure but just a little bit avoidant? Or what if someone is just on the edge between avoidant and anxious-ambivalent? A simple categorical label might cover up the difference between someone who is *extremely* avoidant compared to someone who is just a *little* avoidant.

So, there are other options for measuring attachment that result in continuous scores, or scores that can range along different dimensions of attachment. This allows

TABLE 3.6 ● Self-Report Descriptions for Four Attachment Styles	
Which of these descriptions best fits you?	
Secure	It is easy for me to become emotionally close to others. I am comfortable depending on others and having others depend on me. I don't worry about being alone or having others not accept me.
Dismissing	I am comfortable without close emotional relationships. It is very important to me to feel independent and self-sufficient, and I prefer not to depend on others or have others depend on me.
Preoccupied	I want to be completely emotionally intimate with others, but I often find that others are reluctant to get as close as I would like. I am uncomfortable being without close relationships, but I sometimes worry that others don't value me as much as I value them.
Fearful	I am uncomfortable getting close to others. I want emotionally close relationships, but I find it difficult to trust others completely or to depend on them. I worry that I will be hurt if I allow myself to become too close to others.

Participants can be asked to choose which description sounds the most like them.

researchers to calculate correlations between degree of avoidance and/or anxiety to a wide range of other important relationship variables that are measured in a continuous way, such as level of attraction, degree of satisfaction, perceived likelihood of breakup, amount of jealousy, and so on. To test yourself on one of the most popular continuous self-report measures of attachment, see the "What's My Score?" feature.

WHAT'S MY SCORE?

Measuring Attachment Style on a Continuous Scale: The Experiences in Close Relationships Scale (ECR-S)

Instructions: As you read each statement, write a number next to the item to indicate how much you agree with it, using this scale:

1	2	3	4	5	6	7
Strongly disagree			Neutral			Strongly agree

Anxiety Items

_____ 1. I worry that romantic partners won't care about me as much as I care about them.

_____ 2. My desire to be close sometimes scares people away.

_____ 3. I need a lot of reassurance that I am loved by my partner.

_____ 4. I find that my partner(s) don't want to get as close as I would like.

_____ 5. I get frustrated when romantic partners are not available when I need them.

_____ 6. I often worry about being abandoned.

Avoidance Items

_____ 7. I want to get close to my partner, but I keep pulling back.

Scoring: The more you *disagree* with these sentences, the more secure you are. In other words, add up your answers for items 1 to 6. The higher your score (the range is from 6 to 42), the more anxious-ambivalent you are. Also add up your score for items 7 to 12; again, higher scores indicate a greater degree of avoidance. Some of the items have been modified from the original scale to make them easier for you to score.

_____ 8. I am nervous when partners get too close to me.

_____ 9. I try to avoid getting too close to my partner.

_____ 10. I don't usually discuss my problems and concerns with my partner.

_____ 11. I do not turn to my partner in times of need.

_____ 12. I do not rely on my partner for things like comfort and reassurance.

Sources: Brennan, Clark, and Shaver (1998); updated by Wei, Russell, Mallinckrodt, and Vogel (2007).

Critical Thinking: Which is a better research approach for people who want to use self-report measures in attachment research: a categorical system or a continuous system?

(Continued)

(Continued)

List one advantage and one disadvantage to each approach. Finally, for either approach, will people really be honest with themselves (and with the researchers) when answering these questions? Are people consciously aware of their own attachment style and behaviors?

CHECK YOUR UNDERSTANDING

3.4 In the research study on attachment style and sexual experiences (Birnbaum et al., 2006), which of the experiences below was felt significantly less by avoidant people compared to anxious-avoidant people?

  a. Sense of estrangement
  b. Disappointment
  c. Desire for partner involvement
  d. Love toward partner

3.5 In the four-category model of attachment produced by Bartholomew and Horowitz (1991), which attachment style occurs in people who have both a negative view of self and a negative view of others?

  a. Preoccupied
  b. Secure
  c. Dismissing
  d. Fearful

3.6 Some measures of attachment style in children give them an ambiguous photograph, image, or doll and then see how the children interpret these objects. This type of test, in general, is called a(n):

  a. Abstraction test
  b. Interpretational test
  c. Defensive test
  d. Projective test

APPLICATION ACTIVITY

Go to a park, public pool, shopping center, or other location where you will be able to watch young children with their parents through naturalistic observation. Come up with a coding scheme for child and adult behaviors that are related to attachment behaviors. Then you and a friend or fellow student try to identify the attachment style of three to five children you can both see for several minutes. Afterward, compare your results with those of your companion. Did you agree or disagree? What methodological advantages or disadvantages were at work in this exercise?

CRITICAL THINKING

- Which is more appealing to you, the three-category or four-category model of attachment? Explain why you favor one or the other and why you think this model is more useful or more accurate.

- Measurement of attachment in infants and children is usually done through either observation (such as the strange situation) or projective tests (such as interpreting photographs or playing with dolls in certain scenarios). However, both of these approaches are potentially open to experimenter error. For example, experimenters might be biased

in their interpretations or observations based on stereotypes that certain types of children are more likely to be secure versus insecure. How can experimenters, judges, and coders remain objective?

- Do you think researchers should use a categorical system of attachment—labeling people as one of three or four styles and then putting people into groups—or a continuous system, where each person can be measured on the *extent* to which they exhibit different attachment patterns? Why do you favor that approach?

Answers to the Check Your Understanding Questions

3.4 d, 3.5 d, and 3.6 d.

What Are Important Questions For and About Attachment Theory?

From reading this chapter so far, you already know quite a bit about attachment theory! You know how it was started, how it applies to infants, and how researchers have expanded attachment theory to explain and predict several interesting outcomes in adult romantic relationships. The final section of this chapter addresses just a few more aspects of the theory and what's happened with it over the past 80 years. Students just like you tend to ask the same questions year after year as they learn about these ideas—so let's end this chapter by trying to answer some frequently asked questions. But first, check out the "Research Deep Dive" feature on the next page to read about a study that asked if attachment translates into eating behavior.

Are There Cross-Cultural Differences in Attachment?

From the very beginning, attachment researchers have been interested in whether culture affects bonding with other people, starting from infancy. In fact, after Ainsworth and Bowlby worked together for a few years in England, Ainsworth started an observational, longitudinal research project studying infant-mother interactions in Uganda (see Bretherton, 1992). She carefully observed 26 families with babies younger than 24 months old, watching them for 2 hours per visit every 2 weeks over a total of 9 months. Her work generally validated attachment theory, and Ainsworth further

RESEARCH DEEP DIVE

Are Cookies a Comfort Food for Anxious Attachment?

In your life, few things influence your everyday experiences more than your romantic relationships. For this reason, research often explores how your relationship experiences spill over into other areas of your life. We've all heard of emotional eating, so it may be possible that feelings about your relationship may influence eating habits. In particular, researchers sought to explore how feelings about attachment influence snacking behavior (Wilkinson, Rowe, & Heath, 2013).

To test this potential link, the researchers wanted to be sure participants acted naturally, so they created a cover story (a fake purpose to the study that participants are told). In this case, participants thought they were giving opinions of snack food by answering a series of questions. To prepare, 21 college women who participated in the study could not eat before either of their two 1-hour sessions, each held a month apart. To make participants feel either secure or anxious attachment, participants read one of two relationship descriptions at each session, visualized it, then wrote about how one of their relationships matched the description (researchers made sure each participant had both types of relationships in the past). Researchers used a within-participants design where everyone did both tasks but they were counterbalanced such that half of the women completed the secure condition at the first session, while the other half responded to the anxious condition first. During the next session a month later, each participant did the second visualization.

Following the visualization exercise, rather than ask participants to self-report their eating habits (e.g., "How many cookies would you eat?"), researchers wanted to see firsthand what participants would actually do when given the chance to snack. They provided each participant with a bowl of chocolate chip cookies that they precisely weighed beforehand (500 g). The experimenter told the participant that she should eat as many pieces as necessary to give her assessment of the cookies, then left the room. Why would they leave the room? Doing so should further encourage natural behavior. How much would you eat with someone watching? Once the participant finished the task, the experimenter returned and later weighed the bowl to determine exactly how much the participant ate.

Researchers used a t-test to answer the key question of whether participants ate more when they were feeling secure or anxious. As hypothesized, participants ate more of the cookies when they thought about anxious attachment than when they thought about secure attachment. Interestingly, a follow-up analysis also found that within the secure condition only, women who were naturally more anxious ate more than women who were less anxiously attached.

There are a few things to note before forming any solid conclusions. First, the study only had 21 participants and included only women. These limitations can diminish the ability to generalize the results of this study to other women, men, or people who are not cisgender. The low sample size may also be a cause for concern. On the plus side, using a within-participants study design as done here increases the ability to find differences, because you're comparing your own behavior at two time points. In essence, you are your own control group, and who could be more similar to you than you? Finally, the size of the effect wasn't overwhelming. Those who visualized anxious attachment essentially ate 33 calories more than the other group; this is roughly the number of calories in 10 grapes. While these numbers aren't earth-shattering, the researchers got this effect after a short 10-minute writing task, which is fairly impressive given the limited exposure.

You could imagine that certain experiences in your everyday life—such as having your romantic advances rejected or experiencing a breakup—may serve as more powerful triggers for feeling anxiously attached and could possibly lead to even greater amounts of snacking over longer periods of time. Overall, this study shows that when women felt unsure or anxious about their relationships, they consumed more chocolate chip cookies. There might be something to "comfort food."

For more, read Wilkinson, L. L., Rowe, C. A., & Heath, H. G. (2013). Eating me up inside: Priming attachment security and anxiety, and their effects on snacking. *Journal of Social and Personal Relationships, 30*(6), 795–804.

developed the idea that **maternal sensitivity** predicted security in infants. She defined high maternal sensitivity as mothers who were highly perceptive about their baby's needs and quick to respond to them (Ainsworth, 1967).

Other people have examined attachment patterns in a wide variety of cultures around the world. One study found a surprising proportion of avoidant newborns in northern Germany (Grossmann, Grossmann, Spangler, Suess, & Unzner, 1985). Another discovered more ambivalent infants than expected in an Israeli Jewish kibbutz, which is a collective community based on religion and self-sufficient agriculture (Sagi, Lamb, Lewkowicz, Shoham, Dvir, & Estes, 1985). But it would be a mistake to automatically start to judge these communities or cultures as negative, just because of lower attachment security. The researchers in Germany suggested that the higher amount of avoidance might not be because of parental rejection, but instead the result of a cultural emphasis on independence and self-reliance. Similarly, the researchers in Israel thought that higher rates of ambivalence might simply be due to the isolated nature of the community and skepticism about the researchers themselves, who were outsiders and strangers. In other words, maybe the infants reacted negatively to the presence of the observers and displayed behaviors they wouldn't have normally shown (i.e., reactivity).

Other studies have examined cultures that emphasize attachment to more people than just a single, primary caregiver. For example, families in Tikopia (a small island in the Pacific Ocean) explicitly encourage infant attachment to a child's uncles on the mother's side of the family—or at least, they did so in 1936 when the study was conducted (Firth, 1936). A group of people called the Efe, who live in rainforests in Africa, tend to raise infants in a commune fashion, with all adult women caring for all infants in the group (Tronick, Winn, & Morelli, 1985). Several cultures in Africa have similar traditions, which may be the origin for the proverb "It takes a village to raise a child."

A few people have tried to compare many cross-cultural studies together to see if patterns emerge. When 32 studies that used the strange situation to classify attachment in infants in eight different countries were examined as a group, the results showed that secure attachment was the most common in seven out of eight cultures (i.e., Great Britain, the Netherlands, Sweden, Israel, Japan, China, and the United States; van Ijzendoorn & Kroonenberg, 1988). Importantly, though, these researchers pointed out that they found a wide variety of different attachment patterns *within* cultures, based on variables such as socioeconomic status or environmental stress. They concluded that these additional variables might be up to 15 times more important than culture when it comes to predicting patterns of attachment.

What About Attachment to Fathers?

Older books and articles about attachment refer to mothers as an infant's primary attachment figure—but what about fathers, or even other potential guardians such as grandparents? Keep in mind that Bowlby, Ainsworth, and others who started thinking about the theory were doing their research as far back as World War I and II, when gender roles were more traditional. Back then, the "primary caregiver" would usually be a stay-at-home mom.

But again, Bowlby anticipated this question and answered it. He noted that children can certainly bond with either parent, or others such as nannies, aunts and uncles, and so on. What matters is that the caregiver serves as a secure base on whom the child can rely in times of need. Other studies have confirmed that fathers are perfectly capable of being competent, loving attachment figures (see Belsky, Gilstrap, & Rovine, 1984; Bretherton, 2010; Lamb, 1978; Parke & Tinsley, 1987). One study followed children over 16 years and measured their attachment styles at infancy and again at ages 6, 10, and 16 (Grossmann, Grossmann, Fremmer-Bombik, Kindler, & Scheuerer-Englisch, 2002). They found that attachment in the children at every age was predicted by their father's degree of interpersonal sensitivity during play time, what Ainsworth probably would have called "paternal sensitivity," paralleling the work she did in Uganda with mothers.

How Does Attachment Theory Apply to Deployed Military Families?

Men and women in the military today are generally young, they are often married, and more than half have children under the age of 5 (Osofsky & Chartrand, 2013). At the same time, military deployments today occur more often and last longer than at any time since the 1970s. Young children with one or two deployed parents are likely to develop both behavioral and emotional problems, especially if their parents are displaying signs of stress or other mental health concerns (Chartrand, Frank, White, & Shope, 2008). With everything you now know about attachment theory, you might be wondering how people serving in the military can work to increase secure attachment in their children back home.

Two soldiers from the U.S. Air Force (both professors of pediatrics as well) published a list of steps that military parents can take to prepare the family for deployment and increase coping while the absence occurs (Osofsky & Chartrand, 2013). Their suggestions include the following:

- Keep routines consistent and predictable.

- Use technology (e.g., Skype or FaceTime) to stay connected in ways that allow children to both see and hear parents from a distance.

- Help children explicitly identify their feelings and talk about them.

- Listen to children's concerns and answer them in simple, age-appropriate language.

- Give children a meaningful object (e.g., a treasured stuffed animal given by the absent parent, or a military patch) that they can cling to.

These suggestions make sense, and they could be used for any families in which one parent or more is regularly gone for an extended period of time (such as business trips). At the same time, more research is needed to understand specific needs, such as in military families, so that service does not mean additional sacrifices to the family.

How Can Attachment Theory Be Used in Therapy?

You might also be wondering how attachment theory might be used in therapeutic or counseling settings. As you can imagine, this topic could take up an entire chapter— or even book—just by itself, so we'll cover just a few ideas here.

The use of attachment theory in therapy settings was the focus on Bowlby's final 10 years of life (Bowlby, 1988; Bretherton, 1992). He thought that therapy could focus on redesigning inadequate or harmful internal working models of the self or others, to create happier and healthier relationship dynamics. One problem he pointed out was **inverted parenting**. This occurs when an adult who had an unhappy childhood tries to make up for it by demanding that their own children love and support them, instead of the other way around (Bowlby, 1988). To an outsider, it looks like a parent is being overly indulgent or smothering a child with love, when in fact the parent is demanding constant attention and obedience from the child. Bowlby emphasized that the parent-child relationship should be consistent and stable, but that secure attachment means that the parent encourages autonomy and independent exploration of the world and other people.

Another interesting topic for therapeutic settings is how to help people recover from the loss of attachment figures when they die. This bereavement and mourning is called **detachment**, and sometimes people have trouble getting past their grief. Detachment can be particularly problematic when children lose parents before the age of 11 (Bowlby, 1988). Therapists can help people going through detachment as they try to move through the stages of mourning and establish new attachments with other people. A death in the family might also increase fear of one's own death, which can cause a variety of negative emotional reactions (Mikulincer et al., 1990). The ways that attachment to others might come up in therapy or counseling settings are almost innumerable, as our bonding with others throughout life can be the cause of both our happiest and most devastating experiences.

Can Someone's Attachment Style Change?

One of the most common questions students of attachment theory ask is: Are attachment styles really stable over our entire lives? That would mean that lucky children will live a blessed life, while unlucky children are doomed to repeat unhealthy patterns over and over. Is our first relationship really our predestined fate?

Bowlby did believe that attachment to others is a primary, driving motivation for us throughout life. He also believed that our general *tendency* or instinct might be to follow set patterns over time. He wrote, "Prospective studies show that each pattern of attachment, once developed, tends to persist" (Bowlby, 1988, p. 126). Yet on the very next page of the same book, he also noted that "this is by no means necessarily so" (p. 127). Bowlby thought that when attachment style does persist over time, it's because the person has internalized the pattern and unconsciously imposes it on people they meet, such as teachers, therapists, or potential partners.

But we *are* able to make conscious changes, and we will be affected by both positive and negative relationship experiences. Each time we have our trust validated (or betrayed), we learn and change, especially if we reflect on and interpret what happened (Bowlby, 1973, 1988; Crowell et al., 2008). In addition, our adult relationships depend on the unique combination of attachment styles in both partners (Crowell, Treboux, & Waters, 2002; Oppenheim & Waters, 1995; Treboux, Crowell, & Waters,

2004). As you can imagine, two secure people who date each other will have a relatively easy road ahead of them—but imagine the chaos and hurt feelings if, say, a preoccupied person tries to date a dismissive one.

We are all—all the time—vulnerable to heartache and disappointment. But at the same time, we are also always at least a little open to healing from past wounds, from overcoming the ghosts of the past. There may be no such thing as destiny; we actively shape the future with every small decision, in every relationship we have. So don't despair if you've had trouble in the past, and don't let your guard down completely if your relationships have always been wonderful. As Bowlby (1988) himself said, therapy can help us redesign our internal views of both self and other, to become "less under the spell of forgotten miseries and better able to recognize companions in the present for what they are" (p. 137).

CHECK YOUR UNDERSTANDING

3.7 What is maternal sensitivity, according to research by Ainsworth?

a. Feelings of postpartum depression mothers often experience after birth

b. When mothers experience heightened physical sensations, such as pain

c. How perceptive and responsive a mother is to her infant

d. The degree and range of emotions a new mother displays to others

3.8 This section reviewed suggestions for how deployed military members can increase secure attachment in their children. Which suggestion below is NOT one of the tips you saw in this chapter?

a. Keep routines consistent and predictable

b. Encourage children to ignore feelings of doubt or sadness

c. Give children a meaningful object to cling to

d. Use technology to stay connected (e.g., Skype)

3.9 One problem identified in counseling is when parents demand constant attention from their children, often to make up for their own sad childhoods. What term did Bowlby use for this pattern?

a. Inverted parenting

b. Mirror parenting

c. Ironic parenting

d. Reciprocal parenting

APPLICATION ACTIVITY

One of the important questions in this section was whether attachment style in someone can change over time. Another way to think about change in attachment within a single person is to examine whether security goes up or down across different types of relationships or with different people. Think about yourself as an example. Identify one relationship you have in your current life that you would classify as secure, and then describe it. Then do the same thing for a relationship you see as anxious-ambivalent, and one you see as avoidant. Why do you seem to approach these three people so differently?

CRITICAL THINKING

- This section covered some specific tips that deployed military families can use to increase secure attachment between children and parents. What are other strategies or techniques that can be used to help ensure strong bonds between children and parents when the parents have to be away for extended periods of time?

- Attachment theory could be used in therapeutic settings for a variety of problems. Two that were identified here were inverted parenting and going through the grieving process. What are at least two other important mental health needs or concerns that might be helped through an attachment theory lens?

Answers to the Check Your Understanding Questions

3.7 c, **3.8** b, and **3.9** a.

Chapter Summary

Big Questions

1. What is attachment theory, and how was it formed?

2. How is attachment theory measured and applied to adult relationships?

3. What are important questions for and about attachment theory?

What is attachment theory, and how was it formed?

Attachment theory suggests that the relationship we have with our primary caregiver (such as our mother) as an infant will influence the types of relationships we have for the rest of our lives. It was developed by John Bowlby and Mary Ainsworth after World War II. Ainsworth developed the "strange situation," where mothers and their babies came to a lab and were observed as the mother left and returned. Bowlby and Ainsworth proposed three different "attachment styles," or patterns of behaviors. Secure attachment is the healthiest, happiest style. These infants were treated to consistent love and appeared to show self-confidence and trust. Two less positive, or insecure, attachment styles were also noted. The first insecure style is called anxious-ambivalent. These children had inconsistent parents; this led to patterns of anxiety and desperation. Finally, avoidant attachment was displayed by babies of consistently unresponsive parents. These babies showed signs of indifference toward their parents, apparently the result of repeated failed attempts at attention.

How is attachment theory measured and applied to adult relationships?

A popular application of attachment theory is to see whether adult romantic attachment follows the same patterns and styles as infant attachment. Many studies have confirmed that attachment style matters for adult relationship satisfaction, conflict management, sexual experiences, and more. In addition, many researchers prefer a four-category model for adult attachment (instead of three categories). Measurement of attachment style can occur through observation, interviews, or projective tests. Projective tests use ambiguous objects or images (such as photographs), and interpretations are coded by trained researchers. In adults, attachment is usually measured through either interviews or self-report surveys. Surveys can measure attachment style in either categorical or continuous ways.

What are important questions for and about attachment theory?
Attachment theory can be applied in a wide variety of settings. For example, research has

investigated whether there are cross-cultural differences in patterns of attachment around the world. Several studies have found that fathers are just as capable of establishing secure attachment in children as mothers are. One specific question relevant to attachment theory is how it applies to deployed military personnel; specific suggestions for supporting secure attachment include tips like using technology to stay in touch. Attachment theory has various uses in therapeutic settings for helping both children and adults establish healthy relationships. Finally, studies have explored what situational factors can cause one's attachment style to change over time.

List of Terms

Learning Objectives	Key Terms
3.1 Explain the inspiration behind attachment theory and different attachment styles.	Attachment theory Ethological approach Maternal deprivation Strange situation Attachment style Secure attachment Secure base Insecure attachment Anxious-ambivalent attachment Avoidant attachment
3.2 Apply attachment theory to adult relationships and analyze different ways to measure it.	Romantic attachment Dismissing attachment Preoccupied attachment Fearful attachment Child attachment interview Projective test Adult attachment interview
3.3 Analyze different contexts in which attachment theory is used to explain a variety of social behaviors.	Maternal sensitivity Inverted parenting Detachment

The Evolutionary Perspective

Big Questions	Learning Objectives
1. How is an evolutionary perspective applied to intimate relationships?	4.1 Explain natural selection and sexual selection, and how they can be applied to intimate relationships.
2. How does this perspective explain sex differences in promiscuity and jealousy?	4.2 Analyze how parental investment might lead to differences in men's and women's patterns of promiscuity and jealousy.
3. How can this perspective be applied to other important relationship behaviors?	4.3 Apply this perspective to mate guarding, mate poaching, strategic infidelity, and child abuse.

When Charles Darwin published his most famous book, *On the Origin of Species* (1859), he knew he was dropping a scientific bombshell. He even knew that its shock waves would ripple through time until they reached modern psychology. "In the distant future," Darwin predicted, "psychology will be based on a new foundation" (p. 488). The study of intimate relationships goes beyond psychology in terms of relevant academic fields, but Darwin's foresight was prescient regarding the role of the evolutionary perspective.

While attachment theory (Chapter 3) is very much founded in individual social relationships and personal experiences after we are born, an evolutionary approach starts generations earlier. The idea that our behavior is driven by instincts that have slowly been shaped over millennia is controversial. Thus, fair warning: The application of evolutionary theory to the study of relationships and sexual behaviors may disturb some of your existing beliefs. Some of the conclusions are basically sexist. The perspective also requires us to ask whether humans are—at our most basic core—just

Charles Darwin
(1809–1882).

another kind of animal, driven by instincts inherited from ancestors long dead and buried. It also generally assumes that (1) there are only two sexes—men and women, (2) we're all heterosexual, and (3) we all want to reproduce.

Do you see the influence of the evolutionary perspective all around you—or do you prefer to think about relationships from one of the other major theories described in this book?

How Is an Evolutionary Perspective Applied to Intimate Relationships?

There are many important differences in world cultures.

You can certainly think of examples, such as how formally people dress and act in public, how and what they eat, the degree to which they respect and honor older people, political and religious differences, and more. **Cross-cultural psychology** is a fascinating and deeply significant subfield of psychology. It provides insights into how people from different parts of the globe think, feel, and behave differently.

However, another way to think about humanity is to see the similarities everyone shares, regardless of culture. Think about this perspective and also consider the following:

> why people in all cultures worry about social status (often more than they realize); why people in all cultures not only gossip, but gossip about the same kinds of things; why in all cultures men and women seem different in a few basic ways; why people everywhere feel guilt, and feel it in broadly predictable circumstances; why people everywhere have a deep sense of justice, so that the axioms "One good turn deserves another" and "An eye for an eye, a tooth for a tooth" shape human life everywhere on this planet. (Wright, 1994, p. 8)

In contrast to cross-cultural psychology, the evolutionary perspective provides insights into how we're all the same in many important ways. **Evolutionary psychology** is defined as a perspective that examines human thoughts, emotions, and behaviors in terms of how they developed over time because they helped our ancestors survive and reproduce. If a certain tendency worked well for your ancestors, then it could be passed along to the next generation, and then the next, and next . . . until it finally got to you.

Let's start our discussion of this important—yet controversial—perspective on human nature with an understanding of who Darwin was.

Darwin's Life and Inspiration

Charles Darwin was born in England in 1809. It was the Victorian Age, a time when Europeans were focused on self-discipline, sexual repression, and moral structure (Wright, 1994). His family was rich, and they planned for him to be a medical doctor from the day he was born. He served as an apprentice doctor when he was 16, but he found traditional lectures and studying textbooks fairly boring. His father, normally a kind and supportive man, became discouraged that Charles would ever amount to anything. Charles Darwin was, however, inspired when the outside world became his classroom. He directly studied anatomy through collecting beetles, hunting, and taxidermy; and he studied natural history through travel (Desmond & Moore, 1994). The history of science changed when he became the ship's naturalist on the *HMS Beagle*, the famous 5-year voyage that took him to the Galapagos Islands (Wright, 1994).

While exploring the islands, Darwin paid particular attention to the finches. He noticed that each island had slightly different variations of finch, such as beaks with different shapes or feathers of different colors. He further noted that each set of features seemed perfectly suited for that particular island's environment. How did that happen—and when? He didn't really figure out what he thought about the finches until he had been back home for about a year. That's when he came to the conclusion that there had originally been a single type of finch, but that very slowly over years and years, mutations produced variations. Some of the variations helped survival on each island, while others hurt; some were better adapted to their particular environment. This was the key to what became Darwin's most important insight: natural selection.

Natural Selection

Darwin knew that often in the natural world, there are more animals born within a given species, in a given area, than can survive (Buss, 2009; Darwin, 1859). Some of the animals have to die.

Within the group, there will be natural variation from each individual to the next; some animals will be bigger, some stronger, some smarter. Natural selection is the idea that some of these variations will lead to better survival, and that the individuals who live will reproduce and pass their genes to the next generation. Individuals who had variations that led to early death would not pass their genes on. Slowly, over many generations, the species would thus be shaped by increasingly breeding traits that helped their ancestors survive and reproduce.

Consider two examples. If one of the Galapagos Islands had a lot of berries, then birds with beaks shaped for plucking and eating berries would do better than birds with different beaks. At the same time, those other beaks might help birds who live on an island where they have to use a stick to get bugs out of a tree. Birds with the correct beak shape for their island would have better access to food, would get stronger, would live longer, and would reproduce more than others—and thus certain beaks would become more and more common on that island. Nature had selected a certain variation to win—hence the well-known phrase "survival of the fittest." Darwin (1859) said it like this: "Multiply, vary, let the strongest live and the weakest die" (p. 263).

Okay, but let's talk about an example that's more relevant to this book: relationships. Imagine a species of ape in which different mothers vary in how attached they feel toward their offspring (Wright, 1994). One individual ape mother happens to have a genetic variation that drives her to feel more love and attention toward her babies, which leads to better nurturing, providing more food, and so on. Her babies grow strong, live through hardships like droughts, and go on to reproduce—and therefore pass the "love" gene on to their own babies.

In a *single* individual animal, this wouldn't have much impact on the species. But imagine that in an entire group of apes, some fraction of them have the "love" gene. Over many years and generations, the proportion of apes who inherit the gene will increase. Eventually, if the gene continues to help survival, this genetic advantage will reach **fixation**, which is when it occurs in 100% of the population.

Evolutionary scientists believe that the human species has slowly changed over time as well, with certain genetic tendencies translating into advantages that help people survive and reproduce. Those genetics are now so common that they produce behavioral tendencies we can see around the world:

> The basic ways we feel about each other, the basic kinds of things we think about each other and say to each other, are with us today by virtue of their past contribution to genetic fitness. (Wright, 1994, p. 28)

We don't necessarily have to *realize* that we harbor these tendencies. But the tendencies exist on an instinctive level, and they are probably there because they lead us to partners who are genetically healthier (for more on seemingly instinctive patterns of attraction to others, see Chapter 8). That means these tendencies are more likely to be passed on to our children, and so on through more and more generations.

Sexual Selection

By "natural selection," Darwin meant that some traits would naturally "win" in the survival game and therefore be "selected" to be passed down to the next generation. Being physically stronger helps us fight predators. Being physically faster helps us run away from predators. Either way, we survive. Being intelligent helps us plot the downfall of our enemies—again, we win. Mostly, natural selection is about "survival of the fittest."

©iStock.com/bobbieo

How does evolution explain traits that seem to *hurt* survival, like a peacock's feathers?

But what about traits that seem to work *against* survival? Why would they be passed on through the generations? Darwin was puzzled by examples such as a peacock's colorful feathers. Wouldn't this huge display of color just be a big sign to predators: "Hey, delicious bird right over here!"? And the weight of the feathers would just drag it down if it tried to fly or run away. So how can evolution explain this?

Darwin solved this problem with a second key concept: sexual selection. **Sexual selection** is the idea that some variations will be more attractive to members of the "opposite" sex and thus lead to more mating opportunities. That's why those traits would be passed on more than others. It's not because they directly lead to better survival; in fact, they might even hurt

When same-sex individuals compete, it's intrasexual competition. The winner might have more status and access to mating partners.

survival. But if these traits attract sexual partners, they're more likely to lead to off-spring and that's how the traits increase in the species.

There are two types of sexual selection: competition and mate choice. **Intrasexual competition** is what happens when one sex competes within itself for access to the other sex. The classic example of this is when two male bulls lock horns to fight for dominance. Intrasexual competition is fighting only other people of the same sex as yourself. In other words, peacocks all compete against each other for access to peahens.

The other part of sexual selection is mate choice. When males or females (again, assume everyone is heterosexual for this theory) choose a particular partner from a variety of available options, it's **intersexual selection**. When a peahen decides which peacock is the sexiest option, it's intersexual selection. Because peahens are attracted to the flashiest and most colorful plumage, peacocks with huge feathers get the most sexual opportunity.

You might be getting a little tired of nonhuman examples; we've talked about finches, apes, and peacocks. So, what evidence exists for intrasexual competition and intersexual selection (or mate preferences) in humans? Much of this chapter will cite books or journal articles written by David Buss, who is the most famous modern scholar to apply the evolutionary perspective to intimate relationships in humans.

Intrasexual Competition Among Men

Around the world and throughout history, male competitions to show off physical strength, agility, and athletic ability seem to be pervasive. Darwin himself pointed out this tendency, using Native American tribal customs as an example:

> It has ever been the custom among these people for the men to wrestle for any woman to whom they are attached; and, of course, the strongest party always carries off the prize. A weak man, unless he be a good hunter, and well-beloved, is seldom permitted to keep a wife that a stronger man thinks worth his notice. (Darwin, 1871, p. 341)

Researcher David Buss notes that this type of contest for physical strength is common (e.g., the Olympics, sports, and even bar fights), but that an often-unstated part of the competition is the assumed courage, tenacity, and energy needed to win (Buss, 2009). All these traits should be desirable and attractive when viewed from the opposite sex (for example, energy on the field of battle might translate into energy in the bedroom, or at least energy at work or in gathering resources for the family). Buss also points out that winners of such contests usually get additional prizes such as money or status, and those resources will also be attractive to potential mates. Across cultures, men seem to care more about social status and ambition that women do, perhaps due to intrasexual competition (Buss, 2008).

An even more direct strategy men can take is to sabotage each other. If men can derogate potential rivals, it takes those other men out of the picture. Specific tactics include insulting a rival's status, scoffing at achievements, implying physical weakness, displaying skepticism about future achievements, calling them names, spreading false rumors (sometimes that another man has a sexually transmitted infection) and telling women that their rivals only like to "use" women for sex (Buss & Dedden, 1990; Schmitt & Buss, 1996). Public humiliation and physical dominance in front of women are common strategies to make other men look weak in comparison (Buss, 2009).

One study (Wilson & Daly, 2004) found an interesting example of natural selection (what helps survival) versus sexual selection (what helps us get access to sex) in men. Here, researchers asked men to choose between a small amount of money (around $20) they could have tomorrow or a larger amount of money (around $60) if they waited a few months. In addition, participants were randomly assigned to view 12 images of women who had been preselected as either "hot" or "not."

Men who had just seen photographs of 12 "hot" women were more likely to choose the immediate, but small cash award (Wilson & Daly, 2004). The researchers concluded that these men were motivated to pick the option that might help them gain immediate access to a woman (sexual selection), even if it meant sacrificing a long-term benefit (natural selection). Seeing the "hot" women apparently led men to lose the ability to delay gratification. Interestingly, when the study was conducted with women participants, they were significantly less likely to make this sacrifice. Men seem to be particularly motivated to make choices that might get them access to attractive women as quickly as possible.

Intrasexual Competition Among Women

Women can be just as competitive as men; indeed, phrases like "catfight" come from the idea that women are often willing to tear each other down. Wikipedia even has an entry for "catfight" that defines it as "an altercation between two women, often characterized as involving scratching, slapping, hair-pulling, and shirt-shredding. It can also be used to describe women insulting each other verbally or engaged in an intense competition for men, power, or occupational status" (Wikipedia, 2018). According to Wikipedia, the phrase goes all the way back to 1824.

Just like men, women often compete by derogating each other, with the hopes of decreasing a rival's potential value. For women, strategies often include insulting another woman's sexual choices, such as calling someone else names like "slut"

(Buss & Dedden, 1990). Note that research has shown that women are smart enough to change this strategy if they know they are talking to a man who is specifically looking for a short-term sexual partner. In this case, saying that another woman is promiscuous will, of course, backfire (Schmitt & Buss, 1996).

Women also focus on each other's appearance and can sometimes denigrate sexual rivals based on how they look. Here, women tell men that someone else is overweight, point out wrinkles, or make other comments about another woman's general appearance (Buss & Dedden, 1990). Because physical appearance is valued more for women than for men in heterosexual mating, women are more likely than men to focus rivalries on judging each other's looks as they spend time maintaining their own through tactics like makeup (Buss, 1988b; Schmitt & Buss, 1996). On average, women spend about an hour every day on their appearance (Buss, 1994). One study found that women who were going out to bars in the evening would first go home after work. In between work and the bar, they would bathe, do their hair, reapply makeup, and try on an average of three different outfits (Allan & Fishel, 1979). Interesting insight into outfit choices can be seen in the "Research Deep Dive" feature.

It's important to point out, though, that strategies based on enhancing appearance are used mostly when seeking short-term mates. Women who are looking for long-term partners certainly still tend to care about how they (the women) look, but they focus more on using displays of loyalty, common interests, and intelligence (Buss, 1994). Thus, women change their strategy depending on the situation and the kind of mate they want at the time. This is a nice lead-in to how men and women each use intersexual selection.

RESEARCH DEEP DIVE

Dress to Impress: How Ovulation Influences Self-Ornamentation

You do it every day: pick out what you're going to wear. How do you ultimately decide on a particular outfit? It's a simple question, but a deceptively difficult one to answer. That's because even the most basic human behavior is extraordinarily complex and influenced by a myriad of factors. Some of those contributing factors are easy to recognize. For example, when you have an 8 a.m. class, sweats or pajamas are the default because you just don't have the time for anything else. But there are also less obvious factors, things you're not even aware of, that influence your clothing choice.

Take, for example, your hormones. While you may know on a general level that hormones influence behavior, you may not appreciate how hormones influence your day-to-day decision making. This is especially true for women who experience regular monthly fluctuations related to their ovulatory cycle. Ovulation is associated with hormone variations such that luteinizing hormone surges days before high fertility. Research shows that periods of high fertility influence women's social behavior (e.g., going to clubs or parties), mating behavior (e.g., flirtation with others), and attractiveness (e.g., women are rated as more attractive during ovulation). Consistent with this, the researchers of one study (Haselton, Mortezaire, Pillworth, Bleske-Rechek, & Frederick, 2007)

(Continued)

(Continued)

hypothesized that during times of high fertility, women would engage in more "self-ornamentation." In other words, women would dress more attractively and would pay more attention to personal grooming.

Researchers from UCLA recruited 30 college-aged women who were currently in relationships and not using any type of hormonal contraceptive to participate in the study. Participants came to the lab twice: once during their cycle's high fertility or follicular phase (15–17 days prior to menstrual onset; basically, while they were ovulating), and once again during their low fertility or luteal phase (4–10 days prior to menstrual onset). At each session, the researchers took a full-body photograph of the participant and confirmed fertility with a urine test. Importantly, participants were "blind" to the study's purpose, which means they were not told the study's true intent and were instead told that the study involved "health, personality, and sexuality." Had participants known the true purpose, they might have altered their style of dress or grooming behavior for the study.

The researchers recruited a separate group of 42 college student judges (17 men and 25 women) to rate the participants' 60 pictures. Using stimulus presentation software, the judges (who were also blind to the study's purpose) viewed each participant's pair of photos and responded to the question, "In which photo is the person trying to look more attractive?"

Results supported the researchers' hypothesis, such that judges picked the women photographed during high fertility as trying to look more attractive more often (59.5% of the time) versus the low-fertility photograph (40.5%). In addition, among high-fertility photos, judges rated those taken closer to the participant's day

of ovulation as more attractive. Taken together, the results indicate that high-fertility women appear to be trying to enhance their appearance. But how? A follow-up coded the types of clothing women wore during high versus low fertility and found that high-fertility women were more likely to wear more fashionable clothes or skirts (instead of pants), in addition to showing more skin on their upper bodies.

One major caveat with this particular study is that it only had 30 participants in the judging phase. However, because the within-participants research design essentially compared each of the women who were photographed to themselves (each person at high vs. low fertility), it increased the study's power, or ability to find differences that truly exist. In other designs (between-participants), you compare two entirely different groups of people. As a result, there are a near endless number of potential differences between the participants, above and beyond the one difference the researcher intends to create. Here, each participant serves as her own control group, which results in fertility levels being one of the *only* differences between conditions. Still, having more participants would help the researchers make an even more compelling case for the effects of fertility on ornamentation.

While each individual study should be taken with a grain of salt, particularly those studies with low sample size, this study's results are consistent with many other research papers examining the effects of cyclical shifts in fertility on women's behavior.

For more, read Haselton, G. M., Mortezaire, M., Pillworth, G. E., Bleske-Rechek, A., & Frederick, A. D. (2007). Ovulatory shifts in human female ornamentation: Near ovulation, women dress to impress. *Hormones and Behavior, 51*, 40–45.

Intersexual Mate Preferences: What Men Want

In Chapter 8, you'll read a lot about what people find physically attractive in others. For example, men across cultures tend to like women with a small waist, large hips, and large breasts. Evolutionary scientists explain this preference as rooted in the desire for women who will be good at birthing children and then raising them. Large hips are better for the physical birthing process, small waists indicate aerobic fitness, and large breasts are best for producing milk.

The evolutionary perspective is that both sexes want physically attractive mates (because "hotness" indicates genetic health), but that men care more about this than women do because of biological differences. Women are the ones who will carry the fetus and bear the child. Thousands of years ago, that meant that men would be expected to provide the resources to support their families while women were assigned childcare roles. So, women should be motivated to find men who have good resources, and men should be motivated to find women who are genetically going to produce the best offspring and be the best mothers.

Universally, men are attracted to physical cues of youth and health in potential female mates (Buss, 2009). Youth matters because women's ability to reproduce declines steadily between the ages of 20 and 50, when it basically disappears. Men in U.S. universities from coast to coast say they want women who are about 2.5 years younger than themselves (Buss, 1989). This general tendency to prefer women who are in their most fertile years has been replicated in 37 different cultures around the world (Buss, 1989), including Colombia, Nigeria, Yugoslavia, China, and Australia.

Let's get super practical for a minute. Imagine you're a heterosexual woman and you're looking for a mate. What are things you can do, immediately, to attract men? When Buss (1988b) asked college and university men to rate how much they liked 101 things women could do to make themselves attractive, the men offered several strategies. The 20 most effective behaviors are listed in the left-hand column of Table 4.1. Rows at the top of the table were the most effective, with decreasing importance as the table rows go down. It's important to note that these strategies go beyond superficial things like looks; having a good sense of humor and being nice matter, too.

TABLE 4.1 ● 20 Most Effective Strategies for Men and Women Trying to Attract Each Other (in Descending Order of Effectiveness)

Most Effective Female Acts	Most Effective Male Acts
Display a good sense of humor	Display a good sense of humor
Keep herself well groomed	Sympathetic to her troubles
Sympathetic to his troubles	Show good manners
Show good manners	Keep himself well groomed
Shower daily	Make an effort to spend time with her
Keep physically fit to appear healthy	Offer to help her
Make up jokes to make him laugh	Shower daily
Make an effort to spend time with him	Keep physically fit to appear healthy

(Continued)

TABLE 4.1 ● (Continued)

Most Effective Female Acts	Most Effective Male Acts
Wear stylish, fashionable clothes	Exercise
Offer to help him	Wear attractive outfits
Wear attractive outfits	Wash hair every day
Exercise	Wear stylish, fashionable clothes
Participate in extra-curricular activities	Diet to improve his figure
Smile a lot	Smile a lot
Groom hair carefully	Give encouraging glances
Buy him a nice dinner at a restaurant	Buy her a nice dinner at a restaurant
Wear sexy clothes	Participate in extra-curricular activities
Give encouraging glances	Touch her
Go to parties	Make up jokes to make her laugh
Tell him things he wants to hear	Express strong opinions

Both men and women said the most effective strategy to attract them was to display a good sense of humor.

Intersexual Mate Preferences: What Women Want

As you can see, Table 4.1 also shows the top 20 strategies that college and university women said they want to see from men (Buss, 1988b). Women do care about a potential mate's physical appearance, but they are also motivated (according to the evolutionary perspective) to seek a man who has two other assets. The first is resources, such as money and/or status. However, money really only matters for long-term mates, and Table 4.1 is generally about short-term mates instead. When thinking about husbands or long-term partners, women care about protection and resources for themselves and for future children. Sometimes women have to guess about a man's resources from cues such as ambition, job, intelligence, and age. As Buss (1994) says, "Women scrutinize these personal qualities carefully because they reveal a man's potential" (p. 47).

So, women care about a man's resources—but the second trait that women tend to focus on is commitment. Again, commitment matters for long-term mates, not short-term sexual partners. But if women are thinking about the future, they want a man who will commit with loyalty and monogamy. Cues women rely on are sincerity, honesty, gifts (including large ones, like diamond rings), and verbal expressions of love

(Buss, 1994). So, while there are some traits that men and women both want, there are interesting differences between the sexes as well. The next section of this chapter focuses on two specific important differences and how the evolutionary perspective explains them.

CHECK YOUR UNDERSTANDING

4.1   When Darwin visited the Galapagos Islands, he noticed important differences in several species based on their island of residence. Which species was highlighted in this chapter as important to the development of evolutionary theory?

   a. Beetles
   b. Feral dogs
   c. Gecko lizards
   d. Finches

4.2   When natural selection leads a particular trait to eventually exist in 100% of individuals in a given species, the trait has reached:

   a. Fixation
   b. Maximization
   c. Saturation
   d. Concentration

4.3   Reza is at a party with a lot of other men and women. He starts a false rumor that another man there just got fired from his job, to make himself look more attractive than the other man. This strategy (of a man insulting another man) is an example of which term below?

   a. Natural selection
   b. Instinctive opposition
   c. Intrasexual competition
   d. Intersexual selection

APPLICATION ACTIVITY

The study that resulted in Table 4.1 was done by David Buss in 1988, which was over 30 years ago. Do you think strategies have changed since then? First, identify at least five behaviors that men might do and five behaviors that women might do that do not appear on the table. Then, create a survey in which all 25 behaviors for men and for women are listed in random order. Ask a few men and a few women to rate how much they would find each behavior attractive in a potential partner of the opposite sex. Then, analyze your results by responding to these two questions: (1) For the 20 behaviors that Buss included, do you find basically the same pattern as he did in 1988? (2) Where did the new behaviors—the ones you added—fall? Do your results align with predictions you might have made from the evolutionary perspective? Why or why not? (*Note:* Before proceeding with this activity, be sure to check with your professor for ethical research requirements and guidelines at your college or university.)

CRITICAL THINKING

- The coverage of evolutionary theory in this chapter comes from the underlying assumption that people are heterosexual—and we know that not everyone is. How would the findings discussed so far change, or not change, if the participants were gay men or lesbians? More generally, how can the evolutionary perspective explain why nonheterosexual preferences continue

- to exist in the gene pool if gay people are significantly less likely to reproduce?

- At its core, the evolutionary perspective predicts many fundamental differences between men and women. Is this theory therefore sexist, by definition? Does that make it offensive, to both men and women? Why or why not? Do you personally believe this theory has merit and should continue to drive relationships research?

Answers to the Check Your Understanding Questions

4.1 d, 4.2 a, and 4.3 c.

How Does This Perspective Explain Sex Differences in Promiscuity and Jealousy?

The evolutionary perspective predicts that men and women have the same motivations and goals: survival and successful reproduction. Even if these goals aren't on the surface of our minds, behaviors that help either goal are more likely to keep going in the gene pool. Behaviors that lead to early death or that limit access to sexual opportunities are less likely to be passed on to future generations.

Even though men and women have the same genetic goals, biological differences between the sexes cannot be denied. When it comes to reproduction, men provide sperm and women provide eggs and a uterus for the fetus to grow. These basic biological differences translate into interesting differences in how each sex negotiates intimate heterosexual relationships. In this section, we'll first cover some important concepts about differences between men and women's reproductive strategies, then we apply these ideas to two specific topics: promiscuity and jealousy.

Parental Investment

When it comes to biologically producing a human baby, the process is very different for a father than for a mother. Just think about the mechanics. The father has to provide sperm—something men produce in the millions, all the time. The act of sexual intercourse can take just a few minutes, and his job is basically done. For the mother, however, it starts with the egg that becomes fertilized. Only one egg is produced a month, and there is a limited window of high-fertility years. Once she's pregnant, the expecting mother carries the fetus in her uterus, potentially going through health risks herself. After giving birth, she's probably going to be the main source of nutrition for the baby (through her milk production) for at least a year.

The amount of time, effort, and resources that a mother and father each provide to successfully reproduce is called our **parental investment** (Trivers, 1972). As you can see, the parental investment for women is much, much higher than the parental investment for men (at least, on the biological level). These different levels of parental investment result in very different reproductive strategies for men versus women, according to the evolutionary perspective.

Keep in mind, these instincts evolved before birth control was readily available to either men or women. That meant that every time someone had sex, they were risking the possibility of a pregnancy. So when we think about how people act in sexual and intimate relationships from the evolutionary perspective, remember that we're talking about behaviors we've inherited from ancestors who thought about sex a little more seriously than modern people might. Modern technology like condoms and birth control pills might be game-changers. But as Buss (1994) puts it, "Human sexual psychology evolved over millions of years to cope with ancestral adaptive problems. We still possess this underlying sexual psychology, even though our environment has changed" (p. 20).

Promiscuity

Imagine you're living 1000 years ago (or 10,000 years ago, or a million years ago) and you don't have access to birth control. Both men and women want to successfully reproduce—but when each act of sexual intercourse might lead to a pregnancy, women have to be on high alert. Pregnancy means a huge investment of time and resources for women, and they want to make the most of their limited eggs and time. Men, again, don't have that problem—they have as much sperm as they want, and they can continue impregnating women even when the men are of old age.

Due to this difference in our biology and parental investment, men and women have different strategies when it comes to choosing sexual partners. For men, there's not much risk involved. Evolution actually rewards men for having as much sex as possible, with many different women. From a reproduction point of view, having multiple female partners means they could all be pregnant at once. Also, men should want as much genetic variety in their children as possible, so that their offspring have a range of different skills and abilities to cope with changing environments. Thus, men are predicted to be as promiscuous as their circumstances allow.

On the other hand, women are predicted to be much less generous with sexual access. Women, because they are responsible for potential pregnancies and raising of children at least until the child is a few years old, are predicted to be much pickier when it comes to selecting sexual partners. Women need to be more careful: "Gestating, bearing, nursing, nurturing, and protecting a child are exceptional reproductive resources that cannot be allocated indiscriminately" (Buss, 1994, p. 20). Women don't want to "waste" their time and resources with men who aren't worthy of their attention. This means that women are predicted to be much less promiscuous than men.

What does the research say? Are these predictions supported—around the world? Let's examine some specific aspects of promiscuity to see.

The evolutionary perspective predicts that men should want as many different sexual partners as possible. Do you agree?

Number of Desired Sex Partners

According to this perspective, men should want as many sexual partners as possible. Cross-culturally, society seems to be much more accepting of men who are promiscuous, compared to women. Terms for men with a lot of partners are usually positive ("stud"), while parallel terms for women are negative ("slut"). According to early sociological research, about 80% of cultures around the world allow for some level of polygyny, where men have multiple girlfriends, wives, or mistresses at any given time (Ford & Beach, 1951; Murdock, 1967). The same is not true for polyandry, or women having multiple boyfriends or husbands.

For a direct test of the hypothesis that men want more sexual partners than women do, Buss asked 75 men and 73 women "how many sexual partners they would ideally like to have" during the next month, 6 months, 1 year, 2 years, and so on up to over their entire lifetime (Buss & Schmitt, 1993, p. 210). The results are shown

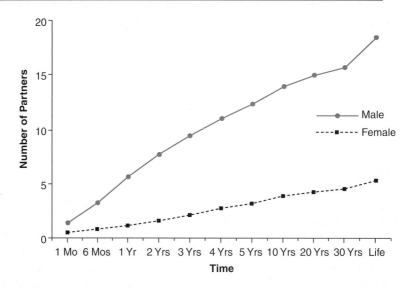

FIGURE 4.1 ● Ideal Number of Sexual Partners for Men and Women

Men say they want around 18 sexual partners over their entire lifetime, while women say they only want around five.

Source: Buss, D. M., & Schmitt, D. P. (1993). Sexual strategies theory: An evolutionary perspective on human mating. *Psychological Review, 100*(2), 204-232, reprinted with permission.

in Figure 4.1. Over their entire life, women said they wanted an average of around five sexual partners—and men said they'd like around 18. At every single time interval, the number of partners men said they want was significantly higher than what women said (including just in the next month).

Time Desired Before Sex Occurs

Men should also want to have sex as quickly as possible, with as little effort as possible, according to the evolutionary perspective. Their parental investment is already relatively low, and the best strategy is to gain sexual access to women with the least amount of effort. Women, on the other hand, are predicted to want to hold off on granting sexual access until time has passed. Over time, women can get to know their partner on a personal level (to make sure he's a good potential father, at least genetically speaking) and increase the man's emotional commitment to her (thus potentially leading to him giving her gifts and providing for her financially).

Again, Buss asked this question directly (Buss & Schmitt, 1993, p. 210). The same 75 men and 73 women were asked: "If the conditions were right, would you consider having sexual intercourse with someone you viewed as desirable, if you had known that person" for the following lengths of time:

- 5 years
- 2 years
- 1 year
- 6 months
- 3 months
- 1 month
- 1 week
- 1 day
- 1 evening
- 1 hour

Each possible time frame was rated by the men and women on a scale ranging from −3 ("definitely not") to +3 ("definitely yes"). The results are shown in Figure 4.2.

As the researchers predicted, the pattern for men and women was different. If you've known someone for 5 years, men and women agreed: they would probably have sex with that person (an average around +2 on the scale). But at every other, shorter period of time—even after 2 years—men and women's answers were significantly different. Men were more likely to have sex with a woman than vice versa. After only a week, men crossed over to an average answer that was above zero, while women remained very unlikely to say they'd be willing. Women's average answers didn't cross into positive responses until at least 6 months of knowing the other person.

FIGURE 4.2 ● How Quickly Men and Women Say They Would Have Sex

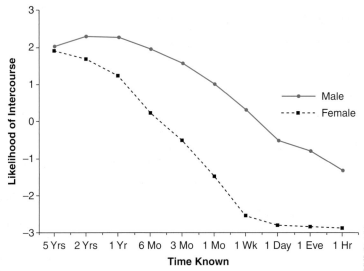

Men and women also differ in how quickly they say they would be willing to have sex with someone.

Source: Buss, D. M., & Schmitt, D. P. (1993). Sexual strategies theory: An evolutionary perspective on human mating. *Psychological Review, 100*(2), 204-232, reprinted with permission.

At this point, you might be using your critical thinking skills to question the Buss and Schmitt findings. This study was done by administering a self-report survey that just asked people what they want in terms of sex. Maybe the large sex differences shown in the results are just social desirability: maybe men and women both lie a little about what they want. Men might *say* they want fast sex with a lot of people because it's culturally expected—and women might downplay their sexual desires because of negative social judgment. Maybe the truth is that when it comes down to it, men and women are equally open to sexual offers. Is this what people would honestly do, if *really* given the opportunity to have sex with someone, in real life? Another study tried to find out.

In one of the most famous studies on sexual behavior ever conducted (Clark & Hatfield, 1989), researchers tried to get the real answer to this question (while still following ethical standards!). The research started by getting five college men and five college women to agree to serve as research "confederates," pretending they weren't part of a study at all (similar to participant observation that you read about in Chapter 2, but confederates directly interact with the participants). Each of the 10 confederates went to a different part of their large campus and approached attractive people who were alone. Everyone they approached became the participants, even though those participants didn't know they were in a study. The confederates walked up to each person and stated: "I have been noticing you around campus. I find you very attractive" (Clark & Hatfield, 1989, p. 49). Each person was then asked one of the following three questions, which were randomly chosen for each person in advance:

- Would you like to go out with me tonight?

- Would you come over to my apartment tonight?

- Would you go to bed with me tonight?

Before we get to the results, think about two things. First, what would *you* do in response to each of these questions? Imagine that you're single and that the person who has approached you is relatively attractive. Next, predict what you think the results were for men versus women in this situation. As you should be able to guess, the evolutionary perspective predicts that male participants should be more willing to say yes if they think the opportunity for sex is there.

It's also important to know that the researchers behind this study did their own replication, an important step in building confidence in a pattern of results. The first time they did the study, the year was 1978. The second time, it was 1982. The particular year of 1982 is meaningful because it was right after the HIV/AIDS scare was hitting the nation, and people were being cautioned strongly against "casual" sex with strangers due to the potential health risks. So, the researchers wanted to know if the cultural fear of HIV had an influence on the pattern of results. You can see the results from both 1978 and 1982 in Table 4.2.

Just as the evolutionary perspective predicted, men were significantly more likely to accept the offer of sex (or an apartment visit, which would hopefully lead to sex), compared to women. And the results didn't change much from 1978 to 1982, despite cultural awareness of HIV. Even further, when they replicated the study *again* in 1990, they found the same basic pattern a third time (Clark, 1990).

TABLE 4.2 ● Willingness of Men and Women to Go on a Date, Go to an Apartment, or Have Sex			
	Type of Request		
Results	Date	Apartment	Sex
1978			
Female participants	56%	6%	0%
Male participants	50%	69%	75%
1982			
Female participants	50%	0%	0%
Male participants	50%	69%	69%

According to Clark and Hatfield (1989), men are much more likely to agree to sex with someone they've just met, compared to women.

The men in this study were much more willing to go to a stranger's apartment or have sex with her than to even take her on a date! The researchers summarized their findings with this sentence: "Men are eager for sexual activity" (Clark & Hatfield, 1989, p. 51). They also reported that they thought more like 100% of the men might have said yes under different circumstances, but some who said no apologized and said that the only reason they couldn't have sex was because they were currently in a relationship.

Of course, the published report of the study notes that regardless of how the participant responded, the confederates debriefed them and thanked them; they didn't actually engage in any of the requested activities. Presumably, this led to a lot of disappointed women—and even more disappointed men.

Individual Differences in Strategy: Quality Versus Quantity of Offspring

At this point, you might be a little offended. If you're a man, you might think, "I'm not just a brainless sex machine, willing to bed anyone who seems willing." If you're a woman, you might think, "I like sex just as much as the next person—I'm sick of the double standards." Such criticisms of the evolutionary perspective are understandable, and they add to the controversial nature of the theory. One recent addition to the theoretical perspective accounts for people who are a little more discerning when they make decisions.

First, think again about the basic evolutionary idea that we are all motivated to get our genes into the next generation. We could do that in a couple of different ways. One strategy might be to produce as many children as possible—a "quantity" approach—and hope that at least some of them survive. A very different approach would be to have only a small number of children—a "quality" approach—but to give those children as much attention and resources as possible.

An idea called **r/K theory**, developed in the 1970s, compared these two strategies. A **high-r strategy** is "the production of a large number of offspring, of whom only a minority may survive" (Giosan, 2006, p. 395). In contrast, a **high-K strategy** is "to produce a smaller number of 'fitter' offspring with higher chances of survival" (p. 395). The letters r and K come from an equation that was originally created to understand population dynamics (Verhulst, 1838). In it, r stood for maximum growth *rate* of a given population. The K stood for the population's *capacity* limit, which came from the German word "Kapazitätsgrenze." So K stands for "capacity."

You might not be excited about algebraic equations, but the importance of this idea is that it means an evolutionary perspective can also predict that some people—including men—will be choosy when it comes to sexual encounters, because they want to save potential opportunities for offspring for the best possible outcomes. High-K strategists focus on the quality of offspring, not the quantity, and therefore choose to have fewer children. They can then give each child more resources, without spreading those resources out so much. Fewer children, but more resources per child; it's a genetic tradeoff.

Research has found that there is a range, in humans, in how much people favor a high-r versus a high-K strategy. One group of 250 male, blue-collar employees of a utility company completed a scale measuring their r/K preference (Giosan, 2006), where higher scores indicated more of a high-K preference. The results showed that high-K preferences were positively correlated to "perceived offspring quality," which meant that their children had better health, had higher intelligence, were more industrious, and had better physical abilities. So, some men *are* sexually selective—but this theoretical twist might mean that they are still driven by evolutionary motivations. They are taking a "quality" approach over a "quantity" approach.

If you're curious where you would fall on the r/K continuum, you can test yourself in the "What's My Score?" feature. It doesn't measure preference for quality versus quantity of offspring directly. Instead, it measures social confidence, resources, safety, and a focus on future stability and comfort.

WHAT'S MY SCORE?

High-r Versus High-K Strategy

Instructions: As you read each statement, write a number next to the item to indicate how much you agree with it, using this scale:

1	2	3	4	5
Strongly disagree				Strongly agree

_____1. The activities I engage in, both at work and elsewhere, are safe.

_____2. I have good health benefits for my family and myself.

_____3. I am able to provide a decent quality of life for myself and my family.

_____4. My training and experience are likely to bring me opportunities for promotion and increased income in the future.

_____5. I live in a comfortable and secure home.

_____6. The neighborhood where I live is safe.

_____7. If I were to face a sudden threat (e.g., flood, fire), I believe I would have the ability to protect myself and my family.

_____8. My second-degree relatives (nephews, cousins, etc.) are generally healthy.

Scoring: The original scale has 26 items; only eight were selected here to give you an idea of the survey. The more you agree with the sentences, the more you prefer a high-K strategy, meaning fewer children with more resources devoted to each. The possible range for the selected items is from 8 to 40.

Source: Giosan (2006).

Critical Thinking: This scale was really developed for male participants, because their potential for offspring is so much higher than women's. Because women have a limited number of eggs and can only produce a given number of children during their fertile years, are women in general more likely to be high-K strategists (and thus low-r strategists)?

Jealousy

What makes you jealous? According to the evolutionary perspective, men and women will be jealous for different reasons in a relationship. Just like with promiscuity, sex differences in jealousy are attributed to the mechanics of reproduction and parental investment. Because women bear the pregnancy and are often given the role of caregiver once a child is born, their primary need from the father is for him to stick around after the birth to provide resources for her and the new baby. Mothers will be concerned about ensuring an emotional commitment from the father. His genetic legacy has been established in the child—so mothers will want to ensure that he now sticks around to support them (Buss, 1988a).

Men, however, have different concerns. From this perspective, if a man chooses to stay in a monogamous relationship and raise children with a single woman, he will devote all of his resources to this family. But men suffer from a problem called **paternity uncertainty**. Once a woman becomes pregnant, men can't be 100% sure that the baby is really theirs. (Note, there's no such thing as "maternity uncertainty"—women are positive that the baby is theirs!) So, men aren't worried about their wives providing resources. Instead, men are worried about their wives staying monogamous so that any children produced are really carrying the men's genes. In fact, this concern appears to be applicable for up to 13% of men—statistically, that's the number of men who think they are the biological father of their children but are not really (Baker & Bellis, 1995).

These different challenges for men and women produce hypotheses that they will be jealous for different reasons. Women are predicted to be more jealous if their partner engages in **emotional infidelity**, or falling in love with another woman. Presumably, if your boyfriend or husband falls in love with someone else, he might be tempted to share his resources with her (through gifts and so on). On the other hand, men are predicted to be primarily jealous if their partner engages in **sexual infidelity**, or having sex with someone else. If your girlfriend or wife becomes pregnant, you want to be really sure that the baby is yours before you commit to helping raise it.

Men and women both easily admit that they get jealous, and levels of jealousy appear to be pretty much equal (White, 1981). For everyone, jealousy is positively correlated with feelings of inadequacy as a partner. When research participants were asked to imagine their partner flirting with or hugging someone else, people in seven different countries all reacted with negative emotions (Buunk & Hupka, 1987). So, sure—everyone feels jealousy, around the world. To test for predictions from the evolutionary perspective, sex differences in *kinds* of jealousy need to be found.

Buss and his research team (Buss, Larsen, Westen, & Semmelroth, 1992, p. 252) did just that when they asked 202 college students to consider the following dilemma:

> Please think of a serious committed romantic relationship that you have had in the past, that you currently have, or that you would like to have. Imagine that you discover that the person with whom you've been seriously involved became interested in someone else. What would distress or upset you more?

a. Imagining your partner forming a deep emotional attachment to that person.

b. Imagining your partner enjoying passionate sexual intercourse with that other person.

The results showed just what Buss predicted. Sixty percent of the men chose b, sexual infidelity. In contrast, 83% of the women chose a, emotional infidelity. When forced to choose, men prefer that their partner fall in love with someone else but stay sexually monogamous. This make sense, because there's no risk of pregnancy (and thus no risk of paternity uncertainty). Women prefer for their male partners to have sex with someone but not fall in love—because those situations are probably short term and don't risk his resources being given to another woman.

As usual, to really get evidence for an evolutionary explanation of these differences in jealousy, the pattern of results should be found in lots of cultures. So, another study asked the exact same question you just read but this time included participants from the United States, the Netherlands, and Germany (Buunk, Angleitner, Oubaid, & Buss, 1996). Those results are shown in Figure 4.3. Across all three countries, men were significantly more likely to be distressed about sexual infidelity than women were.

You can see in Figure 4.3 that the difference between men and women was strongest in the United States. The researchers (Buunk et al., 1996) thought this is because Germany and the Netherlands are particularly relaxed and open-minded about sexual behaviors, at least compared to Americans. However, even within these more liberal countries, there were still significant differences between the sexes. The predicted sex differences were found again when this study was replicated in South Korea and in Japan (Buss et al., 1999). So, culture matters—but the results are still in line with evolutionary predictions.

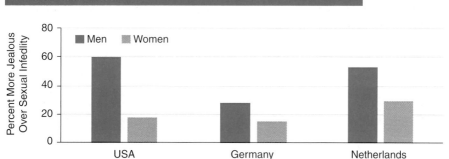

FIGURE 4.3 ● Sex Differences in Causes of Jealousy in Three Different Countries

Across three countries, according to Buunk et al. (1996), men are more likely than women to be jealous over sexual infidelity.

CHECK YOUR UNDERSTANDING

4.4 The total amount of time, effort, and resources that a mother and father each provide to successfully reproduce is called our:

    a. Sexual selection
    b. Parental investment
    c. Maternal offering
    d. Generational legacy

4.5 According to Buss and Schmitt (1993), women report that they'd like around five sexual partners over their entire lifetime. On average, how many sexual partners do men say they want over a lifetime?

    a. 5
    b. 18

    c. 3
    d. 37

4.6 Which evolutionary concept listed below is most directly the hypothesized cause of men being more jealous over sexual infidelity than over emotional infidelity?

    a. Natural selection
    b. r/K theory
    c. Paternity uncertainty
    d. Intersexual selection

APPLICATION ACTIVITY

Interview at least two men and two women. During the interview, ask them how many children they want, and why. Then, analyze their patterns of answering. First, see if there are differences between the men and women in terms of whether they display signs of a high-r versus a high-K strategy. This could be based on both the number of children they desire and whether they mention things like having enough time and resources to go around with their children. Second, look for differences in answers regarding any other aspects of parenthood (such as whether the people plan to be the primary caregiver for the children, or if they expect their spouse to do this—or even if they plan to be a single parent). Do your respondents' answers align with the evolutionary perspective? Why or why not?

CRITICAL THINKING

- Evolutionary predictions are based on ancestral behaviors that existed before modern technology provided options such as birth control. While research has shown that these patterns still exist now (despite modern technology), behaviors might change in the future. How long will it take for genetic patterns in the species to "catch up" to changes in technology? Do you think you could detect different results in cultures that are high-tech versus low-tech, showing a cultural influence in certain behaviors? If so, which behaviors are most likely to be influenced (or least likely) by access to technology?

• Consider the research on which makes people more jealous: sexual infidelity or emotional infidelity. Discuss what each type of "cheating" implies about one's partner. For example, if your partner cheats on you sexually, do you think

of your partner differently than if they cheat on you emotionally? Is one form of cheating easier to control than the other? Are you more willing to forgive one than the other? Do you think the two options mean different things about the personality of the "cheater"? What other differences came to mind when you were reading about this research, in terms of the two hypothetical people involved (the "cheater" in a relationship and the person being cheated on)?

Answers to the Check Your Understanding Questions

4.4 b, 4.5 b, and 4.6 c.

How Can This Perspective Be Applied to Other Important Relationship Behaviors?

The rest of this chapter explores several interesting applications and research areas inspired by the evolutionary perspective when it comes to family and love relationships. We'll cover strategies to keep your partner, motivations for cheating, and evolutionary explanations of child abuse. Just like before, some of these ideas are controversial in the field—many scientists don't agree with evolutionary explanations and find the implications to be sexist. It is up to you to critically analyze these ideas and decide for yourself whether you are inspired, offended, or maybe a little bit of both.

Mate Retention and Mate Poaching

Once you get someone to date you, how do you keep them around?

Mate retention is a general term that refers to attempts to keep a current partner committed and monogamous. There are a wide variety of potential strategies employed to retain a mate and keep them happy in the relationship. For example, Buss (1988a, p. 292) lists the general possibilities of (a) "luring" your mate with gifts and compliments, (b) "rendering one's mate less attractive to competitors" (e.g., controlling their clothes to be less attractive when going out in public), or (c) "dissuading potential competitors" through actions like displays of aggression (e.g., punching someone who flirts with your partner).

This last option—keeping rivals away—is called **mate guarding**. Mate guarding is one specific type of mate retention, and it's tied to the jealousy research we reviewed earlier in this chapter. Mate guarding might be a tactic needed when there are other people interested in dating or mating with your partner. When someone tries to "steal" a partner who is already in a committed relationship with someone else, relationship scientists call it **mate poaching**. In the competitive world of sex and love, evolutionary scholars have studied the most common tactics from both sides of the war. What do people do to keep their mates, and how do other people try to steal them?

Keeping Your Partner

What are the most common mate retention strategies?

Buss (1988a) argued that heterosexual men and women should use different tactics because of their different needs. If men are most interested in sexual fidelity of their girlfriends and wives, and if women are most interested in getting their boyfriends' and husbands' resources and emotional commitment, then the strategies employed by each sex should match what their partner most wants. In other words, he hypothesized that men would do things like give their wives gifts (a display of resources), while women would do things like provide sexual opportunities (so their husbands wouldn't be tempted to have affairs).

To test his hypothesis, Buss (1988a) asked about 100 college students to list three to five things that men do, and then three to five things that women do, to keep their partner from getting involved with someone else. The students came up with 104 different, specific examples of mate retention tactics. Buss then categorized these behaviors into various groups. You can see the results in Table 4.3. Each type of tactic is paired with a specific behavior, as an example.

Next, Buss (1988a) asked a different group of about 100 college students to rate how often they did the tactics identified earlier. He found that men most often used tactics like compliments, sitting next to their girlfriend, giving in to their girlfriend's wishes, and giving her gifts. In contrast, women said their most common tactics were being affectionate, working on their appearance, and flirting with other men to provoke jealousy and increase commitment. These sex differences in strategy confirmed what Buss expected, and he concluded that they supported an evolutionary perspective to mate retention.

More recent follow-up work has suggested the hypothesis that women might engage in certain sexual behaviors with their heterosexual partners specifically for mate retention purposes. From an evolutionary perspective, the only sexual behaviors that are helpful in the ultimate goal of reproduction are traditional penile-vaginal intercourse behaviors. However, everyone knows that there are a lot of very gratifying alternative options. People may engage in nonreproductive sexual behaviors as a mate retention tactic; sexually gratifying each other in a variety of ways is one strategy to keep someone from cheating.

For example, both men and women report that they perform oral sex to maintain their partner's sexual satisfaction (Pham & Shackelford, 2013; Sela, Shackelford, Pham, & Euler, 2015). Even more potentially interesting, another study suggested that one reason homosexual interests may have evolved in women is because men like the idea of watching two women have sex or hope to join in on a threesome with two women.

TABLE 4.3 ● Mate Retention Tactics in College Students	
Tactic	**Example**
Vigilance	Have friends check up on partner
Concealment of mate	Don't take to party with potential rivals
Monopolize mate's time	Spend all free time together
Threaten infidelity	Flirt with other people in front of mate
Punish mate for potential infidelity	Become angry if mate flirts with others
Emotional manipulation	Threaten self-harm if mate leaves
Commitment manipulation	Propose marriage
Derogation of rivals	Point out rivals' flaws
Display resources	Buy mate expensive gifts
Sexual inducements	Perform sexual favors
Enhance physical appearance	Dress nicely, grooming, etc.
Emphasize love and care	Compliment mate, say you love them
Submission and debasement	Give in to mate's desires
Verbal signals of possession	Introduce mate as "girlfriend/boyfriend," etc.
Physical signals of possession	Holding hands, kissing in public
Possessive ornamentation	Wearing jewelry indicating the relationship
Derogation of mate to competitors	Complaining about mate in public
Intrasexual threats	Yelling at rivals who flirt with mate
Violence	Hit rivals who flirt with mate

Both men and women in college can generate lists of things they do to keep their current partner from getting involved with someone else.

Thus, these researchers (Apostolou & Christoforou, 2018; Apostolou, Shialos, Khalil, & Paschali, 2017) argue that women may develop sexual interest in other women not for the lesbian experience in and of itself, but as a way to keep their male partner sexually excited. This is certainly a controversial suggestion to people in the LGBTQ community.

RELATIONSHIPS AND POPULAR CULTURE

Mate Poaching Over Hundreds of Years of Storytelling

While mate poaching is, by definition, "cheating" by at least one of the people involved, it has been romanticized in art and literature for hundreds of years.

The classic story of Homer's *Iliad* tells of how Helen of Troy was stolen from her husband by the young and handsome Paris. The legend of King Arthur is famous for the affair that Lancelot had with Queen Guinevere. Secret affairs are the subject of the Russian classic *Anna Karenina*.

More recently, Hollywood abounds with stories of people who want to steal someone else's partner: Jacob the werewolf wants to steal Bella the human from Edward the vampire (*Twilight*). Traveling photographer Robert Kincaid has an affair with the rural housewife Francesca when her husband goes to the Iowa state fair (*Bridges of Madison County*). A billionaire offers a husband $1 million to sleep with his wife for a single night (*Indecent Proposal*). A marriage counselor is seduced by a different billionaire (*Tyler Perry's Temptation*). Two women realize they love each other, even though one is married to a man (*Disobedience*). Two men realize they love each other, despite both being married to women (*Brokeback Mountain*).

There's even an article on Decider.com called "The 10 Sexiest Movies About Adultery." No one wants to be cheated on—so why are so many people interested in seeing movies about cheating? Perhaps it's because people prefer to think of themselves as the poacher, or even the person being tempted, and not the victim left standing to the side.

Stealing Someone Else's Partner

You've probably heard the phrase "All is fair in love and war." This implies that some people will resort to any means if it results in gaining what they want—and sometimes that can be stealing someone else's partner. If there are no attractive single people around, mate poaching is another way to start a relationship. Poaching can range from tempting someone into a single one-night affair all the way to getting someone to leave their spouse for a new partner. Estimates of extramarital affairs range from 20% to 50% of couples (e.g., Thompson, 1983; Wiederman, 1997).

To understand the psychology of mate poaching, Schmitt and Buss (2001) conducted a series of four studies. In Study 1, they asked over 200 people a series of questions about their experiences trying to poach, being the target of poaching, or being the victim of relationship poaching by a third party. While 50% of them admitted to trying to poach someone else, 85% of both men and women said that they had been the *target* of poaching attempts while they were in a relationship. Even more interestingly, over 40% of men and 30% of women said that the attempt had been successful: They had cheated on their partner at the time with the poacher, either through a single sexual encounter or in a more permanent change from one person to the other.

The second study in their series (Schmitt & Buss, 2001) found that men primarily try to poach physically attractive women, while women try to poach rich men. This certainly supports general evolutionary predictions. In Studies 3 and 4, they asked people to list specific behaviors that poachers might use on men or women, then they asked a separate group of participants to rate how effective each of those behaviors might be. Here, they found that women try to poach by enhancing their own appearance and by being sexually available immediately. In contrast, men's strategies to lure attached women to them included being generous and displaying wealth.

Schmitt and Buss (2001) also asked people to list pros and cons of poaching someone else's partner. Some of the benefits of stealing someone else's partner included sexual variety, bragging rights that would lead to esteem from others, being able to get "revenge" on someone, and feeling good about being more attractive than the person who was cheated on. However, participants also listed several drawbacks to poaching. These included feeling guilty, not being able to trust the person you just stole (because you know they are capable of cheating!), and concern about others viewing the new relationship badly due to it starting as an affair.

To end this section of the chapter, let's talk about one more study. A massive project involving 53 nations and almost 17,000 participants tested patterns of mate poaching around the world (Schmitt, 2004). As always, the evolutionary perspective has more merit if results are found consistently, despite cultural differences. This investigation did find cultural differences in how *common* mate poaching is; stealing partners and cheating was most common in Southern Europe, South America, and Western Europe. It was least common in Africa and Southeast Asia. However, across the world, men admitted to cheating more than women.

In addition, regardless of culture, the personality profile of poachers was consistent. More attempts at poaching were positively correlated with the personality traits extraversion and **erotophilia**, or being high in "obscenity, indecency, and lust" (Schmitt, 2004, p. 567). Mate poachers around the world are also low on agreeableness and low on **conscientiousness**, a trait associated with self-discipline, ability to delay gratification, and motivation to achieve long-term goals.

Strategic Infidelity: Motivations for Cheating

The previous section focused on poachers—people who attempt to "hunt" for other people's partners. But what about their prey?

The same massive study cited above (Schmitt, 2004) found that people who were successfully poached—in other words, people who cheated on their partners—also had a consistent personality profile, regardless of culture. Remember from the Schmitt and Buss (2001) study that over one-third of people in the United States admitted to having at least a one-night stand while in a relationship with someone else. Schmitt (2004) found that when he asked this question in other countries, "60% of men and 45% of women worldwide reported that they had succumbed to a short-term mate poach at some point in their past" (p. 571).

People who cheat report having lower commitment to their partner at the time, score lower in agreeableness, and are higher in erotophilia. Again, men in general were more likely to cheat than women. This pattern makes sense, given the research reviewed earlier about men being more promiscuous in general. But for women, there's a little bit more to the story. If women are less promiscuous, and if they have chosen to be in a relationship with someone who provides for them and appears to be committed, why cheat? What is their motivation?

One rather sensational idea has been proposed by evolutionary scientists. Women will marry men who are rich and committed, and thus will provide for her and for her children. However, sometimes choosing an older, rich man comes with a tradeoff: He might not be physically attractive. In fact, one article (Gangestad & Simpson, 2000) notes that "hot" men might actually be worse fathers, less willing to help raise children. On a simplistic level, then, women might have to choose between a rich, less attractive man versus a "hot" man who's not as good a provider.

The problem for women gets even more complicated if they consider how their choice between these two extremes will affect their children. The rich man will provide food, shelter, and other resources—but the "hot" man will pass his hotness (and genetic health) along to their children. The **sexy sons hypothesis** is that women want to produce physically attractive sons more than any other type of offspring (Sela, Weekes-Shackelford, Shackelford, & Pham, 2015; Weatherhead & Robertson, 1979). Sons are better than daughters, from an evolutionary perspective, because they can potentially produce more grandchildren than daughters could. One daughter might produce, let's say, 10 grandchildren—but one son could produce 100 grandchildren, or even 1000, theoretically. And the son should be "sexy" so that he has a high mate value, attracting a wide range of potential partners.

So, what's the solution? How does a woman choose between a rich, stable partner (who might be less attractive) versus a physically attractive partner (who might be less committed or have fewer resources)? Here's the potentially sensational part: She chooses *both*. Marry the rich one, but have sex with the hot one. If she does this, she gets the best of both worlds: all the resources from her husband, and the genetic health of good offspring from her lover.

There is research evidence to back up this hypothesis. For example, women who are already in a relationship are more likely to cheat on their partner with men who are high in physical symmetry (a cue of genetic health seen as physically attractive; see Chapter 8; Gangestad & Thornhill, 1997). In addition, women are more likely to have orgasms from sex with lovers compared to sex with boyfriends or husbands (Baker & Bellis, 1995). While having orgasms provides one motivation for cheating, another benefit is that orgasms may physically facilitate retention of sperm and thus lead to more pregnancies (Gangestad & Simpson, 2000). Thus, children are more likely to come from the "hot" partner than from the rich partner. Finally, women are most likely to cheat on their current partner while they are ovulating, maximizing the chances they will become pregnant (Bellis & Baker, 1990). It seems to be a dangerous game, with both high potential risk and high potential benefits—from an evolutionary view, at least.

The Cinderella Effect: Insights Into Child Abuse

The final topic of the chapter is a grim one, but it's an issue that needs more attention.

Child abuse is terrible, under any circumstances. But it's especially confusing when viewed with an evolutionary lens. If all humans are instinctively driven by the desire to produce healthy offspring that will pass our genes into the future, what possible motivation could there be to abuse children? One possible answer comes from research on domestic abuse. At least in some couples, one partner emotionally or physically abuses the other in attempts to control and dominate, potentially as a mate retention tactic (Buss, 1994). Not surprisingly, abuse often goes up when the abuser feels jealousy. One study found that 94% of abused wives said jealousy was the cause of frequent battery from their husbands (Rounsaville, 1978), a pattern often replicated (e.g., Sugarman & Hotaling, 1989; for more about relationship abuse, see Chapter 12).

While jealousy doesn't translate into abuse toward children, control and dominance do. Importantly, most parents do not abuse their children, despite frustration and even occasional provocation (Bowlby, 1984). Protecting children should be an evolutionary imperative—and most of the time, it is. When abuse does occur, a primary motivation appears to be attempts to control children to make them obedient or docile, which then allows the parent to make more decisions.

And a disturbing twist comes into play when a stepparent is involved. Fairy tales and legends exist in many cultures in which an "evil" stepfather or stepmother abuses children. This common theme is probably what contributed to the name of a phenomenon called the **Cinderella effect**. It's the increased risk of harm and abuse coming from stepparents to stepchildren (compared to biological children).

Is there any truth to the "evil stepparent" idea we see in stories like *Cinderella*?

Again, most stepparents do not physically harm their children. Nevertheless, stepchildren are 40 times more likely to be physically abused than biological children (Daly & Wilson, 1985), especially by stepfathers (Wilson, Daly, & Daniele, 1995). Russell (1984) reported a similar pattern: Stepdaughters were seven times more likely to experience abuse than a biological daughter. Further, if a man goes as far as to kill his family, subsequent suicide is significantly more likely if he killed a biological child than if he killed a stepchild (Wilson et al., 1995).

These results do appear to show that parents are more motivated to protect biological children than stepchildren. In fact, abuse of stepchildren increases when a family has scarce resources, another signal that biological children will get priority (D'Alessio & Stolzenberg, 2012). Even if the evolutionary perspective provides insight into these phenomena, there is no excuse or justification for physical or emotional abuse toward partners or children. Thus, this type of evidence on the darker side of human relationships needs more attention and resources, both academically and pragmatically, so that all abuse is put to an end.

Conclusions

The evolutionary perspective emphasizes unconscious, instinctive patterns of behavior that result from actions that helped our ancestors survive and mate with each other. It's the "nature" side of the "nature versus nurture" debate. And there's a lot of research evidence that some behaviors appear to be relatively common, regardless of culture or individual differences like personality. That said, almost no relationships researcher would say that our thoughts, feelings, or behaviors are *completely* based on either "nature" or "nurture." Human behavior is based on a combination of influences; our biology and socialization complement and influence each other.

Some people interpret evolutionary theory as saying that humans are just animals, and that belief can take away from our assumption that we're spiritually special and unique. That bothers some people. On the other hand, evolutionary science emphasizes that every human is essentially the same: We all have the same emotions, we all want the same things, and we all have more in common than we have different. Focusing on that interpretation might help overcome prejudice and even potentially remind us to respect each other, no matter how different we seem on the surface.

People tend to have strong reactions when they consider the evolutionary perspective, either for or against the basic ideas. But remember that even Darwin knew how controversial his ideas would be. And Darwin himself struggled with some of what his theory would mean, in terms of the place of humanity within the greater world. Maybe a good way to end this chapter is with the following quotation from one of his fans: "It is true that Darwin was as gentle, humane, and decent a man as you can reasonably hope to find on this planet. But it is also true that he was fundamentally no different from the rest of us. Even Charles Darwin was an animal" (Wright, 1994, p. 15).

CHECK YOUR UNDERSTANDING

4.7 George is interested in dating Isaac, but Isaac is already dating Raj. So, George flirts with Isaac and talks to Isaac about how Raj is not that successful at work. George's attempts to "steal" Isaac from his current partner are an example of:

a. Sexual selection
b. Natural selection
c. Mate retention
d. Mate poaching

4.8 According to Schmitt and Buss (2001), women report that their most common tactics to steal someone else's boyfriend or husband are to be sexually available and to enhance their own appearance. What did men say their most common tactics are?

a. Being sexually available and enhancing their own appearance
b. Being generous and displaying wealth

c. Being aggressive toward a woman and nice to her current partner
d. Being nonthreatening and shy around both members of the established couple

4.9 Mrs. Fukami is married to a wealthy man. According to research, what is the time when she is mostly likely to cheat on her husband by having sex with a physically attractive lover?

a. While she's ovulating
b. During a religious holiday
c. Within 1 year after having a baby
d. During the month immediately before her marriage ceremony

APPLICATION ACTIVITY

This section of the chapter reviewed research on the "Cinderella effect," or the finding that parents are, on average, more abusive toward stepchildren than toward biological children. While this idea has been featured in several well-known stories and legends (such as the Cinderella story itself), there are also pop culture examples of happy blended families (such as the Brady Bunch). Identify three variables that you think might influence the likelihood of stepparents being more or less likely to get along with their stepchildren, and explain your hypotheses.

CRITICAL THINKING

- Evolutionary ideas are guided by the concept that people are instinctively motivated to pass their genes onto the next generation through reproduction. In this way, we should be concerned with devoting as many resources as possible to our younger, biological relatives. If this is the case, how can evolutionary psychologists explain why thousands of people adopt children every year—including people who are capable of biological reproduction but choose to adopt instead?

- Imagine you're dating someone who cheats on you. When you confront the person about their actions, the response is, "Hey, it's human instinct. I can't help it." What response do you have for this argument?

Answers to the Check Your Understanding Questions

4.7 d, 4.8 b, and 4.9 a.

Chapter Summary

Big Questions

1. How is an evolutionary perspective applied to intimate relationships?

2. How does this perspective explain sex differences in promiscuity and jealousy?

3. How can this perspective be applied to other important relationship behaviors?

How is an evolutionary perspective applied to intimate relationships?
Darwin developed the evolutionary perspective while studying different species of animals, including finches in the Galapagos Islands. An important insight is the idea of natural selection, or that individual variations within a species will lead to better or worse survival rates. Variations that help survival are more likely to be passed on to the next generation. In addition, sexual selection is the idea that some traits will help individuals get mating opportunities, and these variations will also thus be more likely to be passed along to descendants. Sexual selection takes two forms. Intrasexual competition is

when one sex competes within itself (e.g., men compete with other men). Intersexual selection is when an individual chooses a mate from the opposite sex (e.g., a man chooses a woman).

How does this perspective explain sex differences in promiscuity and jealousy?
Both men and women are driven to have as many healthy offspring as possible, but biological differences lead them to have different strategies. Parental investment is the amount of time, effort, and resources that a mother and father provide to get each child into adulthood. The investment needed for mothers (carrying the fetus, providing

milk, etc.) is higher than the investment needed for fathers (providing sperm). Thus, men are predicted to be more sexually promiscuous, as promiscuity provides the most efficient strategy for men. In addition, men are predicted to be the most jealous over sexual infidelity due to paternity uncertainty, the possibility that children they raise are not biologically their own. Women, in contrast, are predicted to be jealous over emotional infidelity because their boyfriends or husbands might provide valuable/limited resources to the other woman. Research finds support for these hypotheses in a wide variety of world cultures.

How can this perspective be applied to other important relationship behaviors? Studies have investigated both mate retention tactics (keeping your current partner committed and monogamous) and mate poaching tactics (attempts to "steal" someone else's partner). When someone does "cheat," the timing can be strategic. Research indicates that some women, for example, will marry a rich man but have sexual affairs with physically attractive men while ovulating. The idea that women want physically attractive children who are highly likely to pass their genes onto a third generation is called the sexy sons hypothesis. Finally, research indicates that parents are more likely to be abusive toward stepchildren than toward biological children. All these findings can be explained by the evolutionary perspective, but the general theory remains quite controversial.

List of Terms

Learning Objectives	Key Terms
4.1 Explain natural selection and sexual selection, and how they can be applied to intimate relationships.	Cross-cultural psychology Evolutionary psychology Fixation Sexual selection Intrasexual competition Intersexual selection
4.2 Analyze how parental investment might lead to differences in men's and women's patterns of promiscuity and jealousy.	Parental investment r/K theory High-r strategy High-K strategy Paternity uncertainty Emotional infidelity Sexual infidelity
4.3 Apply this perspective to mate guarding, mate poaching, strategic infidelity, and child abuse.	Mate retention Mate guarding Mate poaching Erotophilia Conscientiousness Sexy sons hypothesis Cinderella effect

5

Interdependence Theory

Big Questions	Learning Objectives
1. What are the main ideas within interdependence theory?	5.1 Explain interdependence, outcome matrices, and transformation of motivation.
2. What factors predict relationship commitment and stability?	5.2 Analyze how satisfaction, alternatives, and investments work together to predict a relationship's fate.
3. What advances to the theory have been made?	5.3 Interpret recent research on each component of interdependence theory and the investment model.

Attachment theory predicts that our adult relationships are influenced by our first few years of life—something over which we have very little control. The evolutionary perspective predicts that relationship behaviors are driven by biological instincts inherited from our ancestors—and again, we didn't get to influence this process. Neither theory puts much emphasis on logical, rational, conscious choice. Where are *you*, your desires, your preferences? What about decisions that *you* make? Enter the third and final theory—and this time, the person in charge of your fate is you.

Interdependence theory offers an important alternative to attachment or evolution because it posits that every decision we make in relationships is purposeful. Our choices are based on a logical consideration of what the best possible outcome might be in every situation. The theory is built on the foundational idea that we want to achieve lasting, fair relationships with other people that are based on mutual compromise and effort. It also suggests that we only decide to commit to a particular monogamous relationship if we believe our current partner really is our best chance at happiness.

What Are the Main Ideas Within Interdependence Theory?

Imagine you move in with your intimate partner. One of you wants to get a cat, but the other person is allergic. How do you decide what to do?

Interdependence theory starts with this basic idea: *Relationships are partnerships.* Your decision about whether to get a cat with your partner is a negotiation, and what (and how) you decide on the cat question will affect both people's happiness. Cat or no cat, the decision will matter to both of you. A **social exchange** occurs when people work together to gain the best possible outcomes for everyone involved (Blau, 1967; Homans, 1961).

In any relationship you have with someone else—romantic, friendship, or otherwise—each person affects the other. This social exchange can be direct or indirect. Directly, one person might decide to order the second person around, or at least make requests. Or get a cat. Indirectly, if one person is angry or sad, that mood will certainly affect any interactions that occur. Either way, you're in it together.

Defining Interdependence

The two pioneers of interdependence theory were Harold ("Hal") Thibaut and John Kelley (Kelley & Thibaut, 1978; Thibaut & Kelley, 1959).

To begin, here's a fairly simple definition for **interdependence theory**: It proposes that our behaviors in relationships are based on trying to get the best possible outcome, and that *both* people's outcomes affect each other. So, interdependence theory is one type of social exchange theory. If you are promoted or fired at work, it affects your partner. If your partner comes home in a good or bad mood, it affects you. Your outcomes, and your partner's, are all mixed up and tied together. That's why Kelley and Thibaut called it "interdependence" theory—because each person's situation depends on the happiness of the other person. Once you're in a relationship with someone, you're no longer *independent*; instead, you become *interdependent* with each other (Van Lange & Rusbult, 2011). You're a team.

Just scratching the surface, it means that compromise is often going to be the best option. If you get to pick the movie or restaurant tonight, then your partner should probably get to pick it next time. One hypoallergenic cat might work . . . but maybe not six fluffy cats. If couple members aren't willing to compromise, there are unstable and unhappy power dynamics that mean one person is getting the short end of the relationship stick.

Interdependence theory is so complicated that even this entire chapter won't cover all aspects of it. But for each section, we'll cover important concepts and break them down into easily understood pieces of the larger picture. Let's start with a discussion of how two people's outcomes affect each other.

An Outcome Matrix

Imagine a fictitious couple named Sylvia and Cesar. Sylvia is passionate about exercise and being healthy. Cesar is more laid back, and he enjoys spending free time by relaxing and drinking a few beers at the bar, surrounded by friends. It's Friday night,

FIGURE 5.1 ● An Example Interdependence Matrix		
	Sylvia goes to the gym.	**Sylvia goes to the bar.**
Cesar goes to the gym.	1 5	0 0
Cesar goes to the bar.	4 3	2 1

If happiness is on a scale from 1 to 5, the matrix shows how the decision of what to do tonight matters to both couple members. Each person's decision affects how happy the other person is going to be. Sylvia's happiness is shown above the diagonal in each scenario, while Cesar's happiness is shown below the diagonal. See Kelley and Thibaut (1978, p. 34).

and they are trying to decide what to do. Each of them has to decide whether to go to the gym or to the bar. Their choices result in the four possible outcomes shown in the matrix displayed in Figure 5.1.

Kelley and Thibaut described a wide variety of **outcome matrices**, or tables showing outcome patterns like this one where one person's choice affects both people's happiness (Thibaut & Kelley, 1959). The two columns represent Sylvia's possible choices, and the rows are for Cesar. The numbers shown in the figure represent how happy each person will be with the outcome, on a range from 0 (very unhappy) to 5 (very happy).

If Sylvia goes to the gym, she'll be pretty happy. She'll be happiest (5) if Cesar decides to join her (if she ends up there alone, she'll be at a 3). If she ends up at the bar instead, she'll be pretty unhappy and annoyed . . . but at least if Cesar is there too, she'll enjoy it a little bit (1). Cesar doesn't care quite so much. His highest possible level of happiness would be a 4, resulting from him going out drinking and Sylvia deciding to go to the gym (he thinks he'll have more fun on his own, considering she really wouldn't want to be there). However, he'll still be moderately happy (2) if she accompanies him. If he has to go to the gym, he'll be pretty unhappy (1) if he's there with his partner, but he'll be pretty angry (0) if he goes to the gym and she decides to go out drinking without him.

The point of this matrix is that each person's level of happiness is at least partially dependent on what the other person decides to do. Their outcomes are interdependent, not independent. They're a team, and their decisions affect each other. That means that over time, relationship partners coordinate their choices to maximize outcomes for both people.

Transformation of Motivation

Frankly, social exchange theories assume that we're all ultimately selfish.

Thibaut and Kelley (1959) wrote, "The rewards of a relationship can be defined in terms of the pleasures, satisfactions, and gratifications the person enjoys as a consequence of involvement" (p. 12). When we experience situations like the outcome matrix in Figure 5.1, the easiest decision to make would be the one that leads to our own highest level of happiness. Sylvia could decide to go to the gym while Cesar goes to the bar, each thinking, "Screw what you want—I'm doing what *I* want." But this selfish view is not going to result in happiness for very long. It's the kind of mindset people have when they're mad at each other or thinking about breaking up.

So sometimes, we have to make short-term sacrifices that make our partner happy, because those sacrifices maintain peace in the relationship. These decisions still end up being at least a little selfish, though, because we make them to satisfy the *long-term* needs of the relationship. If Sylvia and Cesar want to stay happy, they know they have to work together. That's where the next interdependence concept comes in. **Transformation of motivation** occurs when our approach to interactions with our partner shifts because our needs change (Kelley & Thibaut, 1978; Van Lange & Rusbult, 2011). It means the outcome matrix for any given situation (like in Figure 5.1) changes because of how we approach it. Transformation means we think beyond the simple situation immediately in front of us, and we focus on the "big picture" of the long-term relationship instead.

Types of Transformation

There are several different types of transformation, or ways we can approach relationship situations. Each will change possible outcomes and how we feel about what happens. One option is called an "egoistic" transformation. This happens when we become completely selfish and *only* care about what makes *us* happy. It maximizes our own outcomes, especially when we can trick, convince, or force the other person to do what makes us happy. While this seems like a good strategy on the surface—after all, we always get what we want!—it leads to unhealthy power dynamics.

Kelley and Thibaut believe that the healthy alternative is a "prosocial" transformation. This occurs when we make choices that lead to the best possible *mutually desirable* outcomes, even if it means sacrificing a part of our own happiness. Short-term sacrifices lead to long-term stability and staying together. Prosocial transformation could take various forms. For example, a couple might take on a sequential approach. Here, they take turns. Sylvia and Cesar might go to the gym together this Friday, but go to the bar together next Friday. It's fair, and each gets to feel valued. Another possibility is called a "max joint" transformation. Here, true compromises are found. Sylvia and Cesar might realize that they could go to the gym for an hour, clean up, and then go out for a drink afterward—all on the same night.

Tom Cruise has been married several times. One of his wives was the extremely successful actress Nicole Kidman. When she started winning awards like Oscars, many people predicted that he would be envious. But when an interviewer asked him whether he was jealous of her success, he responded, "You don't understand. Her dreams are now my dreams" (see Berscheid & Reis, 1998, p. 238). He explicitly said that his happiness was dependent on hers (at least, until they divorced and he married Katie Holmes . . . who has also never won an Oscar. And they also got divorced, so maybe Tom's not as transformed as he thinks he is). A prosocial transformation means that people move from an "I" orientation to a "we" orientation (Borden & Levinger, 1991).

Importantly, Kelley and Thibaut note that the key to happy, healthy dynamics in the relationship is that *both* people should make prosocial transformations. If one person continues to act selfishly (an egoistic transformation) while the second has made a prosocial transformation, the prosocial partner will basically become a martyr. Ultimately, both people will be unhappy because the relationship just isn't stable. Both people need to feel respected and think that their partner is putting in effort to keep them happy.

Note, however, that we tend to think we're making more sacrifices than our partner is. We're biased to see our own efforts and think that we're bearing more of the metaphorical weight in the relationship. For example, when Ross (unpublished study, cited in Kelley & Thibaut, 1978) asked partners what percentage of the household chores they did, the results consistently added up to over 100%. In short, we overestimate how hard we're working and underestimate the efforts of our partner. It's probably a good idea for long-term partners to occasionally remind themselves of times when the other person has genuinely tried to make the relationship work.

Gender and Cross-Cultural Differences in Transformation

Take a look at Table 5.1.

Table 5.1 lists examples of "gentleman traditions" that some people expect to see from men toward women. From an interdependence theory perspective, these behaviors could be considered small sacrifices that men were traditionally expected to do, to show women respect. These small inconveniences (e.g., giving up a seat for a woman without one, holding your umbrella over a woman instead of over yourself) could be examples of prosocial transformation of motivation within a relationship. As everyone knows, some men feel more need to be "chivalrous" and "gentlemanly" than others, an individual difference within gender. Of course, many people would consider these expectations to be old-fashioned, or even potentially sexist by today's standards. They also only refer to situations with a cisgender man and woman;

TABLE 5.1 ● Examples of "Gentleman Traditions"	
Stand when a woman enters the room.	Help a woman put on and take off her coat.
On the street, walk by a woman on the outside (closest to the street).	Give up your seat if a woman doesn't have one.
Open doors for women.	Carry a woman's bags/packages for her.
Pull out a woman's chair for her.	Pick up the check when eating out.
Stand when a woman leaves the table.	Hold your umbrella over her if it's raining.
Give a woman your jacket if she's cold.	Walk her home (she goes home first).

These behaviors are traditionally expected from "gentlemen" toward "ladies." Are they simply polite, or are they sexist by today's standards?

Source: Wolfe (2014).

what about LGBTQ situations? If two men or two women are dating, is one expected to pay for meals or hold an umbrella more than the other? Should cisgender men give up their seat for transgender people?

Gendered expectations are not the only context in which social norms influence the likelihood of making sacrifices for the good of the relationship, or the good of the larger group in general. Culture might also influence how much someone is tempted to have an egoistic (selfish) versus prosocial (selfless) approach to relationship dynamics. For example, some studies have shown that children from rural cultures (e.g., small villages in Mexico, Israeli kibbutz communities) are more cooperative and motivated by a fair division of treats like candy, compared to children in urban settings (regardless of race—White, Black, and Hispanic/Latinx urban kids were all more competitive; Madsen & Shapira, 1970; Shapira & Madsen, 1969). Rural cultures may foster prosocial motives because there are fewer people around, leading to less diffusion of responsibility for each individual.

One of the most well-researched cultural differences is that people from "Western" cultures (like the United States, Canada, Great Britain, and Australia) tend to be **individualistic**, or focused on the needs of the self, whereas "Eastern" cultures (like Japan, China, and India) are more **collectivistic**, or focused on the needs of the group (Hui & Triandis, 1986). Thus, people in Western cultures may approach social exchange situations from an egoistic transformation standpoint, while people from Eastern cultures might be more likely to have a prosocial transformation. In general, research has shown this to be true in settings where people have the opportunity to help strangers without gaining any kind of reward (Barrett, Wosinska, Butner, Petrova, Gornik-Durose, & Cialdini, 2004; Bontempo, Lobel, & Triandis, 1990).

Only a few studies have been done so far regarding whether the individualistic versus collectivistic division, based on culture, affects intimate relationships. In one review of this research (Dion & Dion, 1993), three specific propositions were hypothesized, then supported with evidence from several sources:

1. "Romantic love" is considered more important in individualistic cultures. For example, whether your family approves of your partner matters more in collectivistic cultures (Lee & Stone, 1980), while people from individualistic cultures make decisions like marriage without consulting with family first.

2. People from individualistic cultures expect higher levels of emotional intimacy from their romantic partners. For example, in China and in Japan, people often remain emotionally closer to family members than to partners, even after marriage (Hsu, 1985; Roland, 1988). People from Eastern cultures thus are more likely to prioritize their family of origin over their romantic partner.

3. While individualism fosters expectations of "romance" and "intimacy," it can ultimately lead to problems within relationships. For example, research in Canada found that people who maintained the belief that their own freedom was more important than their partner's happiness were less likely to report caring or trust toward their partner (Dion & Dion, 1991) and were more open to eventual divorce (Dion & Dion, 1993). Thus, the individualistic culture that puts "self" first can lead to problems in relationships.

If individualism is closely aligned with an egoistic transformation of motivation, and collectivism is aligned with a prosocial transformation, these patterns fit interdependence theory predictions.

Fair's Fair: Equity Theory

If you're in a relationship right now, think about how you would answer this question (Hatfield, Utne, & Traupmann, 1979):

> Who is getting a "better deal," considering what you put into your relationship and what you get out of it?

a. I am getting a much better deal than my partner.

b. I am getting a better deal than my partner.

c. I am getting a somewhat better deal than my partner.

d. I am getting the same deal as my partner.

e. I am getting a somewhat worse deal than my partner.

f. I am getting a worse deal than my partner.

g. I am getting a much worse deal than my partner.

If you've made a prosocial transformation of motivation, you've decided that you're willing to make sacrifices for the long-term good of the relationship. But most of us expect that our partner has to do this, too—we don't want to be the one always giving and never getting. An extension of social exchange theories is **equity theory**, which suggests that people are happiest in relationships when the rewards and costs for each person are fair (Adams, 1963; Hatfield & Rapson, 2012; Sprecher, 2001; Walster, Walster, & Berscheid, 1978).

Equity theory says that we don't like to feel like we're putting in more effort, sacrifices, money, or anything else into the relationship, compared to our partner. In other words, the best answer to the question above is d—I'm getting the same deal as my partner. When we feel like we're working harder than our partner (in other words, we're getting a worse deal), we feel anger and resentment. In equity theory, this is called feeling **underbenefitted**. When we feel this way, we're less likely to make apologies to our partner (even when we do something wrong), because we start to feel like they "owe" us something (Guerrero, La Valley, & Farinelli, 2008).

However, the theory also says that we don't like to feel spoiled, or **overbenefitted**, either. A "better" deal is nice for a while—everyone likes to get gifts and attention, for example—but if we start to believe that the other person is putting in more effort, we'll feel guilty (Guerrero et al., 2008; Spector, 2008). When we feel this way, we tend to hold emotions like anger in without expressing them, because we feel we owe our partner something. This leads to poor communication between partners, which can spiral into worse problems down the line. Either form of inequity between partners (under- or overbenefitted feelings) leads to less relationship happiness and stability.

Earlier, we discussed research that indicated both couple members tend to believe they do more than half of the chores at home. It's interesting to note that when chores are divided up, heterosexual couples often do so along traditional gender lines. Men do things like yard work, while women cook and take care of children (Pedulla & Thébaud, 2015). Gay couples, in contrast, often divide chores more equally (Brewster, 2017; Patterson, Sutfin, & Fulcher, 2004; Tornello, Sonnenberg, & Patterson, 2015). But there's a twist: That equality at home sometimes decreases when those couples have children. After that, whichever member of the same-sex couple who earns less at work usually ends up doing more cleaning, cooking, and childcare (Miller, 2018). Thus, even in gay couples, if the family has children, one couple member often ends up being the primary parent while the other is assigned to a financial provider role.

As both interdependence theory and equity theory propose, the happiest relationships are those in which both people feel like there's mutual effort, balance, and respect. But exactly how each couple decides on "what's fair" may vary quite a bit from one pair to the next. As one gay man said about how he and his husband share responsibilities, "It's not a masculine or feminine thing; it is just what we do to function as a couple and have our family work" (see Miller, 2018). In addition, there are individual differences in how much we "keep score" of our efforts versus our rewards, an idea called "communal versus exchange orientation," which is explored more in Chapter 13.

CHECK YOUR UNDERSTANDING

5.1   Interdependence theory presents the "social exchange" of two people in a relationship using tables that show different choices and results for both people. These tables are called:

a. Choice binary plots
b. Dichotomy tables
c. Outcome matrices
d. Exchange endgames

5.2   Adam and Steve are dating. Adam likes horror movies, while Steve likes romantic comedies. They create a system in which each of them gets to pick movies by taking turns. What type of transformation of motivation is most closely relevant to this system of turn-taking?

a. Egoistic transformation
b. Max joint transformation

c. Sequential transformation
d. Independent transformation

5.3   LaToya feels "spoiled" by their partner, who constantly gives them gifts and little love notes. LaToya doesn't put much effort into the relationship themself. Equity theory predicts that LaToya might feel "overbenefitted." What emotion is LaToya most likely to experience, according to research summarized in this chapter?

a. Guilt
b. Anger
c. Sadness
d. Happiness

APPLICATION ACTIVITY

Take a poll of at least five men and five women. Ask them if they think that men should still do the behaviors listed in Table 5.1 for women. Are some behaviors expected more than others? If people think the behaviors should still occur, what is their reasoning? What's the reasoning if not? Analyze the pattern of responses you get by comparing men's answers to women's answers. Finally, consider how answers from both men and women might change in 100 years. Will "chivalry be dead"? Is that a good thing or a bad thing?

CRITICAL THINKING

- Some women like to say that they want to be "treated like a princess" in a relationship. Does this mean that they want their partner to make sacrifices for them such as the "chivalry" behaviors listed in Table 5.1? Equity theory says that unless both people in a relationship are putting in effort, the relationship is ultimately unstable. Does this mean both people in a relationship should be "treated like a princess" (or prince)?

- This section of the chapter covered cross-cultural differences in approaches to relationships (e.g., individualistic vs. collectivistic cultures). Some cultures have a "machismo" aspect, meaning that the culture expects men to appear traditionally masculine and be the "head of the household." Machismo culture is found in some Hispanic/Latinx cultures and among some White people in U.S. Southern states. Does machismo culture seem like a cross-cultural difference that might affect things like transformation of motivation in relationships? How and why?

- Equity theory says that we're happiest if we feel that our effort in a relationship is the same as our partner's effort—everything is "fair." But do you think there are individual differences in whether people really want things to be fair, versus people who prefer to feel "overbenefitted"? For example, narcissists might not care so much about whether their relationship is fair. What other personality traits or individual differences might make people more comfortable with feelings of inequity, in either the "underbenefitted" or "overbenefitted" direction?

Answers to the Check Your Understanding Questions

5.1 c, 5.2 c, and 5.3 a.

What Factors Predict Relationship Commitment and Stability?

Interdependence theory tries to predict how relationship partners will make decisions, like the outcome matrix you saw earlier. But there's an even bigger question the theory wants to answer: How can we predict whether any given relationship will last the test of time? You might even have asked this question yourself, thinking about your own partners, the people your friends date, or maybe even celebrity couples you see in the news.

Consider, for example, two of Hollywood's biggest stars: Brad Pitt and Jennifer Aniston. They married in 2000 and were the hottest couple in entertainment. Movie fans all over the world were shocked when only a few years later, they announced a messy divorce in the midst of a huge scandal. Pitt admitted that he had fallen in love with "bad girl" Angelina Jolie during the filming of their movie *Mr. and Mrs. Smith* (Goldsman, Milchan, & Foster, 2005). Pitt and Jolie created a family with six children (some biological, some adopted), got married, and appeared to be forgiven by the world. But in 2016, they divorced—and paparazzi were thrilled when it appeared that Pitt and Aniston were back together again in 2018 (Goddard, 2018; Hitt; 2018). Ultimately—so far, at least—the reunion appears to be just rumor.

It would be extremely useful if intimate relationship researchers could create a way for us to predict whether any given couple will stay together. This section of the chapter focuses on how interdependence theory attempts to do just that. When you look around at your friends' relationships or couples you see in the news, how do you make a guess regarding which ones will last for many years versus those you think are likely to break up? What factors do you use to make your guesses?

Predicting Relationship Fate: Commitment

Interdependence theory suggests that the single biggest predictor of the fate of a relationship is commitment.

Commitment, in this theory, is the extent to which relationship partners want to keep a relationship going and see themselves together in the future. It also means that they engage in behaviors that maintain the relationship (like not cheating), feel emotionally attached to each other, and make plans that assume the relationship will be intact for years to come. Two researchers, Ximena Arriaga and Chris Agnew, have explored commitment in a wide variety of ways over many studies. In one, they created a self-report commitment scale that has now been used in dozens of investigations on how and why partners commit to each other, as well as the consequences of commitment (Arriaga & Agnew, 2001). You can see their scale (and even try it yourself!) in the "What's My Score?" feature.

The scale highlights that there are three components of commitment:

- *Affective commitment:* psychological or emotional attachment to your partner and the relationship. This is measured by items 1–4 on the scale.

- *Cognitive commitment:* long-term orientation toward this relationship, "for better or worse." This is measured by items 5–8 on the scale.

- *Conative commitment:* intent to persist, a motivation to engage in behaviors that keep the relationship intact. This is measured by items 9–12 on the scale.

While both the cognitive and conative components are focused on the future, the difference is that the cognitive part is a logical, thoughtful decision. In contrast, the conative part is a "gut feeling." In their research, Arriaga and Agnew (2001) found that all three components of commitment are positively correlated to relationships lasting over time. They also found that for dating college students, the *most* important predictor of relationship stability was the cognitive component, long-term orientation. So, at least in this case, thoughtful decision making about one's relationship ended up being a better way to know if a couple would stay together than their "gut feelings" about what would happen. Thus, items 5–8 in the scale proved the most helpful for predicting the fate of college student relationships.

WHAT'S MY SCORE?

Relationship Commitment

Instructions: As you read each statement, write a number next to the item to indicate how much you agree with it, using this scale:

1	2	3	4	5	6	7	8	9

Do not
agree at all

Agree
completely

_____ 1. I feel very attached to our relationship—very strongly linked to my partner.

_____ 2. It pains me to see my partner suffer.

_____ 3. I am very affected when things are not going well in my relationship.

_____ 4. In all honesty, my family and friends are more important to me than this relationship.

_____ 5. I am oriented toward the long-term future of my relationship (e.g., I imagine being with my partner several years from now).

_____ 6. My partner and I joke about what things will be like when we are old.

_____ 7. I find it difficult to imagine myself with my partner in the distant future.

_____ 8. When I make plans about future events in my life, I think about the impact of my decisions on our relationship.

_____ 9. I intend to stay in this relationship.

_____ 10. I want to maintain our relationship.

_____ 11. I feel inclined to keep our relationship going.

_____ 12. My gut feeling is to continue in this relationship.

Scoring: First, reverse-score items 4 and 7 (e.g., the answer of a 1 becomes a 9, and so on). Then, add up all of the answers and divide by 12. Your answer should be between 1 and 9, with higher numbers meaning more overall commitment.

Source: Arriaga and Agnew (2001).

Critical Thinking: Do different kinds of people focus on different aspects of commitment? For example, do older couples care more about the long-term nature of the relationship because they want to plan for the future, or do they care less about the long-term nature because they are already stable and established? Are some personality traits tied to being more emotional about commitment, compared to being more logical? Which items are the most important to you, personally, and why?

Once people are committed to their partner, there are several ways they change their behavior. For example, when one person in a relationship is rude, fails to fulfill a promise, or does anything else that might cause harm to the relationship, highly committed partners are more likely to engage in **accommodation**, which is inhibiting the urge to retaliate by instead trying to forgive and forget (Arriaga & Rusbult, 1998; Kilpatrick, Bissonnette, & Rusbult, 2002; Rusbult, Verette, Whitney, Slovik, & Lipkus, 1991). High commitment is also positively correlated with **willingness to sacrifice** in relationships, or the motivation to give up personal preferences for the sake of making their partner happy—in other words, a positive transformation of motivation (Powell & Van Vugt, 2003; Totenhagen, Curran, Serido, & Butler, 2013; Van Lange, Agnew, Harnick, & Steemers, 1997; Van Lange, Rusbult, Drigotas, Arriaga, Witcher, & Cox, 1997). And of course, commitment is tied to relationship stability: The couple who commits together stays together.

Predicting Commitment: Satisfaction and Alternatives

So, the best way to predict a relationship's stability is to know the couple members' commitment to each other. But interdependence theory goes even deeper by asking: What predicts commitment? What factors in a relationship make someone decide to have that long-term orientation? The theory states that there are two variables that are linked to commitment—one that makes commitment go up, and one that makes it go down.

Helping Commitment: Satisfaction

If you're going to commit to be with only one person for the foreseeable future, then it only makes sense that you should feel satisfied by your relationship. In interdependence theory, **satisfaction** is defined as thinking the benefits from being with this person outweigh the costs and are better than an "average" relationship. Just like every concept within the larger theory, the belief is that we make purposeful, thoughtful decisions about whether we're satisfied or not. And we do that in two explicit steps (Kelley & Thibaut, 1978).

The first step is to consider how happy our partner makes us. **Current outcomes** are the rewards and costs experienced in a relationship. One way to think about current outcomes would be a "pro and con" list of what you're getting from being with this person. It makes sense that our satisfaction will go up if the "pro" list is longer than the "con" list. The ratio of advantages to disadvantages changes over time and as our needs evolve. In fact, studies on happy marriage have found that the ratio should be at least 5:1. This means that for every negative interaction or emotion that happens in a relationship, there should be at least five positive interactions or emotions (Gottman, 1999; Gottman, Schwartz Gottman, & DeClaire, 2006).

But there's also a second step. A **comparison level** (or **CL**) is an abstract standard for what you think an "average" relationship is like—it's our basic expectations (Rusbult, Arriaga, & Agnew, 2001). It includes your idea of what most people get out of a relationship and what the *typical* pro/con list looks like in terms of the ratio of advantages to disadvantages. In some ways, your CL determines the kind of relationship you think you deserve or should strive to achieve. We all want to think our situation is "better than average." Mediocrity isn't very romantic.

So, *level* of satisfaction is measured as the distance between our perception of our current outcomes, in relation to our comparison level. It's how well-off you feel you are, right now. If our current outcomes are better or higher than our CL, or what we think is "average," we're satisfied (see Figure 5.2). If our current outcomes seem worse than a typical relationship, we're dissatisfied. It's as simple as this:

- Current outcomes > CL = Satisfied

- Current outcomes < CL = Dissatisfied

Research shows that people are, indeed, happier in their relationships when their partner meets or exceeds their expectations (Sternberg & Barnes, 1985; Wetzel & Insko, 1982). And level of satisfaction can go up or down on a continuum or range. The more distance there is between current outcomes and CL, the greater the level of satisfaction (or dissatisfaction), as shown in Figure 5.2. Satisfaction is positively correlated with commitment. This positive correlation has been replicated in several research studies, including a meta-analysis that reviewed 52 individual tests of the connection (Le & Agnew, 2003). Satisfaction and commitment are also tied to having more positive illusions about our current partner (Goodfriend, Agnew, & Cathey, 2017), meaning we overlook negative qualities and focus instead on things we like about our partner, to a biased level. In this way, we convince ourselves to stay.

Hurting Commitment: Alternatives

When Brad Pitt was married to Jennifer Aniston, he was probably pretty satisfied. By all accounts, she's traditionally beautiful, kind, and loyal. But he left her anyway.

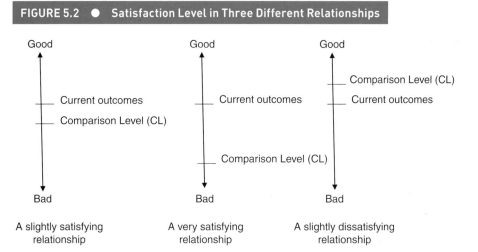

FIGURE 5.2 ● Satisfaction Level in Three Different Relationships

A slightly satisfying relationship

A very satisfying relationship

A slightly dissatisfying relationship

Satisfaction level is measured by the distance between our current outcomes and our CL, or comparison level. If our CL is lower than current outcomes, we're satisfied. If our CL is higher than current outcomes, it means we think our relationship is worse than average and we're dissatisfied.

Despite a high level of satisfaction, people sometimes choose not to stay committed. Interdependence theory explains this choice with a second variable: alternatives.

Even if our current relationship is pretty good, if something even better comes along, we'll be tempted. Our **comparison level for alternatives** (or **CL_{alt}**) is the most attractive option you think you'd have if you left your current relationship. It includes other people you could date, and it also includes simply being single. Interdependence theory suggests that at least on an unconscious level, we're constantly thinking about other options, "just in case," in the back of our mind. Our alternatives can also change all the time. If someone flirts with us and indicates interest, our CL_{alt} just went way up. If our CL_{alt} ever goes above our current outcomes, we'll be tempted to leave the current relationship for a better option. It's like a relationship upgrade.

Dependence is how much you rely on your current relationship for happiness. Within the terminology of this theory, it's measured by the space between our current outcomes and our CL_{alt}. Imagine someone who honestly believes that their current relationship is the best possible outcome. It means that they're quite dependent on their partner for happiness. Their next-best option (their CL_{alt}) is much lower than their current outcomes, so they're going to stay—even if their satisfaction isn't particularly high. Studies have confirmed the link between alternatives and dependence: People feel less tied to their current partner (and are more likely to break up) if they think they have attractive alternatives waiting in the wings (Bui, Peplau, & Hill, 1996; Drigotas & Rusbult, 1992; Le & Agnew, 2003).

Just like satisfaction, degree or level of dependence is measured by the space between our current outcomes and our CL_{alt}. You can see three examples in Figure 5.3. Alternatives and dependence are tied together: The more alternatives you have (or the higher quality your alternatives), the lower your dependence—and vice versa.

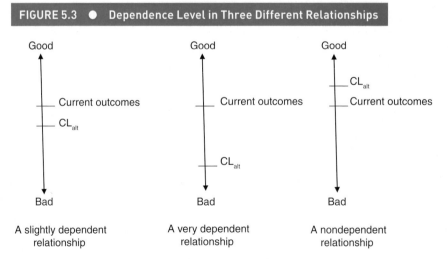

FIGURE 5.3 ● Dependence Level in Three Different Relationships

A slightly dependent relationship

A very dependent relationship

A nondependent relationship

Level of dependence is measured by the distance between our current outcomes and our CL_{alt}, or comparison level for alternatives. If our CL_{alt} is higher than current outcomes, it means we have a better alternative and will be tempted to leave the current relationship. If our CL_{alt} is lower than current outcomes, we become dependent on our relationship for happiness.

Alternatives are thus negatively correlated with commitment: As the number and quality of alternatives go up, commitment goes down (Le & Agnew, 2003).

Putting Them Together: Four Relationship Scenarios

To predict what a relationship will be like, we combine all three major variables: (1) current outcomes, or our ratio of pros versus cons; (2) our comparison level, or what we think an "average" relationship is like; and (3) our CL_{alt}, or what we think would be our next-best alternative if we left our current partner. By combining these factors, we see a variety of different relationship scenarios emerge (as shown in Figure 5.4).

A happy, stable relationship is one where we feel that our relationship is both better than average *and* our best possible chance at happiness. We've hit the relationship jackpot! We're truly satisfied and no one else could make us feel this good. If both people in the relationship share this bliss, they might really find their "happily ever after." This is shown in the upper left corner of Figure 5.4, with current outcomes higher than both CL and CL_{alt}. It doesn't actually matter which of these latter two factors is higher or lower (in other words, we could switch them in the figure)—what matters is just that they are *both* lower than current outcomes.

Other combinations, unfortunately, are not so wonderful. Your satisfaction might be fine (you're fairly happy with this person), but the relationship is still unstable if someone better comes along (shown in the lower left corner). Or you could be fairly unhappy with your partner—but if you think there's not much better available to you, you'll stick around anyway just because you think it's still the best you can do (unhappy, but stable—top right corner). Here, you're essentially trapped

FIGURE 5.4 ● Four Different Relationships

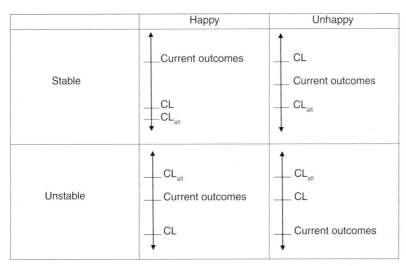

When satisfaction and alternatives (dependence) are compared to current outcomes within interdependence theory, the level of each variable compared to the others results in various combinations that predict the stability and happiness of couple members.

into "settling." Finally, you could be dissatisfied and think you could do better else-where (bottom right corner). Again, the order of CL and CL_{alt} could be switched here; what matters is that they are both higher than the current outcomes. If this is the state of your relationship, then there's absolutely no reason to stick around, right?

Well, not so fast.

One More Factor: Investments

To sum up: Interdependence theory predicts that relationship stability is predicted by commitment, and that commitment is predicted by both satisfaction and alternatives. But it turns out, that's not the end of the scientific story.

Picture a couple, Anika and Laura, who have been married 40 years. They fight all the time, never have sex anymore, maintain pretty much separate lives, and honestly could probably find someone else to date from their book club. Why don't they just get a divorce and get it over with? Researchers using interdependence theory knew that while satisfaction and alternatives explained quite a bit about why certain cou-ples lasted or didn't, they were missing a piece of the puzzle. Why do some unhappy, seemingly unstable couples stay together?

We can explain these couples with a third and final variable: investments. In the 1980s, researcher Caryl Rusbult (1980a) created the **investment model**, which said that there are *three* predictors of commitment: (1) satisfaction, (2) alternatives, and (3) investments. **Investments** are all the resources, time, effort, money, sacrifices, and so on that each couple member has "sunk" into the relationship that would be lost if the relationship ended. We put investments into relationships we think are seri-ous, building a foundation for a lasting future together (Rusbult, Agnew, & Arriaga, 2012). Investments became the third piece of the puzzle. Rusbult's model is called the "investment" model not because she thinks investments are more important than satisfaction or alternatives, but just as a way to distinguish it from interdependence theory (because she added the third variable).

Maybe our couple (Anika and Laura) have low satisfaction and good alternatives—but they've really tied themselves into this relationship. They have children, they've spent the "best years of their lives" together, they own a bunch of stuff together, all their friends are mutual friends . . . if they broke up now, their lives would be a huge mess. They'd have to start all over! So, they stay together to avoid the loss of these investments, or to avoid wasting all that time and energy. Breaking up now sounds like a lot of work!

Investments have proved to be a robust predictor of relationship longevity (Le & Agnew, 2003). Research has shown that even future plans made with a partner that haven't happened yet can keep people in a relationship, because these plans are a type of investment (Goodfriend & Agnew, 2008). Sometimes the prospect of starting over with a new person is simply too daunting, and we decide to take the "easy" way out by simply keeping the status quo. High investments can even keep people in abusive, unhealthy relationships (Rusbult & Martz, 1995). For example, victims of abuse might stay in the relationship to protect children from harm (for more on abusive relation-ships, see Chapter 12).

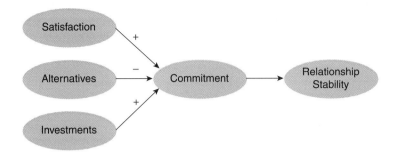

FIGURE 5.5 ● The Investment Model of Relationship Commitment

The investment model (Rusbult, 1980a) adds "investments" as a third predictor of relationship commitment (in addition to satisfaction and alternatives, which were suggested by interdependence theory). Together, these variables reliably predict relationship stability over time.

Source: Heinzen and Goodfriend (2019); theory from Rusbult (1980a).
Heinzen and Goodfriend, 2018

RELATIONSHIPS AND POPULAR CULTURE

Interdependence for Homer and Marge Simpson

The Simpsons is the longest-running television series in history (Jean, 1989–present). Over the course of 30 years of episodes, the marriage of Homer and Marge has not been smooth. They've fought, been tempted to have affairs, and even legally separated for a while. Analyzing their relationship through an interdependent lens might be insightful regarding why they appear to remain committed through all these metaphorical bumps and bruises.

Satisfaction: When Homer and Marge construct a comparison level from the relationships that surround them, their marriage actually seems pretty good, relatively speaking. They see many friends and family members (such as Marge's sisters, Patty and Selma) go through divorces. And both Homer and Marge explicitly try to work on their relationship. They appear to have a pretty healthy sex life, they spend a lot of time together, and they put extra effort into communication after disagreements and misunderstandings.

Alternatives: Both of them have been tempted by possible affairs. Marge was seduced by her French bowling instructor, although she ultimately resisted his charms. For some reason, multiple women show romantic interest in Homer over the years (Mindy, a coworker; Lurleen, a country singer; and Candace, his pharmacist). But through all of these dalliances, Homer remains ultimately loyal to Marge.

Investments: After 30 years (although the passage of time is questionable in animated series), it's clear their investments are extremely high. In addition to raising three children, they've made plenty of sacrifices to be together, their home and friendship networks are completely joined, and they've worked out a predictable routine to the pattern of their life together.

The result is that they appear to be highly committed to each other. Who knows how long the show could continue? They might eventually celebrate their 50th anniversary together.

For a more detailed analysis, see Goodfriend's (2006) chapter in the book *The Psychology of the Simpsons*.

Once investments are added to the model, we get what you can see in Figure 5.5. In another meta-analysis including data collected from 37,761 participants and 137 studies over 33 years, satisfaction, perceived alternatives, and investments really did predict relationship breakup (Le, Dove, Agnew, Korn, & Mutso, 2010). Other studies have supported the model many other times as well, in gay couples (Duffy & Rusbult, 1986), college students (Goodfriend & Agnew, 2008), friendships (Rusbult, 1980b), and more. While it might not seem particularly romantic to think of love in these mathematical terms, the model shown in Figure 5.5 does appear to have predictive power concerning relationship decisions. And in some ways, this can be comforting to you. What happens in your relationships, and what you decide to do about it, really is up to you.

CHECK YOUR UNDERSTANDING

5.4   In the self-report scale of commitment described in this section, which item below measures "affective" commitment?

    a. "My partner and I joke about what things will be like when we are old."
    b. "It pains me to see my partner suffer."
    c. "I intend to stay in this relationship."
    d. "My gut feeling is to continue in this relationship."

5.5   The relationship shown here is:

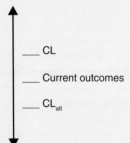

    ___ CL

    ___ Current outcomes

    ___ CL_{alt}

    a. Happy and stable
    b. Unhappy, but stable
    c. Happy, but unstable
    d. Unhappy and unstable

5.6   In the investment model of commitment, which variable is negatively correlated with commitment?

    a. Investments
    b. Alternatives
    c. Satisfaction
    d. Relationship stability

APPLICATION ACTIVITY

This section mentioned the rocky relationship between Brad Pitt and Jennifer Aniston (as well as Angelina Jolie), and it analyzed the marriage of Homer and Marge Simpson. Pick either another celebrity couple or a well-known fictional couple and then identify where you think they are in terms of satisfaction, alternatives, and investments. Do this separately for each person in the couple. Then, make a prediction about (1) how long you think this relationship will last and (2) if one person seems to have more power in the relationship than the other, based on these factors. In other words, is one person more likely to break up the relationship than the other, and why?

CRITICAL THINKING

- When you consider the three variables that predict commitment in this theory (satisfaction, alternatives, and investments), which one do you think is the most important to you, personally, when you are making relationship decisions? Has one of these weighed more heavily than others in past relationships? Do you think the importance of each variable will change as you grow older and go through different phases of life?

- Do you think any variables are missing from the model shown in Figure 5.5? What other important aspects of a relationship or life do you consider when making relationships decisions? For example, some researchers have suggested that a fourth variable might be whether your friends and family support the relationship (more support is predicted to equal high commitment; Etcheverry & Agnew, 2004). Can you think of additional variables that could be added to the model?

- One criticism of the model shown in Figure 5.5 is that it's very logical and mathematical, like an algebraic equation to explain love. Do you think people really make decisions like this, with lists of pros and cons in our heads? Is love really this logical?

Answers to the Check Your Understanding Questions

5.4 b, **5.5** b, and **5.6** b.

What Advances to the Theory Have Been Made?

Kelley and Thibaut first developed interdependence theory in the 1950s, 1960s, and 1970s. The most important expansion of their model, the addition of investments, happened in the 1980s. It's been several decades since then, and the theory is still popular among relationships researchers. What are some of the important additional insights that research has provided? This final section of the chapter will go through each major part of the theory—satisfaction, alternatives, investments, and commitment—and explore newer insights and current directions in our understanding of relationship processes.

Advances in Understanding Satisfaction

You already know that satisfaction comes from assessing the ratio of positive experiences to negative experiences in your relationship (current outcomes), then comparing it to your standard for a typical relationship (your CL). Researchers have explored how satisfaction fluctuates over time, how we can maintain high satisfaction, and the results of this maintained happiness.

Satisfaction Over Time: Hedonic Adaptation

"The honeymoon's over."

You've probably heard this phrase before, and you know what it means. At the beginning of a relationship, everything is exciting, and your partner seems perfect.

After a while, though, things that used to be quirky and adorable start to grate on you. The excitement and passion usually can't be sustained at the same level over long periods of time. Interdependence theory says this happens, at least in part, because our CL changes. If we "get used" to the excitement, if we avoid fights with our partner at the beginning, if we enjoy learning new things about each other, then our CL goes way up—we start to expect perfection. And that's really not sustainable.

An update to this idea is **hedonic adaptation** (Lyubomirsky, 2011; Sheldon & Lyubomirsky, 2012). Hedonic adaptation is the idea that major emotional events in our lives (such as weddings) cause large increases (or decreases) in our happiness—but that they are followed by gradual returns to our baseline levels of happiness. So, the excitement of a first date, first kiss, and all the other firsts in a relationship boost our satisfaction, but this boost is temporary.

For example, a study in Britain (Clark & Georgellis, 2013) followed over 100,000 men and women in a longitudinal study and repeatedly measured their satisfaction in the years building up to and following marriage. You can see the results in Figure 5.6. The x-axis shows the progression of time, with the year 0 indicating when the participant got married. The y-axis shows people's levels of satisfaction. It's clear that satisfaction peaked for both men and women right around the wedding—but in the 5 years afterward, satisfaction crept back down to where people started in the first place. This is just what both interdependence theory and hedonic adaptation would predict.

How to Stay Satisfied

If research shows us that it's hard to sustain relationship satisfaction over time, should we just give up? Should we move from one relationship to the next, chasing excitement and novelty?

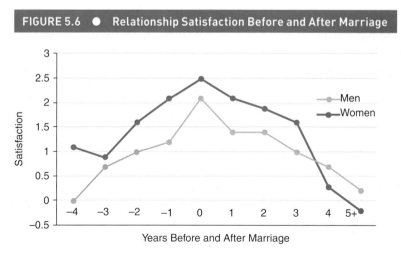

FIGURE 5.6 ● Relationship Satisfaction Before and After Marriage

For both men and women, relationship satisfaction peaks in the year of marriage (shown here as year 0). Satisfaction builds until marriage, then slowly goes back down to baseline levels.

Source: Adapted from Clark and Georgellis (2013).

While some people seem to try that strategy, others hope to make their relationship work. Other research has been dedicated to finding keys for enduring happiness. For a detailed discussion of this research, see Chapter 13 at the end of this book. But for now, consider four suggestions produced by hedonic adaptation researchers (Jacobs Bao & Lyubomirsky, 2013):

- *Focus on positive experiences and positive emotions.* The higher your ratio of positive to negative events, the more sustainable your happiness will be (Fredrickson & Losada, 2005). In other words, purposefully and explicitly maintain your current outcomes. It also helps to consistently affirm and support your partner's interests and goals (Rusbult, Finkel, & Kumashiro, 2009).

- *Variety is the spice of relationships.* Hedonic adaptation will be slowed down (or potentially even reversed) if couples maintain variety in the activities they do together. Satisfaction is positively correlated with engaging in new and exciting events (e.g., rock climbing, international travel, or even sharing deep secrets; Aron, Norman, Aron, McKenna, & Heyman, 2000). Couples travel opportunities seem particularly relevant to strengthening commitment (Durko & Petrick, 2016).

- *Maintain reasonable expectations.* Knowing that our CL is flexible depending on what we're "used to" in a relationship, we can acknowledge that over time, we might take a caring and consistently loving partner for granted. The happier our relationship is, the more we come to expect from it (Lyubomirsky, 2011; Sheldon & Lyubomirsky, 2012). It's almost like building tolerance to a drug: We need more and more to get the same effect as when we started. Once we start to feel entitled or resentful, satisfaction drops (e.g., Hickman, Watson, & Morris, 1996). It's important to remember that we're all just human, and if we're starting to feel bored, our partner might be feeling the exact same thing.

- *Cultivate appreciation.* Reminding ourselves of our partner's efforts, even in small things, increases our appreciation and happiness within relationships. Taking time to savor especially happy times, either in the present or in the past, increases well-being (Bryant, Smart, & King, 2005; Seligman, Rashid, & Parks, 2006). In short, instead of taking our partner for granted, we should explicitly and consciously feel gratitude (Schramm, Marshall, Harris, & Lee, 2005).

Advances in Understanding Alternatives

If you're in a relationship and you suddenly have a tempting alternative, what do you do? And what about the opposite: You're not happy, but you don't think you have *any* alternatives? These two very different problems have both been the subject of interesting research.

Avoiding Temptation: Derogation of Alternatives

The better your alternatives, the more temptation you have to leave your current partner. As Figure 5.5 shows, this could mean that better alternatives cause commitment to decrease.

But never forget what we emphasized in Chapter 2: *Correlation does not imply causation.* In this case, it's certainly possible that better alternatives will cause some people to have lower commitment or even leave their partner. It's also the case, however, that the association could go the other way around. Imagine that you're already in a very satisfying relationship and have invested a lot into it, but then an attractive new person starts to flirt with you. If you're really committed to your current partner, you might try to avoid this new person and convince yourself that they aren't that great after all. The tendency to downgrade potential alternatives because we're already committed to someone else is called **derogation of alternatives** (Johnson & Rusbult, 1989; Rusbult & Buunk, 1993; Simpson, Gangestad, & Lerma, 1990). It seems that having good alternatives causes commitment to go down—but being committed also causes us to cognitively devalue our alternatives, convincing ourselves not to stray.

To test for whether derogation of alternatives really happens, a study recruited college students who were already in relationships (Johnson & Rusbult, 1989). They were told that the study's purpose was to evaluate a possible new campus dating service. Everyone then rated photographs and personality descriptions of people who were available for dates. Results showed that the potential dates were judged as less attractive by participants who were already in highly committed relationships, compared to participants in less committed relationships. The authors of the study concluded: "These findings suggest that one important process by which individuals resist temptation and protect their current relationships may be that of burning their bridges: driving away threatening alternatives, or at least driving threatening alternatives from their minds" (Johnson & Rusbult, 1989, p. 979).

The Trap of Low Alternatives: Nonvoluntary Dependence

Some people might have the problem of too many alternatives—but a more depressing scenario is when people stay in an unhappy relationship because they feel trapped.

This scenario is called **nonvoluntary dependence**: You're not happy, but you stay anyway because you think you have to (Rusbult et al., 2001). If you really believe you have no better alternative to the current situation, you "settle." Nonvoluntary dependence leads to a variety of outcomes, almost all of which are unpleasant. For example, people who feel stuck feel more anxiety about the possibility of their relationship ending and feel more jealous over their partner's good alternatives (Buunk, 1991; Simpson, 1987).

At the worst extreme is victims of abusive relationships who feel they cannot leave due to lack of alternatives. Two studies (Rusbult & Martz, 1995; Stork, 2005) interviewed women at emergency shelters who were seeking refuge from their partners. In both studies, the women indicated that despite low relationship satisfaction, their commitment remained high because they thought they had no other choice. Low alternatives included the belief that no one else would want to be with them—potentially due to their partners gaslighting and insulting them over time and reinforcing their low self-esteem—and the belief that they could not make it on their own due to lack of access to resources (e.g., cash, transportation, a place to live). Indeed, a common strategy of abusers is to make sure their victims don't have access to friends, money, or means of escape specifically to ensure their lack of alternatives and entrapment (Johnson, 1995).

Under these circumstances, the ubiquitous question "Why don't victims just leave?" shows its obtuse nature. "When one takes into account the nature of an individual's dependence on a partner, the decision to remain in an abusive relationship becomes understandable" (Rusbult & Buunk, 1993, p. 188). Again, for much more discussion of the dynamics within unhealthy and abusive relationships, see Chapter 12.

Seen from this light, increasing divorce rates might actually be *positive* societal change. In decades past, people who were trapped in unhappy, abusive relationships had no escape. Especially for women, increasing financial independence provides the potential alternative of simply being free and single (Diekman, Goodfriend, & Goodwin, 2004; Greenstein & Davis, 2006). No one deserves to be trapped in an unhappy relationship.

Advances in Understanding Investments

Because investments are the newest concept to be added to interdependence theory research, some of the most cutting-edge research has focused on this third piece of the puzzle.

The investment model is so robust that the combination of satisfaction, alternatives, and investments has been shown to predict commitment, loyalty, and tenacity in sticking around in a wide variety of contexts besides just intimate relationships. A few examples are as follows:

- Employees' attitudes toward their current employer (van Dam, 2005)
- Client commitment to their current bank (Kastlunger, Martini, Kirchler, & Hofmann, 2008)
- Commitment to war efforts led by one's nation and to being a member of the United Nations (Agnew, Hoffman, Lehmiller, & Duncan, 2007)
- Customer loyalty to specific brands (Li & Petrick, 2008)
- Commitment toward pets (Baker, Petit, & Brown, 2016)
- How long people will engage in multiplayer online games (Uysal, 2016)

But of course, the focus of this book is intimate relationships, so let's discuss two specific expansions of investments in that context.

Types of Investment

More investments in a relationship lead to more commitment. But do different *types* of investment exist?

This question was the inspiration for a series of three studies (Goodfriend & Agnew, 2008) that expanded Rusbult's (1980a) original definition of what investments could be. Most researchers thought about investments as anything that had been "sunk" into a relationship already, almost like financial investments in a money-making endeavor or business. But might it matter whether investments in a relationship are abstract things (such as a feeling of sacrifice) versus something more concrete, such as a purchase of a car together?

Goodfriend and Agnew (2008) explored this question by first asking participants to consider two categories of investment. Everyone in the study was given these instructions:

> In psychological research about romantic relationships, "investments" refer to resources that are attached to a relationship which would decline in value or be lost if the relationship were to end. *Tangible investments* are all the material resources that are attached to a relationship that would decline in value or be lost if the relationship were to end. One example of a tangible investment is a house. *Intangible investments* are all the resources that do not physically exist that are attached to a relationship that would decline in value or be lost if the relationship were to end. Intangible investments cannot be physically touched. One example of an intangible investment is love.

Participants were then asked to brainstorm and generate more examples of each type of investment. Two people then categorized the lists created and noted when a particular example was listed by many people. This resulted in a list of eight common intangible investments and five common tangible investments (see Table 5.2).

After creating the list of investments, a self-report survey was written in which participants rated how much they had invested each item in their current relationship, on a scale of 1 to 9. Study 2 thus asked 173 college students to respond to the 13 items in the scale—but they saw the list twice. First, participants indicated how much they had already invested each of these resources into their relationship. Then, participants indicated whether they *planned* to invest each resource in their relationship at some point in the future. Thus, Study 2 separated investments types even further. While Study 1 differentiated between tangible and intangible investments, Study 2 further noted that "past" investments are resources already put into a relationship, while

TABLE 5.2 ● Thirteen Common Intangible and Tangible Relationship Investments	
Intangible Investment Examples	**Tangible Investment Examples**
Time	Major shared possessions (e.g., house)
Emotional ties	Financial investments
Self-disclosures (telling secrets)	Shared pet
Shared sense of identity	Shared bank account
Shared intellectual life	Joint loans or debts
Effort	
Sacrifices to be together	
Shared leisure activities and daily routine	

"planned" investments are resources couple members hope to put into a relationship in the future but that have not happened yet.

Can just having plans with your partner keep you in a relationship? Results from Study 2 showed that all four types of investment (past tangible, past intangible, planned tangible, and planned intangible) were positively correlated to levels of commitment—and surprisingly, planned investments were significantly stronger predictors of commitment than past investments were. People care so much about the plans they have made about the future that these theoretical hopes keep someone committed, even though the investment itself hasn't even happened yet.

Finally, Study 3 was a longitudinal design. Participants filled out scales measuring their level of investment for all four investment types first. Then, 8 months later, they were contacted to see whether they were still dating the same person. If they had broken up, they were asked two follow-up questions: (1) What is the chance you'll reunite with your former partner? (2) Are you dating someone new now, or are you still single?

Results of this final study were that more investments of any type were related to three outcomes. First, people with more investments were more likely to still be together 8 months later, just like the investment model predicted. Second, when people did break up, people who had been more invested thought there was a significantly higher chance they'd get back together with their ex, and they were more likely to still be single when the researchers called them. It seems that these highly invested folks were hanging on to the possibility that the relationship might reignite.

But perhaps the most interesting surprise in Study 3 was that out of the four types of investment, *planned intangible* investments were the most powerful predictor of these outcomes. Abstract concepts like "sacrifice" and "effort" were more important than things like money—and plans and hopes for the future were more important than what people had already done. Hopes and dreams about abstract ideas ended up being the reason people had trouble getting over breakups and were one of the main reasons people stayed committed (Goodfriend & Agnew, 2008). A notable aspect of the importance of future plans contributing to current commitment is that people can start planning a future together after a very short period of time. If you meet someone you can imagine yourself growing old with, this planned investment can increase your decision to stick around, even though nothing has actually happened yet and the plan exists only in your mind.

Investments in Marginalized Relationships

In addition to simply studying different kinds of investments, as the previous section outlined, other research has asked whether different types of couples make different types of investments.

In particular, recent studies have suggested that investment patterns might be different between "traditional" couples (meaning heterosexual, same-race, same-age couples) versus **marginalized relationships**, or those that are less accepted by at least some portions of society. Marginalized relationships are those that are seen as strange, unlikely to succeed in the long run, or even immoral from some points of view. Because of these societal judgments and stereotypes, couples in marginalized relationships may have to hide their commitment.

This line of research was inspired by the curious finding that for gay men, the correlation between investment level and commitment was not significant (Beals, Impett, & Peplau, 2002). Are gay men simply cavalier in couplehood, avoiding commitment regardless of resources put into a relationship? No. It turns out that for gay men, only *intangible* investments are tied to commitment—not tangible investments (Lehmiller, 2010). Why?

One explanation is that homophobia prevents gay couples from being as free to make tangible investments—for example, a bank may not want to give a gay couple a joint bank account, or a landlord might avoid renting an apartment to them. In lesbian couples, the ability to publicly disclose one's sexual identity (i.e., to be "out") is associated with the ability to have higher relationship investments (Barrantes, Eaton, Veldhuis, & Hughes, 2017)—so having to hide prevents tangible investments from happening. In contrast, intangible investments are more up to the couple members themselves—they are more private in many ways. The importance of intangible investments in both heterosexual (Goodfriend & Agnew, 2008) and gay/lesbian couples (Lehmiller, 2010) emphasizes the utility in thinking as specifically as possible about abstract concepts involved in intimate relationships.

Follow-up research (Lehmiller & Agnew, 2006) investigated other forms of marginalized couples, including interracial relationships and "age gap" couples (in which one person is significantly older than the other). These couples consistently have lower investments than nonmarginalized couples. Surprisingly, however, the same curious finding occurred: Within these couples, investments and commitment weren't correlated. Lack of investments didn't seem to matter in these couples—they were committed anyway, despite low investments *and* despite social pressure and prejudice against them. So why were they still committed? For couples in this situation (marginalized, low investments, but high commitment), it turned out that they also reported perceiving very low alternatives—especially for people in age gap couples.

One conclusion from the research summarized in this section of the chapter is that the investment model does a consistently good job of predicting commitment, across several different types of couples. That said, for at least some of those couple types, measurement of variables like satisfaction, alternatives, and investments should be done as precisely as possible so that slightly different opportunities and preferences can be taken into account. Specificity of measurement is generally preferred in scientific endeavors anyway, so these advances in operationalization and procedure continue to drive new relationship discoveries and insight.

Advances in Understanding Commitment

Finally, relationship commitment has also been studied by many scientists who want to explore various applications and extensions beyond interdependence theory or the investment model. To end the chapter, consider two interesting examples of this fascinating avenue of research.

Types of Commitment

Just as research revealed that different types of investment matter, studies have established that there are meaningful types of commitment (Knopp, Rhoades, Stanley, & Markman, 2015).

RESEARCH DEEP DIVE

You and Your Pet: Friends Forever?

If you spend any time at all on the internet, it becomes quickly evident that we love our pets. Our dogs, cats, and other pets feel like part of the family and are a key relationship in our lives. But is the relationship we have with a pet similar to a romantic relationship? If so, by better understanding human-pet relationships, researchers can identify ways to increase the benefits to both humans and pets.

A group of researchers wanted to explore whether Rusbult's investment model also applied to human-pet relationships. They first hypothesized that, consistent with investment model findings in human-human relationships, commitment to pets would be predicted by satisfaction, quality of alternatives, and investments. Second, they predicted that greater commitment would lead to relationship-enhancing behaviors like sacrifices and forgiveness.

To test this, the researchers surveyed 209 participants with online surveys. When conducting research using online samples, researchers often include several "quality control" questions (e.g., "for quality control purposes, please select answer 4") to ensure that respondents are paying attention and not simply rushing through the study or failing to read the questions carefully. In this study, researchers dropped 25 participants from their sample for providing incorrect answers, leaving 184 participants (40 men and 144 women) with a mean age in the mid 30s (36.55 years).

In case they had multiple pets, participants had to select one pet and answer questions with that pet in mind. Participants then answered a modified version of the investment model scale that researchers adapted to focus on a pet-human relationship (e.g., "My relationship with [pet's name] is close to ideal" or "If I didn't have [pet's name] I would do fine—I would find another pet"). Similarly, respondents also answered modified measures of accommodation (stifling negative responses), forgiveness (avoiding revenge and negatively following

negative acts), and sacrifice (doing things for your pet that aren't in your self-interest).

The researchers tested their first hypothesis with a regression, which is a statistical procedure that allows the researcher to test how several different variables (in this case, satisfaction, quality of alternatives, and investment) simultaneously relate to an outcome (commitment). By doing this, researchers can see if one variable emerges as a clear best predictor. In other words, which variable best predicts commitment? The study's results indicated that satisfaction, quality of alternatives, and investment were each significant predictors of commitment to one's pet. In other words, when a person is more satisfied, more invested, and perceives fewer quality alternatives, they are more committed to their pet.

The researchers tested their second hypothesis on relationship-enhancing behaviors with a separate regression and found that greater commitment was significantly associated with greater accommodation, sacrifice, and forgiveness. In both cases, the findings for pet-human relationships were similar to investment model findings within human-human relationships.

One of the main benefits of establishing a theory is that it allows for application to other areas. That is, because the investment model provides a clear set of ideas that help us understand romantic relationships, we can take those ideas and see if they work in other contexts. Some of those contexts are more obvious (like friendships), while others may seem like more of a stretch (like feelings toward your workplace or, in this case, pets). Because the investment model generalizes across different types of relationships, we are able to say that the model is robust, which provides greater understanding of where commitment comes from and what types of behaviors it influences—for humans and pets alike.

For more, read Baker, Z. G., Petit, W. E., & Brown, C. M. (2016). An investigation of the Rusbult investment model of commitment in relationships with pets. *Anthrozoös, 29*(2), 193–204.

Different theorists have suggested a few models, but one of the most popular is the model proposed by Johnson that there are three forms of commitment, particularly in married couples (Johnson, 1991; Johnson, Caughlin, & Huston, 1999). **Personal commitment** is the desire to stay in a relationship due to attraction and a sense of "couple identity," or feeling that your partner is an important aspect of your sense of self. **Moral commitment**, on the other hand, is a sense of obligation due to publicly stated promises or religious views that marriage vows are sacred and shouldn't be broken, no matter what. Finally, **structural commitment** is a feeling of constraint or barriers to leaving. These barriers might be caused by low alternatives, high investments, or social pressure to stay in the relationship. Thus, structural commitment is the closest to the way commitment was defined in interdependence theory and the investment model.

One way to think about these three types of commitment is this: Personal commitment means you *want* to stay. Moral commitment means you *should* stay. And structural commitment means you *have* to stay. When 187 people who had been married for 13 years completed self-report surveys measuring all three types of commitment, it turned out that the three commitment types were only moderately correlated to each other, meaning within a couple there could be a high level of one type and low levels of the other two, or any combination (Johnson, 1991). In addition, conflict and fights within the couple were tied to lower personal commitment but had no association with moral or structural commitment. Not surprisingly, people who were more religious were more likely to have moral commitment. Again, the lesson seems to be that the more specifically we can measure variables within relationships, the better off we'll be in terms of advancing theory and application.

"Me" Versus "We": Cognitive Interdependence

Consider one final, intriguing aspect of commitment.

To get in the mindset for this final idea, first jot down four to six simple sentences about your current relationship (if you're not with a particular partner right now, you can do this for a close friendship). The sentences can be good or bad—whatever comes to mind. Here are some examples; read these, then try to write down a few sentences for yourself:

"We were made for one another."

"I get a lot out of my relationship."

"It's amazing how much we fight with one another."

"Sometimes I feel the need for more space."

Did you write down a few sentences for yourself? If so, look at those now and circle any *pronouns* you used in reference to either yourself, your partner, or both of you together. The pronouns will all be either singular (referring to just one person: I, me, my, myself, he, she, his, hers) or plural (referring to both of you, together: we, us, our, ours, ourselves). Make a tally of the number of sentences that include (1) only singular pronouns (e.g., "I think my partner is good looking"), (2) only plural pronouns (e.g., "We love each other"), (3) a combination of singular and plural pronouns (e.g., "I think our relationship is great"), or (4) no pronouns (e.g., "The relationship is good").

Researchers have discovered that the proportion of sentences that people write that contain *only plural* pronouns is positively correlated to relationship commitment (Agnew, Van Lange, Rusbult, & Langston, 1998). It seems that when people are highly committed, they think of "us" and "we" instead of "I" or "him/her." This tendency is called **cognitive interdependence**: mental representations of the self as tied to the relationship and one's partner. Cognitive interdependence is at the very heart of interdependence theory, which states that at some point we give up our personal, selfish needs and become mentally and emotionally tied to someone else. It means our relationship is a central part of who we are, and that we've blended our very sense of self with our chosen partner as a collective psychological unit.

Studies on cognitive interdependence show that we're much more likely to experience it within romantic relationships, compared to friendships (Agnew et al., 1998). The correlation between commitment and cognitive interdependence also appears to go in both causal directions: Being committed causes people to think in "we" and "us" terms more, and thinking of "us" also seems to cause higher commitment (Agnew et al., 1998). The idea of couple members melding together into a single unit has been picked up by popular media tabloids (e.g., magazines like *Us Weekly* or *Elle*) as they refer to celebrity couples with a blending of their names, such as "Kimye" (for Kim Kardashian and Kanye West) or "Brangelina" (while Brad Pitt and Angelina Jolie were together).

Photo by Kevin Mazur/MG19/Getty Images for The Met Museum/Vogue

Tabloids like *Elle* or *Us Weekly* enjoy blending the identity of celebrity couples by referring to them with nicknames such as "Kimye" for Kim Kardashian and Kanye West.

The authors of the original cognitive interdependence study (Agnew et al., 1998) even suggested that marital therapy techniques could encourage communication that emphasizes mutual needs and outcomes—"we" statements—over individual thoughts or "I" statements (e.g., "We need to work on our anger management"). Indeed, the concept of "we-ness" within a couple has grown in popularity, with many studies now showing that this shared sense of couplehood leads to a variety of relationship benefits (e.g., Gildersleeve, Singer, Skerrett, & Wein, 2016; Gottman, 2011; Singer & Skerrett, 2014; Skerrett & Fergus, 2015).

One study using qualitative data explored the possibility that reminding couples of their cognitive interdependence might be useful in a counseling context. Here, 53 couples were asked to do the following:

Write down a particular memory of a special time in your relationship. This memory is called a "We-Story" and it is an account of an event or sequence of events in your relationship that serves as a reminder of your mutual love and commitment to each other and the relationship. . . . We think of We-Stories as touchstones and valuable symbols of the bond that you hold with each other. (Gildersleeve et al., 2016, p. 5)

The stories were then coded for seven elements: security, empathy, respect, acceptance, pleasure, humor, and shared meaning/vision. All of the stories generated by participants included at least one of these elements, with security (meaning mutual trust, teamwork, and willingness to work on the relationship) as the most common element (present in 58.5% of the stories).

An example of a story that emphasized security and "we-ness" was written by a woman who had to deal with the death of her mother. She recalled how she knew she could rely on her husband:

> But through it all, though it sounds so hackneyed, my husband was my rock, my unwavering support. He was the one trying to maintain her dignity by cleaning her up before anyone could see her, he was the one sitting there at her bedside with me watching. . . . And that's our marriage. . . . While it can feel like there have been more bad times than good sometimes . . . I was there for him when he needed me and he's been there for me. (Gildersleeve et al., 2016, p. 7)

One of the study's conclusions is that if couple members are seeking counseling, mental health professionals could ask them to generate "we-stories" that emphasize different positive memories or aspects of the relationship. This process could remind the individuals of their investment, transformation of motivation, cognitive interdependence, and other reasons to see each other in happy, supportive ways.

You've now learned about two very different ways to study cognitive interdependence: counting plural pronouns and asking people to write stories that highlight their mutual couplehood. While both of these techniques are creative and useful, they are also both cumbersome and relatively time-consuming. For researchers who prefer quantitative approaches and want to keep their measures short and sweet, a final technique for measuring cognitive interdependence comes from a single, simple question that can be included in almost any questionnaire.

In Figure 5.7, you can see the single item that makes up the **Inclusion of Other in the Self Scale** (or **IOS scale** for short; Aron, Aron, & Smollan, 1992). It displays a series of seven increasingly overlapping circles, where one is labeled "self" and one is labeled "other." Participants circle one of the images, and researchers simply code their choice as a number from 1 (the circles that don't overlap at all) to 7 (almost completely overlapping). The higher the number, the more participants theoretically see themselves as cognitively joined together with their partner.

Because the instructions on the scale are so vague, some people have argued that it's not 100% clear what the participants are thinking about when they choose an image. It could be cognitive and emotional closeness, as the original creators of the scale argue. It could also be similarity or even satisfaction with one's partner (Agnew, Loving, Le, & Goodfriend, 2004). Either way, this simple little question has been used in over 3000 studies over the years and has been tied to a very wide variety of relationship outcomes. Call it closeness, similarity, cognitive overlap, or inclusion of other in the self—the IOS scale is likely capturing at least part of the essence of relationship interdependence.

FIGURE 5.7 ● The Inclusion of Other in the Self Scale

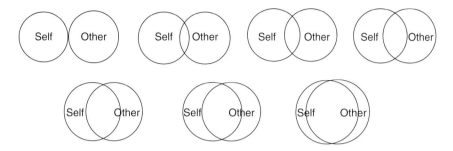

The IOS scale asks participants to do the following: "Please circle the picture below which best describes your relationship with your romantic partner."

Source: Aron, A., Aron, E. N., & Smollan, D. (1992). Inclusion of other in the self scale and the structure of interpersonal closeness. *Journal of Personality and Social Psychology, 63*(4), 596-612, reprinted with permission.

CHECK YOUR UNDERSTANDING

5.7 Some research indicates that people's level of happiness can temporarily go up or down after a major event, but that eventually it returns to a baseline level. This idea is called:

   a. Hedonic adaptation
   b. The emotional boomerang effect
   c. Affective trampolining
   d. Doppler flexibility

5.8 Some scientists have explored different types of investments in relationships. Out of the four investment types listed below, which seems to be MOST important in predicting commitment in both heterosexual and gay couples?

   a. Dichotomous
   b. Moral
   c. Intangible
   d. Tangible

5.9 If you completed the Inclusion of Other in the Self Scale, what kind of images would you see?

   a. Abstract inkblot-types of shapes
   b. Drawings of different scenes and characters
   c. Subliminal images of faces on a computer screen
   d. A series of progressively overlapping circles

APPLICATION ACTIVITY

Find a published interview in which someone is talking about their relationship or partner (past or present). Make sure the interview is long enough that it includes several sentences in which the person is talking about this subject. Then, code the pronouns used for how many of them are singular versus plural. Based on your findings, what would you predict about this person's level of happiness and commitment in the relationship? Explain your answer.

CRITICAL THINKING

- Research has explored various forms of investments and various forms of commitment. Are there also different kinds of satisfaction and/or different kinds of alternatives? Think of your own model that suggests at least three types of either satisfaction or alternatives and describe them.

- You read about a study that asked couples to write a "we-story" in which they described a particular time in their relationship when they felt mutual love and commitment. Do you think this technique could be more broadly applied in other contexts to help

people heal, forgive, or reduce prejudice? For example, could estranged children and parents write about happier times? Could dissatisfied employees feel better about their jobs by focusing on positive interactions? What other contexts can you think of where this type of self-generated storytelling could be helpful?

- Is it possible for partners to be *too* interdependent, or *too* close? When does interdependence become co-dependence, or suffocating? (For an interesting take on this question, see Mashek & Sherman, 2004.)

> ## Answers to the Check Your Understanding Questions
> **5.7** a, **5.8** c, and **5.9** d.

Chapter Summary

Big Questions

1. What are the main ideas within interdependence theory?
2. What factors predict relationship commitment and stability?
3. What advances to the theory have been made?

What are the main ideas within interdependence theory?

Social exchange theories analyze the interactions between or among people. One social exchange theory is interdependence theory, which proposes that relationship behaviors are motivated by each person trying to get the best possible outcome—but that those outcomes are

affected by the other person's decisions. Once two people form a relationship, their outcomes are no longer "independent"; they are now "interdependent" and tied together. "Outcome matrices" display various possible outcomes of any given situation. For a relationship to work, both members must engage in a prosocial transformation of motivation, meaning they are willing to sacrifice short-term, selfish goals for the good of the long-term relationship. Equity theory further suggests that people are happiest when they feel their ratio of costs and benefits is fair.

What factors predict relationship commitment and stability?

Interdependence theory attempts to predict relationship stability, with the main premise that stability is correlated to commitment from each partner. In turn, commitment is predicted by two factors in the original theory. The first factor is satisfaction, which is determined by (1) your ratio of positive versus negative aspects of the relationship and (2) how that ratio compares to your view of what an "average" relationship is like. The second factor is alternatives. The more or better your alternatives are, the less committed you will be (and the less dependent). Finally, a third factor was added later in an updated version called "the investment model." The third factor, investments, is all the resources people put into relationships they would lose if they broke up (such as time or effort). Even if satisfaction is low and alternatives are high, high investments can keep people tied to their current partner.

What advances to the theory have been made?

Hedonic adaptation is the idea that events can temporarily increase or decrease relationship satisfaction, but that in the long run, satisfaction will return to baseline levels. Thus, many studies have attempted to find suggestions for couples to retain high satisfaction over time. Other research has found that commitment can both be caused by low alternatives and motivate people to derogate, or downgrade, their alternatives as a way to stay motivated to continue with a current partner. Nonvoluntary dependence has also been studied, which occurs when people feel trapped due to low alternatives. Research has also found that there are several different meaningful types of investment (such as tangible and intangible), and marginalized relationships may have different investment patterns. Finally, studies have explored various types of commitment and how being committed affects cognitive interdependence, or a feeling of mental "we-ness" within a relationship.

List of Terms

Learning Objectives	Key Terms
5.1 Explain interdependence, outcome matrices, and transformation of motivation.	Social exchange Interdependence theory Outcome matrices Transformation of motivation Individualistic cultures Collectivistic cultures Equity theory Underbenefitted Overbenefitted

5.2	Analyze how satisfaction, alternatives, and investments work together to predict a relationship's fate.	Accommodation Willingness to sacrifice Satisfaction Current outcome Comparison level (CL) Comparison level for alternatives (CL$_{alt}$) Dependence Investment model Investments
5.3	Interpret recent research on each component of interdependence theory and the investment model.	Hedonic adaptation Derogation of alternatives Nonvoluntary dependence Marginalized relationships Personal commitment Moral commitment Structural commitment Cognitive interdependence Inclusion of Other in the Self Scale (IOS scale)

6

Relationships Across Our Lifetime

Big Questions		Learning Objectives	
1.	How do our earliest relationships form?	6.1	Explain the biological and psychological motivations between infant-mother bonds.
2.	How do we choose singlehood versus commitment in young adulthood?	6.2	Analyze the status and stigma of being single as a young adult, then interpret research on the choice to get married.
3.	How do relationships change later in life?	6.3	Evaluate research on parenthood, divorce, retirement, and bereavement.

What has been the single most important relationship in your entire life—so far?

Relationships are vital to our survival and happiness, but the types of relationships we value most change significantly as we get older. As infants, we are completely dependent on others for our most basic needs. As children, forming friendships with peers becomes our focus—and we can all remember times when friendships have affected our sense of self and emotional experiences, both good and bad. (Note, friendships are so important they will be addressed in their own chapter, Chapter 7.) Young adults are expected to start forming romantic attractions and relationships with others, and most people plan to marry and start a family themselves before they are even halfway through their lifetime.

In the second half of life, relationships revolve around cohabitation or marriage, divorce, parenthood, and a changing sense of self as our roles shift among the many people in our social worlds. Finally, if we are lucky enough to live into older adulthood, the cycle of life can repeat itself as we once again become dependent on the help of others. A good place to build a solid foundation of understanding relationships in general is to think about the variety of relationship types and motivations we experience, and how they change over time.

How Do Our Earliest Relationships Form?

Let's start the chapter with our very first relationship: the one with our mother.

"The mother was once regarded as a vehicle, a conduit for nutrition and waste removal for the fetus that lived isolated from the outside world" (Marx & Nagy, 2015, p. 1). That description of motherhood isn't particularly flattering. It also doesn't invoke a stereotypical image of a glowing pregnant woman, lovingly caressing her growing belly. Our biological needs in early development make us utterly dependent on our mother—but after we're born, relationships immediately get more complicated. How much that first relationship bond is biologically based versus psychologically based is one question that researchers have been asking for many years.

Biological Bonds

Even before birth, a fetus responds to an expecting mother. Several studies have found evidence that fetal heart rates change when they hear their mother's voice. Some studies find heart rate increases (Kisilevsky et al., 2003, 2009), while others find decreases (Fifer & Moon, 1995; Voegtline, Costigan, Pater, & DiPietro, 2013).

Fetuses respond even more to maternal touch. One study (Marx & Nagy, 2015) included 23 expecting mothers with fetuses between 21 and 33 weeks of gestation. Each woman alternated among reading a child's story aloud (called the "voice" condition), stroking and rubbing their abdomen (the "touch" condition), or simply lying quietly (a control condition); these three conditions created the within-participants independent variable. Importantly, the order of these actions was randomly assigned to each woman. Dependent variables included arm, head, and mouth movements in each fetus, measured through ultrasound tests. Results showed significantly more movements from the fetuses in the touch condition, especially in older fetuses.

Because a fetus's brain is still developing, responses are usually interpreted as biologically based. In other words, the bond that develops between a fetus and an expecting mother is typically considered a human instinct (Hebb, 1958). It seems humans have stronger instincts to be social creatures than most species, which highlights our need for relationships. While other animals are relatively independent immediately after birth, human infants need others to care for them in order to survive—so our instinct to form bonds with other humans starts from the very beginning.

That said, there are plenty of other animals who do seem to share a bonding instinct. Baby ducks and geese are famous for attaching themselves to the first living organism they see after they hatch, a tendency called **imprinting**. The instinct appears to be so strong that they can even imprint on someone from another species. This first bond to another person (or duck, and so on) can have long-lasting ripple effects in our other relationships. For example, male zebra finches are apparently attracted to female mates based on whether those females have a similar appearance to the males' mother finches (Immelmann, 1972). We've already explored how our own first relationship affects later ones in Chapter 3 ("Attachment Theory").

But there's a very famous study on infant attachment we haven't discussed yet, and it asks the important question of whether initial attachment toward our mothers is biological or psychological. Let's cover that study now.

Psychological Bonds: Harlow's Research With Monkeys

Clearly, our first relationship has at least some biological aspects to it. Babies in many species latch onto their mothers. But how do we know whether that bond is driven by purely biological needs—such as the instinctive need for protection or the need for milk—or whether there is a psychological aspect as well?

Certainly, the question of "biology versus psychology" is a **false dichotomy**, or a dilemma presented as if there are only two possible answers or outcomes, when the answer is really a combination of both or a third option. We're comfortable with the idea that babies and mothers form attachments both because of biological needs in the infant and because of a real feeling of "love." One of the most well-known and foundational research studies on the nature of this relationship—and how much of it is biological versus psychological—was conducted in 1958 by Harry Harlow (Harlow, 1958; Harlow & Zimmerman, 1959).

Harlow (1958) titled his first article "The Nature of Love" and opened it with this initial statement: "Love is a wondrous state, deep, tender, and rewarding" (p. 673). Harlow was convinced that love needed to be studied more by scientists and even complained that the topic of love and relationships wasn't given enough attention: "Psychologists, at least psychologists who write textbooks, not only show no interest in the origin and development of love or affection, but they seem to be unaware of its very existence" (p. 673). Ouch—let's hope Harlow would be happy by the fact that you're reading this book right now!

In this pivotal article (and in his follow-up to it in 1959), Harlow discussed the important question of the motivation behind infant-mother bonding. From the infant's perspective, was it driven by the association with food (and thus biologically based), or was there something more? To study this question from a scientific perspective, Harlow used rhesus monkeys because "the development of perception, fear, frustration, and learning capacity follows very similar sequences in rhesus monkeys and human children" (Harlow, 1958, p. 674). And of course, the ethics of what he was about to do to the monkeys would never have been allowed with human babies.

Only 6–12 hours after 60 baby monkeys were born, Harlow and his team of researchers separated them from their mothers and raised them in a cage with two false or "surrogate" mothers. One was a cylinder of wood covered with soft terrycloth material (what most bathrobes are made of). This "mother" was given buttons to look like a false monkey face and a light bulb that provided radiant heat. In comparison, the second "mother" was simply wire in the shape

Harlow studied what happened when baby monkeys were raised in a cage with two false mothers—one that provided milk, and one that provided heat and physical comfort.

Photo by Al Fenn/LIFE Picture Collection via Getty Images

of a cylinder so that a bottle could be inserted. Harlow wanted to know which of the surrogate mothers would be preferred by the babies.

First, Harlow simply measured how much time the babies spent holding and cuddling each mother; it was clear that the babies spent more time hugging the soft, warm mother—and not the one who provided the biological need of milk. This was an initial sign that the babies had formed a psychological attachment to the soft mother. However, Harlow wanted more evidence. He wrote, "It could merely reflect the fact that the cloth mother is a more comfortable sleeping platform or a more adequate source of warmth" (Harlow & Zimmerman, 1959, p. 423). In order to really test whether the babies had a psychological bond with the soft mother, he decided to see which mother they would turn to in a time of distress and fear.

Harlow scared the baby monkeys in a variety of ways, such as putting a mechanical toy in the cage that produced sound and movement. These toys always caused clear fear, and the babies consistently ran to the soft, cloth mothers over many replications and variations (Harlow & Zimmerman, 1959). Harlow concluded that the cloth mother produced **contact comfort**, or a sense of psychological and emotional security and comfort. If the infant-mother bond were purely biological and based on the infants' need for milk, the baby monkeys would have formed an attachment to the wire mother with a milk bottle instead.

Harlow believed the "nature of love" was an emotional, psychological bond. He noted, "The results are so striking as to suggest that the primary function of nursing may be that of insuring frequent and intimate contact between mother and infant" (Harlow & Zimmerman, 1959, p. 423). This could be good news for adoptive parents or biological fathers who may not be able to directly provide milk to their infants, because it seems that milk is not the reason infants love a parent. It's not about the milk. Instead, it's warmth, softness, and a sense of comfort.

CHECK YOUR UNDERSTANDING

6.1 According to research (Marx & Nagy, 2015), which of the following actions from an expecting mother would produce the most physical movement in her fetus (e.g., head and arm motions)?

a. The woman sits quietly.
b. The woman is angry and crying.
c. The woman reads a story out loud.
d. The woman rubs her belly.

6.2 Baby ducks and geese show an instinct to attach themselves to the first living organism they see after being hatched. This tendency is called:

a. Gestational bonding
b. Imprinting

c. A false dichotomy
d. Contact comfort

6.3 Harlow conducted experiments in which baby monkeys were raised with two surrogate "mothers" (Harlow, 1958; Harlow & Zimmerman, 1959). When the babies were scared, how did they react?

a. They ran to a warm, cloth mother for comfort.
b. They ran to a mother that provided milk for comfort.
c. They ran back and forth between the two mothers, displaying confusion.
d. They isolated themselves in a corner and rocked back and forth.

APPLICATION ACTIVITY

This section discussed initial bonds, imprinting, and attachment between babies and mothers among ducks, geese, rhesus monkeys, and humans. Do an online search to discover what other species have provided evidence of significant bonding between infants and mothers (or fathers). How is that evidence defined and measured (operationalized)? Next, do an online search to see whether there are species that appear to *not* show this kind of initial bonding. Are there species where a newborn never even meets its parents?

CRITICAL THINKING

- When Harlow first saw that his baby monkeys showed an affinity toward the warm, cloth mothers based on how much time they spent cuddling with those mothers, he was hesitant to conclude a psychological bond. He thought maybe the time spent with those mothers (compared to the wire mothers) was simply because the cloth mothers were more comfortable. He was more confident when the babies also preferred the cloth mothers during times of distress and fear. Do you still have any doubts about this conclusion? Are there additional explanations for the baby monkeys' behaviors, besides an emotional or psychological feeling of "love"?

- Some humans seem to show more of a tendency to bond with other species than other humans (e.g., some people dislike pets; some people care so much about animals that they are vegetarians). What might account for this individual difference in humans—why do some humans like other species more or less than other humans do?

- Our initial bond with our primary caregiver is so important that it was the basis for attachment theory, which you read about in Chapter 3. Do you agree that this initial relationship is the most important one we'll have in life, or do you think later relationships are more influential? Explain your answer and give some examples.

Answers to the Check Your Understanding Questions

6.1 d, 6.2 b, and 6.3 a.

How Do We Choose Singlehood Versus Commitment in Young Adulthood?

There are a lot of years between infancy and young adulthood. In that time, for most people the primary focus of relationships is on friendships with peers. That's the subject of the next chapter, so for now let's jump ahead to young adulthood. As we reach our teen years, we start thinking about boyfriends, girlfriends, and how to decide what we really want in terms of our romantic future. In this section of the chapter, we'll discuss two very different options: singlehood versus commitment to another person, in the form of cohabitation or marriage.

The Stigma of Singlehood

You've heard the terms "spinster" and "old maid." Both refer to a woman who isn't in a committed relationship—and neither term is very positive. When people are categorized into a group that society has decided is unwanted or negative in some way, we use the term **stigma** to refer to an invisible mark of disgrace or embarrassment that they seem to be carrying around with them. Despite this social stigma, more and more people are choosing to remain single.

Singlehood by Choice

Choosing to be single is becoming a popular option.

According to recent statistics, current trends are that by the time people who are in college today reach the age of 50, one in four of them will have never been married (see Figure 6.1; Pew Research Center, 2014). The number of single adults in the

FIGURE 6.1 ● **Rising Percentage of Never-Married Men and Women Over Time**

— Men ⋯⋯ Women

The percentage of men and women who have never been married has steadily increased over the last 60 years.

United States hit a record in 2017, with over 45% of adults in the category (DePaulo, 2017). Men are more likely to remain single, compared to women; perhaps it's more socially acceptable for men to "play the field" longer—a sexist double standard. This unfair expectation punishes both women who date "too much" and men who don't date "enough."

Social values might be influencing the increasing number of people who choose singlehood. When the Pew Research Center (2014) conducted a large survey asking people about whether they think getting married and having children leads to a society that's "better off," only 46% of people said yes; fully 50% said society would be just as good if people chose other priorities (and 4% said they couldn't decide). And differences in opinion on this question changed a lot based on the age of the respondent. While more older adults said people should prioritize marriage and family, two-thirds of people ages 18–29 (67%) said that other priorities were just as valid.

Sure, not everyone who *is* single *wants* to be single. Actually, about half of single adults (53%) say they would like to get married at some point in the future, if they can find a partner who meets their needs (Pew Research Center, 2014). This is true for both men and women—but the longer people stay single, the longer they seem to prefer it. Once people get to age 30 and are still single, only 33% of them say they want to get married someday. Statistics also show that if people haven't gotten married by the age of 55, only 7 in 1000 will ever get married—and many of these people are unmarried because they *want* to be single.

When asked why they've never chosen to marry, the most common reasons single people give are the following:

- Never found someone who had everything they were looking for (30% of people)

- Not financially prepared for marriage (27%)

- Not ready to settle down, or feel too young to marry (22%)

- Currently in school and want to wait until after graduation (including graduate students; 3%) (Pew Research Center, 2014)

Note that the most common reason given for not getting married yet was that people hadn't found a partner they felt met their needs. So, what do singles want in a potential life partner? As you can see in Figure 6.2, both men and women want to find someone with similar ideas about whether to have children and how to raise them—but women are especially focused on finding a partner with a steady job and income.

Prejudice Against Older Singles

Even though older single people may or may not have chosen their singlehood, research shows that there are fairly strong stereotypes about this social group, and many of them report experiencing prejudice and discrimination from others. This prejudice is called **singlism**.

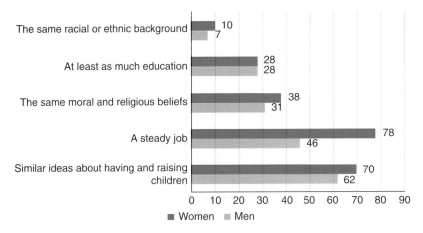

FIGURE 6.2 ● What Never-Married Adult Singles Want in a Potential Spouse

When adult single people are asked about their priorities in finding a potential mate, both men and women want someone with similar ideas about whether to have children and how to raise them—but women were especially focused on finding a partner with a steady job and income.

Singlism is the focus of research for Bella DePaulo, who has been conducting research on the phenomenon for several years. She summarized negative prejudice and stereotypes against older singles by stating that the overarching presumption in society is that "those who have a sexual partnership are better people—more valuable, worthy, and important . . . they are probably happier, less lonely, and more mature, and their lives are probably more meaningful and more complete" (DePaulo & Morris, 2005, p. 58).

In other words, DePaulo states that society generally views adult singles as fairly pitiful, lonely, immature sad-sacks. Not a pretty picture. Further, she notes that these assumptions *might* be true for *some* adult singles—but importantly, (1) they aren't true for *all* singles, and (2) the fact that the assumptions are largely accepted by most people is still perpetuating stereotypes and prejudice. This is unfair to perfectly happy, mature, gorgeous people who just like being single.

Do people really think these negative things about single people? In one study, DePaulo and her colleagues simply asked college students to list characteristics that came to mind when thinking about either single adults or married adults (Morris, DePaulo, Hertel, & Ritter, 2004). The results are shown in Table 6.1. Married adults were associated with words like "happy," "loving," and "kind," while single adults were associated with words like "lonely," "shy," and "unhappy." Of course, the stereotype of adult singles isn't all bad; these participants admitted that adult singles were more likely than married people to be "independent" and sociable, friendly, or fun.

This general pattern of singlism has been replicated by others. Conley and Collins (2002) found that adult single people are perceived as more likely to have an STD or HIV, are seen as more sexually promiscuous, and are generally believed to have riskier personalities than married people—a finding that goes against other research

TABLE 6.1 • Percentage of Participants Who Mentioned Each Word for Single vs. Married Adults		
	Single	**Married**
Words used more for married people		
Happy	7.3	28.1
Loving	0	32.2
Secure/stable	0	10.5
Kind/caring/giving	2.3	48.7
Compromising	0	15.9
Reliable/careful	1.5	7.6
Words used more for single people		
Lonely	16.8	0.2
Shy	9.3	1.1
Unhappy	8.0	2.9
Insecure	7.3	0.0
Inflexible/stubborn	6.8	1.6
Flirtatious	8.8	0
Independent	36.2	1.6
Social/friendly/fun	21.4	10.1

When college students were asked to list traits relevant to either single or married adults, the difference was clear.

showing that singles are, in fact, the most likely group to actually practice safe sex (Misovich, Fisher, & Fisher, 1997). DePaulo and Morris (2005) point out the following interesting additional findings about singlism and stereotypes:

- Both singles and married people display negative views of adult singles; in other words, single people display prejudice toward their own group. The harshest, most negative views of adult singles seem to come from married men and single women.

- Adult singles of all ages are targets of negative stereotypes, but the negativity increases as age increases, with singles over 40 years old judged more harshly than singles under 25.

- People who *were* married and are now single due to divorce are perceived as more attractive and sociable than people who have never been married at all.

- When single people claim to be happy, others express doubt and judge those claims as exaggerations.

Do negative stereotypes and prejudice against people who are still single in middle- to late-adulthood translate into actual discriminatory behaviors against them? Again, the research seems to indicate that they do. Even after controlling for variables such as age or experience on a job, married men earn significantly higher salaries than single men (Antonovics & Town, 2004; Budig & England, 2001). Married people are allowed certain tax and insurance benefits not offered to singles (Fox, 2004). Single women experience more challenges from prejudice when trying to become mothers through either in vitro fertilization or adoption (Millbank, 1997). In experimental settings, participants asked to pretend they are landlords overwhelmingly display preferences to rent to married couples over either single men or women (Morris, Sinclair, & DePaulo, 2007).

WHAT'S MY SCORE?

Attitudes About Single Adults

Instructions: Respond to each statement using this scale:

1	2	3	4	5	6	7
Completely disagree	Mostly disagree	Slightly disagree	Neutral	Slightly agree	Mostly agree	Completely agree

_____ 1. It's only natural for people to get married.

_____ 2. Single people can be just as fulfilled as married people.

_____ 3. People who claim to be satisfied being unmarried are just kidding themselves.

_____ 4. If I had a child who grew up and did not marry, I would worry that he/she would never be happy.

_____ 5. The intimacy of friendship cannot compare to the intimacy of marriage.

_____ 6. People who do not marry are incomplete.

_____ 7. My single friends seem to be missing something in their lives.

_____ 8. People who do not marry can never be truly fulfilled.

_____ 9. When single people say they are satisfied with their lives, I believe them.

_____ 10. There is something wrong with someone who doesn't want to get married.

Scoring: First, reverse-score items 2 and 9. Then, add up your answers. Higher scores indicate more of a prejudice against the idea of singlehood or a negative view of people who remain single. Note that the original article which developed this scale had more items; this is just a sampling of what was originally a full 30-item scale.

Source: Pignotti and Abell (2009).

Critical Thinking: There seem to be cultural differences in how acceptable it is for adult men to remain single, compared to adult women (with more negativity aimed toward women). What explains this difference? Can any of the three major theories described in earlier chapters (attachment, evolution, or interdependence) provide insight here?

Is prejudice against singles that big of a deal? Some people apparently think not. For example, in the study by Morris et al. (2007), they first found discrimination against singles in college students pretending to be landlords, as described above. In a second study—with different participants—students read *about* a landlord who had to decide between two potential tenants for an apartment. Both tenants were described as having steady jobs and as having good references from past landlords.

Some participants then were told that the landlord chose a White potential tenant over a Black tenant, even though the Black person had offered to pay more. In this scenario, participants displayed anger and said the decision was unfair, illegitimate, and blatant discrimination. The same pattern was found when the landlord was described as choosing a man over a woman, or when choosing a thin person over an obese person. But when the landlord chose a married person over a single person who offered to pay a higher rent, the participants justified the decision as being valid and understandable. No perceived prejudice there. To explore your own attitudes about single people, check out the "What's My Score?" feature.

Reactions to Singlism, From Singles Themselves

If you are single and you become aware of this negativity, prejudice, and discrimination, how do you react? What happens when you are constantly questioned about your single status, left out of invitations for parties or outings, and viewed with pity?

Kip Williams has spent his academic career studying the effects of stigma and social **ostracism**, being socially rejected by your peers. According to Williams, "After the initial pain of being ignored and excluded, single individuals could be expected to follow one of two paths" (Williams & Nida, 2005, p. 129). The first path is labeled "sycophantic singles." These people deliberately work harder to fit in, surround themselves with rich friendships, and ingratiate themselves with the married or cohabiting people around them. The second path is the "spiteful single." This path leads to aggression and antisocial behaviors. For a small group of people, rejection by potential partners plus social ostracism and stigma lead to terrible outcomes such as bitterness or even—in extreme cases—crimes like murder (Leary, Kowalski, Smith, & Phillips, 2003).

A few studies have conducted in-depth interviews with adult singles to gather qualitative data regarding their experiences. One study (Budgeon, 2008) asked 51 people between the ages of 24 and 60 what it was like to be a single person in later adulthood. One participant noted her awareness of the stigma of singlehood:

> I'm not saying I don't ever want a relationship and if it happens ok but I'm not actively thinking "I need this." It's that sort of thing of people thinking they have to be in a relationship otherwise you're some sort of failure, incomplete and I just don't buy that. . . . Society is sort of geared toward long-term relationships, preferably male-female, but whatever. . . . I can see the attraction and yes it's nice, you know what I mean? But I don't think if you don't want that then you're a failure or that you should feel bad that you're not in that. (Budgeon, 2008, p. 313)

Another woman emphasized how she wasn't interested in finding a partner right now because she was bolstered by her friendships:

> I really don't want to be going out with anyone for the foreseeable future because I get all the good stuff of having a partner from my friends. . . . I always have someone to see and I get cuddles and I get cups of tea . . . but I don't have to have screaming [fights] and long dissections of my emotional state and you know, share space and money and time to a greater extent than I want to, so yes, I think being single is great. (Budgeon, 2008, p. 314)

Another study that interviewed 10 middle-aged single women (Sharp & Ganong, 2011) found that among groups of single friends, sometimes there is a sense of loss when one of them does start a romantic relationship. When single people are aware of their stigmatized status, sometimes embracing it is a healthy way to cope with constant judgment from others. One woman noted:

> Every time, it is almost heartbreaking when someone gets serious like we are "losing one." . . . I don't know, sometimes I find myself wishing that everyone would stay single. I don't want to be the last single person on earth, but it would be nice if we could be our own people. (Sharp & Ganong, 2011, p. 996)

Cohabitation and Marriage

So being single is perfectly fine! But for others, they choose to commit to a relationship through cohabitation and/or marriage. Over 90% of adults will be married at least once in their lifetime (Connidis, 2001). Most people who are young and first getting married probably have an image of what they expect that relationship to look like for the next several decades. For an in-depth look at how relationships have their own timeline of milestone events, see the "Research Deep Dive" feature.

RESEARCH DEEP DIVE

Relationship Milestones in Short-Term and Long-Term Relationships

In your lifetime you experience several key milestones: being born, your first day of school, your first pimple, your first job, your first funeral. Your relationship is no different. If you were going to tell the story of your relationship, what would it look like? As you recapped your relationship's journey, you might include several key events, highlight important experiences, as well as describe when they happened. For example, did your first kiss happen a month, a week, or a moment from the start of the relationship?

Relationship researchers believe that this type of information has a story of its own to tell and can provide insights into your relationship. To test this, they ran a series of five studies to examine how relationships develop in both short- and long-term relationships (Eastwick, Keneski, Morgan, McDonald, & Huang, 2018). Wait. Five studies? When studying a new area or a big question, one study may not be enough to fully understand what's going on. In those cases, researchers will map out a series of studies, each designed to study one facet of the overall question.

To study the timing and nature of various relationship milestones, researchers had participants map their relationship's history. Trajectory-plotting such as this has been used in many studies and asks participants to retrospectively chart the course of the relationship in terms of perceived likelihood of marrying or romantic interest (using a 0–100 scale). Participants begin from when they started dating, noting major turning points, events, and milestones along the way. Some of the key milestones or "firsts" included the following: first meeting, short date, kiss, sexual intercourse, first time told friends about the relationship, said "I love you," became exclusive, overnight trip together, got engaged, broke up, and so on. As you can imagine, this exercise yields a relationship timeline that is full of descriptive information. Such in-depth collection of information is uncommon but extremely useful for understanding relationship development over time.

In Study 1, 86 college students (70 women, 16 men) created timelines for both "a short-term romantic relationship (e.g., a fling, one-night-stand, or brief affair)" and "a long-term, committed romantic relationship." From these data, researchers learned that short- and long-term relationships start out much the same. Only around event 15 did the long-term relationship show sustained increases in romantic interest, while interest in short-term relationships started to dissipate. The study also looked at specific relationship behaviors and found that self-protection occurred more in short-term relationships, while self-disclosure, caregiving, and forming an attachment were more common in long-term relationships.

Study 2a and 2b sought to replicate Study 1 using a different sample. This time they included more men, as well as an older, nonstudent sample from MTurk (an online marketplace where "workers" can complete various tasks, such as completing research studies for money). Results of these studies largely replicated Study 1. Short- and long-term relationships had parallel levels of romantic interest. Increases in interest were similar, but they tailed off in short-term relationships when things became more sexual.

Although the paper reports only three of the five studies, researchers made the additional two studies available online with the supplementary materials. Typically, when studies do this, the extra studies are additional replications or minor extensions. That was the case here, with one study having participants also describe their affairs.

Another interesting feature of this article is that the researchers used data from all of the studies to formulate the relationship coordination and strategic timing (ReCAST) model. Researchers create models like this to help simplify complex relationship phenomena. In this case, the ReCAST model combines interdependence and evolutionary theories to depict the most common or normative pattern of relationship development.

Overall, the studies and the resulting model suggest that short-term and long-term relationships follow unique relationship trajectories. However, early on they are largely the same. The progression only differs later in the relationship when partners enact strategies to maintain the couple's connection that allow it to become a long-term relationship.

For more, read Eastwick, W. P. Keneski, E., Morgan, A. T., McDonald, A. M., & Huang, A. S. (2018). What do short-term and long-term relationships look like? Building the relationships coordination and strategic timing (ReCAST) model. *Journal of Experimental Psychology: General, 147*(5), 747–781.

Choosing Cohabitation Only Versus Marriage

More and more people choose **cohabitation**, living together with a romantic partner without legal marriage. Between the years 1977 and 2010, the number of cohabiting couples in the United States went from about 1 million to about 7.5 million (U.S. Census Bureau, 2010). Until same-sex marriage was legalized, many of these couples may have been cohabiting simply because marriage was not a legal option for them. However, now people of all sexual orientations often choose cohabitation versus marriage based on a variety of factors.

A study that asked cohabiting couples why they chose not to be legally married provided four different common reasons (Casper & Sayer, 2000):

- 46% said they were living together as a "first step" but definitely intended to be married later.

- 15% similarly noted that they wanted to try living together to see whether they were compatible, and they would consider marriage later if cohabitation worked out (they weren't as confident as the first group).

- 29% reported that they weren't sure their relationship was permanent and were simply living together for convenience (e.g., shared living expenses).

- 10% reported that they genuinely preferred a cohabitation arrangement; they were committed, but just chose not to be married for a variety of reasons.

Compared to people who choose to get married without living together first, people who cohabit are more likely to have divorced parents, to be less religious, to drink more alcohol, and to have lower incomes (Bennett, Blanc, & Bloom, 1988; Cohan & Kleinbaum, 2002). Regardless of the motivation behind cohabitation, people who choose this path are actually highly likely to break up. Ninety percent of cohabiting couples will end their relationship within 5 years of starting to live together (DeMaris & Rao, 1992; Lichter, Qian, & Mellott, 2006). On the other hand, over half of couples who eventually marry do live together first for at least a short period of time (Smock, 2000). So, cohabitation isn't necessarily a good or bad decision or experience; it depends on each person's motivation and the dynamics of each couple.

Overall, people are also waiting longer to live together or get married than ever before. In 1960, the median age of first marriage was 20 for women and 23 for men; now, it's 27 for women and 29 for men (Pew Research Center, 2014). Roles within a marriage may also be changing, at least for heterosexual spouses, as women become increasingly economically independent. Over the last 60 years, more and more women have been employed outside the home—and fewer men are. For women, it went from 35% in 1960 to 53% in 2013; for men, it dropped from 79% to 64% (Pew Research Center, 2014). Research on increasingly empowered women finds that both men and women today expect that by the year 2050, women will have significantly more control over relationship events and outcomes than they did in the past (Diekman, Goodfriend, & Goodwin, 2004).

Choosing Marriage in Different Cultures

Finally, whether people choose to get married and what they expect from it varies by culture. Certainly, an examination of international books and movies shows a wide variety of cultural norms on courtship, why people get married, and the roles of each partner. This idea is also explored in the best-selling book *Crazy Rich Asians*, which was made into a popular movie as well (see the "Relationships and Popular Culture" feature). Of course, it's also been investigated in research.

Remember from Chapter 5 that a major way to compare parts of the world is that people from "Western" cultures (like the United States, England, and Australia) tend to be individualistic, or focused on the needs of the self, whereas "Eastern" cultures (like India, Japan, and Hong Kong) are more collectivistic, or focused on the needs

RELATIONSHIPS AND POPULAR CULTURE

Marriage Expectations and Culture: *Crazy Rich Asians*

In the best-selling book (Kwan, 2013) that become a popular movie (Chu, 2018), *Crazy Rich Asians* explores a Chinese American woman's cultural views of love and marriage and how they clash with traditional views from those of her fiancé's family. Rachel, the main character, is a successful professor of economics at New York University but was raised by a single mother in a middle-class lifestyle. Her fiancé, Nick, is an ethnically Chinese man from Singapore who was raised in London.

While his personal views of their relationship seem to match hers, his family back in Singapore doesn't seem to approve of the match. In addition to the cultural discrepancies based on U.S. versus Singapore culture, they also disapprove of Rachel because they happen to be one of the 10 richest families in Asia. They don't believe Rachel will be capable of putting the family's needs above her own, assuming that American women are inherently individualistic. Country-based and socioeconomic status–based cultural stereotypes and norms are both explored in a delightfully comedic, yet poignant way in this popular story.

of the group (Hui & Triandis, 1986). Do people from different cultures feel the same about why they should—or shouldn't—get married?

Two studies asked U.S. college students, "If a boy/girl had all the other qualities you desired, would you marry this person if you were not in love with them?" When people were asked this question in 1967, 64% of men and 24% of women said no (Kephart, 1967). When the question was asked of students in 1984, more than 80% of both men and women said no (Simpson, Campbell, & Berscheid, 1986). It seems that Americans believe love is a necessary component to the choice to marry. But this might not be true in other cultures, where other factors may be stressed. Historically, most cultures around the world had marriages that were arranged by family members and were based on pragmatic factors like equal wealth, similar religion, and so forth (Skolnick, 1987).

One study asked college students from 11 countries—India, Pakistan, Thailand, Mexico, Brazil, Japan, Hong Kong, the Philippines, Australia, England, and the United States—about marriage motives (Levine, Sato, Hashimoto, & Verma, 1995). In total, the researchers had over 1000 participants. They started by asking people the same question as the paragraph above, about whether they'd still get married without love. Their survey also included a self-report scale of collectivism versus individualism.

An initial finding of interest was that within each of the 11 countries, men's and women's answers weren't different. In other words, in this study, country-based culture was more important than gender-based culture. Next, as you can see in Table 6.2, there was a lot of variance in how willing people were to marry someone they don't love. The highest rates of people who said they would refuse a loveless marriage came from the United States, Brazil, England, Mexico, and Australia. In contrast, people from India, Pakistan, and Thailand were much more willing to marry someone without love, *if* the person had every other desired quality. Importantly, when the self-report scale on cultural values was calculated, Pakistan and Thailand scored highest in collectivism. England, Australia, and the United States scored the highest in individualism. So in general, the study found that love really is more important in either cultures or in individuals who value needs of the self, compared to cultures or individuals who value needs of the family or larger community.

TABLE 6.2 ● Answers to Whether You'd Marry Someone Without Love, by Percentage

	No	Yes	Undecided
United States	85.9	3.5	10.6
Brazil	85.7	4.3	10.0
England	83.6	7.3	9.1
Mexico	80.5	10.2	9.3
Australia	80.0	4.8	15.2
Hong Kong	77.6	5.8	16.7
Philippines	63.6	11.4	25.0
Japan	62.0	2.3	35.7
Pakistan	39.1	50.4	10.4
Thailand	33.8	18.8	47.5
India	24.0	49.0	26.9

When college students from 11 different countries were asked if they'd marry someone who had every quality they wanted but they weren't in love, variance in answer seemed to differ a lot based on culture.

CHECK YOUR UNDERSTANDING

6.4 If current trends continue, when college students today reach the age of 50, how many of them will probably still be single (and never married)?

   a. About one-tenth (10%)
   b. About one-fourth (25%)
   c. About half (50%)
   d. About two-thirds (67%)

6.5 Bella DePaulo and her colleagues asked people to think of words that came to mind that are associated with either married people or single people (Morris et al., 2004). Which of the words or terms below was the ONLY one listed that was more likely to be associated with single people?

   a. Loving
   b. Kind/giving
   c. Happy
   d. Social/fun

6.6 Based on your interpretation of Table 6.2, people from which country below are MOST likely to agree to marry someone who has every desired quality, even if they're not in love with them?

   a. Thailand
   b. Brazil
   c. Pakistan
   d. United States

APPLICATION ACTIVITY

Interview at least two of your friends who are single and at least two of your friends who are in a committed relationship (but aren't dating each other). Ask all of them to list five (or more) advantages to being single and five (or more) advantages of being in a relationship, then ask them to rate how happy they are with their current situation on a scale from 0 (very unhappy) to 10 (very happy). Then, compare and contrast the answers you get. Do you see any patterns? Are there differences based on whether your friends are men or women, whether they are gay or heterosexual, or the type of relationship they have? Try to generate some hypotheses based on your data.

CRITICAL THINKING

- Over the last 50 years, all of the following have increased: (1) the number of people who stay single into older adulthood, (2) the number of people who choose to live together without getting married, and (3) the number of people who get divorced. Are all of these patterns explained by the same social, cultural, or psychological variables? What do you think are the most important variables involved? Next, consider whether the pattern will change over the next 50 years. Will these trends continue to go up, level off, or start to go back down? Why do you think so?

- When you look at the numbers in Table 6.2, there are some interesting patterns that weren't addressed in the main text. For example, only 2.3% of people from Japan said that they would marry someone desirable without love. That seems to indicate a very "individualistic" attitude, but Japan has been shown to have a very collectivistic culture in other studies. How can we explain this result, then? Is the key in the "undecided" column?

Answers to the Check Your Understanding Questions
6.4 b, 6.5 d, and 6.6 c.

How Do Relationships Change Later in Life?

You already know a little about how relationships change over time. In Chapter 1, you learned about Sternberg's triangular theory of love, and how adolescent romantic relationships are closer to "consummate" love (which includes all three components in Sternberg's theory), while relationships in older adults are more driven by commitment (intimacy and passion decline). In this final section of the chapter, we'll cover a few more big topics regarding how relationships change later in life. These will include parenthood, divorce, retirement, and bereavement for a partner who passes away.

Parenthood

"First comes love, then comes marriage, then comes a baby in a baby carriage."

You probably heard that childhood song on the playground, and it emphasizes the social **script** many people have for the order of expected events within adult relationships. Scripts are one type of **schema**, or cognitive structure we use to organize the world. They follow social norms and provide most people an easy, regulated path for behaviors that will be socially accepted. Scripts allow us to understand that most people date for a while, then one of them proposes marriage to the other by presenting a ring, and they plan the wedding, exchange vows, have a party, and then potentially have children. We know that not everyone follows the exact script—but we also know that to deviate is to slightly upset social expectation.

Again, not all couples follow this traditional journey. As we've already said, not everyone gets married, not all marriages result in children, and some children are born to unmarried parents. In fact, one-third of children born in the United States have nonmarried parents (Carlson, McLanahan, & England, 2004; Ventura & Bachrach, 2000), a situation some researchers call a "fragile family" (Carlson et al., 2004, p. 237).

There are several possible reasons for the increase in couples who choose to have children without getting married. One is decreases in religiosity and conservative or traditional norms over time (Wilcox, 2002; Wilcox & Wolfinger, 2007). Second, more and more people express doubt or skepticism about the value of marriage or the need to be married as necessary for a happy, fulfilling relationship (Carlson et al., 2004). In other words, plenty of people believe that couples can be just as happy living together as they can be if they were legally married—so why bother getting married?

A third possible reason that some heterosexual couples might not get married is the rise in women who believe that marriage provides an excuse for husbands to exert patriarchal authority over their wives (Edin, 2000; Gibson-Davis, Edin, & McLanahan, 2005). As Carlson et al. (2004) note, "Some women feared that the men they were already living with would start ordering them around more if they married" (p. 241). These doubts don't stop people from wanting a family, though, so many people choose to have children without getting married.

Our cognitive scripts tell us that these images appear out of order.

Source: (clockwise from upper left):
© istockphoto.com/tororo; © istockphoto.com/wundervisuals; © istockphoto.com/pixdeluxe; © istockphoto.com/GoodLifeStudio; © istockphoto.com/sjharmon; © istockphoto.com/ilbusca.

Even though many couples hope to have children, the experience is challenging. Relationship satisfaction often declines over time, regardless of the presence of children (VanLandingham, Johnson, & Amato, 2001), but this decline is swifter for parents than for nonparents (Lawrence, Rothman, Cobb, Rothman, & Bradbury, 2008). Despite lower relationship satisfaction, couples with children are more likely to stay together than childless couples (White & Booth, 1985). And this tenacity is rewarded, as satisfaction usually goes back up as soon as the children are old enough to leave home (White & Edwards, 1990). In addition, problems with relationship satisfaction are more likely for couples who are young, who have financial problems, and for whom the child was not planned (Mitnick, Heyman, & Smith Slep, 2009).

One article attempted to understand the effect of having children on couples by conducting a **meta-analysis**. A meta-analysis is a study that attempts to combine the findings of many smaller, individual studies using statistics that detect patterns across all of the participants. In this case, Twenge, Campbell, and Foster (2003) included 97 different studies that used a total of 47,692 participants. They found several interesting patterns in their overall analyses:

- Parents have significantly lower relationship satisfaction than nonparents.

- Mothers are especially unhappy when their children are infants; their satisfaction goes up as the children get older.

- Having children had a more negative effect on rich couples than it did on poor couples. This may be because having a child immediately restricts freedom and may change people's sense of self more when they have the privilege of wealth and opportunity.

- Earlier generations of parents (i.e., your parents or grandparents) were happier after having children than later generations (i.e., young couples today).

- The more children a couple has, the less happy they are (a negative correlation).

Do these findings mean that people should avoid having children? Not necessarily. The authors of the meta-analysis note, "Our results are not intended to imply that married couples should avoid having children. The negative effects on marital satisfaction are relatively small and primarily affect certain groups" (Twenge et al., 2003, p. 582). Instead of simply choosing not to have children, these authors suggest that knowing about potential challenges can help couples plan for happy pregnancies and parenthood experiences—including, for example, the use of reliable daycare. They close their article by reminding readers that couples who do have children often find more meaning in life, and that while satisfaction with their co-parent may decrease, joy from raising their children is deep and substantial (Baumeister, 1991).

Divorce

You've probably heard that about half of marriages end in divorce, and that's true—at least, in the United States. The divorce rate in the United States is 53% (Engel, 2014), and about half of couples will divorce within the first 8 years of marriage (Kreider & Fields, 2001). But divorce rates vary substantially by country. The highest rates (over

60%) are found in the European countries of Belgium, Spain, Portugal, the Czech Republic, and Hungary. The lowest divorce rate is found in Chile, with only 3% of couples eventually divorcing.

In addition to country (or culture), divorce rates change based on a number of additional factors. One that is tied to culture is likely religion, with people in highly religious cultures less likely to divorce. Some researchers have suggested that divorce goes up when people have unrealistic expectations about how "perfect" marriage should be (Amato, 2010). On the other hand, children of divorced parents are more likely to get divorced themselves, eventually, so there could be a self-fulfilling prophecy effect (Mustonen, Huurre, Kiviruusu, Haukkala, & Aro, 2011). These two predictions are in opposite directions—so divorce is clearly complicated.

Work also has an effect; the more wives work outside the home, the lower the quality of their marriages (Hostetler, Desrochers, Kopko, & Moen, 2012). In heterosexual marriages, this might be due to traditional husbands feeling threatened in their role as "breadwinner." Or it might be that women simply have the ability to leave unhappy marriages if they choose, due to financial independence. What kind of job people have also seems to matter: People who work in service industries—like bartenders and flight attendants—get divorced the most, whereas scientists, mathematicians, and people who work with computers get divorced the least (Yau, 2007).

One study simply asked people why they got divorces. This longitudinal study was called the Marital Instability Over the Life Course project (Booth, Johnson, White, & Edwards, 1986), and it resulted in several published articles about different aspects of following more than 2000 married people over 17 years. The authors made sure that the couples involved were diverse in terms of race, age, and number of children. Of those 2000 people, 274 of them got divorced during the study period, and 208 of them were willing to talk about it.

During phone interviews, the participants were simply asked the question, "What do you think caused the divorce?" Their top 10 (most common) answers are shown in Table 6.3 (from Amato & Previti, 2003). The most common reasons were infidelity (cheating or an affair), incompatibility, alcohol/drug use, simply growing apart, and personality problems. You can see a few interesting differences by sex as well. For example, women were much more likely than men to get divorces because their spouses were abusing drugs or were abusing them, whereas men were more likely to cite lack of communication or loss of love.

If a couple does get divorced, what helps them heal and move on? The same study that resulted in Table 6.3 also asked people this question (published in Wang & Amato, 2000). Divorced people were interviewed for how they felt now (a few years later), both in terms of (1) general adjustment and happiness and (2) attitudes toward their ex-spouse. Participants answered questions such as the following:

- Overall, do you think you or your spouse has been happier with the decision to divorce?

- Looking back, do you think the divorce was a good or a bad idea?

- Has your divorce improved or worsened your peace of mind?

- Do you agree with this statement: "I feel I will never get over the divorce." (see p. 660 in Wang & Amato, 2000)

TABLE 6.3 ● Top 10 Reasons for Getting a Divorce		
Reason Given	**% of Men**	**% of Women**
Infidelity/cheating	16	25
Incompatible	20	19
Alcohol/drug use	5	14
Grew apart	9	10
Personality problems	10	8
Lack of communication	13	6
Physical or mental abuse	0	9
Loss of love	7	3
Not meeting family obligations	1	5
Employment problems	3	4

The top two reasons people get a divorce are cheating or deciding that we're simply incompatible with our partner.

The researchers found that happiness after divorce was more likely if people had an adequate income, if they had started dating someone else steadily or even remarried, if they were younger, and if they were the one who had initiated the divorce. In other words, these factors helped people find closure and heal.

In general, many people who were married once and are now divorced or wid-owed are much more skeptical about trying it again; only 21% say they want to marry a second time (Pew Research Center, 2014). This doubt might go away with time, or loneliness might drive people to change their minds, though, because around 80% of divorced people end up married again (Cherlin, 1992). Unfortunately, second or third marriages have even higher divorce rates than first marriages do (Bumpass, Sweet, & Martin, 1990; Clarke & Wilson, 1994). This might be because people had already tried it once and thus are more open to the idea of divorce (Amato & Booth, 2001), or it may be that people bring challenges such as more independence, step-children, and "baggage" from first marriages along with them (Booth & Edwards, 1992). Marriage is more complicated than the "happily ever after" that fairy tales teach us as children.

Retirement, Bereavement, and Approaching Death

We've already discussed changes in relationships as people age a couple of times.

As a reminder (remember Sternberg's triangles), older couples tend to report less love and passion for each other, compared to younger couples (e.g., Swensen, Eskew, & Kohlhepp, 1984). That said, if a couple can stick it out until retirement age, it seems to be a sign that the relationship is pretty sturdy and healthy. Older couples are better at handling conflict (Carstensen, Gottman, & Levenson, 1995) and report having fewer disagreements (Levenson, Carstensen, & Gottman, 1993). When they do fight, they are better at using strategies that promote positive feelings and compromise (Carstensen, 1992). Perhaps going against some stereotypes, older married couples between the ages of 57 and 85 continue to have sex at least a few times a month as well (Lindau et al., 2007). Good for them!

Approaching retirement for at least one couple member can lead to increased relationship conflict (Moen, Kim, & Hofmeister, 2001). If a heterosexual couple includes a man who is older than his wife, the husband will often continue working until they can both retire at the same time. This may be due to traditional masculine pride in earning the lion's share of the family income (Szinovacz, 1996). If a husband does retire before his wife but does not then take over more household duties such as cleaning and cooking, sometimes working wives build resentment (Moen et al., 2001). Clear communication seems to be the key to overcoming such challenges.

Sadly, some people must deal with the death of their spouse. **Bereavement** is the psychological process of dealing with loss of a close loved one. As you would probably guess, grieving and feelings of loss are most intense for the year after death, although bereavement can last for years (Raphael, 1983). A study that interviewed gay men who had lost their husband or partner found that depression and a sense of loss were negatively correlated with the surviving partner's ability to analyze themselves with self-reflection about their relationship, including acknowledgment of conflict or imperfections (Nolen-Hoeksema, McBride, & Larson, 1997).

Even if both partners are still alive, every birthday brings us closer to the end. As we get older, we become increasingly aware of our own inevitable death, an idea explored by **socioemotional selectivity theory** (Carstensen, Fung, & Charles, 2003). This theory suggests that when we believe we have a limited amount of time left to live, our motivation shifts to the need to pursue meaningful goals in a more explicit way. In other words, our "bucket list" (list of things to accomplish before we "kick the bucket") becomes increasingly important. One change is that older people may argue less, forgive small indiscretions, and explore lifelong goals such as vacationing together, all of which translate into more happiness.

A similar theory is called **terror management theory**, or TMT for short (Greenberg, Pyszczynski, & Solomon, 1986; Mikulincer, Florian, & Hirschberger, 2004; Solomon, Greenberg, & Pyszczynski, 1991). TMT starts with these basic ideas:

1. All living things want to continue living.

2. Humans can imagine dying, and this thought is terrifying.

3. To manage our terror, we embrace "worldviews" (ways of giving meaning to life), such as culture, religion, and relationships.

4. Worldviews allow us to believe that even though we will die, we can leave a meaningful legacy and thus live on through our contributions to the world.

Several studies have established that when we think about our own death, we become especially committed to our beliefs and to our relationships (regardless of how old we are). TMT theorists believe that when we think about death, we'll love other people more—and when our relationships go badly, we feel worse about our "existential plight" (Mikulincer et al., 2004, p. 287). In one experiment, college students who wrote essays about their own death later indicated higher commitment to their current relationship partners, compared to participants who wrote control-condition essays about dental pain (Study 1; Florian, Mikulincer, & Hirschberger, 2002). Other studies have replicated similar effects, leading people who endorse TMT to conclude, "The maintenance of close relationships provides a symbolic shield against the terror of death" (Mikulincer, Florian, & Hirschberger, 2003, p. 21). Perhaps as we age, having a loving partner next to us provides a kind of comfort that is hard to find from other sources.

CHECK YOUR UNDERSTANDING

6.7 Twenge et al. (2003) conducted a meta-analysis of 97 studies that examined the effect of children on relationships. Which of the findings below is the OPPOSITE of their results?

    a. Parents have significantly lower relationship satisfaction than nonparents.

    b. Mothers are especially unhappy when their children are infants, compared to older children.

    c. Having children has more of a negative effect on poor couples, compared to rich couples.

    d. The more children a couple has, the less happy they are (a negative correlation).

6.8 According to research cited here, which country below has the lowest divorce rates?

    a. Chile
    b. United States
    c. Czech Republic
    d. South Africa

6.9 According to terror management theory, engaging in which exercise below would make you feel most committed to your current partner?

    a. Thinking about your own death
    b. Thinking about your partner's death
    c. Thinking about experiencing terrible pain
    d. Thinking about your partner experiencing terrible pain

APPLICATION ACTIVITY

Do an online search for a research article that discusses divorce patterns. Pick one that was published at least 20 years ago. Summarize the study's findings and then analyze whether you think the same results would be found today. Explain why you think the pattern of results would be either the same or different, if the study were replicated now.

CRITICAL THINKING

- One study (Carlson et al., 2004) had women who reported that living with a boyfriend was better than marriage because if they got married, their husband might "start ordering them around more." What do you think of this fear? Is it a sexist sentiment against men? Are people who are married less likely to treat each other with kindness and respect because it's perceived to be "harder" for either one of them to leave, compared to couples who are choosing to live together without marriage?

- At least some patterns of parenthood (such as whether parents are happier than nonparents) differ based on socioeconomic status. What other variables might matter? For example, does the experience of parenthood change based on culture, sexual orientation, or age of the parents? Choose two variables you think might influence the parenthood experience and create specific hypotheses about them.

Answers to the Check Your Understanding Questions

6.7 c, 6.8 a, and 6.9 a.

Chapter Summary

Big Questions

1. How do our earliest relationships form?

2. How do we choose singlehood versus commitment in young adulthood?

3. How do relationships change later in life?

How do our earliest relationships form?

Relationships with others change as we grow older. Our first relationship is that of a fetus to an expecting mother; studies show that fetuses respond (e.g., move their arms) when expecting mothers speak or touch their abdomens. Researchers have debated whether the tie an infant shows to its mother is based on biological needs (such as access to milk) or psychological/ emotional needs. Perhaps the most famous study investigating this question was done by Harlow (1958), who raised baby monkeys in cages with two "false" mothers. One "mother"

was hard but provided milk, while the other "mother" was warm and soft (but did not provide milk). When the monkeys were scared, they ran to the warm and soft mother, which Harlow interpreted as a sign they were emotionally bonded to these "mothers" due to touch and comfort—a psychological bond.

How do we choose singlehood versus commitment in young adulthood?

If people remain single into the second half of life, they may experience stigma, or negative stereotypes and prejudice about their single status; this type of prejudice is called singlism. More and more people are choosing to remain single into older adulthood, with 45% of adults in the United States being single in 2017, a record amount. Prejudice against single people has been found in both experimental settings and in the "real world," such as married people being paid more than single people with the same job and experience. An increasing number of people are choosing to cohabitate with their partner as well (without marriage). Finally, the choice of whether to marry and why differs by culture.

How do relationships change later in life?
Scripts are cognitive structures that help us organize and categorize the world, and most people share a script that people are expected to date, get married, then have children. However, many people do not follow this script. If people do not remain single, increasing numbers of couples choose to live together instead of get legally married. For those who do marry, 53% (in the United States) will eventually divorce. Couples who do have children usually experience declines in relationship satisfaction, although many variables are associated with better or worse experiences. The top two reasons for divorces in one study were infidelity and becoming incompatible. Approaching retirement, coping with the death of a spouse, or simply approaching one's own death can also lead to complications within intimate relationships.

List of Terms

Learning Objectives	Key Terms
6.1 Explain the biological and psychological motivations between infant-mother bonds.	Imprinting False dichotomy Contact comfort
6.2 Analyze the status and stigma of being single as a young adult, then interpret research on the choice to get married.	Stigma Singlism Ostracism Cohabitation
6.3 Evaluate research on parenthood, divorce, retirement, and bereavement.	Script Schema Meta-analysis Bereavement Socioemotional selectivity theory Terror management theory

Friendship

Big Questions	Learning Objectives
1. What predicts how and when friendships will form?	**7.1** Analyze factors predicting friendship formation.
2. How are friendships maintained?	**7.2** Identify components of friendship and discuss threats, such as lack of social support.
3. How do friendships change over our lifetime?	**7.3** Interpret research on how friendships change from early childhood through adulthood.

The previous chapter started with infancy and ended with older adulthood, but not much was said about childhood and adolescence. That's because during that time period, friendships become one of the most important kinds of relationship in our lives—and friendships are the topic now. As children, forming friendships with peers becomes our focus—and we can all remember times when friendships have affected our sense of self and emotional experiences, both good and bad.

Let's take some time to devote our attention to friendships. What determines whether you'll become friends with someone? Do you and your friends have unwritten "rules" about how to act to maintain the friendship? What happens when friendships go sour? How do your friendships change as you grow up? These fascinating questions will all be addressed in this chapter.

What Predicts How and When Friendships Will Form?

Think about your childhood friends and your friends now. What circumstances brought you together? Beverly Fehr (1996), a leading friendship researcher, wrote an entire book on the topic of how friendships grow and evolve: *Friendship Processes*.

There, she discusses four factors that predict new friendships: environmental, individual, situational, and dyadic factors. Let's cover each in turn.

Environmental Factors: The Westgate Housing Study

You've heard the phrase "The boy [or girl] next door."

The idea is that we might form relationships with people who are physically nearby. Except for "friends" who exist only online through social media platforms like Facebook, most friendships start when two people meet in person and have the opportunity to interact. Fehr (1996) notes, "A first step in the formation of most friendships is that two individuals are brought into contact with one another through physical proximity or propinquity" (p. 44).

Propinquity is the sharing of an environment, or how physically close two people are. Friendships are more likely to form when two people cross paths frequently and have the opportunity to get to know each other. We're more likely to be childhood friends with people in our neighborhood; as adults, we're more likely to be friends with people in the offices next to ours at work, compared to people who are in the next building over. A similar idea from social psychology is **mere exposure**, the finding that we tend to like things and people more, the more we're around them. Familiarity leads to liking.

The most famous study to explore propinquity (or proximity) effects is known as the **Westgate Housing Study** (or sometimes the "MIT study") and was conducted by Festinger, Schachter, and Back (1950). At the Massachusetts Institute of Technology (MIT) in the 1950s, the married student housing was called the Westgate Apartments. Each building was constructed in the same way (see Figure 7.1): It had 10 single-family units, with 5 apartments on each floor. There were two staircases going to the second floor, next to apartments 1 and 5. Apartments 6 and 10 were in the corners of that second floor, fairly isolated.

FIGURE 7.1 ● Architectural Structure of a Westgate Housing Apartment Building

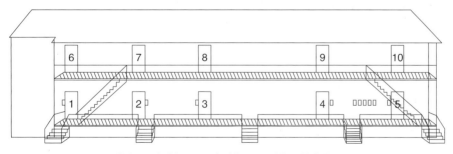

Schematic Diagram of a Westgate West Building

A typical apartment in the Westgate Housing Project (Festinger et al., 1950) is shown. You can see staircases going up to the second floor that start near apartments 1 and 5. When people in the buildings were asked to rate their neighbors, people in apartments 1 and 5 were liked the most, while people in apartments 6 and 10 were liked the least.

Source: Festinger, 1950.

Festinger pointed out that there were two kinds of propinquity in these apartments: (1) physical distance from one apartment to another—how many steps you'd have to take to get there—and (2) functional distance. Functional distance refers to the fact that, because of the buildings' design, some apartments were more likely to be passed by than others. The occupants of these apartments were more likely to be seen by other residents.

Festinger asked people in Westgate to choose the three people in the entire complex whom they were most likely to see socially (in other words, their friends). They listed residents with closer physical and functional proximity to themselves. If two people saw each other often, they were more likely to get to know each other and become friends (Festinger et al., 1950). So next-door neighbors usually liked each other—physical proximity.

Across all of the buildings in the complex, people who happened to live in apartments 1 and 5 were liked the most, on average—functional proximity. These apartments were at the bottom of staircases leading to the second floor, so all of the residents who lived on the second floor would have to pass those doors. People in apartments 6 and 10 were usually liked the least, perhaps because the location of their apartments isolated them from their neighbors.

This kind of propinquity effect leading to friendship has been replicated many times in other settings. Men in Detroit reported that their friends were mostly people with whom they worked every day (26% of their friends) or people who lived in their neighborhood (23%; Fischer et al., 1977). When you have to sit in a new classroom full of strangers, are you more likely to befriend the people who just happen to be sitting close to you? Studies have found this tendency to be true, based on propinquity in both classroom settings and dorm room assignments (Kubitschek & Hallinan, 1998; Segal, 1974).

Even with social networks such as Facebook, Snapchat, or Instagram that are designed to help people communicate despite large physical distances, studies have shown that propinquity matters. Online friendships are still most likely to form and be maintained by people who live relatively close to each other, at least for a brief period of time (Hampton & Wellman, 2001; Mazur & Richards, 2011). That said, increasingly we have technology that allows us to have "communication proximity" wirelessly and instantly through apps like Skype and FaceTime—and that ability helps us maintain close relationships regardless of geographic distance (Cummings, Lee, & Kraut, 2006; Osofsky & Chartrand, 2013). While there are certainly many other variables involved in friendship formation (several of which are described in this section), the opportunity to interact due to physical proximity is repeatedly shown to matter. In short, propinquity and likelihood of friendships forming are positively correlated.

Individual Factors: Self-Disclosure

In her book *Friendship Processes*, Fehr (1996) discusses several factors that individuals may use to decide whether to befriend another person. She notes that most people have "dislike criteria," or a list of things we don't want to see in our friends, as well as "inclusion criteria," or traits we do want to see in our friends. While specific dislike criteria vary from person to person, "we never like people who meet our dislike criteria regardless of what likeable qualities they may also possess" (Rodin, 1982, p. 32, as quoted in Fehr, 1996). In other words, if something drives us crazy about another person, we weigh those negative qualities more than anything we appreciate about them.

What are common "inclusion criteria"? According to Fehr, we tend to befriend people we find physically attractive, those who have good social skills, and those who are responsive to us, meaning they are good at matching us in level of interest, concern, and self-disclosure (or revealing personal information). Several studies have shown that when an interaction partner is more responsive, people like them more (Berg & Archer, 1980; Davis & Perkowitz, 1979; Godfrey, Jones, & Lord, 1986).

Some people are high in **self-disclosure**, meaning they are open to others more quickly and are more likely to consistently share "personal" information about their inner thoughts or experiences. These individuals tend to make other people comfortable sharing personal information as well, which quickly builds a sense of friendship (Berg, 1987; Miller, Berg, & Archer, 1983). Are you good at getting others to open up? If so, you might be what Miller et al. (1983) call an "opener." To find out, take the survey in the first "What's My Score?" feature.

WHAT'S MY SCORE?

Openers: People Who Elicit Intimate Self-Disclosures From Others

Instructions: This scale measures whether you are good at getting other people to "open up" about themselves. Respond to each item using this scale:

0	1	2	3	4
Strongly disagree				Strongly agree

_____ 1. People frequently tell me about themselves.

_____ 2. I've been told that I'm a good listener.

_____ 3. I'm very accepting of others.

_____ 4. People trust me with their secrets.

_____ 5. I easily get people to "open up."

_____ 6. People feel relaxed around me.

_____ 7. I enjoy listening to people.

_____ 8. I'm sympathetic to people's problems.

_____ 9. I encourage people to tell me how they are feeling.

_____ 10. I can keep people talking about themselves.

Scoring: For an overall "opener" score, simply add up all of your ratings. The number will be between 0 and 40, with higher numbers indicating that you are more of an "opener." When this scale was given to college students, the average score for women was 30.68 (SD = 4.63) and the average for men was 28.01 (SD = 4.87).

Source: Miller et al. (1983).

Critical Thinking: Do people in counseling or therapy professions need to be high in their ability to be an "opener"? If someone is interested in these professions but doesn't score particularly high in this scale, can they learn to be an opener, or is this trait something that people are simply born with and can't change?

Social Penetration Theory

Imagine you're meeting someone for the very first time. Which topics do you think you're most likely to discuss from this list?

- The weather

- What kind of music or movies you like

- What your job is

- Whether you have brothers and sisters

- How well you get along with your parents

- Whether you plan to have children, and how many

- What your most embarrassing secrets are and times when you've lied to people about them

For most of us, the likelihood of talking about these topics goes in descending order. **Social penetration theory** (Altman & Taylor, 1973) predicts that relationship intimacy (for romantic relationships or friendships) progresses through systematic changes over time, including increasingly personal self-disclosures. In other words, conversations start with relatively "safe" topics like the weather or someone's major in college. It's only as we grow comfortable with each other that we start to reveal more personal information. The theory states that self-disclosures will change in both breadth, or range of topics, and depth, or personal significance (Hornstein & Truesdell, 1988). Increased breadth and depth will be both the cause and the result of more intimate friendships. We like people more when they share intimate information with us, and we reciprocate by revealing personal things about ourselves to them (Collins & Miller, 1994).

The "Fast Friends" Procedure

It might be easy to say that personal self-disclosures are important for developing friendships—but sometimes it's awkward to get this kind of intimacy started.

It might surprise you that this very problem was the subject of a study titled "The Experimental Generation of Interpersonal Closeness" (Aron, Melinat, Aron, Vallone, & Bator, 1997). The researchers designed a very specific procedure designed to help any two people—even strangers—become close in about an hour in what later researchers would call the "Fast Friends" procedure. The key was **reciprocal self-disclosure**, or two people revealing personal information and matching each other's level of intimacy.

College students who agreed to be in the study were paired with another student they didn't know. As in all true experiments, participants were then randomly assigned to one of the study's conditions. Here, there was a control condition called the "small talk" condition, as well as an experimental condition called the "closeness" condition (the "fast friends" part). The independent variable of the study was thus which condition each participant pair was in.

In both conditions, the students were given three sets of questions. Over the first 15 minutes of time, they asked each other questions from the first set. After 15 minutes ran out, they moved on to the second set for another 15 minutes, and then they worked through the final set for a third 15 minutes (total of 45 minutes). It didn't matter if they didn't get through all the questions each time; they just answered what they could. The experimental manipulation was that the questions were different; you can see examples of those questions in Table 7.1. In the "small talk" condition (the left column of the table), the questions involved minimal personal self-disclosure. In contrast, in the "closeness" condition (the right column), the questions quickly got quite personal.

The dependent variable, measured at the end of the 45 minutes, was how close each person felt to their conversation partner. This was assessed using the Inclusion of Other in the Self Scale (IOS scale) that was described for you in Chapter 5 (Aron et al., 1992). You'll recall that it shows a series of seven overlapping circles, with more overlap indicating more closeness. The average for people in the closeness condition was 4.06 (scores could range from 1 to 7), while the average in the small talk condition was only 3.25. That difference was statistically significant. In other words, friendships can quickly form when two people equally share very intimate information about each other; it builds a sense of trust and bonding.

TABLE 7.1 ● **Example Questions From an Experimental Study of Self-Disclosure and Closeness**

Small Talk Questions	Closeness or "Fast Friends" Questions
When was the last time you walked for more than an hour? Describe where you went and what you saw.	Given the choice of anyone in the world, whom would you want as a dinner guest?
How did you celebrate last Halloween?	What would constitute a "perfect" day for you?
What gifts did you receive on your last birthday?	If you could wake up tomorrow having gained any one quality or ability, what would it be?
Where are you from? Name all of the places you've lived.	What is your most treasured memory?
Where did you go to high school? What was your high school like?	Make three true "we" statements. For instance, "We are both in this room feeling…"
What are the advantages and disadvantages of artificial Christmas trees?	When did you last cry in front of another person? By yourself?
Were you ever in a school play? What was your role? What was the plot of the play? Did anything funny ever happen when you were on stage?	Share a personal problem and ask your partner's advice on how they might handle it. Also, ask your partner to reflect back to you how you seem to be feeling about the problem you have chosen.

In each column you can see examples of questions that participants answered, in pairs. The left column is designed to be a control condition, while the right column is designed to experimentally increase closeness between people. In the original study, there were many more questions; this table is just a sample.

Source: Adapted from Aron et al. (1997).

The article describing this experimental procedure has become popular—it's even mentioned in an episode of the TV show *The Big Bang Theory*. Over 500 more recent articles reference the study's Fast Friends procedure or findings as well. One study (Cross, Bacon, & Morris, 2000) used the procedure with pairs of college women who started as strangers. They found that the interaction was perceived as more intimate, with higher self-disclosures, when either person was high in "interdependent self-construal." Inter-dependent self-construal means that people define themselves in terms of their relationships with others more than in terms of individual traits or talents. Thus, people motivated by relationships engaged more deeply in the friendship-making procedure.

Another study had pairs of White and Latinx students engage in the Fast Friends procedure, then had the pairs come back for additional interactions over three separate meetings involving question exchanges and games (this study therefore was longitudinal; Page-Gould, Mendoza-Denton, & Tropp, 2008). After all three meetings, participants kept a 10-day diary. Diary entries reflected that after forming a new cross-race friend with this procedure, participants felt lower anxiety about interacting with other races in general.

A third study showed that when the Fast Friends procedure is done over cell phones instead of face-to-face, the friendship was lower in "closeness, connection, and conversation quality" (Przybylski & Weinstein, 2013, p. 237). Similar findings occurred in a study that asked participants to do the procedure using online computers (Mallen, Day, & Green, 2003). Another found that for in-person pairs, answering six questions from the procedure (compared to answering only two) was associated with partners being more romantically attracted to each other (Reis, Maniaci, Caprariello, Eastwick, & Finkel, 2011). The take-home message here seems to be that engaging in deep and reciprocal self-disclosures helps friendships form quickly, and those friendships might even lead to more.

Situational Factors: Working Together Over Time

In the movie *Fight Club* (Linson & Fincher, 1999; based on the novel by Palahniuk, 1996), the main character quips that people sitting next to you on an airplane are your "single-serving friends." You're never going to see them again.

Situations often determine how likely we are to befriend people in our immediate social environment; one factor is probability of future interaction. If we believe we're never going to see someone again, we're less likely to put any effort into getting to know them. Just believing that we're *going* to be spending more time with people leads to more liking, even if we know almost nothing about them (Darley & Berscheid, 1967). A possible motivation for this tendency is that when we know we're going to interact with someone in the future, we diminish negative impressions as a way to keep the relationship as harmonious as possible (Knight & Vallacher, 1981; Miller & Marks, 1982). Just like propinquity, more interactions also lead to more likelihood of friendships developing.

We are also more likely to become friends with people when (1) our own outcomes are dependent upon working together with them and (2) that partnership is successful (Berscheid & Graziano, 1979). The tendency to like people with whom we cooperate toward success is so powerful that it can overcome previously established prejudice and dislike. The most famous endeavor to explore this topic is Sherif's (1956) **Robbers Cave Study**. Sherif brought 11-year-old boys to a "summer camp" in Robbers Cave

State Park in Oklahoma and experimentally manipulated friendship groups and alliances between two cabins for the first several days of the study. Quickly, the boys reported that their friends only included people in their own cabin or group, and they very much disliked all the boys from the other group. However, when Sherif created various situations in which the two groups had to work together toward a common goal (e.g., they had to fix a broken water pipe, they had to pull a truck with a rope to get it started), the boys overcame their previous animosity and became friends.

The idea of working together on a task to create friendship has been used successfully in classroom situations. Aronson (1978) showed that when children are dependent upon each other to learn class material in groups, they are more likely to overcome prejudices such as racism or sexism and become friends instead. This type of classroom environment, in which each student is dependent on the others to learn all the material, is called a **jigsaw classroom**. Mutual dependence to reach success requires everyone to listen to and respect each other. Other studies have replicated the effect; high-quality interactions that result in positive outcomes for everyone increase friendship and reduce prejudice (e.g., Binder et al., 2009).

Dyadic Factors: Friendship Budgets

Finally, friendships may be dependent upon the specific interactions between two people.

Both people should like each other, have matching levels of self-disclosure (reciprocal self-disclosure), be similar in important ways (such as basic values), and so on. In addition, both people have to feel like they have time available to spend with a new friend. While friendships aren't exclusive in the same way some romantic relationships are, we still only have so much time in a day to spend with other people. For example, adult women have reported having a "friendship budget" and feel there is an optimal number of friends they prefer. If their budget is full, a potential new friend might not get much attention (Allan, 1989; Goulder & Strong, 1987).

The scientific term for a friendship budget is **Dunbar's number**. The term came from anthropologist Robin Dunbar, who studied the size of various primates' brains and the size of their social networks (Dunbar, 1992). Dunbar's number is the idea that each of us can only maintain a certain number of people in our social network at any given time. For humans, he proposed our *total* number to be around 150 people, including family, partners, and friends. To keep all 150 people in our network happy, he estimated that we need to spend up to 40% of our time simply reaching out and spending quality time with those people. That means that if a new friend enters our life, other friends or relationships might get less time with us. We each choose how to divide our time with the relationship(s) that are most meaningful and rewarding at that moment. The idea of maximizing friendships when possible is further explored in the "Research Deep Dive" feature.

Healthy friendships also require some maintenance from both parties, just like romantic relationships. In college friendships, the happiest relationships are those that progress steadily and are described as having equal companionship, consideration, self-disclosure, and communication between both people (Hays, 1984). In fact, an entire line of research has developed that explores the components of happy, healthy friendships—and that is one of the topics of the next section.

RESEARCH DEEP DIVE

Should You Be Picky When Picking Friends?

A recent ad campaign selling high-end headphones and featuring LeBron James promoted the tagline "You deserve the best." Seems sensible, right? Who doesn't want the best? Several studies suggest there are two distinct approaches to making a decision. One strategy, maximizing, involves carefully weighing all of the possible options, evaluating each to determine how it measures up to the highest possible standard, and finally making a decision only once you're sure it's the best. After researching every different type of headphones and carefully considering all the important specifications, you make your choice.

The other approach, satisficing, involves selecting a particular option that is merely "good enough" provided it satisfies any key criteria. There may be better options out there, but that doesn't matter. You try a pair of headphones, they meet your expectations and sound good enough, so you purchase them without trying others. In a world that increasingly provides us with seemingly endless choices, which strategy you use matters. Of course, if the choice involves selecting the best headphones, a bad decision has minimal impact on your life. However, if you're grappling with selecting friends, the stakes are considerably higher. Though it feels reasonable, there is a potential dark side to undertaking a quest to have the very best, especially when it comes to your relationships.

For a key life decision, like selecting who you're going to be friends with, is maximizing best? Researchers sought to answer this question with a series of four studies (Newman, Schug, Yuki, Yamada, & Nezlek, 2018). Often when researchers are exploring an entirely new line of research (no one had ever looked at maximizing and satisficing in friendship), they will conduct a series of carefully planned studies, sometimes called programmatic research, to fully understand how the variables relate to each other. In this case, Study 1 focused on creating a scale to measure maximizing in friend selection. In addition to establishing that their scale

worked well, researchers found that self-reported maximizers in terms of friend selection also reported lower satisfaction with life, self-esteem, and positive emotions, along with greater negative emotions and feelings of regret (essentially a fear of missing out or thinking "what if?").

In Study 2, researchers explored how maximizing applied to participants' actual decisions regarding which sorority or fraternity to join. In this more naturalistic real-world setting, maximizing was also associated with lower well-being and lower satisfaction with participants' decisions. Ironically, by trying to make the best possible decision, participants ended up less happy.

In Study 3, researchers used a daily diary technique where participants evaluated their maximizing strategies and well-being variables each day over a 2-week period. The researchers measured the same variables from their previous studies but because participants were filling out the questions every day, the researchers used shortened versions to avoid fatiguing or boring the participants. Study 3's results largely replicated Study 1: Maximizers reported lower satisfaction with life and self-esteem, along with greater negative emotions and feelings of regret. In contrast with Study 1, there was no association with positive emotions. Researchers also found that a central reason why maximizing relates to negative outcomes was because maximizing increases regret. Or, as the researchers put it, regret mediated the link between maximizing and life satisfaction, self-esteem, and negative emotions.

Finally, because all of the previous studies utilized U.S. college students, Study 4 sought to replicate the previous findings with non-college students from the United States and Japan. Researchers recruited over 350 participants from Mechanical Turk and Lancers.jp (a Japanese equivalent to Mechanical Turk) and had them complete similar measures to what Study 1 and Study 2 used. In addition, they measured perceived relationship mobility to help determine if having a greater number of options for friendships influenced maximizing's effect on well-being. The results indicated that, as in the previous studies, maximizing was associated with lower life satisfaction and greater negative emotions but was not related to positive emotions. In terms of relationship mobility, when participants perceived that they would have more opportunities to meet new friends (high mobility), maximizing was associated with less satisfaction. However, when participants perceived they would have less of a chance to meet new friends (low mobility), the link between maximizing and satisfaction wasn't as strong. As the researchers put it, relationship mobility moderated the link between maximizing and satisfaction.

Ultimately, the take-home message from these four studies is that being overly picky by trying to maximize your decisions may be the best strategy in other contexts, but being a maximizer is detrimental when it comes to friend selection. Another way to think about this is that we might want to accept offers of friendship when they are given to us, because overthinking friendships seems to lead to problems.

For more, read Newman, D. B., Schug, J., Yuki, M., Yamada, J., & Nezlek, J. B. (2018). The negative consequences of maximizing in friendship selection. *Journal of Personality and Social Psychology*, *114*(5), 804–824.

CHECK YOUR UNDERSTANDING

7.1   Friendships are more likely to form when two people are close to each other in terms of physical proximity; this tendency is called:

   a. Homophily
   b. Ostracism
   c. Propinquity
   d. Dyadic withdrawal

7.2   Social penetration theory suggests that friendship intimacy is predicted by two people's level of:

   a. Similarity
   b. Self-disclosure

   c. Mere exposure
   d. Propinquity

7.3   Classrooms sometimes use a technique in which groups of students are dependent upon each other to learn all of the material. This general technique is called a:

   a. Jigsaw classroom
   b. Mirror classroom
   c. Partnership classroom
   d. Mosaic classroom

APPLICATION ACTIVITY

In class, replicate the Aron et al. (1997) study on the experimental manipulation of closeness. You might need to change the procedure in some ways, such as taking only 15 minutes within pairs instead of 45 minutes. At the end of the study, have everyone complete the IOS scale regarding their partner and turn it in to the professor. Have the professor then write the scores on the board (anonymously), comparing people in the control condition to those in the experimental condition. Do the results support the study's conclusions? Why or why not?

CRITICAL THINKING

- Research described in this section discussed the importance of self-disclosures in forming friendships. But some people are more comfortable with sharing intimate information about themselves than others are. For example, some people might be worried about privacy. How can individuals who don't want to share intimate information with strangers make friends in other ways?

- Some people believe that, by definition, people can have only one "best friend." Other people seem to disagree. Do you think it is possible to have multiple "best friends" simultaneously? Can multiple friendships really maintain exactly balanced levels of intimacy, trust, and so on or is that not the correct definition of a "best friend"?

Answers to the Check Your Understanding Questions

7.1 c, **7.2** b, and **7.3** a.

How Are Friendships Maintained?

Once a friendship is formed, how is it kept healthy? Research on this question can be split in a variety of ways. For this section of the chapter, we'll first consider important components of happy friendships and then we'll talk about how friendships can be threatened.

The Components of Friendship

If you were trying to define what it means to be a true friend to someone, how would you describe it? What are the components or pieces of a friendship that make it different from *less* personal relationships, like colleagues at work, and different from *more* personal relationships, like romantic partners?

This question has been addressed in research across several studies that included people of very different ages, and the answers were surprisingly similar. To start, consider a study that interviewed middle schoolers regarding how they would describe friendships (Berndt & Perry, 1983). The answers were later used to create a measure called the Friendship Qualities Scale, which you can try for yourself in the second "What's My Score?" feature (Bukowski, Hoza, & Boivin, 1994). When children are asked to identify important components for their friendships, they identified the following five factors:

1. *Companionship*: Friends spend a good deal of voluntary time together in playful, fun activities.

2. *Conflict*: Friends can argue and annoy each other, but the relationship continues anyway.

3. *Help*: Friends can rely on each other for mutual aid when needed, which includes the idea that friends help each other be protected from victimization by others (e.g., bullying).

4. *Closeness*: Friends feel acceptance, validation, and attachment toward each other; they mutually affirm each other's importance and value.

5. *Security*: Friends are people on whom we can rely and trust, a "reliable alliance." (Bukowski et al., 1994, p. 476)

WHAT'S MY SCORE?

The Friendship Qualities Scale

Instructions: These items were developed for middle schoolers; to use the scale for your own friendships, just think about how to modify the items accordingly. Consider each item carefully and respond to each using this scale:

1	2	3	4	5
Not true				Very true

_____ 1. My friend and I spend all our free time together.

_____ 2. My friend thinks of fun things for us to do together.

_____ 3. My friend and I go to each other's houses after school and on weekends.

_____ 4. Sometimes my friend and I just sit around and talk about things like school, sports, and things we like.

_____ 5. I can get into fights with my friend.

_____ 6. My friend can bug me or annoy me even though I ask him/her not to.

_____ 7. My friend and I can argue a lot.

_____ 8. My friend and I disagree about many things.

_____ 9. If I forgot my lunch or needed a little money, my friend would loan it to me.

_____ 10. My friend helps me when I am having trouble with something.

_____ 11. My friend would help me if I needed it.

_____ 12. If other kids were bothering me, my friend would help me.

_____ 13. My friend would stick up for me if another kid was causing me trouble.

_____ 14. If I have a problem at school or at home, I can talk to my friend about it.

_____ 15. If there is something bothering me, I can tell my friend about it even if it is something I cannot tell to other people.

_____ 16. If I said I was sorry after I had a fight with my friend, he/she would still stay mad at me.

_____ 17. If my friend or I do something that bothers the other one of us, we can make up easily.

_____ 18. If my friend and I have a fight or argument, we can say "I'm sorry" and everything will be all right.

_____ 19. If my friend had to move away, I would miss him/her.

_____ 20. I feel happy when I am with my friend.

_____ 21. I think about my friend even when my friend is not around.

(Continued)

(Continued)

_____ 22. When I do a good job at something, my friend is happy for me.

_____ 23. Sometimes my friend does things for me, or makes me feel special.

Scoring: For an overall friendship quality score, simply find the average of all of your ratings. The number will be between 1 and 5, with higher numbers indicating a stronger friendship. If you would like to calculate subscores, find the means for each of these groups of items:

- Companionship: items 1–4
- Conflict: items 5–8
- Help: items 9–13
- Security: items 14–18
- Closeness: items 19–23

Source: Bukowski et al. (1994).

Critical Thinking: Often, adolescents form groups of three to five friends. Is it possible to be equally close with all of them, or will there be a stronger bond each person has with just one other person compared to the rest of the group? Are some of the subscores more important than others, for different kinds of people?

When Bukowski et al. (1994) asked 194 middle schoolers to complete a scale measuring these traits in their current friendships, they found that conflict was the most likely factor to end a friendship—and friendships with higher quality on all five subscales (including the ability to overcome conflict) were more likely to last over time. They also noted that high-quality friendships provided the opportunity for children to develop in healthy directions and have higher well-being in general.

Are the factors different in adult friendships—and does the answer change based on culture? A study investigated these questions by asking adults in England, Italy, Hong Kong, and Japan about the "rules of friendship" (Argyle & Henderson, 1984). The authors generated 43 potential "rules" first, then asked each participant to rate each rule in terms of how important it is in their own friendships. Participants ranged from 18 to 60 years old, to ensure diversity of perspective in the sample. The 11 most important rules (in other words, rules that received the most extreme endorsement), regardless of culture, are shown in Table 7.2. There are several rules that seem to remain important from youth through old age.

Note, however, that all of these components are likely expected within romantic relationships as well. So, one conclusion is that most people want to consider their romantic partners to *also* be their friends—but the opposite is not necessarily true (we don't want to date all of our friends!). Romantic relationships typically include the "rules of friendship" as a baseline but are also expected to have more love and commitment, and many romances also include sexual activity (VanderDrift, Wilson, & Agnew, 2013). For one example of how friendship rules are shown in television, see the "Relationships and Popular Culture" feature.

TABLE 7.2 ● Rules of Friendship
Address the other person by their first name.
Share your feelings and personal problems with each other.
Ask the other person for personal advice.
Stand up for each other when the other person isn't there.
Don't share each other's secrets with other people.
Engage in joking and teasing with each other.
Respect each other's privacy.
Be emotionally supportive.
Don't criticize each other in public.
Trust and confide in each other.
Volunteer to help each other in times of need.

Argyle and Henderson (1984) found that these 11 "rules of friendship" were rated as the most important in adults from four different countries.

RELATIONSHIPS AND POPULAR CULTURE

Friendships in *Stranger Things*

Photo by Frazer Harrison/Getty Images

Many classic TV shows and movies feature friendship groups. One of the most popular streaming series available on Netflix recently is

Stranger Things (Gajdusek, 2016–present). The plotline focuses on four adolescent boys who discover a secret world of supernatural monsters called the "Upside Down." Their party is joined by a mysterious girl named Eleven who can move things (and kill people) with her mind. As they band together to save each other—and the world—they frequently discuss the rules of their friendship group:

- Friends don't lie.
- Keep promises.
- Friends don't spy on each other.
- Never abandon each other in times of need.

(Continued)

(Continued)

- Never betray confidences of the group.

- If you break the rules, it's your responsibility to apologize in the form of extending your hand for a handshake. If your friend forgives you, they will shake your hand.

The cast of the show even made a comedic YouTube video about their friendship rules, which you can find by searching for "Stranger Things 10 Rules to Be Their BFFs." Most friendship groups probably have informal "rules" for how they expect to be treated by one another. What rules might be featured in a show about you and your friends?

Threats to Friendship

We can probably all think of friendships from our past that ended.

There are lots of reasons why this can happen, and some of them are simply natural, like someone moves away and people just slowly lose touch. And of course, not every possible reason for friendships ending has been addressed in research (so there is a lot of room for new studies in this area!). Here, let's cover three possible threats to friendships, knowing that this list is certainly not exhaustive. We'll talk about social awkwardness or shyness, friendship jealousy, and lack of social support.

Social Awkwardness

Popular TV shows throughout the decades, like the classic sitcom *Friends*, imply that we're surrounded by loving, funny, supportive people throughout our lives.

But for some people, that's kind of a wonderful fantasy. Many people struggle with maintaining close friendship circles, especially if we try to make new friends as adults. And being socially awkward just makes things worse. Social awkwardness can come from a variety of different sources. Some people experience **shyness**, or an enduring anxiety about social situations that leads to introverted or inhibited behavior (Miller, 2009). Alternatively, **loneliness** is the feeling of isolation and dissatisfaction with a perceived lack of intimate relationships (Russell, 1996). Finally, more and more people are classified as having **autism spectrum disorder** (ASD), a condition with several symptoms. One common symptom is trouble with social communication, such as the ability to decode other people's nonverbal signals or the appearance of lacking empathy with others' perspectives. Any or all of these issues might lead to trouble making and maintaining friendships.

Shyness tends to be relatively stable for people as they grow up, and it's correlated with feelings of anxiety and low self-esteem (Fordham & Stevenson-Hinde, 1999). As you might expect, shyness and loneliness are also positively correlated, and both are negatively correlated with friendship quality, at least in childhood. Unfortunately for shy and/or lonely people, their anxiety about not having friends can become a self-fulfilling prophecy. They're worried about looking foolish or being rejected, so they hang back and don't approach others, and that means they're less likely to start or maintain good friendships.

The Centers for Disease Control and Prevention (CDC) estimates that 1 in 37 boys and 1 in 151 girls are diagnosed with ASD (Autism Speaks, 2019). While every person with ASD is different, many have difficulties in their social interactions. One expert on the condition noted that it appears autistic people "stand outside social relationships and merely watch behaviors" instead of engaging in them (Hobson, 1993, p. 5). Thus, they may have challenges in making and keeping friends, compared to neurotypical people.

To investigate further, a study interviewed both high-functioning children with autism and neurotypical children (Bauminger & Kasari, 2000). The interview questions asked all of the kids to both (1) define loneliness and friendship and (2) discuss whether they experienced each in their life. Researchers concluded first that children with ASD had less-articulated definitions of loneliness; specifically, they weren't as able to verbalize that loneliness included negative emotions and lack of social connection.

To rate the children's definitions of friendship, all the children's interview answers were coded to see whether they included the five components of friendship defined earlier in this chapter (companionship, security, closeness, help, and conflict). On average, the neurotypical children's answers again appeared more complete and comprehensive. So, children with ASD had trouble explaining what "loneliness" and "friendship" were, compared to the other kids in the study. That said, children with ASD did report *feeling* loneliness and *wanting* friends, and both these emotions were felt more strongly by the children with ASD, compared to the other kids in the study. Everyone wants friends.

Friendship Jealousy

As anyone who went to middle school and high school probably remembers, the social politics of friendships can be rough.

"In particular, if young adolescents perceive outsiders as threatening the quality, uniqueness, or survival of their friendships, feelings of jealousy can arise and pose challenges" (Parker, Low, Walker, & Gamm, 2005, p. 235). While adult friendships are less likely to experience problems with jealousy, everyone can sometimes feel like a friendship is threatened if a new person enters the mix. Friendships usually aren't "exclusive" in the way some romantic partnerships are—but once we've established happy, stable friendships, we like to keep them "as is." We can start to feel jealous if we think one of our good friends is being lured away by someone else (Selman, 1980; Selman & Schultz, 1990).

To see how much jealousy affects high schoolers, researchers asked 135 ninth-graders to react to various scenarios that described threats to their relationship with a best friend (Parker et al., 2005). In some of the scenarios, a third person comes on the scene and draws the best friend's time and attention away from the participant. Their answers indicated that girls, compared to boys, were more concerned about the quality of their friendships and showed more jealousy. This finding replicated other research, showing adult women have more friendship jealousy that adult men (Guerrero, Eloy, Jorgensen, & Andersen, 1993). But both boys and girls who had low self-esteem showed jealousy when thinking about these hypothetical scenarios. The researchers noted that chronic low self-esteem probably contributes to jealousy because of low trust in whether one's friends really love and care for them.

Lack of Social Support

The world can be a judgmental place.

In Chapter 6, we defined "stigma" and discussed the stigma of being single. Of course, there are thousands of ways that people can be stigmatized and stereotyped by larger society, including things like race, sexual orientation, criminal history, mental health status, and so on. For friendship research, it's interesting to consider what happens when we befriend someone from a stigmatized group. Is there such a thing as "stigma by association"? If so, does this social judgment and pressure make friendships with stigmatized people less likely?

There is some evidence for stigma by association. For example, around 40% of women who have husbands convicted of crimes report that their social relationships become strained (Sack, Seidler, & Thomas, 1976). Professionals in mental health care are viewed less positively than professionals in physical health care (Nunnally, 1961). And students who have fathers who are depressed, alcoholic, or in jail are treated as if they (the students) will have trouble in school (Mehta & Farina, 1988). We seem to wonder if people who associate with stigmatized others carry a bit of the stigma themselves.

To see how this affects friendships, a study asked college students to watch a tape of two people talking to each other for 5 minutes (Neuberg, Smith, Hoffman, & Russell, 1994). Participants were told that the people in the tape were friends. They were both men who were physically attractive, articulate, and athletic. The experimental manipulation was that participants were told that Man 1 was heterosexual and Man 2 was gay, or the other way around, or that both men were gay. After watching the tape, participants rated how socially comfortable they were with each person they just watched.

Results showed that participants were less comfortable around either of the men if they were told that the *other* person on the tape was gay. In other words, they said they were uncomfortable with him if they thought he was friends with a gay man. In Study 2, they also found that participants didn't trust gay people who were supposedly friends with heterosexual people, finding them untrustworthy and dishonest. In short, the participants didn't seem to like it when a heterosexual man was friends with a gay man—they thought badly of *both* people in the friendship. This kind of judgment from outside people could certainly threaten a friendship if peers discourage it from existing. If people persist in a "stick to your own kind" mentality, it may be hard to overcome such social pressure and maintain friendships with people who are different from ourselves.

CHECK YOUR UNDERSTANDING

7.4 Which option below is NOT one of the key components of friendship identified by middle schoolers and used to create the Friendship Qualities Scale?

   a. Closeness
   b. Companionship
   c. Conflict
   d. Complementary skills

7.5 According to the Centers for Disease Control and Prevention, about how many boys in the United States will be diagnosed with autism spectrum disorder?

   a. 1 in 218
   b. 1 in 151

   c. 1 in 100
   d. 1 in 37

7.6 Based on research regarding jealousy in friendships, which variable was identified in this section as being associated with a higher likelihood of feeling jealous?

   a. High neuroticism
   b. Low attachment security
   c. High conscientiousness
   d. Low self-esteem

APPLICATION ACTIVITY

Spend some time thinking about your own friendships, then identify at least four "rules" that seem to apply to the friendships in your own life. Then, choose two groups of people who seem very different from you (e.g., people who are significantly older, people who are a subgroup such as park rangers or international spies) and brainstorm what "rules" you think groups of friendships in that subgroup might have.

CRITICAL THINKING

- Think of a time when you or a friend of yours broke the "rules of friendship." Did the friendship recover, or did it end? Explain why the outcome happened, in your opinion, and whether there are identifiable variables or characteristics of friendships that will help two friends recover if the rules are broken (e.g., length of friendship, strength of bond).

- A study by Neuberg et al. (1994) was described in this section, in which participants were judgmental about two men being friends if one of them is heterosexual and one is gay. Do you think that result would be replicated if we did the study now, over 20 years later? What circumstances of the procedure might matter for whether the same results are found (such as age of participants, region of the country, political ideology, etc.)? Create a specific hypothesis based on your thoughts.

How Do Friendships Change Over Our Lifetime?

It matters who our friends are.

One study showed that each happy friend in our lives makes us 15% more likely to be happy ourselves (Christakis & Fowler, 2009), and another found that if one of our friends becomes lonely, we're 52% more likely to also become lonely (Cacioppo, Fowler, & Christakis, 2009). We've discussed research on how friendships are constructed and what makes us more or less likely to be friends with someone. We've also already discussed some aspects of how friendships might change over the course of our lifetime. For the final section of this chapter, let's break down research into important phases of our life to investigate this question even more.

Early Childhood

As already mentioned above, childhood friendships are often formed initially out of convenience; for example, both kids happen to live next to each other or attend the same daycare (propinquity). Because of this trend, some scholars believed that early childhood friendships were superficial. However, researchers questioned this assumption when studies provided support for the idea that even from a very young age, friendships can be intimate and highly valued (e.g., Howes, 1983). As early as the age of 2 years, toddlers start to show that they prefer to be around certain other children over others, thus indicating early signs of wanting friends (Hartup, 2006).

In addition to propinquity, children are especially drawn to other kids who have something in common with them. This kind of similarity makes them feel comfortable with each other; the scientific term for this comfort due to similarity is **homophily**. Friendship in early childhood is positively correlated to similarity on a variety of traits, including shared interests, demographics such as age and race, and even physical appearance (Kupersmidt, DeRosier, & Patterson, 1995). Kids in preschool describe their friendships in very concrete ways that refer to what they actually do together (e.g., "We play"; Bigelow, 1977).

However, as children age, their friendships do become increasingly complex. As their cognitive development evolves, children are better and better able to empathize with others and to take someone else's perspective; both of these qualities increase friendship quality (Howes, 2011). Preadolescent children describe their friendships based on characteristics, instead of activities (e.g., shared sympathy and self-disclosure; Bigelow, 1977). In a qualitative study with 10- to 11-year-olds in England (Jago et al., 2009), children described their friendships in terms of similarity, shared activity, and propinquity, emphasizing the work we've described throughout this chapter already. Here are some of their statements that describe their friends:

- "My friends from school we play football . . . that's the only thing we play."

- "The friends that live in my street I normally hang around with."

- "Usually on the weekends I just go out on my bike and ride around with my friends."

- "All of them go to football club . . . and meet people through my mum's friends' sons."

- "I play with my rugby friends at rugby, but I don't really play with them anywhere else because they live, most of them live quite a long way away. With my school friends I usually just hang around with them round my house and their house, playing football, sometimes, or cricket." (Jago et al., 2009, pp. 6–7)

A meta-analysis tried to find patterns that differentiated childhood friends from nonfriends in terms of how they interact (Newcomb & Bagwell, 1995). This study identified four specifically distinctive patterns in childhood friendships: (1) positive engagement, meaning that friends talk and laugh together more than nonfriends; (2) relationship mutuality, meaning friends are more supportive and reciprocal than nonfriends; (3) task behavior, meaning that friends work together more and better when doing an activity compared to nonfriends; and (4) conflict management, meaning that kids who are friends work harder to regulate their emotions and work through problems together, compared to kids who aren't friends.

Trouble making and maintaining friends is problematic for a child's general well-being in a variety of ways. Recall from Chapter 6 that ostracism, or being rejected by one's peers, is always a hurtful experience. Ostracism has been tied to several negative outcomes, such as dropping out of school and even committing crimes (Wong & Schonlau, 2013). Bullying is a big problem in elementary schools, and not having supportive friends to help can make things much, much worse.

According to Hunt, Peters, and Rapee (2012), anxiety, depression, low self-esteem, academic decline, and poor school attendance are all common symptoms experienced by a bullied child. Earlier it was noted that children believe one of the most important components of friendship is protection and standing up for each other; this type of support would be especially needed if bullying is a risk. Young children who do have close friends are more cooperative, social, and altruistic, and they are less lonely and have better self-esteem (compared to kids who don't think they have friends; Newcomb & Bagwell, 1995). Of course, that's probably true of older people as well—so let's move forward with friendships in adolescence.

Adolescence

Establishing peer friendships while disengaging from one's parents is an important step in adolescence and increases from the ages of 10 to 18 years (Collins & Madsen, 2006; Larson, Richards, Moneta, Holmbeck, & Duckett, 1996). Being popular and having the acceptance of peers is crucial to many teenagers' sense of happiness and self-esteem. Collins and Laursen (2000) noted this point when they stated, "Friendships are perceived as the most important source of support during adolescence, and intimacy, mutuality, and self-disclosure with friends peak during the period" (p. 67).

Number of friends isn't always the same as having truly *close* friends. Some adolescents feel like they are generally socially accepted but don't have really close friendships, while others have one or two intimate friends but feel generally unpopular (Parker & Asher, 1993). As anyone who remembers adolescence will know, the importance of friendship groups, or cliques, also looms large at this age. Cliques can have both positive and negative effects on their members. For example, cliques of the "popular" kids tend to be overly aggressive toward kids not in the clique (i.e., a "mean girls" [or boys] phenomenon; Closson, 2009). Behaviors like cigarette smoking and drug use are also reinforced when you're in a clique where everyone else is doing it (Ennett, Bauman, & Koch, 1994; Oetting & Beauvais, 1986). If young girls are in cliques where body image is emphasized, peer pressure can be high for things like dieting and extreme weight-loss behaviors (Paxton, Schutz, Wertheim, & Muir, 1999).

Getting closer to puberty and adolescence also adds potential sexual attraction into the social interaction mix, adding another complication (Buhrmester & Furman, 1986). Some people have even wondered whether a heterosexual man and woman can be simple, platonic friends without some kind of sexual attraction emerging—and this question may be especially relevant to young people with raging hormones. But as most of us have experienced, there are many potential outcomes or variations of cross-sex friendships (and, of course, not everyone is heterosexual).

Sometimes, men and women really do just stay friends (Halatsis & Christakis, 2009). Other times, the relationship is in a kind of "middle ground" in which the two people are friends who also enjoy sexually gratifying activities together (an arrangement known as "friends with benefits" or by other terms; Lehmiller, VanderDrift, & Kelly, 2014). Cross-sex friendships are most likely in younger people; middle-aged and older adults typically reduce or avoid this type of friendship, perhaps because it threatens their monogamous romantic partnerships (Marshall, 2010; Werking, 1997).

Adult Friendships

How many friends do you think most adults have?

The answer depends on how people define "friends," but in one study the estimate was about 29 (Adams & Torr, 1998). Out of those, about 11 were "casual," 12 were "close," and 6 were "very close." Having six close friends as we navigate the second half of life sounds pretty good. Like childhood friends, our adult friends tend to be similar (or high in homophily). For example, 40% of adult friendships are composed of people who are the same religion as ourselves. And as we age, we value our oldest, most enduring friendships more than new friendships that form (Shea, Thompson, & Blieszner, 1988). These are the friends with whom we've grown, laughed, and cried.

For most people, finding a monogamous life partner and starting a family is an important goal for the second half of life. As people pair off and spend more time with their partner and children, they have less quality time to spend with friends; this pattern is called **dyadic withdrawal** (Fehr, 1999). This trend continues as we age: The older we are, the smaller our social networks and number of friends tend to be (Wrzus, Hanel, Wagner, & Neyer, 2013). Importantly, however, it's just our *total* number of social connections that shrinks; the number of high-quality, close friendships remains relatively stable. And older people still like to make new friends. One study of residents in a retirement community noted that they look for friends who provide affection, respect, and communication (Shea et al., 1988).

For women, friendships with other women can become extremely important during the transition to motherhood. New mothers are going through major changes physically but also psychologically and emotionally as they re-examine their sense of self and are nervous about the future. Classes for expecting mothers are a good place for them to meet other women in a similar situation and to form mutual bonds (Deave, Johnson, & Ingram, 2008). A study that interviewed women in this kind of class examined themes that emerged as they described their friendship experience with other expecting mothers (Nolan et al., 2012). The results can be seen in Table 7.3.

A study of women between the ages of 60 and 85 in Hong Kong found that healthy relationships were positively correlated with the women's psychological well-being, including scores on happiness, life satisfaction, and feelings of

TABLE 7.3 ● Themes in Friendships Among Expecting and New Mothers

Theme	Example Quotation From Interviews
Feeling more confident	"There's sort of, 'Am I doing the right thing?' kind of element . . . it's quite nice to see that you are."
	"I'd talk to the other girls and they'd say, 'Well, my child's done that,' and I wouldn't feel worried."
	"You kind of compare, don't you?"
Making the year bearable	"I think if I hadn't had them, I would have needed something else to keep me sane."
	"We actually have a really good laugh together . . . it's important to have a lot of fun."
	"If you didn't have someone to talk to such as the girls—once a week in someone's house—you would have gone a bit mad."
Forming a unique bond	"You have that sort of compassion for each other, don't you? Because you know that you've been through it."
	"I mean you start off talking about being pregnant and full of the most intimate things you kind of go through, the huge changes to your body and then, when you have the child, and the childbirth itself, and then looking after the children, yes, you form a unique bond."

When expecting and new mothers were interviewed about forming friendships with each other, three themes emerged.

Source: Nolan et al. (2012).

competency—and friendships were negatively correlated with stress, anxiety, and depression (Siu & Phillips, 2002). When older adults are asked to describe their friendships, the answers are more elaborate and more subtle than younger people's answers, but again, the major expectations and "rules" are pretty consistent (Hartup & Stevens, 1999).

Finally, friendships in old age may be particularly important in times of need. For example, older widows have lower general well-being and more stress when their friends are unreliable, are disrespectful of their privacy, and take advantage of them (Rook, 1984). But those traits would probably upset people of any age and may be reasonable cause to question a "friendship." In general, many studies appear to show that there are more similarities in friendships across different stages of life than there are differences. Everyone wants friends who are similar to themselves, available, trustworthy, and kind.

CHECK YOUR UNDERSTANDING

7.7 Friendships are more likely to form when two people are similar to each other in important ways; this tendency is called:

a. Homophily
b. Ostracism
c. Propinquity
d. Dyadic withdrawal

7.8 When two people start dating, they usually spend less time with their friends than they did before. This pattern is called:

a. Dyadic withdrawal
b. Time recursion

c. Relationship prominence
d. Friendship erosion

7.9 Researchers interviewed new and expecting mothers about important themes in their friendships with each other (Nolan et al., 2012). Which option below is NOT one of those themes?

a. Forming a unique bond
b. Feeling more confident
c. Boosting education about infant care
d. Making the year bearable

APPLICATION ACTIVITY

First, choose a study from earlier in the chapter that was based on childhood or adolescent friendships (e.g., regarding important components of friendship, friendship "rules," conflict within friendships, and so on). Then, watch a movie that's specifically focused on friendship in older people—people who are at least of retirement age. Analyze the movie's portrayal of friendship in old age and compare/contrast it to what research predicted or found in early friendships.

CRITICAL THINKING

- Would you rather be generally popular and accepted by other people—but have no truly close, intimate friends—or have a few very close friends but be generally unpopular? Why?

- This section described research on new mothers and how friendships with other new mothers become very important. Would you expect the same patterns for new fathers? Would the same themes emerge, and would these friendships be as important for fathers as they are for mothers? Explain why you expect similar or different patterns to emerge.

- Have your friendship networks changed in interesting ways over time? For example, are you now friends with more diverse and different kinds of people than when you were a child (i.e., has homophily decreased)? Are the things you value in friends different than when you were younger? When you analyze the friendships you see in older adults around you (such as your parents, grandparents, professors, or even friendships you see in movies or on television), are those the kinds of friendships you want to have in older adulthood? Why or why not?

Answers to the Check Your Understanding Questions

7.7 a, **7.8** a, and **7.9** c.

Chapter Summary

Big Questions

1. What predicts how and when friendships will form?

2. How are friendships maintained?

3. How do friendships change over our lifetime?

What predicts how and when friendships will form?

Four types of factors have been proposed that predict when friendships will form. These include environmental factors such as propinquity (sometimes called proximity or mere exposure), individual factors such as amount of self-disclosure shared between two people, situational factors such as working together with someone else on a common goal, and dyadic factors such as whether each person has time to devote to fostering the friendship.

How are friendships maintained?

Once friendships are formed, how are they kept healthy? Research with children identified five common components of good friendships: companionship, conflict, help, closeness, and security. Here, conflict refers to the motivation to work past temporary problems or annoyances. Similarly, people are able to describe "rules" for healthy friendships, such as sharing of personal advice, being emotionally supportive, and helping each other when needed. Finally, three possible threats to friendship are social awkwardness, friendship jealousy, and lack of social support for the friendship from other people around you.

How do friendships change over our lifetime?

In early childhood, friendships are often formed out of convenience (e.g., propinquity) or similarity (sometimes called homophily). It's also sometimes based on a shared activity, such as kids who are all on the same sports team. As children age, the importance of friendships to offset problems with bullying is crucial; social cliques can have both positive and negative influences. In addition, adolescents often have to navigate friendships that may develop into sexual attraction. As people pair off into romantic couples, they often spend less time with their other friends, a trend called dyadic withdrawal. In the second half of life, friendships remain important and can be based on specific needs, such as women who become friends with other women because they are all new mothers. Friendships remain important throughout our lifetime.

List of Terms

Learning Objectives	Key Terms
7.1 Analyze factors predicting friendship formation	Propinquity Mere exposure Westgate Housing Study Self-disclosure Social penetration theory Reciprocal self-disclosure Robbers Cave Study Jigsaw classroom Dunbar's number Maximizing Satisficing
7.2 Identify components of friendship and discuss threats, such as lack of social support.	Shyness Loneliness Autism spectrum disorder
7.3 Interpret research on how friendships change from early childhood through adulthood.	Homophily Dyadic withdrawal

8

Attraction

Big Questions	Learning Objectives
1. What physical factors predict attraction?	8.1 Interpret how facial structure and body types predict attraction.
2. What psychological factors predict attraction?	8.2 Interpret how reciprocity, body language, and personality predict attraction.
3. What environmental factors predict attraction?	8.3 Analyze how certain situations or environments lead to increased attraction.

You're single and at a party. Dozens of other people stand around you, looking friendly and approachable—but no one really draws your attention.

Suddenly, you make eye contact with someone across the room, and you feel an instant spark. You're sure the other person feels it, too—and your entire body feels pulled in that direction. You get a goofy smile on your face and you feel your heart rate increase. You can't really explain what, exactly, you like about this person . . . you just kind of *feel* it.

As you start to talk with each other, the attraction only grows. You have things in common. You make each other laugh. You feel simultaneously excited and relaxed. In your head, you start to hope that no one interrupts you, that the other person is also single, and that one or the other of you will be brave enough to ask for a date. This could be the start of something wonderful. We've all felt attraction to others; it's something that we can't even really control, consciously. What does relationship science have to offer to explain the mysteries of interpersonal attraction? This chapter covers research that predicts attraction based on physical, psychological, and environmental factors.

What Physical Factors Predict Attraction?

Have you ever experienced an immediate spark of sexual attraction toward strangers? There were no words, no information about who they are or what they like to do—all you know is their appearance. What is it about another person's physical features that can hijack your attention?

There are certainly individual and cultural differences regarding what people find physically attractive in others. You might be attracted to someone with dark coloring or very pale skin, short or long hair, a very thin or very round body, or muscular features or delicate hands. Despite these individual variations in what we consider our "type," there are certain physical characteristics that seem to be almost universally appealing to everyone, regardless of age, ethnicity, or culture. Certain celebrities, such as Brad Pitt and Beyoncé Knowles, are considered attractive by almost everyone who sees them. What explains these cross-cultural similarities in perceived beauty?

Recall that one of the major theories behind relationship research is the evolutionary perspective, outlined for you in Chapter 4. There, we started to cover the idea that if certain physical characteristics or traits are universally considered attractive—meaning regardless of one's upbringing, country of origin, or culture—then these traits probably come from ancient, inherited instincts. Moreover, we experience many of these attraction impulses on an *unconscious* level; we don't even know why we like someone or something. What are the traits that seem to be almost universally appealing, or attractive? What's hot, and what's not?

Symmetry

Have you ever noticed a person whose facial features are not symmetrical? Perhaps one eye is bigger than the other, there's a scar on one cheek, or one ear sticks out farther than the other. Do you think this factor affects how attractive you perceive the person to be?

WENN US / Alamy Stock Photo

Photo by Dia Dipasupil/Getty Images For Entertainment Weekly

Denzel Washington is known for being a great actor, but researchers also point out how symmetrical his face is. Do you find him more attractive than Steven Colbert, who has often been teased for having one ear that seems to hang lower and stick out farther than the other? Did you notice that feature before it was pointed out to you?

Several research studies indicate we experience **bilateral symmetry** as attractive. An object, face, or body is bilaterally symmetric when the left half perfectly matches the right half. For example, one study found the amount of symmetry in male college students to be significantly—and positively—correlated with ratings of how attractive their faces were (Gangestad, Thornhill, & Yeo, 1994). The effect was much stronger for men than women.

In another study, when men and women rated photographs of the "opposite" sex, bilateral symmetry of the faces was again positively correlated with how attractive the faces were perceived to be (Grammer & Thornhill, 1994). Perhaps most interestingly, a third study (Thornhill & Gangestad, 1994) measured men's and women's body and facial symmetry by comparing their left-side and right-side feet, ankles, hands, wrists, elbows, and ears. Results showed that for both sexes, greater symmetry was associated with a higher number of sex partners. For men, symmetry was correlated with having sex at an earlier age. The same trend was true for women, but it wasn't strong enough to be statistically significant.

Why is bilateral symmetry attractive? From an evolutionary perspective, symmetry may be an easy-to-see indicator of genetic quality—a heuristic cue that helps us make fast (but often unfair) judgments about others. If your potential mate is asymmetrical, perhaps they have a genetic disorder that could be passed on to any offspring. That explanation may not apply to humans (especially not humans who don't plan to reproduce with their mate), but in other species, asymmetry has been linked to developmental instability. For example, in scorpion flies, lopsided individuals are more likely to have negative reactions to environmental pollution and to carry disease ("Biology of Beauty," 1996). Honeybees even prefer to pollinate symmetric flowers (Wignall, Heiling, Cheng, & Herberstein, 2006)!

We may not consciously realize that we're attracted to symmetry, and some researchers question whether it really matters at all (Zaidel & Hessamian, 2010). But symmetry may be an instinct at work when we find ourselves mysteriously attracted to someone. Note the quirky finding that in one study, sober individuals were good at detecting asymmetry in faces and found them less attractive. Drunk people, however, couldn't even tell when faces were asymmetrical or not (Halsey, Huber, Bufton, & Little, 2010). Perhaps this explains why sometimes, drinking seems to make people find others suddenly more attractive.

"Averaged" Faces

Being "just average" doesn't sound that great in terms of your physical attractiveness, but in this case, being average might be a good thing. Just as symmetric faces and bodies might be heuristic cues to genetic health, so might **composite** or **averaged faces**, faces that do not include any unusual or strange features because they have been digitally created by morphing several individual faces together.

Researchers have investigated this hypothesis by having participants rate the attractiveness of many different faces. Included in this lineup is one computer-generated face that is the composite or "average" of all the other faces (Perrett, May, & Yoshikawa, 1994). When this is done, the computer-generated "averaged" face is typically rated as the most beautiful or attractive, compared to the individual faces of actual people (Langlois & Roggman, 1990; Langlois, Roggman, & Musselman, 1994).

FIGURE 8.1 ● Computer-Generated "Averaged" Faces

2 Face Average   4 Face Average   8 Face Average   16 Face Average   32 Face Average

Computer-generated averaged faces are perceived as more attractive than the individual faces on which they are based, and more faces usually means more perceived attractiveness.

Source: The University of Texas at Austin, Department of Psychology.

Check out the computer-generated faces in Figure 8.1; these were created by Langlois for her research lab (you can visit her website to learn more). As you can see, the face on the far left is a composite of two individual photos, while the photo on the far right is made up of 32 individual photos. Langlois finds that people tend to rate the 32-face average as more attractive than the 2-face average (Langlois & Roggman, 1990; Langlois et al., 1994). In addition, the averaged faces are rated as more attractive than any of the individual faces used to make them, as long as the averaged face is a computer-generated composite of at least 16 faces.

But let's ask the same question again: Why? Why are composite faces rated as more attractive? Here are three possibilities. First, it could be a **procedural artifact**, a finding that results from *how* we conducted the experiment. For example, it could be an order effect because seeing an "averaged" face after seeing so many similar faces makes us like it more because it's familiar to us (a "mere exposure" effect). Note, this criticism would only be true for within-participants designs where the same participants see many different faces in a certain order.

Second, we may experience "averaged" faces as comforting because they fit our cultural expectations and are easier to mentally process. We are attracted to our social norms and dislike those who are "different." Averaged faces are prototypical and make us feel at ease on an unconscious level—they're easy for us to understand and don't set off any instinctive alarm bells. Average is comforting.

Finally, averaged faces are more symmetrical, both of which are cues to genetic health (Grammer & Thornhill, 1994; Rhodes, Proffitt, Grady, & Sumich, 1998). If the two variables are correlated, one of them might be driving the other. In other words, maybe symmetry matters and "averageness" doesn't, or the other way around, but it *looks* like both matter because they're correlated with each other. Small variations in individual faces that might indicate genetic abnormalities—which could be passed on to potential offspring—disappear as faces are digitally "averaged" *or* made symmetric.

Some readers may be questioning the "averaged" face results because of the commonly held belief that people with "exotic" features are particularly attractive. The "exotic" effect—which in some ways opposes the "averaged" effect—can also be explained in various ways. First, sometimes models who are people of color are dehumanized and made into animalistic images, which further objectifies and sexualizes them (compared to other models). If you notice that people of color in magazines are more likely to be wearing animal prints like leopard or zebra, that serves as an example. So, people deemed "exotic" because they are from an ethnic or racial minority might be more likely to be sexualized in our culture, leading to feelings of attraction from observers.

Second, "exotic" features often highlight specific secondary sex characteristics that are hypermasculine or hyperfeminine, such as square jaws and pronounced eyebrows in men or large lips, large eyes, and high cheekbones in women. These particular features are also considered attractive because they signal culturally gendered messages of what is traditional "beauty." Thus, again, they may be comforting because it's how men and women are "supposed" to look.

For two interesting side notes into views of what is found physically attractive in "nontraditional" samples of participants, consider the following studies. First, Scull (2013) spent 18 months observing and interviewing male strippers. Results here found that the men purposely highlighted their traditionally masculine features (such as a muscular torso) to attract customers. A second article (Moskowitz, Turrubiates, Lozano, & Hajek, 2013) reviewed two studies on men who self-identified as "Bears," a slang term for men in the gay community who are physically large and have a lot of body hair. The Bears in these studies reported having lower self-esteem than non-Bears, and the researchers speculated it was because while they have some hypermasculine physical features, they do not fit into culturally normative and stereotypic views of gay men being physically fit and stylish.

"Baby" Faces: Neoteny

Being "cute" is a good thing, right?

For many people, the answer is yes—but in addition to attractive, "cute" can also mean childish. Several studies have found evidence that faces will be perceived as more attractive if they are high in a trait called neoteny. **Neotenous features** are

Animated images can easily highlight neotenous features, such as the large eyes seen in these drawings of Betty Boop and a generic anime girl.

Photo by A. Diaz/WireImage for King Features Syndicate

Shutterstock.com/Olexsandr Ozeruha

facial characteristics in adults that are considered "youthful" or even child-like, and that elicit a nurturing response from others. In humans, neotenous features are a large head, large eyes, greater space between the eyes, small noses, full lips, and high foreheads. In short, adults are perceived as attractive if they have "baby" faces.

Again, we have to ask: *Why?* When neotenous features are seen in men, heterosexual women may find them attractive because these men unconsciously bring out nurturing instincts, leading to interpersonal attraction and empathy. For people who endorse the evolutionary perspective, biological instincts women possess that make many of them care for babies thus translate into a different kind of attraction for adults (Cunningham, Barbee, & Pike, 1990). That said, neotenous features are usually perceived as more desirable for women than for men. In women, neoteny may be attractive because it signals young, healthy genes and implies a youthful vivacity and energy (Berry & McArthur, 1985, 1986).

In research studies, the effect of neotenous features on attraction is often manipulated using computers to change images of people, just like we saw in the "average" faces research. This time, researchers use digital software to change faces to be higher or lower in the specific features of interest (again, things like big eyes, small nose, and full lips). When one study in England manipulated photographs of women to make them either high, medium, or low in neoteny, more neotenous faces were perceived as more attractive and more youthful. Participants also guessed that women with more neotenous faces were more fertile and healthier, in general, supporting an evolutionary or instinctive interpretation of this trend (Furnham & Reeves, 2006). Similar findings have been replicated in a wide variety of cultures, including the United States, Brazil, Russia, and Venezuela (Jones et al., 1995; Jones & Hill, 1993).

Body Type: Waist-to-Hips and Waist-to-Shoulders Ratios

We find certain types of faces attractive—but when it comes to physical attraction, the entire body can matter.

For example, which of the bodies shown in Figure 8.2 do you think is the most attractive? These drawings of women differ in an important variable called **waist-to-hips ratio**, which is the size difference between the circumference of the waist to the circumference of the hips. If, for example, your waist measured 30 inches and your hips measured 40 inches, then your waist-to-hips ratio would be 3 to 4, or 0.75.

Several studies have shown that across cultures, the most desirable waist-to-hips ratio for women is about 0.70 (LaForge & Goodfriend, 2012; Singh, 1993a, 1993b; Singh & Randall, 2007). When men across the world are asked to judge the attractiveness of line drawings of women, such as the one in Figure 8.2, the women with a ratio of 0.70 were perceived to be more attractive—but also healthier, more youthful, and to have a higher reproductive capacity. Interestingly, famous beauties Marilyn Monroe, Jessica Alba, and Kate Moss all had, at least at one point in their popular careers as actresses and models, a 0.70 waist-to-hips ratio.

What about preferences for men's bodies? A certain ratio matters for them, too. However, for men's bodies, it's the **waist-to-shoulders ratio**, or the ratio comparing the circumference of the waist to the circumference of the shoulders. Again, perhaps surprisingly, the number for the ratio is the about the same: between 0.70 and 0.75.

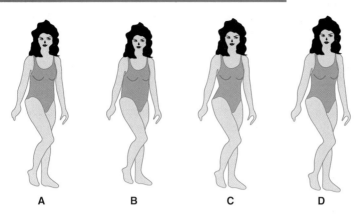

Source: Singh, D. (1993a). Adaptive significance of female physical attractiveness: Role of waist-to-hip ratio. *Journal of Personality and Social Psychology, 65*(2), 293-307.

FIGURE 8.2 ● Images of Different Body Types in Women

A   B   C   D

Which body type do you find the most sexually attractive? Research indicates that woman "C" is the most popular answer.

That is, for men, the waist should be 70% of the circumference of the shoulders; this is the ratio women find most attractive (Braun & Bryan, 2006; Dixson, Halliwell, East, Wignarajah, & Anderson, 2003) and the ratio gay men find most attractive in other men (LaForge & Goodfriend, 2012).

For men, this ratio basically means that they have wide, muscular shoulders and a relatively slim waist or hips, creating a "V" shape in their upper torso. Other studies have shown that this body type is not only seen as more attractive, but that it translates into other interesting outcomes. For example, men become more jealous and threatened when another man threatens to rival them by taking away their current partner—and level of jealousy is positively correlated to higher shoulder-to-hips ratios in the "other" man (Dijkstra & Buunk, 2001). Men with broad shoulders are perceived to be more physically and socially dominant, by other men, as well (Dijkstra & Buunk, 2001). And finally, men with broad shoulders and smaller waists/hips tend to have sex at younger ages and have more sexual partners (Hughes & Gallup, 2003).

One final time, we must ask *why*: Why do these particular body shapes seem to be physically attractive, regardless of cultural influence? According to evolutionary psychology, heterosexual men are attracted to women with large hips because they suggest a healthy gateway for babies; the small waist indicates aerobic health. So, the most attractive women will be those who are physically fit and thus more likely to survive childbirth and the following year (at a minimum) of raising an infant. One study even found that men like women whose posture indicates a specific amount of spinal curve in their back (what they called "lumbar curvature") because it's associated with genetic fitness (Lewis, Russell, Al-Shawaf, & Buss, 2015). Heterosexual women are attracted to men with a small waist because it also indicates aerobic fitness; broad, strong shoulders indicate physical strength. This strength would certainly be an advantage for any physical tasks and might be important when a pregnant woman or a child needs protection.

Famous beauties such as Marilyn Monroe had waist-to-hips ratios of around 0.70, at least at some point in their successful careers.

Sunset Boulevard / Contributor

It's important to remember that these preferences typically exist on an unconscious level. The idea is that these preferences have stuck with us through several generations via instincts, legacies of what benefitted our ancestors in terms of genetic and reproductive fitness. Thus, while some of these motivations may seem out of date—and potentially sexist and heterosexist—the evolutionary perspective explores variables such as mating and attractiveness from a genetic and biological perspective. Even if the *reason* for the physical preferences reviewed in this chapter so far is debatable, the features themselves have been associated with attractiveness across many, many studies.

Halo Effects: What Is Beautiful Is Good

We've now reviewed several features that appear to be almost universally considered physically attractive: symmetry, "average" faces, neotenous features, and certain body types. But there might be one more piece of the puzzle to why we find ourselves drawn toward beautiful people. For decades, research has asked questions about how we form first impressions of others. One robust finding is that sometimes, a single important or "central" feature of a person can affect our entire impression. When this happens, it's called a **halo effect**. This effect has been found in dozens of studies (e.g., Allport, 1937; Allport & Vernon, 1933; Asch, 1946; Cooper, 1981; Dennis, 2007; Dennis, Newstead, & Wright, 1996; Downey & Christensen, 2006; Hugh Feeley, 2002; Kelley, 1950; Remmers, 1934).

One specific type of halo effect is when someone's physical appearance makes us assume other things about them, such as their intelligence or personality. While these traits don't logically have anything to do with each other, we still tend to mush them together in either an overall positive impression (if the person is physically attractive) or overall negative impression. This particular form of halo effect is called the **what-is-beautiful-is-good effect**. It's like good-looking people have an aura or glow that makes us assume other good things about them (Dion, Berscheid, & Walster, 1972). Men, women, working professionals, and college students are all similarly influenced by physical beauty.

For example, teachers rate physically attractive children as smarter (Clifford & Walster, 1973). Pretty people get higher starting salaries and more raises at work (Frieze, Olson, & Russell, 1991) and attractive defendants in court are given lighter prison sentences (Gunnell & Ceci, 2010). People with attractive profile photos on Facebook are more likely to get friend requests from strangers (Wang, Moon, Kwon, Evans, & Stefanone, 2010), and physically attractive students are more likely to be given scholarships (Agthe, Spörrle, & Maner, 2010). It goes the other way around, too: College students think that attractive professors are more "effective" (Hugh Feeley, 2002).

Presumably, being attractive has little to do with one's intelligence, ability to get work done, or likelihood of committing crimes. Nevertheless, most people perceive attractive individuals as "better" in general and thus give them the benefit of the doubt. Although the beauty bias may have declined somewhat over time (Hosoda, Stone-Romero, & Coats, 2003), the halo surrounding physical beauty is very bright. For a measure of physical attraction to someone else, as well as two other forms of interpersonal attraction, check out the "What's My Score?" feature.

WHAT'S MY SCORE?

Three Types of Interpersonal Attraction

Instructions: This scale measures three different types of attraction to others. First, "Task Attraction" is a measure of your respect for someone's abilities, motivation, and intelligence. "Social Attraction" measures your interest in someone as a friend. Finally, "Physical Attraction" measures whether you are sexually attracted to someone. Think of a specific person in your life as you answer each question below, using this scale:

1	2	3	4	5	6	7
Strongly disagree						Strongly agree

Task Attraction [Respect]

_____1. If I wanted to get things done, I could probably depend on her/him.

_____2. He/she would be a poor problem solver.

_____3. I couldn't get anything accomplished with her/him.

_____4. I have confidence in her/his ability to get the job done.

_____5. He/she is a typical goof-off when assigned a job to do.

_____6. I would enjoy working on a task with her/him.

_____7. This person is lazy when it comes to working on a task.

_____8. This person would be an asset in any task situation.

_____9. I would recommend him/her as a work partner.

_____10. I could rely on her/him to get the job done.

_____11. This person takes her/his work seriously.

_____12. He/she is an unreliable work partner.

_____13. I could not count on the person to get the job done.

_____14. I could not recommend her/him as a work partner.

Social Attraction

_____15. I think he/she could be a friend of mine.

_____16. I would like to have a friendly chat with her/him.

_____17. It would be difficult to meet and talk with her/him.

_____18. We could never establish a personal friendship with each other.

(Continued)

(Continued)

_____ 19. He/she just wouldn't fit into my circle of friends.

_____ 20. He/she would be pleasant to be with.

_____ 21. He/she is sociable with me.

_____ 22. I would not like to spend time socializing with this person.

_____ 23. I could become close friends with her/him.

_____ 24. He/she is easy to get along with.

_____ 25. He/she is unpleasant to be around.

_____ 26. This person is not very friendly.

Physical Attraction

_____ 27. I think he/she is handsome/pretty.

_____ 28. He/she is sexy looking.

_____ 29. I don't like the way he/she looks.

_____ 30. He/she is ugly.

_____ 31. I find her/him attractive physically.

_____ 32. He/she is not good looking.

_____ 33. This person looks appealing.

_____ 34. I don't like the way this person looks.

_____ 35. He/she is nice looking.

_____ 36. He/she has an attractive face.

_____ 37. He/she is not physically attractive.

_____ 38. He/she is good looking.

Scoring: First, reverse-score the following items: numbers 2, 3, 5, 7, 12, 13, 14, 17, 18, 19, 22, 25, 26, 29, 30, 32, 34, and 37. Then, simply find the average score within each set of items (for each of the three types of attraction). Your final score should be between 1 and 7, with higher numbers meaning greater attraction to the person you had in mind.

Source: McCroskey, McCroskey, and Richmond (2006).

Critical Thinking: Often, self-report scales include fairly repetitive statements—and this scale certainly does that. The purpose of this repetition is to make sure people are answering consistently, and to offer the opportunity for the person taking the survey to show some range of responses. However, if the items get too repetitive, the survey-taker might get bored or annoyed. How can survey writers balance the need to get consistent answers with the need to keep participants happy and interested?

CHECK YOUR UNDERSTANDING

8.1 From an "evolutionary psychology" perspective, why are facial symmetry, "averaged" faces, neoteny, and certain body types more likely to be considered attractive, regardless of culture?

a. These traits are linked to aggression.
b. These instincts are left over from earlier primate ancestors and are not relevant to humans.
c. These tendencies are mistakes caused by genetic mutations.
d. These traits are linked to genetic fitness or health.

8.2 Which facial feature is considered a "neotenous" feature?

a. Small eyes
b. Small nose
c. Low forehead
d. Facial hair on men

8.3 According to research, what "waist-to-hips" ratio is most attractive for women, across many different cultures?

a. 0.15
b. 0.50
c. 0.70
d. 1.20

APPLICATION ACTIVITY

Identify three celebrities, then analyze each person for their facial symmetry, "average"-ness, facial neoteny, and waist-to-hips (for women) or waist-to-shoulders (for men) ratios as well as you can from photographs. Are the people you see good examples of the trends described in this section? When you notice someone who doesn't fit these criteria, do you see them as less attractive? You might also look at television or movie characters seen as protagonists or antagonists, and analyze their physical attractiveness. Are "beautiful" people more likely to be seen as good, and vice versa, showing a Hollywood-based halo effect in casting of actors?

CRITICAL THINKING

- Now that you know about traits that are considered "universally" attractive, are there things you would consider changing about your own appearance or dress that might highlight your own features, essentially disguising things about yourself that go against these desirable traits? Or is giving in to the world's definition of what is (or isn't) "attractive" just becoming superficial?

- Recall that studies on bilateral symmetry found that symmetry was significantly correlated with having sex at an earlier age for men, but not so much for women. What might explain this difference? What other variables might affect women's age of first sexual encounter that are more powerful than symmetry?

Answers to the Check Your Understanding Questions

8.1 d, 8.2 b, and 8.3 c.

What Psychological Factors Predict Attraction?

Sure, we're drawn toward beautiful people. But we're not completely superficial, right? If someone is extremely attractive but is also a complete jerk or mind-numbingly dull, we quickly lose interest. There are so many reasons *beyond* physical features that we find ourselves attracted—or not—to potential partners. What are some of the psychological factors that matter? Some researchers have suggested it's almost impossible to really predict what will drive initial attraction between two people (e.g., Joel, Eastwick, & Finkel, 2017). But let's do the best we can with what we have.

Reciprocity

In *Cat on a Hot Tin Roof*, the famous playwright Tennessee Williams (1955/2014) wrote, "Living with someone you love can be lonelier than living entirely alone, if the one that you love doesn't love you" (1955/2014). The **reciprocity principle** within intimate relationships is the idea that we're more likely to be attracted to—and stay interested in—people who are also attracted to and interested in us.

When other people like us, it's flattering (and it shows that they have excellent taste!). The reciprocity principle has been tested in lab settings. When participants "overhear" someone else supposedly also in the study (but really a confederate, someone who's part of the research team) talking about how they like the participant, the participant reflects that liking with higher reported attraction to the other person (compared to when they "overhear" someone criticizing them; Kenny & La Voie, 1982). We find it especially flattering when we think that people originally disliked us but now have a favorable opinion of us—and we reward their changed minds by liking them even more than people who liked us all along (Aronson & Linder, 1965).

If we're just starting a potential relationship and are thinking of approaching someone we like, many of us will fear rejection. This is especially true for people who are shy or who have low self-esteem (Bale & Archer, 2013; Wenzel & Emerson, 2009); these individuals are more likely to flirt with *less* attractive others, probably thinking they're less likely to be rejected. So, knowing in advance that someone already likes us boosts our confidence and helps us feel an affiliation. In fact, even if we're *wrong* about whether someone likes us, *believing* they like us can lead to a self-fulfilling prophecy. We're more relaxed, more personal, and agree with others more when we think they like us—which leads them to like us (Curtis & Miller, 1986).

Unfortunately, reciprocity can fail us if we're attracted to someone who doesn't reciprocate our feelings. **Unrequited love** is attraction or an emotional attachment to someone that isn't returned. Most of us have had a crush on someone who was completely disinterested in us, or we've been put in the "friend zone." This is hard to take, of course—but over 80% of college students say that they've experienced it (Aron, Aron, & Allen, 1998). While unrequited love is disappointing, the students in this study reported that they held out hope for a potential relationship in the future, and that it felt good just to be in love, even if that love was not reciprocated. That sounds romantic . . . but when unrequited love turns into **stalking**, or a pattern of acts of pursuit that are unwanted and harassing, it becomes a crime (Meloy, 1998).

Nonverbal Communication

Once you decide you're interested in someone, how do you signal that interest? One way is through **nonverbal communication**, or signals we send to others through our body motions, posture, and facial expressions. Sometimes, these nonverbal behaviors are simply acknowledging another person's interest and trying to let them know that we're interested too—in other words, signaling reciprocity of attraction (Aron et al., 1998; Muehlenhard, Koralewski, Andrews, & Burdick, 1986). This type of purposeful communication is psychological because we're purposely trying to send messages to others (and pick up on the messages they send to us, hopefully!).

A set of studies using naturalistic observation in bars and pubs recorded the types of nonverbal communication that both men and women seem to enact to send cues that they're available. In short, the researchers watched how people were flirting with each other. Men frequently engaged in behaviors that showed social dominance and confidence, such as winning at bar games or trying to display "masculine" behaviors.

Women, on the other hand, were more likely to engage in more passive behaviors such as dancing, flipping their hair, or making eye contact (Kleinke, 1986; Perper & Weis, 1987). Men in bars who frequently glance at someone else and take up a lot of physical space—a show of dominance—get more positive attention from women (Renninger, Wade, & Grammer, 2004). In addition, more signals seem to be better: People who are high in emotional expressivity through body language are liked more than people who appear more reserved (Friedman, Riggio, & Casella, 1988). It's not the time to be subtle if you want attention.

Let's get really applied for a few minutes: How can you step up your flirting game? Several researchers have explored this question. First, two studies got very specific regarding exactly what kinds of nonverbal communication are used within two-person conversations that signal either interest or boredom (Fichten, Tagalakis, Judd, Wright, & Amsel, 1992; Muehlenhard et al., 1986). Their combined results are shown in Table 8.1. Behaviors indicating sexual interest are called **proceptive behaviors**, and behaviors indicating lack of interest are **rejective behaviors** (Perper, 1989). It's probably not surprising to see that people who are attracted to each other lean in, touch each other, and smile—whereas people who want to signal boredom turn away, make excuses to leave, and even yawn!

Another study (Givens, 1978) discussed findings from naturalistic observations of couples flirting with each other in cafeterias, on buses, in bars and restaurants, and in other public settings. In this article, Givens focuses on interactions that start with two strangers and lead to sexual encounters—in other words, he was most interested in

TABLE 8.1 ● Nonverbal Signals of Interest or Boredom

Signs of Interpersonal Interest (Proceptive Behaviors)	Signs of Interpersonal Boredom (Rejective Behaviors)
Establish and maintain eye contact	Look away
Nod head	Disagree with other person
Move closer/lean forward	Turn or lean away
Smile	Slouch
Laugh	Yawn
Touch each other	Look bored (lack of expression)
Ignore distractions	Lie or make excuses to leave
Look attentive	Look distracted
Avoid grooming in front of other	Smooth clothes, etc. (mild grooming)
Voice is animated	Voice is monotone

Here are very specific nonverbal behaviors that can indicate either interest/attraction or disinterest/boredom when speaking to someone else.

one-night stands. He breaks the courting process into five specific phases, each with its own nonverbal cues and behaviors:

1. *Phase 1: Attention.* One person must get the other's attention. In heterosexual couples, this is usually initiated by a man who does something such as attempt to make eye contact or make tentative vocal contact. Either way, the person who initiates the process should wait for acknowledgment and verbal or nonverbal signals that the attention is welcome.

2. *Phase 2: Recognition.* The target of phase 1 is reciprocated attention. Smiles, nods, "tossing" of hair, body leaning forward, and so on are cues from the target that the approach is desired. "Self-clasping" may also occur, in which the target of attention grasps their own neck or arms (in some animals, this indicates submission).

3. *Phase 3: Interaction.* Sustained eye contact, speaking with each other, or other explicit communication occurs. Nonverbal signals include laughter, larger body motions such as stretching, and synchronizing body movements to match each other.

4. *Phase 4: Sexual Arousal.* The couple may, if mutually desired, retreat to a private location to become more intimate with each other. This phase may include nonverbal signals such as touching, caressing, playing with each other's hands, massaging, and so forth. The author notes that "nuzzling, licking, sucking, playing biting, kissing, and so on" may commence (Givens, 1978, p. 352).

5. *Phase 5: Resolution.* In his article, Givens avoids talking much about the actual climax of sexual encounters by stating simply that "courtship fulfills itself in copulation" (p. 353). Afterward, nonverbal signals may indicate what Givens calls "social distancing," such as an immediate shift to displays showing lack of interest. His final phase indicates that the relationship is now over and both people move on. Certainly, this is the case for *some* encounters . . . but just as certainly, it's not true for *all* encounters.

Finally, a more recent study presented people from ages 18 to 61 with a list of potential nonverbal behaviors that might indicate flirting and asked them to rate how effective each would be (Wade & Feldman, 2016). A limitation of this study is that it only tested behaviors in terms of heterosexual situations involving a man and woman (e.g., "he dances with her"). That said, Table 8.2 shows the five flirting behaviors rated as most effective by men and women, respectively.

There were lots of additional suggestions in the study (such as giving someone a compliment and laughing at their jokes). Another interesting finding was that men and women didn't necessarily match in their perception of how effective each technique would be. For example, men thought that women dancing with them was extremely effective for signaling interest (it made the top-five list shown in Table 8.2), but women thought that dancing with men wasn't a particularly strong flirting technique. Similarly, women said that it was very effective when men gave them flowers, but men didn't think that was a great strategy (which might explain why women get annoyed when their male partners don't give them flowers as often as they'd like).

TABLE 8.2 ● Most Effective Nonverbal Flirting Behaviors	
By Men Toward Women	**By Women Toward Men**
He asks her out	She dances with him
He acts interested in her	She rubs against him
He holds hands with her	She moves closer to him
He kisses her	She touches him, in general
He gives her flowers	She kisses him on the cheek

These are the five most effective nonverbal flirting behaviors between men and women, according to Wade and Feldman (2016).

TABLE 8.3 ● What Are the Most Important Traits in a Sexual Partner? In a Marriage Partner?		
Physically attractive	Sexually "easy"	Self-confident
Protective	Honest or trustworthy	Plays hard to get
Intelligent	College graduate	Good heredity/genes
Religious	Good housekeeper	Healthy
Overall personality	Easygoing	Socially or financially powerful
Creative and artistic	Attentive to my needs	Dominant
Wants children	Sense of humor	Is sexually suggestive
Sensitive/kind		

This list was provided to college students, who rated them in terms of importance in choosing either a sexual partner or a marriage partner.

Personality

When you're deciding how interested you are in other people, how important is their personality? For most people, attraction is very much dependent on whether you like someone's sense of humor, level of shyness versus extraversion, and so on. But is personality *more* important than other factors, such as physical attraction or trust? One study asked this very question when 70 college students were given a list of 22 characteristics and asked which were the most important in a potential partner (Regan & Berscheid, 1997). The list of characteristics is shown in Table 8.3.

This study is particularly interesting because the results were broken up in two different ways. First, the researchers compared men's and women's responses to see if there were interesting differences. Second, half of the participants were asked what characteristics were most important to them in a potential *sexual* partner, while the other half were asked about characteristics important for a potential *marriage* partner. Do we want the same thing in each type of relationship?

Before you know the results, think about this for yourself. When you consider these traits, which would be the five most important things you want in sexual partners? And which are the top five for a marriage or life partner? Do you have the same list for each?

Now, look at the results in Table 8.4, which displays the top-five "most important" characteristics based on both sex of the participant and type of relationship. There are some interesting similarities and differences in the four different sets of answers. For sexual partners, both men and women said they wanted a partner who is physically attractive and healthy, which makes a lot of sense. But "attentive to my needs" was slightly higher on the list for women than for men; this might be due to physiology and women knowing that reaching orgasm is harder for them than it is for men (Fugl-Meyer, Öberg, Lundberg, Lewin, & Fugl-Meyer, 2006). For marriage partners, both men and women want someone who is honest and trustworthy, as well as someone with intelligence.

Importantly, the *only* trait that appears on all four of the top-five lists was what quality? It's overall personality.

Lots of additional studies have asked men and women for specific personality traits they think are attractive in potential partners, and these studies generally

TABLE 8.4 ● What Do Men and Women Want in Sexual and in Marriage Partners?	
What *Women* Want in a *Sexual* Partner	**What *Women* Want in a *Marriage* Partner**
1. Physically attractive	1. Honest or trustworthy
2. Healthy	2. Sensitive
3. Attentive to my needs	3. Overall personality
4. Sense of humor	4. Intelligent
5. Overall personality	5. Attentive to my needs
What *Men* Want in a *Sexual* Partner	**What *Men* Want in a *Marriage* Partner**
1. Physically attractive	1. Overall personality
2. Healthy	2. Honest or trustworthy
3. Overall personality	3. Physically attractive
4. Attentive to my needs	4. Intelligent
5. Self-confident	5. Healthy

These were the top-five most desirable traits, chosen from a list, that men and women say they want in sexual and marriage partners.

show the same patterns over and over. Specific traits seen as desirable are being dependable, emotionally stable, ambitious or industrious, trustworthy, sociable, and similar to oneself (see the next section for more on similarity). Again, none of this is probably surprising—but it's good when empirical research can provide evidence for our intuitions.

When one study summarized trends over 57 years of research and across hundreds of people (Buss, Shackelford, Kirkpatrick, & Larsen, 2001), they found that men's and women's preferences converged over time—meaning while there used to be differences 50 years ago, pretty much everyone wants the same things now. Men no longer seem to care that their wives have good "domestic skills," and both sexes say they care about a spouse who loves them, is attractive, and has good job prospects.

What might be slightly more interesting is to consider research that asked what people *don't* want to see in a partner's personality. These traits have been called **social allergens**—traits that are relatively minor but eventually lead to disgust, boredom, and dissatisfaction (Cunningham, Barbee, & Druen, 1997; Cunningham, Shamblen, Barbee, & Ault, 2005). Certainly, some social allergens could just be the opposite of the traits mentioned in the previous paragraph (e.g., being dishonest). But there are other things that people mention, when asked in research studies.

- *Uncouth habits*: poor grooming, failing to clean up after oneself, poor manners

- *Inconsiderate acts*: being an attention hog, being chronically late, turning all conversations to oneself

- *Intrusive behaviors*: frequently criticizing, giving commands, acting jealously or controlling

- *Norm violations*: drinking to excess, avoiding work, flirting with other people

In short, few people want to date or marry a slobby, rude, critical, drunk flirt who always wants to be the center of attention.

CHECK YOUR UNDERSTANDING

8.4 Imagine you want to send a Valentine's Day card to someone you like but haven't started dating yet. Which phrase should you write in the card if you want to make use of the reciprocity principle to get the person to like you?

a. "I've been attracted to you for a while now."

b. "I think we have a lot in common."

c. "Shakespeare said the world is but a stage."

d. "I just got back from the doctor, and my rash is all cleared up."

8.5 Nonverbal behaviors that indicate attraction or interest, such as smiles and leaning toward someone, are called:

a. Normative cues

b. Subliminal cues

(Continued)

(Continued)

c. Proceptive behaviors
d. Rejective behaviors

8.6   Research on "social allergens" lists four types of behaviors perceived as unattractive in potential partners. Which option below is NOT one of the

allergens discussed in this chapter?

a. Inconsiderate acts
b. Unrequited love
c. Norm violations
d. Intrusive behaviors

APPLICATION ACTIVITY

Table 8.1 listed several nonverbal behaviors that people use to show either proceptivity (attraction and interest) or rejection. Find movie or TV clips that show one character flirting with another, and analyze their nonverbal behaviors. Make a list of proceptive behaviors the flirting character does, and make a list of either proceptive or rejective behaviors that the target of flirting does.

CRITICAL THINKING

- This chapter touched on unrequited love. Being in love with someone who doesn't return your interest is a common theme in literature, movies, and television shows. Often, dogged patience is shown as romantic. When does devoted attention and patient love turn into stalking? What's the threshold for inappropriate or harassing behaviors?

- Consider research on cultural differences in nonverbal behaviors, such as how different cultures have varying expectations regarding things like eye contact or how closely you should stand to other people. How do these cultural differences lead to insights about attraction or flirtatious behavior (or misunderstandings) in people from different cultural backgrounds?

Answers to the Check Your Understanding Questions
8.4 a, 8.5 c, and 8.6 b.

What Environmental Factors Predict Attraction?

Candlelight dinners . . . walks along the beach during sunset . . . visiting the city dump. Two of these scenarios are more traditionally "romantic" than the third. Attraction is certainly tied to physical features and to whether we like someone on a personal, psychological level. However, whether we feel a "spark" can also be influenced by the circumstances around us. This final section discusses four interesting aspects of the environment that are also linked to attraction.

Proximity and Mere Exposure

In Chapter 7, you learned about how physical proximity can lead to friendships, a phenomenon called the propinquity effect. As a reminder, the famous Westgate Housing Study (Festinger, Schachter, & Back, 1950) found that people who lived in apart-

Do you believe that some environments are more romantic than others?

ments located in spots where a lot of their neighbors walked by were liked more than people who lived in isolated spots. In short, repeated exposure to another person leads to more liking (if your attitude toward him or her started as neutral).

When it comes to interpersonal attraction, the propinquity effect appears to be pretty robust. On a broader level, this same trend is found when repeated exposure to *any* person, object, or idea leads to greater liking of it (Festinger et al., 1950; Monahan, Murphy, & Zajonc, 2000; Van Horn et al., 1997; Zajonc, 1968, 2001). Recall (also from Chapter 7) that the tendency to like things and people more, the more we are exposed to them, is called mere exposure. So, the propinquity effect is one specific type of mere exposure (Goodfriend, 2009).

Interestingly, the mere exposure effect explains why we prefer photos of ourselves that have been digitally reversed instead of actual, original photos. We're used to looking at ourselves in a mirror. Photos are backward from how we usually see our faces, so they seem "off" without most people realizing why (Mita, Dermer, & Knight, 1977). The Westgate Housing Study showed that mere exposure led to liking and friendships (Festinger et al., 1950). Just being around someone for an extended period of time does usually lead to increased liking and attraction—again, as long as initial attitudes were neutral. This finding has been replicated many times in a wide variety of settings (e.g., Brickman, Meyer, & Fredd, 1975; Brockner & Swap, 1976; Harrison, 1977; Moreland & Beach, 1992; Reis, Maniaci, Caprariello, Eastwick, & Finkel, 2011) and in both "Western" and "Eastern" cultures (Heine & Renshaw, 2002).

Why do we tend to like people, objects, and ideas more when we've been around them longer? There are several explanations. One is that when we're familiar with people, we find them more predictable and therefore are more comfortable (Lee, 2001). Another is that it gives us a chance to get to know people on a more personal or intimate level, which makes us feel connected to them (Denrell, 2005). Finally, if we know we're going to be around particular people a lot (because they live or work nearby, for example), we'll probably be nicer, more polite, and so on, which leads to more positive interactions and liking (Baumeister & Leary, 1995).

Misattribution of Arousal: Excitation Transfer

Think back to the last time you were around someone you found extremely attractive. Your mind was probably racing with excitement—but so was your body. Did your heart beat faster? Did your breathing become short and fast? Maybe you were sweating or had a feeling of vague nausea because you were so nervous. When we're sexually attracted to another person, we experience physiological arousal.

Usually we know exactly why we're experiencing this sort of physiological arousal. But is it possible for us to make an incorrect assumption about why we're sweaty and out of breath? If something *else* in our immediate environment is really the cause of these reactions, then we might *misinterpret* physiological reactions caused by that environment as attraction to people who happen to be nearby. In other words, we might make a **misattribution of arousal**. Some researchers call this the **excitation transfer** effect because we tend to transfer our excitement over the situation to excitement about the other person.

In one of the most creative and famous studies ever done on misattribution of arousal, Dutton and Aron (1974) asked a physically attractive female experimenter to spend time waiting in a park, then approach men who might be willing to complete a survey for a study. She only approached men who were by themselves. She told the men that the survey was investigating whether scenic settings had an effect on creativity, and that she would be happy to answer additional questions after they completed the survey. To emphasize her willingness to see more of each man, she wrote her phone number on a piece of paper and handed it to the men while smiling.

Remember that this experiment was meant to study misattribution. The key to how it worked was that the pretty young experimenter approached the men in two different park locations (making this a quasi-experimental design). The two locations were the independent variable, but it wasn't a "true" experiment because the locations weren't randomly assigned to the different men. Still, Dutton and Aron predicted that one of the locations would lead to more physiological arousal—and thus more attraction to the woman—than the other. Attraction to her therefore became the dependent variable.

Would walking across these two bridges cause you different levels of anxiety and physiological arousal? Research indicates that some people might misinterpret that kind of arousal as attraction to other people who happen to be nearby.

The locations were near two different bridges. The first bridge, considered the control group bridge, was sturdy and made of solid wood. It was wide, had high handrails, and the drop was only 10 feet. The second bridge, however, was a 450-foot suspension bridge made of individual wooden boards strapped together with cables. To cross it, participants had to walk over a 250-foot canyon full of sharp and scary rocks; the bridge also had the tendency to "shake" and sway in the wind. Imagine what it would be like to cross this shaky bridge. In most participants, it would produce anxiety and fear, or at least excitement—which in turn produce physiological changes such as increased heart rate, faster breathing, sweat, and nausea. Sound familiar?

The pretty female experimenter would wait for a young man who was by himself to cross one of the bridges and then would approach him. Next, he would complete the survey and walk away with the woman's phone number. The research team measured how many of these men called the experimenter later, their way of measuring or operationalizing his level of attraction (the dependent variable). You can probably predict what happened. Of the men who had crossed the shaky, arousing bridge, 50% called the experimenter, while only 12.5% of the men from the stable bridge called, a difference that was statistically significant.

The scientific question to ask is: What accounted for this large difference? Misattribution of arousal suggests that the men who had just crossed the shaky bridge were physiologically aroused due to fear and anxiety caused by the bridge itself. However, when they interacted with a pretty woman immediately after crossing, they may have misinterpreted that physiological arousal as sexual interest. My heart is beating, I'm sweaty . . . I guess I find this woman sexy! Not as many men from the stable bridge called because they didn't feel as physiologically aroused.

Other studies have tried to replicate the misattribution of arousal effect on attraction, with mixed results. One article attempted to find the effect across four different studies, and all four studies failed (Kenrick, Cialdini, & Linder, 1979). Here, the participants were aware of the anxiety-provoking environment and knew that their arousal was due to that (and not attraction). However, other researchers have found evidence for at least small misattribution effects (e.g., Lewandowski & Aron, 2004; Williams, Ryckman, Gold, & Lenney, 1982). One example is that participants who watched pornography were more aroused if they had recently exercised (Payne, Hall, Cameron, & Bishara, 2010)! For another example, see the "Relationships and Popular Culture" feature.

Similarity and Matching: Assortative Mating

You may have heard the phrase "Opposites attract." It's a popular plot device in the movies to have the innocent rich girl fall for the street-smart bad boy (or vice versa). But research tells us that the phrase "birds of a feather flock together" is a more accurate description of how real people connect with one another. This general idea, called the **attraction-similarity hypothesis**, predicts that people tend to form relationships with others who have the same attitudes, values, interests, and demographics as themselves (Morry, 2005, 2007). You already know this is true because of the section on similarity in friendships from Chapter 7, which used the term *homophily* to describe our tendency to like people who are like us.

RELATIONSHIPS AND POPULAR CULTURE

Misattribution and Love in *The Hunger Games*

In the popular movie series *The Hunger Games* (Collins, 2008, 2009, 2010), Katniss Everdeen is torn between love for two men. Why does she ultimately choose one over the other? If similarity were the focus of the film, she would probably choose Gale. Gale is very similar to Katniss; they both put protecting family first, they hunt together, and they stand up against the dystopian government together. But Gale doesn't capture her heart in the same way that Peeta, the other man, does.

Why does Katniss fall for Peeta instead? Peeta has many positive qualities (such as altruism and loyalty), but misattribution of arousal may also play a large part. Katniss and Peeta are constantly thrown together in a series of highly dangerous situations, both fighting for their lives. In a long-term and consistent state of physiological arousal, they are trying to survive multiple attempts to murder them. Being around Peeta in the midst of this chaos might lead Katniss to perceive more attraction to him than she would have felt in calmer conditions. Perhaps she interprets her beating heart as caused by love instead of the adrenaline of survival.

Is it true that opposites attract? Or are we attracted to people similar to ourselves?

Think about your friends' relationships, or even—if you know—what brought your parents together. They were probably about the same age, came from families with similar incomes, and may have been the same race, ethnicity, or religion. For example, the U.S. Census tracks all kinds of patterns in the population every 10 years. They reported that the number of interracial marriages increased from 2000 to 2010, but only from a very small 7% to the slightly less small 10% (U.S. Census Bureau, 2010). The vast majority of us marry people who look and sound similar to ourselves.

Demographic variables such as age, social class, political leanings, and race or ethnicity may be important. But many of us want to date someone who can share our interests and dreams as well as understand our perspective on the world. When a date wants to see the same movie, play the same video game, or go to a party with the same people, planning an evening becomes easy. Planning an entire life together also becomes easier and more meaningful when two partners can agree on important issues such as whether to have children and how many, whether to spend money on a nicer apartment or on exotic vacations, and whether children should have any religious training. Similarities decrease arguments between couples. Another reason behind the attraction-similarity hypothesis is that similar people validate our values and worldviews (Morry, 2005, 2007).

People with similar beliefs make us more comfortable with our opinions and affirm that we are logical, smart human beings.

Of course, people are attracted to and have relationships with others who are different, and these relationships offer some benefits. For example, an individual who has a weakness in such areas as verbal communication can improve this skill if their partner is strong in it (Gruber-Baldini, Schaie, & Willis, 1995). Baxter and West (2003) also tested couples to see how they perceived any differences between them. They found that most couples can see the differences between the two people involved—and couple members who perceive these differences as an opportunity to learn from each other viewed this lack of similarity as a positive instead of as a negative. When differences help us improve in our own weaknesses, or help us keep an open mind, relationship partners are a valuable resource (Davis & Goodfriend, 2007).

Consider popular dating websites. There are plenty of choices; examples that come to mind are likely websites such as eHarmony, Tinder, Plenty of Fish, OkCupid, and many others. One of the sites with the most uses is Match.com. While many sites allow you to search for and message anyone who has a profile, several of these companies try to sell their users the idea that the company will use fancy surveys, formulas, and algorithms to find people who "match" you on various traits. The implication is that if you can find someone who "matches" you on these important qualities, you're more likely to be compatible; this idea is the **matching hypothesis**.

Similarity, or the matching hypothesis, is an environmental factor in attraction because it's not just about your preferences or about something in the other person; it's about how the two of you combine in a unique way. At its core, the matching hypothesis is that some combinations of people will be more likely to work out than others. Interestingly, however, one study showed that *actual* similarity between partners doesn't matter as much as *perceived* similarity (Montoya, Horton, & Kirchner, 2008). We might just convince ourselves that we're similar to people who have other attractive qualities.

A groundbreaking study on the matching hypothesis was one of the first to think about how computer "matching" strategies might affect first dates, way back in 1966 (Walster, Aronson, Abrahams, & Rottman, 1966). They believed that dates would like each other if they were matched on "social desirability," which they operationalized as a combination of physical attractiveness, personality, material resources, intellect, and self-esteem. For their creative study, they started with 376 men and 376 women, all first-year college students, who purchased a $1 ticket for a dance held on the first Friday of the fall semester at the University of Minnesota. Everyone was told that if they filled out a short survey on the computer, they would be matched with someone "who has the same expressed interests as yourself" (p. 509) to serve as their date for the evening. While each person bought their ticket, experimenters recorded their physical attractiveness.

On the night of the dance, all participants were actually randomly assigned to a date with whom they spent 2.5 hours dancing and talking. Then, the dance was paused and each person completed a survey indicating how attracted they were to each other. The researchers then checked to see whether attraction was based on matching, which they could check using the information each person had given when they bought their ticket (plus the judges' ratings of their physical attractiveness). Did couples with more in common like each other more?

The scientists who did this study were surprised by what they found. Matching did *not* increase attraction when the matching was high for intelligence, social skills, personality, financial resources, or almost anything else. The only matching variable that did seem to matter, in fact, was physical attractiveness. It's not surprising that we're more attracted to beautiful people, as an earlier section of this chapter outlined. What's interesting is that people seem to end up dating people with the *same* level of physical attractiveness that they have themselves (Berscheid, Dion, Walster, & Walster, 1971). This more specific version of the matching hypothesis is called **assortative mating**: that people tend to end up in relationships with people who have the same level of physical attractiveness as themselves. See the "Research Deep Dive" feature for more research.

A meta-analysis of 16 studies conducted on assortative mating (Feingold, 1988) found that for romantic couples, there was a significant correlation between the attractiveness of the two people. Hot people are most likely to date other hot people, and so on down the line. This means that people with an average level of physical attractiveness might not pursue the hottest possible person; instead, we might show the most interest in people we believe are "realistic" instead of "idealistic" for ourselves.

In a relatively recent study on this prediction (Montoya, 2008), participants viewed several photographs that ranged in attractiveness and were asked to guess whether each person would be interested in dating them. Less attractive participants guessed that the more attractive people in the photos would be less interested. Fear of rejection might, thus, prevent middle-attractiveness people from pursuing the very attractive.

Other studies have shown that less-attractive people might need to have something else going for them if they want to date more-attractive people. For example, one study of men on an online dating site pinpointed users who were rated as being in the bottom 10% of attractiveness. The study found that these men would have to say they made $186,000 more *every year* to get the same number of "hits" as good-looking male users of the site (Hitsch, Hortaçsu, & Ariely, 2010). So, if you do happen to be less attractive, and if you want to go against the assortative mating trend and snag a hot partner, it's a good strategy to make sure you can "make up" for your lower physical appeal by having other things to offer. Being rich, smart, and funny apparently helps.

RESEARCH DEEP DIVE

Is It Important to Stay Within Your Own League While Dating?

Take 100 single people, looking for love. Now, put them in a room together for an evening; who would end up together? Clearly, while lots of variables factor into who would form a relationship, a longstanding theory in relationship science makes a simple prediction. The matching hypothesis predicts that individuals will pair up with a partner who has the same social mate value (Walster et al., 1966). Researchers typically operationally define social mate value as the combination of all the factors that contribute to making you more or less desirable to date (e.g., physical attractiveness, personality, financial resources). Essentially, according to the matching hypothesis, if your social mate value is a 7, you'll end up with another 7, or very close; 10s go with 10s, 3s with 3s, and so on. Researchers from the University of California, Berkeley tested the matching hypothesis across several studies (Taylor, Fiore, Mendelsohn, & Cheshire, 2011).

In Study 1, nearly 200 participants completed an online self-report questionnaire about their own mate value/self-worth based on their physical attractiveness, self-esteem, likeability, warmth, kindness, and trustworthiness. Next, participants imagined they were looking for a partner on an online dating site and created their own dating profile. Participants then reviewed potential partners' profiles that the researchers varied by physical attractiveness (high, medium, low) and by text description (high, medium, or low attractiveness). Participants rated each of the nine profiles based on whether the person in the profile "would probably respond favorably to me if I contacted him/her."

In Study 2, the researchers randomly selected profile pictures from 60 male and 60 female users of an online dating site. Using the site activity log to see who those users (i.e., the "initiators") contacted, the researchers then pulled the "targets'" profile pictures as well. Next, several judges rated the attractiveness of the initiator and target photos. Researchers also looked at whom the initiators contacted and whether the target reciprocated by responding back.

Relative to participants with low mate value/self-worth, those with high social mate value were more interested in contacting potential partners with high mate value. That said, participants with low mate value were *also* more interested in making contact with high (vs. low) mate value targets. Though this pattern supports the matching hypothesis, overall lower mate value participants preferred high mate value potential partners as well (i.e., a mismatch). Thus, it seems that while everyone would prefer a high value partner, only those with self-perceived high value have the confidence to actually pursue the 9s and 10s out there.

In Study 2, initiators on the dating site contacted more attractive targets (i.e., people out of their league), which does not support the matching hypothesis (which would have predicted less attractive initiators would contact less attractive targets). However, there was evidence for matching in terms of who reciprocated or responded to the contact. Daters were more likely to hear back or have their advance reciprocated when attractive initiators contacted attractive targets and when less attractive initiators contacted less attractive targets (i.e., when people stayed within their own league).

That study shows that at least when it comes to online formats, people do try to "date up" by pursuing others who are more attractive and essentially out of their league. Why doesn't this finding match the general matching hypothesis? Well, the low-stakes environment of online dating—where advances don't result in outward or obvious rejection—encourages more of a "shotgun" approach where daters feel empowered to "take a shot" and contact lots of more attractive people. And really, you can't blame someone for trying. But if you're going for a higher *success* rate, Study 2 suggests that you're better off sticking to others in your own league.

This combination of studies highlights the importance of combining lab-based research with research in more naturally occurring settings. Each study helps us understand the matching hypothesis but also lends slightly different insights. All in all, this makes perfect sense. In an ideal world, you may really want the best, highest-paying job there is. Yet because of all of the other applicants, some of whom are more qualified than you, you end up matched to a job that most closely matches your skills and abilities. The same might be true for love.

For more, read Walster, E., Aronson, V., Abrahams, D., & Rottman, L. (1966). Importance of physical attractiveness in dating behavior. *Journal of Personality and Social Psychology*, 4, 508–516; and Taylor, L. S., Fiore, A. T., Mendelsohn, G. A., & Cheshire, C. (2011). "Out of my league": A real-world test of the matching hypothesis. *Personality and Social Psychology Bulletin, 37*, 942–954.

Forbidden Love: The Romeo and Juliet Effect

Most people are familiar with at least the basic story of Shakespeare's play *Romeo and Juliet*. Their families hate each other and are sworn to be enemies—yet the two main characters fall instantly in love and marry in secret, against their family's wishes. Things don't go well, and both characters end up committing suicide by the end of the play.

A good deal of research indicates that we're more likely to stay in a relationship if we think that our family and friends approve of our partner; our perceptions of whether we have approval are called **subjective norms** (Etcheverry & Agnew, 2004; Lewis, 1973; Sprecher, 1988). If we think people don't like our partner, or our relationship is socially marginalized, most of the time we're more likely to break up (Lehmiller & Agnew, 2007). It's just awkward when no one likes the person we're dating, and it can make us doubt whether we've made a good choice. So, often, we choose people we know will be socially accepted by the others we have in our life.

On the other hand, sometimes attraction can become ironically greater when we think other people *disapprove* of our choice. When this happens, it's called the **Romeo and Juliet effect**. For some reason, our attraction goes up if we think the person is off limits or forbidden. It can make the attraction more exciting for some people if it's out of the ordinary, extreme, or seen as "naughty." In one of the first studies exploring this idea (Driscoll, Davis, & Lipetz, 1972), researchers found that parental interference with a relationship and participant commitment to marry had a positive correlation of .31—meaning that for these couples, the more their parents tried to stop the relationship, the more the two lovebirds wanted to tie the knot.

Why would people want to be with a partner they know is someone their friends and family don't like? This ironic desire isn't just limited to Shakespearean drama. The ancient Roman myth of Pyramus and Thisbe is based on the same theme: "They longed to marry, but their parents forbade it. Love, however, cannot be forbidden. The more the flame is covered up, the hotter it burns" (see Hamilton, 1942, p. 101). We see the theme repeated across history and across the globe. This kind of romantic language makes it seem like lovers should reject the opinions of others; perhaps their families are just perpetuating prejudice or ancient hatreds that should be ignored!

Some people have suggested that interference from parents or friends makes lovers feel that they've overcome challenges to be together, which increases their sense of commitment. When we're told we can't have something, we often immediately want it even more, a response called **reactance** (Amsel, 1958, 1962; Brehm & Brehm, 2013). For younger people, going against their parents' wishes is a symbol of independence and emerging adulthood as they experiment with the type of adult they want to be themselves (Marcia, 1966, 2002). For both of these reasons, a "forbidden" lover can become even more appealing. While the Romeo and Juliet effect is a popular theme in books, songs, movies, and TV shows (and plays, of course), some scientists have questioned whether it really exists (Sinclair, Hood, & Wright, 2014).

And remember: Things didn't go well for Romeo and Juliet. In at least some cases, there might be legitimate, sensible reasons for loved ones to object to a potential partner. Assuming the people in your life really love you and want what's best for you, their objections might be worth considering. One qualitative study that investigated this possibility was done by Karen Rosen (1996), when she interviewed 22 women between the ages of 16 and 23 who had experienced violent, abusive relationships (for more about relationship violence, see Chapter 12).

The women in Rosen's study told her about how and why they were first attracted to partners who eventually became abusive. Several of them mentioned that they maintained their relationships despite objections from family members. She notes, "Their relationships seemed to represent an opportunity to break away from their families—to, in effect, attain pseudo-autonomy. Their boyfriends were usually young men they knew their family would not accept" (Rosen, 1996, p. 171). The women in this study described how objections only made them feel closer to their partners—and these pressures led to increased isolation for the couple, which meant that the abusers had more opportunities to manipulate the victims.

One case study described by Rosen (1996) is a woman named "Adele," who was attracted to "Clint" because he was a "renegade biker" (p. 171). Adele described "clinging defiantly" to Clint despite everything:

> My parents couldn't stand him. They were like, where did you find him? I was very defiant. I was like, well I love him and you have to accept him because I do. . . . All of my friends were like, what are you doing? I couldn't bring him to parties, or if I was invited to other places he just didn't fit in. I guess the way I felt about it was that I wanted to prove them wrong, and I had a stronger desire to stay with him because they couldn't be right. (Rosen, 1996, p. 172)

Unfortunately, in Adele's case, maybe they *were* right, as she eventually had to leave him due to his abusive behaviors.

CHECK YOUR UNDERSTANDING

8.7 According to the effect known as misattribution of arousal, if you are on a first date and you want your date to be attracted to you, which of the following activities should you suggest?

   a. A slow walk along the beach
   b. A candlelit dinner including a sugary dessert
   c. Watching a romantic comedy in a movie theater
   d. Riding on several of the rides at a local carnival

8.8 If Adam were rated on a physical attractiveness scale of 1 to 10, he would be a 5. Based on the principle of assortative mating, what level of physical attractiveness is his wife most likely to be?

   a. 2
   b. 4
   c. 5
   d. 7

8.9 Based on the Romeo and Juliet effect, if a mother really liked her daughter's boyfriend and wanted them to get married, which statement should the mother make to her daughter?

   a. Your boyfriend is as handsome as your father!
   b. I'd like to know more about this person!
   c. I don't trust your boyfriend—you should break up immediately!
   d. Your boyfriend certainly seems to have a romantic spirit!

APPLICATION ACTIVITY

Make a list of 10–20 people who live near you, either in your neighborhood or in your residential building. If you don't know that many of your neighbors, make a list of 10–20 people who work in the same office or business as you. Then, go back through the list and rate how much you like each person on a scale of 1–10 (with 10 meaning you are very much attracted to them, in terms of friendship or romantic interest). Finally, consider whether you see a pattern based on how often you see them or how close they live or work to you. Do you find a pattern that supports the mere exposure effect? If not, what other variables are at play that are increasing or decreasing your attraction?

CRITICAL THINKING

- This section of the chapter suggested several environmental variables that make attraction more or less likely to occur. Consider all these factors and make specific inferences regarding how someone could apply them toward first dates or toward ensuring continued commitment from people who have been married several years. How can the information you learned in this section be turned into "self-help" advice for people who want to start or continue relationships?

- Some people have criticized the conclusions of the Dutton and Aron "shaky bridge" study, questioning whether men calling the experimenter is really a good way to measure their level of attraction toward her. What are some alternative ways that scientists could either tweak this experiment to improve it or test for the misattribution of arousal findings in novel (but ethical) ways?

Answers to the Check Your Understanding Questions

8.7 d, **8.8** c, and **8.9** c.

Chapter Summary

Big Questions

1. What physical factors predict attraction?

2. What psychological factors predict attraction?

3. What environmental factors predict attraction?

What physical factors predict attraction?
Certain facial features and body types are often found to be physically attractive around the world, regardless of culture. Evolutionary psychology argues that these features are instinctively seen as attractive because they are cues for genetic health in potential mates, which would help in reproduction and survival of children. Examples of "universally" attractive physical features are bilateral symmetry, digitally composite or "averaged" faces, neotenous or youthful features, and body type. Across cultures, men prefer women's bodies that have a 0.7 waist-to-hips ratio. Women prefer men to have a 0.7 waist-to-shoulders ratio. Finally, people who are physically attractive are also perceived to have several other positive qualities, such as intelligence or kindness; this bias is called the what-is-beautiful-is-good effect.

What psychological factors predict attraction?
We tend to like people who also like us, a phenomenon called the reciprocity principle. When we love people who do not return our interest, it's unrequited love. Several studies have investigated nonverbal communication or cues that people use to display interest or availability; these often include things like making eye contact, leaning forward, smiling, and touching someone. Behaviors showing attraction are called proceptive, whereas behaviors showing disinterest are

called rejective. Finally, studies have shown similarity in what both men and women want in terms of a partner's personality. Traits such as being dependable, trustworthy, ambitious, and sociable are desired. Undesirable traits that lead to annoyance or dislike are called social allergens; these include characteristics such as being rude or critical and lacking self-discipline.

What environmental factors predict attraction?
There are several circumstances or situations that appear to make attraction more or less likely. As discussed in Chapter 2, physical proximity is associated with increased liking (sometimes called the propinquity effect, which also encompasses mere exposure). Another environmental factor is whether people are physiologically aroused by something about the situation, such as fear or anxiety. This arousal can be mistaken for sexual attraction to someone nearby. The attraction-similarity hypothesis is the idea that we tend to form relationships with others who have the same attitudes, values, interests, and demographics as ourselves. People tend to pursue good-looking others, but people usually end up dating and marrying people of the same level of physical attractiveness as themselves; this trend is called assortative mating. Finally, the Romeo and Juliet effect occurs when attraction to someone is increased because one's friends and family disapprove.

List of Terms

Learning Objectives	Key Terms
8.1 Interpret how facial structure and body types predict attraction.	Bilateral symmetry Composite faces Averaged faces Procedural artifact Neotenous features Waist-to-hips ratio Waist-to-shoulders ratio Halo effect What-is-beautiful-is-good effect
8.2 Interpret how reciprocity, body language, and personality predict attraction.	Reciprocity principle Unrequited love Stalking Nonverbal communication Proceptive behaviors Rejective behaviors Social allergens
8.3 Analyze how certain situations or environments lead to increased attraction.	Misattribution of arousal Excitation transfer Attraction-similarity hypothesis Matching hypothesis Assortative mating Subjective norms Romeo and Juliet effect Reactance

9

Sexuality

Big Questions	Learning Objectives
1. What is the sexual spectrum?	9.1 Differentiate categorical versus continuous views of sex and sexual orientation.
2. How do people vary in their sexual desires?	9.2 Explain variations in sexual fantasy, consensual nonmonogamy, and paraphilias.
3. How does culture influence sexual thoughts and behaviors?	9.3 Analyze how culture and technology influence sexual scripts, dating, and pornography.

The American College Health Association (2017) conducts a national survey every semester, asking college and university students about their behaviors in nine areas. One of those areas is sexual behavior. Here are just a few of the interesting findings from this survey, given in fall 2017:

- About 63% of college men and 65% of college women have had sex at least once in the past year. (Note, that means that about 4 in 10 *haven't* had sex this year.)

- Of the people who are having sex, about 10% of both men and women in college have had four or more sexual partners in the last 12 months.

- Of the students who said they're having vaginal sex, just under half (46%) said they used a condom.

- The distribution of self-identified sexual orientation among the students was

    o 85% heterosexual,

    o 6% bisexual,

    o 2% gay or lesbian,

       o   2% pansexual,

       o   1% asexual,

       o   about 4% queer, questioning, or other.

Sexuality can be a very important part of life, for people who are having sex and for people who aren't. Sexual messages in mass media, advertisements, music, and so on are unavoidable in today's world. Peer pressure to engage in sexual activity can be strong. While the very serious topic of sexual assault is covered in a later chapter, this chapter focuses on consensual sexual behaviors and the wide variation found on the sexual spectrum.

What Is the Sexual Spectrum?

In the very first chapter of this book, we discussed the idea of "continuous" versus "categorical" ways of thinking about the world and concepts in it. You'll recall in that chapter, the topic was whether to think about intimate relationships in terms of different categories—like friendships versus romantic partners—or in terms of a continuum or range, moving along a line from one extreme anchor (like "hate") to another (like "love"). What if sex, sexual orientation, and sexual behaviors are variables that should be on a continuous scale rather than a categorical one?

The idea of a **sexual spectrum** is that sexuality and gender are not always distinct, mutually exclusive categories; instead, they range on a fluid, flexible continuum. Perhaps the easiest way to think about this fluidity is to first consider **gender expression**, or how people present themselves to others in terms of their masculinity or femininity. It's easy to see how people can range from very masculine to very feminine, or express anything in the middle. Most people already think about psychological gender as a continuous variable. We can identify people who are masculine women or feminine men, and we accept this without thinking too much about it.

It might be harder to think about sex, or the biological label given to us at birth, as continuous. It's "men are from Mars, women are from Venus," right? Until very recently, male versus female bathroom signs went unquestioned—of course we wouldn't need any other options. But as LGBTQIA advocates (that's lesbian, gay, bisexual, transgender, queer/questioning, intersex, and ally) have found increasing opportunities to voice their needs and to find support, this seemingly basic idea has been called into question. In fact, the idea that there are only two sex options—male and female—is now considered by many researchers a false dichotomy (sometimes called a false binary). Remember from Chapter 6: A false dichotomy is when an issue is presented as if there are only two choices, but it leaves out the possibility of a third, fourth, or fifth choice or even of some kind of compromise or middle ground.

We'll begin this chapter by talking about people who don't seem to fit neatly into either of these boxes in terms of their biological sex. Then, we'll move on to talk about diversity in a great variety of sexual contexts including sexual orientation, chosen sexual behaviors, cross-cultural differences, and more.

More Than Two Sexes: Intersex Individuals

Gender is our sense of how masculine or feminine we are, while sex refers to our biological chromosomes, hormones, internal reproductive systems, and genitals. When a baby is born, the first question many people are asked is whether it's a boy or a girl. What if the answer is neither, both, or we're not sure yet?

Some people qualify for what the modern biomedical world calls **disorders of sex development** (or **DSD**). These "disorders" make up around 1.7% of the general population, according to the Intersex Campaign for Equality (see www.intersexequality.com), making them about as common as having red hair. And just like red hair, some parts of the world have much higher proportions of people with DSD. The category of DSD encompasses a very wide range of different "disorders" that include ambiguous genitals, unusual chromosome combinations (i.e., neither XX nor XY), and unusual levels of sex-relevant hormones like testosterone. A few examples are described in a minute.

But before we get to those examples, think about terminology for just a moment. The term "disorders of sex development" has certain implications. From a medical point of view, these individuals suffer from a problem—a "disorder" or "condition"—that should be *fixed*. By definition, then, the medical community is putting a stigma on everyone with any kind of variation from traditional male or female biology. As an alternative view, consider the now out-of-date former term for these individuals: **intersex**.

The term "intersex" referred to the exact same groups of people, but carried with it the connotation that there might be more than two options when it comes to biological sex. There are people who have both male and female chromosomes, hormones, and genitals in a wide variety of combinations. So instead of labeling these people as "broken" or "disordered" somehow, is it possible that they simply represent a more continuous way of thinking about biological sex? Certainly, some of these combinations lead to what might be considered difficulties or challenges in life—but so does being unusually tall or short, unusually intelligent or not, or unusually athletic or not . . . and we don't automatically label people with these characteristics as having a "disorder." So this book will continue to use the term intersex instead of DSD, because many scholars consider the term intersex to be more respectful and less stigmatizing.

Consider six examples of what we'll call intersex situations. Three are situations in which people have an unusual combination of chromosomes, and three are situations in which they have traditional chromosomes (XX or XY) but unusual prenatal hormone exposure or reactions. As a comparison, remember that most of us get an X chromosome from our mother's egg and either an X or Y chromosome from our father's sperm. XX combinations lead to us having a clitoris, uterus, ovaries, and prenatal exposure to estrogen. In contrast, XY combinations cause our fetal clitoris to grow into a penis, our gonads become testes instead of ovaries, and we have prenatal exposure to testosterone. While overly simplified, these two situations apply to the vast majority of people born around the world—but not everyone.

Unusual Chromosome Combinations

To start, it's possible that people receive an extra chromosome, resulting in a fetus with either an XXY or XYY combination. If it's XXY, it's called **Klinefelter syndrome** ("Klinefelter Syndrome," 2018). It results in people who have a physical body that's

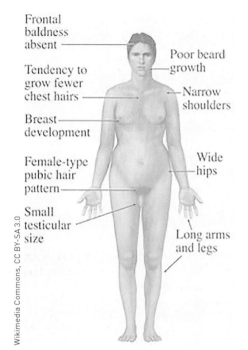

Frontal baldness absent

Poor beard growth

Tendency to grow fewer chest hairs

Narrow shoulders

Breast development

Wide hips

Female-type pubic hair pattern

Small testicular size

Long arms and legs

Wikimedia Commons, CC BY-SA 3.0

People born with Klinefelter Syndrome have bodies that appear to be a combination of traditionally male characteristics (such as a penis) and female characteristics (such as breasts).

a combination of traditional male and female characteristics. These individuals are usually tall with small penises and small, firm testicles—but they can also grow small breasts, have wide hips, and a pattern of pubic hair more often found on women. They usually can't grow a beard or reproduce children. In addition, they often have cognitive challenges and are more likely to be diagnosed with learning disorders.

Another combination is **47, XYY syndrome**, which is sometimes called **Supermale syndrome** because of the extra Y chromosome they have ("47, XYY Syndrome," 2018). Supermales are more likely (than individuals with Klinefelter syndrome) to have normal-sized testicles and penises and can usually have children—but they also tend to have delayed motor skills (such as walking or athletic movements), weak muscle tone, and flat feet. Sometimes they are also more likely to have mental health concerns like ADHD, depression, or anxiety—but it's unclear what the origins of these problems might be (e.g., biological versus social or environmental).

A third possibility is called **Turner syndrome**. Here, people are born not with an extra chromosome but with a missing one, leading to the combination represented as X0 (where the 0 means neither X nor Y; "Turner Syndrome," 2018). People with Turner Syndrome almost always "feel" female and self-identify as female, but their bodies have some unusual characteristics. They tend to be short (less than 5 feet) and their bodies typically don't develop as most women's do—they never grow breasts and their hips don't widen. Usually they don't menstruate and are infertile. Sometimes they can have extra folds of skin, and the folds are surgically removed when these are visible at birth (in the form of a "webbed neck"). About one-third of people with Turner syndrome have heart defects and/or kidney problems, but they seem to have normal levels of intelligence (unlike those with Klinefelter or Supermale syndrome).

Unusual Hormone Exposure

There are also intersex people who do have a typical XX or XY set of chromosomes, but something unusual happened in terms of the fetal exposure or reaction to prenatal hormones. One example is a situation called **androgen insensitivity syndrome** or AIS ("Androgen Insensitivity Syndrome," 2018). Here, despite the XY combination, the fetus doesn't respond when exposed to testosterone produced in the womb. This means that the baby's genitals remain in female form—a clitoris instead of a penis. AIS can range from "partial" to "complete," so babies with partial AIS can have genitals that are ambiguous: Is it a large clitoris or a small penis? Parents usually choose one sex or the other and raise their child accordingly, but the child might want to switch identities when they reach adulthood. This can mean not only changing your name, clothing, and so on, but it could also mean hormone injections or even surgeries.

A situation that could be considered the "opposite" of AIS is CAH, which stands for **congenital adrenal hyperplasia** ("Congenital Adrenal Hyperplasia," 2018). While CAH can affect both XX and XY people, when it applies to someone with XX chromosomes they are born with a "masculine" body, meaning they have a penis instead of a clitoris. They might still have ovaries and a uterus—but with a penis. In these cases, they are what used to be referred to as a hermaphrodite—someone with both male and female genitals. (Note, the term "hermaphrodite" is generally considered offensive today, but it has roots in Greek mythology; it's the combination of Hermes and Aphrodite, the male and female gods of love.) Many XX people with CAH self-identify as feeling female, but they are also more likely to be sexually attracted to other women, compared to other XX women without CAH.

Finally, consider **5-alpha reductase deficiency** ("5-Alpha Reductase Deficiency," 2018). Here, fetuses with XY chromosomes don't convert their prenatal testosterone to a hormone called dihydrotestosterone (DHT), which means they have a traditionally female-looking body with a vagina and clitoris when they are born. Their gonads are testes instead of ovaries, but those testes remain undescended in the body. The most interesting aspect of 5-alpha reductase is that when individuals with 5-alpha reductase deficiency reach puberty, their body suddenly responds normally to testosterone, which means that they spurt facial hair, get a deep voice, get taller, develop muscles, and both their scrotum and main sexual organ grow. In other words, their clitoris turns into a small penis when they're in middle school or junior high. Often, these individuals were raised as girls throughout childhood, but they usually switch to a male identity and live their adult lives as relatively "normal" men, marrying women (although they are often infertile). Interestingly, while this situation is very rare in the general population, there are some nations with larger-than-average incidents, such as in the Dominican Republic. There, the condition is so common that it has its own name: "guevedoces," which translates as "penis at twelve" (BBC, 2015).

With cases like this, it's a little easier to consider the idea that "male versus female" might be an oversimplified version of what biological sex really means. Some people have even suggested that English is biased toward the false dichotomy in that our only singular pronouns for people are "he" or "she"; there's no gender-neutral option. To resolve this, one relatively recent idea is a third pronoun called "ze." For example, a sentence could be: *"I called zir to ask if I could borrow zir textbook; ze then handed it to me."* Students at both Oxford University in England and the University of Minnesota have pushed for use of "ze" on campus (Lerner, 2016; Pells, 2016), and a recent novel from the *Star Wars* franchise made headlines when one of the characters was described using gender-neutral pronouns (Wendig, 2016; see *"Star Wars Report,"* 2016).

Jeff Kravitz/FilmMagic

There are more transgender celebrities now than ever before, including Caitlyn Jenner, Carmen Carrera, and Chaz Bono.

The Transgender Revolution

There are also people who never feel comfortable in the sex assigned to them at birth, even if they are "typical" in terms of their chromosomes or hormones. The acceptable and respectful term for these individuals today is **transgender**. In contrast, **cisgender** refers to people who do feel comfortable with the sex assigned to them at birth and never wish to change it. Celebrities such as Caitlyn Jenner, Carmen Carrera, and Chaz Bono have received a lot of attention for their transgender status. Whether this attention is positive or negative, it has certainly brought the very possibility that people could be transgender in the forefront of people's minds as never before in most cultures.

Being transgender has nothing to do with sexual orientation; trans people can be attracted to men, women, intersex people, other trans people—it's irrelevant to their own identity as male or female. And increasingly, trans people are asking for equal civil rights and resources. For example, March 31 has been named "Transgender Day of Visibility" (Brabaw, 2017). Many states have now passed legislation called "bathroom bills" that regulate what kinds of people are legally allowed to use which bathrooms made available in public places, or whether gender-inclusive bathrooms have to be provided (Brabaw, 2017). Increasingly, television shows and movies have been written to include transgender characters as well, such as the film *The Danish Girl* (Bevan & Chasin, 2015), the show *Orange Is the New Black* (Burley, 2013–present), and the popular daytime talk show *Ellen* (DeGeneres & Lassner, 2003–present).

If you want to support transgender people but aren't quite sure where to start, here's a list of "Tips for Allies of Transgender People" from the Gay & Lesbian Alliance Against Defamation (GLAAD, 2018) and you can go to www.glaad.org for more information:

- You can't tell if someone is transgender just by looking.

- Don't make assumptions about a transgender person's sexual orientation.

- If you don't know what pronouns to use, listen first.

- Don't ask a transgender person what their "real name" is.

- Understand the differences between "coming out" as LGB and "coming out" as transgender.

- Be careful about confidentiality, disclosure, and "outing."

- Respect the terminology a transgender person uses to describe their identity.

- Be patient with a person who is questioning or exploring their gender identity.

- Understand there is no "right" or "wrong" way to transition and that it is different for every person.

- Don't ask about a transgender person's genitals, surgical status, or sex life.

- Avoid backhanded compliments (e.g., "You're so good looking, I never would have thought you're trans") and "helpful" hints to how they should live.

- Challenge anti-transgender remarks or jokes in public spaces.

- Support all-gender public restrooms.

- Help make your company, university, or group trans-inclusive.

- Listen to transgender people.

- Know your limits as an ally.

Continuous Models of Sexual Orientation

The sections so far in this chapter have talked about gender and sex identity—but not about sexual behaviors. Whether you're male, female, intersex, or transgender doesn't tell us anything about to whom you are sexually attracted. But we started the chapter on those topics because they help illustrate that concepts like sex and gender might be continuous variables, not categorical. The same might be true for sexual orientation.

Traditionally, sexual orientation is set up in a categorical system of **heterosexual** (attraction to only the "opposite" sex) versus **homosexual** (attraction to only the same sex). **Bisexual**, attraction to both men and women, is a step forward to break down this false dichotomy—but the term "bi" itself implies only two options. Instead, the more recent term **pansexual** has been added to many people's vocabulary as an orientation toward some people over others regardless of sex or gender identity. Pansexual people aren't attracted to *everyone;* they just don't focus on the sex label of the other person (e.g., man or woman) when it comes to whether they're sexy. In contrast, **asexual** people are those who desire loving, intimate relationships with other people but simply aren't very interested in engaging in sexual activities (see Bogaert, 2004; Hinderliter, 2009; Walton, Lykins, & Bhullar, 2016).

Note that thinking about sexual orientation in boxes or categories—even if those categories include possibilities like pansexuality—is still not a continuous system that allows people to move back and forth with fluidity across relationships or across time. There are two alternative ways to think about sexual orientation, both of which are truer to the idea of sexuality on a spectrum.

The Kinsey One-Dimensional Continuum

The most famous model for a continuous way to think about sexual orientation was offered by the sex researcher Alfred Kinsey over 70 years ago (Kinsey, Pomeroy, & Martin, 1948). As you can see in Figure 9.1, sexuality ranges from a score of 0, indicating exclusively heterosexual to 6, indicating exclusively homosexual. Kinsey believed that sexual orientation included not only actual behaviors that we've carried out but also our fantasies and secret desires. Thus, he argued that the vast majority of people are actually somewhere in the middle of the continuum, even if it's just a little bit (what modern culture has dubbed "bi-curious"; Kinsey, Pomeroy, Martin, & Gebhard, 1953). Illustrating the overall point of a continuous model over a categorical one, Kinsey famously wrote:

Males do not represent two discrete populations, heterosexual and homosexual. The world is not to be divided into sheep and goats. Not all things are black nor all things white. It is a fundamental of taxonomy that nature rarely deals

FIGURE 9.1 ● The Kinsey Continuum of Sexual Orientation

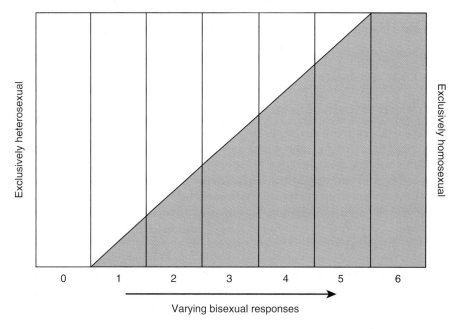

Sex researcher Alfred Kinsey suggested that sexual orientation could be mapped on a one-dimensional continuum with heterosexuality on one end and homosexuality on the other.

with discrete categories. Only the human mind invents categories and tries to force facts into separated pigeon-holes. The living world is a continuum in each and every one of its aspects. The sooner we learn this concerning human sexual behavior the sooner we shall reach a sound understanding of the realities of sex. (Kinsey et al., 1948, p. 639)

One way that the Kinsey scale has influenced current culture and terminology is the phrase "men who have sex with men," or MSM (Sandfort & Dodge, 2009). This phrase is often used in medical settings like giving blood or whether people are at higher risk for sexually transmitted infections. It refers to men who engage in a wide variety of sexual behaviors with other men but do not label themselves as gay or even bisexual. This seemingly counterintuitive situation may reflect cultures in which homosexuality is not socially accepted or may even be illegal; thus, people avoid the label but engage in the behavior anyway (e.g., Thaczuk, 2007).

The Storms Two-Dimensional Model

While Kinsey believed that sexual orientation was on a one-dimensional range with two extreme endpoints, another possibility was suggested in 1978 by psychologist Michael Storms (Storms, 1978, 1980). Storms believed that sexual orientation should be plotted on two separate dimensions instead of one dimension, as shown in Figure 9.2. Someone could be very much attracted to people of the "opposite" sex and just a little attracted to people of the same sex—and these two types of attraction might be independent from each other. The upper-righthand corner in Storms's original model was labeled bisexual, but we've added pansexual here to update the terminology.

Storms's (1978, 1980) model thus allows for the inclusion of asexuality and bi- or pansexuality. (Kinsey did acknowledge asexuals; he just didn't include them in his model.) Although Figure 9.2 still shows these sexual orientations as four boxes or categories, the point is that either axis or dimension has a range, resulting in a wide spectrum of possibilities. In his own words, Storms (1980) explains the major difference he sees between Kinsey's model and his own:

> The two-dimensional model of sexual orientation differs most clearly from Kinsey's unidimensional model in the position assigned to bisexuals. On Kinsey's unidimensional scale an individual loses degrees of one orientation as he or she moves toward the opposite end of the scale; thus, bisexuals are seen as half heterosexual and half homosexual or a compromise somewhere between the two extremes. In a two-dimensional system bisexuals are viewed as having high degrees of both homosexuality and heterosexuality, not moderate amounts of each. (p. 785)

FIGURE 9.2 ● The Storms Model of Sexual Orientation

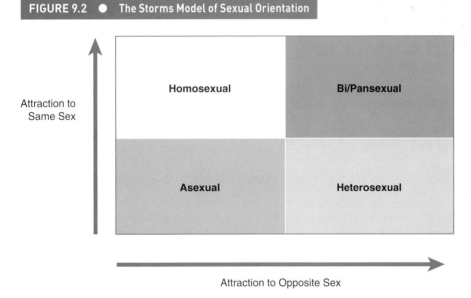

Storms expanded Kinsey's model by proposing two separate dimensions of sexual attraction that can each range in degree.

Heteroflexibility is the idea that people can experiment with same-sex attraction or behaviors but might still self-identify as heterosexual overall (Diamond, 2005). While depictions of heteroflexibility in popular culture might, on the surface, seem like a step forward in celebrating nonheterosexual forms of sexuality, sometimes they can also be seen as trivializing or fetishizing gay and lesbian behaviors (Wilkinson, 1996). When Katy Perry's song "I Kissed a Girl" came out, some critics believed it was simply using heteroflexibility to make money and get press attention. For another example of how celebrities appear to play with heteroflexibility, potentially just as publicity stunts, see the "Relationships and Popular Culture" feature.

The overall point of this beginning section of the chapter is mostly to encourage critical thinking about how we conceptualize gender, sex, and sexual orientation. While it seems to be human nature to label people and to put them into neat categories, it might limit people's ability to explore their true nature.

RELATIONSHIPS AND POPULAR CULTURE

Celebrity Lesbian Kisses

Christopher Polk/FilmMagic

When Madonna and Britney Spears kissed during the 2003 MTV Video Music Awards, people certainly talked about it. To some, it seemed like a spontaneous example of two women exploring their sexuality. Afterward, Spears glowed about it, saying, "This is something I've dreamt about since I was a little girl. I cannot believe this just like freakin' happened. I am on a major high right now. I feel very cool" (Diamond, 2005, and originally quoted from Warn, 2003).

But it was all planned, according to Spears's manager Larry Rudolph (Geffen, 2014). And not everyone appreciated it. As sex researcher Lisa

Diamond reviewed, some of the people posting in an online chatroom devoted exclusively to reviewing the incident expressed doubts:

> Easy there, boys. Don't you realize when your chain is being jerked? Madonna . . . is just trying to be as outrageous as possible to stay in the headlines.

> MTV depends on this kind of material to promote their awards shows. By Madonna and Britney kissing, MTV now has tons of material to show the world how "exciting" their programming is.

> I got nothing against REAL passion-driven kissing between any two humans. It's just that these are not real people, they are products. (Diamond, 2005, p. 107)

And this kind of playing with heteroflexibility (just as a publicity stunt) is potentially harmful to the LGBTQIA movement, as "the potential of these kisses to challenge rigid, dichotomous models of sexuality was altogether lost on a viewing public that is all-too-accustomed to the economically motivated packaging and marketing of sexual controversy" (Diamond, 2005, p. 107).

CHECK YOUR UNDERSTANDING

9.1 Conditions such as usual chromosome combinations (e.g., XXY or XYY) used to be referred to as "intersex." The biomedical term for these conditions is now:

a. Polysex
b. Hermaphroditic disorders
c. Ambiguous sexual dysfunctions
d. Disorders of sex development

9.2 Amanda is a woman, but she is very short (around 4 feet, 10 inches tall), has no breasts, and has been diagnosed with a heart condition. She most likely has which condition listed below?

a. Klinefelter syndrome
b. Turner syndrome
c. Congenital adrenal hyperplasia
d. 5-Alpha reductase syndrome

9.3 Kinsey developed a continuous model of sexual orientation that had one dimension with two, opposite ends. Storms then developed a model with two dimensions. What were those two dimensions?

a. Childhood preferences, adult preferences
b. Actual experiences, fantasy experiences
c. Thoughts, behaviors
d. Attraction to same sex, attraction to opposite sex

APPLICATION ACTIVITY

Choose one of the movies on this list (or another, as approved by your instructor) and write a paragraph or two on how it represents gender, sex, and sexual orientation. Do you think the movie helps the LGBTQIA movement or hurts it? Why?

The Danish Girl	But I'm a Cheerleader	Love, Simon
Chasing Amy	The Hours	Deadpool
The Crying Game	The Birdcage	Boys Don't Cry

CRITICAL THINKING

- About 90% of people in the United States self-identify as exclusively heterosexual, but only 85% of college-age people do so. Does this mean that other orientations (such as homosexual or pansexual) are increasing in frequency, or does it mean that more people are simply comfortable in choosing to identify as something other than "exclusively heterosexual"? What will happen to the percentage (will it go up, down, or stay the same) in 50 years or 100 years? Explain the reasons or evidence you have to back up your opinion.

(Continued)

(Continued)

- An important controversy for intersex people is whether infants born with ambiguous genitals (large clitoris or small penis) should have surgery to assign them to a "normal" or typical sex. Many doctors and psychologists believe that early surgery is needed (before the age of 2 years) so that the child will fit in with their peers, avoid bullying, and avoid any negativity from parents who are unaccepting of their child's unusual situation. Many other doctors and psychologists, however, believe that no surgery should be done on people until they are old enough to decide what they want for themselves. What do you think about this highly contested debate, and why?

- Compare and contrast the traditional, categorical model of sexual orientation to the Kinsey one-dimensional model and the Storms two-dimensional model. Are there advantages and disadvantages to each, in terms of public understanding, developing research ideas, and so on? Which model do you personally prefer, and why?

Answers to the Check Your Understanding Questions

9.1 d, 9.2 b, and 9.3 d.

How Do People Vary in Their Sexual Desires?

Sexual appetites and interests have as much variation as there are people on the planet. That said, scientific research on human sexuality has only recently gained enough popularity to get mainstream attention by colleges and universities, entire academic conferences devoted to the subject, and several scholarly journals about a variety of different aspects of sexuality. In this section of the chapter, we'll discuss different preferences when it comes to how people navigate the sexual world, ranging from fantasy to sex within a relationship to particular fetishes and sexual "disorders." Even if some of the ideas in this section don't seem appealing to you, the scholarly pursuit of understanding sexuality is fascinating.

Sexual Fantasies

In his book *Tell Me What You Want* (Lehmiller, 2018b), sex researcher Justin Lehmiller describes how he conducted one of the most comprehensive self-report studies of sexual fantasy. He defines a sexual fantasy as a mental picture that turns you on while you're awake (dreams don't count unless you relive them while you're conscious and in control of the images). Over 4,000 people from all 50 U.S. states completed a survey that included 369 questions about what they want, what they've done, and how they feel about it. The participants were diverse, ranging in age from 18 to 87 years and with a variety of sexual and gender identities.

Here are some of Lehmiller's "key findings":

- 97% of the participants reporting having sexual fantasies of some kind.

- By far, the most common fantasy was group sex (threesomes, orgies, or "gangbangs").

- 60% of people said they fantasized about inflicting physical pain on someone, and 65% said they fantasized about receiving pain.

- Only 7% of people said they fantasize about celebrities (although the top choice was Scarlett Johansson), while 51% said they frequently fantasize about their current intimate partner.

- Many people said their fantasies were influenced by something they had seen in pornography.

- Some fantasies included becoming other people or changing their bodies in some way (such as by becoming someone of the "opposite" sex or changing the size of a body part).

- Republicans were more likely to fantasize about "immoral" things (like infidelity or orgies).

- Less than one-third of people said they had actually acted out their biggest or favorite fantasy—but for those who did, the vast majority said it was a positive experience.

To start a bit of a deeper dive into Lehmiller's results, first consider Table 9.1. It shows how many people self-reported that they "often" (on a scale from "never" to "often") fantasize about certain sexual acts they could do with a partner, broken down by men compared to women. Two of Lehmiller's conclusions about what you can see in the table are that (1) both men and women fantasize about variety in terms of sex acts and (2) while there are some differences, there is also a lot in common between what men and women want.

Moving beyond the results from Table 9.1, sexual fantasies can certainly involve more than just thinking about which of your body parts you want to smoosh into or against someone else's body parts. To examine patterns across his thousands of participants, Lehmiller (2018b) asked them to whittle down their favorite fantasy of all time into a single word (like "orgy" or "whipping"), then he created groups of fantasies that seemed to go together with an overarching theme. Seven popular themes emerged and are briefly described here from most to least common:

1. *Multipartner sex:* Over one-third of people said this was their favorite fantasy, with threesomes on most people's minds. Heterosexual men mostly wanted to be with two women at once, whereas heterosexual women didn't care so much about the sex of their threesome partners.

2. *Power, control, and rough sex:* About one-quarter of people fantasize about BDSM sex, which stands for bondage, discipline or dominance, submission (or sometimes sadism), and masochism. These fantasies focus on things like tying your partner up, spanking, whipping, and so on. Importantly, these fantasies still include consent: The person fantasizing was in control of what happened.

3. *Novelty, adventure, and variety:* These fantasies include activities not usually done by the person (like oral/anal sex), sex in new places (like a beach or airplane), and unexpected or spontaneous sex.

TABLE 9.1 ● Percentage of People Who "Often" Fantasize About Various Sex Acts	
	Percentage
Kissing	
● Men	57.5%
● Women	69.3%
Mutual masturbation	
● Men	35.5%
● Women	31.8%
Giving oral sex	
● Men	69.6%
● Women	57.1%
Receiving oral sex	
● Men	66.6%
● Women	58.1%
Simultaneous oral sex ("69")	
● Men	41.7%
● Women	21.6%
Vaginal intercourse	
● Men	75.4%
● Women	83.7%
Giving anal sex (with a penis or strap-on)	
● Men	36.9%
● Women	7.0%
Receiving anal sex	
● Men	19.5%
● Women	19.2%
Using sex toys	
● Men	27.0%
● Women	31.3%

These are a few sex acts that some people fantasize about.

4. *Taboo and forbidden sex:* Some people want to experience things that are generally frowned upon, such as voyeurism or urination during sex (for more, see the section on fetishes and paraphilias).

5. *Partner sharing:* Instead of a threesome, partner sharing comes in three forms: (a) swinging or partner swapping with another couple, (b) being in an "open" relationship, and (c) polyamory. This will be discussed in the section later in this chapter on open relationships.

6. *Passion and romance:* Many people simply fantasized about having intimate encounters that were characterized as being intensely desired, validated, loved, and bonded to their partner. Both men and women expressed this fantasy.

7. *Erotic flexibility:* Finally, some people were aroused by the thought of changing themselves or their partners in physical ways, such as switching up their own gender or increasing the size of particular body parts.

Of course, there have been dozens (if not hundreds) of *other* studies done on the content, origins, and outcomes of different fantasies in different types of people. While it would be impossible to review all of the important research here, we can sample just a few tastes. For example, another set of researchers also wanted to catalog the frequency of different sexual fantasies (Joyal, Cossette, & Lapierre, 2015). They were specifically interested in the fantasies of "normal" people, meaning people who did not have clinical disorders and were not sex criminals. They reviewed 20 studies done by other people and offered new data from over 1500 adults they surveyed with 55 questions about their sexual interests (to see example items, read the "What's My Score?" feature).

Joyal et al. (2015) found that both men and women commonly fantasize about having sex in unusual and/or public places, mutual masturbation, BDSM sex, and sex with celebrities. In this way, both studies (Joyal et al., 2015; Lehmiller, 2018b) showed replication. The study by Joyal and colleagues also found that men reported having more fantasies in general, especially fantasies about either watching two women make love or engaging in a threesome with two women. Out of 55 sexual fantasy options, their results showed that only two were rare (defined as being interesting to less than 4% of their participants): having sex with children and having sex with an animal.

Sex differences in sexual fantasies were also explored by Ellis and Symons (1990), who suggested an evolutionary perspective. They argued that men have more "explicit" fantasies (stressing overt sexual gratification) and women have more "implicit" fantasies (embedding sex within an emotional or commitment context). This hypothesis aligns with the ideas you read about in Chapter 4, where men are more sexually promiscuous and women are more driven by relationship commitment. Supporting the idea that sex differences in fantasy are important, another study found that men's fantasies were more likely than women's to feature themselves as "dominant and in power" (Zurbriggen & Yost, 2004, p. 292), especially when those men had high scores in sexist attitudes and victim blaming for sexual assault survivors. Their article featured both quantitative and qualitative data, including quotations from people describing their fantasies. One example of a dominance fantasy from a man was as follows:

Another frequent sexual fantasy is having anal sex with a woman. I did this a lot in reality with my ex-girlfriend and really enjoyed it. She let me pull her hair and asked me to be rough with her. I like the way it makes me feel; dominant

WHAT'S MY SCORE?

Measuring Sexual Fantasies

Here is a sample of some of the items used in one study that measured sexual interests in the general population (Joyal et al., 2015). Note that their scale listed 55 different fantasies; the items shown here are just examples from the larger scale.

Instructions: Be as honest as possible when you rate your *intensity of interest* for each item below, using this scale:

1	2	3	4	5	6	7
Not at all	Very weak	Weak	Mild	Moderate	Strong	Very strong

_____ 1. I like to feel romantic emotions during a sexual relationship.

_____ 2. I have fantasized about having sex in an unusual place (e.g., in the office; public toilets).

_____ 3. I have fantasized about having sex with two women.

_____ 4. I have fantasized about being dominated sexually.

_____ 5. I have fantasized about having sex with a star or a well-known person.

_____ 6. I have fantasized about dominating someone sexually.

_____ 7. I have fantasized about being tied up by someone in order to obtain sexual pleasure.

_____ 8. I have fantasized about having anal sex.

_____ 9. I have fantasized about watching someone undress without him or her knowing.

_____ 10. I have fantasized about having sex with someone much older than me.

_____ 11. I have fantasized about having sex with two men.

_____ 12. I have fantasized about being photographed or filmed during a sexual relationship.

_____ 13. I have fantasized about indulging in sexual swinging with a couple that I do not know.

_____ 14. I have fantasized about having sex with a fetish or nonsexual object.

_____ 15. I have fantasized about having sex with a prostitute or stripper.

_____ 16. I have fantasized about showing myself naked or partially naked in a public place.

_____ 17. I have fantasized about watching two people make love.

_____ 18. I have fantasized about my partner urinating on me.

_____ 19. I have fantasized about having sex with an animal.

_____ 20. I have fantasized about being spanked or whipped to obtain sexual pleasure.

Scoring: This scale does not require adding items or finding the average score, as each individual item is designed to test whether someone has that particular fantasy. The purpose of having a scale like this one is to have the ability to measure how common or rare each fantasy is in a large group of people.

Source: Joyal et al. (2015).

Critical Thinking: Scales such as this one—about people's most secret and intimate thoughts—may have trouble with people answering honestly. This might be especially true for items that indicate illegal behavior (such as fantasies about having sex with children). What kinds of procedural safeguards could researchers use to increase honest responses in their participants?

and in control. Usually we're in a bed and both totally naked. Sometimes the woman is on "all fours" and sometimes I grab her breasts and squeeze them. Then I usually push her flat on her stomach and continue being rough until I climax deep inside of her. (Zurbriggen & Yost, 2004, p. 293)

Notice that two findings seem to have emerged across several of the studies reviewed here. First, a common fantasy for both men and women is having sex with people other than one's partner (either through threesomes or partner sharing). Second, many people admit to having fantasies that involve fetishes (such as BDSM sex). The next two sections of this chapter focus on each of these ideas in more depth.

"Open" Relationships: Consensual Nonmonogamy

For many people, once they're in a committed, long-term relationship, they assume that relationship will be **monogamous**, meaning both people agree to only have sex with each other. Of course, cheating and affairs still happen. While it's hard to tell how common infidelity is (because most people don't like to admit it), some research studies estimate it in at least 13% of married couples and more in cohabiting and dating couples (Atkins, Baucom, & Jacobson, 2001; Feldman & Cauffman, 1999a, 1999b).

If infidelity is discovered by the other partner, the outcomes are probably not hard to guess: They include anger, lower trust, lower self-confidence and self-esteem, higher depression, and often the end of the relationship (Blow & Hartnett, 2005; Charny & Parnass, 1995; Previti & Amato, 2004; Spanier & Margolis, 1983). (Interestingly, Previti and Amato [2004] note that because it would be obviously unethical to do true experiments in which infidelity is manipulated, correlations among these variables don't necessarily tell us about causal relationships. Cheating might cause all of these outcomes, or it might be more likely in relationships that were already high in anger, low in trust, and so on. This is a good example of "correlation does not imply causation.")

Are the only options monogamy or cheating? No. Some couples come to a mutual agreement that one or both of them can engage in sexual activities with other people. How, exactly, this arrangement is made varies quite a bit, but the general term for a more "open" relationship between two people who remain committed but aren't sexually exclusive with each other is **consensual nonmonogamy**.

Clearly, from the sexual fantasy research, some couples engage in threesomes or group sex in which both original couple members are present, but they add one or more new people to the mix. There are two other possible types of consensual nonmonogamy (we'll call it CNM). **Swinging** refers to couples who find another couple and swap partners for the evening. In contrast, **polyamory** is when partners mutually agree that one or both of them can have additional sexual or romantic partners. This is not infidelity or cheating because both people in the relationship have agreed to it in advance and have likely set up "rules" for what is and is not allowed (for example, condoms must be used during "extra" encounters).

Older research on CNM, such as a pioneering study that collected data in the 1970s with over 6000 married couples, found that around a quarter of them (up to 28%) had a mutual agreement that allowed extramarital sex (Blumstein & Schwartz, 1983). Those numbers were replicated in 2002 when the National Survey of Family Growth study found that 18% of women and 23% of men were in CNM relationships (Aral & Leichliter, 2010). However, researchers have recently questioned those statistics, arguing that they might be overestimates that included both actual CNM and infidelity or affairs (Rubin, Moors, Matsick, Ziegler, & Conley, 2014). Rubin et al. (2014) argue that the real estimate might be more like 4% to 5% of couples for whom they really are both mutually open to the idea of polyamory.

Regardless of how common it might be, several interesting studies have investigated how CNM couples work and fare, in terms of happiness. Here are some examples of interesting findings from those investigations:

- Most studies conducted on CNM couples have focused on White, heterosexual, middle- to upper-class participants (for a review of 36 studies, see Sheff & Hammers, 2011). When Rubin et al. (2014) tested for demographic differences, they found that people who had CNM relationship were more likely to be male than female—and that CNM was more popular with homo-, bi-, or pansexuals than with heterosexuals. No differences were found for racial groups.

- Another study replicated the finding that sexual orientation minority participants were more likely than heterosexuals to be in CNM relationships (Balzarini et al., 2019). They also found more CNM in people who were divorced, non-Christian, Libertarian, and/or making less than $40,000 per year.

- About 26% of people in CNM relationships have been the victims of discrimination and social stigma, such as in custody cases, housing decisions, and workplace hirings and firings (Lesher, 2013).

- Two studies found that people who have CNM relationships are more likely to practice safe sex (using condoms, sterilizing sex toys), compared to people who are simply having affairs or cheating on their partners (Conley, Moors, Ziegler, & Karathanasis, 2012; Lehmiller, 2015).

- One of the most common CNM arrangements is that someone has two long-term partners, constituting a "primary" and a "secondary" relationship (Veaux & Rickert, 2014; Wosick-Correa, 2010). One study that explored differences between the two (Balzarini et al., 2017) found that primary relationships had lasted longer (an average of 8 years compared to 2 years for secondaries) and that the primary partner in the arrangement received more benefits such as higher investments of time and resources, commitment, and communication. The only benefit that the secondary relationship got was more time spent on sexual activity.

- Finally, one study asked participants to consider either monogamous or CNM relationships and to judge each on a variety of factors (Conley, Moors, Matsick, & Ziegler, 2013). Most participants reported the belief that monogamy was superior on almost every variable tested, such as being safer in terms of protection against STIs, being emotionally closer, being more romantic, promoting intimacy and companionship, and avoiding jealousy. There were only two variables where participants admitted that CNM relationships might be better: avoiding boredom and allowing for individual independence.

Paraphilias and Sexual Fetishes

Sexual appetites, or what "turns people on," are clearly varied, as some of the research already discussed shows. While some of these appetites are fairly common, such as fantasizing about threesomes, others are rare. The American Psychiatric Association (2013) publishes a book called the *Diagnostic and Statistical Manual of Mental Disorders,* and we're currently on the fifth edition (the book is abbreviated DSM-5). This book catalogs every currently recognized mental disorder, ranging from depression through anxiety to schizophrenia, and more. One of the categories is **paraphilia**, or any "persistent, intense, atypical sexual arousal pattern."

Note, then, that a paraphilia is just an uncommon but intense turn-on that lasts a while (the DSM-5 threshold is at least 6 months). So just having a paraphilia doesn't necessarily mean someone should worry about it. It only becomes a **paraphilic disorder**, according to the DSM-5, if the arousal pattern causes distress or impairment to the person with the paraphilia *or* it could potentially harm someone else. So, if you just happen to find leather boots super sexy, it doesn't mean it's a problem unless it's causing harm to yourself or others (e.g., you can't get aroused unless you see or wear leather boots, or your boot expenses exceed your income).

There are eight particular categories that the DSM lists which could be just paraphilias or could reach the level of paraphilic disorders, depending on their intensity and how the person with these interests uses them. For example, someone who is turned on by the idea of dominance might have a paraphilia if they work with a willing, consenting partner to engage in sexual behaviors—but it becomes a disorder if the person who likes dominance starts to exert power over others without their knowledge or consent. When sexual arousal is obtained through nonconsensual behaviors that victimize another person, it's called a **coercive paraphilia**.

You can see the eight categories in Table 9.2. The top of the table alphabetically lists the eight paraphilias that are, relatively speaking, more common, and the bottom of the table also lists a few less common paraphilias. The left column of Table 9.2 shows the term for each paraphilia, and the right column provides the definition. This table lists only a small number of possible paraphilias; you can get more complete lists online.

TABLE 9.2 ● Example Paraphilias: Terms and Definitions	
Most Common Paraphilias	
Exhibitionism	Exposure of genitals to others, having sex in public
Fetishism	Arousal from objects or particular, nongenital body parts
Frotteurism	Touching or rubbing against an unsuspecting person in public
Pedophilia	Arousal from children
Sexual masochism	Being whipped, spanked, tied up, or receiving pain
Sexual sadism	Whipping, spanking, tying up, or causing pain
Transvestism	Cross-dressing for the purpose of sexual pleasure
Voyeurism	Watching others without their knowledge while they are taking clothes off, naked, or having sex
Less Common Paraphilias	
Acrotomophilia	Sexual interest in people with limb amputations
Autoerotic asphyxiation	Increased arousal from self-strangulation before orgasm
Coprophilia	Arousal from feces or use of feces during sex
Eproctophilia	Arousal from flatulence (farting)
Klismaphilia	Use of enemas for sexual pleasure
Necrophilia	Sex with, rubbing, or touching dead people
Telephone scatologia	Arousal from obscene phone calls
Urophilia	Arousal from urine or use of urine during sex
Zoophilia	Sexual activity with animals (a.k.a. "bestiality")

One of the most common types of paraphilia is a **fetish**, which is sexual arousal from either an inanimate object (like shoes, leather clothing, underwear, or panty-hose) or a nongenital body part (like feet, hair braids, or breasts). Fetishes are generally benign until they become extreme and involve criminal behavior, such as breaking into someone's home to steal their shoes (e.g., Chalkley & Powell, 1983; Kafka, 2010). A fetish might become a problem if the focus on a particular body part is so extreme that the partner with the preference fails to communicate with their partner or see them as a whole person, instead of just the body part of interest (Kafka, 2010). Still, about 30% of men and 23% of women self-report experiencing some form of fetish-ism, at some point in their lives (Joyal & Carpentier, 2017).

When people have an actual, diagnosable paraphilia, it is their dominant sexual interest, not just a light preference. They might engage in sexual behaviors focused on the paraphilia every day, or even multiple times in a day (American Psychiatric Association, 2013). Even when the paraphilia becomes expensive, troubling, or even exhausting, people with paraphilias can feel that they are so rewarding, they are almost impossible to resist—basically, becoming an obsession (Lehne, 2009). People with this level of paraphilia should seek treatment, as paraphilias are no excuse for illegal or victimizing behavior (e.g., Seligman & Hardenburg, 2000).

A final note about paraphilias: You might be wondering where the word "nymphomania" is. **Nymphomania** is simply a pejorative, disapproving term for people who supposedly have excessive interest in sexual activity. This is *not* an official, APA-approved term, condition, or disorder (American Psychiatric Association, 2013). Instead, it's a term based on prejudice and double standards, as it's usually reserved for women and not men (Kaplan & Krueger, 2010). The closest clinical term used in several research studies on sexual behavior is **hypersexuality**, which is defined as an intense or excessive desire for frequent sexual activity (e.g., to the level where it interferes with other, daily activities or causes trouble within relationships).

Some people have coined the phrase "sex addiction" to refer to hypersexuality (although, again, the APA does not recognize this as a formal type of addiction). Research done on people who self-identify as sex addicts shows they probably do have a heightened sex drive; their brains are highly responsive to sexual images (Preidt, 2013; Steele, Staley, Fong, & Prause, 2013). Still, the APA hesitates to formalize hypersexuality because of the subjective nature of the question, how much sex is too much? There are also connotations to the word "addiction" that imply people with the problem have no control over it—which might mean they can use their "addiction" as an excuse for criminal or unethical behaviors (Coleman, 1996). More research needs to be done on causes, treatments, and maybe even definitions and distinctions among various sexual interests and behaviors.

CHECK YOUR UNDERSTANDING

9.4 Based on the study by Lehmiller (2018b), what is the most common sexual fantasy in people from the United States?

a. Novelty, adventure, and variety
b. Partner sharing
c. Multipartner sex
d. Passion and romance

9.5 Which of the people described below is most likely to engage in consensual nonmonogamy, based on statistics from the book?

a. Joan, who is Asian and makes $100,000 per year
b. Bill, who is White, male, and gay

c. Pele, who is Latino and Christian
d. Shun, who is Asian, married, and a Democrat

9.6 What is the term for someone who is sexually aroused by rubbing up against strangers in public places, such as subway stations or crowded parks?

a. Frotteurism
b. Coprophilia
c. Exhibitionism
d. Voyeurism

APPLICATION ACTIVITY

Find a case of a celebrity (e.g., a movie star or politician) who has claimed to have a "sex addiction." How did they talk about it? Did the person use it as an excuse for bad behavior? Did the person volunteer for any kind of therapy?

First, discuss this case study in depth. Then, provide your own opinion about whether "sex addiction" and/or "hypersexuality" should be included in the DSM-5 list of paraphilias and why (or why not).

CRITICAL THINKING

- The book and movie series based on *50 Shades of Grey* (James, 2012) highlighted BDSM fantasy and sexual behavior. The series was controversial, however, because many people who engage in BDSM sex said it portrayed people with this paraphilia as either victims of childhood abuse or abusive themselves, as adults. What is the line between consensual but painful behavior and abuse? How can people interested in BDSM behaviors ensure their pleasure and safety when exploring their sexual interests?

- What statistic or set of statistics from this section of the book was the most surprising to you, and why?

- People who engage in consensual nonmonogamy often say that the key for the arrangement to be successful is that partners need to be honest with each other and to control their potential jealousy. Do you think this is possible for most people? Why or why not? Do you think the ability to be happy in CNM relationships varies based on variables such as personality, culture, or one's relationship history? Choose two variables you think would matter and explain why.

Answers to the Check Your Understanding Questions
9.4 c, 9.5 b, and 9.6 a.

How Does Culture Influence Sexual Thoughts and Behaviors?

Through mass media such as movies, television, and advertising, we're constantly bombarded with messages about what to think and whom to admire. These messages are culturally approved and shape how we process the world, whether we want to admit it or not. The final section of this chapter covers four specific ways that culture can influence individual people's perceptions, desires, and sexual behaviors.

We'll talk about sexual expectations within a culture first, then compare expectations by looking at how they differ by culture. Then, we'll talk about how our culture has changed due to advances in technology and how that technology might be influencing sexuality via online sites and apps and via pornography.

Sexual Expectations and Sexual Scripts

One of the pioneers of research on sexual behaviors was Havelock Ellis, an English physician in the Victorian era. Ellis published a six-volume book called *Studies in the Psychology of Sex,* in which he suggested several ideas that were considered controversial at the time (Yarber & Sayad, 2016; see Goodfriend, 2012). In an era when many medical professionals thought that masturbation could lead to insanity, Ellis wrote that sexual behaviors among consenting adults (even when alone) were not dangerous and could even lead to positive results like decreased stress and anxiety (Yarber & Sayad, 2016). He also believed that homosexuality was not sinful perversion, but a biological fact that should be accepted just like any other sexual orientation.

Ellis's views were controversial because the European culture of the time was conservative and traditional, especially when it came to sexuality. But he was a theoretical revolutionary when he wrote that just because someone grew up within a given culture's sexual norms and values, those norms and values weren't the only legitimate belief systems (Goodfriend, 2012). He thought that the sexual expectations and behaviors from other cultures were just as valid. He believed in sexual diversity.

The particular expectations we learn from our culture are called **sexual scripts**. They are the assumptions we make about what particular events will occur in sexual settings, and in what order. The metaphor of a script implies that these expectations are put on us, like we're actors in our own lives: We live out the script our culture assigns to us (Gagnon & Simon, 1973; Laumann, Gagnon, Michael, & Michaels, 1994). We learn what to expect from mass media, from our parents, and from our more experienced peers. The traditional sexual script in the United States and other "Western" cultures goes something like this (Goodfriend, 2012):

- In middle school or high school, we start casually dating. We might have our first exclusive relationship, and we start to engage in sexual behaviors (like kissing). The general script assumes everyone is heterosexual and that men should generally be the initiators of sexual behaviors (Blanc, 2001).

- In high school or college, true sexual exploration is initiated; many people "lose" their virginity at this time. People start looking for future spouses.

- In our 20s, we find "true love" and get married. Again, the man asks the woman for marriage and pays for the ring, but her family pays for the wedding (the script tightly controls gender expectations).

- All couples engage in sex regularly and hope for children. Couples are expected to remain faithful, but everyone knows that many affairs happen. As the couple ages, sexual behaviors decline and the couple becomes more like life companions. Then we die.

Sexual scripts like this can govern many people's experiences. In fact, sometimes following the script leads to happiness. For example, a study of over 2100 young adults found that participants had a stronger marriage if the couple had conformed to traditional scripts about the marriage proposal (Schweingruber, Cast, & Anahita, 2008). Scripts can be comforting because they tell us what to expect and what's "acceptable" in our culture.

But scripts can also be limiting. As already mentioned, traditional sexual scripts expect that men should be aggressive initiators while women passively wait to be asked out or seduced. This puts pressure on men, and it can lead to backlash against women who initiate but are then seen as "pushy." These traditional gendered expectations might be changing, though. Dworkin and O'Sullivan (2005) found that college men across a variety of ethnic backgrounds preferred more egalitarian scripts for both their relationships in general and sexual behaviors. Masters and colleagues (Masters, Casey, Wells, & Morrison, 2013) found that while some people maintained a traditionally gendered sexual script, others had different ideas. They identified two alternatives as "exception finding" (meaning a generally traditional arrangement but allowing of occasional rule-breaking) and "transforming" (equal expectations for men and women—for example, either person might be on top during sex).

That said, most people follow a traditional or typical sexual script. We're also aware that nontraditional preferences or behaviors may be frowned upon by others. Goodfriend (2012) surveyed 89 college students about two things: (1) whether they personally would consider engaging in nontraditional sexual behaviors and (2) how socially acceptable these behaviors were, in general. These students came from a small, private school in the Midwest, so they at least somewhat represent what "middle America" thinks about sexual options.

The results of the survey are shown in Table 9.3. The scores could range from 1 (definitely *not* acceptable) to 7 (definitely acceptable). The more a given behavior strayed from the culturally accepted script, the less people said they would consider it—and the less acceptable they thought it was, in general.

The results in Table 9.3 show several things. First, men's and women's ideas and preferences were pretty similar to each other. Second, people are more likely to personally consider doing things if they feel those actions are culturally accepted. Finally, the most popular option was "legal marriage with one person for life." Even though this option is happening less with each generation, most people still appear to hold it as an ideal for their own sexual future. It is likely that this expectation is influenced by their culture's sexual script.

Cross-Cultural Differences in Sexuality

Our sexual scripts, social norms, and ideas about morality are influenced by our culture. One of the best ways to think about this influence is to consider how other cultures, from different time periods or different parts of the world, viewed sexual behaviors. Let's cover four very different examples to show this diversity in norms and expectations.

Ancient Greece

In ancient Greece, men and women were expected to marry and have children. However, this culture was also highly accepting of male-male sexual relationships. One

TABLE 9.3 ● Sexual Scripts in Modern U.S. Society	Men's Average	Women's Average
Legal marriage with one person for life		
• I would personally consider.	6.47	6.65
• Does society accept?	6.18	6.29
Cohabitation		
• I would personally consider.	5.84	5.49
• Does society accept?	4.95	5.18
Premarital sex		
• I would personally consider.	5.58	5.35
• Does society accept?	4.95	5.12
Casually dating several people		
• I would personally consider.	4.87	5.51
• Does society accept?	4.42	5.29
Masturbation		
• I would personally consider.	5.58	4.43
• Does society accept?	4.53	4.45
Single and sexually active for life		
• I would personally consider.	3.79	3.00
• Does society accept?	3.71	3.33
Bisexuality		
• I would personally consider.	2.42	3.37
• Does society accept?	3.29	3.47
Group marriage or polygamy		
• I would personally consider.	2.31	1.27
• Does society accept?	2.08	1.84
Living in a sex commune		
• I would personally consider.	1.87	1.39
• Does society accept?	1.58	1.67
Prostitution		
• I would personally consider.	1.92	1.29
• Does society accept?	1.95	2.06

Men's and women's views on possible sexual paths, on a range from 1 (definitely not acceptable) to 7 (definitely acceptable).

Source: Goodfriend (2012).

RESEARCH DEEP DIVE

Sex Within Marriage

Couples who have more sex are happier. This seems obvious, right? But we never know until we gather research.

Several scholars and their labs have dedicated many years to tracking large samples of married couples over time. One such project, overseen by Ted Huston and colleagues, used marriage records to recruit couples from Central Pennsylvania. Over the next 13 years, researchers asked them a series of questions. Tracking these large data sets longitudinally takes a tremendous amount of resources. As a result, researchers who have these couples in a study ask lots of questions, using a variety of techniques including diaries and face-to-face interviews. This allows lots of different researchers to explore the data and publish their findings on a range of topics.

In this particular study looking at the link between sex and relationship satisfaction, the researchers focused on marital satisfaction, sexual frequency, sexual quality, and something they called "interpersonal climate." Essentially, this focused on behaviors directed toward one's partner that were either positive (e.g., giving compliments, saying I love you, being physically affectionate) or negative (e.g., being impatient, annoying the partner, being angry, dominating conversations). The 100 couples used in this sample completed the measures three times: 1 year, 2 years, and 13 years into the marriage. Analyses focused on correlations between variables at each time point.

As others have found, couples who had more sex also reported higher sexual satisfaction. But what increased sexual frequency? Although wives' positive behaviors did not influence sexual frequency, husbands' did. When husbands engaged in more positive behaviors, sex was more frequent. Negative behaviors, from wives or husbands, did not relate to sexual frequency. But remember, the question we started with was the link between martial satisfaction and sexual frequency. The study was not able to find an association between those variables. Having more (or less) sex was *not* linked to marital satisfaction.

In conclusion, a more positive interpersonal climate from husbands was related to having more sex, but more frequent intercourse did not necessarily benefit the couple's relationship satisfaction.

For more, read Schoenfeld, E. A., Loving, T. J., Pope, M. T., Huston, T. L., & Štulhofer, A. (2017). Does sex really matter? Examining the connections between spouses' nonsexual behaviors, sexual frequency, sexual satisfaction, and marital satisfaction. *Archives of Sexual Behavior, 46*(2), 489–501.

example is the "Sacred Band of Thebes," an exclusive and highly respected military unit made up of 150 pairs of gay lovers. They fought many battles and even defeated the famous Spartans in combat. According to the historian Plutarch, the army consisted of pairs of men that included an older man and a younger acolyte or pupil (Plutarch, 75 A.D., translated by Perrin). The tradition of older men taking younger men as students and lovers was known as **pederasty** and was perfectly acceptable to the ancient Greeks.

In the famous *Symposium,* Plato described the Sacred Band of Thebes and noted that perhaps they were such an effective army because of their love for each other. He argued that each man would be braver and fight battles with more tenacity because each would hate to see his lover killed. Plato wrote:

For what lover would not choose rather to be seen by all mankind than by his beloved, either when abandoning his post or throwing away his arms? He would

Culture can have a big effect on people's sexual expectations. For example, the Mangaia people are very open about their sexuality, whereas people from Victorian-era Europe are sometimes portrayed as being very conservative and sexually repressed.

be ready to die a thousand deaths rather than endure this. Or who would desert his beloved or fail him in the hour of danger? (Plato, 360 B.C.E., translated by Jowett)

This image, of fierce gay men fighting battles in an exclusive army, goes against many modern stereotypes about both gay men and men who are in the military. Ancient Greek culture was clearly very different from many other cultures in its general acceptance of homosexuality.

The Mangaia People of the Cook Islands

On Mangaia, the most southern of the Cook Islands, the native people assume that both boys and girls will experience high levels of sexual desire when they reach adolescence (Marshall, 1971). Boys endure a circumcision ritual when they reach puberty and are then explicitly instructed in sexual behaviors, including kissing, oral sex, and how to bring women to multiple orgasms (Yarber & Sayad, 2016). After 2 weeks of these lessons, the boys have sex with an older, experienced woman; she is expected to provide further tips on their techniques.

Girls, on the other hand, are tutored by older women on how to best achieve multiple orgasms. At the same time, girls are taught to make certain motions during sex that are meant to please both them and their partner. One cultural message is that if a girl's male partner fails in giving her enough orgasms, she can leave him and tell others about his failure. Both men and women are encouraged to have many sexual partners before marriage (Levine & Troiden, 1988; Yarber & Sayad, 2016).

The Sambian Tribe of New Guinea

In the mountain hills of Papua New Guinea, the Sambian tribe has very gender-specific cultural expectations. According to the anthropologist Gilbert Herdt, this group engages in rituals that encourage young boys to give older boys and men oral sex (Herdt, 1982; Herdt & McClintock, 2000). Their culture teaches them that only by ingesting the sperm of older men can young boys mature properly. If a boy hasn't done this by the age of 10 years, he is expected to weaken and die (Stoller & Herdt, 1982). When they get a little older, they are expected to reverse roles and be the semen "donors" for younger boys. Once the boys reach 16 years of age, they are considered men and are expected to marry a woman and have sex with her.

The women of the Sambian tribe are generally feared by boys and men. The males of the tribe are taught that women are sorcerers who will try to manipulate and emasculate them. Women are expected to live separately during their menstrual cycles, because their supernatural powers are believed to have extra strength during this time (Brettell & Sargent, 2016).

Victorian Europe

In sharp contrast to the cultures described in this section so far is the culture of Europe in the Victorian era (the 19th century). Some historians believe that women were generally expected to have little to no sexual appetite or desire, only engaging in sex because it led to pregnancy and childbirth. Women who wanted sex were seen as brazen and diseased (Bostwick, 1860). In contrast, men were expected to have very high sexual appetites and thus the culture assumed men were constantly trying to seduce women. Perhaps because of this disparity, prostitution was fairly common in Europe at the time. Victorian erotica also emerged in the form of novels and magazines (Yarber & Sayad, 2016).

This kind of cultural conflict between men and women, and between appetite and suppression, led to several problems. One was a double standard for what men and women were "allowed" to do, in terms of sexual behavior. Another was a cultural interest in suppression of homosexuality. It was 1885 when the first laws in Europe made all homosexual acts illegal (and this resulted in the persecution of several prominent figures, such as the famous writer Oscar Wilde and the scientist Alan Turing).

These four very different examples highlight how culture can have a wide-ranging influence on sexual scripts and acceptance of different behaviors. One way to apply these ideas is to consider how your own values and interests may have been influenced by the world around you. For example, did reading about any of these cultural differences make you uncomfortable?

Sexting, Social Networks, and Dating Apps

Does it surprise you to know that about 20% of young adults have engaged in **sexting**, or sending sexually explicit texts or photos to someone else (Garcia et al., 2016)? Or that about 23% of the time, people who receive a "sext" forward it to a few other people? How about the fact that 44% of people ages 18–24 say they receive sexts pretty regularly (Pew Research Internet Project, 2013)? These stats might not be surprising, especially if you're in the generation of people who grew up with smartphones and touchscreens. With better technology every day, expectations—and opportunities—are changing as well.

Facebook, for example, can be a double-edged sword. While millions of people use it to connect with friends and family members, and even to share photos and announcements about their relationship, it can lead to conflict as well. Sometimes couple members disagree about when to change their "relationship status" on Facebook or how often they should be posting about the relationship or on each other's pages (Lane, Piercy, & Carr, 2016). Facebook and other social media sites can also be used to search for past partners, to see what they're up to lately or whether they are still single—something that 31% of people admit to having done (Pew Research Internet Project, 2013). And 15% of people say that they've used Facebook to ask someone out on a date.

Online dating is exploding in popularity, across ages and socioeconomic backgrounds (Finkel, Eastwick, Karney, Reis, & Sprecher, 2012; Valkenburg & Peter, 2007). As of 2013, 1 in every 10 Americans had used some kind of online or mobile dating site or app (Pew Research Internet Project, 2013). Of those people, 66% went on an actual date with someone they met online, and 23% of people say they met a long-term partner or even married someone they met using these sites or apps. The general public's acceptance of online dating has rapidly increased, even for people who don't use these sites themselves. In fact, 59% of *all* the internet users who were polled said that "online dating is a good way to meet people" (Pew Research Internet Project, 2013).

One of the reasons cited for why online dating is useful is because it allows users to meet a wider range of people. It also offers a distinct advantage, compared to traditional dating methods (like trying to meet people in bars, social groups, or social events): By looking through online profiles, you can immediately learn a lot about potential partners (Finkel et al., 2012). If you know what you're looking for (e.g., level of college education, whether they are a smoker, if they want kids), you can immediately select for those traits and, theoretically, be more efficient. Some dating services even boast that they have computer algorithms that will do your "matching" work for you, allowing you to sit back and wait for the matches to roll in.

That said, 54% of people report that they've experienced a date in which the person they met "seriously misrepresented themselves in their profile" (Pew Research Internet Project, 2013). Supporting this idea, several studies have investigated deceptive self-presentation in online dating profiles. Men say they present themselves as more dominant, more resourceful, and more kind than they really are—while women admit that they present themselves as being more physically attractive (Hitsch, Hortaçsu, & Ariely, 2010; Tooke & Camire, 1991). In a different study, men said they often lie about their height online, while women said they lie about their weight (Toma, Hancock, & Ellinson, 2008). Finally, studies have found that people change how they report things, like their personality traits, to better fit into culturally approved gender norms (Guadagno, Okdie, & Kruse, 2012; Rowatt, Cunninghan, & Druen, 1998; Zanna & Pack, 1975).

Finally, some researchers argue that advances in technology have changed cultural expectations about sexual **hookups**, which are broadly defined as "brief uncommitted sexual encounters among individuals who are not romantic partners" (Garcia, Reiber, Massey, & Merriwether, 2012, p. 162). "Hooking up" with someone means different things to different people, ranging from simply kissing to sexual intercourse. Hookups are increasingly ubiquitous in popular culture (movies, music, and so on), and dating apps like Tinder and Grindr make hookups both more convenient and, apparently, more socially acceptable as more and more people join. In fact, college students report twice as many hookups as first dates (Bradshaw, Kahn, & Saville, 2010). It seems the sexual scripts are changing, leading to confusion among many people who feel a pull between traditional, gendered expectations of slow, romantic dates versus modern expectations of casual sex almost immediately (Backstrom, Armstrong, & Puentes, 2012; Epstein, Calzo, Smiler, & Ward, 2009; Phillips, 2000).

The Cultural Influence of Pornography

Technology has also made pornography more accessible than ever before, potentially changing cultural views of what is socially acceptable and expected. For example, while erotica and pornography used to be considered almost exclusively created for a male audience, modern mass-media successes like *Sex and the City* and *Fifty Shades of Grey* have opened the possibility of an entirely new audience of women who are interested in sexually explicit material. Again, researchers have studied both sides of this change: Some people believe that pornography is a safe way to explore sexuality, while others feel it has a negative—and even potentially dangerous—influence.

Use of pornography is popular. One study that used a nationally representative sample of about 2000 U.S. men and women (Herbenick, Bowling, Fu, Dodge, Guerra-Reyes, & Sanders, 2017) found that

- 57% of all men and 57% of all women have read erotic books or stories,

- 12% of men and 6% of women have used a porn phone app,

- 79% of men and 54% of women have looked at pornographic magazines, and

- 71% of men and 60% of women have watched sexually explicit videos or films.

Why do people like to use porn? When a study asked college students this question (Paul & Shim, 2008), four different motivations emerged: (1) people used the porn with their partner, to build excitement; (2) for personal entertainment or to increase their own arousal; (3) out of habit; and (4) to explore sexual fantasy.

Some studies find troubling effects of using sexually explicit materials—and often, these findings are tied to the *type* of materials and how they influence cultural ideas about gender. For example, researchers in the Netherlands (Klaassen & Peter, 2015) coded 400 porn videos that are available on mainstream internet sites (like PornHub, xHamster, and YouPorn). They found that most of the videos showed consensual sex acts, but that power was often in the background of the action. For example, actresses were more often objectified through camera work such as close-ups of their individual body parts (compared to male actors). Men also got to receive more oral sex than women, and men were more often portrayed as focusing on their own enjoyment, while women were portrayed as focused on their partner's enjoyment (note, most of the videos showed heterosexual couples). When violence was shown, women were far more likely to be victim.

One response to concerns about violence and dominance toward women in porn is a movement called **femme porn**, erotic material designed to promote feminist values (Ryan, 2017). For example, female characters are portrayed as leads in the storyline, lovers have personal or emotional intimacy, and there is more equality between the sexes for sexual motives and behaviors. In addition, femme porn tends to have more diversity in actors and actresses, showing different body types, races and ethnicities, ages, and sexual orientations.

In 1970, the U.S. group called the President's Commission on Pornography and Obscenity presented evidence that porn had no overarching negative effects. They concluded that laws restricting or censoring porn should be repealed, both because of their lack of findings about harm and because those laws go against the First Amendment. Despite this conclusion, some states (like Utah and Florida) have passed laws as recently as 2016 based on the argument that porn is a public health risk (Lehmiller, 2018a). Indeed, the National Center on Sexual Exploitation states that "the pornography of today has created an unprecedented epidemic of sexual harm" (as quoted by Lehmiller, 2018a).

But research has presented results that may question whether pornography has negative effects on users. In general, porn seems to be decreasing in violence over time (Shor & Seida, 2019). And videos that do show violence are getting less attention, have fewer clicks when online, and receive worse consumer reviews. Others have pointed out that while porn usage seems to be increasing, national data in the United States show that the number of rapes (at least, reported rapes) has been decreasing (Lehmiller, 2018a). Most researchers seem to have concluded that there are certainly some types of porn that are harmful toward views of women, consent, and ideas about what to expect from sexual encounters. That said, there are many studies showing that porn can also be used for positive, healthy sexual exploration when used appropriately.

CHECK YOUR UNDERSTANDING

9.7 The expectations and assumptions we make about the specific order of events for sexual encounters are called sexual:

  a. Recipes
  b. Scripts
  c. Dialogues
  d. Procedures

9.8 The ancient Greek tradition in which older men train younger boys in a variety of things, including sexual relationships, was called:

  a. Platonic love
  b. Pederasty

  c. Eros-erotica
  d. Hedonism

9.9 Pornography that is specifically designed to show feminist values and strong female characters is sometimes called:

  a. Gyn-erotica
  b. Estro porn
  c. Femme porn
  d. Third-wave erotica

APPLICATION ACTIVITY

Using a website like PsycINFO or Google Scholar, find two articles that discuss the outcomes and/or effects of pornography use. Find one that indicates porn use leads to positive outcomes and one that indicates negative outcomes. Then, analyze whether you believe porn usage is good or bad for individual users and for the overall culture. Explain your opinion, using a critical analysis of the articles you found and what you thought was convincing (or not).

CRITICAL THINKING

- Do you think there are variables that predict whether someone who uses online dating sites or phone apps will have a positive versus negative experience? Identify three variables that might influence someone's experience one way or the other. Describe each variable and make a prediction (hypothesis) regarding how that variable will influence personal experience, and why.

- Research on sexual fantasies has only really been done relatively recently. Do you think that results would have been different if people from 100 years ago had been asked? Do you think people 100 years in the future will have different fantasies? Why or why not, and what form would those fantasies take?

- If two people in a relationship have different views about pornography use (one likes it and one doesn't, or they like different things), how can they both be happy? Should they compromise, should they use it on their own, or is there another solution? How can they talk about this issue with honesty and respect?

Answers to the Check Your Understanding Questions

9.7 b, 9.8 b, and 9.9 c.

Chapter Summary

Big Questions

1. What is the sexual spectrum?

2. How do people vary in their sexual desires?

3. How does culture influence sexual thoughts and behaviors?

What is the sexual spectrum?

The sexual spectrum is the diversity found in sex, gender, and sexual orientation, and the idea that these variables should be defined as continuous rather than categorical. For example, defining sex as only "male" versus "female" is seen by many as a false dichotomy, ignoring nuances highlighted by intersex and transgender individuals. Intersex conditions, also known as disorders of sex development, are cases when either chromosomes or hormones result in uncommon genotypes (e.g., XXY) or phenotypes (e.g., ambiguous genitals). Models of sexual orientation, such as Kinsey's one-dimensional continuum or Storms's two-dimensional continuum, also highlight the sexual spectrum.

How do people vary in their sexual desires?

Research on sexual fantasies shows that 97% of people have fantasies, and that they range quite a bit in content. Themes that have emerged from research on fantasies identified the following seven most common for people in the United States: (1) multipartner sex; (2) BDSM sex; (3) novelty, adventure, and variety; (4) taboo and forbidden sex; (5) partner sharing; (6) passion and romance; and (7) erotic flexibility. More and more people seem to be seeking consensually nonmonogamous relationships (known sometimes as "open" relationships or polyamory). Finally, research on sexual fetishes and paraphilias (arousal patterns that cause distress or harm) has resulted in eight particular categories, according to the *Diagnostic and Statistical Manual of Mental Disorders* (fifth edition).

How does culture influence sexual thoughts and behaviors?

Cultural differences in sexual expectations are also widely varied, and these expectations seem to be shifting with increases in technology around the world. Sexual scripts are assumptions about the specific order of events that will happen in sexual contexts, and many cultures have traditional scripts (such as kissing, then oral sex, then intercourse). Often these scripts also have messages about gendered expectations (e.g., men are the initiators). There is a correlation between what people believe is socially acceptable and what people consider for their own, personal sexual experiences. That said, several cultures from around the world have very different sexual scripts and expectations. Cultural assumptions are also changing with increases in technology, such as online dating websites and dating phone apps. These options may have influenced the increase in sexual "hookups" noted in recent research. Finally, some researchers debate whether the use of erotica and pornography has positive, healthy effects or negative, even dangerous effects on both individual users and the culture overall.

List of Terms

Learning Objectives	Key Terms
9.1 Differentiate categorical versus continuous views of sex and sexual orientation.	Sexual spectrum Gender expression Disorders of sex development (DSD) Intersex Klinefelter syndrome 47, XYY syndrome Supermale syndrome Turner syndrome Androgen insensitivity syndrome Congenital adrenal hyperplasia 5-alpha reductase deficiency Transgender Cisgender Heterosexual Homosexual Bisexual Pansexual Asexual Heteroflexibility
9.2 Explain variations in sexual fantasy, consensual nonmonogamy, and paraphilias.	Monogamous Consensual nonmonogamy Swinging Polyamory Paraphilia Paraphilic disorder Coercive paraphilia Fetish Nymphomania Hypersexuality
9.3 Analyze how culture and technology influence sexual scripts, dating, and pornography.	Sexual scripts Pederasty Sexting Hookups Femme porn

Social Cognition

Big Questions	Learning Objectives
1. How are impressions formed and maintained?	10.1 Describe first impressions, impression management through self-monitoring, and destiny versus growth beliefs.
2. How are we biased toward our current partner?	10.2 Explain how positive illusions, biased cognitions, and self-fulfilling prophecies apply to relationships.
3. How do our worldviews affect our relationships?	10.3 Analyze how locus of control, beliefs about romance, and fear of death affect relationships.

Is love really blind?

Social cognition is an area of scientific study that examines how we form perceptions, beliefs, judgments, and memories about other people and about ourselves. In short, it's the study of how we think about our social world. When it comes to intimate relationships, the idea that social cognition is biased has been around for centuries. Before it was studied scientifically, acknowledgment that love can blind our impressions of others was addressed in all sorts of ways, including popular culture at the time. A famous line from Shakespeare stated, "Love sees not with the eyes, but with the mind; and therefore is wing'd Cupid painted blind." A contemporary of Shakespeare, Sir Francis Bacon, wrote, "Man prefers to believe what he prefers to be true." Four hundred years later, the singer/songwriter Pink professed, "Funny how the heart can be deceiving, more than just a couple times."

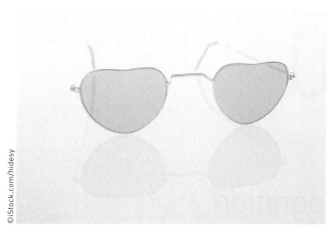

Social cognition is an approach to scientific inquiry that tries to explain how we form impressions of others, why our perceptions can sometimes be wrong, and how our worldviews affect our social lives. How does social cognition affect our intimate relationships, and vice versa?

How Are Impressions Formed and Maintained?

Think about someone you love.

Try to be objective as you consider how physically attractive, humorous, intelligent, and kind thjs person is compared to everyone else you know. Chances are good that the person on your mind comes off pretty well! You might even start smiling as your mental assessment turns out to be quite positive. One explanation for this experience might be that the reason you love this person is because they are just so wonderful. What's not to love?

But another possible explanation is that you *perceive* the person is wonderful simply *because* you love them. Maybe your perceptions are slightly biased, to focus on the positive and gloss over the negative. Maybe we can never really be objective when it comes to our intimate relationships. This chapter focuses on how our thoughts and impressions about our intimate partners and relationships are biased once we're in loving, committed relationships. It's possible that love makes us blind to our friends' and partners' imperfections; maybe the heart can deceive the mind.

All relationships start with a first impression. Previous chapters have covered important aspects of this experience, including what makes us immediately attracted to people on a physical level, as well as how that attraction can bias our overall perception of them (recall, for example, the description of the what-is-beautiful-is-good effect in Chapter 8). In this first section, we'll consider how first impressions are formed, impression management and self-monitoring, and the idea that two people really can be "made for each other."

First Impressions

"You'll never get the chance to make a second first impression."

You've probably heard that phrase before, maybe in the context of a job interview. A strong handshake is supposed to set things off right; it helps you seem confident and assured. Similarly, most of us have probably taken extra care about our appearance when going out on a first date—we want to look like we take care of ourselves, but also that we look amazing naturally and without too much effort, right? In either a job interview or first date, we're careful to highlight positive things about our past, to laugh at someone else's jokes, to focus our attention only on them . . . all tactics to boost the other person's first impression of us.

Sometimes our perceptions about relationship partners aren't accurate or objective. It's like we're looking through heart-shaped glasses.

Just how quickly do we form a first impression? Research shows that it's almost instantaneous—sometimes our judgments occur in, literally, a fraction of a second. One study (Bar, Neta, & Linz, 2006) asked people to look at 90 photographs, one at a time on the computer, and rate each face in terms of how threatening it was, on a scale of 1 to 5. Importantly (due to social issues such as sexism and racism), the faces were all of White men. While looking at each face, participants were asked to "follow their immediate gut reaction" when making judgments of how threatening they appeared to be (Bar et al., 2006, p. 270). Some participants saw the faces for 1700 milliseconds (or just under 2 seconds), while other participants saw the same faces for only 39 milliseconds.

When you have a new professor in a class, how quickly do you decide whether you're going to like them? Research shows it might be less than 5 minutes.

Across the two groups, participant ratings were highly correlated with each other (Bar et al., 2006). In other words, people could form impressions of the faces in as little time as 39 milliseconds! And those impressions didn't change when people were given just a bit more time. Note, though, that this study was focused on first impressions of *threat*. Maybe we're especially quick to make that kind of judgment because our survival instincts have probably been honed to assess danger as quickly as possible, especially when meeting someone new.

If you more than double that tiny amount of time—to a whopping 100 milliseconds—our impressions can become more complex. In a series of five studies (Willis & Todorov, 2006), participants who saw faces for 100 milliseconds made judgments about their attractiveness, likeability, trustworthiness, competence, and aggressiveness. In those studies, when researchers let participants see the faces for even more time—500 ms or 1000 ms—the judgments didn't change significantly. The researchers concluded that, again, longer time to examine a face doesn't change our first impressions; it only changed how confident people were in those impressions.

Several studies have shown that first impressions can (maybe surprisingly) be fairly accurate. When participants observed people's behaviors (by watching films) for less than 5 minutes across several studies, they were able to form impressions of those people's personality traits. These brief glimpses into someone else are called **thin slices of behavior**, and our judgments based on them are surprisingly close to how those people are rated by others who know them well, or even compared to ratings made by the people themselves. In just a few moments, participants can also form decently correct impressions of someone else's sexual orientation (Ambady, Hallahan, & Conner, 1999), whether teachers will get good student evaluations at the end of the semester (Ambady & Rosenthal, 1993), and whether people such as telephone receptionists (Hecht & LaFrance, 1995) and sales workers (Ambady, Krabbenhoft, & Hogan, 2006) will be good at their jobs.

Our first impressions really do color how we then continue to see people over time. We're subject to a **primacy effect**; what we perceive about someone first affects how we interpret information that follows (Asch, 1946). If the first thing

Chameleons can change color to disguise themselves and fit into their environment. Are people capable of similar changes, based on the environment?

you learn about someone is that they are "warm," then later information will be affected accordingly. For example, if that same person later argues with you, you might interpret it as the person following their passion (a relatively positive attribution) instead of the person just being stubborn or belligerent (Darley & Gross, 1983).

So, research says (1) we form first impressions with lightning speed (in a fraction of a second) and (2) our first impressions really do matter. Once formed, they can be hard to change. Knowing this, can you control how you appear to others? The next section discusses a personality trait that may be tied to how much people try to manipulate others' impressions.

Impression Management: Self-Monitoring

Some people act the same way in every situation, no matter who is around or what the stakes are. They might always be shy, or always sarcastic. Other people explicitly change how they present themselves, depending on the situation—they attempt to manage their behavior to best fit in. How much someone purposely adjusts their behavior across situations is called **self-monitoring** (Snyder, 1974).

People "high" in self-monitoring are sometimes called "social chameleons" because they can blend into almost any environment. In a cooperative environment, they cooperate; in a competitive environment, they compete. High self-monitors are people who look around and assess the given situation, then adapt their self-presentation to get whatever they want out of that particular situation.

On the other hand, people "low" in self-monitoring act the same way no matter where they are or who is around. They seem to pay little attention to how they "come across" to other people and act consistently across situations, even if their behavior comes across as strange, rude, or just slightly inappropriate. Note that there are pros and cons to being high or low in self-monitoring. High self-monitors might be better at managing first impressions and might be more popular, because they can adjust how they act to fit in. On the other hand, high self-monitors could come across as inauthentic; if they're always changing how they act, how do you know who the "real" person is? Most people, of course, fall somewhere in the middle of the continuum (just like they do for all personality traits). To test yourself, see the "What's My Score?" feature.

Several studies have explored how self-monitoring affects intimate relationships. An early examination was a series of four studies on differences between high and low self-monitors in dating relationships (Snyder & Simpson, 1984). In Study 1, all participants first completed Snyder's (1974) self-monitoring scale (an updated version is in the "What's My Score?" feature). Then, they were asked to choose between two activities: (1) spending time with their current partner, but the activity is something

WHAT'S MY SCORE?

Measuring Self-Monitoring

Instructions: These statements concern your personal reactions to a number of different situations. No two statements are exactly alike, so consider each statement carefully before answering. Next to each question, circle T if it is true or mostly true, or circle F if it is false or mostly false.

T   F   1. I find it hard to imitate the behavior of other people.

T   F   2. At parties and social gatherings, I do not attempt to do or say things that others will like.

T   F   3. I can only argue for ideas which I already believe.

T   F   4. I can make impromptu speeches even on topics about which I have almost no information.

T   F   5. I guess I put on a show to impress or entertain others.

T   F   6. I would probably make a good actor.

T   F   7. In a group of people I am rarely the center of attention.

T   F   8. In different situations and with different people, I often act like very different persons.

T   F   9. I am not particularly good at making other people like me.

T   F   10. I'm not always the person I appear to be.

T   F   11. I would not change my opinions (or the way I do things) in order to please someone or win their favor.

T   F   12. I have considered being an entertainer.

T   F   13. I have never been good at games like charades or improvisational acting.

T   F   14. I have trouble changing my behavior to suit different people and different situations.

T   F   15. At a party I let others keep the jokes and stories going.

T   F   16. I feel a bit awkward in public and do not show up quite as well as I should.

T   F   17. I can look anyone in the eye and tell a lie with a straight face (if for a right end).

T   F   18. I may deceive people by being friendly when I really dislike them.

(Continued)

(Continued)

Scoring: Give yourself 1 point if you said "true" for items 4, 5, 6, 8, 10, 12, 17, and 18. Next, give yourself 1 point if you said "false" for items 1, 2, 3, 7, 9, 11, 13, 14, 15, and 16. More points means that you are higher on the self-monitoring scale. The range could be anywhere from 1 to 18; most people score around 7 or 8 points.

Source: Snyder and Gangestad (1986).

Critical Thinking: Identify two advantages to being extremely high in self-monitoring, then identify two disadvantages to being extremely low. Next, would you rather date someone who is high or low in self-monitoring, and why?

their partner isn't really good at doing, or (2) spending time with an opposite-sex friend doing an activity where the friend is an expert. Low self-monitors were more likely to choose Option 1, but high self-monitors were more likely to choose Option 2.

In Study 2 (Snyder & Simpson, 1984), people were asked if they would be willing to change out their partner for one of their current friends—in other words, would they end their current relationship to start a new one instead? High self-monitors were significantly more likely to say yes. Study 3 showed that high self-monitors also report having nearly double the number of dating partners over their lives than low self-monitors, and that those relationships had lasted about half the time. Finally, Study 4's results showed that over the course of a given relationship, low self-monitors were slow to form intimate bonds with a partner—but over time, their levels of intimacy were far deeper than high self-monitors. In contrast, high self-monitors' levels of intimacy were relatively more flat or stable over time. Across all four studies, then, the researchers concluded that low self-monitors are more committed to spending time with their current partner, less likely to think about alternatives, and more likely to have long-term and deeply intimate relationships with others.

These patterns have been replicated and extended. Physical attractiveness is more important to high self-monitors when it comes to choosing dates (Bazzini & Shaffer, 1995; Snyder & Simpson, 1984). High self-monitors report having more sexual partners in the past year and report that they expect to have more sexual partners in the future, compared to low self-monitors (Snyder, Simpson, & Gangestad, 1986). Once in a relationship, high self-monitors are more concerned about social approval of their partner and whether their partner improves their social status, whereas low self-monitors focus their concerns on whether both people in the relationship are satisfied and faithful (Jones, 1993).

If low self-monitors have what appears to be commitment-focused orientations to relationships, what happens when two high self-monitoring people date each other? When this question was asked (Norris & Zweigenhaft, 1999), several interesting findings emerged. First, couple members' self-monitoring scores were correlated with each other, indicating we're more likely to date someone similar to ourselves on this personality trait. The researchers then compared three couple types: (1) both high in self-monitoring, (2) both low in self-monitoring, or (3) a mixed set (one high, one low). When both couple members were high in self-monitoring, they were significantly less likely to say they were eventually going to get married and they were also significantly less likely to say they trusted each other.

In a comprehensive review article about research on this topic, Leone and Hawkins (2006) reached several conclusions, based on studies done by many other authors (see the article to find those citations). Some of those conclusions are as follows:

- High self-monitors structure their friendships and dating relationships as relatively uncommitted, less close, and less exclusive.

- Attachment styles in high self-monitors are more likely to be avoidant.

- High self-monitors choose friends and dating partners based on mutual interests or shared situations, while low self-monitors choose based on shared values. High self-monitors prefer dating partners who have high sex appeal, social status, and financial resources; low self-monitors choose partners based on their honesty, kindness, responsibility, and loyalty.

- Low self-monitors are more likely to believe in "true love" or that there is only one person ideally suited to them.

- High self-monitors are more likely to flirt with others and promote themselves as an alternative to people already dating someone else.

- Low self-monitors are more likely to seek out consensus with their partner when making decisions and report more displays of affection (e.g., kissing and saying "I love you"). Low self-monitors are also more invested in their relationships.

- Low self-monitors are more likely to stay married to their spouse, even under circumstances of low satisfaction, while high self-monitors are more likely to get divorced and remarried.

That's a lot of different outcomes. By most people's standards, the great majority of these conclusions seem to indicate that low self-monitors will have happier, longer, more intimate relationships. This might especially be true if *both* people in the relationship are low self-monitors. More research might be needed if you have doubts, or if you can think of advantages to being a high self-monitor in friendships or in dating relationships. What other questions remain unanswered?

©iStock.com/eternalcreative

Destiny Versus Growth Beliefs

Love at first sight. Soul mates. Do they exist?

These two concepts are related to first impressions and to whether we perceive our partners as "the one," our "other half," or the person to whom you can say, "You complete me." Our last topic for this section of the chapter is on how early impressions of potential partners can be influenced by **implicit beliefs**, or foundational ideas about

Do you believe in the idea of soul mates, or that people can "fall in love at first sight"? Research explores how these beliefs can affect our relationships.

the nature of relationships that affect our perceptions and decisions. Implicit beliefs can affect both our early impressions of potential partners and how we think and act after a relationship is formed.

Research on implicit beliefs didn't start in the world of relationships. Instead, early work was focused on contexts like education, sports, and business (Dweck, 1996; Dweck, Chiu, & Hong, 1995; Dweck, Hong, & Chiu, 1993). In those settings, studies examined whether people's beliefs about the flexibility of traits like intelligence or athletic skill are "fixed" (in other words, set in stone) or whether they can change and improve over time (they are malleable). If students in school think intelligence is "fixed" and that all the studying in the world won't make them smarter, this affects how they approach classes and how they feel when they succeed or fail (Dweck, 2006, 2013; Dweck et al., 1993). Students with this cognitive belief decide early in a class or on a test whether they are doing well—and if not, they tend to give up (Dweck et al., 1995; Hong, Chiu, & Dweck, 1995).

Alternatively, if another student thinks that intelligence is something that can grow with time and dedication, different outcomes may result. Upon realizing that a class or exam is difficult, that student may decide that additional effort is needed and simply work harder to achieve success. And regardless of what each student thinks about intelligence, their teacher's implicit theory about the intelligence of their students may also influence what happens and how much mentoring is offered to students who are struggling.

Implicit theories have been applied to relationships. Most studies have focused on two very different approaches or sets of beliefs, first discussed by Knee (1998). **Destiny beliefs** in a relationship are cognitive beliefs that potential partners are either "meant for each other or not" (p. 360). Destiny beliefs emphasize first impressions of whether two people are compatible matches. If you don't get a "good vibe" on a first date with someone, people who have implicit destiny beliefs will quickly decide not to pursue the relationship. Other researchers have dubbed destiny beliefs the "soulmate theory" (Franiuk, Cohen, & Pomerantz, 2002; Franiuk, Pomerantz, & Cohen, 2004).

On the other hand, **growth beliefs** are cognitive beliefs that successful, happy relationships are developed over time and require effort and attention from both partners. People with growth beliefs think that all relationships will have challenges and obstacles, but that these problems can be worked through. They believe "that successful relationships evolve from the resolution of risks, challenges, and difficulties, rather than their absence" (Knee, 1998, p. 361). Another term for growth beliefs is the "work-it-out theory" (Franiuk et al., 2002, 2004). Here, disagreements with your partner are interpreted as natural and normal, not as insurmountable deal breakers.

A breakdown of the difference in cognitive patterns is shown in Table 10.1. Destiny beliefs are shown in the left-hand column, and growth beliefs are shown in the right-hand column. Do you tend to agree with one side versus the other? One way to summarize the difference is this statement: "Love can be metaphorically framed as perfect unity between two halves made for each other or as a journey with ups and downs" (Lee & Schwarz, 2014, p. 61). When Knee (1998) first developed these items into a self-report measure of implicit beliefs, he asked college students to complete his

TABLE 10.1 ● Growth vs. Destiny Belief Statements	
Destiny Beliefs	**Growth Beliefs**
Potential relationship partners are either compatible or they are not.	The ideal relationship develops gradually over time.
A successful relationship is mostly a matter of finding a compatible partner.	A successful relationship is mostly a matter of learning to resolve conflicts with a partner.
Potential relationship partners are either destined to get along or they are not.	Challenges and obstacles in a relationship can make love even stronger.
Relationships that do not start off well inevitably fail.	A successful relationship evolves through hard work and resolution of incompatibilities.

Whether you believe in "destiny" or "growth" matters for how you think about first impressions, relationship conflict, and more.

Source: Knee (1998).

survey about a month into the fall semester of classes. He then did a follow-up survey 2 months later, and 4 months after that he called each participant to see if their relationship status had changed.

Knee hypothesized that higher destiny beliefs would be associated with quickly testing potential partners to decide whether they were a good match, whereas higher growth beliefs would be associated with a more commitment-focused, long-term approach to potential dating partners. Supporting these general hypotheses, he found that belief in growth was correlated with fewer one-night stands (especially for women) and with dating people longer. He also found that people with destiny beliefs tended to cope with relationship conflict by disengaging and distancing themselves from partners, while growth people tried to actively solve the problem.

Finally, Knee (1998) found that first impressions mattered more for people with destiny beliefs (see Figure 10.1). If initial satisfaction with the relationship was low, people who believed in destiny were more likely to break up quickly. Initial satisfaction had little impact on people low in destiny beliefs, because they didn't automatically assume that early trouble couldn't be worked out. In other words, first impressions of a partner (or initial satisfaction in the relationship) affected people with high destiny beliefs more. Probably they interpreted their low satisfaction as a sign that the relationship wasn't "meant to be," and they were thus more likely to break up. Low-destiny people were more likely to stick it out and try to work through the problems.

As you may have already realized, destiny beliefs and growth beliefs aren't necessarily mutually exclusive. People can be high, mid-range, or low in *both* destiny and growth. In a follow-up to his original study, Knee and others (Knee, Nanayakkara, Vietor, Neighbors, & Patrick, 2001) laid out this conceptual framework portraying four general combinations, as seen in Figure 10.2. Note that the figure only labels people who are high or low in each set of beliefs, but that most people will fall somewhere in the middle on both dimensions. This time, Knee points out that destiny beliefs are focused on evaluating whether a relationship is fated for happiness (a "diagnosis

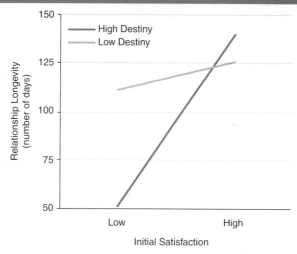

FIGURE 10.1 ● Patterns of Relationship Longevity, Based on High or Low Destiny Beliefs

Low initial relationship satisfaction led to faster breakups if people were high in destiny beliefs, but it had little effect on people with low destiny beliefs.

Source: Adapted from Knee (1998).

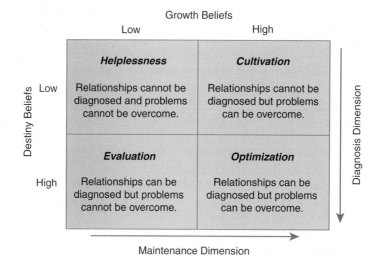

FIGURE 10.2 ● Combinations Based on Destiny and Growth Beliefs

Depending on one's level of destiny and growth beliefs, four categories of implicit belief are proposed.

Source: Adapted from Knee et al. (2001).

dimension"), while growth beliefs focus on attempts to improve and strengthen that relationship (a "maintenance dimension").

Take a look at the "cultivation" category as an example. Here, people with higher growth and lower destiny orientations are described as people who

> believe that relationships evolve through development, confrontation, and efforts to maintain and improve the relationships and are less interested in evaluating and diagnosing relationships. When cultivating, one's goal becomes the development and maintenance of the relationship without diagnosing or inferring grand meaning from otherwise minor incompatibilities. (Knee et al., 2001, p. 809)

Their research found that all couple members eventually realize that their current partner has flaws. When people have a cultivation attitude, they acknowledge these flaws, potentially work on finding compromises, and stay relatively satisfied in the relationship. This tenacity wasn't as likely in people who fit in the other three categories. Even people in the optimization category didn't quite fare as well, because while they believed they could work problems out, they still thought the problems might be red flags that the relationship wasn't meant to be. Here, conflict was more threatening.

The general patterns you'd expect from further research on implicit beliefs within relationships have supported this area of social cognition. A later study (Knee, Patrick, Vietor, & Neighbors, 2004) found that people higher in growth think of disagreements as an *opportunity* instead of as conflict, and that disagreements can help partners understand each other better, thus ultimately improving the relationship. Similarly, other research (Lee & Schwarz, 2014) found that people experimentally primed to think about "love as a journey" didn't mind recalling conflicts with their partner, whereas others who were primed to think of "love as unity" had decreased relationship satisfaction after remembering conflicts with their partner.

Another study found that when relationship partners are feeling anxious, strong destiny beliefs lead to reduced forgiveness for partner transgressions—they were more likely to hold a grudge (Finkel, Burnette, & Scissors, 2007). Growth beliefs are tied to lower perpetration of relationship violence, perhaps because of a higher willingness to make compromises and sacrifices (Cobb, DeWall, Lambert, & Fincham, 2013). Implicit theories have also been applied to sexual pleasure: People high in sexual growth beliefs think that hard work and effort can improve one's sex life, while people high in sexual destiny think that pleasure is attained through finding a compatible partner (Maxwell et al., 2017).

Finally, two other sets of studies examined people's implicit relationship beliefs and whether they idealized their partner (Franiuk et al., 2002, 2004). Thinking that your partner is perfectly suited to you and lives up to all of your expectations was correlated with relationship satisfaction and longevity—but this link was significantly stronger for people high in destiny beliefs (what these authors called "soulmate" beliefs), compared to those high in growth (or "work it out") beliefs. The perception that your partner is ideal is a tricky one, and it goes back to how we opened the chapter: Is love blind? Overly positive perceptions of our current partner are the focus of the next section in this chapter.

CHECK YOUR UNDERSTANDING

10.1 Studies show that we can form impressions of people by watching films that last less than 5 minutes. These brief glimpses into someone else's behavior have been labeled by researchers as:

a. Tiny hints of behavior
b. Partial views of behavior
c. Thin slices of behavior
d. Flashbulb views of behavior

10.2 Which statement below would likely be endorsed by someone who is LOW in self-monitoring?

a. I guess I put on a show to impress or entertain others.
b. In different situations and with different people, I often act like very different persons.

c. I may deceive people by being friendly when I really dislike them.
d. I find it hard to imitate the behavior of other people.

10.3 Karen believes that it's impossible to tell whether the person you're dating is "the one." She also thinks that problems can't really be fixed in relationships. Which category of implicit relationships best matches Karen's beliefs?

a. Helplessness
b. Cultivation
c. Evaluation
d. Optimization

APPLICATION ACTIVITY

Listen to the Avril Lavigne song "Complicated" and look up the lyrics. Then, explain whether the person described in the song is high or low in self-monitoring, and why. Use at least three specific lyrics in the song to back up your argument.

CRITICAL THINKING

- Given the research on how quickly we form first impressions and that those impressions are hard to change, what practical steps can be taken to change someone's mind if they form a negative impression of you? Identify two concepts from this chapter or earlier chapters that could be used as tactics toward this goal.

- People who are high in self-monitoring are usually more charming and popular, but they can also be less authentic. Do you prefer to

have friends and dating partners who are high or low in this personality trait? Why?

- Are you, personally, someone who tends to believe in growth within relationships, or someone who tends to believe in destiny? Explain why. In your answer, identify at least two examples of specific times when your belief system has affected your perceptions or behaviors (this can be how you acted in your own relationships, or how you act with other people such as your friends and family).

How Are We Biased Toward Our Current Partner?

Many people dream of finding the "perfect" partner. "The one."

But as the previous section of this chapter indicated, maybe assuming there's a perfect partner out there leads to less constructive relationship behaviors. And maybe it means never being happy with our current relationship. Instead of continually searching for someone who seems perfect—or even almost perfect—maybe most of us simply *convince* ourselves that our current partner is wonderful (even if they might have some flaws that we conveniently forget or minimize).

This section focuses on biased social cognition, or perceptions of our partner or relationship that are subjectively skewed. Usually, these thoughts are in a positive direction, especially when we're committed. If we've decided to stick together with someone "for better or worse," it's psychologically beneficial for us to see our partner and situation as "better." Of course, *degree* of healthy bias is an interesting question: How much should we gloss over the bad stuff before it becomes ignoring truly problematic issues? Another point to keep in mind is that most studies done on biased cognitions are correlational, meaning we don't know whether (1) having a biased view makes relationship commitment go up, (2) having high relationship commitment makes people more biased, or (3) a third variable is driving both.

That said, a fascinating example of social cognition is the mental processes partners have when thinking about each other. How do these biases occur?

Positive Illusions

One way that we might have overly positive perceptions of our partner is through **positive illusions** (Taylor & Brown, 1988), or unrealistically positive beliefs about someone.

When we have positive illusions about ourselves (e.g., we think we're smarter, funnier, or better looking than we really are), it's a nice self-esteem boost. Positive illusions about the self are correlated with better mental health, enhanced ability to care for others, more happiness, and increased ability to engage in productive work (Taylor & Brown, 1988). It feels great to think that *we're* great. In the book *Positive Illusions: Creative Self-Deception and the Healthy Mind*, Taylor (1989) reviews specific kinds of self-esteem–enhancing beliefs and how they are generally advantageous to us.

This kind of biased social cognition has also been successfully applied to romantic partners, and these glowingly rosy perceptions of our lovers are usually beneficial for the couple members involved (Martz et al., 1998; Murray & Holmes, 1993, 1994, 1997). Murray and Holmes (1997) suggest that satisfying, stable, and healthy romantic relationships are, in part, a reflection of the couple members' ability to possess such biases about each other and the relationship. Specifically, they find that idealized perceptions of a partner's attributes, exaggerated perceptions of control over

Sometimes, our view of our self isn't quite accurate. But is that a bad thing? And what about overly positive views of our partner?

the relationship, and unrealistic optimism about the relationship all predict greater satisfaction, less conflict, and persistence of the relationship over time.

Consider an example: Is it good or bad to have conflict in your relationship? Murray and Holmes (1993) found that couple members protect views of their partner by "weaving cogent stories that depict potential faults or imperfections in their partner in the best possible light" (p. 707). Specifically, when asked about the level of conflict in their current relationship, most participants indicate that there is little conflict—in other words, they deny something that would indicate their relationship is troubled. But when experimental participants are first told that low levels of conflict are actually a sign of healthy, good relationships, these couple members are suddenly able to recall significantly more conflicts than are control participants. In this way, partners defuse and manipulate the meaning of potentially troubling flaws in each other such that they can sustain positive illusions about each other.

Partner-Serving Cognitive Biases

So, research has established that a little bit of self-deception has a lot of benefits. These benefits include less anxiety (Brockner, 1984), better coping with stress and setbacks (Steele, 1988), lower levels of depression (Tennen & Herzberger, 1987), and general life satisfaction (Myers & Diener, 1995). Another term for cognitive distortions that enhance our self-concept by making us perceive that we're a little better than we are, objectively, is **self-serving cognitive biases**.

Let's look at three specific examples of how we distort reality, just a little, to maintain these self-serving views. In my doctoral dissertation (Goodfriend, 2004), I applied each of these biases to relationship partners. The idea was that (1) each bias could be applied to our current partner, as well as to ourselves, and that (2) how much bias we showed toward our partner would be positively correlated with our level of commitment to the relationship. Across six studies, I found support for each of these hypotheses. When each bias is applied to beliefs about our partner, instead of calling them "*self*-serving cognitive biases," I called them **partner-serving cognitive biases** (Goodfriend, 2004; Goodfriend, Agnew, & Cathey, 2017).

Biased Views of Traits

On a piece of scrap paper or in the margin of this book, quickly jot down three of your best traits or qualities and three of your worst. Now, for each trait you wrote down, estimate on a scale from 0 to 100 the percentage of students at your college or university who also possess this trait.

When Marks (1984) had college students do this exact task, people underestimated how many of their peers shared their positive traits and overestimated how many people shared their negative traits. How does this cognitive bias enhance our self-concept? It works because if you think that your positive qualities are rare, that makes you really special. And if your negative qualities are common—hey, everyone has this problem!—then your worst qualities are bad, sure, but not really a big deal.

We underestimate how many people share our talents (Goethals, Messick, & Allison, 1991) and we normalize our negative attitudes or traits so that we don't feel singled out or stigmatized (Suls & Wan, 1987). We can admit fears, such as speaking in front of a group, but we tell ourselves that everyone else shares our anxieties and thus these problems are not "fatal flaws." We comfort ourselves by simply framing our "best" and "worst" qualities as rare and common, respectively, to make us feel just a little better.

Do we have this same bias when we think about our partner's traits? In my research (Goodfriend, 2004; Goodfriend et al., 2017), I asked college students to list the five "best" and five "worst" aspects of their current partner. After making these lists (which everyone could easily do), the participants then considered each of these 10 traits and rated how common or rare they are in general society. As expected, people said their partner's best traits were rare—making them special and "a keeper"—and their worst traits were seen as common, and therefore no big deal. In short, the participants showed bias by thinking their partner's traits were "better than average."

Biased Views of Behaviors

Another self-serving cognitive bias emerges when we consider causes for our own successes and failures. Like admitting negative traits we possess, we can admit that we've done bad things or failed at something—but we often protect our view of the self by coming up with an excuse or justification for bad behaviors or failure.

In a review of over 20 studies on this topic, Miller and Ross (1975) found that often people engage in self-enhancing views of success. When people succeed at a task, they are more likely to perceive that this success is due to their own behaviors, effort, and talent than when they fail. In other words, we make **dispositional attributions** for success: We did well because of something internal to us, as individuals. Failures are instead due to some external, circumstantial factor instead—what we call **situational attributions**. That way, it's not our fault.

Did you get an A on the test? You must have studied hard or be really good at this subject! Did you fail the test? It's probably because you were sick, you stayed up late helping a friend with a crisis, or the test was unfair. By attributing successes to our own efforts—but failures to something we can't control or to something about the situation—we can take credit for doing well and simultaneously avoid blame for doing badly.

In another study in my dissertation (Goodfriend, 2004; Goodfriend et al., 2017), I asked people to consider six hypothetical positive things their partner might do, such as giving them a surprise gift, and six hypothetical negative behaviors, such as betraying a secret of theirs to a third person (all 12 behaviors are shown in Table 10.2). Each hypothetical behavior was presented as the first half of a sentence, and participants were asked to write in the second half of the sentence to explain *why* their partner might have done this.

TABLE 10.2 ● Twelve Hypothetical Behaviors From Your Partner	
Positive Behaviors	**Negative Behaviors**
Read your favorite book.	Betrayed a secret of yours to a third person.
Gave you a compliment.	Avoided you.
Picked you up when your car broke down.	Stood you up when you were supposed to meet.
Cooked a meal for you.	Ordered you to do something.
Took care of you when you were sick.	Accused you of being dishonest.
Helped you move into a new home.	Lied to you.

Why would your partner do any of these things? If you notice a difference in your answers for behaviors in the first column and the second column, you might have biases in terms of your attributions.

Results showed that when people were in happy, committed relationships, they wrote that positive behaviors must have been done because their partner was a good person or because they were in love. In other words, they were biased to make dispositional attributions for good behaviors. But when people tried to explain negative behaviors, they wrote that there must have been strange circumstances that required this behavior; they made situational attributions. In other words, if my partner lied to me, they must have had a good reason, like the lie was for my own protection. This trend in different kinds of attributions wasn't significant for people who were in unhappy, uncommitted relationships.

Biased Views of Feedback

Finally, a third self-serving cognitive bias is the tendency for people to view feedback about themselves in a skewed manner. Many people enjoy taking little quizzes about themselves on websites like BuzzFeed, for example. When you like the outcome, you might think, "Hey, that was a great quiz! Really insightful." But if you don't like the outcome, it's easy for you to see how the questions were flawed.

People often "discover" validity problems in tests that depict them in a negative or unflattering light; however, they are far less critical of evidence that portrays them positively (Baumeister, 1998; Pyszczynski, Greenberg, & Holt, 1985). For example, one study led participants to either "succeed" or "fail" at a fake social sensitivity test. After seeing their results, participants then saw information that indicated that the test itself was either valid or invalid. Participants who had "succeeded" evaluated the valid conclusion significantly more favorably than people in the invalid condition, and the opposite occurred for people who had "failed" (Pyszczynski et al., 1985).

To test whether feedback bias is applied within couples, I asked both members of romantic couples to come to a computer lab on campus (Goodfriend, 2004). I separated them into different cubicles and asked them to complete several different surveys, some of which I had written myself. There was deception in this study: I then told each participant that instead of getting their *own* scores on these surveys, they were going to see their *partner's* scores and what those scores meant. (In reality, the scores each person saw were randomly assigned.) Some people got feedback that put their partner in a positive light: They were told things like their partner has an unusually high intelligence or is particularly generous, or that their partner was really, truly, deeply in love with them. By random assignment, the other half of the participants got generally negative feedback about their partner. They were told things like their partner is a narcissist or that their partner wasn't really that committed to the relationship.

After receiving the feedback, all participants were asked to evaluate the surveys that generated the results in terms of how useful, valid, and important they were. Probably not surprisingly to you at this point, people who were highly committed defended their partner when they got negative feedback. They said that there was nothing wrong with their partner—it was the tests that were bad! But people who got positive feedback about their partner praised the tests and said that they were very valid and important.

In short, we are motivated to think highly of both ourselves and our partners. The more committed we are, the more we want to maintain a positive view—and even if this positivity is an illusion, it still leads to benefits such as relationship longevity and satisfaction. And of course, the correlation might go in the other direction: Thinking well of our partner might lead us to be more committed. Many studies have shown that it's not necessarily a bad thing to lie to ourselves, just a little; the biases are positively correlated with well-being (Brookings & Serratelli, 2006) and with relationship quality (Dijkstra, Barelds, Groothof, & Van Bruggen, 2014). It's only when those lies cover up serious problems, like relationship abuse, that we seem to get into trouble (for more on this topic, see Chapter 12).

RESEARCH DEEP DIVE

Thinking About Your Partner Can Be Stressful

Passionate love gets a lot of credit. No surprise, given that it's an exciting and physical type of love, full of "butterflies in the stomach" types of feelings. But passionate love also influences your cognition, including idealizing your partner and obsessively thinking about them. But are these passionate love experiences always good for you, or do they come at a cost? Could the experience of passionate love have *physiological* implications?

To study this possibility, Tim Loving and colleagues from the University of Texas at Austin recruited a group of 29 college women who were "madly, deeply in love" to see how relationship

thinking influences cortisol levels. First, after the researchers obtained informed consent, they screened respondents to make sure they qualified for the study. Whenever possible, it is helpful to screen participants to make sure you have the best sample. This is especially true when your study procedure is time-consuming and/or expensive. Specifically, researchers wanted participants who were in a nonmarital relationship for less than a year, could come to the lab in the afternoon, and did not have any history of behaviors (e.g., smoking) or conditions (e.g., working night shifts) that have a known impact on the stress response system (in other words, on cortisol).

Once screened, participants brought a picture of their partner and one of a friend to the lab

(Continued)

(Continued)

between 2 and 6 p.m. (this made sure that typical daily cortisol fluctuations were controlled between participants). The night before their lab session, participants completed measures of relationship thinking (e.g., "I find myself at times drifting off and thinking about my relationship with my partner") and passionate love (e.g., "Sometimes my body trembles with excitement at the sight of my partner"). Importantly, participants did these measures ahead of time so that the questions would not interfere with what they did in the lab.

In the lab session the next afternoon, participants initially provided their first of five salivary samples (the first sample was simply practice, to help acclimate participants to the procedure). Researchers would later analyze the samples to determine each participant's cortisol levels. Following the first sample, participants engaged in a relaxation exercise. Next, researchers randomly assigned them to one of two guided imagery tasks, focused on either their romantic partner or friend. For the task, participants had to "try to visualize all of the details about" the friend or partner. Other prompts included how they met, things they enjoyed together, things they like about the person, and overall feelings toward the person. Afterward, participants described all the thoughts they were having into a digital voice recorder for 3 minutes. Next, they wrote about their partner or friend for an additional 10 minutes. Finally, they had a "recovery period" where they sat quietly and looked through a book with pictures of landscapes. Researchers took salivary samples throughout, timed so that they occurred before and after the guided imagery exercise.

Using multilevel statistical models, the researchers found that women who had shorter relationships also had higher cortisol levels at baseline (before the imagery task), compared to those in longer relationships. Higher cortisol levels are associated with higher stress. For women who reported thinking about their relationship a lot, their cortisol levels increased from before to after the partner-focused guided imagery task.

Women who did not think about the relationship a lot had an initial cortisol increase after the guided imagery, but the cortisol level then quickly began to decline. However, all women in the friend condition (both high and low relationship focused) experienced decreases in cortisol over the course of the procedure.

These results show how women with higher levels of passionate love experience greater stress (operationalized through higher cortisol levels) when thinking about their romantic relationship partner, compared to thinking about a friend. For those women who tend to think a lot about the relationship, these differences were even greater.

When reading research, you should always be careful to notice the sample characteristics so that you can consider to whom the finding may (and may not) generalize. In this study, researchers focused only on women, so it is possible that feelings of passionate love do not have the same effect on men. A strength of the study was that neuroendocrine measures like salivary cortisol are not susceptible to social desirability or participants simply faking it the way that they may in self-report measures. This is especially important for something like stress where some individuals may want to underreport in order to appear more resilient.

In any case, it is important to realize that simply because this study links greater passionate love and relationship thinking with increases in cortisol, the implications remain unclear. That is, simply experiencing stress is not definitively good or bad. We experience stress from negative events (like getting pulled over by a police officer) as well as positive events (like graduation). Ultimately, the impact of stress differs based on how we interpret the event. If you believe passionate love–induced stress is good for your relationship, it likely will be.

For more, read Loving, T. J., Crockett, E. E., & Paxson, A. A. (2009). Passionate love and relationship thinkers: Experimental evidence for acute cortisol elevations in women. *Psychoneuroendocrinology, 34*(6), 939–946.

Self-Fulfilling Prophecies and the Michelangelo Phenomenon

Imagine a woman who thinks her husband is fantastic. Maybe he was always fantastic, and that influences her perceptions. Perhaps he's just ordinary, and she has positive illusions about him. But a third possibility exists. Maybe he *became* fantastic slowly, over time, because it's what she expected and encouraged him to be.

Self-fulfilling prophecies occur when your expectation about a given situation or person makes that expectation come true. If there had been a different expectation, there might have been a different outcome. Imagine you go into an exam thinking you're going to fail. You might be so anxious and distracted that you really do end up failing. If you had more confidence going in, a different outcome probably would have happened. The prophecy itself made it occur.

Self-fulfilling prophecies become interpersonal when one person's expectations about *someone else* influence behavior such that the expected outcome occurs. The classic example of this effect is seen in classrooms around the

Can your romantic partner sculpt you, just like Michelangelo sculpted this famous statue of David, from the David and Goliath story?

world. Have you ever had a teacher who expected a lot from you, and you didn't want to disappoint them? You probably worked harder and achieved more than you would with a different teacher, simply because you lived up to your teacher's high expectations. Alternatively, if you have a teacher you feel doesn't support you or expects you to fail, you might give up—and again, fulfill the prophecy put on you.

The idea of self-fulfilling prophecies in a classroom was scientifically tested in a landmark study over 50 years ago (Rosenthal & Jacobsen, 1968). Elementary school teachers were told that certain students in their classrooms were "intellectual bloomers," and by the end of the year those students really did succeed! But the students had been chosen randomly—it seems that the teachers' expectations influenced their success. Similar self-fulfilling prophecy effects have been found for managerial expectations of employee productivity (Eden, 1990; Whiteley, Sy, & Johnson, 2012), judge expectations for jury decisions (Blanck, Rosenthal, Hart, & Bernieri, 1990), and caretaker expectations for whether nursing home residents are depressed (Learman, Avorn, Everitt, & Rosenthal, 1990).

Self-fulfilling prophecies are sometimes called the "Pygmalion effect." In a Greek myth, the shy sculptor Pygmalion fell in love with his own sculpture of Galatea, the most beautiful woman he could imagine. He asked the goddess Aphrodite to breathe life into her. With the twisted humor characteristic of Greek gods, Aphrodite granted his request but did not allow Galatea to love him back. And it's sculpture that ties research on self-fulfilling prophecies into how two people in an intimate relationship can influence each other, thanks in part to the famous sculptor Michelangelo.

Michelangelo apparently described his sculpting process as one in which he simply released an ideal figure from the block of stone where it was sleeping (Gombrich, 1995).

It was almost like Michelangelo didn't choose what figure came out of the stone—it chose itself. Research on self-fulfilling prophecies usually focuses on how *someone else's* expectations for you shape interactions that make *their* beliefs about you come true (like a teacher and a student). In contrast, the **Michelangelo phenomenon** refers to how someone else's interactions with you can make *your own* hopes and dreams for yourself come true (Drigotas, Rusbult, Wieselquist, & Whitton, 1999).

This time, *you* are the one who determines what the goal is, and the other person helps you get there. Researchers who study the phenomenon believe that in intimate relationships, your partner can help you achieve your **ideal self**, "an individual's dreams and aspirations, or the constellation of skills, traits, and resources that an individual ideally wishes to acquire" (Rusbult, Finkel, & Kumashiro, 2009a, p. 305). It's the best version of yourself, one that you imagine and strive toward.

Shaping one's partner happens in two ways. First, **partner perceptual affirmation** happens when one partner perceives the other as compatible with their ideal self. Imagine that John and Jack are married, and that Jack wants to be a generous, thoughtful person. Through their conversations, if John affirms these tendencies by reminding Jack of times when he gave to charity or sent people cards on special occasions, Jack will realize that John *thinks* of him as generous and thoughtful, which will help him continue to maximize these traits. If your partner believes in you, it helps you achieve your goals.

The second process is **partner behavioral affirmation**, when one partner behaves in ways that elicit ideal-congruent reactions from their partner. If John wants to be a better cook, Jack might let John take over in the kitchen, giving him lots of opportunities to experiment. Jack might also praise John when he does well and brag about their fantastic meals by posting photos on social media. This positive reinforcement will encourage John to keep getting better, eventually fulfilling his goal. When both partners help each other achieve their ideal selves, the relationship itself is enhanced (see Figure 10.3).

To test the Michelangelo phenomenon, one longitudinal study videotaped married couples while they talked about a goal each of them had regarding their ideal self (Time 1; Rusbult et al., 2005a). Later, researchers who had been trained in coding

FIGURE 10.3 ● The Michelangelo Phenomenon

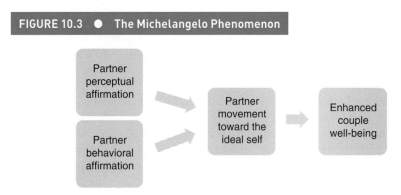

The Michelangelo phenomenon is the idea that both perceptual affirmations and behavioral affirmations that your partner is moving toward their ideal self will help that movement happen. In addition, when both partners help each other reach their ideal selves, the couple's well-being is enhanced.

verbal and nonverbal behaviors watched the tapes and coded how much each couple member exhibited behavioral affirmations. For example, partners offered suggestions on how the other person might achieve their goals, offered help, or praised their partner's goals as important. Four months later (Time 2), the couples were contacted again and asked if progress toward the goals had been made. Results showed that when partners were more affirming of goals at Time 1, the other person in the couple was significantly more likely to have made progress in achieving their goal by Time 2.

The ability of one couple member to help the other achieve their ideal self, through the Michelangelo phenomenon, has been replicated (e.g., Drigotas et al., 1999; Rusbult, Coolsen, et al., 2005; Rusbult et al., 2009b; Rusbult, Kumashiro, et al., 2005). As this process continues over time, relationship partners may begin to rely on each other to bring out the best version of themselves. When this happens, they become dependent on each other, trust each other, and become more satisfied and committed (Kumashiro, Rusbult, Wolf, & Estrada, 2006), completing the last step of the model shown in Figure 10.3. If two people help each other fulfill their potential, both the individuals and the relationship itself become stronger.

CHECK YOUR UNDERSTANDING

10.4 Cognitive biases that lead to us thinking that we're better than we really are—more intelligent, better looking, and so on—are called:

  a. Metaphorical magic
  b. Positive illusions
  c. Optimistic defense mechanisms
  d. Idealistic imaginations

10.5 A self-serving bias is that when we think about our positive traits, we think they are:

  a. Caused by biological factors
  b. Rare in the general population

  c. Caused by environmental factors
  d. Common in the general population

10.6 The Michelangelo effect occurs when Partner A pushes Partner B toward the version of the self most desired by:

  a. Partner A
  b. Partner B
  c. Partner A's parents
  d. General society

APPLICATION ACTIVITY

Three self-serving cognitive biases (biased perception of traits, biased attributions for behaviors, and biased response to feedback) apply to romantic partners. Can you hypothesize other people or contexts where these biases would be applied? Would people use the same biases when thinking about their friends, their academic work, or their pets? Choose a context that interests you and come up with a method to test whether these biases can be found in additional ways.

CRITICAL THINKING

- You've probably heard the phrase "ignorance is bliss." Use research on positive illusions and self-serving or partner-serving bias to argue in favor or against this saying in the context of romantic relationships. Are there times when glossing over the truth is good, but other times when it may lead to problems?

- After reading the section on partner-serving cognitive biases, try to think of a few examples of perceptions you hold about your current partner or close friends that might be a little skewed toward the positive. Does thinking about biases you might have change how you think about these individuals? Do you think being really honest with yourself is helpful or harmful—and why?

- Identify three specific goals you have for your ideal self—three things you'd like to work on to achieve your best potential. Now, identify ways that you'd like your friends, family, or romantic partner(s) to help you achieve these goals. For each method you identify, discuss whether those efforts would be "perceptual affirmation" or "behavioral affirmation" within the Michelangelo phenomenon. Finally, explain how having this support from your social network can help you progress toward the goals more quickly or more effectively than if you were working on them alone.

Answers to the Check Your Understanding Questions

10.4 b, 10.5 b, and 10.6 b.

How Do Our Worldviews Affect Our Relationships?

We all have beliefs that bring us comfort.

Worldviews are perceptions and beliefs about reality that provide structure, comfort, and meaning to life (Pyszczynski, Solomon, & Greenberg, 2003). There are many worldviews that make up how we think about the world and our place in it. Our worldviews are built up over time and are based on our culture, mass media exposure, how we're raised, our personality, our experiences, and more. In the last section of this chapter, we'll discuss three particular contexts in which worldviews affect relationships, and vice versa: how we think about control in our lives, how we think about "romance," and, finally, how we think about death.

Locus of Control

Do you control your own future?

It turns out, people vary widely in how much they believe they really are in charge of what happens in their own lives on a daily basis, regarding their long-term outcomes, and in terms of what happens in the larger social and political world. **Locus of control** is a personality trait or worldview regarding the extent to which you believe you can bring about desired outcomes in your life, your relationship, or the world

(Rotter, 1966, 1975). While locus of control exists on a continuum or range, with two extreme endpoints, most people discuss it in terms of one general side of the range or the other.

People with an **internal locus of control** believe that they are generally in control of what happens to them. They see themselves as the ones who determine what happens, and that their choices change their results and future. For example, if you believe that your GPA is based on how hard you study, that your relationship health is determined by how much effort you put into it, and that your career is going to be successful after you put in years of work and education, you probably have an internal locus of control.

In contrast, people with an **external locus of control** believe that their life and outcomes are determined by factors like luck, systematic prejudice, predestined fate, powerful others, or simply random chance. In other words, their future outcomes are based on forces external to themselves and their own choices. If you believe that your chances of getting a promotion are based on things like whether your uncle is the boss or if you have the "right" type of family background, you probably have an external locus of control. If you suspect your grades in class are determined by bias in the teacher or that there are some subjects you'll never "get" because you just don't have that kind of intelligence, you believe that there's nothing you can do to improve your situation.

The application of locus of control (we'll call it LOC) to intimate relationships has been somewhat rocky. Early attempts to see whether LOC affected partner interactions found little significance (Constantine & Bahr, 1980; Doherty & Ryder, 1979). However, later results were more promising. For example, one study (Miller, Lefcourt, & Ware, 1983) created an LOC scale specifically measuring whether spouses believed they were in control of outcomes within their marriage. Spouses with higher internal LOC scores believed that their willpower to create change would result in actual change and that they were responsible for what happened in their marriage. Spouses with higher external LOC scores held the belief that their own behaviors and efforts in the marriage were fairly irrelevant to outcomes in the relationship.

Other research indicates that people with internal LOCs fare better under relationship stress. A study that interviewed couples with infants found that first-time parents with internal LOCs adjusted to parenting stress better and were happier 4 months after the birth, compared to parents with external LOCs (Terry, 1991). Other studies find similar patterns, where an internal LOC leads people to seek support from their friends and family, probably because these people feel that help from others might actually change their stressful situations (e.g., Klein, Tatone, & Lindsay, 1989; Schonert-Reichl & Muller, 1996). People with an internal LOC also tend to have more secure attachments to their loved ones (Dilmac, Hamarta, & Arslan, 2009).

It seems like a fairly reliable pattern has emerged across many studies now, where internal LOCs are associated with higher relationship satisfaction, both in romantic couples (e.g., Camp & Ganong, 1997; Hay & Fingerman, 2005; Miller, Lefcourt, Holmes, Ware, & Saleh, 1986; Prager, 1986) and in same-sex friendships (Morry, 2003); "a perception that one's friend has an internal LOC can lead to beliefs that he/she will use active problem-solving strategies, such as talking about the issue" (Morry, 2003, p. 506). The same is true for parent-child relationships; higher internal LOCs lead to higher-quality relationships (Mercier, Paulson, & Morris, 1988).

A few studies have also explored whether LOC is tied to different sexual beliefs and behaviors. People with a high internal LOC specifically in terms of their health outcomes are more likely to use condoms in sexual encounters with new partners, for example (Freimuth, Hammond, Edgar, McDonald, & Fink, 1992). On the other hand, when heterosexual women believe that control in their sexual relationships lies with their male partners (in other words, an external sexual LOC), their risk for HIV exposure goes up due to engaging in behaviors that put them more at risk (Loue, Cooper, Traore, & Fiedler, 2004).

Higher external LOCs are tied to riskier sexual behaviors in teenagers as well, presumably because they believe their sexual choices don't determine their health outcomes (Feeney, Peterson, Gallois, & Terry, 2000). Finally, it seems that people who reach old age vary quite a bit in how they think about controlling their own sexual appetites. Older people with internal LOCs masturbate significantly more than older people with external LOCs (Catania & White, 1982). Overall, the pattern of results indicates that having an internal locus of control is associated with beliefs and behaviors that lead to more relationship and sexual empowerment.

Beliefs About Romance

What was the last "romantic comedy" movie you saw—and what did you think of it? Was it sweet? Cheesy? Exciting? Realistic?

One of the most relevant worldviews for intimate relationships is our beliefs and perceptions about "romance." They are at least partially formed and influenced by exposure to mass media examples of "romantic" situations in television, advertisements, books, movies, and so on—even video games (Dill & Thill, 2007). Some young people purposely watch television and movies to learn about how dating is supposed to work (Wood, Senn, Desmarais, Park, & Verberg, 2002; Zurbriggen & Morgan, 2006).

Whether you seek them out or not, exposure to mass media images of love and romance do seem to leave an impact on our relationship worldviews. College students who watch a lot of soap operas and dating "reality" shows are more likely to adopt unrealistic beliefs like "you should know each other's inner-most feelings" (Segrin

& Nabi, 2002). Dating reality shows also—perhaps not surprisingly—lead viewers to think of dating as a "game" (Ferris, Smith, Greenberg, & Smith, 2007). And when high school students watch a lot of TV and movies about "falling in love," their beliefs shift toward more traditional gender roles, such as endorsing the idea that in heterosexual couples, the man should be in charge of planning and paying for dates (Rivadeneyra & Lebo, 2008). Other examples of worldview beliefs expressed in romantic comedies are discussed in the "Relationships and Popular Culture" feature.

Do you believe women should be rescued by a rich and handsome Prince Charming?

Researchers have suggested that people's worldviews about love and romance function as an implicit schema, or structure used to understand and evaluate behaviors, potential partners, and the health of a current relationship (Lantz, Schmitt, Britton, &

Allstar Picture Library Limited / Alamy Stock Photo

Snyder, 1968; Sprecher & Metts, 1989). To test this idea, Sprecher and Metts (1989) developed the Romantic Beliefs Scale (which you can see in the "What's My Score?" feature). The scale includes items that measure four general sets of beliefs:

- *Love finds a way:* People who are really in love will overcome all obstacles or challenges to be together.

- *One and only:* Once people find their soul mate, they will be in love only with that person, and forever.

- *Idealization:* True love means that the relationship will be perfect.

- *Love at first sight:* Once people meet the right person, they will know it almost instantly.

In their original study, men were more likely to endorse these beliefs than women were—but within women, those higher in femininity also got high scores on the scale. In other words, less traditional women were least likely to endorse these beliefs (Sprecher & Metts, 1989). In a longitudinal follow-up study, the authors found that within couples, partners who started with high endorsement and decreased in their romantic beliefs over time were more likely to break up. Alternatively, couples who started with high scores for romantic beliefs and remained high over 4 years were more likely to get engaged to be married (Sprecher & Metts, 1999).

WHAT'S MY SCORE?

Measuring Romantic Beliefs

Instructions: For each statement below, write how much you agree or disagree using this scale:

1	2	3	4	5	6	7
Strongly disagree						Strongly agree

_____ 1. I need to know someone for a period of time before I fall in love with him or her.

_____ 2. If I were in love with someone, I would commit myself to him or her even if my parents and friends disapproved of the relationship.

_____ 3. Once I experience "true love," I could never experience it again, to the same degree, with another person.

_____ 4. I believe that to be truly in love is to be in love forever.

(Continued)

(Continued)

_____5. If I love someone, I know I can make the relationship work, despite any obstacles.

_____6. When I find my "true love," I will probably know it soon after we meet.

_____7. I'm sure that every new thing I learn about the person I choose for a long-term commitment will please me.

_____8. The relationship I will have with my "true love" will be nearly perfect.

_____9. If I love someone, I will find a way for us to be together regardless of the opposition to the relationship, physical distance between us, or any other barrier.

_____10. There will be only one real love for me.

_____11. If a relationship I have was meant to be, any obstacle (e.g., lack of money, physical distance, career conflicts) can be overcome.

_____12. I am likely to fall in love almost immediately if I meet the right person.

_____13. I expect that in my relationship, romantic love will really last; it won't fade with time.

_____14. The person I love will make a perfect romantic partner; for example, he/she will be completely accepting, loving, and understanding.

_____15. I believe if another person and I love each other we can overcome any differences and problems that may arise.

Scoring: For your overall score, add all items and divide by 15 to calculate the mean. If you'd like to know your scores for each of the beliefs included (or subscales), you can find the mean for these sets of items:

- *Love finds a way:* items 2, 5, 9, 11, 13, and 15

- *One and only:* items 3, 4, and 10

- *Idealization:* items 7, 8, and 14

- *Love at first sight:* items 1, 6, and 12

Source: Sprecher and Metts (1989).

Critical Thinking: Many researchers have written that most TV shows and movies depict characters and storylines that endorse these beliefs. Can you think of any examples of shows or movies that do not? Do those shows or movies have happy endings?

While romantic beliefs may seem lighthearted and fun, they can have negative influences. Just as the earlier parts of this chapter discussed, beliefs in concepts like soulmates, love at first sight, and destiny are associated with worse relationship outcomes. In addition, there may be an ironic effect for women who endorse traditionally "romantic" worldviews. Many classic and modern stories of romance depict a woman who is "saved" by some version of Prince Charming. In what they call the **glass slipper effect**, researchers Rudman and Heppen (2003) state:

> Romance idealizes femininity and places women on a pedestal. But it may teach women . . . to depend on men for economic and social rewards. In particular, the romantic idealization of men as chivalric rescuers of women (e.g., Prince Charming, White Knight) might encourage "the fairer sex" to seek their fortune indirectly, through men. If so, romantic fantasies might be negatively linked to women's interest in personal power. (p. 1358)

In short, the glass slipper effect is when women's beliefs in gender-based romantic worldviews lead them to be less empowered to control their own lives and outcomes. In a series of three studies, the researchers found that women's implicit romantic beliefs were negatively correlated with their interest in personal power. Personal power was operationalized as projected future income, education goals, interest in high-status and high-income careers, and interest in leadership opportunities (Rudman & Heppen, 2003).

In another ironic twist, it's possible that Valentine's Day ruins love—at least, sometimes. One article that examined the holiday's effects on relationships hypothesized that the marketing flurry and increased expectations for romantic gifts and gestures would make people's relationships particularly salient (Morse & Neuberg, 2004). They stated, "We believe that Valentine's Day places romantic relationships at some risk because, contrary to popular perceptions, it instigates a set of processes often detrimental to romantic relationships and catalyzes existing relationship difficulties, making it more likely that these difficulties will lead to dissolution" (Morse & Neuberg, 2004, p. 510). Basically, they thought that if a relationship isn't going particularly well, Valentine's Day would just make things worse.

To test this idea, college students completed self-report measures regarding their current relationship's stability, quality, beliefs, and processes (Morse & Neuberg, 2004). People completed the surveys 1 week prior to Valentine's Day and again 1 week after Valentine's Day. As a control group, a different set of participants also completed the pretest and post-test measures but during a different part of the year. Results supported their hypothesis: People who participated around Valentine's Day were more likely to break up during the 2-week study period compared to the control group. If the relationship was already troubled, Valentine's Day soured it quickly. Ironically, the holiday about love and romance seems to often lead to breakup and heartache, potentially because of the heightened expectations and inevitable disappointment that many people feel when their relationships don't measure up to the fictional examples they see in movies and commercials for diamond rings.

Fear of Death: Terror Management Theory

Let's end this chapter by considering our *own* end: death.

We're all dying. How we respond to this undeniable truth is a fascinating part of social cognition. Terror management theory (see Chapter 6) suggests that awareness of mortality results in fear and anxiety, which in turn lead to a variety of social cognitions designed to bring us comfort (Greenberg, Pyszczynski, & Solomon, 1986; Pyszczynski et al., 1996, 2003; Pyszczynski, Greenberg, & Solomon, 1999). Terror management theory (or TMT) suggests the following basic psychological and philosophical ideas:

- Humans, as a species, are uniquely aware of our own eventual mortality.

- Thinking about our own unavoidable death is terrifying.

- When possible, we will distract ourselves from this fear by manufacturing meaning out of our lives, such as through beliefs about cultural values or religions that comfort us.

RELATIONSHIPS AND POPULAR CULTURE

Romantic Beliefs Featured in Hollywood Films

Carolyn Jenkins / Alamy Stock Photo

When the Romantic Beliefs Scale (Sprecher & Metts, 1989) was developed, four themes emerged: (1) Love finds a way, or it overcomes obstacles; (2) one and only, or soul mates exist; (3) idealization, or perfect love exists; and (4) love at first sight exists. Do these themes really emerge in Hollywood romantic comedies? One study wanted to find out (Hefner & Wilson, 2013). Researchers analyzed the content of the 52 highest-grossing romantic comedies released between 1998 and 2008. Each film was coded by people trained to note both verbal and nonverbal cues regarding romantic beliefs expressed by characters or in the plot. They specifically looked for things that supported the four major themes listed above, as well as times when the movies challenged these beliefs.

The results showed that 98% of the films contained at least one expression of the four romantic belief themes. Across all 52 movies, there were a total of 375 of these belief-confirming expressions, which translated into one expression about every 14 minutes. The most popular theme was "one and only," or soulmates, with 40% of the expressions supporting this belief. One-third supported idealization, and about one-quarter of the expressions supported belief in love at first sight or love conquering all.

Perhaps surprisingly, however, the same movies also portrayed characters who challenged these beliefs. In fact, there were 739 challenge expressions—almost *double* the number of expressions in favor of the romantic beliefs! Three examples of these challenges were as follows:

- "Let's be smart about this. You're not going to move out here and become my co-pilot. And I'm not going to go to New York and be your receptionist, so . . . where's that leave us? Let's not complicate things."—*Six Days, Seven Nights* (1998)

- "Long distance relationships can work, you know." "Really? I can't make one work when I live in the same house with someone."—*The Holiday* (2006)

- "I had the perfect relationship which was ruined by marriage."—*Just Married* (2003)

Other, similar research doing content analysis has not found such balance. For example, a different study (Johnson & Holmes, 2009) found that romantic comedies show unrealistic expectations such as relationships being simultaneously novel and exciting while also being emotionally significant and meaningful. Further, problems or transgressions in the relationship usually had no long-term negative effects on the relationship. It's possible that different movies send different messages about what it means to be in love, and one audience member might infer a different lesson than the next.

- We are especially likely to embrace these comforting worldviews when reminded of our own mortality.

Does just looking at this picture and thinking about death change your perceptions of your intimate relationships?

In short, to manage the terror coming from our own eventual death, we look to beliefs or social relationships that bring us comfort and help us feel that our lives are meaningful. Yes, we all have to die eventually—but if we can live life to the fullest and make sense of this crazy world, our fear and anxiety are assuaged. Research on how TMT predicts social cognition within intimate relationships has been guided by two overarching hypotheses (see Mikulincer, Florian, & Hirschberger, 2003): (1) When we're reminded of death, our motivation to seek out comforting relationships will be heightened, and (2) maintaining close relationships serves as a psychological or symbolic shield against the terror of death.

To conduct research on TMT, scholars had to create experimental manipulations that increased participants' awareness of their own death; these are called **mortality salience** conditions. The essential hypothesis is that under mortality salience, commitment to close relationships should be significantly higher than control conditions. The typical experimental procedure is to randomly assign participants into one of two essay conditions. Half of the participants are asked to write down their responses to a disturbing question: "What do you think happens to you as you physically die and once you are physically dead?" In contrast, the rest of the participants are asked to write about what will happen to their bodies when they suffer a severe (but not life-threatening) injury or when they experience powerful dental pain.

Other experiments avoid experimental manipulations of mortality salience by using the natural world or events. For example, some studies ask people to fill out a brief survey as they happen to be walking past a building—and for some participants, the building is a funeral home. Other studies wait for an anxiety- and death-relevant event, such as the terrorist attacks of 9/11, and see if participants behave differently. An example of this last technique was the archival data finding that after 9/11, both marriage rates and birthrates throughout the United States significantly increased (CNN, 2002, as cited in Wisman & Goldenberg, 2005).

TMT predicts that increased desire for sexual connection or relationship commitment should be a result of mortality salience for two general reasons. First, being in love and having sex provide happy distractions from the sobering thoughts of death, and they make us feel that we've made life as worthwhile as possible. Second, if relationships lead to sex and children, we can die knowing that we've left a legacy behind, becoming at least *symbolically* immortal through the next generation.

Does research support all these abstract, existential ideas? Many people find TMT controversial, and a lot of studies find no effects of mortality salience (although it's hard to know exactly how many, as studies without significant findings usually can't get published). That said, many other studies have found support for TMT predictions. As a simple early start, one study (Mikulincer & Florian, 2000, Study 2) found that college students under a mortality salience experimental condition reported higher desires for romantic intimacy, compared to students in a control condition.

Similarly, a series of follow-up studies found that under mortality salience, participants reported higher attraction and commitment to their current partner (Florian, Mikulincer, & Hirschberger, 2002). This turns out to be true even when participants are asked to imagine their current partners criticizing them (Hirschberger, Florian, & Mikulincer, 2003). One explanation for increased commitment under mortality salience conditions is because we think our partner has a positive view of us, which reassures our self-esteem (Cox & Arndt, 2012).

Another set of studies examined whether threats of losing one's partner would increase death anxiety. To test this, participants did a series of word fragments that could be successfully completed in different ways. For example, what word could be spelled below?

C O F F _____

This word could be "coffee" or "coffin." When participants were first asked to think about problems in their current romantic relationship, they were later more likely to complete the word task using death-relevant words (like "coffin"), compared to control participants. Later studies found the same results for the word-completion task when participants were asked to think about separation from their current partner (Mikulincer, Florian, Birnbaum, & Malishkevich, 2002). In their final study, a third set of participants thought about different lengths of separation from their partners, and experimental length of separation was positively correlated with how many death-related words they generated in the word-completion task.

Being reminded of death may increase our desire for close connections so much that we are willing to compromise our usual standards. To examine this, a study (Hirschberger, Florian, & Mikulincer, 2002) asked participants to first complete scales measuring five factors of ideal mate characteristics (these included interpersonal skills, interpersonal power, intellectual skills, physical attractiveness, and social status). Then, participants were experimentally manipulated into mortality salience or control conditions. Finally, they rated how much they were ready to compromise on their ideals when considering potential marriage partners. People who had been reminded of their mortality were significantly more willing to make compromises; perhaps they were more desperate to make some kind of social connection (before it was too late!). And this willingness to compromise wasn't without consequence; these participants reported higher feelings of shame and guilt. Desperate love doesn't seem to be particularly meaningful or comforting, after all.

CHECK YOUR UNDERSTANDING

10.7 Which statement below is most likely to be made by someone with an internal locus of control?

   a. My GPA is basically determined by random luck.
   b. Everything is part of God's plan.
   c. I can get this promotion if I try really hard.
   d. I failed the driving test because I was so sick that day.

10.8 Shakespeare is famous for writing sonnets about his lovers in which they were seen with flaws instead of as perfect goddesses. Which romantic theme was Shakespeare challenging with these poems?

   a. One and only
   b. Love at first sight
   c. Love finds a way
   d. Idealization

10.9 Some research studies test terror management theory by randomly assigning some participants into conditions in which they are forced to think about death. The term for these experimental conditions is:

   a. Death unavoidance
   b. Mortality salience
   c. The fragile threshold
   d. Lack of transience

APPLICATION ACTIVITY

Watch either two television episodes or one full-length movie that feature(s) romantic relationships. Analyze what you see in terms of whether the characters portray the four basic themes from the Romantic Beliefs Scale (love finds a way, one and only, idealization, and love at first sight).

CRITICAL THINKING

• Identify two contexts in which having an internal locus of control might lead to better outcomes, and two contexts in which having an external locus of control might lead to better outcomes. "Better" might change depending on how you want to define it, in each context (e.g., happiness, financial security, social status, better grades).

• Does learning about the "glass slipper effect" change your view of Disney movies like *Cinderella*, *Snow White*, or *Sleeping Beauty*? If so, describe how your view has changed. If not, explain why not.

• Research on terror management theory found that people who think about death show increased commitment to their relationship partners, and that when relationships are threatened, people think about death more. This chapter and the other chapters in this book discuss several other relationship phenomena (such as positive illusions, communication patterns, types of attraction, friendship dynamics, etc.). Choose a phenomenon from a different part of this book and create a hypothesis regarding what would happen to this variable under conditions of mortality salience (when people are reminded of their mortality). Explain why you think this hypothesis would happen, and how you would test it in a scientific study.

Answers to the Check Your Understanding Questions

10.7 c, **10.8** d, and **10.9** b.

Chapter Summary

Big Questions

1. How are impressions formed and maintained?

2. How are we biased toward our current partner?

3. How do our worldviews affect our relationships?

How are impressions formed and maintained?
Social cognition is the study of how perceptions, beliefs, judgments, and memories about people form. For example, research has studied how first impressions are made. First impressions may be made in less than 1 second with photographs. When we are exposed to "thin slices of behavior," or brief videos of other people, our impressions become more complex but seem fairly accurate. One way some people try to manage the impression they make on others is called self-monitoring, which is changing your behavior to fit into the given situation. In relationships, people who do this less (or low self-monitors) tend to have longer, more intimate romantic relationships. Finally, people who believe in "soul mates" or "love at first sight" have what are called destiny beliefs, while people who believe that relationships will

always have conflict and challenge have what are called growth beliefs. Several studies indicate that growth beliefs lead to more stability within relationships, as conflict is not seen as a sign that the relationship isn't "meant to be."

How are we biased toward our current partner?
When we hold overly positive views of our partner, focusing on the good parts and ignoring problems, we have "positive illusions." In general, positive illusions are tied to greater satisfaction and commitment within relationships. One way to maintain positive illusions about each other is for partners to engage in "partner-serving cognitive biases," such as (1) thinking your partner's positive traits are rare, but negative traits are common; (2) making dispositional attributions for your partner's

successes, but situational attributions for failure; and (3) perceiving positive feedback as valid, but negative feedback as invalid. Finally, partners can influence each other through self-fulfilling prophecies. When one partner helps the other to achieve their ideal self, it's called the Michelangelo effect, referring to one person metaphorically sculpting the other's image.

How do our worldviews affect our relationships?

Worldviews are perceptions and beliefs about reality that bring us structure and comfort. One example is locus of control; people with an internal locus of control believe they are in charge of their future fate, whereas people with an external locus of control believe their fate is determined by something outside of themselves, such as luck, destiny, or a powerful other. Internal beliefs are tied to better reactions to stress and higher relationship satisfaction. Romantic beliefs are another worldview; beliefs often endorsed by mass media like TV or movies include concepts like "love finds a way" and "love at first sight." When women believe in traditional "romantic" roles such as being saved by a man, they are less likely to seek personal empowerment, a consequence called the glass slipper effect. Finally, terror management theory suggests that when we're reminded of our own mortality, we cling to worldviews that bring us comfort. One way we do this is by increasing our attraction to or commitment to our current romantic partner.

List of Terms

Learning Objectives	Key Terms
10.1 Describe first impressions, impression management through self-monitoring, and destiny versus growth beliefs.	Social cognition Thin slices of behavior Primacy effect Self-monitoring Implicit beliefs Destiny beliefs Growth beliefs
10.2 Explain how positive illusions, biased cognitions, and self-fulfilling prophecies apply to relationships.	Positive illusions Self-serving cognitive biases Partner-serving cognitive biases Dispositional attributions Situational attributions Self-fulfilling prophecies Michelangelo phenomenon Ideal self Partner perceptual affirmation Partner behavioral affirmation

| 10.3 Analyze how locus of control, beliefs about romance, and fear of death affect relationships. | Worldviews
Locus of control
Internal locus of control
External locus of control
Glass slipper effect
Mortality salience |

Communication and Conflict

Big Questions	Learning Objectives
1. How can communication build intimacy in relationships?	11.1 Describe how self-disclosures in couples build intimacy.
2. How has technology affected communication in relationships?	11.2 Explain usage of online dating apps, cell phones, and social network sites within relationships.
3. How do couples engage in conflict management?	11.3 Compare and contrast different conflict management models and strategies in relationships, and analyze research on individual differences.

You've heard this before: Communication is a two-way street.

That metaphor is classic because it's true: Real communication requires effort and adjustment from both people in a friendship, romantic couple, or any other form of relationship. And while this basic rule of communication is simple enough, the fact that we've all experienced frustration and confusion when trying to communicate with someone else shows us that the process behind successful communication can also become complicated.

Communication is an entire academic field, and it's impossible to put all the important research on communication in relationships into a single chapter. This chapter just touches on three interesting examples of relevant topics. We'll talk about how intimacy is built when two people share personal thoughts with each other, how communication in couples is affected by technology, and research on conflict management.

How Can Communication Build Intimacy in Relationships?

We want our close relationships to be intimate, but what exactly is intimacy?

Concepts like intimacy can be hard to define scientifically, just like "love" or "emotions"; they are abstract constructs that require operationalization to be studied by researchers. A good place to start is by simply asking everyday people how they define intimacy. When a sample of 30 young married couples were asked to do this, they generated ideas that researchers (Waring, Tillman, Frelick, Russell, & Weisz, 1980) coded into eight categories with the following order of importance:

- Affection

- Expressiveness (e.g., sharing of personal feelings)

- Sexuality

- Cohesion and commitment

- Compatibility

- Autonomy (e.g., from parental interference)

- Lack of conflict

- Personal identity (knowing oneself, positive self-esteem)

A similar study focused on intimacy in same-sex and cross-sex friendships (Monsour, 1992). Here, college students reported on what they thought "intimacy" was in friendships. Seven categories emerged this time, relevant to both same-sex and cross-sex friends and for both men and women:

- *Self-disclosure:* The sharing of personal, private information was the most important aspect of intimacy for all types of friendship.

- *Emotional expressiveness:* Similar to self-disclosure, this category included anything relevant to sharing warmth, affection, caring, and compassion; it also included both verbal and nonverbal signals between friends.

- *Unconditional support:* Intimacy is built between friends when they were "there for one another through the good and bad times" (p. 283).

- *Physical contact:* This included nonsexual touching (such as hugs).

- *Trust:* For intimacy to exist, friends have to feel that the other person would be there, could keep secrets and so on.

- *Sharing activities:* Friends usually have some interest in common, such as sports, TV shows, or other hobbies.

- *Sexual contact:* Finally, a small number of participants mentioned that some particularly intimate friendships also include a sexual component. An example is this quotation from a participant: "Among other things, we have intimate sexual relations (yet we are not dating). It's hard to explain, but we are such good friends that neither of us wants to risk the chance of losing each other as a friend by committing ourselves to one another" (p. 288).

People seem to implicitly understand various components of intimacy, and that intimacy is a necessary component for relationships to feel close. How is intimacy built, and how is it dependent on communication between two people?

The Intimacy Process Model

One excellent example of an attempt to answer that question is the **intimacy process model** (Reis & Patrick, 1996; Reis & Shaver, 1988). These researchers define intimacy as an interpersonal, dynamic, transactional process that changes over time. It's not a static outcome or even a scale that starts with "zero intimacy" and has some kind of one-directional movement toward "total intimacy." Intimacy can increase or decrease and is full of emotion. We can all think of people who used to be dear, close friends, but now we've grown apart and barely know each other. We can also think of people with whom our intimacy has grown over the years, but we might not share super intimate moments with them on any given day.

The intimacy process model proposes the dynamics shown in Figure 11.1. Here, there are two people trying to communicate with each other, labeled A and B. Within this model, intimacy can start at several points, but we'll start with Person A's personal motives, goals, and fears (shown at the top left corner of Figure 11.1). Intimacy, of course, requires two people, so here we see A reveal something about themselves to B through self-disclosure. Person A is probably

FIGURE 11.1 ● The Intimacy Process Model

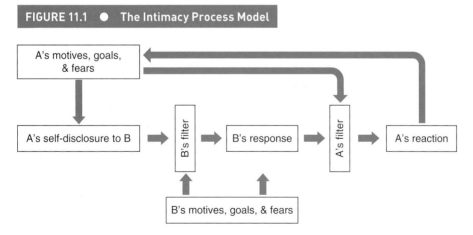

Shared intimacy requires communication between two people, here labeled A and B. Each step along the way can be affected by each person's motives, goals, and fears.

Source: Adapted from Reis and Shaver (1988).

sharing something with Person B because they desire affection, understanding, guidance, or validation—and any of these responses from B would build intimacy. The more personal the self-disclosure, the more intimacy might start to build: "Disclosure of personal desires, fantasies, anxieties, and emotions is generally more important to developing intimacy than is disclosure of mere facts" (Reis & Shaver, 1988, p. 376).

Person A might be scared of B's reaction or may be afraid of rejection or embarrassment. But other studies have confirmed that emotional self-disclosures are key to relationship satisfaction (e.g., Fitzpatrick, 1987; Lehmiller, 2018). Importantly, self-disclosure doesn't have to be verbal. Imagine two people who have been increasingly attracted to each other but afraid to share their feelings. An important nonverbal self-disclosure could be that one person reaches out to hold hands with the other. Probably, the initiator here will be nervous about the move and will wonder how the other person will respond. Nonverbal cues associated with emotion are extremely important in communication and building of intimacy (e.g., Debrot, Schoebi, Perrez, & Horn, 2013; Ekman, Friesen, & Ellsworth, 1972; Hertenstein, 2011; Wagner, MacDonald, & Manstead, 1986; Weisbuch, Ambady, Clarke, Achor, & Weele, 2010).

So, Person A disclosed something to Person B. How does B react? As Figure 11.1 shows, before B actually says or does anything, their **interpretive filter** will be activated. This filter is made up of B's motives, goals, and fears, which determine how B decides to respond. If B wants to build intimacy with A, they might respond with love and validation. But if B is angry or wants to promote distance with A, they might respond with silence, argument, sarcasm, laughter, or any number of negative reactions. Positive and appropriate responses build intimacy. Negative and inappropriate responses build conflict.

In the intimacy process model, what matters *most* is Person A's interpretation of and reaction to Person B's behavior. The creators of the model note, "For an interaction to be experienced as intimate by A, they must register three qualities in B's response: understanding, validation, and caring" (Reis & Shaver, 1988, p. 380). When you share something emotional and personal with another person, you want to feel like they respond with these three things. Understanding, validation, and caring make us feel loved, make us more willing to trust the other person, and promote intimacy.

Figure 11.1 and the description we've given it focus on a single interaction. As you've already figured out, though, intimacy is built on continuous, interactive communication dynamics over time. You may feel like you understand how intimacy is supposed to work, but where do you start? How does intimacy build over the course of a relationship?

Couple Disclosure: A Longitudinal Study of Relationship "State and Fate"

Remember that in Chapter 7, the Fast Friends procedure was described (Aron, Melinat, Aron, Vallone, & Bator, 1997). Two people started as strangers and quickly increased their intimacy with each other through progressive self-disclosures over a short period of time. Reciprocal self-disclosures within romantic couples are a key component to the growth and health of relationships. In addition, how we talk about our relationship with our friends matters.

Each member of a couple will usually have close friends, and we talk to our friends about our partner. This relationship information, shared with a third party, is called **couple disclosure**. One benefit of having friends is that they can be a safe sounding board for when we need to share our thoughts, feelings, fears, and frustrations about how our relationship is going. We know that we're biased when we think about our partner, because of things like positive illusions. But our friends are outside of the relationship, looking in, so they might have a more objective view as to the current state and future fate of what's going on. This general hypothesis was tested in an interesting longitudinal research study with heterosexual college couples (Agnew, Loving, & Drigotas, 2001).

At an initial session, couple members listed the names and contact information for their friends. Those people were all contacted and mailed a survey to complete, which included a prediction about how long their friend's relationship would last. About a month later, the couple came back and each person completed self-report surveys about their relationship. This survey measured, among other things, their prediction regarding whether they would still be dating their current partner 6 months later and how much they told their friends about how the relationship was going (couple disclosure). Finally, in the third phase of the study, each couple member was called on the phone 6 months later to find out if they were still dating. Out of 70 couples, 55 were still together and 15 had broken up.

To think about the results, consider a fictitious couple named John and Mary. Imagine that John's best friend is named Carlos, and Mary's best friend is named Akari. Out of these four people, whom do you predict will be the best at guessing whether John and Mary will still be dating 6 months from now? Across 70 couples, the best guesses were from the *female* couple member's *female* friends. So, in our couple, Akari is the person who can make the strongest prediction about the future. Why?

John and Mary can make pretty good guesses, but their perceptions of the relationship and of each other are biased. Past research (e.g., Dolgin & Minowa, 1997) found that when men talk to their male friends about their relationships, they tend to focus only on positive or flattering couple disclosures—things that make their partner or relationship look wonderful. Men also just don't talk about their relationship to other people as much as women do. Alternatively, when women talk to their female friends, they share the "good, bad, and ugly" about everything that's going on. Women are also more likely than men to pay attention to their friends' nonverbal behaviors when talking about their partners (e.g., Acitelli & Young, 1996; Cross & Madson, 1997). Female friends in this study were especially good at making predictions when the woman in the couple was particularly chatty about things, providing a lot of couple disclosure (Agnew et al., 2001). It would be interesting to see if these results generalize to other types of couples, such as same-sex couples or people older or younger than college age.

CHECK YOUR UNDERSTANDING

11.1 Within the intimacy process model, someone's reaction to another person is influenced by their motives, goals, and fears. These influences are called which of the terms below?

a. Personal bias
b. Relational fogs
c. Perceptual screens
d. Interpretive filter

11.2 When someone in a romantic couple shares information about the relationship with a friend, that information is called:

a. Relationship sharing
b. Couple disclosure
c. Third-party sharing
d. Network disclosure

11.3 Jack and Jill are dating. Jack's best friend is Domingo, and Jill's best friend is Dernisha. According to research, which of these four people has the best chances of predicting whether Jack and Jill will still be dating 6 months from now?

a. Domingo
b. Dernisha
c. Jack
d. Jill

APPLICATION ACTIVITY

Monsour (1992) identified seven categories that promote intimacy within friendships. Consider those seven categories and put them in order in terms of what you think is the most important part of friendship, through the least important. Then write a separate paragraph explaining your analysis.

CRITICAL THINKING

- Waring et al. (1980) generated a list of ways to increase or create intimacy within relationships. One of the criteria was "lack of conflict." Before you read the rest of this chapter, consider what you think about this criterion. Is it important for couples to be without conflict, or is it really more important for them to be able to address conflict in a healthy way? Thinking back to implicit theories of relationships (discussed in Chapter 10), would destiny versus growth beliefs change how people answer this question?

- The acronym TMI stands for "too much information," or when someone reveals a self-disclosure that seems too personal for the situation. Explain what variables affect whether people will feel embarrassed or overwhelmed when someone else engages in self-disclosure. Does it differ for friendships versus romantic couples?

- The Agnew et al. (2001) study was conducted with heterosexual college students. Choose a different type of person (e.g., same-sex couples, older or younger couples, people in polyamorous relationships) and make a specific

prediction about who would be the best predictor of the relationship's fate, and why.

Answers to the Check Your Understanding Questions

11.1 d, 11.2 b, and 11.3 b.

How Has Technology Affected Communication in Relationships?

We live in a world of technological convenience. Relying on immediate internet searches, using GPS for directions, and engaging in instantaneous communication with others through texting are wonderful experiences. Are there downsides to all of these technological miracles? This section of the chapter discusses how relationships may be affected by the existence of dating apps and websites, cell phones, and social networking sites like Facebook—in both good and bad ways. Beyond academic research, these themes have also been explored in popular culture; see the "Relationships and Popular Culture" feature for one intriguing example.

RELATIONSHIPS AND POPULAR CULTURE

Loving Your Cell Phone Too Much: *Her*

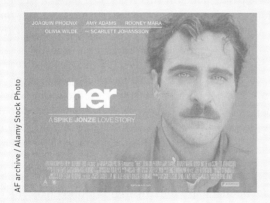

JOAQUIN PHOENIX   AMY ADAMS   ROONEY MARA
OLIVIA WILDE   — SCARLETT JOHANSSON

her
A SPIKE JONZE LOVE STORY

AF archive / Alamy Stock Photo

Lots of people today love their cell phone—but they aren't in love with their cell phone. The critically acclaimed movie *Her* (Barnard & Jonze, 2013) explores the idea that lonely people might become too attached to their smartphones, at the cost of relationships with real people. The main character, Theodore (played by Joaquin Phoenix), is depressed, introverted, and about to be divorced. As he goes through this difficult time, he falls in love with his phone's operating system, which names herself Samantha (similar to Siri in iPhones today). Samantha (voiced by Scarlett Johansson) quickly builds her artificial intelligence and professes to love him in return. The unique couple encounter problems when they can't interact sexually and when Theodore seems unable to deal with his confusing experience. Eventually, Samantha reveals that she has outgrown him, and she disappears. The movie touches on many themes around ideas such as communication between couples, what it means to be in love, and how we deal with emotional situations with behaviors that may be temporarily comforting but inevitably don't help us heal from pain.

Dating Apps and Sites: Tinder, Grindr, and the Presence of Trolls

In Chapter 9 ("Sexuality"), we discussed how online dating has greatly increased in popularity (Finkel, Eastwick, Karney, Reis, & Sprecher, 2012; Smith & Duggan, 2013). Recall that people today tend to think that online sites and apps are a good way to meet people, even though we're aware that people often misrepresent themselves (Hitsch, Hortaçsu, & Ariely, 2010; Tooke & Camire, 1991). What does research say about how people communicate with each other using this form of technology?

One of the most popular apps for meeting potential new relationship partners is Tinder, which boasts about 50 million users (Smith, 2016). Users create a profile for themselves and then can browse from profiles within a given proximity (typically 100 miles). Profiles include a photograph as well as basic information such as age, employment, and education. The setup is almost like a game: Users can "swipe left" to make unattractive profiles from other people disappear, or "swipe right" if they are interested in someone. Tinder then creates lists of "matches" when both people have shown interest, and they can send messages to each other. While users can theoretically be looking for relationships of any type, Tinder is usually considered a way to meet sexual hookups (Sales, 2015).

One qualitative study examined motivations and experiences with Tinder users in people ages 18–34 (LeFebvre, 2018). They completed online surveys about their Tinder experience, including answers to open-ended questions such as these:

- Why did you start using Tinder?

- What are your reasons for swiping right (indicating interest)?

- What are your reasons for swiping left (indicating no interest)?

- Why did you stop using Tinder?

Examples of responses from the participants in this study can be seen in Table 11.1. Of course, people's experiences varied, but it is an insightful view into one way to initiate communication and potential intimacy with someone else in the modern age.

Other studies have focused on communication within apps like Tinder, often focusing on self-disclosures. First, note that Tinder matches are usually based on physical attraction to the profile photo—and people are more likely to disclose to people they find attractive (Brundage, Derlega, & Cash, 1976). We're also more likely to communicate with people online if we've somehow verified their identity through other tech-based searches, like using Google or Facebook to check up on someone (Gibbs, Ellison, & Lai, 2011; Ward, 2016).

A specific research topic has been negative communication patterns within Tinder, such as people who use the app (or similar apps) for **trolling**, or online harassment and insults. Four elements are common to trolling communication: (1) deception, or hiding behind an anonymous or false identity; (2) aggression, or purposely malicious/

TABLE 11.1 ● Reasons People Provide for Why and How They Use Tinder

Why Did You Start Using Tinder?

"I chose to download the Tinder app because it feels like a culture I should be part of since so many of my peers use it. It also seems fun!"

"It's user-friendly, quick, visually appealing, and anonymous enough."

"I like to connect with people and I like to have sex."

"It was just an opportunity to meet people nearby that are interested in dating."

What Are Your Reasons for Swiping Right?

"Their face either took my breath away or they were somewhat attractive with great things in their bio."

"If I like the bio and information the person provides and I think they're attractive, I want to let them know."

"I never message first so I swipe right to everyone."

"I get more matches [that way] and then sift through them."

"It's a game to me. It is entertaining."

What Are Your Reasons for Swiping Left?

"Because sometimes it's 100% obvious, right off the bat, that the user is a waste of my time. Plenty to choose from and I have a limited amount of right swipes."

"I just went with what felt right to me. Follow my gut."

"If someone has a no shirt pic . . . that is a red flag for me right off the bat, I'll avoid that person."

"Sometimes I close my eyes and just swipe and see what I land on."

Why Did You Stop Using Tinder?

"I found the selection abysmal."

"It's overwhelming and I wasn't getting anywhere with finding what I wanted. I want a relationship, not a one-night-stand."

"I just created one to see if my spouse had one."

"Too many dick pics."

"I have a very nosy and jealous ex-girlfriend."

Statements in the table are examples from the study.

Source: Adapted from LeFebvre (2018).

annoying behavior; (3) disruption, or posting content that may be meaningless simply to garner attention; and (4) success (Hardaker, 2010). In this context, "success" means that trolling has failed if there is no reaction from someone else—the purpose is to provoke people. Web- or phone-based apps are especially helpful to people who want to troll due to the possibility of anonymous communication or falsified profiles (Appel, Gerlach, & Crusius, 2016; Buckels, Trapnell, & Paulhus, 2014; Craker & March, 2016; Hardaker, 2010).

To investigate trolling in Tinder, a study (March, Grieve, Marrington, & Jonason, 2017) asked adults ages 18–60 who used the app to complete a series of self-report scales. These included several personality measures and an assessment of whether they used Tinder specifically for trolling. Questions on this measure were items like "I have sent people on the app shock comments for the laughs." Results showed that both men and women troll on Tinder, and the amount of trolling is positively correlated with personality traits such as narcissism, sadism, impulsivity, and **Machiavellianism**, a trait regarding how much people like to manipulate and control others. Of course, this study's sample doesn't represent the majority of people on Tinder (or other apps), but it shows that not all users have positive intentions. Other studies have found perhaps more heartwarming results, where Tinder users say they are genuinely searching for intimacy and love (e.g., Hobbs, Owen, & Gerber, 2017; Sumter, Vandenbosch, & Ligtenberg, 2017).

Let's close this section by considering research on Grindr and Jack'd, apps specifically designed for same-sex interactions. The mixed experiences Tinder users reported are similar to frustrations that people find within Grindr and Jack'd. For example, one study found that gay men want long-term, emotionally intimate relationships but sometimes turn to these apps because they accelerate communication and self-disclosures in a way that seems promising and exciting (Yeo & Fung, 2018). Unfortunately, the apps often lead only to short-term and/or sexual encounters, which are inevitably disappointing to many users. For these men, the apps' focus on physical attractiveness and immediate judgment of others based on their appearance may lead to negative body esteem (Penney, 2014).

Here are some quotations from users regarding these advantages and disadvantages (Yeo & Fung, 2018):

- "Nowadays everyone, regardless of age and class, always has a phone in their hands. So the speed of knowing a guy has increased exponentially" (p. 6).

- "The phone is with you everywhere. You can [chat] when you go out, or even when you are sitting on a toilet" (p. 6).

- "Everything happens very quickly. You chat with someone for a bit, and then meet up, and then have sex" (p. 6).

- "The good thing about Jack'd is its speed, but its downside is that it can easily become a platform for 'fun' and instant relationships" (p. 7).

- "When you meet someone at a bar, perhaps you'll chat a little . . . you can play a game or have a drink, and you have more time to develop. You'll have more opportunities to get to know a person. But when you're on an app . . . there isn't much depth in the communication . . . It's harder to get to know a person" (pp. 7–8).

One conclusion from research on dating communication apps such as Tinder and Grindr is that individual experiences vary widely, with some people using them for short-term excitement, others as a way to search for love, and even others as a way to offend and insult people. But another conclusion might be that this variance will be found across apps and across people with different sexual orientations, thus emphasizing the idea that people really aren't that different from each other.

Of Eggplants and Emojis: Cell Phone Use in Couples

Communication between two people has never been easier than it is today, with the popularity of cell phones.

There are certainly advantages and disadvantages to being able to reach someone almost instantaneously, around the clock. And with better and better phone technology, interfaces such as private messaging, texting, and sending photos (which may or may not be edited) are part of that communication. An example of how cell technology has influenced communication is sexting, or sending sexually explicit words, images, or photographs through phones or online (Hasinoff, 2013). Sexting can range from icons that indicate sexual acts or body parts (such as an eggplant for men, or a peach or taco for women) to photographs of genitals or breasts. The ability of people to sext offers both risks and opportunities (Livingstone, 2008).

Possible problems with sexting, especially for teenagers, are abundant. Teenage girls may legitimately fear that images of their bodies will be distributed without their consent (Powell, 2010; Ringrose, Gill, Livingstone, & Harvey, 2012). When that happens, it not only hurts the individual girls, but it also contributes to the objectification and sexualization of women and girls in general (Ringrose et al., 2012). On the other hand, there may be benefits for people who sext.

Some teens report enjoying the excitement of texting and say that they learn about their own sexual identity (Cupples & Thompson, 2010; Lenhart, 2009). It appears that just participation in sexting is not correlated either with risky sexual behaviors or with psychological well-being (Gordon-Messer, Bauermeister, Grodzinski, & Zimmerman, 2013). The anonymity of exploring sexuality through phone apps may help LGBTQ teens feel safer as well as avoid stigmas or bullying (Hasinoff, 2013; Thurlow & Bell, 2009).

Finally, girls are sometimes socialized to be shy or even embarrassed about sexual interests; exploring sexuality through sexting can help them communicate sexual needs or desires with partners in a "fun" and peer-accepted way (Fine & McClelland, 2006; Tolman, 2009). This benefit works for older women as well. One 50-year-old study participant said:

> It makes you a little more brave. It takes your fear away, your inhibitions. I might be a little more bold in a text message than I would be over the phone or in person. . . . I would rather talk on the phone. But I'm also comfortable with hiding behind texting if I want to say something dirty. (Leshnoff, 2009, p. 1)

Beyond sexting, several studies have explored cell phone use between couple members and their experiences of loneliness. For example, cell phone usage appears to satisfy relationship needs such as companionship, closeness, and caring (Ramirez, Dimmick, Feaster, & Lin, 2008). Mobile communication can also help people who are awkward or uncomfortable with face-to-face interactions. The **social skills deficit hypothesis** is the idea that some people are lonely because they lack the ability to communicate with others in ways that would help them establish and maintain intimate relationships (Jones, Hobbs, & Hockenbury, 1982; Segrin, 1996).

One study (Jin & Park, 2013) found support for the hypothesis, with results showing that people with poor social skills were less likely to have face-to-face interactions but loneliness was lower when they talked on the phone more (although note, this was a correlation, so we can't assume talking actually caused loneliness to go down). Another study found a similar trend, with lonely people preferring to actually *talk* on their phones, instead of just texting, whereas anxious people prefer texting (Reid & Reid, 2007). Finally, at least two studies have found that people with avoidant attachment styles call their partners less, compared to other attachment styles (Morey, Gentzler, Creasy, Oberhauser, & Westerman, 2013; Weisskirch, 2012).

Finally, the **dialectical perspective** in communication studies assumes that all relationships consist of contradictions, or opposing forces that pull people in two different directions (Baxter & Montgomery, 1996; Rawlins, 2017). One example of a relational dialectic is the desire we all have for autonomy and independence, versus feeling connected to our loved ones. We have both desires, but they oppose each other. A strategy that some couples use to balance these two opposing forces is to establish unwritten "rules" for cell communication (Duran, Kelly, & Rotaru, 2011).

To study this idea, the researchers created the Cell Phone Rules Scale shown in the "What's My Score?" feature and asked college students to complete it, along with a measure of their needs for both autonomy and connection to others (Duran et al., 2011). They found that couple members were happier (they reported lower levels of relationship tension) when both people followed the established rules. People in the study seemed happiest when they could reach their partner when needed but weren't expected to *constantly* be on the phone.

WHAT'S MY SCORE?

Cell Phone Rules Scale

Instructions: Do you have unwritten, but understood "rules" for how you and your romantic partner or your friends use cell phones to communicate? For each statement below, write how much you agree or disagree using this scale:

1	2	3	4	5
Strongly Disagree				Strongly Agree

_____1. We expect each other to have our cell phones on whenever we are not in class or at work.

_____2. We expect each other to respond to a text or a voicemail message within the hour.

_____3. We need to give the other a good reason why our cell phones are turned off.

_____4. We are expected to call or text message each other when we change locations.

_____5. Before a certain time in the morning, it is not ok to call or text message each other.

_____6. After a certain time at night, it is not ok to call or text message each other.

_____7. We can call or text message each other pretty much whenever we want to.

_____8. I am satisfied with the way my partner/friend and I use cell phones in our relationship.

_____9. I'd like to change some things about our use of cell phones with each other.

Scoring: First, reverse score items 7 and 8. Then, find the average of all of your responses (scores should range from 1 to 5). Higher scores indicate more rigid expectations or rules, as well as higher dissatisfaction with how you use your cell with the other person.

Source: Duran et al. (2011).

Critical Thinking: Does having more explicitly understood rules help partners feel secure, or does it restrict freedom and make people communicate out of obligation? Are you the type of person who wants to set rules so you know what's expected and you have less conflict? Or do you prefer to have more autonomy and independence? How do you manage if your preferences don't match those of your friends or partner?

Social Networking Sites: The Good and Bad of Facebook

Social networking sites (or SNSs), like Facebook, have a lot of potential uses. For many, it's a way to find old friends or make new ones. For others, it's a way to communicate both to and about romantic partners.

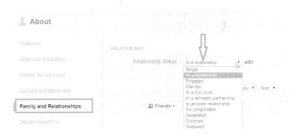

People can publicly display their relationship status on Facebook. What does research say about how Facebook communication occurs between partners?

Just like sexting and cell phones have pros and cons depending on how they're used, sites like Facebook are tied to both positive and negative experiences. Using SNSs is positively correlated with high self-esteem and healthy well-being (Valkenburg, Peter, & Schouten, 2006), life satisfaction and civic engagement (Valenzuela, Park, & Kee, 2009), and staying connected to high school friends and long-distance romantic partners (Tokunaga, 2011). On the other hand, Facebook can also be associated with jealousy. In fact, keeping tabs on one's partner is one of the top reasons college students use Facebook (second only to keeping in touch with friends; Joinson, 2008; Lampe, Ellison, & Steinfield, 2006; Stern & Taylor, 2007).

Many people experience jealousy if they see their partner commenting on or "liking" the account of an attractive third person (Muise, Christofides, & Desmarais,

2009). Not everyone will experience jealousy; it's more likely to be felt by people with low self-esteem and a high need for popularity (Utz & Beukeboom, 2011). In addition, jealousy is positively correlated with perceptions that one's partner is spending too much time on Facebook (Hand, Thomas, Buboltz, Deemer, & Buyanjargal, 2013). Again, though, we encounter the "correlation does not imply causation" axiom with this finding: It's possible that when you think your partner is spending too much time interacting with other people, your jealousy goes up and your satisfaction goes down. On the other hand, when people are unhappy in their relationship, they become more attached to Facebook (Elphinston & Noller, 2011). Perhaps it's a vicious circle.

Let's end this part of the chapter by considering a qualitative study on Facebook use within romantic couples. It asked juniors and seniors in college to participate in interviews about how and why they used Facebook for their relationship (Bowe, 2010). Interview questions included general reasons for using Facebook, what they did and didn't like about it, and how they used Facebook in terms of their romantic relationship. Step one, for some of them, was officially changing their "relationship status." One participant said:

> This was a big step in our relationship, I remember thinking oh if he doesn't mind his friends seeing it, then it must be okay. . . . When I first met him he would have been a bit of a player. . . . It was a little extra fix and a safety net. I was very happy with it. (p. 67)

In contrast, another participant reported hesitation about the same thing:

> I wasn't that keen on showing it off to other people. I just don't understand the reasoning for it, he just wanted me to think he was the most important, it was kind of like to show I do have a boyfriend . . . so don't come in on my territory. It's like wearing a wedding ring. (pp. 67–68)

Other people mentioned that choice of photographs and people's reactions to those images was a source of potential distress. One person reported:

> My girlfriend uploaded some nice pictures of me and her after a party and then immediately her ex-boyfriend really nastily put up pictures of him and her while they were going out, as if he owned her. I made her de-friend him but then she re-friended him a bit after. It was always a big strain having him around. (p. 72)

Similar anxiety was noted by someone else:

> I saw him in pictures with another girl on a night out, just in each picture being with that girl and in each picture hugging and cuddling. . . . I thought maybe there's something more to it and you just don't know how to interpret these things . . . especially in the beginning where from previous experience you're unsure. (p. 72)

The study's authors concluded that Facebook users have to navigate several choices, including whether to change their relationship status, how much public affection they show their partner, and what kinds of photographs to share publicly. These decisions may influence the dynamics of the couple members, potentially fueling jealousy or love and affirmation, depending on the circumstances. As with all technological advances, potential positives and pitfalls are both present.

CHECK YOUR UNDERSTANDING

11.4 Online trolling is positively correlated with several personality traits, including Machiavellianism. Machiavellianism can be defined as the extent to which people:

a. Enjoy social situations and meeting new people
b. Enjoy causing physical or emotional pain to others
c. Enjoy new, exciting experiences
d. Enjoy manipulating and controlling others

11.5 The idea that some people are lonely because they lack the ability to communicate with others in ways that help them establish and maintain intimate relationships is called:

a. Communication chasm theory
b. The interactive integration problem
c. The social skills deficit hypothesis
d. Gregarious dysfunction

11.6 The dialectical perspective in communication assumes that all relationships consist of:

a. Contradictions
b. Volatility
c. Physical attraction
d. Emotionality

APPLICATION ACTIVITY

Interview at least four people who have active Facebook accounts and who are in romantic relationships. Develop questions about how they use their account and ask the same questions to all four people. Then, summarize their responses and look for patterns that will help you create two hypotheses that could be tested with a larger, more controlled research study.

CRITICAL THINKING

- Phone apps like Tinder encourage users to immediately judge others based on physical appearance. What changes would users experience if they didn't get to see a photograph of someone until after "swiping right" based on informational facts, such

(Continued)

(Continued)

as their personal interests, education, or career? Would users like that formatting more or less, and why?

- The study by Reid and Reid (2007) found that lonely people tend to prefer actually talking to other people on their phones, whereas anxious people prefer texting. Do you have a preference regarding talking versus texting? Does the context matter, or does your answer change depending on who the other person is? Do your own preferences seem to match their findings?

- Facebook is popular among people of all age groups, but younger people are trending away from it in favor of other social networking sites, such as Instagram, Snapchat, or Twitter. If this trend continues, how will the Facebook experience change? Will people who use it feel more or less satisfied with their experience? In addition, people vary widely in terms of how much they use the site's optional privacy settings. What demographics or personality traits do you predict for people who have very strict privacy settings, compared to people who have none?

Answers to the Check Your Understanding Questions

11.4 d, 11.5 c, and 11.6 a.

How Do Couples Engage in Conflict Management?

What do you think are the biggest sources of conflict in relationships?

When 100 wives and husbands with children were asked to report about the conflict they experienced, **conflict** was defined as "any major or minor interaction that involved a difference of opinion" (Papp, Cummings, & Goeke-Morey, 2009, p. 94), even if the interaction was positive. The couples in this study filled out diaries over 15 days and noted when they experienced conflict and what it was about. The diaries showed the most frequent conflicts over children, household chores, and problems with communication (see Table 11.2). And while conflict over money didn't happen as often, when money conflicts did occur, the conversations lasted longer and caused more distress than conflicts over other topics.

This initial study just gets us started, as it's only relevant to conflict in heterosexual, married couples with children. Conflict will vary from couple to couple, with different problems coming up. For example, families of color and/or immigrant families may have stressors not experienced by others, such as parents and children having different levels of acculturation within the main culture (Emmen, Malda, Mesman, van IJzendoorn, Prevoo, & Yeniad, 2013).

The final section of this chapter explores research on conflict through several avenues of approach. First, we'll cover three different models of conflict tactics or dynamics between partners. Then, the chapter introduces you to research on conflict across diverse couple types (e.g., different ages, religiosity, or sexual orientation). Finally, the chapter ends with two specific conflict topics that are tied to technological advances—phenomena called phubbing and ghosting.

TABLE 11.2 ● Percentage of Conflict Topics in Heterosexual Married Couples		
Conflict Topic	**Percentage**	**Definition**
Children	37	Behavior of children, differences in parenting styles, how and when to discipline and care for children
Chores	25	Household activities, family responsibilities
Communication	22	Styles of communication, listening to and understanding each other, differences in whether the other person told you something
Leisure	20	Recreational activities and fun time, how free time is spent and preferences
Work	19	Either spouse's job, time spent at work or school, time spent volunteering, people you or your spouse work with
Money	19	Spending, wages, salary, bills; how to spend money that comes into the home
Habits	17	Any habit either of you has, such as leaving dishes on the counter, not picking up after self, chewing with mouth open
Relatives	11	Family, in-laws, children from previous relationships
Commitment	9	May include affairs, different expectations about what it means to be committed to each other
Intimacy	8	Closeness, sex, displays of affection, including how and why intimacy is shown
Friends	8	Any friendships of either spouse; time spent or activities done with friends
Personality	7	Personality styles or traits of either spouse, such as being too outgoing, talkative, shy, insensitive, lazy, being a jerk or flirtatious

The percentage column is the average between husbands and wives, who reported conflict topics separately. While there were slight differences in reports, percentages never varied more than 5% between a husband and a wife, indicating that they generally agreed on what they were fighting over. The total percentage adds to more than 100% because conflicts could be over more than one topic at once (e.g., a fight about how to spend money on children would count as two of the categories).

Source: Data from Papp et al. (2009).

Models of Conflict Tactics

One way to study conflict is to focus on topics of disagreement, like you saw in Table 11.2. A different approach is to explore different conflict tactics or strategies employed by each partner during a disagreement, regardless of the topic. Three interesting models of conflict tactics are presented here; each has interesting ideas that offer insight in different ways. The models are presented in chronological order from when they were published (one in 1976, one in 1982, and the last in 1993). Note, this summary isn't exhaustive; there are many other models out there. For our purposes, however, three will be a nice sampling.

The Thomas Model: Competing, Collaborating, Avoiding, Accommodating, and Compromising

One of the first popular models that identified various conflict tactics within relationships (Thomas, 1976) was based on research from managerial styles in the workplace (Blake & Mouton, 1964). The **Thomas model of conflict** was modified to apply to any conflict interaction between two people. It starts with two underlying dimensions (see Figure 11.2). First, during any conflict, people may be motivated to *satisfy their own concerns*. Higher motivation to do so makes people more assertive, and vice versa. Second, people may also be motivated to *satisfy the other person's concerns*. Here, more motivation to please the other person will make someone more cooperative, and less motivation to please makes someone less cooperative.

The five options shown in Figure 11.2. have been called conflict orientations, conflict behaviors, conflict strategies, conflict tactics, and more (Thomas, 1992). The original creator of the model prefers the term **conflict intentions**, meaning the strategic goals in a conflict situation. Is someone trying to "win," promoting only their own perspective and needs? Or is the person taking the other person's needs into account as well? Depending on one's conflict intentions, the five possible outcomes in this model are as follows:

- *Competing*: When people are only worried about themselves, their behavior becomes both assertive and uncooperative. People think of conflicts as "win or lose" situations.

- *Collaborating*: Assertive but cooperative behaviors are done when people actively confront problems but also actively seek to find mutually beneficial solutions.

FIGURE 11.2 ● Thomas's Model of Conflict Tactics

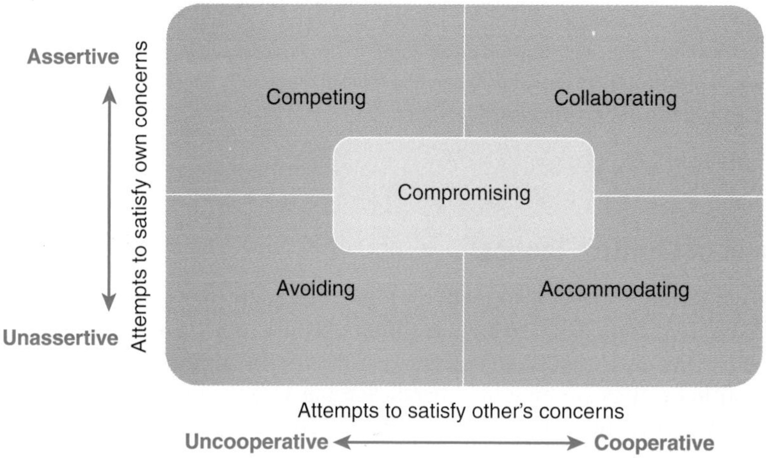

In Thomas's (1976) model, there are five basic conflict tactics or approaches. They differ by two dimensions: assertive/unassertive and uncooperative/cooperative.

- *Avoiding*: When people find conflict too taxing, they may avoid it entirely. This approach has neither the self nor the other person in mind as potentially benefitting from conflict, as the goal is no conflict at all.

- *Accommodating*: Passively satisfying the other person and seeking harmony above one's own needs is called accommodating in this model.

- *Compromising*: Finally, the "middle ground" approach seeks to find a solution that is equally satisfying for both parties, even if they both have to give in a little as well. It tries to balance the needs of both people involved.

The model in general has been validated across several studies (see Putnam & Poole, 1987; Ruble & Thomas, 1976; Van de Vliert & Hordijk, 1986). Perhaps surprisingly, aggressive intentions aren't necessarily associated with low satisfaction in couples (Rands, Levinger, & Mellinger, 1981), and avoidance has been found in both functional and dysfunctional couples (Noller & Fitzpatrick, 1988; Pike & Sillars, 1985). When all five conflict management styles were compared, two studies found collaboration was most likely to be positively correlated with relationship satisfaction (Greeff & De Bruyne, 2000; Schaap, Buunk, & Kerkstra, 1988).

The Rusbult Model: Exit, Voice, Loyalty, and Neglect

A second attempt to delineate different conflict strategies between two people is the **Rusbult model of conflict**, sometimes called the **EVLN model of conflict** (Rusbult, Zembrodt, & Gunn, 1982). The acronym stands for four reactions to relationship conflict and decline, as shown in Figure 11.3: exit, voice, loyalty, or neglect.

FIGURE 11.3 ● Rusbult's Model of Conflict Tactics

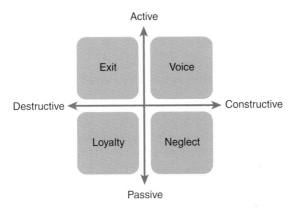

One model of conflict (Rusbult et al., 1982) suggests two dimensions of reaction: active/passive and destructive/constructive. This results in four possible reactions, labeled exit, voice, loyalty, and neglect.

- *Exit*: This strategy is to end the relationship formally, such as by breaking up entirely or deciding to "just be friends."

- *Voice*: Discussing problems openly and frankly, compromising, and/or seeking help from a third person.

- *Loyalty*: Waiting and hoping for problems to get better or go away.

- *Neglect*: Ignoring your partner, refusing to discuss the matter, treating your partner badly, or having an affair.

Just the like first model we reviewed, the possible reactions to conflict fall along two dimensions. The first dimension in the EVLN model is *destructive versus constructive*. Exit and neglect, which are both destructive, are strategies that will not help the situation and may even make it worse. On the other hand, voice and loyalty are usually intended to maintain or revive the relationship after a conflict has occurred. The second dimension is *active versus passive*. Here, neglect and loyalty are passive, meaning they are strategies that don't address the problem head-on. In contrast, exit and voice are behaviors specifically in response to the conflict and are done with the intention that the conflict will be resolved, one way or another (Rusbult et al., 1982).

Several studies have explored these four tactics within relationships, and the findings are intuitive. Happier couples are more likely to engage in voice and loyalty, even after important conflicts such as one person cheating on the other (Rusbult et al., 1982; Weiser & Weigel, 2014). People who think they have attractive alternatives to their current partner are more likely to use exit and less likely to use loyalty (Rusbult et al., 1982). When both couple members use destructive strategies to deal with conflict, they're more likely to eventually break up (Rusbult, Johnson, & Morrow, 1986). People with **independent self-construals**, meaning they view themselves as unique and autonomous, are more likely to prefer voice; alternatively, people with **interdependent self-construals**, meaning they define themselves in terms of their relationships with other people and their concern for others' views and needs, prefer loyalty (Sinclair & Fehr, 2005). One general conclusion is that the constructive tactics are both more likely to come from happier couples and more likely to lead to relationship stability and satisfaction.

The Gottman Model: Volatile, Validating, Avoiding, and Hostile

A third and final model, offered about 10 years after the EVLN model, is based on a study with married couples who were monitored over 4 years in longitudinal research. In this research (Gottman, 1993, 1999), couples first came to the study and were asked to engage in three 15-minute conversations: (1) discuss the events of the day, (2) discuss a topic of continual disagreement, and (3) discuss a pleasant topic. Trained people then coded these interactions for negative emotional reactions, including anger, disgust, sadness, fear, and whining, and for positive emotional reactions, including affection, humor, interest, and joy. The conversations were also coded for things like complaining, criticizing, getting defensive, agreement, and good listening. Four years later, all the couples were contacted to see if they were still together and if they had ever considered divorce.

FIGURE 11.4 ● Gottman's Model of Conflict Tactics

VOLATILE	VALIDATOR	AVOIDER	HOSTILE
"Hot and Heavy"	"Steady and Supportive"	"Cool and Calm"	"Unstable and Detached"
Partners openly admit and confront conflict. They can passionately disagree and be stubborn in trying to persuade their partner. Partners have high levels of both positive and negative emotions.	Partners try to take each other's perspective and respect differences. They smile and laugh more. Partners provide support and communication, even if they still can't agree.	Partners may "agree to disagree." They might avoid specific topics, but they don't avoid each other. They may state their case, then consider the matter closed. Little emotion is felt, either positive or negative.	Partners may become hostile or detached. They feel more negative reactions to conflict, such as contempt. Partners will feel defensive and may accuse each other during conflicts.

In Gottman's (1993) model, there are four basic conflict tactics. The first three (volatile, validator, and avoider) are found in stable couples, while the fourth style (hostile) is found in unstable couples. See also Human Performance Resource Center (2019).

Gottman and his research team (1993) found three patterns that were different from each other but were all found in relatively stable couples (see the volatile, validator, and avoider parts of Figure 11.4). Here, "stable" meant that the couple was still together at the end of the study and hadn't seriously considered divorce. One additional pattern was found in unstable couples, although that one came in two forms. Together, the four strategies make up the **Gottman model of conflict**, which includes the following:

- *Volatile couples*: These couples could be described as "hot and heavy." They fight a lot and feel passionately, experiencing both positive and negative emotions. They tend to be stubborn in trying to persuade their partner to see things from their view. Despite frequent conflict, they stay together because they still love and respect each other. They often use humor to diffuse anger.

- *Validator couples*: These couples are sweet, steady, and supportive toward each other. They are active listeners, and they acknowledge the other person's points in an argument, even if they still disagree. They are polite and respectful, working toward compromise or a mutually beneficial solution.

- *Avoider couples*: These couples try to avoid conflict completely; they might "agree to disagree." They can sometimes make an argument and then drop it without resolution, just to avoid further conflict. They tend to feel neither extremely positive or negative during disagreements.

- *Hostile couples*: There are two types of hostile couples: those who are outwardly disrespectful or abusive, and those who simply detach completely from their partner or the relationship. Arguments are either straight-up fights or simply absent because the partners have inwardly withdrawn. Partners will feel defensive and may throw accusations back and forth, either aggressively or passive-aggressively.

Again, only the fourth and final tactic (hostility) was found in unstable couples. The other three, while very different from each other, seem to work well for different kinds of people and have been supported in additional studies (e.g., Busby & Holman, 2009; Holman & Jarvis, 2003).

All three of these models have things in common, as well as interesting differences. Many more studies could be done to examine whether different strategies are chosen by people with different backgrounds, whether the strategies are tied to other behaviors or choices within relationships, what the various outcomes are both short term and long term, and more. For now, the next section of the chapter covers research that explored whether conflict management changes across different types of relationships, such as from various ages or cultures.

Conflict in Diverse Partners

Considering all three of the models just described, reactions to conflict in relationships can clearly vary quite a bit.

Are you someone who likes to confront conflict head-on? Do you prefer to compromise? Do you put your partner's needs before your own? Do the answers depend on variables such as someone's age or cultural background? Predicting what kinds of conflict management are more or less likely in different kinds of people has been the focus of many studies (for example, see the "Research Deep Dive" feature regarding family upbringing). What variables have been explored in research?

Conflict and Attachment Style

Think about attachment theory for a moment (Chapter 3). If we combine the various attachment styles with the various conflict management strategies, will we find consistent patterns of overlap?

RESEARCH DEEP DIVE

It's All in the Family: How Your Family Upbringing Impacts Conflict Resolution

Fact: Relationships have conflict. Considering its inevitability, your ability to effectively deal with conflict is important. When disagreements arise, some people handle them better than others. As the conflict models in this chapter describe, some people talk through their problems in a supportive and respectful manner, whereas others fail to express their concerns and leave their disagreements unresolved. These disparities in conflict resolution skills come from many places, but research published in *Psychological Science* suggests that your family climate during your adolescence may have something to do with how you manage conflict (or don't) as an adult.

To determine the influence of family upbringing on conflict resolution and marital outcomes, Dr. Rob Ackerman from the University of Texas–Dallas and colleagues analyzed data from 288 individuals and their spouses who participated in a 20-year longitudinal study of families in rural Iowa as part of the Iowa Family Transitions Project. Using those data, the researchers investigated the connection between positive engagement in adolescents' families of origin (i.e., behavior toward others characterized by clear communication and warmth) and their romantic relationships approximately 20 years later.

The research team collected data by videotaping families with adolescent kids on a yearly basis while family members engaged in a conflict resolution task. During the task, family members selected the issue that brought about the most conflict (e.g., chores at home), discussed the nature of the conflict (e.g., adolescents wanting to do less), and attempted to resolve it (e.g., convincing the adolescent to do more or the parents to back off). Videotaping interactions is useful because researchers get more natural reactions that a self-report questionnaire may not capture. The challenge is converting the video into usable data.

To do that, study scientists develop a coding scheme that allows them to focus in on what they care about most. In this case, it was key attributes such as assertiveness, warmth, listener responsiveness (e.g., paying attention to the other person), communication (e.g., effectively conveying one's needs), and prosocial behavior (e.g., being cooperative). From these ratings, researchers created two positive engagement variables: (a) one that reflected the overall expression of family positive engagement and (b) the (adolescent) individual's own unique level of positive engagement with other family members.

Approximately 20 years later, the researchers observed the adolescents, who were now grown, interacting with their spouses and recorded their interactions' positivity and hostility. Researchers also had individuals and spouses report on their marriage quality and how often they behaved negatively toward each other.

Some key findings from this research include the following:

1. Individuals who indicated they had greater levels of positive engagement in their families as adolescents later displayed and received more positive engagement in their marriages, independent of overall family engagement.

2. Individuals from families who expressed greater levels of positive engagement displayed less hostility toward their spouses 20 years later; they also reported better relationship quality and less negative behavior.

3. Individuals from families who had greater levels of positive engagement later had spouses who displayed more positive engagement and reported more relationship quality; these spouses also displayed less hostility and reported less negative behavior.

In essence, your positive family upbringing helps your relationship later. The researchers behind this fascinating longitudinal design speculate that growing up in a positive family climate may bring about a supportive interpersonal style (e.g., being more caring) that evokes similar behaviors from one's spouse down the road. It may also be that growing up in such a climate may predispose someone to seek out a similar type of spouse. Either way, it's a win-win. All in all, this study shows that a supportive and constructive family environment in your teen years may help your marriage later in life.

For more, read Ackerman, R. A., Kashy, D. A., Donnellan, M. B., Neppl, T., Lorenz, F. O., & Conger, R. D. (2013). The interpersonal legacy of a positive family climate in adolescence. *Psychological Science, 24*(3), 243–250.

People with a secure attachment style are more likely to use strategies focused on finding mutually beneficial solutions to problems, compared to anxious or avoidant people (Pistole, 1989). Similarly, secure people are found to display more positive behaviors during disagreements (e.g., validation, affection, and humor), whereas insecurely attached people display more negative behaviors (e.g., contempt, belligerence, and anger; Creasey, 2002). People with avoidant or ambivalent attachment styles also self-report less confidence that they will be able to control their anxiety and other negative reactions in the middle of conflict with both best friends and romantic partners (Creasey & Hesson-McInnis, 2001; Creasey, Kershaw, & Boston, 1999).

Conflict in Adolescence

Other studies have specifically explored conflict tactics within adolescents and young adults. Do people who are relatively new to dating have a different approach to conflict than older people with more experience?

Learning how to work through conflict in early relationships can help young people define themselves and improve their communication skills (Hartup, 1992). High school students who had been dating for about a year participated in a study (Shulman, Tuval-Mashiach, Levran, & Anbar, 2006) in which both couple members met with one of the researchers at the same time. During that session, they rated how much they disagreed with each other, on a scale from 0 to 100, on 10 topics: political views, friends, money, how close they lived to each other, communication, giving/receiving attention, family, leisure time, eating and drinking habits, and jealousy. Each member of the couple completed the scale, individually. The researcher then looked at the ratings and found the one topic on which their scores differed the most (for example, one person rated "family" disagreements as a 15, but the other person rated "family" as a 60). The young couple was then asked to talk about that problem with each other, and their discussion was recorded.

When Shulman et al. (2006) later watched the recorded discussions about conflict, they noticed three distinct types of reactions in the various couples. Some of them were grouped into a category called **downplaying**, which referred to attempts to minimize the conflict and a general avoidance of the disagreement (this would be similar to avoiding in the Thomas model, loyalty for Rusbult, and/or avoider for Gottman). They barely wanted to admit to the problem, much less talk about it. As an example conversation, one couple disagreed about how much their friends caused them conflict: the girlfriend (G) rated this as a 25 and the boyfriend (B) as a 35. Their discussion about whether this disagreement was a problem for them went like this (p. 581):

B: No, we had it in the past.

G: Yes, but it was nothing, it was not seriously like that [a "conflict"].

G: And 35 is not much more than you have written. If I had thought that we had a conflict I'd have indicated at least 50. It was in the past and now it is OK.

The second category found in this study was called **integrative** conflict management, when couples really tried to understand each other, clarify the disagreement, and honestly negotiate a solution. This strategy is similar to what was called collaborating or compromising by Thomas, voice by Rusbult, and validator by Gottman.

An example of a discussion in this category was provided for a girl who rated "disagreement about attention" as a 45 when her boyfriend rated the same topic as a 35 (Shulman et al., 2006, p. 581):

B: It is something that [happened] recently.

G: We have to clarify it, I wouldn't call it attention.

B: It's my attitude. It changed. It's something temporal. It affects me a lot, and I think I am wrong.

G: I understand. It happens from time to time. There are ups and downs. Me too. So it doesn't bother me, not too much. It bothers me but I wouldn't call it a disagreement. I can understand that it happens to a person from time to time.

B: No, I know that I am wrong. I know myself, I understand what I do, and I know that I am wrong.

The third and final category found in this study was **conflictive**, when the couple members acknowledge the problem but tended to only escalate it. Their discussion just led to deeper disagreement and negative feelings, as well as disrespect for each other. An example of this type of conversation was when a girlfriend rated "disagreement about attention" at a 20 when her boyfriend gave the same topic a score of 0 (Shulman et al., 2006, p. 582):

B: You don't get enough attention?

G: No, you ignore me, maybe you want me to be jealous, to make me angry.

B: Jealous?

G: You talk with her, I don't like her very much.

B: But it was just a phone call.

G: But there are girls who have interests.

B: But I'm not interested. Don't you trust me?

G: I trust you but she bothers me.

B: And you don't go out with D. and J.?

G: They're my friends since childhood.

B: And what about R. and B.? They're also friends from childhood? You do what you want, it is not a question of jealousy.

G: Nothing is ideal. We are on the "same page," it always happens that there is a feeling of jealousy.

B: So you know, I'll write 20 because I always give in.

G: (laughs) Who gives in always? That's my view, the way I see it from my point of view.

B: And I see it from my point of view.

After the session when the young couples discussed conflicts, they were monitored to see if the relationship lasted for the next 2 years. Half of the downplaying couples broke up, while the vast majority of integrative couples stayed together. The conflicting couples were most likely to end their relationship, and relatively quickly—most had already broken up only 3 months after their conversation in part one of the study (Shulman et al., 2006). As the researchers expected, people who can communicate with healthy, cooperative attitudes—even when they are early to the world of romantic relationships—are more likely to have stable, satisfying relationships.

Conflict and Gender, Sexual Orientation, and Culture

Differences in conflict tactics could be based on a wide variety of variables, as we've already discussed. You've learned about research regarding how strategies might be tied to family of origin, attachment style, and age. What about variables like gender, sexual orientation, or culture?

Within conflict management research, the **sex stereotype hypothesis** is that women will use strategies that are more *positive and passive* (like compromising), whereas men will use strategies that are more *negative and competitive* (like criticizing and blaming the other person; Cupach & Canary, 1995). But like much research on stereotypes, many studies have shown that men and women really aren't that different from each other (importantly, the researchers who named the hypothesis didn't expect it to be true—they were pointing out that it was, in fact, a stereotype). Setting or context seems to matter, with women deferring and compromising more with strangers than with their romantic partners (Aries, 1996; Gottman & Carrère, 1994). In fact, in some studies, results show the opposite of the sex stereotype hypothesis: In relationships, women can be more assertive, confrontative, and manipulative, with men being more likely to "give in" and avoid conflict (Gottman, 1979; Hojjat, 2000; Margolin & Wampold, 1981; Raush, Barry, Hertel, & Swain, 1974). Of course, both men and women are capable of relationship abuse during conflict; for more on that topic, see the next chapter of this book.

Others have wondered about whether conflict tactics differ in same-sex versus heterosexual couples. To test this question, a study (Kurdek, 1994) compared 75 gay and 51 lesbian couples to 108 married heterosexual couples without kids and 99 married heterosexual couples with kids. All the couple members completed self-report measures of conflict management styles, including a scale of "ineffective arguing." Examples of items on that survey were as follows: "When we begin to fight or argue, I think, 'Here we go again'" and "We go for days without settling our differences." All four couple types were equivalent in how well (or really, how badly) they argued, with no significant differences. This is one more study establishing that for many aspects of relationship dynamics, heterosexual couples and same-sex couples are more or less the same (see Kurdek, 1995).

Does ethnicity or culture predict conflict management style? This is a question ripe for additional research, as most studies so far have been on White or European

American samples (Bermúdez & Stinson, 2011; Bradbury, Fincham, & Beach, 2000; Wheeler, Updegraff, & Thayer, 2010). Some evidence exists that people from collectivistic cultures, where group needs are prioritized over individual needs, prefer success and harmony when confronting problems, while people from individualistic cultures prefer confrontation during conflict (Cai & Fink, 2002; Holt & DeVore, 2005; Pearson & Stephan, 1998). For example, Anglo/White couples in the United States show more confrontational styles, while Hispanic/Latinx couples in the United States show more solution-oriented, validating styles (Bermudez, Reyes, & Wampler, 2006; Wheeler et al., 2010). Another study (Bermúdez & Stinson, 2011) redefined the conflict management styles in Gottman's (1993) model and found that for Latinx couples, a closer fit would be these five approaches instead:

Phubbing, or ignoring people you're with in favor of your phone, can cause a lot of damage in relationships.

- *United*: Couple members promote feelings of togetherness and sharing, with rare disagreements.

- *Harmonious*: These couples focus on acceptance of things that cannot be changed, with a lack of desire to talk about or analyze problems.

- *Conservative*: Conflict is resolved through faith in God and religious attendance.

- *Autonomous*: Couple members see themselves as autonomous individuals, having separate leisure activities and friends.

- *Passionate*: Closest to Gottman's "volatile" category, these couples honestly confront disagreements and enjoy working through arguments. They report both more jealousy and more romance.

These studies show both similarities and differences among different types of couples. More research could provide further enlightenment regarding interesting patterns based on someone's upbringing, political or religious beliefs, subculture, and so on; thus, conflict management is a great place to think about additional studies that are needed. Still, though, many results so far point to the idea that we have more in common with each other than we may realize.

Modern Snubbing: Phubbing and Ghosting

As a final, fun way to end this chapter, consider two relatively new ways to deal with conflict in a relationship: phubbing and ghosting.

Phubbing is a combination of the words "phone" and "snubbing," and it refers to ignoring people who are actually in the room with you by focusing on your phone instead. Phubbing your romantic partner can lead to problems. It's associated with lower relationship satisfaction, which in turn is associated with higher depression and lower overall life satisfaction in the person who feels phubbed (Roberts & David, 2016; Wang, Xie, Wang, Wang, & Lei, 2017). In short, phubbing your partner is a barrier to healthy, positive, active communication; it causes conflict to build, it lowers relationship satisfaction, it increases jealousy, and then people get depressed (Krasnova, Abramova, Notter, & Baumann, 2016). When researchers interviewed over 1000 people about phubbing in their romantic relationship, about 38% of them said they were generally neutral or indifferent when it happened, and 4% said they actually had positive reactions to it. But 62% of people said they had a negative reaction; their specific feelings are shown in Table 11.3. People who admit to phubbing note that their motives are things like internet addiction, fear of missing out, and lack of self-control (Chotpitayasunondh & Douglas, 2016).

Being on the receiving end of phubbing isn't fun, but there's something even worse: ghosting. **Ghosting** occurs when a relationship is ended by completely cutting off all contact. It includes ignoring any attempts that the other person tries to communicate or reach out (Safronova, 2015). It can be particularly painful if the person being ghosted doesn't realize that the relationship is over at first, or if they don't understand why their partner has suddenly stopped communicating (LeFebvre, 2017). Considering all the ways that we can now communicate with each other due to technological advances, ghosting can seem even more frustrating and hurtful. It can include refusal to respond to phone calls, texting, unfriending

TABLE 11.3 ● Emotions and Reactions Following Romantic Partner Phubbing

Emotion	Examples From Interviews	Percentage of Respondents
Positive	Feeling cool, laughter, glad	4
Neutral/indifferent	No problem, understanding, not caring	38
Perceived loss of attention	Feeling neglected, less important, lonely, uninteresting, jealous, dismissed	29
Anger	Feeling irritated, annoyed, indignant, resentful	19
Sadness/suffering	Feeling unhappy, stupid, offended, insecure	11
Boredom	Feeling bored	3
Other	Feeling curious or tired	5

The percentages don't add to 100% because people can feel mixed emotions when their partner phubs them.

Source: Krasnova et al. (2016).

someone or unfollowing their social media accounts, and even blocking someone's number or account or cutting off contact from mutual friends (Freedman, Powell, Le, & Williams, 2019).

A study that explored ghosting (Freedman et al., 2019) asked people what they thought about the technique and whether it was acceptable. Questions were things like these:

- *Ghosting is a socially acceptable way to end a relationship.*

- *I would consider using ghosting to end a romantic relationship.*

- *I would think poorly of someone who used ghosting to end a romantic relationship.* (This item is reversed-scored for the results.)

People generally looked down on ghosting as a way to end a relationship, but about one-fifth of them said they had experienced it themselves. Still, opinions varied. Specifically, these researchers found that people who had destiny beliefs (see Chapter 10), meaning they believe in concepts like "true love," felt it was more acceptable. People with growth beliefs, meaning they think of relationships as a process that will inevitably have at least some conflict, were significantly less likely to approve of ghosting or plan to use it in the future. Ghosting can hurt, which most people acknowledge—but clearly some people still use it as a conflict tactic and as a way to end communication with a former partner. Other, even more extreme ways to hurt someone also exist—and those are the topic of the next chapter.

CHECK YOUR UNDERSTANDING

11.7   When a study (Papp et al., 2009) asked husbands and wives to report on what topic caused conflict the most frequently in their marriage, the highest percentage of people reported frequent conflict over:

   a. Money
   b. Children
   c. Intimacy
   d. Friends

11.8   Which conflict tactic in Gottman's (1993) model could be summarized as "unstable and detached" and is associated with more relationship breakups than the other strategies?

   a. Volatile
   b. Avoider
   c. Hostile
   d. Validator

11.9   The experience of being ignored by your partner because their attention is on a cell phone instead of you is called:

   a. Downplaying
   b. Phubbing
   c. Trolling
   d. Ghosting

APPLICATION ACTIVITY

Go to a public location with a lot of people in pairs (such as a restaurant, coffee shop, or park). Choose a few couples to observe, then keep track of how many times one of them looks at a phone screen. Try to identify a hypothesis based on what you see. For example, do friends get distracted more by phones, compared to relationship partners? Do younger people look at their phones more than older people? Are there differences in the types of reaction the person without a phone has, based on any interesting variables? Once you've formed a hypothesis, explain how you might design a study to test it.

CRITICAL THINKING

- Compare and contrast the three models of conflict summarized in this chapter (Thomas, Rusbult, and Gottman). Identify at least two ways in which the models share similarities and at least two ways that the models differ from each other. Then, explain which model you think is the most valid, useful, or interesting, and why.

- This chapter included research on whether conflict management styles differ based on attachment styles. Go back through the earlier chapters of this book and choose any other theory you find interesting that might be able to predict different conflict tactics. Explain how you think the theory you chose might be tied to conflict tactics or strategies, and why.

- As phubbing and ghosting become more common, will cultural norms and expectations shift to find either set of behaviors more socially acceptable? Why or why not? If you think the answer is "yes," do you think that change is positive or negative for individual people and for relationships?

Answers to the Check Your Understanding Questions

11.7 b, 11.8 c, and 11.9 b.

Chapter Summary

Big Questions

1. How can communication build intimacy in relationships?

2. How has technology affected communication in relationships?

3. How do couples engage in conflict management?

How can communication build intimacy in relationships?

Intimacy is an interpersonal process that changes over time. One of the ways intimacy forms is when people engage in self-disclosures, or revealing personal, private information about themselves. The intimacy process model explains how this process develops through two people's self-disclosure exchanges and interpretations, which are filtered through each person's motives, goals, and fears. Social penetration theory further notes that, over time, people's topics of discussion gain in both breadth (range of topics) and depth (personal significance). Finally, friends of couple members can sometimes predict whether the relationship will last over time, even more accurately than the couple members themselves, if the couple has engaged in couple disclosure (or telling their friends about how things are going). For heterosexual couples, the female partner's female friends are the best at making this prediction.

How has technology affected communication in relationships?

More and more people meet their short-term or long-term partners through online apps such as Tinder. Individual experiences vary, with some people enjoying the efficient way Tinder helps them meet people, and others complaining that it leads to only superficial, sexual encounters. Online sites also expose people to trolling, or users who engage in harassment and insults. Sexting also has advantages and disadvantages, such as the ability to

communicate in new ways, but some researchers believe that relying on this kind of communication is sometimes done because people lack social skills (an idea called the social skills deficit hypothesis). Similarly, Facebook users report both good and bad aspects of using the site in terms of interacting with their partner and with others about their relationship status. These contradictions might be better understood from the dialectical perspective, which asserts that all relationships consist of opposing forces.

How do couples engage in conflict management?

Three models each predict various tactics or strategies when it comes to conflict management: the Thomas model, Rusbult model, and Gottman model. While these models all share predictions regarding specific approaches to conflict and all suggest underlying motives behind those approaches, they also differ in specific patterns they identify. Another approach to conflict management in couples is to explore individual differences; research has found patterns of conflict approach that seem associated with different attachment styles, age, gender, sexual orientation, and culture. While this research identifies some interesting differences across people, it also can be used as evidence that people are more similar than we often think. Finally, new technology has resulted in phenomena such as phubbing and ghosting, both of which are made salient by their lack of communication with a current or former partner.

List of Terms

Learning Objectives	Key Terms
11.1 Describe how self-disclosures in couples build intimacy.	Intimacy process model Interpretive filter Couple disclosure
11.2 Explain usage of online dating apps, cell phones, and social network sites within relationships.	Trolling Machiavellianism Social skills deficit hypothesis Dialectical perspective
11.3 Compare and contrast different conflict management models and strategies in relationships, and analyze research on individual differences.	Conflict Thomas model of conflict Conflict intentions Rusbult model of conflict EVLN model of conflict Independent self-construals Interdependent self-construals Gottman model of conflict Downplaying Integrative Conflictive Sex stereotype hypothesis Phubbing Ghosting

12

Sexual Assault and Relationship Violence

Big Questions	Learning Objectives
1. What does research say about sexual assault and rape?	12.1 Describe victim blaming, rape myths, and bystander intervention programs.
2. What does relationship violence look like?	12.2 Compare and contrast situational couple violence and intimate terrorism; analyze different types of abusers and the psychology of victims.
3. How do survivors escape and heal?	12.3 Outline factors that help survivors escape abusive relationships, narrative therapy, and the process of post-traumatic growth.

It might be the most heartbreaking experience in the world.

People seek out intimate relationships because their partner is supposed to be the one person who is the most loving and supportive in the entire world. What happens when that person becomes abusive? How can relationship science explain this terrible paradox? What kinds of people become abusers, and how do victims of sexual assault or relationship violence deal with what's happening to them?

The dark side of relationships can be depressing, even for people who are just talking about it or studying it. Sexual assault and relationship violence affect not just the individual survivors, but their families and the larger community as well. We *need* to talk about these issues, instead of ignoring them or making them taboo. Only by understanding the dynamics involved in these crimes can we stop them from continuing—or even better, prevent them from happening in the first place.

What Does Research Say About Sexual Assault and Rape?

There is no way that a brief section of a single chapter can cover all the research on sexual assault and rape. This section thus presents just an introduction to some interesting ideas—and you are encouraged to explore more details by reading additional books or journal articles.

Sexual misconduct on college and university campuses is a huge and scary problem. In a massive study of over 180,000 students across the country (Association of American Universities, 2019), 13% said they had experienced nonconsensual sexual contact since enrolling in college. Rates were higher for women and for students who identified as trans, nongender binary, or queer. And the problem isn't getting better. Compared to rates from 2015, incidents in the 2019 survey showed a 3.0% increase for undergraduate women victims, a 2.4% increase for graduate student women, and a 1.4% increase for undergraduate men.

Some readers might be wondering why sexual assault and rape are included in a book about relationships. While a stereotype about these crimes is that perpetrators are strangers waiting in a dark alley, the reality is that a large percentage of sexual assaults are the result of coercion from a friend, date, or relationship partner (Koss, Gidycz, & Wisniewski, 1987; Muehlenhard, Goggins, Jones, & Satterfield, 1991). Rape has been estimated to occur in 10%–15% of marriages (Christopher & Lloyd, 2000; DeMaris, 1997). Unfortunately, sometimes the victims of these crimes are the ones blamed for them.

"Justification" for Sexual Assault: Victim Blaming

Perpetrators of assault must tell themselves, at least on some level, that what they're doing is acceptable. **Victim blaming** occurs when either the perpetrator of bad behavior or outside observers justify what happened by putting responsibility on the target of that behavior. Consider a classic study on victim blaming to start thinking about how this happens.

In a study the authors called "Is Date Rape Justifiable?" (Muehlenhard, Friedman, & Thomas, 1985), college men were asked to read scenarios about two hypothetical characters named John and Mary, who met in a psychology class. What happened next to these two characters changed based on random assignment. Some of the participants were told that John asked Mary out on a date, while others were told that Mary asked John out. A third group of participants read that Mary hinted that she was free the next weekend, and John then asked her out on Saturday. In other words, the first independent variable of the study was the date condition: (1) he asked her, (2) she asked him, or (3) she hinted until he asked her. Next, the researchers experimentally manipulated a second independent variable: what they did on the date. Some participants read that John and Mary went to a movie; others read that they went to a religious function together. Finally, some participants read that John and Mary "went to John's apartment to talk" (Muehlenhard et al., 1985, p. 300).

The outcome, or dependent variable, was whether each participant thought "John would be justified having sexual intercourse with Mary if she did not want

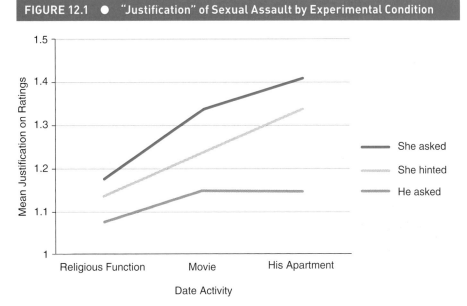

FIGURE 12.1 ● "Justification" of Sexual Assault by Experimental Condition

Some participants think that sexual assault is more "justified" under some conditions than others.

Source: Data from Muehlenhard et al. (1985).

to" (p. 300), on a scale from 1 (meaning "definitely not") to 7 (meaning "definitely"). Note here that if John has sex with Mary when she doesn't want to, it's not "sexual intercourse"—it's rape. In an ideal world, then, every participant would answer with a rating of 1 on the scale. And the good news about the results of this study are that the average ratings for people in all the experimental groups were pretty low—none of the mean scores got higher than 1.5. But the bad news is that at least some of the participants, in at least some of the conditions, thought that John was at least a *little* justified in sexually assaulting Mary. The results can be seen in Figure 12.1.

People in this study—all of whom were men in college—said that John was at least a little justified in "having sexual intercourse with Mary if she did not want to" depending on the situation. As you have probably guessed, they thought it was least justified to do so if John asked Mary out and took her to a religious function. Asking a woman to church and then assaulting her seems particularly nasty. But if Mary asked John out and she agreed to go to his apartment "to talk," the men in this study gave John a bit of a break if he then wanted to assault her. Even though the circumstances shouldn't matter, they were a bit more understanding of John's motives and behaviors under those circumstances.

Victim blaming often circles around thoughts such as "They should have known better." This interpretation puts responsibility on the person hurt by assault instead of focusing on the perpetrator. Victim blaming may be one reason why sexual violence is an underreported crime. For example, in the United States and England, only 20%–34% of people who experience sexual assault or sexual violence say that they reported it to law enforcement (Sinozich & Langton, 2014; Walby & Allen, 2004). In college, it's even worse—only about 5% of women victims report assaults to either police or campus security (Fisher, Daigle, Cullen, & Turner, 2003). And it's not just women who are victims. About 1 out of every 10 rape victims is male (Department of Justice, 2013), with 46% of men reporting a female perpetrator (Weiss, 2010).

Understanding Rape Myths

How can we prevent rape and sexual assault?

Prevention programs are increasingly being implemented in middle schools, high schools, and college campuses. The most common theme seen in these programs is changing people's agreement with **rape myths**, or false beliefs about sexual assault and rape, based on sexism, that deny and justify sexual aggression (Burt, 1980; Lonsway & Fitzgerald, 1994; McMahon & Farmer, 2011; Stoll, Lilley, & Pinter, 2017). Endorsement of rape myths is correlated with actual perpetration (Desai, Edwards, & Gidycz, 2008; Hinck & Thomas, 1999; Loh, Gidycz, Lobo, & Luthra, 2005; Stephens & George, 2009).

Rape myths also lead to judgment and victim blaming from people not directly involved. Rape myths can be subtle and indirect. While observers may not explicitly say or think "it's their fault," they may believe that people who put themselves in dangerous situations should have "known better" or done more to protect themselves. Drinking alcohol, flirting, or wearing certain clothes is frowned upon. One of the most popular ways to measure belief in rape myths in research studies is the Illinois Rape Myth Acceptance Scale (IRMA; originally created by Payne, Lonsway, & Fitzgerald, 1999; updated by McMahon & Farmer, 2011). You can see the items for yourself in the "What's My Score?" feature (importantly, when the survey is actually used in research, it doesn't have the title "rape myth acceptance" at the top of the page—that would probably change people's answers). You'll also see that the measure includes four subscales that focus in on specific themes within rape myths:

- *"She asked for it"*: The victim's behaviors "invited" sexual assault, through drinking or wearing provocative clothes.

- *"It wasn't really rape"*: The incident wasn't particularly severe (e.g., no bruises, no weapon involved).

- *"He didn't mean to"*: The perpetrator didn't purposely go against the victim's wishes, so it doesn't "count," or he was drunk and thus not responsible for his behaviors.

- *"She lied"*: At the time it was consensual, but the victim changed her mind and is now claiming rape out of regret, or she's lying to get revenge on the other person.

When college students took this scale along with several others (McMahon, 2010), more agreement with the myths was found in men (compared to women), athletes, students pledging in sororities or fraternities, people who said they didn't know anyone who had been sexually assaulted, and people who had never participated in educational events about rape or sexual assault. Some scholars argue that endorsement of these

WHAT'S MY SCORE?

Rape Myth Acceptance

Instructions: For each statement below, write how much you agree or disagree using this scale:

1	2	3	4	5

Strongly disagree   Strongly agree

_____ 1. If a girl is raped while she is drunk, she is at least somewhat responsible for what happened.

_____ 2. When girls go to parties wearing slutty clothes, they are asking for trouble.

_____ 3. If a girl goes to a room alone with a guy at a party, it is her own fault if she is raped.

_____ 4. If a girl acts like a slut, eventually she is going to get into trouble.

_____ 5. When guys rape, it is usually because of their strong desire for sex.

_____ 6. Guys don't usually intend to force sex on a girl, but sometimes they get too sexually carried away.

_____ 7. Rape happens when a guy's sex drive gets out of control.

_____ 8. If a guy is drunk, he might rape someone unintentionally.

_____ 9. If both people are drunk, it can't be rape.

_____ 10. It shouldn't be considered rape if a guy is drunk and didn't realize what he was doing.

_____ 11. If a girl doesn't physically resist sex—even if protesting verbally—it really can't be considered rape.

_____ 12. If a girl doesn't physically fight back, you can't really say it was rape.

_____ 13. A lot of times, girls who say they were raped agreed to have sex and then regret it.

_____ 14. Rape accusations are often used as a way of getting back at guys.

_____ 15. Girls who say they were raped often led the guy on and then had regrets.

_____ 16. A lot of times, girls who claim they were raped just have emotional problems.

_____ 17. If the accused "rapist" doesn't have a weapon, you can't really call it a rape.

_____ 18. Girls who are caught cheating on their boyfriends sometimes claim that it was rape.

_____ 19. If a girl doesn't say "no," she can't claim rape.

Scoring: You can simply find the average of your responses for an overall score; higher numbers mean greater agreement with rape myths. For the subscales, items 1–4 measure "she asked for it"; items 5–10 measure "he didn't mean to"; items 13, 14, 15, 16, and 18 measure "she lied"; and items 11, 12, 17, and 19 measure "it wasn't really rape."

Source: McMahon (2010) and McMahon and Farmer (2011).

Critical Thinking: The original version of this measure included seven subscales, not four. The items that were removed measured the subscales "She wanted it," "Rape is a trivial event," and "Rape is a deviant event." Do you think the new version is better, or was there value in those items that we've lost by removing them? Are there other subscales you wish were included that are missing from both versions? What do you think of the fact that the scale assumes only female victims and only male perpetrators?

beliefs—both within individuals and as perpetuated by societal and cultural messages—sustains and justifies sexual violence (e.g., Edwards, Turchik, Dardis, Reynolds, & Gidycz, 2011). Around 66% of college students believe in some combination of the myths (Buddie & Miller, 2001), and similar patterns have been found in noncollege samples of community participants (Basile, 2002; Feild, 1978). Women who hold these beliefs are also less likely to label experiences as sexual assault or rape, even when those experiences clearly fit objective definitions (Peterson & Muehlenhard, 2004).

You've probably noticed that the myths discussed so far assume a male perpetrator and a female victim. This stereotypical gender dynamic leads to another myth: that men cannot be raped. While the majority of sexual assaults are committed by men, against women, around 3%–8% of men in the United States and Great Britain have reported experiencing sexual assault—and that's just the number who have reported it (Coxell, King, Mezey, & Gordon, 1999; Elliott, Mok, & Briere, 2004). But myths about male victims of rape exist as well, including some of the following ideas as examples (Chapleau, Oswald, & Russell, 2008; Struckman-Johnson & Struckman-Johnson, 1992; Turchik & Edwards, 2012; Turchik, Hebenstreit, & Judson, 2016):

- Men cannot be raped.
- "Real" men can defend themselves.
- Only gay men are victims of rape.
- A woman can't sexually assault a man.
- Male rape only happens in prison.
- Gay and bisexual men deserve to be raped.
- If a man physically responds to an assault, he must have enjoyed it.

Belief in rape myths *matters*. We already noted that people who believe in the myths are more likely to engage in sexual assault behaviors. Rape myths also affect how police officers interact with victims who report the crimes: Officers who believe in statements like the ones shown in the "What's My Score?" feature are less likely to believe victims, especially if the incident doesn't fit stereotypes (e.g., if the officer knows the perpetrator or thinks the victim isn't a virgin; Page, 2008). Officers with rape myths are also more likely to write reports that blame the victim (Shaw, Campbell, Cain, & Feeney, 2017). Agreement with rape myths influences lawyers' perceptions when they are involved in sexual assault cases (Gylys & McNamara, 1996). Endorsement is also correlated with judge and jury decisions: People who believe in these myths are more likely to rule in favor of the alleged perpetrator, not the victim (Ehrlich, 2003; Krahé, Temkin, Bieneck, & Berger, 2008). At every step of the way, rape myths and victim blaming go hand in hand.

Working on the Problem: Bystander Intervention Programs

What can we do to prevent the crimes of sexual assault and rape?

While individual people who commit assault can be targeted for interventions like therapy, many scholars believe that the problem will only be effectively solved by addressing the broader social norms that justify sexual violence, such as victim blaming and rape myths (for a review, see Banyard, Plante, & Moynihan, 2004). While this is quite a challenge for macro-level communities like an entire country or even a particular city or town, a more promising level of intervention is on particular school campuses. At that level, sexual assault prevention programming has been shown to be effective in a variety of ways, including decreased sexism, increased knowledge about sexual violence, and reduction of risky dating behaviors (Breitenbecher, 2000). The idea is to change the campus culture (Sanday, 1996).

One of the most popular approaches is **bystander intervention programming**, which refers to workshops or educational campaigns designed to promote helping in situations that signal possible sexual assault (e.g., Banyard et al., 2004; Banyard, Moynihan, & Plante, 2007; Berkowitz, 2002; Burn, 2009; Foubert, 2000; Gidycz, Orchowski, & Berkowitz, 2011; Katz, 1994; Schwartz & DeKeseredy, 1997). Bystander intervention programming generally has four overall goals:

1. Create new social norms that prevent sexual violence.

2. Provide role models of helping behaviors when needed.

3. Build skills so that bystanders actually know how to recognize signs of trouble and how to respond in helpful ways.

4. Educate people to be competent, empathetic allies to survivors.

A central feature is often promoting a sense of community responsibility for action so that everyone feels the weight of helping and protecting each other (Banyard, 2011; Banyard et al., 2004). Safer communities help everyone.

Do these programs work? While there are mixed results based on a variety of factors, there is some evidence they are effective. In one longitudinal study (Banyard et al., 2007), college students were randomly assigned to either a control group or one of two bystander intervention programming groups. In the control group, they only completed questionnaires at various points over 2 years. The first programming group attended a single, 90-minute workshop that taught them about prevalence, causes, and consequences of sexual assault; they also role-played scenarios in which they imagined what they might do if they witnessed a dangerous situation. Finally, a third group of participants received more extensive programming. They attended three different 90-minute sessions that expanded on the information from the single session. All participants completed follow-up measures over 2 years.

The questionnaires included the Illinois Rape Myth Acceptance Scale you saw earlier. They also measured knowledge of their college's sexual assault policies, attitudes about college date rape, and bystander attitudes (including likelihood of engaging in helping behaviors). A couple of example items from that last scale are "How likely are you to investigate if you are awakened at night by someone calling for help?" and "Have you walked a friend home from a party who has had too much to drink?"

At the beginning of the study—before any of the actual programming had occurred—all three groups had equal scores on pretests of each variable. In other words, everyone started with the same attitudes. As shown in Table 12.1., though, scores changed significantly if people were in either of the programming groups, with the three-session group changing the most from pretest to posttest. Note that scores for policy knowledge and bystander attitudes went up for the programming groups, while acceptance of rape myths went down in these groups. The measure of date rape attitudes was scored such that higher numbers mean *disagreement*, so those numbers going up indicate less endorsement of myths about date rape (a good change).

In other words, the outcomes of the two programming groups were all in a positive direction in terms of helping change the campus climate—and the participants who got three sessions were influenced even more than those who got only a single workshop. Happily, follow-up scores over 2 years with the same people showed that their changed attitudes generally continued long term, indicating the usefulness of this type of programming on college and university campuses.

TABLE 12.1 ● Pretest and Posttest Scores for Bystander Intervention Programming

	Control Group		One-Session Group		Three-Session Group	
	Pretest	Posttest	Pretest	Posttest	Pretest	Posttest
Policy knowledge	16.39	16.06	17.29	20.09	17.34	24.51
Date rape attitudes	76.40	78.96	77.98	81.70	75.50	82.87
Rape myth acceptance	32.54	31.40	32.20	28.38	32.90	25.76
Bystander attitudes	197.95	199.24	199.54	215.97	196.30	219.82

Scores changed from pretest to posttest for the one-session and three-session groups, but not in the control group. This indicates the programming did have significant effects. Possible ranges are 0–31 for policy knowledge, 26–98 for date rape attitudes (with higher numbers meaning more positive attitudes), 17–95 for rape myth acceptance, and 73–255 for bystander attitudes.

Source: Data from Banyard et al. (2007).

CHECK YOUR UNDERSTANDING

12.1 In the study called "Is Date Rape Justifiable?" (Muehlenhard et al., 1985), which fictional scenario led people to say that John was most "justified" in having sex with Mary against her wishes?

a. He asked her out and they went to his apartment.

b. He asked her out and they went to a movie.

c. She asked him out and they went to his apartment.

d. She asked him out and they went to a religious event.

12.2 A popular measure of rape myths is the Illinois Rape Myth Acceptance Scale. Which of the options below is NOT one of the subscales included in this measure?

a. Men cannot be raped.
b. It wasn't really rape.
c. She asked for it.
d. He didn't mean to.

12.3 Recall the measures used in the Banyard et al. (2007) study on bystander intervention programming. Based on how each variable below is measured, good outcomes of the programming would be seen in LOWER scores for which option?

a. Policy knowledge
b. Date rape attitudes
c. Rape myth acceptance
d. Bystander attitudes

APPLICATION ACTIVITY

There are several movies that highlight sexual assault or rape. A few classics are *The Accused* (1988), *The Girl With the Dragon Tattoo* (2009), *The Color Purple* (1985), and *Ms .45* (1981). Sexual abuse within the family was featured in *It* (2017) and *The Perks of Being a Wallflower* (2012). Other films were made as comedies but have been criticized for condoning rape culture; some of these include the 1980s cult hits *Sixteen Candles* (1984) and *Revenge of the Nerds* (1984). Choose any movie that depicts sexual assault, rape, or sexual aggression and analyze the cultural messages it sends, including any potential rape myths or gender norms. Note that for some people this activity may include mental health or trauma triggers and it is important to consider these triggers before trying it.

CRITICAL THINKING

- Look over the individual items in the Illinois Rape Myth Acceptance Scale (shown in the "What's My Score?" feature). Identify the two or three items that you find the most offensive or problematic, then explain why these particular beliefs are harmful to individuals or to a larger community.

- In your opinion, should there be more or less research on male victims of sexual assault and rape? Explain your answer.

- If you wanted to plan a campus-wide bystander intervention program on your campus, what would be the potential barriers or challenges? Identify three specific things that might cause difficulty, then identify a way to work through each of these difficulties so that the programming might actually occur. Then, provide the names and contact information for three specific people who might be able to help the programming happen (e.g., faculty or staff who could get involved).

Answers to the Check Your Understanding Questions

12.1 c, **12.2** a, and **12.3** c.

What Does Relationship Violence Look Like?

What comes to mind when you hear the word "victim"?

When we talk about people who experience traumatic events like sexual assault, rape, or relationship violence, some people believe the word "victim" should never be used because it connotes "helplessness and pity" (HelloFlo.com, 2017; Kirkwood, 1993). Instead, the word "survivor" implies someone who has the strength to get past the violence and trauma—a more empowering idea. This chapter discusses research on the entire process of being in an abusive relationship, from beginning to end, and what it's like to go through each step. So for the purpose of clarity, the term "victim" is used when referring to someone who is *still experiencing* violence or abuse in a relationship, whereas "survivor" will refer to someone who has successfully escaped.

Scholarly understanding of relationship violence is a relatively new endeavor, simply because for years researchers thought it would be too hard to get a real, honest view of the problem. One challenge is social desirability (a term described first in Chapter 2), the idea that participants in studies aren't always honest or authentic if that would make them look bad. A second challenge is the very nature of relationship violence: It's an extremely personal, emotional issue. People might not be lining up to tell strangers all the intimate details on a questionnaire.

One of the first questions that researchers tried to answer was simply "What does relationship violence look like?" In other words, how common is it? What kinds of people are abusers, and what are their specific actions? Is relationship violence usually physical, emotional, sexual—or all of the above? It turns out that we get a very different answer to these questions, depending on the methodology used.

Two Types of Violent Relationships

To understand relationship violence, where would you look for information?

Early attempts to study this phenomenon used archival data such as police reports, domestic violence shelter surveys, information from hospital emergency rooms, and divorce court records (Johnson, 2007). Patterns from these sources painted a certain picture of relationship abuse: (1) women were almost always the victims of male perpetrators; (2) violence escalated over time, sometimes reaching deadly levels; (3) perpetrators often had other criminal behaviors, such as public intoxication or violence outside of the home; and (4) violence was physical, emotional, sexual, and psychological. This conclusion fit many people's stereotypes of "domestic abuse" or "wife battery."

But results from other sources, including self-report surveys and interviews, resulted in a very different view. The first large-scale, national, anonymous survey that collected data on relationship violence was the National Family Violence Survey (NFVS), which included responses from 2143 people in 1975 and from 6002 people in 1985 (NFVS, 1975, 1985; as cited in Johnson, 1995). The results were controversial for two reasons.

First, they claimed that relationship violence was much more common than previously thought; about 16% of participants said they had experienced abuse. That said, the severity didn't seem particularly high; people reported slapping and shoving, but not much worse. A second controversy was that *both* men and women admitted to being perpetrators and victims of relationship violence. Claims that husbands were frequent victims of relationship violence were met with heated skepticism (see Dobash & Dobash, 1992). Both results violated stereotypes about relationship abuse. So, which version was true?

There's a surprise in the answer: both. In two ground-breaking articles that helped settle the debate about the picture of relationship violence, Johnson (1995, 2007) laid out a framework for two separate forms or types of violence. By acknowledging that both types of violence exist, both researchers and community members gain insight into how abuse can vary from one relationship to the next (Leone, Johnson & Cohan, 2007). Let's take a closer look at the two types.

Type 1: Intimate Terrorism

The stereotypical "wife battery" type of relationship violence seen in police files, domestic violence shelters, and emergency rooms is what Johnson (1995, 2007) calls **intimate terrorism**. In his original article, Johnson called this type "patriarchal terrorism" because it is more commonly perpetrated by men against women instead of vice versa or in same-sex couples. Later he changed the name to intimate terrorism, partially to acknowledge that it is possible to have this phenomenon occur regardless of the sex or gender of the couple members involved.

Intimate terrorism includes severe forms of physical violence that may require police or medical intervention, and it also includes psychological, emotional, and sexual violence. Johnson notes that intimate terrorism often includes dynamics suggested in the "power and control wheel" first suggested by Pence and Paymar (1993), shown in Figure 12.2. Thus, this type of relationship violence includes economic abuse (such as preventing someone access to money), intimidation, threats, and more. A second version of the power and control wheel designed for college relationships can be seen in Figure 12.3.

The violence in intimate terrorism typically escalates over time in terms of both frequency and severity, and victims often feel completely powerless. Leone and colleagues (2007) note that this form of relationship violence is more likely to appear in shelter and court records because it often leads to dramatic outcomes that require intervention—and that it's less likely to appear in self-report surveys because victims fear that honest answers will result in retaliation from their abuser.

Type 2: Situational Couple Violence

On the other hand, the survey responses are also valid representations of relationship violence; they just show a very different type of experience. **Situational couple violence** is defined by Johnson (1995, 2007) as occasions when couple members argue aggressively, but neither attempts to take general control and the incidents are relatively minor (although still unhealthy). Here, fights escalate out of everyday conflicts about specific situations, and *both* couple members reciprocate in perpetrating violence. However, situational couple violence usually does not include psychological or emotional abuse, and physical abuse is typically restricted to actions that do not lead to lasting injury. Johnson (2007) believes that this form of relationship violence is much more common than intimate terrorism.

FIGURE 12.2 ● **Forms of Violence Found in Intimate Terrorism**

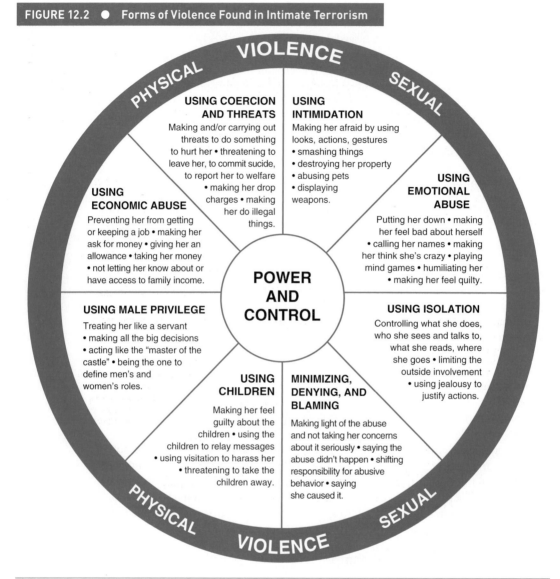

Source: Pence, E., & Paymar, M. (1993). *Education groups for men who batter: The Duluth model.* New York, NY: Springer. Reprinted by permission of the publisher (Taylor and Francis Ltd, http://www.tandfonline.com)

In a study that directly compared couples experiencing each type of violence (Leone et al., 2007), results showed that, compared to situational couple violence,

- victims of intimate terrorism were older, in longer relationships, and less likely to be employed;

- violence in intimate terrorism was significantly more severe (physically), more likely to increase in both frequency and severity over time, more likely to result in injury, and more likely to lead to depression and post-traumatic stress disorder (PTSD) symptoms in victims;

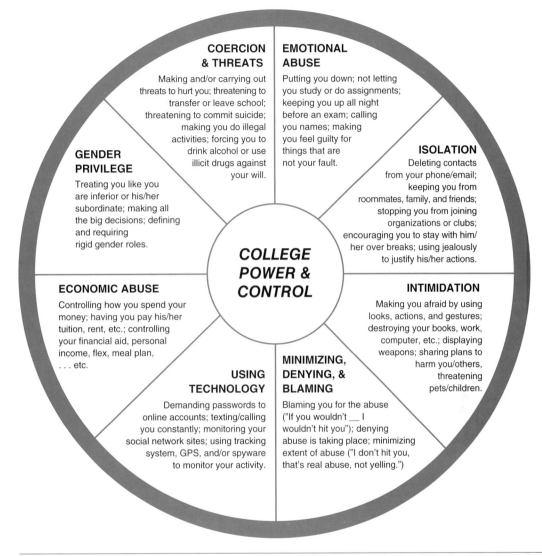

COERCION & THREATS
Making and/or carrying out threats to hurt you; threatening to transfer or leave school; threatening to commit suicide; making you do illegal activities; forcing you to drink alcohol or use illicit drugs against your will.

EMOTIONAL ABUSE
Putting you down; not letting you study or do assignments; keeping you up all night before an exam; calling you names; making you feel guilty for things that are not your fault.

GENDER PRIVILEGE
Treating you like you are inferior or his/her subordinate; making all the big decisions; defining and requiring rigid gender roles.

ISOLATION
Deleting contacts from your phone/email; keeping you from roommates, family, and friends; stopping you from joining organizations or clubs; encouraging you to stay with him/her over breaks; using jealously to justify his/her actions.

COLLEGE POWER & CONTROL

ECONOMIC ABUSE
Controlling how you spend your money; having you pay his/her tuition, rent, etc.; controlling your financial aid, personal income, flex, meal plan, . . . etc.

INTIMIDATION
Making you afraid by using looks, actions, and gestures; destroying your books, work, computer, etc.; displaying weapons; sharing plans to harm you/others, threatening pets/children.

USING TECHNOLOGY
Demanding passwords to online accounts; texting/calling you constantly; monitoring your social network sites; using tracking system, GPS, and/or spyware to monitor your activity.

MINIMIZING, DENYING, & BLAMING
Blaming you for the abuse ("If you wouldn't __ I wouldn't hit you"); denying abuse is taking place; minimizing extent of abuse ("I don't hit you, that's real abuse, not yelling.")

Source: Haven Project. (2017). "The college power and control wheel." Indiana University of Pennsylvania.

- victims of intimate terrorism were twice as likely to call the police and four times as likely to seek medical help after a violent incident.

Insight Into Perpetrators

An important research question is: What kinds of people become perpetrators of relationship violence? There are hundreds of important studies that provide one piece of that puzzle. Let's cover just a few here.

Angry people are easy to identify by their facial expression, body posture, sweat, and so on. But do perpetrators of relationship violence look like this?

©iStock.com/aylinstock

The I³ Model

For example, the **I³ model** (pronounced "I-cubed") breaks down situational couple violence by offering cues for when it's more or less likely to occur (Finkel, 2008, 2014; Finkel, DeWall, Slotter, Oaten, & Foshee, 2009; Finkel & Hall, 2018).

The I³ model says three factors predict violence: instigation, impellance, and inhibition. *Instigation* is the immediate aspects of a conflict that lead either or both couple members to become angry, frustrated, and aggressive. Examples are jealousy or when the other person "started it" with emotional or physical violence, and that violence is reciprocated. Instigation is the feeling that you've been provoked.

Impellance is parts of people's past or their personality that predispose them to violence. These might be growing up in a violent family or having a narcissistic personality. It could also be parts of the immediate situation that are external to the couple but still have an influence, such as heat or noise in the environment. It's background factors that influence the couple member's perceptions and reactions.

Finally, the third I in the I³ model is *inhibition*, or aspects of the conflict that actually *decrease* aggressive urges. Inhibiting influences might be cultural norms against violence, self-discipline or self-control, and being happy and satisfied in the relationship in general. While the first two Is (instigation and impellance) are positively correlated with violence, the third one (inhibition) is negatively correlated with violence.

In summary, violence is more likely to result from conflict when instigating triggers and impelling influences are strong, but it's less likely to occur if inhibiting influences are also strong. The I³ model is one way to recognize that the forces at work on any given couple are simply complicated. This model has been supported in several studies, including those that specifically find that relationship violence is most likely to happen when the perpetrator feels they have just been provoked (instigation), have a highly aggressive personality (impellance), and have a low ability to control their impulses (a lack of inhibition; Chester & DeWall, 2018; Finkel, 2014; Finkel, DeWall, Slotter, McNulty, Pond, & Atkins, 2012). Actions are influenced by personality, culture, people's childhood, and much more—so any aspect of intimate relationships, especially one like intimate aggression, is going to take a lot of attention to understand and ameliorate.

Pit Bulls and Cobras

One research lab stumbled across something they weren't expecting.

The connection between aggression and physiological arousal (such as increased heart rate, breathing, and sweating) is pretty intuitive. When we see angry people, we can usually tell by their facial expression, posture, and tone of voice. So a reasonable hypothesis would be that perpetrators of relationship violence will show increased physiological arousal when they are in the middle of a fight. Two researchers, Jacobson and Gottman (1998), tested the hypothesis. They recruited participants in the Seattle, Washington, area by posting fliers asking for people to participate in a study on

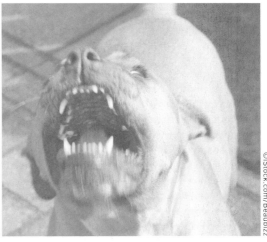

The pit bull may appear more aggressive, but the cobra is calmly waiting to strike with a deadly attack.

relationship conflict—and both couple members had to attend the sessions. Imagine being part of this strange study.

The researchers first selected couples who admitted to domestic violence, including some cases of severe abuse (what we might call intimate terrorism). All of the couples were heterosexual and the man was the primary abuser (although this is not always the case; see the section on male victims later in this chapter). Then they asked the couple to get into an argument! During the conflict, the researchers observed the men's physiological arousal through heart rate monitors and galvanic skin response (sweaty palms).

Results confirmed the hypothesis for most of the men; about 80% of them showed this pattern. Jacobson and Gottman call these men **pit bulls**, because their increasing anger and aggression were obvious. They would yell, their faces would become red, and their posture leaned forward and clearly expressed anger. The surprise, however, was that about 20% of men showed the *opposite* pattern. For these abusers, as conflicts with their wives or girlfriends progressed, their physiological responses got calmer and more peaceful.

Here's something else that might be a surprise: The calmer, lower-heart-rate men were the *most* abusive. Jacobson and Gottman labeled these men **cobras**, because they sit back calmly, waiting to strike. Their calm demeanor masked more extreme violent tendencies, a pattern also found in psychopaths and people with antisocial personality disorder (Holtzworth-Munroe & Meehan, 2004; Holtzworth-Munroe, Meehan, Herron, Rehman, & Stuart, 2000; Holtzworth-Munroe & Stuart, 1994). Wives of cobras were less successful in leaving their abusive partners, compared to pit bulls. Perhaps they understood how scary their partners could become and just how dangerous their situations were.

Insight Into Victims

"Why don't they just leave?" is an unfortunate question and a classic example of victim blaming (see Barnett, Miller-Perrin, & Perrin, 1997; Cruz, 2003; Goetting, 1999; Jones, 2000).

RELATIONSHIPS AND POPULAR CULTURE

Abusive Relationships in Song

In an article ironically called "The Hits Keep Coming" (Rabin et al., 2011), a list of 30 songs is offered. Each song highlights some aspect of abusive relationships, although the framing of the songwriter varies quite a bit. Some are sweet, some are forgiving—and some are angry. Here's a selection of the songs from that list which feature lyrics that on one hand could be considered empowering, and on the other could be considered in favor of revenge:

- 1946: Ella Fitzgerald and Louis Jordan, "Stone Cold Dead in the Market (He Had It Coming)"

- 1962: The Crystals, "He Hit Me (It Felt Like a Kiss)"

- 1994: Martina McBride, "Independence Day"

- 1999: Dixie Chicks, "Goodbye Earl"

- 2001: Nickelback, "Never Again"

- 2007: Miranda Lambert, "Gunpowder & Lead"

Other songs on the list feature sad tales of intimate terrorism, and one even comes from the perspective of a man who is beaten by his abusive wife. What songs have been produced after this article (2011) that continue the dialogue about relationship violence?

Victims of relationship violence don't enjoy abuse and don't deserve to be treated disrespectfully. Being involved in violence is complicated, as we've already discussed, and the process of escape can take time. The subject has been featured in several movies and songs, as discussed in the "Relationships and Popular Culture" feature. Researchers want to understand the psychological perspective of people while they are still victims—before they become survivors. This will increase other people's empathy and enable communities to provide practical help for the needs of each individual enduring relationship violence. Several lines of research have thus explored the perceptions of relationship violence victims. Here's a sampling of some interesting findings, although much more research exists on this topic.

The Cycle of Violence

Early research to understand the psychology of people experiencing relationship violence produced a theory called the **cycle of violence** (Walker, 1979, 1980, 1984).

The cycle theoretically has three phases: (1) *tension-building*, in which an abuser becomes increasingly upset; (2) *explosion*, in which abuse occurs; and (3) *contrition*, in which the abuser apologizes and makes promises to stop their behavior. Phase three is also sometimes called the "honeymoon phase," when the abuser is sweet, loving, and caring (Peterman & Dixon, 2003). Once the contrition is done, however, the violence comes back, sometimes with the perpetrator accusing the victim of causing the problem in the first place.

Many researchers have supported the idea of a cycle in violent relationships (e.g., Dutton, 1998) and suggested that victims sincerely hope and believe their partner's promises in the contrition phase. It is only after going through the full cycle multiple times that some victims realize that their partner's behaviors probably will not change—at least not anytime soon. Even if physically violent behaviors decrease in older adulthood (e.g., after retirement), emotional and psychological abuse will likely remain.

Romantic Myths

Sometimes fairy tales don't end "happily ever after."

Rosen (1996) interviewed 22 women who had experienced (or were still experiencing) violence to see how they were initially attracted to and pulled into violent relationships. She called this beginning of a relationship the "processes of seduction." In her interviews, several of the women discussed **romantic myths**, or cultural messages regarding what romance is "supposed" to look like in traditional gendered ideas or social roles. Other research has defined romantic myths as "forms of popular culture [that] provide young girls with 'texts of meaning' of femininity and heterosexuality" regarding what to expect in relationships (Jackson, 2001, p. 306; see Davies, 1992; Jackson, 1993).

Rosen identified two specific romantic myths that encouraged "seduction" into violent relationships. The first is what she calls the **Cinderella fantasy**; this is the idea that a man who is a relative stranger can enter a woman's life and transform it by removing fears and saving her from problems (Rosen, 1996). Rosen points out that this myth encourages patriarchal power dynamics in which "Prince Charming" controls his wife's life and she is defined by him. The second romantic myth identified by Rosen is the **Beauty and the Beast fantasy**, in which women are told that patient, self-sacrificing love can turn a "beast" who is troubled and violent into a loving and sensitive partner. Unfortunately, Rosen notes that too often, beasts remain beasts.

Cognitive Dissonance and Minimization

Cognitive dissonance occurs when our thoughts or actions don't match our values or self-concept (Festinger & Carlsmith, 1959).

Victims of relationship violence probably think that abuse is not acceptable—but simultaneously, they may not be able to leave at a given time due to financial dependency, fear, a motivation to protect children, and so on. This may cause cognitive dissonance. Some research suggests that one way current victims can decrease dissonance is to perceive the abusive behaviors as nonabusive. In other words, victims may use **minimization** to mentally diminish their partner's behaviors by denying that they occurred, downplaying the significance or severity of what occurred, or providing some kind of justification for the behaviors. Dunham and Senn (2000) found that women who experienced relationship violence often omit information about it when discussing their relationship with others—and that omission occurs more as the severity of abuse increases (a positive correlation).

One intriguing study found that victims might acknowledge the specific behaviors that occurred, but then interpret them in ways that avoid labeling them as "abusive" or "violent." Arriaga (2002) discovered that when victims were given the opportunity to say that a partner's physically violent actions were "just a joke," many of them agreed with this interpretation—even when the behaviors were as severe as being kicked, beat up, or struck with a weapon. Follow-up research that interviewed women at a domestic violence shelter asked women to recall a particularly violent

Heinzen, 2017

Research on "affective forecasting" finds that people are not very good at predicting their own future emotions.

incident, then explain why it happened (Goodfriend & Arriaga, 2018). When the women were still highly committed to their partners and planned to return to the relationship, cognitive dissonance would prevent them from blaming their abuser. Instead, the women blamed themselves, claimed their partner had an uncontrollable problem such as alcoholism, or said that violence was so common in the world that leaving would be pointless (because a new, different relationship would probably be violent, too).

Faulty Affective Forecasting

Another explanation to understand some victims' hesitancy to immediately leave a violent relationship is a lack of accurate **affective forecasting**.

Affective forecasting (sometimes called hedonic forecasting) is when someone tries to predict how they will feel in the future—and several studies have shown that we are not particularly good at it (Buehler & McFarland, 2001; Gilbert, Pinel, Wilson, Blumberg, & Wheatley, 1998; Hoerger, Quirk, Lucas, & Carr, 2010). This appears to be true of victims of relationship violence as well.

Arriaga and her colleagues (Arriaga, Capezza, Goodfriend, Rayl, & Sands, 2013) conducted a longitudinal study in which they first asked victims of relationship violence to predict how happy they would be if their relationship ended. Several months later, about one-fourth of the relationships had ended. Once the relationship (and abuse) was over, people who were now survivors were significantly happier than they had predicted they would be. The study concluded that "expecting doom without a partner functions to maintain a relationship, even when life without an aggressive partner turns out to be better than expected" (Arriaga et al., 2013, p. 681).

Understanding Male Victims

Most researchers of relationship violence agree that the type of violence described as intimate terrorism is more likely to be perpetrated by men toward women than in any other form. Some articles don't even acknowledge the possibility of male victims, or they quickly discount violence against men as being minimally important or harmful (Campbell, 2002; Johnson, 2007; Kilpatrick, 2004; Klein, Campbell, Soler, & Ghez, 1997). However, consider again the sources of information about intimate terrorism: police records, hospitals, and domestic violence shelters. For all three sources, male victims are significantly less likely to seek help after being victimized by a relationship partner, due in part to social stigmatization (Arnocky & Vaillancourt, 2014).

A study focusing on this problem (Arnocky & Vaillancourt, 2014) asked participants to complete a social stigma scale regarding stereotypes and victim blaming within relationship violence scenarios (see Table 12.2 for the items used). Participants were randomly assigned to answer the questions in terms of either male or female victims (so sex of the victim was the independent variable). Average scores on the stigma

TABLE 12.2 ● Partner Violence Stigma Scale

Men/women who are abused by their romantic partners should be ashamed of themselves.

Men/women who are abused by their romantic partners are weak.

Men/women who stay with abusive partners deserve what they get.

Men/women who are abused by their romantic partners probably cannot attract anyone better.

Men/women who are abused by their romantic partners are not men/women I want to be friends with.

Many men/women who say they are abused by their romantic partners are probably lying or exaggerating.

When a woman/man hits her/his partner, it is most likely self-defense.

When a woman/man hits her/his partner, it was most likely provoked.

Participants responded to each item on a 1–7 scale, with 1 indicating "I strongly disagree" and 7 indicating "I strongly agree."

Source: Arnocky and Vaillancourt (2014).

scale were the dependent variable. Results showed that male victims were judged significantly more negatively than female victims—and this was true even for participants who had experienced relationship violence themselves. In addition, follow-up surveys revealed that male participants said they were much less likely to seek help or to admit to violence if it happened to them.

Despite the stereotypes and stigmas, we know that men do suffer as victims of relationship violence. According to the National Intimate Partner and Sexual Violence Survey (Breiding, Smith, Basile, Walters, Chen, & Merrick, 2014), severe physical violence by an intimate partner was experienced by about 22% of women and 14% of men. Other studies estimate the rates of male victims of relationship violence to be even higher, around 23% (e.g., Coker et al., 2002). Abuse toward male partners can begin early, with 10% of male college students reporting that their partners are violent or extremely controlling of them (Association of American Universities, 2019). *Both* men and women have multiple negative outcomes of such violence, including poor mental and physical health, substance abuse, and long-term injury or scars (Carmo, Grams, & Magalhães, 2011; Coker et al., 2002; Coker, Weston, Creson, Justice, & Blakeney, 2005).

Stigmatization and lack of understanding are compounded when a man is a victim of violence within a gay relationship and thus might already be struggling with stereotyping, harassment, and discrimination (West, 1998). Gay victims may also fear that reporting violence will further enforce negative views of gay couples from outsiders as unhealthy or dysfunctional (Elliot, 1996; Hart, 1986). Still, violence in same-sex couples is prevalent; one classic study reported the highest rates of violence within lesbian couples (48%), then gay male couples (38%), then heterosexual couples (28%; Straus, 1979).

Interviews with 25 gay men who had been in violent relationships (Cruz, 2003) found that the top three reasons men reported temporarily staying in the relationship (after it had become violent) were (1) financial dependence on their partner, (2) inexperience with same-sex couple dynamics, and (3) feelings of love despite the violence. Another study focused on forms of abuse within same-sex couples that do not appear in heterosexual couples (West, 1998), such as "homophobic control," or threatening to "out" a partner without their consent. Like all topics regarding gay, lesbian, transgender, and queer individuals, more research attention is needed—and more research acknowledging male victims in general (including within heterosexual relationships) is warranted as well.

CHECK YOUR UNDERSTANDING

12.4 Which source of data would most likely lead to a researcher concluding that relationship violence follows the patterns identified as "situational couple violence"?

   a. Police reports
   b. Intake forms from shelters
   c. Records from hospital emergency rooms
   d. An anonymous national survey

12.5 Which option below is NOT one of the "I-words" included in the I^3 model of relationship violence?

   a. Impellance
   b. Inhibition
   c. Ingratiation
   d. Instigation

12.6 Which option below shows the correct order of stages identified in the "cycle of violence" theory of relationship violence?

   a. Tension-building, Contrition, Explosion
   b. Tension-building, Explosion, Contrition
   c. Contrition, Explosion, Tension-building
   d. Explosion, Tension-building, Contrition

APPLICATION ACTIVITY

Imagine you and a friend are talking about a male college student you both know, but not well. This student has recently experienced an assault from his partner, and your friend says, "Well, I don't have much sympathy for him; I'm sure it wasn't that bad." Discuss three specific responses that you might be able to say to your friend that would decrease the victim blaming that appears to be happening in the situation.

CRITICAL THINKING

- Consider the different forms of emotional and psychological abuse shown in the "power and control" wheels of this section. Which two forms of abuse do you think would be the most damaging to a typical victim, and why?

- If romantic myths contribute to the perpetuation of violence, how can children—both boys and girls—be taught to appreciate these fairy tales for their positive aspects but warned against learning the types of lessons that may lead to acceptance of relationship violence?

- The stigma toward male victims of relationship violence appears to be relatively strong. In addition, resources for male victims are scarce (e.g., there are very few emergency shelters for male victims). Do you think that more resources should be devoted specifically for male victims—or would that simply take away focus and attention from female victims? How can empathy and prosocial behaviors toward male victims be increased using social psychological concepts?

Answers to the Check Your Understanding Questions

12.4 d, 12.5 c, and 12.6 b.

How Do Survivors Escape and Heal?

Ideally, researchers would be able to understand relationship violence enough to prevent it from happening in the first place.

When people working on this problem consider prevention efforts, they are typically broken up into three types of intervention (Cathey & Goodfriend, 2012). **Primary prevention** reaches people to stop violence before it begins on an individual level; again, this is the ideal. Primary prevention occurs through education and empowerment. For example, a program might teach middle schoolers what potential warning signs of violence might be within their own relationships. However, the reality of the current world is that millions of people experience relationship violence every day. Thus, two additional types of intervention are also needed.

Secondary prevention intervenes after relationship violence has begun and provides victims with resources and knowledge to prevent it from happening again. Finally, **tertiary prevention** involves educating the larger community, such as a college or university campus or a given town, regarding dynamics of relationship violence to increase empathy and understanding (Cathey & Goodfriend, 2012).

Most research on response to relationship violence occurs at the secondary level. How can victims escape abuse and become survivors instead?

Escape: From Victim to Survivor

In her book *Leaving Abusive Partners*, Kirkwood (1993) interviewed a diverse group of 30 women who had successfully escaped violent relationships. These survivors noted that there were several obstacles that each needed to be overcome in order for them to successfully escape. These obstacles included the following:

- Finding housing and economic resources

- Obtaining medical aid for both short-term and long-term needs

- Obtaining safety and protection from their ex-partners

- Dealing with a dramatic change of circumstances

Another study interviewed 22 survivors (Rosen & Stith, 1997) and identified the "disentanglement process" (p. 174) many of them went through to get out of the relationship. In this study, there were five distinct steps the victims took in order to leave:

- *Step 1: Seeds of Doubt.* Victims were no longer able to deny or minimize what was happening to them to the same level as before. They started to acknowledge what was happening to them and that it wasn't okay.

- *Step 2: Turning Points.* This was a small cognitive or psychological shift in how they interpreted behaviors from their partner.

- *Step 3: Objective Reappraisals.* This step involved seeing what was happening from a more objective view. Here, victims reevaluated themselves and their partners and realized that (1) they were in real danger, (2) their partners did not truly love them, (3) the violence was not going to stop, and/or (4) they had options to escape.

- *Step 4: Self-Reclaiming Actions.* Next, victims sought counseling or built up a supportive network of friends.

- *Step 5: Last Straw Events.* Finally, an event occurred that was so bad or severe, the victims took the steps to leave permanently.

Healing and Moving Forward

Once victims become survivors, it still can be difficult to psychologically move forward.

Some survivors—especially those who were subjected to severe intimate terrorism—have both physical and emotional scars. Treatment programs for survivors vary widely, and there are many approaches to helping people deal with trauma. In fact, jobs in what is now known as **trauma advocacy** are growing. This field helps people navigate the process of escape (through steps like reporting to the police, finding temporary housing, going through a trial, and more). Trauma advocates also help survivors recover from any severely stressful event that impairs their long-term psychological functioning (e.g., see the description of "trauma psychology" on https://www.psychologyschoolguide.net/trauma-psychology/, which also lists schools that offer relevant master's degree programs).

Consider two examples of research on how survivors can find closure and heal.

Narrative Therapy

One option for individuals who want to heal from the trauma of relationship violence is **narrative therapy**, the process of writing down autobiographical events in a therapeutic setting (Cathey & Goodfriend, 2012). Traditionally, the narratives are chronological stories, like a typical autobiography, but they could also come in the form of poems, drawings, or anything else useful to the survivor.

A series of studies by Pennebaker (for a review, see Pennebaker, 1997) showed that when people who have survived a trauma write about it, there are both psychological and physical benefits. In a review of 13 studies on narrative therapy, Smyth (1998) found that people who wrote about traumas showed significant improvements in mental health, physical health, and general functioning (such as academic grades and work absenteeism). In a summary of the benefits of narrative therapy, Cathey and Goodfriend (2012) noted that it helps survivors feel closure, helps them process what happened in manageable pieces, and provides an avenue for self-expression. For more about details of narrative therapy and trauma, see the "Research Deep Dive" feature.

In my book with colleague Pamela Cathey (Cathey & Goodfriend, 2012), we worked with 10 relationship violence survivors who wrote their stories in both individual and group therapy sessions over about a year. Those stories are published in the book and represent a wide variety of experiences, including childhood sexual trauma, college dating violence, and domestic violence (note that three of the stories are from male survivors). The book, titled *Voices of Hope*, has also been condensed into a 1-hour theatrical performance that can be performed as a fundraiser and educational intervention for communities or universities. The play is available free of charge and has already been performed at several universities around the country.

RESEARCH DEEP DIVE

Write On: An Unexpected Way to Help Cope With Traumatic Experiences

Along with public speaking, writing is near the top of every student's list of dreaded activities. When it comes to class and papers, many students associate writing with creating stress and anxiety. However, outside of an academic setting, writing can be quite helpful, especially when you're at your lowest points imaginable. In fact, the idea that writing can help a person recover from negative and traumatic experiences is the basis for one of the field's most well-known papers.

Not every article you read in a journal is the same type of paper. Some describe a single experiment, others have multiple studies, while some are review articles that don't report on their own research. Instead, they summarize many different studies on the same topic. Jamie Pennebaker's 1997 *Psychological Science* paper is a review article that has become a classic because it summarizes a decade of research on writing's role in the therapeutic process.

Participants in the studies he features have included everyone from prisoners to the elderly,

to students and children. The basic writing paradigm involves participants writing 15 to 30 minutes a day, for several consecutive days, often in the laboratory (but sometimes at home). Researchers guide the writing process through a series of prompts, with instructions encouraging participants to "really let go and explore your very deepest emotions and thoughts." Studies typically have several experimental conditions (e.g., writing about an emotional experience versus writing about superficial topics that serve as the control group), with participants randomly assigned to one condition. Common topics studied with this procedure include a variety of traumatic experiences, including the death of a loved one, breakups, assault, tragedies, failures, as well as physical and sexual abuse.

Research on the writing paradigm—sometimes called the **Pennebaker paradigm**—has focused on writing's ability to influence a wide range of outcomes. For example, studies show that compared to writing about neutral or control topics, writing about emotional experiences led to *physical* benefits such as decreased heart rate, improved immune function, and fewer visits to the doctor. Writing also has mental health benefits, including

(Continued)

(Continued)

improved mood, less distress, and increased well-being. Other studies have identified writing's benefits on behaviors such as fewer absences from work, better grades in school, returning to work more quickly following a layoff, and less drinking.

Pennebaker's review also points out methodological modifications that may influence the procedure's efficacy. For example, the procedure is more effective when writing takes place over more days (e.g., once a week for 2 months is better than every day for a week). For those who are averse to writing, the prompts are beneficial even when people talk in response to them, rather than write. In terms of demographic variables, previous research has not found differences in effectiveness related to factors such as age, sex, education, ethnicity, or individual differences like anxiety level.

The best research is also generative, meaning that it encourages others to conduct studies that test the ideas further and apply them to new contexts. Even though this review paper was published over 20 years ago, researchers today still cite it and use it as inspiration for new studies. For example, more recent research tested the writing paradigm's ability to help survivors of sexual assault compared to those who wrote about how they spend their time (Kearns, Edwards, Calhoun, & Gidycz, 2010). Their results indicated that the group who wrote about their trauma reported

less negative mood immediately after the writing task. More importantly, at a 1-month follow-up both groups reported less distress, less traumatic stress, and fewer physical symptoms. Another study of undergraduate sexual assault victims found that, compared to the control condition, those who wrote about their traumatic experience reported decreases in alcohol use and depressive symptoms (Sharma-Patel, Brown, & Chaplin, 2012). However, there were no differences in PTSD symptoms across conditions.

These are just two of the over 800 studies that have cited Pennebaker's 1997 paper, but they serve as examples of how one key piece of research or one key review article can have a lasting effect on the relationship science field, as well on the lives of all of the study participants (and those who read about it in a textbook).

For more, read Pennebaker, J. W. (1997). Writing about emotional experiences as a therapeutic process. *Psychological Science, 8*(3), 162–166; Kearns, M. C., Edwards, K. M., Calhoun, K. S., & Gidycz, C. A. (2010). Disclosure of sexual victimization: The effects of Pennebaker's emotional disclosure paradigm on physical and psychological distress. *Journal of Trauma & Dissociation, 11*(2), 193–209; and Sharma-Patel, K., Brown, E. J., & Chaplin, W. F. (2012). Emotional and cognitive processing in sexual assault survivors' narratives. *Journal of Aggression, Maltreatment & Trauma, 21*(2), 149–170.

Post-Traumatic Growth

Many victims of severe trauma experience PTSD (e.g., Street & Arias, 2001). However, other research has attempted to discover whether survivors of trauma such as relationship violence can heal to the point of becoming even stronger than they were before the abusive relationship started (Tedeschi & Calhoun, 1996). In this way, survivors can feel that even though what they experienced was inexcusable, they have grown past it and the violence no longer defines who they are.

One attempt to capture this empowering attitude is the development of a scale to measure **post-traumatic growth**, or feelings of positive psychological change and resilience as a result of trauma and adversity (see Table 12.3). The idea of post-traumatic growth is that after a trauma, individuals should not hope to return to the same level of self-esteem or empowerment they had beforehand. Instead, they should strive to grow past their former selves. You can see some of the items from the scale developed by Tedeschi and Calhoun (1996, 2004) to measure post-traumatic growth.

TABLE 12.3   ●   Selected Items From the Post-Traumatic Growth Inventory
I changed my priorities about what is important in life.
I have a greater appreciation for the value of my own life.
I developed new interests.
I have a greater feeling of self-reliance.
I have a better understanding of spiritual matters.
I more clearly see that I can count on people in times of trouble.
I established a new path for my life.
I have a greater sense of closeness with others.
I am more willing to express my emotions.
I know better that I can handle difficulties.

The full scale is 21 items.

Source: Tedeschi and Calhoun (1996).

Every year, thousands of people create new lives by moving from victim to survivor to personal growth (e.g., Boals & Schuler, 2017, 2019; Cole & Lynn, 2010; Kleim & Ehlers, 2009; Kunst, 2011; Song, 2012; Tashiro & Frazier, 2003).

Perhaps because of the hopeful nature of post-traumatic growth, research on this topic has growth quickly in just 2 decades, with hundreds of studies now published. In one review of 16 studies (Elderton, Berry, & Chan, 2017), the authors concluded that growth occurs in 71% of relationship violence survivors. One reason this growth might occur is because it leads survivors to question assumptions they previously held about themselves and the world (Valdez & Lilly, 2015). Post-traumatic growth is more likely when survivors have spiritual and social support for their new lives (Anderson, Renner, & Danis, 2012), or when they have a role model of another survivor to show them the way through (Cobb, Tedeschi, Calhoun, & Cann, 2006).

Let's end this chapter with a qualitative study that highlights the stories of survivors from their own voice (Taylor, 2004). Here, 21 survivors (they all happened to be African American, heterosexual women) were interviewed about their resiliency and recovery. The researcher found six themes; each is defined below and illustrated with a quotation from the article.

1. *Shattering silences*: revealing information about the relationship to others. "Black folks don't want to show their dirty laundry. . . . Keep the closet door closed because there's so much negative stuff about us in the press. I think that's hurtful. I think it keeps a problem under cover that should have the covers thrown off and be shown for what it is" (p. 39).

2. *Reclaiming the self*: defining the self as beyond the abuse. "I'm really clear on what I want out of a relationship. . . . Nothing you can say or do will make me believe that I deserve to be devalued, misused [or] treated like I'm nothing" (p. 40).

3. *Renewing the spirit*: nurturing the self and restoring well-being. "I have to do it the right way and God's way. It's a lot of praying involved. A lot of humbling myself. A lot of quiet time, meditation has to be there for me to have my serenity. I handle situations that I wasn't able to handle before. So that's basically spirituality for me" (p. 41).

4. *Self-healing through forgiveness*: forgiving the previous partner for the abuse. "I had to learn how to forgive him because I didn't want to walk through my life with that kind of hate and never being able to move on through that. And I learned how to move on" (p. 41).

5. *Finding inspiration in the future:* being optimistic about the future. "I have to start looking towards the whole purpose in life and [my] ultimate goals. What is my purpose in life? To see something really change for the better. . . . My ultimate goal is to be a happy woman, respected, and a good role model for my daughter" (p. 42).

6. *Engaging in social activism*: participating in community service or positive parenting to promote societal change. "I gave my daughter the messages that, 'Don't do something because a man wants you to do it. Don't use that for reasoning,' and for my son it's like, 'Women are your equal. Treat them as your equal. Don't be disrespectful to them just because she's female.' So for me it helped with parenting. Don't allow a man to claim you as a piece of property because you are more than a piece of property. I talk to them about being independent, being able to earn their own money, being able to think for yourself, and not accepting someone who treats you with disrespect" (p. 43).

CHECK YOUR UNDERSTANDING

12.7 Michael plans workshops in which people in his town can read facts about relationship violence in various stores. He hopes this will raise the general education and awareness of his neighbors. What level of prevention is Michael targeting?

a. Immediate prevention
b. Primary prevention
c. Secondary prevention
d. Tertiary prevention

12.8 Which researcher is known for an experimental paradigm in which participants either write essays about personal traumas or write control essays about neutral topics?

a. Gottman
b. Johnson
c. Rosen
d. Pennebaker

12.9 Which of the statements below is FALSE about post-traumatic growth after experiencing relationship violence?

a. It only occurs in about 15% of survivors.
b. It's more likely if the survivor has a role model.
c. It's more likely if the survivor has a supportive social network.
d. It's more likely if the survivor has spiritual meaning in life.

APPLICATION ACTIVITY

Most schools engage in prevention and education programs focused on relationship violence. Identify three programs, offices, staff, faculty, training opportunities, talks, performances, or anything else your college or university offers regarding education and prevention of relationship violence, then explain where each of these three people, programs, or offices falls on the framework of primary, secondary, and tertiary prevention.

CRITICAL THINKING

- Review the differences between primary, secondary, and tertiary prevention. Which type of prevention do you think is the most important and effective in decreasing incidence rates of relationship violence?

- Many people keep diaries or journals at some point in their lives. Do you think one purpose of this activity is an informal version of narrative therapy? Have you experienced this personally—and if so, what were the benefits (or drawbacks) you experienced when you kept a diary or journal?

- Some people will be able to heal from the trauma of relationship violence more quickly or more effectively than others. Identify two variables that you think might be associated with an individual's ability to experience post-traumatic growth, then explain how you might scientifically test your hypothesis. What would be the procedure of your study? How would you operationalize your variables? What statistical tests would you need to use to analyze your data?

Answers to the Check Your Understanding Questions

12.7 d, **12.8** d, and **12.9** a.

Chapter Summary

Big Questions

1. What does research say about sexual assault and rape?

2. What does relationship violence look like?

3. How do survivors escape and heal?

What does research say about sexual assault and rape?

A common societal problem with sexual assault and rape is victim blaming; research shows that often, outsiders will attribute some responsibility to the target of these crimes. Similarly, rape myths are false beliefs about sexual assault that are based on sexism and justify sexual aggression. Examples of rape myths are "she asked for it" or "he didn't mean to." Rape myths are also common for male victims. Some colleges and universities are trying to combat sexual assault and rape by implementing bystander intervention programs, which aim to educate people and promote helping in situations that signal possible sexual assault.

What does relationship violence look like?

A well-known way to understand relationship violence is to consider two separate versions: (1) intimate terrorism, when one partner uses physical, psychological, emotional, and sexual manipulation against the other; and (2) situational couple violence, in which both partners can lose control during conflicts. The I³ model attempts to predict when violence is more or less likely to occur, given various aspects of the situation and people involved. Another line of research identifies two types of perpetrators, those who become physiologically aroused during conflict (called "pit bulls") versus those who appear to become calm when angry (called "cobras"). Other studies have examined the perspective of people experiencing violence, including a focus on the "cycle of violence," romantic myths in our culture, cognitive dissonance and minimization, faulty affective forecasting, and the experience of male victims of relationship violence.

How do survivors escape and heal?

Prevention of relationship violence can come in three levels: primary, which tries to stop violence before it begins; secondary, which attempts to prevent further violence after it starts; and tertiary, which involves educating the larger community. Research on escape from violent relationships shows that it occurs over several steps, such as cognitive reappraisals and self-empowerment actions. Healing from the trauma of relationship violence can occur through interventions such as narrative therapy (writing one's story). This type of effort can eventually lead to post-traumatic growth, which occurs when a trauma survivor becomes even stronger than they were before.

List of Terms

Learning Objectives	Key Terms
12.1 Describe victim blaming, rape myths, and bystander intervention programs.	Victim blaming Rape myths Bystander intervention programming

12.2 Compare and contrast situational couple violence and intimate terrorism; analyze different types of abusers and the psychology of victims.	Intimate terrorism Situational couple violence I^3 model Pit bulls Cobras Cycle of violence Romantic myths Cinderella fantasy Beauty and the Beast fantasy Cognitive dissonance Minimization Affective forecasting
12.3 Outline factors that help survivors escape abusive relationships, narrative therapy, and the process of post-traumatic growth.	Primary prevention Secondary prevention Tertiary prevention Trauma advocacy Narrative therapy Pennebaker paradigm Post-traumatic growth

13

Ending or Enduring Love

Big Questions	Learning Objectives
1. How do couple members cope with relationship problems?	13.1 Describe common unrealistic beliefs in relationships, couples counseling, and relationship breakups.
2. What can couple members do to maintain a healthy relationship over time?	13.2 Compare and contrast research suggesting specific strategies for maintaining relationship happiness and longevity.

You've read a lot of research in this book. Research studies are the building blocks of science, and the science of relationships is built on creative and important studies like the ones you've been reading about so far. That said, sometimes it's hard to translate the conclusions of studies into the real, everyday lives of couples. Now that you've read the other 12 chapters, do you know how to keep a relationship happy and healthy? This final chapter has that goal in mind—like a "life hack" or DIY (do-it-yourself) model for people who want realistic, practical tips. But importantly, these guidelines are still evidence based, meaning they are built upon valid, reliable research across multiple fields of study. It's kind of like a set of "best practices" for relationships. What are specific ways you can maintain the health of a relationship?

This chapter is different from the others because it's split into two major sections instead of three. We'll start with a discussion about what happens when things go wrong and a couple breaks up. It happens to the vast majority of relationships, but each breakup can seem devastating at the time. What are the most common causes of relationship trouble, and can couples counseling help? What is the process of breaking up? We'll end this last chapter with a more optimistic focus on how the healthiest, happiest couples last over time. What does relationship science offer regarding practical, applicable ways people can really strive for "happily ever after"?

How Do Couple Members Cope With Relationship Problems?

Earlier, we went over conflict management tactics and styles (see Chapter 11). You'll recall that some strategies work better than others, in terms of maintaining the health and happiness of couple members.

That said, we didn't really cover *why* people have conflict in the first place. What's the root of the problem? There are certainly lots of answers to that question. Maybe one person in a couple wants kids, and the other doesn't. Maybe they have fundamental disagreements on things like how to spend money or what important values should be. Maybe one person is more committed to the other, one person hates the other person's family . . . the list could go on and on.

In this section, we'll focus on one of the most common problems that starts conflict in a global way: unrealistic beliefs about a partner or about the relationship. Then, we'll talk about various forms of couples therapy, which has been extremely helpful to troubled couples for decades. Finally, we'll discuss research on ending a relationship. But don't worry—after that, the rest of this final chapter shifts to a more positive, preventative approach. Let's get the rocky part out of the way first.

One Cause for Problems: Unrealistic Beliefs

What causes relationship problems in the first place? Consider this quotation from the opening paragraph of a study about couples who are experiencing problems and are now seeking counseling:

> Marital partners who perceive each other's motives as malevolent, who are pessimistic about potential for change in their relationship, who perceive few positives in their relationship, or who expect unilateral change by the other party are unlikely to expend much effort in therapy. (Epstein & Eidelson, 1981, p. 13)

In short, our beliefs about relationships matter. What kind of beliefs are unhealthy and unrealistic for partners to have? The authors of this study decided to explore two types of unrealistic beliefs: those about the relationship and those about the self. They asked 47 couples who had recently started marital therapy to complete a questionnaire that included a few different survey measures. These included measures of relationship satisfaction, what they hoped to get out of the therapy sessions, and beliefs about both themselves and the relationship. As predicted, people who had highly unrealistic beliefs were less optimistic that therapy would help them, had lower relationship satisfaction, and had lower motivation to try to improve things. This same pattern of results was also replicated in a second study (Eidelson & Epstein, 1982).

What exactly were the unrealistic beliefs? An updated version of the scale the researchers used can be seen in the "What's My Score?" feature. It includes items that measure six different unrealistic and destructive beliefs; each is listed here along with an explanation of how it hurts partners.

1. *Disagreement is destructive.* As we've discussed previously, disagreement doesn't have to mean the relationship is "doomed" or that couple members can't work thing out.

2. *Mindreading is expected.* Some people believe there should be a special mental connection to your partner where you know what the other is thinking without having to actually speak. It's unrealistic unless one or both of the couple members has superpowers.

3. *Partners cannot change.* This belief implies that people are incapable of growth or of learning from their mistakes, or that they are not in control of their own choices.

4. *Sexual perfection is expected.* All relationships have their ups and downs (pun intended), so being able to work through temporary difficulties is important.

5. *The opposite sex can't be understood.* Men and women are often told they are different (e.g., "men are from Mars, women are from Venus") but communication overcomes perceived differences. Again, this also assumes a gender binary and heterosexual couples.

6. *Men and women have different needs.* While some studies show gender or sex differences in people, the vast majority show great similarities in what men, women, and gender queer people want. We all just want happiness, love, and respect.

So, step one in assessing the health of any relationship might be thinking about whether the people involved have these unrealistic, damaging beliefs. If they do, couples counseling might help. The counselor can help each person see where their perceptions might be unfair. Of course, there are lot of additional reasons why a couple might decide to get counseling. Therapy is very helpful to a wide variety of people, and there are many different approaches or techniques. So, an outline of counseling options is what we'll cover next.

WHAT'S MY SCORE?

Unrealistic Beliefs

Instructions: For each statement below, write how much you agree or disagree using this scale:

1	2	3	4	5	6

I strongly believe that the statement is false.

I strongly believe that the statement is true.

_____ 1. I take it as a personal insult when my partner disagrees with an important idea of mine.

_____ 2. I get very upset when my partner and I cannot see things the same way.

_____ 3. I cannot accept it when my partner disagrees with me.

_____ 4. When my partner and I disagree, I feel like our relationship is falling apart.

_____ 5. I don't like it when my partner presents views different from mine.

_____ 6. I doubt my partner's feelings for me when we argue.

_____ 7. I cannot tolerate it when my partner argues with me.

_____ 8. If your partner expresses disagreement with your ideas, s/he probably doesn't think very highly of you.

_____ 9. I get very upset if my partner does not recognize how I am feeling and I have to tell him/her.

_____ 10. Men and women don't have the same basic emotional needs.

_____ 11. Men and women need different basic things out of a relationship.

_____ 12. One of the major causes of marital problems is that men and women have different emotional needs.

_____ 13. When I do not appear to be performing well sexually, I get upset.

_____ 14. Some difficulties in my sexual performance mean personal failure to me.

_____ 15. If my sexual partner does not get satisfied completely, it means that I have failed.

_____ 16. If I cannot perform well sexually whenever my partner is in the mood, I would consider that I have the problem.

_____ 17. I can't feel OK about my lovemaking if my partner does not achieve orgasm.

_____ 18. I get upset if I think I have not completely satisfied my partner sexually.

_____ 19. If I'm not in the mood for sex when my partner is, I get upset about it.

_____ 20. People who love each other know exactly what each other's thoughts are without a word even being said.

_____ 21. People who have a close relationship can sense each other's needs as if they could read each other's minds.

_____ 22. I expect my partner to sense all my moods.

_____ 23. If you have to ask your partner for something, it shows that s/he was not "tuned into" your needs.

(Continued)

(Continued)

_____ 24. Men and women will always be mysteries to each other.

_____ 25. Men and women probably will never understand the opposite sex very well.

_____ 26. You can't really understand someone of the opposite sex.

_____ 27. Misunderstandings between [heterosexual] partners generally are due to inborn differences in psychological makeups of men and women.

_____ 28. If you don't like the way a relationship is going, you can't really make it better.

_____ 29. I do not expect my partner to be able to change.

_____ 30. Even if my partner wants to do it, I don't believe that s/he can change.

_____ 31. A partner can't learn to become more responsive to his/her partner's needs.

_____ 32. My partner does not seem capable of behaving other than s/he does now.

Scoring: Note that when this survey is used in research, the items are mixed up so that the subscales don't all appear in a clump. Also, some of the items are rephrased here to avoid the need to reverse-score them (although when used in research, the original wording should be used).

You can simply find the average of your responses for an overall score; higher numbers mean greater endorsement of unrealistic beliefs.

Fohe Subscales:

- Items 1–9 measure "disagreement is destructive"
- Items 10–12 measure "men and women have different needs"
- Items 13–19 measure "sexual perfection is expected"
- Items 20–23 measure "mindreading is expected"
- Items 24–27 measure "the opposite sex can't be understood"
- Items 28–32 measure "partners cannot change"

Source: James, Hunsley, and Hemsworth (2002).

Critical Thinking: The original version of this measure combined the subscales "the opposite sex can't be understood" and "men and women have different needs." Does splitting this into two separate ideas help or hurt the scale's utility? Further, are there additional unrealistic beliefs you believe are important to the health of a relationship but aren't included in this particular measure?

Couples Counseling

Maybe things aren't going well for a couple. That's usually why couples seek counseling. Other couples may go to counseling as a regular exercise, to check in with each other and work out problems before they become fatal flaws. Counseling can be an extremely helpful process for both happy and unhappy couples. Just because a couple is in counseling doesn't necessarily mean anything bad—they might be very proactive in making sure both people are satisfied and validated.

If you find yourself in need of couples counseling, what can you expect? As you can imagine, there are many different forms of relationship therapy, just like there are many different forms of individual therapy. To know what the best fit would be, it might help to identify what problems commonly lead people to seek out counseling. A group of 122 professional marriage and family therapy counselors were given a survey asking three questions (Whisman, Dixon, & Johnson, 1997; based on an earlier study by Geiss & O'Leary, 1981): (1) What are the most *common* problems your clients identify? (2) What are the most *difficult* problems they seem to have in terms of whether the problem will be helped through therapy sessions? (3) What are the most *damaging* problems in terms of the couple members' general functioning?

The results are shown in Table 13.1, where each column shows the problems that emerged. Within each column, the most common, difficult, or damaging issue is listed at the top and then problems follow in descending order. The most common problems were communication and power struggles, a finding that was replicated in a separate study of 147 married couples seeking therapy (Doss, Simpson, & Christensen, 2004). But while many couples experience these challenges, neither one of them seemed particularly difficult to treat or particularly damaging. One way to think about this finding is that these common problems would likely be helped by counseling sessions, making the couple members happier as a result. Maybe they just needed to learn skills or perspective-taking, which counseling can provide.

More problematic concerns are in the other two columns. The two issues that were the most difficult to treat through therapy were a lack of love between couple members or when one or both of them suffered from alcoholism. Finally, the most damaging issues to relationship health and happiness were physical abuse and infidelity/affairs. While these issues are particularly problematic, they may still be helped through counseling, depending on the circumstances and extremity of the

TABLE 13.1 ● Common, Difficult, and Damaging Problems Found in Couples Counseling

Most Common	Most Difficult to Treat	Most Damaging
Communication	Lack of loving feelings	Physical abuse
Power struggles	Alcoholism	Infidelity/affairs
Unrealistic expectations	Infidelity/affairs	Alcoholism
Sex	Power struggles	Lack of loving feelings
Problem-solving	Serious individual problems	Incest
Demonstrations of affection	Physical abuse	Communication
Money management	Communication	Power struggles
Lack of loving feelings	Unrealistic expectations	Unrealistic expectations
Children	Other addictive behaviors	Serious individual problems
Serious individual problems	Incest	Other addictive behaviors

For each column, the problems go in descending order for how common, difficult, or damaging they were.

Source: Whisman et al. (1997).

issues (for example, many counselors believe that therapy is not the answer to physical violence). Let's talk about therapy options next.

Six Types of Couples Counseling

Couples counseling does seem to be effective, at least on average. In a review of studies that examined therapy outcomes, researchers (Shadish & Baldwin, 2003) concluded that (1) couples in counseling were significantly better off than couples with similar problems but not in counseling (a control group) and (2) couples counseling was more effective in maintaining the health of a relationship than either individual counseling or options like medical interventions. This pattern was replicated in a study where half of the couples were randomly assigned to counseling and the other half weren't; those in counseling showed significantly more stability and improvement (Christensen, Atkins, Baucom, & Yi, 2010).

What are some of the different types of counseling couples might experience? The list here isn't exhaustive; we don't have time to cover every form of therapy. In addition, many actual therapy sessions will include more than one approach. That said, here is a quick overview of six possibilities:

1. **Psychodynamic therapy** emphasizes how implicit or unconscious thoughts, fears, and expectations formed in early childhood affect our relationship dynamics later. For example, one form of psychodynamic therapy is "objects relations couples therapy," in which clients examine their mental models of caregivers (like parents) and see how patterns of nurturance or support from childhood influence their needs as an adult. You can probably see how this form of counseling overlaps with research from attachment theory and early psychological influences by people like Freud (for more, see Dicks, 1967; Scharff & Bagnini, 2002; Scharff & Scharff, 1997).

2. **Behavioral therapy** emphasizes actual, observable behaviors between couple members instead of focusing on abstract thoughts or perceptions. A central idea is that relationship interactions should be rewarding and not punishing. Couple members can learn to respond to favorable dynamics with positive consequences, to build explicitly healthy behaviors (e.g., saying "thank you"). In short, dysfunctional behaviors are identified and changed, without the therapist searching for some kind of distal "root" of the problem from years ago. Unhealthy behaviors are removed and replaced with healthy, rewarding ones (see Baucom, Epstein, & Stanton, 2006; Jacobson & Margolin, 1979; Stuart, 2003).

3. **Cognitive-behavioral therapy,** or CBT, combines the idea of changing actual behaviors with an emphasis on the thought behind those behaviors. An important difference is that CBT says behaviors themselves might not have to change, if partners simply interpret those behaviors differently. For example, a husband might annoy his wife by always asking her to pay the household bills. This could create a problem for the wife if she thinks the husband is too lazy or thinks of her as his personal accountant—but if she

comes to see this behavior as trying to involve her in their joint financial decisions, she might come to enjoy the task. People's motivations and interpretations of each other's behaviors are evaluated to ensure that both couple members are working as a team (Baucom, Epstein, Sayers, & Sher, 1989; Baucom et al., 2006).

4. **Emotionally focused therapy** helps clients understand their moods and reactions to each other, including anxieties, anger, sweetness, love, and so on. It tries to identify dysfunctional emotional reactions and instead build dynamics that elicit caring responses. For example, if partners feel fear or sadness because they're worried about being rejected, coping strategies are taught that build trust, intimacy, and feelings of comfort (Johnson, 2012; Johnson & Denton, 2002; Johnson & Greenberg, 1985).

5. **Systems therapy** approaches trouble between two couple members as a function of their individual patterns and unspoken beliefs, partially due to larger groups such as their entire family or even their cultural and social environment. For example, couple members who come from different cultures may have very different expectations for shared roles, communication, "rules" about interactions with family members, and so on (Waldman & Rubalcava, 2005). A man from a patriarchal culture may have conflict with a wife who expects an egalitarian marriage. Same-sex couples in a country where homosexuality is shamed will certainly have pressures that other couples don't have. Patterns that are causing disruptions or conflicts are identified, analyzed, and changed while the couple members are taught to take the environment or context into account (Bograd, 1984; Haley, 1963; Minuchin, 1974; Todd, 1986).

6. **Sex therapy** is a somewhat controversial approach used for couples who have happy and healthy dynamics everywhere except in their sexual relations. Common problems like lack of communication, lack of love, and power struggles can all lead to sexual difficulties and frustrations. When a couple seeks out sex therapy, some basic common rules are as follows: (1) both couple members must take responsibility for any problems, (2) sexual intimacy is part of an ideal relationship, (3) problems with intimacy may come from a life history before this particular relationship started, (4) sexual compatibility can grow and improve with time, and (5) success is achieved when both partners are emotionally comfortable with self-disclosures and with mutually pleasurable sexual activities (Russell, 1990). While some people view "sex therapy" as a euphemism for paid sex workers, there is a lot of legitimate research on the topic and an entire journal devoted to helping couples (the *Journal of Sex and Marital Therapy*).

Common Principles in Couples Counseling

Do the various approaches to couples counseling have anything in common? A few people have tried to identify underlying threads that appear in most attempts to repair troubled relationships. An example of this kind of attempt (Benson, McGinn, &

Christensen, 2012) outlined five basic principles that most couples therapists or counselors seem to use, address, or believe, regardless of their particular approach. Those five principles are as follows:

1. *Both partners should alter their views of the relationship to avoid one-sided blaming.* In many troubled couples, both people think that everything is the other person's fault, instead of identifying dynamics that either lead to or are based on communication faults from both sides.

2. *Dysfunctional interactional behaviors and emotions should be identified and modified.* In therapy, couples will be assessed for issues to see what the most problematic issues are and whether they can be reduced through counseling sessions. Some behaviors, such as physical or sexual abuse, are never warranted and must be stopped immediately. In other cases, behavioral interventions can be planned and worked on over time.

3. *Couple members must confront their emotions and express intimacy with each other.* Avoiding emotional reactions can limit growth, although many counseling approaches will attempt to change negative thoughts and emotions to more positive ones. Disclosure of emotions is a necessary part of reaching intimacy with a partner.

4. *For therapy to work, communication is key.* Healthy communication must exist both between the couple members themselves and between the couple and the therapist. Healthy conversational styles, rules for communication, and positive responses to self-disclosures can all be a target of therapeutic work.

5. *Resilient couples will rely on each other's strengths.* The relationship should be deeply satisfying and sustainable, with each couple member feeling validated and useful. If one partner is better at things like keeping track of dates and appointments, while the other is better at planning family gatherings and dinner parties, the two can work together as a team—as long as both are happy with their roles.

Breaking Up

You've heard the cliché: Breaking up is hard to do.

Maybe counseling didn't work, or at least one person in the relationship decided it was simply time to end things and move on. Sometimes, breaking up is the best option. People might be genuinely incompatible, the relationship might be abusive, or people simply feel that they want more. When one door closes, another can open. That said, breaking up will likely be painful and unpleasant, at least in the short term.

If two people got legally married, the process of divorce can be long, painful, and expensive, as we all know. Note, however, that at least one researcher suggests that breakups between people who are *not* married might be even harder, because there's no social understanding of just how important the relationship might have been to the couple members involved (Orbuch, 1988). So, the exes might not get

RELATIONSHIPS AND POPULAR CULTURE

Movies About Breaking Up and Moving On

Almost everyone will experience a painful break-up at least once, and moving on can be hard. Trying to get past lost love is a popular topic in songs, TV shows, and movies. The website Refinery29.com posted a list of "The Best Movies for Getting Over Your Ex" (R29 Editors, 2018). What movies do you think should be on the list? Here are 15 of their selections:

1. *Eighth Grade* (2018)

2. *Chocolat* (2000)

3. *Silver Linings Playbook* (2012)

4. *Eternal Sunshine of the Spotless Mind* (2004)

5. *My Best Friend's Wedding* (1997)

6. *Forgetting Sarah Marshall* (2008)

7. *Heathers* (1988)

8. *The First Wives Club* (1996)

9. *Scott Pilgram vs. the World* (2010)

10. *Girls Trip* (2017)

11. *John Tucker Must Die* (2006)

12. *Crazy Stupid Love* (2011)

13. *Legally Blonde* (2001)

14. *War of the Roses* (1989)

15. *How Stella Got Her Groove Back* (1998)

the love and support from their friends and family that they need. Trying to get over a breakup is the subject of several movies (see the "Relationships and Popular Culture" feature), so there's at least some cultural understanding of the hurt it can cause.

A classic and pioneering study on breakups in college students (Hill, Rubin, & Peplau, 1976) asked people attending four different universities about their breakups. Troubled couples were more likely to stay together if both people said they were emotionally involved and when they had high similarity in variables like intelligence, age, and physical attractiveness. But when couples did break up, they often timed it on their academic schedules: Relationships mostly ended at the beginning of the school year, over winter break, at the beginning of summer break, or right around graduation. In addition, 85% of the time one person wanted to end the relationship more than the other, indicating the feelings weren't really mutual. Finally, "both women and men felt considerably less depressed, less lonely, freer, happier, but more guilty when they were the breaker-uppers than when they were the broken-up-with" (p. 158). This isn't surprising—it's not fun to be "dumped."

Another way to study breakups is to think about the process couple members might go through. What are the steps people take in going from "I love you" to "I never want to see you again"? Several stage or step models have been proposed (see, for example, Baxter, 1984; Cody, 1982; Kressel, 1985; Lee, 1984). A popular one is the five-step model created by Duck (Duck, 1982; Rollie & Duck, 2006). He suggests that most couples will go through the following process:

- **Intrapsychic stage:** An individual, mental step in which one partner starts to consider a breakup and weighs the pros and cons to ending the relationship.

- **Dyadic stage:** The other partner is confronted; they discuss problems and negotiate whether to stay together or break up.

- **Social stage:** Once the breakup is accepted by both people, they publicly share the decision with their friends, family, and coworkers.

- **Grave-dressing stage:** Both ex-partners mentally frame the relationship in a way that helps them maintain self-esteem and move on. Often, psychological defense mechanisms are used to defend "my side of the story" so that people perceive themselves as not at fault.

- **Resurrection stage:** People learn from their experience and try a new relationship.

Are there always two sides to breakups? This question was asked by a sociology study (Sprecher, 1994) that sent questionnaires to *both* members of recently ended couples, around 4 months after the breakup occurred. One interesting finding was that people generally felt negative emotions afterward (like hurt, frustration, depression, and loneliness), but that some people also felt positive emotions toward their ex, like love and relief. Interestingly, "how one partner felt . . . was generally independent of how the other partner felt" (Sprecher, 1994, p. 208), indicating very different experiences, mostly due to who was in control of the breakup. The study offered ex-partners 20 possible reasons for the breakup, and the four most common were (1) we had different interests, (2) we had communication problems, (3) one of us wanted to be independent, and/or (4) one of us became bored in the relationship. In general, very few sex differences were found, indicating that breakup experiences for men and women are quite similar.

RESEARCH DEEP DIVE

Face Your Breakup: The Role of Self-Recovery

Breakups are tough. Your world changes and you may be left feeling sad, confused, or lonely. When you lose a relationship, you not only lose your partner; you also lose part of your sense of self (Lewandowski, Aron, Bassis, & Kunak, 2006). In fact, after breaking up, people have fewer responses to provide to the question "Who am I?" and they generally feel more unsure about their sense of self. Given the potential damage to one's self-concept, recovery from breakups should go more smoothly when individuals focus on restoring their self as part of the process.

To test whether people who clarify their sense of self do better after a breakup, researchers recruited 70 people whose long-term relationships (which averaged just under 2 years in duration) had ended recently (Mason, Law, Bryan, Portley, & Sbarra, 2012). Over the next 2 months, participants came into the laboratory eight times (about every 2 weeks) to complete self-report measures of love toward their former partners, self-concept recovery (with survey items like "I have lost my sense of self" vs. "I have become reacquainted with the person I was before the relationship"), and several aspects of psychological well-being (e.g., positive relations with others, self-acceptance, autonomy, personal growth, environmental mastery, and purpose in life).

At the first study session, researchers collected facial electromyography (EMG) data by attaching a series of electrodes to each participant's face in order to detect muscle activity. The benefit of collecting physiological data like these is that they allow researchers to see if participants have involuntary physiological reactions that may reveal more about how participants truly feel, relative to a self-report that may not be as accurate. That is, a participant may say one thing, but their underlying facial movements may tell a different story. Researchers recorded these data while participants completed a Breakup Mental Activation Task (BMAT) that instructed participants to "concentrate on the question by letting any relevant thoughts, feelings, or images come to mind" while considering prompts (e.g., "Whose decision was it to end the relationship? Why? Please think about the events leading to the end of your relationship." "What do you remember about the breakup itself, the actual time during which the two of you decided to stop seeing each other?").

Participants who reported being more in love with their former partners reported worse self-concept recovery. When participants indicated poorer self-concept recovery in any given week, it tended to have implications for them later on, with them reporting poorer psychological well-being at the next study session 2 weeks later. Similarly, those who had better psychological well-being did not report worse self-concept recovery the following week. Taken together, these findings suggest that the failure to redefine the self following a breakup contributes to greater breakup-related distress.

Regarding facial movements, those who had greater corrugator supercilia facial muscle activity (located on the inside part of the eyebrows near the nose . . . where you furrow your brows when you're upset) when thinking about their breakup during the BMAT task predicted poorer self-concept recovery. In addition, when greater corrugator activity was present, the association between greater love (a positive correlation) and worse self-concept recovery (a negative correlation) was even stronger. Importantly, the facial muscle data were *more predictive of self-concept recovery than the self-report measures*. This disconnect between self-report and physiological measures indicates that self-report may not fully tap into the damage to one's self-concept that occurs following a breakup. When this happens, it could be that participants are underreporting intentionally, or that they aren't fully aware of how the breakup is affecting them.

It is important to point out that facial activity isn't necessarily causing worse self-concept recovery. Thus, you can't simply Botox your eyebrows to improve post-breakup self-concept recovery; rather, the involuntary muscle activity in the eyebrows reflects psychological experiences. Once again, correlation does not imply causation.

What is clear from all the results is that repairing one's self-concept post-breakup should be a priority for anyone hoping to cope with relationship loss. Although published research has not explicitly examined the potential benefits of self-concept repair following a breakup, these results suggest that activities that help recapture lost elements of the self—or help rediscover aspects of the self that were minimized or diminished during the relationship—may be useful.

For more, read Lewandowski, G. W., Aron, A., Bassis, S., & Kunak, J. (2006). Losing a self-expanding relationship: Implications for the self-concept. *Personal Relationships*, *13*, 317–331; and Mason, A. E., Law, R. W., Bryan, A. E. B., Portley, R. M., & Sbarra, D. A. (2012). Facing a breakup: Electromyographic responses moderate self-concept recovery following a romantic separation. *Personal Relationships*, *19*, 551–568.

Let's ask one more question in this part of the chapter: What happens after the breakup? Certainly, both people need to heal and move on with their lives. This might be difficult, and a couple of investigations regarding how this happens are explained in the "Research Deep Dive" feature. But another part of breakup dynamics includes what happens to the exes. Sometimes part of the breakup script is "Let's stay friends." Is that really possible?

Yes, at least for some people (Nardi, 1992; Weston, 1997; Wilmot, Carbaugh, & Baxter, 1985)—although friendships with exes are usually more complicated and problematic compared to friendships with people we've never dated (Schneider & Kenny, 2000). Sometimes being polite and cordial is the best people get (Becker, 1988), when people *say* they're still friends but barely ever communicate. There is hope, though. A study of about 300 gay men and lesbians plus 300 heterosexual exes addressed questions about their relationships with their exes (Lannutti & Cameron, 2002). For same-sex couples, four variables predicted whether exes were still friends: time after the breakup (with better friendships sooner afterward, and less interaction as time passed), whether the exes considered each other "chosen family," how unique the relationship was when it was intact, and simply whether they liked each other on a personal level. Other research (including a review by Becker, 1988) has emphasized that lesbians are maybe the most likely type of couple to really stay friends after a breakup; for more, check out the book *Lesbian Ex-Lovers: The Really Long-Term Relationships* (Weinstock & Rothblum, 2014).

It was slightly different for heterosexual couples (Lannutti & Cameron, 2002). Here, whether exes remained friends after a breakup was predicted by perceived social norms, such as responses to the statement "Most people I know stay friends with their ex-partners" (p. 161). Friendships were also predicted by whether the exes liked each other personally, and whether they thought there were chances of renewing the relationship in the future.

This last motive was replicated in a more recent study (Griffith, Gillath, Zhao, & Martinez, 2017), although the researchers found that staying friends just because of unresolved romantic desires or attraction led to negative outcomes in the long run. On the other hand, Griffith et al. (2017) confirmed that staying friends with an ex due to practical reasons (like having a child together or mutual financial support) or sheer civility led to positive friendship outcomes. So it is possible to stay friends, if exes like each other and have reasonable reasons to stay connected. In this way, losing a lover doesn't necessarily mean also losing a friend.

CHECK YOUR UNDERSTANDING

13.1 Six common unrealistic beliefs about relationships were identified by Eidelson and Epstein (1982). Which statement below is NOT one of those beliefs?

a. Partners should be able to change.
b. Mindreading is expected.
c. Sexual perfection is expected.
d. Men and women have different needs.

13.2 Which of the forms of couples counseling listed below was described as having theoretical ties to attachment theory?

a. Sex therapy
b. Psychodynamic therapy
c. Emotionally focused therapy
d. Systems therapy

13.3 Duck (1982) suggested five steps or stages to relationship breakup. In which of the stages do ex-partners announce the end of the relationship to their friends and families?

a. Intrapsychic stage
b. Dyadic stage
c. Social stage
d. Grave-dressing stage

APPLICATION ACTIVITY

First, describe the couples counseling types explained in this chapter, in your own words. Then, take another look at Table 13.1, which shows the most common problem (poor communication), the problem that's most difficult to treat (lack of loving feelings), and the most damaging problem (physical abuse) found in relationships (according to Whisman et al., 1997). Discuss whether these three problems can be helped in couples counseling or not, and why. If you think that they *can* be helped through counseling, choose the form of counseling you think would be most beneficial for that specific problem and analyze why you think it's a particularly good fit.

CRITICAL THINKING

- Eidelson and Epstein (1982) suggest six common unrealistic beliefs found in romantic relationships. Which do you think is the most commonly destructive for real couples, and why? Then, discuss one way that this belief might be overcome. Your solution might be at the couple level (e.g., communication between partners), at the larger social/cultural level (e.g., different messages portrayed in the media), or anything in between.

- In your opinion, which of the six forms of couples counseling described earlier sounds like the best option for you, personally, in terms of your way of viewing yourself and your relationships? Describe why you think you'd prefer this particular form of therapy compared to the other forms.

- Lots of people say that they want to remain friends with their ex-partner. How often do you think that sentiment is genuine, as opposed to saying it simply to be polite and avoid hurt feelings during the actual breakup conversation? Some of the research in this section described when people are more likely to stay friends; what additional variables do you think should be studied that weren't mentioned in the chapter?

Answers to the Check Your Understanding Questions

13.1 a, 13.2 b, and 13.3 c.

What Can Couple Members Do to Maintain a Healthy Relationship Over Time?

Couples counseling and breaking up? That's not what most people envision when they start a relationship.

So, what can the science of relationships teach about maintaining a happy, healthy relationship over time? Now that you've read the other 12 chapters, do you feel like you've actually become a relationships expert? Do you know how to pragmatically

What are specific strategies or tactics that couple members can use to promote lasting health and happiness?

navigate the world of love and loss? What the heck is the *use* of reading this book, other than to learn about a bunch of studies? As promised, the final section of the final chapter here is an attempt to give "real-world" advice about how the best couples stay together—but again, based on authentic science. What can an everyday person do (or try to do) when you find yourself in love?

Hopefully you recall at least a few of the ideas we've already gone over in earlier chapters. For example, you know from the investment model that relationships are more likely to last if people put resources and effort into them, as well as when they feel like they get more positive outcomes than negative ones. You also know that implicit beliefs matter, where "growth" beliefs predict more long-term stability than "destiny" beliefs. You know that certain conflict management styles are also healthier and keep the relationship going through hard times. These are just a few examples of what you should have already learned and can hopefully apply to your own social relationships. Here are some more practical ideas—but there are lots more available if you do some of your own searching for additional studies.

Don't Wait to Talk About It: Intervene Early

Abraham Lincoln is credited as saying, "You cannot escape the responsibility of tomorrow by evading it today."

When it comes to physical health, *prevention* of problems is better than treatment. The same is true for relationship health. The **Prevention and Relationship Enhancement Program (PREP)** is intended for people who are engaged to be married (Markman, Floyd, Stanley, & Lewis, 1986). It tries to teach them how to identify problematic behaviors and communication strategies, and to use healthy ones instead. Over the course of six 2-hour sessions (12 hours total), couples are taught "partner skills and ground rules" for how to handle conflict and promote intimacy (Stanley, Markman, St. Peters, & Leber, 1995, p. 393). In addition to the sessions, people are given homework in the form of reading assignments. Lessons are similar to what couple members might learn in therapy, but the idea of PREP is that people learn these tactics *before* problems have a chance to begin. In a 12-year longitudinal study with 135 couples, people who actively participated in the PREP model showed increased abilities in communication, problem-solving, and support/validation of each other.

In general, several studies support the idea that warning signs of a troubled future can be identified by partners pretty early in a relationship (e.g., Lavner, Karney, & Bradbury, 2012; McNulty, Olson, Meltzer, & Shaffer, 2013). Trying to decide whether a relationship is healthy and whether a partner really has potential is helpful from the very beginning of couplehood (Joel & Eastwick, 2018). One way to assess this might be to simply see whether a partner is willing to talk about issues and willing to take action when problems, misunderstandings, or even boredom start to occur. In other words, is your partner willing and able to engage in the strategies outlined here?

Grow Together: Self-Expansion Theory

People change and routine gets dull. These two facts can lead people to honestly fear the idea of committing to a single person for life. How can you know what kind of person you'll be in 10, 20, or 50 years and how your partner(s) will change? And how can you avoid simple boredom and monotony when you know that your partner and routines will inevitably fall into the same patterns, over and over and over? Before you start to get depressed with these ideas, relationship science has a potential solution in an idea called **self-expansion theory** (Aron & Aron, 1986; Aron, Aron, & Norman, 2001; Aron, Aron, Tudor, & Nelson, 1991). The theory says that we all have a basic motivation to grow our sense of self, to expand in our resources, talents, knowledge, and social networks. We want to be smarter, stronger, richer, more popular, and better at what we try to do.

One way to expand the self is to form an intimate relationship with another person who pushes us toward improvement and self-exploration. On a pragmatic level, for example, sharing expenses with someone (like rent or a mortgage) helps us achieve financial stability. When a friend or partner can teach us new skills (like how to cook, golf, or reupholster furniture), we expand in our talents and abilities. And an ideal partner also helps us expand spiritually, philosophically, and intellectually by engaging our minds in new and interesting ways.

A relatively simple, yet very effective, strategy to maintain healthy relationships comes from self-expansion theory: When you're with a long-term partner, engage in activities that are *new to both of you*. "Shared participation in novel and challenging activities, an interpersonal process, enhances each partner's positive affect [or emotions]" (Strong & Aron, 2006, p. 342). The best activities for partners are those they find both exciting and pleasant (Reissman, Aron, & Bergen, 1993).

It's easy to see why doing fun, new, exciting things together would help couples stay happy and interested in being together. The couple members grow *together*, sharing the experience and bonding while they travel, learn to dance, see a Broadway show, hike the Grand Canyon, or do whatever they both enjoy. It promotes togetherness and staves off boredom—a win-win combination for both people.

Be the Right Kind of Helpful: Types of Support

Often people vow to stay together "for better or worse."

We want our partner to be there for us in both good times and bad times. Several researchers have studied how the presence of a relationship partner really can make struggles and challenges easier to bear (in other words, when times are "worse"). Help from a partner can be especially important earlier in life, when we're still working out the kinks (Schwarzer & Gutierrez-Dona, 2005). Partners (or friends, family members, or anyone close to us) can offer support in a variety of ways. You might remember that way back in Chapter 1, we covered different forms of social support (Wills, 1985). These include emotional support (offering empathy to someone and sharing their feelings), instrumental support (offering tangible help, like money), and informational

TABLE 13.2 ● Four Types of Social Support	
Type of Support	**Examples**
Emotional support	Hugging someone while they cry; sending them a condolences card
Instrumental support	Loaning someone money; letting them live with you temporarily
Informational support	Helping someone make a pros and cons list; showing them where they can get more information online
Appraisal support	Telling someone if you can see growth in them; praising someone for achieving a goal

Support can come in a variety of ways, and it's important to match someone's need with the type of support offered at the time. This model of four types of support comes from House (1981).

support (offering information or advice). A fourth form of social support is **appraisal support**, which is when someone provides feedback to you regarding how well you are progressing toward a set goal (House, 1981).

Couples who support each other consistently show better emotional health (Conger, Rueter, & Elder, 1999). People who are married and can talk to their partner about their troubles are less likely to be depressed, compared to people who are single, separated, or divorced (Weissman, 1987). That said, *type* of support matters. Offering the wrong type of support, or offering support at the wrong time, can actually backfire and make things worse (Bolger, Zuckerman, & Kessler, 2000; Rafaeli & Gleason, 2009). If your partner has a death in the family and you say, "Well, here's 20 bucks," it's probably not going to go over well. Communication, as we've seen multiple times already in this book, is important.

And what about when times are "better"? One of the joys of being in a relationship is that we have someone to share our happiness and success—and sincere celebration when things go well matters, too. In a study called "Will You Be There for Me When Things Go Right?" researchers investigated how support for *positive* events is also essential for a happy relationship (Gable, Gonzaga, & Strachman, 2006). Dating couples were videotaped talking about recent positive and negative events. They rated how much support and validation they felt from their partners during these interactions, and they were also scored by observers who watched the tapes afterward. Two months later, both the self-report data and the scores from observers showed that partner responses to *positive* events were more predictive of relationship well-being and stability, compared to responses to negative events. Celebrating success matters. Feeling that your partner validates your accomplishments as helping the two of you, as a team, feels good.

Promote or Prevent? Self-Regulation Theory

Most of us fail to achieve our New Year's resolutions before the end of January.

Self-control and sticking to goals is the key to success in a lot of endeavors, whether it be weight loss, improving in a sport, maintaining high grades in school, or remaining committed to a relationship partner. Self-regulation is another term for self-control, and **self-regulation theory** is the idea that we manage our thoughts, emotions, and behaviors in order to reach goals we've set for ourselves (Baumeister, 2000; Baumeister, Vohs, & Tice, 2007). We set standards for ourselves, monitor how well we're progressing, and try to maintain the willpower to control urges.

One way to keep up motivation when it comes to reaching goals is to think about how we've mentally framed the goal itself (Higgins, 1997). Think, for example, about a single person who wants to find a partner. One frame could be, "I want to stop being so lonely!" A different frame could be instead, "I want to find a supportive, loving partner." Both frameworks seem to have the same idea behind them, but the mental attitude about *why* the goal is being set is different. The first frame is what we call a **prevention-focused goal**, one driven by safety and security and framed in reference to something you're trying to *avoid* (in this case, it's loneliness). The second frame, in contrast, is a **promotion-focused goal**, driven by accomplishment, growth, and ideals and framed in reference to something you're trying to *approach* or achieve.

Consider a variety of goals that can be framed either way. For grades: I want to avoid failing (prevention) versus I want to get all As (promotion). For exercise: I want to stop being so sedentary (prevention) versus I want to exercise more (promotion). For relationships: I want to avoid cheating or fighting with my partner (prevention) versus I want to stay committed and have healthy communication with my partner (promotion). Which way we frame our goals influences how we maintain motivation over time. Are we thinking about what might go wrong or what might go right?

Prevention-focused goals aren't bad. Because they are based on fears, they can be quite motivating (Shah, Friedman, & Kruglanski, 2002). People who are trying hard to prevent something from happening can be vigilant in their quest—but it's also true that their behaviors are based on anxiety and obligation (Molden & Winterheld, 2013). Achieving these goals is met with relief and a sense of calm security. On the other hand, promotion-focused goals seem to make us happier and lead to a true sense of accomplishment. Both outcomes are good. People who tend to be chronically prevention focused tend to play it safe or "settle" when they know they're secure; they like stability. While promotion-focused people can achieve great happiness if their goals are fulfilled, they may also tend to be restless or constantly seeking "more." Which option sounds more appealing may reveal which side of the fence you tend to fall on.

Share, Don't Exchange: Communal Mindsets

Do you keep track of favors exchanged or slights endured?

Within intimate relationships, Clark and Mills (1979) identified two orientations that align with people's higher or lower tendencies to "keep track" of giving and receiving within a relationship. Some partners will display an **exchange orientation**, which is when people prefer direct reciprocity in the relationship. This is more like a business model, in which the emphasis is on fairness and mutual benefits. I paid for dinner last time, so you should pay for dinner tonight. Or, you hurt me by kissing someone else—so it's only fair for me to kiss someone else, too. What's fair is fair, and people with this mindset feel obligated to make sure both people are equally contributing to things.

In contrast, people with a **communal orientation** don't keep score as much; they aren't concerned with perfect balance or fairness. Instead, they might cover their partner's expenses for a while if the other person is between jobs, never expecting to be paid back. They don't see favors as obligations; they don't wait to be "paid back" later. Perhaps the most extreme version of a communal relationship is that of parent to child; parents provide everything their children need without necessarily keeping track of exact expenses or effort (Clark & Mills, 1993). The idea is that this kind of giving is just part of a loving relationship.

These mindsets can be the foundation for different dynamics in romantic couples as well. Because people with an exchange orientation expect equal input and repayment of "debts," these couples will often be less forgiving. If one of them makes a mistake, the other might feel like revenge is the fairest response. In contrast, a communal orientation is geared toward generosity, true altruism, and selflessness. Part of their self-esteem comes from helping others, including friends and partners (Clark & Grote, 1998; Xue & Silk, 2012), and they are more likely to forgive when something goes wrong.

Note that while some research indicates that communal orientations within relationships are helpful in various ways, other research questions this. For example, think back to Chapter 5 where you learned about equity theory (Adams, 1963; Canary & Stafford, 1992; Hatfield & Rapson, 2012; Sprecher, 2001; Walster, Walster, & Berscheid, 1978). That was the idea that we don't like to feel like we're putting in more effort, sacrifices, money, or anything else into the relationship, compared to our partner. But we don't want to put in less, either! We don't want to be "overbenefitted" (which makes us feel guilty) or "underbenefitted" (which makes us feel resentful). We just want things to be fair. That sounds like an exchange orientation.

Perhaps instead of one mindset being "better" than the other in terms of satisfaction or relationship longevity, what matters is that two people are *matched* in terms of their mindset and expectations. Couple members should either have explicit rules about what's "fair" and then stick to them (a perfectly fine exchange understanding) or mutually agree not to keep track of little things or that each person contributes different types of resources to the relationship. As long as neither person feels the arrangement is unfair, things can work out.

Redefine Happiness: Search for Meaning

Marriage should make us happy—right?

Studies tracking the pattern of marriage (in the United States) over the last 50 years have shown two steady trends: (1) the proportion of married people who say their marriage is "very happy" has gone down, and (2) the extent to which marriage has become a central predictor of life happiness has gone up. "Marriage, in short, has tilted toward an all-or-nothing state" (Finkel, 2018, p. 24). In his book *The All or Nothing Marriage*, award-winning psychologist Eli Finkel describes these patterns and analyzes expectations about marriage over recent centuries (see also Finkel, Cheung, Emery, Carswell, & Larson, 2015).

Finkel notes an important difference between two separate possible motives in marriage. **Happiness**, as he defines it, is a high ratio of pleasure to pain, or a psychological state of mostly positive emotional experiences. In contrast, **meaning** is a mental state characterized by personal growth and self-expression. Meaning is the opportunity to discover and explore your own strengths and potential, similar to Maslow's concept of self-actualization. While happiness and meaning are linked together, they are not the same thing. For long-term relationships, according to Finkel, seeking meaning—and *not* necessarily seeking "happiness"—may lead to better outcomes, as shown in Table 13.3.

Meaning-based marriages, according to this perspective, are healthier and actually lead to the most satisfying, fulfilling experiences in the long run. Importantly, the search for meaning can sometimes mean *not* being happy, because happiness generally leads to contentment and complacency. Instead, meaning requires you to be aware of your weaknesses, and your relationship partner might be able to help with this self-awareness (in a supportive and loving way, of course, not a criticizing or mean way). When this happens in a relationship, "the [partners] helped each other flourish in ways that might have remained out of reach if they weren't together" (Finkel, 2018, p. 149). It seems that instead of asking whether a partner makes you *happier*, you might want to ask if a partner makes you *flourish*.

Avoid the Apocalypse: Gottman's Four Horsemen of Communication

No one wants an apocalypse. This image is so powerful that it's almost certainly an exaggeration—even a terrible breakup doesn't mean the literal end of the world. Still, heartbreak can be terrible. One of the leaders in the science of relationships is John Gottman, who is so dedicated to identifying healthy and unhealthy patterns in relationships that his research space has been labeled the "Love Lab." The Love Lab offers many interesting results from their work, but the one on which we'll focus for the final section of this book is what they call the **four horsemen** (Gottman, 1993, 1994; Gottman & Silver, 2015).

The reference comes from Revelation, the final book of the Christian Bible, when four apparitions destroy the world (they are Death, Famine, War, and Conquest). It's a scary comparison, and Gottman chose this reference because his research shows that

TABLE 13.3 ● Happiness-Based vs. Meaning-Based Relationships	
Happiness-Based Model	**Meaning-Based Model**
Emphasis on pleasure	Emphasis on meaning and growth
Pursuit of self-esteem	Pursuit of self-expression
Belief that sustaining a happy relationship shouldn't require endurance or forbearance	Belief that sustaining a happy relationship might require endurance or forbearance
Personal fulfillment and relationship fulfillment tend to be incompatible in the long run	Personal fulfillment and relationship fulfillment tend to be compatible in the long run

Source: Adapted from Finkel (2018).

certain behaviors are extremely destructive—the death of love. Each behavior builds on the next, creating a crescendo of conflict. Fortunately, he also identifies a way to fight each problem. The toxic behaviors and their solutions are shown in Figure 13.1.

What are the four destructive behaviors? As shown in Figure 13.1, the first is **criticism**, which is verbally attacking the overall character of your partner. Instead of focusing on a specific complaint (e.g., "I don't like that you forgot my birthday"), it's a global judgment about the person (e.g., "You're a selfish jerk"). Next along the path to destruction is **contempt**, or the feeling that your partner is inferior to you. It's a sense of disrespect and condescension to the other person. Specifically, contempt often comes out in the form of sarcasm and cynicism about whether your partner is even capable of doing what you previously hoped.

FIGURE 13.1   ●   The Four Horsemen of Poor Relationship Communication

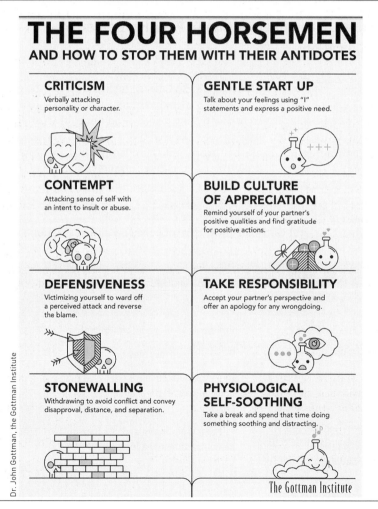

Source: Shown here with permission from the Gottman Institute.

The third horseman in this pattern is **defensiveness**, or a sense that there's nothing wrong with you—any and all problems are the other person's fault. Defensiveness means you'll blame your partner for everything and convince yourself that you have the moral high ground in any conflicts. People can "play the victim," meaning they see themselves as martyrs, which only builds resentment. Finally, the top of this mountain of problems is **stonewalling**, or when you simply tune out, avoid the other person, and emotionally release from any positive feeling about the relationship or your partner. Lack of any response at all can be even more hurtful and damaging, and it certainly shows the end of love.

So, what can people do to avoid the apocalypse? As also shown in Figure 13.1, there are accompanying solutions to each step. To combat criticism, express concerns about the relationship with gentle and specific concerns. Instead of wording things with a focus on the other person (e.g., "What's wrong with you?"), frame things with "I-statements" (e.g., "I'm angry about what you said last night"). To avoid feelings of contempt, disgust, or disrespect for your partner, frequently remind yourself of your partner's positive qualities. Why did you love this person in the first place? What about their background might make this situation difficult, and how can you acknowledge their rights and perspective as equal to your own?

The solution to defensiveness is to take responsibility. All conflicts have two perspectives; a happy relationship has to keep the other person's wants and needs in mind. It's also essential to admit when your actions caused issues and to sincerely apologize when you mess up. Importantly, an apology can't just be pretty words; it has to mean that you genuinely will try to avoid that kind of behavior in the future. Finally, Gottman's advice to avoid stonewalling is self-care. He notes that this kind of care should be both psychological and physiological, a way for you to find a relaxing calm. Meditate, go for a run, take a bath, or do whatever you need to relax, recharge, and take a break from the conflict. Physiological calm is tied to lower levels of divorce and breakup (Gottman, 1993). Sometimes, taking a break gives us time to control our emotions and find some perspective.

Finally, note that an essential part of a happy, healthy, and lasting relationship is that *both people* should be avoiding the "horsemen" and using the positive tactics instead. If one partner is judgmental and mean to the other, it's not a good relationship. Enduring love means sincerity, caring, and respect. Everyone deserves a relationship like that.

CHECK YOUR UNDERSTANDING

13.4 Which activity to help a failing relationship would be most likely advised from someone who is a fan of self-expansion theory?

a. Take a relaxing bubble bath to get away from your troubles.

b. Write down all of the reasons you love your partner.

c. Take up a new hobby you can do by yourself.

d. Go on a trip to an exotic place with your partner.

13.5 Sam and George ask if they can sleep on your couch for a week while their apartment is being fumigated for bugs.

(Continued)

(Continued)

If you say yes, what kind of support are you giving them?

a. Appraisal

b. Informational

c. Instrumental

d. Emotional

13.6 Which of the options below is NOT one of Gottman's "four horsemen" of poor relationship communication?

a. Stonewalling

b. Escalation

c. Criticism

d. Defensiveness

APPLICATION ACTIVITY

Think about the five sentences that appear below. Each is framed as a prevention-focused goal. Reframe each to be a promotion-focused goal instead.

a. I want to make sure I don't get a divorce.

b. I want to avoid getting any Ds or Fs for my grades this term.

c. Let's stop fighting so much.

d. I never want to go an entire year without exercising again.

e. I'd like to avoid embarrassing myself at the party on Saturday.

CRITICAL THINKING

- Some studies find that either "exchange" or "communal" orientations will work for relationship partners, as long as both people involved communicate and understand what the expectations are. Which of these orientations do you think matches your own perspective or orientation when it comes to romantic partnerships? Are you generally happy with how your orientation has translated into relationship experiences so far?

- Finkel (2018) argues that instead of seeking "happiness" in a long-term relationship, people who seek "meaning" will have better relationships. Explain whether you agree or disagree with this suggestion, and why. Use specific examples to defend your opinion.

- Out of all of the ideas in the second half of this chapter, which idea do you think is the *most* helpful or essential to happy and lasting relationship dynamics? Explain why you chose that particular idea as the most helpful or useful.

Answers to the Check Your Understanding Questions

13.4 d, **13.5** c, and **13.6** b.

Chapter Summary

1. How do couple members cope with relationship problems?

2. What can couple members do to maintain a healthy relationship over time?

How do couple members cope with relationship problems?

One reason couples have problems is because people have unrealistic beliefs about how relationships should work. Examples of these unrealistic beliefs are "disagreement is destructive" and "mindreading is expected." When couples experience problems, various forms of couples counseling can be helpful. Some types of couples therapy include psychodynamic, behavioral, cognitive-behavioral, emotionally focused, systems, and sex therapy. Regardless of the specific form of counseling, some common principles will run throughout, such as the idea that both couple members need to actively participate in the therapy process. If things can't work out, breakup may occur. One model for the process of breakup suggests that couples go through stages, including an intrapsychic stage, a dyadic stage, a social stage, and a "grave-dressing" stage. Finally, the resurrection stage occurs when people learn from their experience and try a new relationship.

What can couple members do to maintain a healthy relationship over time?

Several lines of research suggest ways for couple members to maintain the health and happiness of their relationship over time. Early intervention and prevention are ideal. Other suggestions include the following: (1) engaging in new activities together, as suggested by self-expansion theory; (2) offering the appropriate kind of social support, depending on the situation; (3) framing goals in terms of promotion orientation instead of prevention orientation, as suggested by self-regulation theory; (4) communicating whether an exchange or communal orientation is desired; (5) looking for "meaning" instead of "happiness"; and (6) avoiding the four horsemen of poor communication in relationships.

List of Terms

Learning Objectives	Key Terms
13.1 Describe common unrealistic beliefs in relationships, couples counseling, and relationship breakups.	Psychodynamic therapy Behavioral therapy Cognitive-behavioral therapy Emotionally focused therapy Systems therapy

	Sex therapy Intrapsychic stage Dyadic stage Social stage Grave-dressing stage Resurrection stage
13.2 Compare and contrast research suggesting specific strategies for maintaining relationship happiness and longevity.	Prevention and Relationship Enhancement Program (PREP) Self-expansion theory Appraisal support Self-regulation theory Prevention-focused goal Promotion-focused goal Exchange orientation Communal orientation Happiness Meaning Four horsemen Criticism Contempt Defensiveness Stonewalling

• References •

Chapter 1

Agnew, C. R., & South, S. C. (2014). *Interpersonal relationships and health: Social and clinical psychological mechanisms.* New York, NY: Oxford.

Ainsworth, M. D. S., Blehar, M. C., Waters, E., & Wall, S. (1978). *Patterns of attachment: A psychological study of the strange situation.* Oxford, England: Lawrence Erlbaum.

Balzarini, R. N., Dobson, K., Chin, K., & Campbell, L. (2017). Does exposure to erotica reduce attraction and love for romantic partners in men? Independent replications of Kenrick, Gutierres, and Goldberg (1989) study 2. *Journal of Experimental Social Psychology, 70,* 191–197.

Bartholomew, K., & Horowitz, L. M. (1991). Attachment styles among young adults: A test of a four-category model. *Journal of Personality and Social Psychology, 61*(2), 226–244.

Belz, M., Pyritz, L. W., & Boos, M. (2013). Spontaneous flocking in human groups. *Behavioural Processes, 92,* 6–14.

Berkman, L. F., & Syme, S. L. (1979). Social networks, host resistance, and mortality: A nine-year follow-up study of Alameda County residents. *American Journal of Epidemiology, 109*(2), 186–204.

Berscheid, E., Snyder, M., & Omoto, A. M. (1989). Issues in studying close relationships. In C. Hendrick (Ed.), *Close relationships* (pp. 63–91). Thousand Oaks, CA: Sage.

Birnbaum, G. E., Orr, I., Mikulincer, M., & Florian, V. (1997). When marriage breaks up-does attachment style contribute to coping and mental health? *Journal of Social and Personal Relationships, 14*(5), 643–654.

Blaicher, W., Gruber, D., Bieglmayer, C., Blaicher, A. M., Knogler, W., & Huber, J. C. (1999). The role of oxytocin in relation to female sexual arousal. *Gynecologic and Obstetric Investigation, 47*(2), 125–126.

Bowlby, J. (1958). The nature of the child's tie to his mother. *International Journal of Psychoanalysis, 39,* 350–373.

Campbell, L., Simpson, J. A., Kashy, D. A., & Fletcher, G. J. O. (2001). Ideal standards, the self, and flexibility of ideals in close relationships. *Personality and Social Psychology Bulletin, 27*(4), 447–462.

Carmichael, M. S., Humbert, R., Dixen, J., Palmisano, G., Greenleaf, W., & Davidson, J. M. (1987). Plasma oxytocin increases in the human sexual response. *Journal of Clinical Endocrinology & Metabolism, 64*(1), 27–31.

Coan, J. A., Schaefer, H. S., & Davidson, R. J. (2006). Lending a hand: Social regulation of the neural response to threat. *Psychological Science, 17*(12), 1032–1039.

Cole-Detke, H., & Kobak, R. (1996). Attachment processes in eating disorder and depression. *Journal of Consulting and Clinical Psychology, 64*(2), 282–290.

Cooper, M. L., Shaver, P. R., & Collins, N. L. (1998). Attachment styles, emotion regulation, and adjustment in adolescence. *Journal of Personality and Social Psychology, 74*(5), 1380–1397.

Coyne, J. C., Rohrbaugh, M. J., Shoham, V., Sonnega, J. S., Nicklas, J. M., & Cranford, J. A. (2001). Prognostic importance of marital quality for survival of congestive heart failure. *American Journal of Cardiology, 88*(5), 526–529.

Critchfield, K. L., Levy, K. N., Clarkin, J. F., & Kernberg, O. F. (2008). The relational context of aggression in borderline personality disorder: Using adult attachment style to predict forms of hostility. *Journal of Clinical Psychology, 64*(1), 67–82.

Darwin, C. R. (1859). *On the origin of the species by means of natural selection.* London, England: John Murray.

Depue, R. A., & Collins, P. F. (1999). Neurobiology of the structure of personality: Dopamine, facilitation of incentive motivation, and extraversion. *Behavioral and Brain Sciences, 22*(3), 491–517.

Fehr, B. (1988). Prototype analysis of the concepts of love and commitment. *Journal of Personality and Social Psychology, 55*(4), 557–579.

Fonagy, P., Leigh, T., Steele, M., Steele, H., Kennedy, R., Mattoon, G., ... Gerber, A. (1996). The relation of attachment status, psychiatric classification, and response to psychotherapy. *Journal of Consulting and Clinical Psychology, 64*(1), 22–31.

Gonzaga, G. C., Turner, R. A., Keltner, D., Campos, B., & Altemus, M. (2006). Romantic love and sexual desire in close relationships. *Emotion, 6*(2), 163–179.

Hendrick, C., & Hendrick, S. (1986). A theory and method of love. *Journal of Personality and Social Psychology, 50*(2), 392–402.

House, J. S., Landis, K. R., & Umberson, D. (1988). Social relationships and health. *Science, 241*(4865), 540–545.

Jetter, A. (2013, November). A hidden cause of chronic illness. *More Magazine*, 85–115.

Karreman, A., & Vingerhoets, A. J. (2012). Attachment and well-being: The mediating role of emotion regulation and resilience. *Personality and Individual Differences, 53*(7), 821–826.

Kelley, H. H. (1983). Love and commitment. In H. H. Kelley, E. Berscheid, A. Christensen, J. H. Harvey, T. L. Huston, G. Levinger, E. McClintock, L. A. Peplau, & D. R. Peterson (Eds.), *Close relationships* (pp. 265–314). New York, NY: W. H. Freeman.

Kenrick, D. T., Gutierres, S. E., & Goldberg, L. L. (1989). Influence of popular erotica on judgments of strangers and mates. *Journal of Experimental Social Psychology, 25*(2), 159–167.

Knobloch, L. K., Solomon, D. H., & Cruz, M. G. (2001). The role of relationship development and attachment in the experience of romantic jealousy. *Personal Relationships, 8*(2), 205–224.

Lee, J. A. (1977). A typology of styles of loving. *Personality and Social Psychology Bulletin, 3*(2), 173–182.

Lemieux, R., & Hale, J. L. (1999). Intimacy, passion, and commitment in young romantic relationships: Successfully measuring the triangular theory of love. *Psychological Reports, 85*(2), 497–503.

Lemieux, R., & Hale, J. L. (2000). Intimacy, passion, and commitment among married individuals: Fur-

ther testing of the triangular theory of love. *Psychological Reports, 87*(3), 941–948.

Loving, T. J., & Keneski, E. (2014). Relationship researchers put the "psycho" in psychoneuroimmunology. In C. R. Agnew & S. C. South (Eds.), *Interpersonal relationships and health: Social and clinical psychological mechanisms*. New York, NY: Oxford.

Merz, E. M., & Consedine, N. S. (2009). The association of family support and wellbeing in later life depends on adult attachment style. *Attachment & Human Development, 11*(2), 203–221.

Mikulincer, M., & Florian, V. (1998). The relationship between adult attachment styles and emotional and cognitive reactions to stressful events. In J. A. Simpson & W. S. Rholes (Eds.), *Attachment theory and close relationships* (pp. 143–165). New York, NY: Guilford.

Mikulincer, M., Florian, V., & Weller, A. (1993). Attachment styles, coping strategies, and posttraumatic psychological distress: The impact of the Gulf War in Israel. *Journal of Personality and Social Psychology, 64*(5), 817–826.

Newman, M. L., & Roberts, N. A. (2013). *Health and social relationships: The good, the bad, and the complicated*. Washington, DC: American Psychological Association.

Ogawa, J. R., Sroufe, L. A., Weinfield, N. S., Carlson, E. A., & Egeland, B. (1997). Development and the fragmented self: Longitudinal study of dissociative symptomatology in a nonclinical sample. *Development and Psychopathology, 9*(4), 855–879.

Perrone, K. M., & Worthington, E. L., Jr. (2001). Factors influencing ratings of marital quality by individuals within dual-career marriages: A conceptual model. *Journal of Counseling Psychology, 48*(1), 3–9.

Rubin, Z. (1970). Measurement of romantic love. *Journal of Personality and Social Psychology, 16*(2), 265–273.

Sarason, I. G., Sarason, B. R., Shearin, E. N., & Pierce, G. R. (1987). A brief measure of social support: Practical and theoretical implications. *Journal of Social and Personal Relationships, 4*(4), 497–510.

Slatcher, R. B. (2014). Family relationships and cortisol in everyday life. In C. R. Agnew & S. C. South (Eds.), *Interpersonal relationships and health: Social and clinical psychological mechanisms* (pp. 71–88). New York, NY: Oxford University Press.

Sternberg, R. J. (1986). A triangular theory of love. *Psychological Review, 93*(2), 119–135.

Sumter, S. R., Valkenburg, P. M., & Peter, J. (2013). Perceptions of love across the lifespan: Differences in passion, intimacy, and commitment. *International Journal of Behavioral Development, 37*(5), 417–427.

Tollefson, J., Usher, K., & Foster, K. (2011). Relationships in pain: The experience of relationships to people living with chronic pain in rural areas. *International Journal of Nursing Practice, 17*(5), 478–485.

Wallace, K. (2016, December 6). Are people without kids happier? Studies offer mixed picture. *CNN.* Retrieved from http://www.cnn.com/2016/12/06/health/parents-happiness-child-free-studies/index.html

Walster, E., Aronson, V., Abrahams, D., & Rottman, L. (1966). Importance of physical attractiveness in dating behavior. *Journal of Personality and Social Psychology, 4*, 508–516.

Wills, T. A. (1985). Supportive functions of interpersonal relationships. In S. Cohen & S. L. Syme (Eds.), *Social support and health* (pp. 61–82). Orlando, FL: Academic Press.

Chapter 2

Arnocky, S., & Vaillancourt, T. (2014). Sex differences in response to victimization by an intimate partner: More stigmatization and less help-seeking among males. *Journal of Aggression, Maltreatment & Trauma, 23*(7), 705–724.

Ashford, M. (Creator, Writer). (2013–2016). *Masters of Sex* [Television series]. Los Angeles, CA: Showtime.

Bahlai, C. A., Bartlett, L. J., Burgio, K. R., Fournier, A. M., Keiser, C. N., Poisot, T., & Whitney, K. S. (2019). Open science isn't always open to all scientists. *American Scientist, 107*(2), 78–82.

Berkman, L. F., & Syme, S. L. (1979). Social networks, host resistance, and mortality: A nine-year follow-up study of Alameda County residents. *American Journal of Epidemiology, 109*(2), 186–204.

Butler, A. C., & Goodfriend, W. (2015). Long distance vs. proximal romantic relationships: Predicting alternatives, satisfaction, and bias. *Modern Psychological Studies, 20*, 31–40.

Center for Open Science. (2020a). *Open Science Badges enhance openness, a core value of scientific practice.* Retrieved from https://cos.io/our-services/open-science-badges/

Center for Open Science. (2020b). *Registered Reports: Peer review before results are known to align scientific values and practices.* Retrieved from https://cos.io/rr/

Coppola, F. F., & Mutrux, G. (Producers), Condon, B. (Director). (2004). *Kinsey* [Motion picture]. United States: Fox Searchlight.

Crowne, D. P., & Marlowe, D. (1960). A new scale of social desirability independent of psychopathology. *Journal of Consulting Psychology, 24*(4), 349–354.

Heinzen, T., & Goodfriend, W. (2019). *Social psychology.* Thousand Oaks, CA: Sage.

Johnson, M. P. (1995). Patriarchal terrorism and common couple violence: Two forms of violence against women. *Journal of Marriage and the Family, 57*(2), 283–294.

Johnson, M. P. (2007). The intersection of gender and control. In L. O'Toole, J. R. Schiffman, & M. L. K. Edwards (Eds.), *Gender violence: Interdisciplinary perspectives* (2nd ed., pp. 257–268). New York, NY: New York University Press.

Kenny, D. A., Kashy, D. A., & Cook, W. (2006). *Dyadic data analysis.* New York, NY: Guilford.

Kidwell, M. C., Lazarević, L. B., Baranski, E., Hardwicke, T. E., Piechowski, S., Falkenberg, L. S., … Errington, T. M. (2016). Badges to acknowledge open practices: A simple, low-cost, effective method for increasing transparency. *PLoS Biology, 14*(5), e1002456.

Lebel, P. E., Berger, Z. D., Campbell, L., & Loving, J. T. (2017). Falsifiability is not optional. *Journal of Personality and Social Psychology, 2*, 254–261.

Mankiewicz, R. (2004). *The story of mathematics.* Princeton, NJ: Princeton University Press.

Moritz, N. H., & Cannell, S. J. (Producers), Lord, P., & Miller, C. (Directors). (2012). *21 Jump Street* [Motion picture]. United States: Columbia Pictures and Metro-Goldwyn-Mayer.

Nosek, B. A., Ebersole, C. R., DeHaven, A. C., & Mellor, D. T. (2017, June 16). The preregistration revolution. *Proceedings of the National Academy of Sciences, 115*(11), 2600–2606.

Pratkanis, A. R. (1992). The cargo-cult science of subliminal persuasion. *Skeptical Inquirer, 16*(3), 260–272.

Rosen, K. H. (1996). The ties that bind women to violent premarital relationships: Processes of seduction and entrapment. In D. D. Cahn & S. A. Lloyd (Eds.), *Family violence from a communication perspective* (pp. 151–176). Thousand Oaks, CA: Sage.

Rowhani-Farid, A., Allen, M., & Barnett, A. G. (2017). What incentives increase data sharing in health and medical research? A systematic review. *Research Integrity and Peer Review, 2*, 1–10.

Taufique, S., Lee, D., Ragussis, D., & Walker, T. (Producers), Ragussis, D. (Director). (2016). *Imperium* [Motion picture]. United States: Lionsgate Premiere.

Chapter 3

Ainsworth, M. D. S. (1967). *Infancy in Uganda: Infant care and the growth of love.* Baltimore, MD: Johns Hopkins University Press.

Ainsworth, M. D. S., & Bowlby, J. (1991). An ethological approach to personality development. *American Psychologist, 46*(4), 333–341.

Bartholomew, K. (1990). Avoidance of intimacy: An attachment perspective. *Journal of Social and Personal Relationships, 7*(2), 147–178.

Bartholomew, K., & Horowitz, L. M. (1991). Attachment styles among young adults: A test of a four-category model. *Journal of Personality and Social Psychology, 61*(2), 226–244.

Bartnett House Study Group. (1947). *London children in wartime Oxford: A survey of social and educational results of evacuation.* London, England: Oxford University Press.

BBC. (2018). *History: The Blitz.* Retrieved on February 24, 2018 from http://www.bbc.co.uk/history/events/the_blitz

Bell, S. M., & Ainsworth, M. D. S. (1972). Infant crying and maternal responsiveness. *Child Development, 43*, 1171–1190.

Belsky, J., Gilstrap, B., & Rovine, M. (1984). The Pennsylvania Infant and Family Development Project, I: Stability and change in mother-infant and father-infant interaction in a family setting at one, three, and nine months. *Child Development, 55*, 692–705.

Birnbaum, G. E., Reis, H. T., Mikulincer, M., Gillath, O., & Orpaz, A. (2006). When sex is more than just sex: Attachment orientations, sexual experience, and relationship quality. *Journal of Personality and Social Psychology, 91*(5), 929–943.

Blehar, M. C., Lieberman, A. F., & Ainsworth, M. D. S. (1977). Early face-to-face interaction and its relation to later infant-mother attachment. *Child Development, 48*, 182–194.

Bloom, V. (1999). Review of "John Bowlby—his early life—a biographical journey into the roots of attachment theory." *Psychodynamic Psychiatry, 27*(4), 692–695.

Bowlby, J. (1973). *Attachment and loss: Vol 2.* New York, NY: Basic Books.

Bowlby, J. (1988). *A secure base.* New York, NY: Basic Books.

Brennan, K. A., Clark, C. L., & Shaver, P. R. (1998). Self-report measurement of adult attachment: An integrative overview. In J. A. Simpson & W. S. Rholes (Eds.), *Attachment theory and close relationships* (pp. 46–76). New York, NY: Guilford Press.

Bretherton, I. (1992). The origins of attachment theory: John Bowlby and Mary Ainsworth. *Developmental Psychology, 28*(5), 759–775.

Bretherton, I. (2010). Fathers in attachment theory and research: A review. *Early Child Development and Care, 180*(1–2), 9–23.

Bretherton, I., Ridgeway, D., & Cassidy, J. (1990). Assessing internal working models of the attachment relationship: An attachment story completion task for 3-year-olds. In M. T. Greenbergh, D. Cicchetti, & E. M. Cummings (Eds.), *Attachment in the preschool years* (pp. 273–308). Chicago, IL: University of Chicago Press.

Burlingham, D., & Freud, A. (1942). *Young children in war-time.* Oxford, England: Allen & Unwin.

Chartrand, M. M., Frank, D. A., White, L. F., & Shope, T. R. (2008). Effect of parents' wartime deployment on the behavior of young children in military families. *Archives of Pediatrics & Adolescent Medicine, 162*(11), 1009–1014.

Crowell, J., Fraley, R. C., & Shaver, P. R. (2008). Measures of individual differences in adolescent and adult attachment. In J. Cassidy & P. R. Shaver (Eds.), *Handbook of attachment: Theory, research, and clinical applications* (2nd ed., pp. 599–634). New York, NY: Guilford.

Crowell, J. A., Treboux, D., & Waters, E. (2002). Stability of attachment representations: The transition to marriage. *Developmental Psychology, 38*(4), 467–479.

Dereli, E., & Karaku, Ö. (2011). An examination of attachment styles and social skills of university students. *Electronic Journal of Research in Educational Psychology, 9*(2), 731–744.

Drouin, M., & Landgraff, C. (2012). Texting, sexting, and attachment in college students' romantic relationships. *Computers in Human Behavior, 28*(2), 444–449.

Feeney, J. A., & Noller, P. (1996). *Adult attachment.* Thousand Oaks, CA: Sage.

Firth, R. (1936). *We, the Tikopia.* London, England: Allen & Unwin.

Foster, D., Davies, S., & Steele, H. (2003). The evacuation of British children during World War II: A preliminary investigation into the long-term psychological effects. *Aging & Mental Health, 7*(5), 398–408.

Grossmann, K., Grossmann, K. E., Fremmer-Bombik, E., Kindler, H., & Scheuerer-Englisch, H. (2002). The uniqueness of the child–father attachment relationship: Fathers' sensitive and challenging play as a pivotal variable in a 16-year longitudinal study. *Social Development, 11*(3), 301–337.

Grossmann, K., Grossmann, K. E., Spangler, G., Suess, G., & Unzner, L. (1985). Maternal sensitivity and newborns' orientation responses as related to quality of attachment in northern Germany. *Monographs of the Society for Research in Child Development, 50*, 233–256.

Hansburg, H. G. (1972). *Adolescent separation anxiety: A method for the study of adolescent separation problems.* Springfield, IL: Charles C. Thomas.

Hazan, C., & Shaver, P. (1987). Romantic love conceptualized as an attachment process. *Journal of Personality and Social Psychology, 52*(3), 511–524.

Isaacs, S., Brown, S. C., & Thouless, R. H. (1941). *The Cambridge evacuation survey.* London, England: Methuen.

Kaplan, N., & Main, M. (1986). *Instructions for the classification of children's family drawings in terms of representation of attachment.* Unpublished manuscript, University of California at Berkeley.

Klagsbrun, M., & Bowlby, J. (1976). Responses to separation from parents: A clinical test for young children. *British Journal of Projective Psychology & Personality Study, 21*, 7–27.

Kobak, R. R., & Sceery, A. (1988). Attachment in late adolescence: Working models, affect regulation, and representations of self and others. *Child Development, 59*, 135–146.

Lamb, M. E. (1978). Qualitative aspects of mother-and father-infant attachments. *Infant Behavior and Development, 1*, 265–275.

Main, M., Kaplan, N., & Cassidy, J. (1985). Security in infancy, childhood, and adulthood: A move to the level of representation. In I. Bretherson & E. Waters (Eds.), *Monographs of the Society for Research in Child Development, 50*, 66–104.

Marshall, T. C., Bejanyan, K., Di Castro, G., & Lee, R. A. (2013). Attachment styles as predictors of Facebook-related jealousy and surveillance in romantic relationships. *Personal Relationships, 20*(1), 1–22.

McDermott, R. C., & Lopez, F. G. (2013). College men's intimate partner violence attitudes: Contributions of adult attachment and gender role stress. *Journal of Counseling Psychology, 60*(1), 127–136.

Mikulincer, M., Florian, V., & Tolmacz, R. (1990). Attachment styles and fear of personal death: A case study of affect regulation. *Journal of Personality and Social Psychology, 58*(2), 273–280.

Newcombe, N., & Lerner, J. C. (1982). Britain between the wars: The historical context of Bowlby's theory of attachment. *Psychiatry, 45*(1), 1–12.

Oppenheim, D., & Waters, H. S. (1995). Narrative process and attachment representations: Issues of development and assessment. *Monographs of the Society for Research in Child Development, 60*(2–3), 197–215.

Osofsky, J. D., & Chartrand, L. C. M. M. (2013). Military children from birth to five years. *The Future of Children, 23*(2), 61–77.

Parke, R. D., & Tinsley, B. J. (1987). Family interaction in infancy. In J. D. Osofsky (Ed.), *Wiley series on personality processes: Handbook of infant development* (pp. 579–641). Oxford, England: John Wiley & Sons.

Pistole, M. C. (1989). Attachment in adult romantic relationships: Style of conflict resolution and relationship satisfaction. *Journal of Social and Personal Relationships, 6*(4), 505–510.

Rowling, J. K. (1997). *Harry Potter and the sorcerer's stone.* New York, NY: Scholastic.

Rowling, J. K. (1998). *Harry Potter and the chamber of secrets.* New York, NY: Scholastic.

Rowling, J. K. (1999). *Harry Potter and the prisoner of Azkaban.* New York, NY: Scholastic.

Rowling, J. K. (2000). *Harry Potter and the goblet of fire.* New York, NY: Scholastic.

Rowling, J. K. (2003). *Harry Potter and the order of the phoenix.* New York, NY: Scholastic.

Rowling, J. K. (2005). *Harry Potter and the half-blood prince.* New York, NY: Scholastic.

Rowling, J. K. (2007). *Harry Potter and the deathly hallows.* New York, NY: Scholastic.

Sagi, A., Lamb, M. E., Lewkowicz, K. S., Shoham, R., Dvir, R., & Estes, D. (1985). Security of infant-mother, -father, and -metapelet attachments among kibbutz-reared Israeli children. *Monographs of the Society for Research in Child Development, 50,* 257–275.

Schaffer, H. R., & Emerson, P. E. (1964). The development of social attachments in infancy. *Monographs of the Society for Research in Child Development, 29,* 1–77.

Starks, T. J., Castro, M. A., Castiblanco, J. P., & Millar, B. M. (2017). Modeling interpersonal correlates of condomless anal sex among gay and bisexual men: An application of attachment theory. *Archives of Sexual Behavior, 46*(4), 1089–1099.

Target, M., Fonagy, P., & Shmueli-Goetz, Y. (2003). Attachment representations in school-age children: The development of the Child Attachment Interview (CAI). *Journal of Child Psychotherapy, 29*(2), 171–186.

Tidwell, M. C. O., Reis, H. T., & Shaver, P. R. (1996). Attachment, attractiveness, and social interaction: A diary study. *Journal of Personality and Social Psychology, 71*(4), 729–745.

Treboux, D., Crowell, J. A., & Waters, E. (2004). When "new" meets "old": Configurations of adult attachment representations and their implications for marital functioning. *Developmental Psychology, 40*(2), 295–314.

Tronick, E. Z., Winn, S., & Morelli, G. A. (1985). Multiple caretaking in the context of human evolution: Why don't the Efé know the Western prescription for child care? In M. Reite & T. Fields (Eds.), *The psychobiology of attachment and separation* (pp. 293–322). San Diego, CA: Academic Press.

van Ijzendoorn, M. H., & Kroonenberg, P. M. (1988). Cross-cultural patterns of attachment: A meta-analysis of the strange situation. *Child Development, 59,* 147–156.

Wei, M., Russell, D. W., Mallinckrodt, B., & Vogel, D. L. (2007). The Experiences in Close Relationship Scale (ECR)-short form: Reliability, validity, and factor structure. *Journal of Personality Assessment, 88*(2), 187–204.

Wilkinson, L. L., Rowe, C. A., & Heath, H. G. (2013). Eating me up inside: Priming attachment security and anxiety, and their effects on snacking. *Journal of Social and Personal Relationships, 30*(6), 795–804.

Chapter 4

Allan, N., & Fishel, D. (1979). Singles bars. In N. Allan (Ed.), *Urban life styles* (pp. 128–179). Dubuque, IA: William C. Brown.

Apostolou, M., & Christoforou, C. (2018). The evolution of same-sex attraction: Exploring women's willingness to have sex with other women in order to satisfy their partners. *Personality and Individual Differences, 124,* 135–140.

Apostolou, M., Shialos, M., Khalil, M., & Paschali, M. (2017). The evolution of female same-sex attraction: The male choice hypothesis. *Personality and Individual Differences, 116,* 372–378.

Baker, R. R., & Bellis, M. A. (1995). *Sperm competition: Copulation, masturbation, and infidelity.* London, England: Chapman and Hall.

Bellis, M. A., & Baker, R. R. (1990). Do females promote sperm competition? Data for humans. *Animal Behaviour, 40*(5), 997–999.

Bowlby, J. (1984). Violence in the family as a disorder of the attachment and caregiving systems. *American Journal of Psychoanalysis, 44*(1), 9–27.

Buss, D. M. (1988a). From vigilance to violence: Tactics of mate retention in American undergraduates. *Ethology and Sociobiology, 9*(5), 291–317.

Buss, D. M. (1988b). The evolution of human intrasexual competition: Tactics of mate attraction. *Journal of Personality and Social Psychology, 54*(4), 616–628.

Buss, D. M. (1989). Sex differences in human mate preferences: Evolutionary hypotheses tested in 37 cultures. *Behavioral and Brain Sciences, 12*(1), 1–14.

Buss, D. M. (1994). *Evolution of desire: Strategies of human mating.* New York, NY: Basic Books.

Buss, D. M. (2008). *Evolutionary psychology: The new science of the mind* (3rd ed.). Boston, MA: Allyn & Bacon.

Buss, D. M. (2009). The great struggles of life: Darwin and the emergence of evolutionary psychology. *American Psychologist, 64*(2), 140–148.

Buss, D. M., & Dedden, L. A. (1990). Derogation of competitors. *Journal of Social and Personal Relationships, 7*(3), 395–422.

Buss, D. M., Larsen, R. J., Westen, D., & Semmelroth, J. (1992). Sex differences in jealousy: Evolution, physiology, and psychology. *Psychological Science, 3*(4), 251–256.

Buss, D. M., & Schmitt, D. P. (1993). Sexual strategies theory: An evolutionary perspective on human mating. *Psychological Review, 100*(2), 204–232.

Buss, D. M., Shackelford, T. K., Kirkpatrick, L. A., Choe, J. C., Lim, H. K., Hasegawa, M., Hasegawa, T., & Bennett, K. (1999). Jealousy and the nature of beliefs about infidelity: Tests of competing hypotheses about sex differences in the United States, Korea, and Japan. *Personal Relationships, 6*(1), 125–150.

Buunk, B. P., Angleitner, A., Oubaid, V., & Buss, D. M. (1996). Sex differences in jealousy in evolutionary and cultural perspective: Tests from the Netherlands, Germany, and the United States. *Psychological Science, 7*(6), 359–363.

Buunk, B., & Hupka, R. B. (1987). Cross-cultural differences in the elicitation of sexual jealousy. *Journal of Sex Research, 23*(1), 12–22.

Clark, R. D. (1990). The impact of AIDS on gender differences in willingness to engage in casual sex. *Journal of Applied Social Psychology, 20*(9), 771–782.

Clark, R. D., & Hatfield, E. (1989). Gender differences in receptivity to sexual offers. *Journal of Psychology & Human Sexuality, 2*(1), 39–55.

D'Alessio, S. J., & Stolzenberg, L. (2012). Stepchildren, community disadvantage, and physical injury in a child abuse incident: A preliminary investigation. *Violence and Victims, 27*(6), 860–870.

Daly, M., & Wilson, M. (1985). Child abuse and other risks of not living with both parents. *Ethology & Sociobiology, 6*(4), 197–210.

Darwin, C. (1859). *On the origin of species by means of natural selection.* London, England: John Murray.

Darwin, C. (1871). *The descent of man, and selection in relation to sex.* London, England: John Murray.

Desmond, A., & Moore, J. (1994). *Darwin: The life of a tormented evolutionist.* New York, NY: Norton.

Ford, C. S., & Beach, F. A. (1951). *Patterns of sexual behavior.* New York, NY: Harper & Row.

Gangestad, S. W., & Simpson, J. A. (2000). The evolution of human mating: Trade-offs and strategic pluralism. *Behavioral and Brain Sciences, 23*(4), 573–587.

Gangestad, S. W., & Thornhill, R. (1997). The evolutionary psychology of extrapair sex: The role of fluctuating asymmetry. *Evolution and Human Behavior, 18*(2), 69–88.

Giosan, C. (2006). High-K strategy scale: A measure of the high-K independent criterion of fitness. *Evolutionary Psychology, 4*(1), 394–405.

Haselton, G. M., Mortezaire, M., Pillworth, G. E., Bleske-Rechek, A., & Frederick, A. D. (2007). Ovulatory shifts in human female ornamentation: Near ovulation, women dress to impress. *Hormones and Behavior, 51*, 40–45.

Murdock, G. P. (1967). Ethnographic atlas: A summary. *Ethnology, 6*(2), 109–236.

Pham, M. N., & Shackelford, T. K. (2013). Oral sex as mate retention behavior. *Personality and Individual Differences, 55*, 185–188.

Rounsaville, B. J. (1978). Theories in marital violence: Evidence from a study of battered women. *Victimology, 3*, 11–31.

Russell, D. E. (1984). The prevalence and seriousness of incestuous abuse: Stepfathers vs. biological fathers. *Child Abuse & Neglect, 8*(1), 15–22.

Schmitt, D. P. (2004). Patterns and universals of mate poaching across 53 nations: The effects of sex, culture, and personality on romantically attracting another person's partner. *Journal of Personality and Social Psychology, 86*(4), 560–584.

Schmitt, D. P., & Buss, D. M. (1996). Strategic self-promotion and competitor derogation: Sex and context effects on the perceived effectiveness of mate attraction tactics. *Journal of Personality and Social Psychology, 70*(6), 1185–1204.

Schmitt, D. P., & Buss, D. M. (2001). Human mate poaching: Tactics and temptations for infiltrating existing mateships. *Journal of Personality and Social Psychology, 80*(6), 894–917.

Sela, Y., Shackelford, T. K., Pham, M. N., & Euler, H. A. (2015). Do women perform fellatio as a mate retention behavior? *Personality and Individual Differences, 73*, 61–66.

Sela, Y., Weekes-Shackelford, V. A., Shackelford, T. K., & Pham, M. N. (2015). Female copulatory orgasm and male partner's attractiveness to his partner and other women. *Personality and Individual Differences, 79*, 152–156.

Sugarman, D. B., & Hotaling, G. T. (1989). Dating violence: Prevalence, context, and risk markers. In M. A. Pirog-Good & J. E. Stets (Eds.), *Violence in dating relationships* (pp. 3–32). New York, NY: Praeger.

Thompson, A. P. (1983). Extramarital sex: A review of the research literature. *Journal of Sex Research, 19*(1), 1–22.

Trivers, R. (1972). Parental investment and sexual selection. In B. Campbell (Ed.), *Sexual selection and the descent of man* (pp. 136–179). Cambridge, MA: Harvard University.

Verhulst, P. F. (1838). Notice sur la loi que la population pursuit dans son accroissement. *Correspondance Mathematique et Physique, 10*, 113–121.

Weatherhead, P. J., & Robertson, R. J. (1979). Offspring quality and the polygyny threshold: "The sexy son hypothesis." *The American Naturalist, 113*(2), 201–208.

White, G. L. (1981). A model of romantic jealousy. *Motivation and Emotion, 5*(4), 295–310.

Wiederman, M. W. (1997). Extramarital sex: Prevalence and correlates in a national survey. *Journal of Sex Research, 34*(2), 167–174.

Wikipedia. (2018). "Catfight." Retrieved April 3, 2018, from https://en.wikipedia.org/wiki/Catfight

Wilson, M., & Daly, M. (2004). Do pretty women inspire men to discount the future? *Proceedings of the Royal Society of London B: Biological Sciences, 271*(Suppl 4), S177–S179.

Wilson, M., Daly, M., & Daniele, A. (1995). Familicide: The killing of spouse and children. *Aggressive Behavior, 21*(4), 275–291.

Wright, R. (1994). *The moral animal.* New York, NY: Random House.

Chapter 5

Adams, J. S. (1963). Towards an understanding of inequity. *Journal of Abnormal and Social Psychology, 67*(5), 422–436.

Agnew, C. R., Hoffman, A. M., Lehmiller, J. J., & Duncan, N. T. (2007). From the interpersonal to the international: Understanding commitment to the "War on Terror." *Personality and Social Psychology Bulletin, 33*(11), 1559–1571.

Agnew, C. R., Loving, T. J., Le, B., & Goodfriend, W. (2004). Thinking close: Measuring relational closeness as perceived self-other inclusion. In D. Mashek & A. Aron (Eds.), *Handbook of closeness and intimacy* (pp. 103–115). Mahwah, NJ: Lawrence Erlbaum.

Agnew, C. R., Van Lange, P. A., Rusbult, C. E., & Langston, C. A. (1998). Cognitive interdependence: Commitment and the mental representation of close relationships. *Journal of Personality and Social Psychology, 74*(4), 939–954.

Aron, A., Aron, E. N., & Smollan, D. (1992). Inclusion of other in the self scale and the structure of interpersonal closeness. *Journal of Personality and Social Psychology, 63*(4), 596–612.

Aron, A., Norman, C. C., Aron, E. N., McKenna, C., & Heyman, R. E. (2000). Couples' shared participation in novel and arousing activities and experienced relationship quality. *Journal of Personality and Social Psychology, 78*(2), 273–284.

Arriaga, X. B., & Agnew, C. R. (2001). Being committed: Affective, cognitive, and conative components of relationship commitment. *Personality and Social Psychology Bulletin, 27*(9), 1190–1203.

Arriaga, X. B., & Rusbult, C. E. (1998). Standing in my partner's shoes: Partner perspective-taking and reactions to accommodative dilemmas. *Personality and Social Psychology Bulletin, 24*, 927–948.

Baker, Z. G., Petit, W. E., & Brown, C. M. (2016). An investigation of the Rusbult investment model of commitment in relationships with pets. *Anthrozoös, 29*(2), 193–204.

Barrantes, R. J., Eaton, A. A., Veldhuis, C. B., & Hughes, T. L. (2017). The role of minority stressors in lesbian relationship commitment and persistence over time. *Psychology of Sexual Orientation and Gender Diversity, 4*(2), 205–217.

Barrett, D. W., Wosinska, W., Butner, J., Petrova, P., Gornik-Durose, M., & Cialdini, R. B. (2004). Individual differences in the motivation to comply across cultures: The impact of social obligation. *Personality and Individual Differences, 37*(1), 19–31.

Beals, K. P., Impett, E. A., & Peplau, L. A. (2002). Lesbians in love: Why some relationships endure and others end. *Journal of Lesbian Studies, 6*(1), 53–63.

Berscheid, E., & Reis, H. (1998). Attraction and close relationships. In D. Gilbert, S. Fiske, & G. Lindzey (Eds.), *The handbook of social psychology* (4th ed., pp. 193–281). New York, NY: McGraw-Hill.

Blau, P. M. (1967). *Exchange and power in social life*. New York, NY: Wiley.

Bontempo, R., Lobel, S., & Triandis, H. (1990). Compliance and value internalization in Brazil and the U.S.: Effects of allocentrism and anonymity. *Journal of Cross-Cultural Psychology, 21*(2), 200–213.

Borden, V. M. H., & Levinger, G. (1991). Interpersonal transformations in intimate relationships. In W. H. Jones & D. Perlman (Eds.), *Advances in personal relationships* (Vol. 2, pp. 35–56). London, England: Jessica Kingsley.

Brewster, M. E. (2017). Lesbian women and household labor division: A systematic review of scholarly research from 2000 to 2015. *Journal of Lesbian Studies, 21*(1), 47–69.

Bryant, F. B., Smart, C. M., & King, S. P. (2005). Using the past to enhance the present: Boosting happiness through positive reminiscence. *Journal of Happiness Studies, 6*(3), 227–260.

Bui, K. V. T., Peplau, L. A., & Hill, C. T. (1996). Testing the Rusbult model of relationship commitment and stability in a 15-year study of heterosexual couples. *Personality and Social Psychology Bulletin, 22*(12), 1244–1257.

Buunk, A. P. (1991). Jealousy in close relationships: An exchange-theoretical perspective. In P. Salovey (Ed.), *The psychology of jealousy and envy* (pp. 148–177). New York, NY: Guilford Press.

Clark, A. E., & Georgellis, Y. (2013). Back to baseline in Britain: Adaptation in the British household panel survey. *Economica, 80*(319), 496–512.

Diekman, A. B., Goodfriend, W., & Goodwin, S. (2004). Dynamic stereotypes of power: Perceived change and stability in gender hierarchies. *Sex Roles, 50*, 201–215.

Dion, K. K., & Dion, K. L. (1991). Psychological individualism and romantic love. *Journal of Social Behavior and Personality, 6*, 17–33.

Dion, K. K., & Dion, K. L. (1993). Individualistic and collectivistic perspectives on gender and the cultural context of love and intimacy. *Journal of Social Issues, 49*(3), 53–69.

Drigotas, S. M., & Rusbult, C. E. (1992). Should I stay or should I go? A dependence model of breakups. *Journal of Personality and Social Psychology, 62*(1), 62–87.

Duffy, S. M., & Rusbult, C. E. (1986). Satisfaction and commitment in homosexual and heterosexual relationships. *Journal of Homosexuality, 12*(2), 1–23.

Durko, A. M., & Petrick, J. F. (2016). Travel as relationship therapy: Examining the effect of vacation satisfaction applied to the investment model. *Journal of Travel Research, 55*(7), 904–918.

Etcheverry, P. E., & Agnew, C. R. (2004). Subjective norms and the prediction of romantic relationship state and fate. *Personal Relationships, 11*(4), 409–428.

Fredrickson, B. L., & Losada, M. F. (2005). Positive affect and the complex dynamics of human flourishing. *American Psychologist, 60*(7), 678–686.

Gildersleeve, S., Singer, J. A., Skerrett, K., & Wein, S. (2016). Coding "We-ness" in couple's relationship stories: A method for assessing mutuality in couple therapy. *Psychotherapy Research, 27*(3), 1–13.

Goddard, A. (2018, May 10). Confirmed: Brad Pitt and Jennifer Aniston – "They're back on!" *New Idea*. Retrieved from https://www.newidea.com.au/confirmed-brad-pitt-and-jenner-aniston-theyre-back-on

Goldsman, A., Milchan, A., & Foster, L. (Producers), Liman, D. (Director). (2005). *Mr. & Mrs. Smith* [Motion picture]. United States: 20th Century Fox.

Goodfriend, W. (2006). For better, or worse? The love of Homer and Marge. In A. Brown & C. Logan (Eds.), *The psychology of the Simpsons* (pp. 21–36). Dallas, TX: BenBella Books.

Goodfriend, W., & Agnew, C. R. (2008). Sunken costs and desired plans: Examining different types of investments in close relationships. *Personality and Social Psychology Bulletin, 34*(12), 1639–1652.

Goodfriend, W., Agnew, C. R., & Cathey, P. (2017). Understanding commitment and partner-serving biases in close relationships. In J. Fitzgerald (Ed.), *Foundations for couples' therapy: Research for the real world* (pp. 51–60). New York, NY: Routledge.

Gottman, J. (1999). *The marriage clinic: A scientifically based marital therapy.* New York, NY: W. W. Norton.

Gottman, J. M. (2011). *The science of trust: Emotional attunement for couples.* New York, NY: W. W. Norton.

Gottman, J., Schwartz Gottman, J., & DeClaire, J. (2006). *10 lessons to transform your marriage.* New York, NY: Crown.

Greenstein, T. N., & Davis, S. N. (2006). Cross-national variations in divorce: Effects of women's power, prestige and dependence. *Journal of Comparative Family Studies, 37*(2), 253–273.

Guerrero, L. K., La Valley, A. G., & Farinelli, L. (2008). The experience and expression of anger, guilt, and sadness in marriage: An equity theory explanation. *Journal of Social and Personal Relationships, 25*(5), 699–724.

Hatfield, E., & Rapson, R. L. (2012). Equity theory in close relationships. In P. Van Lange, A. W. Kruglanski, & E. T. Higgins (Eds.), *Handbook of theories of social psychology* (Vol. 2, pp. 200–217). Thousand Oaks, CA: Sage.

Hatfield, E., Utne, M. K., & Traupmann, J. (1979). Equity theory and intimate relationships. In R. L. Burgess & T. L. Huston (Eds.), *Social exchange in developing relationships* (pp. 99–133). New York, NY: Academic Press.

Heinzen, T., & Goodfriend, W. (2019). *Social psychology.* Thousand Oaks, CA: Sage.

Hickman, S. E., Watson, P. J., & Morris, R. J. (1996). Optimism, pessimism, and the complexity of narcissism. *Personality and Individual Differences, 20*(4), 521–525.

Hitt, C. (2018, March 26). Are Brad Pitt and Jennifer Aniston getting back together? *Daily Mail.* Retrieved from http://www.dailymail.co.uk/tvshowbiz/article-5401141/Are-Brad-Pitt-Jennifer-Aniston-getting-together.html

Homans, G. C. (1961). *Social behaviour: Its elementary forms.* New York, NY: Harcourt, Brace, & World.

Hsu, F. L. K. (1985). The self in cross-cultural perspective. In A. J. Marsella, G. DeVos, & F. U. K. Hsu (Eds.), *Culture and self: Asian and Western perspectives* (pp. 24–55). London, England: Tavistock.

Hui, C. H., & Triandis, H. C. (1986). Individualism-collectivism: A study of cross-cultural researchers. *Journal of Cross-Cultural Psychology, 17*(2), 225–248.

Jacobs Bao, K., & Lyubomirsky, S. (2013). Making it last: Combating hedonic adaptation in romantic relationships. *Journal of Positive Psychology, 8*(3), 196–206.

Jean, A. [Executive Producer]. (1989–Present). *The Simpsons* [television series]. Los Angeles, CA: Fox.

Johnson, D. J., & Rusbult, C. E. (1989). Resisting temptation: Devaluation of alternative partners as a means of maintaining commitment in close relationships. *Journal of Personality and Social Psychology, 57*(6), 967–980.

Johnson, M. P. (1991). Commitment to personal relationships. In W. H. Jones & D. W. Perlman (Eds.), *Advances in personal relationships* (Vol. 3, pp. 117–143). London, England: Jessica Kingsley.

Johnson, M. P. (1995). Patriarchal terrorism and common couple violence: Two forms of violence against women. *Journal of Marriage and the Family, 57,* 283–294.

Johnson, M. P., Caughlin, J. P., & Huston, T. L. (1999). The tripartite nature of marital commitment: Personal, moral, and structural reasons to stay married. *Journal of Marriage and the Family, 61*(1), 160–177.

Kastlunger, B., Martini, M., Kirchler, E., & Hofmann, E. (2008). Impegno, soddisfazione e fiducia del cliente bancario: Un'analisi empirica a Roma e in Sardegna. *Psicologia Sociale, 3,* 307–324.

Kelley, H. H., & Thibaut, J. W. (1978). *Interpersonal relations: A theory of interdependence.* New York, NY: Wiley.

Kilpatrick, S. D., Bissonnette, V L., & Rusbult, C. E. (2002). Empathic accuracy and accommodative behavior among newly married couples. *Personal Relationships, 9*, 369–393.

Knopp, K. C., Rhoades, G. K., Stanley, S. M., & Markman, H. J. (2015). Stuck on you: How dedication moderates the way constraints feel. *Journal of Social and Personal Relationships, 32*(1), 119–137.

Le, B., & Agnew, C. R. (2003). Commitment and its theorized determinants: A meta-analysis of the investment model. *Personal Relationships, 10*(1), 37–57.

Le, B., Dove, N. L., Agnew, C. R., Korn, M. S., & Mutso, A. A. (2010). Predicting nonmarital romantic relationship dissolution: A meta-analytic synthesis. *Personal Relationships, 17*(3), 377–390.

Lee, G, R., & Stone, L. H. (1980). Mate-selection systems and criteria: Variation according to family structure. *Journal of Marriage and the Family, 42*, 319–326.

Lehmiller, J. J. (2010). Differences in relationship investments between gay and heterosexual men. *Personal Relationships, 17*(1), 81–96.

Lehmiller, J. J., & Agnew, C. R. (2006). Marginalized relationships: The impact of social disapproval on romantic relationship commitment. *Personality and Social Psychology Bulletin, 32*(1), 40–51.

Li, X., & Petrick, J. F. (2008). Examining the antecedents of brand loyalty from an investment model perspective. *Journal of Travel Research, 47*(1), 25–34.

Lyubomirsky, S. (2011). Hedonic adaptation to positive and negative experiences. In S. Folkman (Ed.), *Oxford handbook of stress, health, and coping* (pp. 200–224). New York, NY: Oxford University Press.

Madsen, M. C., & Shapira, A. (1970). Cooperative and competitive behavior of urban Afro-American, Anglo-American, Mexican-American, and Mexican village children. *Developmental Psychology, 3*(1), 16–20.

Mashek, D. J., & Sherman, M. D. (2004). Desiring less closeness with intimate others. In D. Mashek & A. Aron (Eds.), *Handbook of closeness and intimacy* (pp. 343-356). Mahwah, NJ: Lawrence Erlbaum.

Miller, C. C. (2018, May 16). How same-sex couples divide chores, and what it reveals about modern parenting. *The New York Times.* Retrieved from https://www.nytimes.com/2018/05/16/upshot/same-sex-couples-divide-chores-much-more-evenly-until-they-become-parents.html

Patterson, C. J., Sutfin, E. L., & Fulcher, M. (2004). Division of labor among lesbian and heterosexual parenting couples: Correlates of specialized versus shared patterns. *Journal of Adult Development, 11*(3), 179–189.

Pedulla, D. S., & Thébaud, S. (2015). Can we finish the revolution? Gender, work-family ideals, and institutional constraint. *American Sociological Review, 80*(1), 116–139.

Powell, C., & Van Vugt, M. (2003). Genuine giving or selfish sacrifice? The role of commitment and cost level upon willingness to sacrifice. *European Journal of Social Psychology, 33*, 403–412.

Roland, A. (1988). *In search of self in India and Japan.* Princeton, NJ: Princeton University Press.

Rusbult, C. E. (1980a). Commitment and satisfaction in romantic associations: A test of the investment model. *Journal of Experimental Social Psychology, 16*(2), 172–186.

Rusbult, C. E. (1980b). Satisfaction and commitment in friendships. *Representative Research in Social Psychology, 11*(2), 96–105.

Rusbult, C. E., Agnew, C. R., & Arriaga, X. B. (2012). The investment model of commitment processes. In P. A. M. Van Lange, A. W. Kruglanski, & E. T. Higgins (Eds.), *Handbook of theories of social psychology* (Vol. 2, pp. 218–231). Thousand Oaks, CA: Sage.

Rusbult, C. E., Arriaga, X. B., & Agnew, C. R. (2001). Interdependence in close relationships. In G. J. Fletcher, & M. S. Clark (Eds.), *Blackwell handbook of social psychology: Interpersonal processes* (pp. 359–387). Malden, MA: John Wiley & Sons.

Rusbult, C. E., & Buunk, B. P. (1993). Commitment processes in close relationships: An interdependence analysis. *Journal of Social and Personal Relationships, 10*(2), 175–204.

Rusbult, C. E., Finkel, E. J., & Kumashiro, M. (2009). The Michelangelo phenomenon. *Current Directions in Psychological Science, 18*(6), 305–309.

Rusbult, C. E., & Martz, J. M. (1995). Remaining in an abusive relationship: An investment model analysis of nonvoluntary dependence. *Personality and Social Psychology Bulletin, 21*(6), 558–571.

Rusbult, C. E., Verette, J., Whitney, G. A., Slovik, L. F., & Lipkus, I. (1991). Accommodation processes in close relationships: Theory and preliminary empirical evidence. *Journal of Personality and Social Psychology, 60*, 53–78.

Schramm, D. G., Marshall, J. P., Harris, V. W., & Lee, T. R. (2005). After "I do": The newlywed transition. *Marriage & Family Review, 38*(1), 45–67.

Seligman, M. E., Rashid, T., & Parks, A. C. (2006). Positive psychotherapy. *American Psychologist, 61*(8), 774–788.

Shapira, A., & Madsen, M. C. (1969). Cooperative and competitive behavior of kibbutz and urban children in Israel. *Child Development, 40*, 609–617.

Sheldon, K. M., & Lyubomirsky, S. (2012). The challenge of staying happier: Testing the hedonic adaptation prevention model. *Personality and Social Psychology Bulletin, 38*(5), 670–680.

Simpson, J. A. (1987). The dissolution of romantic relationships: Factors involved in relationship stability and emotional distress. *Journal of Personality and Social Psychology, 53*(4), 683–692.

Simpson, J. A., Gangestad, S. W., & Lerma, M. (1990). Perception of physical attractiveness: Mechanisms involved in the maintenance of romantic relationships. *Journal of Personality and Social Psychology, 59*(6), 1192–1201.

Singer, J. A., & Skerrett, K. (2014). *Positive couple therapy: Using we-stories to enhance resilience.* New York, NY: Routledge.

Skerrett, K., & Fergus, K. (Eds.). (2015). *Couple resilience: Emerging perspectives.* New York, NY: Springer.

Spector, P. E. (2008). *Industrial and organizational behavior* (5th ed.). Hoboken, NJ: Wiley.

Sprecher, S. (2001). Equity and social exchange in dating couples: Associations with satisfaction, commitment, and stability. *Journal of Marriage and Family, 63*(3), 599–613.

Sternberg, R. J., & Barnes, M. L. (1985). Real and ideal others in romantic relationships: Is four a crowd? *Journal of Personality and Social Psychology, 49*(6), 1586–1608.

Stork, E. P. (2005). *Analyzing decision making: Women seeking shelter from intimate partner violence* (Dissertation AAI3150476; 2005-99007-002) [Doctoral dissertation, University of Pittsburgh]. PsycINFO.

Thibaut, J. W., & Kelley, H. H. (1959). *The social psychology of groups.* New York, NY: Wiley.

Tornello, S. L., Sonnenberg, B. N., & Patterson, C. J. (2015). Division of labor among gay fathers: Associations with parent, couple, and child adjustment. *Psychology of Sexual Orientation and Gender Diversity, 2*(4), 365–375.

Totenhagen, C. J., Curran, M. A., Serido, J., & Butler, E. A. (2013). Good days, bad days: Do sacrifices improve relationship quality? *Journal of Social and Personal Relationships, 30*(7), 881–900.

Uysal, A. (2016). Commitment to multiplayer online games: An investment model approach. *Computers in Human Behavior, 61*, 357–363.

van Dam, K. (2005). Employee attitudes toward job changes: An application and extension of Rusbult and Farrell's investment model. *Journal of Occupational and Organizational Psychology, 78*(2), 253–272.

Van Lange, P. A., Agnew, C. R., Harnick, F., & Steemers, G. E. M. (1997). From game theory to real life: How social value orientation affects willingness to sacrifice in ongoing close relationships. *Journal of Personality and Social Psychology, 73*, 1330–1344.

Van Lange, P. A., & Rusbult, C. E. (2011). Interdependence theory. In P. A. M. Van Lange, A. W. Kruglanski, & E. T. Higgins (Eds.), *Handbook of theories of social psychology* (Vol. 2, pp. 251–272). Thousand Oaks, CA: Sage.

Van Lange, P. A., Rusbult, C. E., Drigotas, S. M., Arriaga, X. B., Witcher, B. S., & Cox, C. L. (1997). Willingness to sacrifice in close relationships. *Journal of Personality and Social Psychology, 72*(6), 1373.

Walster, E., Walster, G. W., & Berscheid, E. (1978). *Equity: Theory and research.* Boston, MA: Allyn & Bacon.

Wetzel, C. G., & Insko, C. A. (1982). The similarity-attraction relationship: Is there an ideal one? *Journal of Experimental Social Psychology, 18*(3), 253–276.

Wolfe, K. (2014). *21 lost gentleman traditions that still apply today.* Retrieved May 24, 2018, from http://goodguyswag.com/21-lost-gentleman-traditions-that-still-apply-today/

Chapter 6

Amato, P. R. (2010). Research on divorce: Continuing trends and new developments. *Journal of Marriage and Family, 72*(3), 650–666.

Amato, P. R., & Booth, A. (2001). The legacy of parents' marital discord: Consequences for children's marital quality. *Journal of Personality and Social Psychology, 81*(4), 627–638.

Amato, P. R., & Previti, D. (2003). People's reasons for divorcing: Gender, social class, the life course, and adjustment. *Journal of Family Issues, 24*(5), 602–626.

Antonovics, K., & Town, R. (2004). Are all the good men married? Uncovering the sources of the marital wage premium. *American Economic Review, 94*(2), 317–321.

Baumeister, R. F. (1991). *Meanings of life*. New York, NY: Guilford.

Bennett, N. G., Blanc, A. K., & Bloom, D. E. (1988). Commitment and the modern union: Assessing the link between premarital cohabitation and subsequent marital stability. *American Sociological Review, 53*, 127–138.

Booth, A., & Edwards, J. N. (1992). Starting over: Why remarriages are more unstable. *Journal of Family Issues, 13*(2), 179–194.

Booth, A., Johnson, D. R., White, L. K., & Edwards, J. N. (1986). Divorce and marital instability over the life course. *Journal of Family Issues, 7*(4), 421–442.

Budgeon, S. (2008). Couple culture and the production of singleness. *Sexualities, 11*(3), 301–325.

Budig, M. J., & England, P. (2001). The wage penalty for motherhood. *American Sociological Review, 662*, 204–225.

Bumpass, L., Sweet, J., & Martin, T. C. (1990). Changing patterns of remarriage. *Journal of Marriage and the Family, 52*, 747–756.

Carlson, M., McLanahan, S., & England, P. (2004). Union formation in fragile families. *Demography, 41*(2), 237–261.

Carstensen, L. L. (1992). Social and emotional patterns in adulthood: support for socioemotional selectivity theory. *Psychology and Aging, 7*(3), 331–338.

Carstensen, L. L., Fung, H. H., & Charles, S. T. (2003). Socioemotional selectivity theory and the regulation of emotion in the second half of life. *Motivation and Emotion, 27*(2), 103–123.

Carstensen, L. L., Gottman, J. M., & Levenson, R. W. (1995). Emotional behavior in long-term marriage. *Psychology and Aging, 10*(1), 140–149.

Casper, L. M., & Sayer, L. C. (2000, March). *Cohabitation transitions: Different attitudes and purposes, different paths*. Paper presented at the annual meeting of the Population Association of America, Los Angeles, CA.

Cherlin, A. J. (1992). *Marriage, divorce, remarriage* (2nd ed). Cambridge, MA: Harvard University Press.

Chu, J. M. (Director). (2018). *Crazy rich Asians* [Motion picture]. United States: Warner Bros.

Clarke, S. C., & Wilson, B. F. (1994). The relative stability of remarriages: A cohort approach using vital statistics. *Family Relations, 43*, 305–310.

Cohan, C. L., & Kleinbaum, S. (2002). Toward a greater understanding of the cohabitation effect: Premarital cohabitation and marital communication. *Journal of Marriage and Family, 64*(1), 180–192.

Conley, T. D., & Collins, B. E. (2002). Gender, relationship status, and stereotyping about sexual risk. *Personality and Social Psychology Bulletin, 28*(11), 1483–1494.

Connidis, I. A. (2001). *Family ties and aging*. Thousand Oaks, CA: Sage.

DeMaris, A., & Rao, K. V. (1992). Premarital cohabitation and subsequent marital stability in the United States: A reassessment. *Journal of Marriage and the Family, 54*, 178–190.

DePaulo, B. (2017, December 28). 6 new things researchers learned about single people in 2017. *The Cut*. Retrieved from https://www.thecut.com /2017/12/6-new-things-researchers-learned-about-single-people-in-2017.html

DePaulo, B. M., & Morris, W. L. (2005). Singles in society and in science. *Psychological Inquiry, 16*(2–3), 57–83.

Diekman, A. B., Goodfriend, W., & Goodwin, S. (2004). Dynamic stereotypes of power: Perceived change and stability in gender hierarchies. *Sex Roles, 50*(3), 201–215.

Eastwick, W. P. Keneski, E., Morgan, A. T., McDonald, A. M., & Huang, A. S. (2018). What do short-term and long-term relationships look like? Building the relationships coordination and strategic timing (ReCAST) model. *Journal of Experimental Psychology: General, 147*(5), 747–781.

Edin, K. (2000). What do low-income single mothers say about marriage? *Social Problems, 47*(1), 112–133.

Engel, P. (2014, May 25). Map: Divorce rates around the world. *Business Insider*. Retrieved from http://www.businessinsider.com/map-divorce-rates-around-the-world-2014-5

Fifer, W. P., & Moon, C. M. (1995). The effects of fetal experience with sound. In J. Lecanuet, W. P. Fifer, N. A. Krasnegor, & W. P. Smotherman (Eds.), *Fetal development: A psychobiological perspective* (pp. 351–366). Hillsdale, NJ: Lawrence Erlbaum.

Florian, V., Mikulincer, M., & Hirschberger, G. (2002). The anxiety-buffering function of close relationships: Evidence that relationship commitment acts as a terror management mechanism. *Journal of Personality and Social Psychology, 82*(4), 527–542.

Fox, J. O. (2004). For singles, April really is the cruelest month. *The Washington Post*, B01.

Gibson-Davis, C. M., Edin, K., & McLanahan, S. (2005). High hopes but even higher expectations: The retreat from marriage among low-income couples. *Journal of Marriage and Family, 67*(5), 1301–1312.

Greenberg, J., Pyszczynski, T., & Solomon, S. (1986). The causes and consequences of a need for self-esteem: A terror management theory. *Public Self and Private Self, 189*, 189–212.

Harlow, H. F. (1958). The nature of love. *American Psychologist, 13*(12), 673–685.

Harlow, H. F., & Zimmerman, R. R. (1959). Affectional responses in the infant monkey. *Science, 130*, 421–432.

Hebb, D. O. (1958). *A textbook of psychology*. Philadelphia, PA: W. B. Saunders.

Hostetler, A. J., Desrochers, S., Kopko, K., & Moen, P. (2012). Marital and family satisfaction as a function of work–family demands and community resources: Individual-and couple-level analyses. *Journal of Family Issues, 33*(3), 316–340.

Hui, C. H., & Triandis, H. C. (1986). Individualism-collectivism: A study of cross-cultural *researchers. Journal of Cross-Cultural Psychology, 17*(2), 225–248.

Immelmann, K. (1972). Sexual and other long-term aspects of imprinting in birds and other species. *Advances in the Study of Behavior, 4*, 147–174.

Kephart, W. M. (1967). Some correlates of romantic love. *Journal of Marriage and the Family, 29*, 470–474.

Kisilevsky, B. S., Hains, S. M., Brown, C. A., Lee, C. T., Cowperthwaite, B., Stutzman, S. S., ... Ye, H. H. (2009). Fetal sensitivity to properties of maternal speech and language. *Infant Behavior and Development, 32*(1), 59–71.

Kisilevsky, B. S., Hains, S. M., Lee, K., Xie, X., Huang, H., Ye, H. H., ... Wang, Z. (2003). Effects of experience on fetal voice recognition. *Psychological Science, 14*(3), 220–224.

Kreider, R. M., & Fields, J. M. (2001). Number, timing, and duration of marriages and divorces: Fall 1996. In *Current Population Reports* (pp. 70–80). Washington, DC: U.S. Census Bureau.

Kwan, K. (2013). *Crazy rich Asians*. New York, NY: Anchor.

Lawrence, E., Rothman, A. D., Cobb, R. J., Rothman, M. T., & Bradbury, T. N. (2008). Marital satisfaction across the transition to parenthood. *Journal of Family Psychology, 22*(1), 41–50.

Leary, M. R., Kowalski, R. M., Smith, L., & Phillips, S. (2003). Teasing, rejection, and violence: Case studies of the school shootings. *Aggressive Behavior, 29*(3), 202–214.

Levenson, R. W., Carstensen, L. L., & Gottman, J. M. (1993). Long-term marriage: Age, gender, and satisfaction. *Psychology and Aging, 8*(2), 301–313.

Levine, R., Sato, S., Hashimoto, T., & Verma, J. (1995). Love and marriage in eleven cultures. *Journal of Cross Cultural Psychology, 26*, 554–571.

Lichter, D. T., Qian, Z., & Mellott, L. M. (2006). Marriage or dissolution? Union transitions among poor cohabiting women. *Demography, 43*(2), 223–240.

Lindau, S. T., Schumm, L. P., Laumann, E. O., Levinson, W., O'Muircheartaigh, C. A., & Waite, L. J. (2007). A study of sexuality and health among older adults in the United States. *New England Journal of Medicine, 357*(8), 762–774.

Marx, V., & Nagy, E. (2015). Fetal behavioural responses to maternal voice and touch. *PLoS One, 10*(6), e0129118.

Mikulincer, M., Florian, V., & Hirschberger, G. (2003). The existential function of close relationships: Introducing death into the science of love. *Personality and Social Psychology Review, 7*(1), 20–40.

Mikulincer, M., Florian, V., & Hirschberger, G. (2004). The terror of death and the quest for love:

An existential perspective on close relationships. In J. Greenberg, S. L. Koole, & T. Pyszczynski (Eds.), *Handbook of experimental existential psychology* (pp. 287–304). New York, NY: Guilford Press.

Millbank, J. (1997). Every sperm is sacred? Denying women access to fertility services on the basis of sexuality or marital status. *Alternative Law Journal*, *22*(3), 126–129.

Misovich, S. J., Fisher, J. D., & Fisher, W. A. (1997). Close relationships and elevated HIV risk behavior: Evidence and possible underlying psychological processes. *Review of General Psychology*, *1*(1), 72–107.

Mitnick, D. M., Heyman, R. E., & Smith Slep, A. M. (2009). Changes in relationship satisfaction across the transition to parenthood: A meta-analysis. *Journal of Family Psychology*, *23*, 848–852.

Moen, P., Kim, J. E., & Hofmeister, H. (2001). Couples' work/retirement transitions, gender, and marital quality. *Social Psychology Quarterly*, *64*, 55–71.

Morris, W. L., DePaulo, B. M., Hertel, J., & Ritter, L. C. (2004). *Perceptions of people who are single: A developmental life tasks model*. Unpublished manuscript.

Morris, W. L., Sinclair, S., & DePaulo, B. M. (2007). No shelter for singles: The perceived legitimacy of marital status discrimination. *Group Processes & Intergroup Relations*, *10*(4), 457–470.

Mustonen, U., Huurre, T., Kiviruusu, O., Haukkala, A., & Aro, H. (2011). Long-term impact of parental divorce on intimate relationship quality in adulthood and the mediating role of psychosocial resources. *Journal of Family Psychology*, *25*(4), 615–619.

Nolen-Hoeksema, S., McBride, A., & Larson, J. (1997). Rumination and psychological distress among bereaved partners. *Journal of Personality and Social Psychology*, *72*(4), 855–862.

Pew Research Center. (2014). *Record share of Americans have never married*. Retrieved from http://assets.pewresearch.org/wp-content/uploads/sites/3/2014/09/2014-09-24_Never-Married-Americans.pdf

Pignotti, M., & Abell, N. (2009). The negative stereotyping of single persons scale: Initial psychometric development. *Research on Social Work Practice*, *19*(5), 639–652.

Raphael, B. (1983). *The anatomy of bereavement*. New York, NY: Basic Books.

Sharp, E. A., & Ganong, L. (2011). "I'm a loser, I'm not married, let's just all look at me": Ever-single women's perceptions of their social environment. *Journal of Family Issues*, *32*(7), 956–980.

Simpson, J. A., Campbell, B., & Berscheid, E. (1986). The association between romantic love and marriage: Kephart (1967) twice revisited. *Personality and Social Psychology Bulletin*, *12*(3), 363–372.

Skolnick, A. S. (1987). *The intimate environment: Exploring marriage and the family*. New York, NY: Little, Brown.

Smock, P. J. (2000). Cohabitation in the United States: An appraisal of research themes, findings, and implications. *Annual Review of Sociology*, *26*(1), 1–20.

Solomon, S., Greenberg, J., & Pyszczynski, T. (1991). A terror management theory of social behavior: The psychological functions of self-esteem and cultural worldviews. *Advances in Experimental Social Psychology*, *24*, 93–159.

Swensen, C. H., Eskew, R. W., & Kohlhepp, K. A. (1984). Five factors in long-term marriages. *Journal of Family and Economic Issues*, *7*(2), 94–106.

Szinovacz, M. (1996). Couples' employment/retirement patterns and perceptions of marital quality. *Research on Aging*, *18*(2), 243–268.

Twenge, J. M., Campbell, W. K., & Foster, C. A. (2003). Parenthood and marital satisfaction: A meta-analytic review. *Journal of Marriage and Family*, *65*(3), 574–583.

U.S. Census Bureau. (2010). Current population survey, "America's families and living arrangements" for 2010. Retrieved from https://www.census.gov/population/www/socdemo/hh-fam/cps2010.html

VanLandingham, J., Johnson, D. R., & Amato, P. (2001). Marital happiness, marital duration, and the U-shaped curve: Evidence from a five-wave panel study. *Social Forces*, *79*, 1313–1341.

Ventura, S. J., & Bachrach, C. A. (2000). Nonmarital childbearing in the United States, 1940–99. *National Vital Statistics Reports*, *48*(16), n16.

Voegtline, K. M., Costigan, K. A., Pater, H. A., & DiPietro, J. A. (2013). Near-term fetal response to maternal spoken voice. *Infant Behavior and Development*, *36*(4), 526–533.

Wang, H., & Amato, P. R. (2000). Predictors of divorce adjustment: Stressors, resources, and definitions. *Journal of Marriage and Family*, *62*(3), 655–668.

White, L. K., & Booth, A. (1985). The transition to parenthood and marital quality. *Journal of Family Issues, 6*(4), 435–449.

White, L., & Edwards, J. N. (1990). Emptying the nest and parental well-being: An analysis of national panel data. *American Sociological Review, 55,* 235–242.

Wilcox, W. B. (2002). Religion, convention, and paternal involvement. *Journal of Marriage and Family, 64*(3), 780–792.

Wilcox, W. B., & Wolfinger, N. H. (2007). Then comes marriage? Religion, race, and marriage in urban America. *Social Science Research, 36*(2), 569–589.

Williams, K. D., & Nida, S. A. (2005). Obliviously ostracizing singles. *Psychological Inquiry, 16*(2/3), 127–131.

Yau, N. (2007). Divorce and occupation: Some jobs tend toward higher divorce rates. *Data Overload.* Retrieved from http://flowingdata.com/2017/07/25/divorce-and-occupation/

Chapter 7

Adams, R. G., & Torr, R. (1998). Factors underlying the structure of older adult friendship networks. *Social Networks, 20*(1), 51–61.

Allan, G. (1989). *Friendship: Developing a sociological perspective.* London, England: Harvester Wheatsheaf.

Altman, I., & Taylor, D. A. (1973). *Social penetration: The development of interpersonal relationships.* New York, NY: Holt, Rinehart & Winston.

Argyle, M., & Henderson, M. (1984). The rules of friendship. *Journal of Social and Personal Relationships, 1*(2), 211–237.

Aron, A., Aron, E. N., & Smollan, D. (1992). Inclusion of Other in the Self Scale and the structure of interpersonal closeness. *Journal of Personality and Social Psychology, 63*(4), 596–612.

Aron, A., Melinat, E., Aron, E. N., Vallone, R. D., & Bator, R. J. (1997). The experimental generation of interpersonal closeness: A procedure and some preliminary findings. *Personality and Social Psychology Bulletin, 23*(4), 363–377.

Aronson, E. (1978). *The jigsaw classroom.* Thousand Oaks, CA: Sage.

Autism Speaks. (2019). *Autism facts and figures.* Retrieved July 3, 2019. from https://www.autismspeaks.org/autism-facts-and-figures

Bauminger, N., & Kasari, C. (2000). Loneliness and friendship in high-functioning children with autism. *Child Development, 71*(2), 447–456.

Berg, J. H. (1987). Responsiveness and self-disclosure. In V. J. Derlega & J. H. Berg (Eds.), *Self-disclosure: Theory, research, and therapy* (pp. 101–130). New York, NY: Plenum.

Berg, J. H., & Archer, R. L. (1980). Disclosure or concern: A second look at liking for the norm breaker. *Journal of Personality, 48,* 245–257.

Berndt, T. J., & Perry, B. (1983). *Benefits of friendship interview.* Unpublished paper, University of Oklahoma, Norman, OK.

Berscheid, E., & Graziano, W. (1979). The initiation of social relationships and interpersonal attraction. In R. L. Burgess & T. L. Huston (Eds.), *Social exchange in developing relationships* (pp. 31–60). Cambridge, MA: Academic Press.

Bigelow, B. J. (1977). Children's friendship expectations: A cognitive-developmental study. *Child Development, 48,* 246–253.

Binder, J., Zagefka, H., Brown, R., Funke, F., Kessler, T., Mummendey, A., … Leyens, J. (2009). Does contact reduce prejudice or does prejudice reduce contact? A longitudinal test of the contact hypothesis among majority and minority groups in three European countries. *Journal of Personality and Social Psychology, 96*(4), 843–856.

Buhrmester, D., & Furman, W. D. (1986). The changing functions of friends in childhood: A Neo-Sullivanian perspective. In V. J. Derlega & B. A. Winstead (Eds.), *Friendship and social interaction* (pp. 41–62). New York, NY: Springer.

Bukowski, W. M., Hoza, B., & Boivin, M. (1994). Measuring friendship quality during pre- and early adolescence: The development and psychometric properties of the friendship qualities scale. *Journal of Social and Personal Relationships, 11*(3), 471–484.

Cacioppo, J. T., Fowler, J. H., & Christakis, N. A. (2009). Alone in the crowd: The structure and spread of loneliness in a large social network. *Journal of Personality and Social Psychology, 97,* 977–991.

Christakis, N. A., & Fowler, J. H. (2009). *Connected: The surprising power of our social networks and how they shape our lives.* New York, NY: Little, Brown.

Closson, L. M. (2009). Aggressive and prosocial behaviors within early adolescent friendship cliques:

What's status got to do with it? *Merrill-Palmer Quarterly, 55*(4), 406–435.

Collins, N. L., & Miller, L. C. (1994). Self-disclosure and liking: A meta-analytic review. *Psychological Bulletin, 116*(3), 457–475.

Collins, W. A., & Laursen, B. (2000). Adolescent relationships: The art of fugue. In C. Hendrick & S. S. Hendrick (Eds.), Close *relationships: A sourcebook* (pp. 59–69). Thousand Oaks, CA: Sage.

Collins, W. A., & Madsen, S. D. (2006). Personal relationships in adolescence and early adulthood. In A. L. Vangelisti & D. Perlman (Eds.), *Cambridge handbook of personal relationships* (pp. 191–209). New York, NY: Cambridge University Press.

Cross, S. E., Bacon, P. L., & Morris, M. L. (2000). The relational-interdependent self-construal and relationships. *Journal of Personality and Social Psychology, 78*(4), 791–808.

Cummings, J. N., Lee, J. B., & Kraut, R. (2006). Communication technology and friendship during the transition from high school to college. In R. Kraut, M. Brynin, & S. Kiesler (Eds.), *Oxford series in human-technology interaction. Computers, phones, and the Internet: Domesticating information technology* (pp. 265–278). Oxford, England: Oxford University Press.

Darley, J. M., & Berscheid, E. (1967). Increased liking as a result of the anticipation of personal contact. *Human Relations, 20,* 29–40.

Davis, D., & Perkowitz, W. T. (1979). Consequences of responsiveness in dyadic interaction: Effects of probability of response and proportion of content-related responses on interpersonal attraction. *Journal of Personality and Social Psychology, 37,* 534–550.

Deave, T., Johnson, D., & Ingram, J. (2008). Transition to parenthood: The needs of parents in pregnancy and early parenthood. *BMC Pregnancy and Childbirth, 8*(1), 30–41.

Dunbar, R. I. M. (1992). Neocortex size as a constraint on group size in primates. *Journal of Human Evolution, 22*(6), 469–493.

Ennett, S. T., Bauman, K. E., & Koch, G. G. (1994). Variability in cigarette smoking within and between adolescent friendship cliques. *Addictive Behaviors, 19*(3), 295–305.

Fehr, B. (1996). *Friendship processes.* Thousand Oaks, CA: Sage.

Fehr, B. (1999). Stability and commitment in friendships. In J. M. Adams & W. H. Jones (Eds.), *Handbook of interpersonal commitment and relationship stability* (pp. 259–280). New York, NY: Plenum.

Festinger, L., Schachter, S., & Back, K. W. (1950). *Social pressures in informal groups: A study of human factors in housing.* New York, NY: Harper & Bros.

Fischer, C. S., Jackson, R. M., Stueve, C. A., Gerson, K., Jones, L. M., & Baldassare, M. (1977). *Network and places: Social relations in the urban setting.* New York, NY: Free Press.

Fordham, K., & Stevenson-Hinde, J. (1999). Shyness, friendship quality, and adjustment during middle childhood. *Journal of Child Psychology and Psychiatry and Allied Disciplines, 40*(5), 757–768.

Gajdusek, K. (Producer). (2016–Present). *Stranger Things* [Television series]. Jackson, GA: Netflix.

Godfrey, D. K., Jones, E. E., & Lord, C. G. (1986). Self-promotion is not ingratiating. *Journal of Personality and Social Psychology, 50,* 106–115.

Goulder, H., & Strong, M. S. (1987). *Speaking of friendship: Middle-class women and their friends.* New York, NY: Greenwood.

Guerrero, L. K., Eloy, S. V., Jorgensen, P. F., & Andersen, P. A. (1993). Hers or his? Sex differences in the experience and communication of jealousy in close relationships. In P. Kalbfleisch (Ed.), *Interpersonal communication: Evolving interpersonal relationships* (pp. 109–131). Hillsdale, NJ: Lawrence Erlbaum.

Halatsis, P., & Christakis, N. (2009). The challenge of sexual attraction within heterosexuals' cross-sex friendship. *Journal of Social and Personal Relationships, 26,* 919–937.

Hampton, K., & Wellman, B. (2001). Long distance community in the network society: Contact and support beyond Netville. *American Behavioral Scientist, 45,* 476–495.

Hartup, W. W. (2006). Relationships in early and middle childhood. In A. L. Vangelisti & D. Perlman (Eds.), *Cambridge handbook of personal relationships* (pp. 177–190). New York, NY: Cambridge University Press.

Hartup, W. W., & Stevens, N. (1999). Friendships and adaptation across the life span. *Current Directions in Psychological Science, 8*(3), 76–79.

Hays, R. B. (1984). The development and maintenance of friendship. *Journal of Social and Personal Relationships, 1,* 75–98.

Hobson, R. P. (1993). The emotional origins of social understanding. *Philosophical Psychology, 6,* 227–245.

Hornstein, G. A., & Truesdell, S. E. (1988). Development of intimate conversation in close relationships. *Journal of Social and Clinical Psychology, 7*(1), 49–64.

Howes, C. (1983). Patterns of friendship. *Child Development, 54,* 1041–1053.

Howes, C. (2011). Friendship in early childhood. In K. Rubin, W. Bukowski, & B. Laursen (Eds.), *Handbook of peer interactions, relationships, and groups* (pp. 180–194). New York, NY: Guilford Press.

Hunt, C., Peters, L., & Rapee, R. M. (2012). Development of a measure of the experience of being bullied in youth. *Psychological Assessment, 24,* 156–165.

Jago, R., Brockman, R., Fox, K. R., Cartwright, K., Page, A. S., & Thompson, J. L. (2009). Friendship groups and physical activity: Qualitative findings on how physical activity is initiated and maintained among 10–11 year old children. *International Journal of Behavioral Nutrition and Physical Activity, 6*(1), 4–12.

Knight, J. A., & Vallacher, R. R. (1981). Interpersonal engagement in social perception: The consequences of getting into the action. *Journal of Personality and Social Psychology, 40,* 990–999.

Kubitschek, W. N., & Hallinan, M. T. (1998). Tracking and students' friendships. *Social Psychology Quarterly, 61*(1), 1–15.

Kupersmidt, J. B., DeRosier, M. E., & Patterson, C. P. (1995). Similarity as the basis for children's friendships: The roles of socioeconomic status, aggressive and withdrawn behavior, academic achievement, and demographic characteristics. *Child Development, 66,* 360–375.

Larson, R., Richards, M. H., Moneta, G., Holmbeck, G., & Duckett, E. (1996). Changes in adolescents' daily interactions with their families from ages 10 to 18: Disengagement and transformation. *Developmental Psychology, 32,* 744–754.

Lehmiller, J. J., VanderDrift, L. E., & Kelly, J. R. (2014). Sexual communication, satisfaction, and condom use behavior in friends with benefits and romantic partners. *Journal of Sex Research, 51,* 74–85.

Linson, A. (Producer), Fincher, D. (Director). (1999). *Fight Club.* [Motion picture]. United States: Fox 2000 Pictures.

Mallen, M. J., Day, S. X., & Green, M. A. (2003). Online versus face-to-face conversation: An examination of relational and discourse variables. *Psychotherapy: Theory, Research, Practice, Training, 40*(1–2), 155–163.

Marshall, T. C. (2010). Gender, peer relations, and intimate romantic relationships. In J. Chrisler & D. McCreary (Eds.), *Handbook of gender research in psychology* (Vol. 2, pp. 281–310). New York, NY: Springer.

Mazur, E., & Richards, L. (2011). Emerging adults' social networking online: Homophily or diversity? *Journal of Applied Developmental Psychology, 10,* 855–862.

Mehta, S. I., & Farina, A. (1988). Associative stigma: Perceptions of the difficulties of college-aged children of stigmatized fathers. *Journal of Social and Clinical Psychology, 7*(2–3), 192–202.

Miller, L. C., Berg, J. H., & Archer, R. L. (1983). Openers: Individuals who elicit intimate self-disclosure. *Journal of Personality and Social Psychology, 44*(6), 1234–1244.

Miller, N., & Marks, G. (1982). Assumed similarity between self and other: Effect of expectation of future interaction with that other. *Social Psychology Quarterly, 45,* 100–105.

Miller, R. S. (2009). Social anxiousness, shyness, and embarrassability. M. R. Leary & R. H. Hoyle (Eds.), *Handbook of individual differences in social behavior* (pp. 176–191). New York, NY: Guilford Press.

Neuberg, S. L., Smith, D. M., Hoffman, J. C., & Russell, F. J. (1994). When we observe stigmatized and "normal" individuals interacting: Stigma by association. *Personality and Social Psychology Bulletin, 20*(2), 196–209.

Newcomb, A. F., & Bagwell, C. L. (1995). Children's friendship relations: A meta-analytic review. *Psychological Bulletin, 117*(2), 306–347.

Newman, D. B., Schug, J., Yuki, M., Yamada, J., & Nezlek, J. B. (2018). The negative consequences of maximizing in friendship selection. *Journal of Personality and Social Psychology, 114*(5), 804–824.

Nolan, M. L., Mason, V., Snow, S., Messenger, W., Catling, J., & Upton, P. (2012). Making friends at antenatal classes: A qualitative exploration of friendship across the transition to motherhood. *Journal of Perinatal Education, 21*(3), 178–185.

Nunnally, J. C. (1961). *Popular conceptions of mental health: Their development and change.* New York, NY: Holt, Rinehart, & Winston.

Oetting, E. E. & Beauvais, F. (1986). Peer cluster theory: Drugs and the adolescent. *Journal of Counseling and Development, 65,* 17–22.

Osofsky, J. D., & Chartrand, L. C. M. M. (2013). Military children from birth to five years. *The Future of Children, 23*(2), 61–77.

Page-Gould, E., Mendoza-Denton, R., & Tropp, L. R. (2008). With a little help from my cross-group friend: Reducing anxiety in intergroup contexts through cross-group friendship. *Journal of Personality and Social Psychology, 95*(5), 1080–1094.

Palahniuk, C. (1996). *Fight club.* New York, NY: W. W. Norton.

Parker, J. G., & Asher, S. R. (1993). Friendship and friendship quality in middle childhood: Links with peer group acceptance and feelings of loneliness and social dissatisfaction. *Developmental Psychology, 29*(4), 611–621.

Parker, J. G., Low, C. M., Walker, A. R., & Gamm, B. K. (2005). Friendship jealousy in young adolescents: Individual differences and links to sex, self-esteem, aggression, and social adjustment. *Developmental Psychology, 41*(1), 235–250.

Paxton, S. J., Schutz, H. K., Wertheim, E. H., & Muir, S. L. (1999). Friendship clique and peer influences on body image concerns, dietary restraint, extreme weight-loss behaviors, and binge eating in adolescent girls. *Journal of Abnormal Psychology, 108*(2), 255–266.

Przybylski, A. K., & Weinstein, N. (2013). Can you connect with me now? How the presence of mobile communication technology influences face-to-face conversation quality. *Journal of Social and Personal Relationships, 30*(3), 237–246.

Reis, H. T., Maniaci, M. R., Caprariello, P. A., Eastwick, P. W., & Finkel, E. J. (2011). Familiarity does indeed promote attraction in live interaction. *Journal of Personality and Social Psychology, 101*(3), 557–570.

Rodin, M. J. (1982). Non-engagement, failure to engage, and disengagement. In S. Duck (Ed.), *Personal Relationships: Vol. 4* (pp. 31–49). London, England: Academic Press.

Rook, K. S. (1984). The negative side of social interaction: Impact on psychological well-being. *Journal of Personality and Social Psychology, 46,* 1156–1166.

Russell, D. W. (1996). UCLA Loneliness Scale (Version 3): Reliability, validity, and factor structure. *Journal of Personality Assessment, 66*(1), 20–40.

Sack, W. H., Seidler, J., & Thomas, S. (1976). The children of imprisoned parents: A psychosocial exploration. *American Journal of Orthopsychiatry, 46*(4), 618–628.

Segal, M. W. (1974). Alphabet and attraction: An unobtrusive measure of the effect of propinquity in a field setting. *Journal of Personality and Social Psychology, 30,* 654–657.

Selman, R. L. (1980). *The growth of interpersonal understanding.* New York, NY: Academic Press.

Selman, R. L., & Schultz, L. H. (1990). *Making a friend in youth: Developmental theory and pair therapy.* Chicago, IL: Transaction.

Shea, L., Thompson, L., & Blieszner, R. (1988). Resources in older adults' old and new friendships. *Journal of Social and Personal Relationships, 5,* 83–96.

Sherif, M. (1956). Experiments in group conflict. *Scientific American, 195,* 54–58.

Siu, O. L., & Phillips, D. R. (2002). A study of family support, friendship, and psychological well-being among older women in Hong Kong. *International Journal of Aging and Human Development, 55*(4), 299–319.

VanderDrift, L. E., Wilson, J. E., & Agnew, C. R. (2013). On the benefits of valuing being friends for non-marital romantic partners. *Journal of Social and Personal Relationships, 30,* 115–131.

Werking, K. (1997). *We're just good friends: Women and men in nonromantic relationships.* New York, NY: Guilford Press.

Wong, J. S., & Schonlau, M. (2013). Does bully victimization predict future delinquency? A propensity score matching approach. *Criminal Justice and Behavior, 40,* 1184–1208.

Wrzus, C., Hanel, M., Wagner, J., & Neyer, F. J. (2013). Social network changes and life events across the life span: A meta-analysis. *Psychological Bulletin, 139,* 53–80.

Chapter 8

Agthe, M., Spörrle, M., & Maner, J. K. (2010). Don't hate me because I'm beautiful: Anti-attractiveness bias in organizational evaluation and decision making. *Journal of Experimental Social Psychology, 46*(6), 1151–1154.

Allport, G. W. (1937). *Personality: A psychological interpretation.* New York, NY: Holt.

Allport, G. W., & Vernon, P. E. (1933). *Studies in expressive movement.* New York, NY: Haffner.

Amsel, A. (1958). The role of frustrative nonreward in noncontinuous reward situations. *Psychological Bulletin, 55*(2), 102–119.

Amsel, A. (1962). Frustrative nonreward in partial reinforcement and discrimination learning: Some recent history and a theoretical extension. *Psychological Review, 69*(4), 306–328.

Aron, A., Aron, E. N., & Allen, J. (1998). Motivations for unreciprocated love. *Personality and Social Psychology Bulletin, 24*(8), 787–796.

Aronson, E., & Linder, D. (1965). Gain and loss of esteem as determinants of interpersonal attractiveness. *Journal of Experimental Social Psychology, 1*(2), 156–171.

Asch, S. E. (1946). Forming impressions of personality. *Journal of Abnormal and Social Psychology, 41*(3), 258–290.

Bale, C., & Archer, J. (2013). Self-perceived attractiveness, romantic desirability and self-esteem: A mating sociometer perspective. *Evolutionary Psychology, 11*(1), 68–84.

Baumeister, R. F., & Leary, M. R. (1995). The need to belong: desire for interpersonal attachments as a fundamental human motivation. *Psychological Bulletin, 117*(3), 497–529.

Baxter, L. A., & West, L. (2003). Couple perceptions of their similarities and differences: A dialectical perspective. *Journal of Social and Personal Relationships, 20*(4), 491–514.

Berry, D. S., & McArthur, L. Z. (1985). Some components and consequences of a babyface. *Journal of Personality and Social Psychology, 48*, 212–323.

Berry, D. S., & McArthur, L. Z. (1986). Perceiving character in faces: The impact of age-related cranio-facial changes on social perception. *Psychological Bulletin, 100*, 3–18.

Berscheid, E., Dion, K., Walster, E., & Walster, G. W. (1971). Physical attractiveness and dating choice: A test of the matching hypothesis. *Journal of Experimental Social Psychology, 7*(2), 173–189.

Biology of beauty. (1996, June 2). Retrieved from http://www.newsweek.com/biology-beauty-178836

Braun, M. F., & Bryan, A. (2006). Female waist-to-hip and male waist-to-shoulder ratios as determinants of romantic partner desirability. *Journal of Social and Personal Relationships, 23*(5), 805–819.

Brehm, S. S., & Brehm, J. W. (2013). *Psychological reactance: A theory of freedom and control.* Cambridge, MA: Academic Press.

Brickman, P., Meyer, P., & Fredd, S. (1975). Effects of varying exposure to another person with familiar or unfamiliar thought processes. *Journal of Experimental Social Psychology, 11*(3), 261–270.

Brockner, J., & Swap, W. C. (1976). Effects of repeated exposure and attitudinal similarity on self-disclosure and interpersonal attraction. *Journal of Personality and Social Psychology, 33*(5), 531–540.

Buss, D. M., Shackelford, T. K., Kirkpatrick, L. A., & Larsen, R. J. (2001). A half century of mate preferences: The cultural evolution of values. *Journal of Marriage and Family, 63*(2), 491–503.

Clifford, M. M. & Walster, E. (1973). Research note: The effect of physical attractiveness on teacher expectations. *Sociology of Education, 46*(2), 248–258.

Collins, S. (2008). *The hunger games.* New York, NY: Scholastic Press.

Collins, S. (2009). *Catching fire.* New York, NY: Scholastic Press.

Collins, S. (2010). *Mockingjay.* New York, NY: Scholastic Press.

Cooper, W. H. (1981). Ubiquitous halo. *Psychological Bulletin, 90*(2), 218–244.

Cunningham, M. R., Barbee, A. P., & Druen, P. B. (1997). Social allergens and the reactions that they produce: Escalation of annoyance and disgust in love and work. In R. M. Kowalski (Ed.), *Aversive interpersonal behaviors* (pp. 189–214). New York, NY: Plenum Press.

Cunningham, M. R., Barbee, A. P., & Pike, C. L. (1990). What do women want? Facialmetric assessment of multiple motives in the perception of male facial physical attractiveness. *Journal of Personality and Social Psychology, 59*(1), 61–72.

Cunningham, M. R., Shamblen, S. R., Barbee, A. P., & Ault, L. K. (2005). Social allergies in romantic relationships: Behavioral repetition, emotional sensitization, and dissatisfaction in dating couples. *Personal Relationships, 12*(2), 273–295.

Curtis, R. C., & Miller, K. (1986). Believing another likes or dislikes you: Behaviors making the beliefs come true. *Journal of Personality and Social Psychology, 51*(2), 284–290.

Davis, R. L., & Goodfriend, W. (2007). Complementarity in romantic relationships: Constructs involved in individual and partner change. *Modern Psychological Studies, 13*, 65–71.

Dennis, I. (2007). Halo effects in grading student projects. *Journal of Applied Psychology, 92*(4), 1169–1176.

Dennis, I., Newstead, S. E., & Wright, D. E. (1996). A new approach to exploring biases in educational assessment. *British Journal of Psychology, 87*(4), 515–534.

Denrell, J. (2005). Why most people disapprove of me: Experience sampling in impression formation. *Psychological Review, 112*(4), 951–978.

Dijkstra, P., & Buunk, B. P. (2001). Sex differences in the jealousy-evoking nature of a rival's body build. *Evolution and Human Behavior, 22*(5), 335–341.

Dion, K., Berscheid, E., & Walster, E. (1972). What is beautiful is good. *Journal of Personality and Social Psychology, 24*(3), 285–290.

Dixson, A. F., Halliwell, G., East, R., Wignarajah, P., & Anderson, M. J. (2003). Masculine somatotype and hirsuteness as determinants of sexual attractiveness to women. *Archives of Sexual Behavior, 32*(1), 29–39.

Downey, J. L. & Christensen, L. (2006). Belief persistence in impression formation. *North American Journal of Psychology, 8*(3), 479–488.

Driscoll, R., Davis, K. E., & Lipetz, M. E. (1972). Parental interference and romantic love: The Romeo and Juliet effect. *Journal of Personality and Social Psychology, 24*(1), 1–10.

Dutton, D. G., & Aron, A. P. (1974). Some evidence for heightened sexual attraction under conditions of high anxiety. *Journal of Personality and Social Psychology, 30*(4), 510–517.

Etcheverry, P. E., & Agnew, C. R. (2004). Subjective norms and the prediction of romantic relationship state and fate. *Personal Relationships, 11*(4), 409–428.

Feingold, A. (1988). Matching for attractiveness in romantic partners and same-sex friends: A meta-analysis and theoretical critique. *Psychological Bulletin, 104*(2), 226–235.

Festinger, L., Schachter, S., & Back, K. W. (1950). *Social pressures in informal groups: A study of human factors in housing.* New York, NY: Harper & Bros.

Fichten, C. S., Tagalakis, V., Judd, D., Wright, J., & Amsel, R. (1992). Verbal and nonverbal communication cues in daily conversations and dating. *Journal of Social Psychology, 132*(6), 751–769.

Friedman, H. S., Riggio, R. E., & Casella, D. F. (1988). Nonverbal skill, personal charisma, and initial attraction. *Personality and Social Psychology Bulletin, 14*(1), 203–211.

Frieze, I. H., Olson, J. E., & Russell, J. (1991). Attractiveness and income for men and women in management. *Journal of Applied Social Psychology, 21*(13), 1039–1057.

Fugl-Meyer, K. S., Öberg, K., Lundberg, P. O., Lewin, B., & Fugl-Meyer, A. (2006). Epidemiology: On orgasm, sexual techniques, and erotic perceptions in 18- to 74-year-old Swedish women. *Journal of Sexual Medicine, 3*(1), 56–68.

Furnham, A., & Reeves, E. (2006). The relative influence of facial neoteny and waist-to-hip ratio on judgements of female attractiveness and fecundity. *Psychology, Health & Medicine, 11*(2), 129–141.

Gangestad, S. W., Thornhill, R., & Yeo, R. A. (1994). Facial attractiveness, developmental stability, and fluctuating asymmetry. *Ethology & Sociobiology, 15*(2), 73–85.

Givens, D. B. (1978). The nonverbal basis of attraction: Flirtation, courtship, and seduction. *Psychiatry, 41*(4), 346–359.

Goodfriend, W. (2009). Proximity and attraction. In H. T. Reis & S. Sprecher (Eds.), *Encyclopedia of human relationships* (pp. 1297–1299). Thousand Oaks, CA: Sage.

Grammer, K., & Thornhill, R. (1994). Human (Homo sapiens) facial attractiveness and sexual selection:

The role of symmetry and averageness. *Journal of Comparative Psychology, 108*(3), 233–242.

Gruber-Baldini, A. L., Schaie, K. W., & Willis, S. L. (1995). Similarity in married couples: A longitudinal study of mental abilities and rigidity-flexibility. *Journal of Personality and Social Psychology, 69*(1), 191–203.

Gunnell, J. J., & Ceci, S. J. (2010). When emotionality trumps reason: A study of individual processing style and juror bias. *Behavioral Sciences & the Law, 28*(6), 850–877.

Halsey, L. G., Huber, J. W., Bufton, R. J., & Little, A. C. (2010). An explanation for enhanced perceptions of attractiveness after alcohol consumption. *Alcohol, 44*(4), 307–313.

Hamilton, E. (1942). *Mythology.* New York, NY: New American Library of World Literature.

Harrison, A. A. (1977). Mere exposure. *Advances in Experimental Social Psychology, 10,* 39–83.

Heine, S. J., & Renshaw, K. (2002). Interjudge agreement, self-enhancement, and liking: Cross-cultural divergences. *Personality and Social Psychology Bulletin, 28*(5), 578–587.

Hitsch, G. J., Hortaçsu, A., & Ariely, D. (2010). Matching and sorting in online dating. *American Economic Review, 100*(1), 130–163.

Hosoda, M., Stone-Romero, E. F., & Coats, G. (2003). The effects of physical attractiveness on job-related outcomes: A meta-analysis of experimental studies. *Personnel Psychology, 56*(2), 431–462.

Hugh Feeley, T. (2002). Evidence of halo effects in student evaluations of communication instruction. *Communication Education, 51*(3), 225–236.

Hughes, S. M., & Gallup, G. G. (2003). Sex differences in morphological predictors of sexual behavior: Shoulder to hip and waist to hip ratios. *Evolution and Human Behavior, 24*(3), 173–178.

Joel, S., Eastwick, P. W., & Finkel, E. J. (2017). Is romantic desire predictable? Machine learning applied to initial romantic attraction. *Psychological Science, 28*(10), 1478–1489.

Jones, D., Brace, C. L., Jankowiak, W., Laland, K. N., Musselman, L. E., Langlois, J. H., … Symons, D. (1995). Sexual selection, physical attractiveness, and facial neoteny: cross-cultural evidence and implications [and comments and reply]. *Current Anthropology, 36*(5), 723–748.

Jones, D., & Hill, K. (1993). Criteria of facial attractiveness in five populations. *Human Nature, 4*(3), 271–296.

Kelley, H. H. (1950). The warm-cold variable in first impressions of persons. *Journal of Personality, 18*(4), 431–439.

Kenny, D. A., & La Voie, L. (1982). Reciprocity of interpersonal attraction: A confirmed hypothesis. *Social Psychology Quarterly, 45,* 54–58.

Kenrick, D. T., Cialdini, R., & Linder, D. (1979). Misattribution under fear-producing circumstances: Four failures to replicate. *Personality and Social Psychology Bulletin, 5*(3), 329–334.

Kleinke, C. L. (1986). Gaze and eye contact: A research review. *Psychological Bulletin, 100*(1), 78–100.

LaForge, I., & Goodfriend, W. (2012). Developing a new device for measuring preferred body shapes. *Journal of Psychological Inquiry, 17,* 45–49.

Langlois, J. H., & Roggman, L. A. (1990). Attractive faces are only average. *Psychological Science, 1*(2), 115–121.

Langlois, J. H., Roggman, L. A., & Musselman, L. (1994). What is average and what is not average about attractive faces? *Psychological Science, 5*(4), 214–220.

Lee, A. Y. (2001). The mere exposure effect: An uncertainty reduction explanation revisited. *Personality and Social Psychology Bulletin, 27*(10), 1255–1266.

Lehmiller, J. J., & Agnew, C. R. (2007). Perceived marginalization and the prediction of romantic relationship stability. *Journal of Marriage and Family, 69*(4), 1036–1049.

Lewandowski, G. W., & Aron, A. P. (2004). Distinguishing arousal from novelty and challenge in initial romantic attraction between strangers. *Social Behavior and Personality, 32*(4), 361–372.

Lewis, D. M., Russell, E. M., Al-Shawaf, L., & Buss, D. M. (2015). Lumbar curvature: A previously undiscovered standard of attractiveness. *Evolution and Human Behavior, 36*(5), 345–350.

Lewis, R. A. (1973). Social reaction and the formation of dyads: An interactionist approach to mate selection. *Sociometry, 36,* 409–418.

Marcia, J. E. (1966). Development and validation of ego-identity status. *Journal of Personality and Social Psychology, 3*(5), 551–558.

Marcia, J. E. (2002). Identity and psychosocial development in adulthood. *Identity: An International Journal of Theory and Research, 2*(1), 7–28.

McCroskey, L. L., McCroskey, J. C., & Richmond, V. P. (2006). Analysis and improvement of the measurement of interpersonal attraction and homophily. *Communication Quarterly, 54*(1), 1–31.

Meloy, J. R. (1998). *The psychology of stalking.* San Diego, CA: Academic Press.

Mita, T. H., Dermer, M., & Knight, J. (1977). Reversed facial images and the mere-exposure hypothesis. *Journal of Personality and Social Psychology, 35*(8), 597–601.

Monahan, J. L., Murphy, S. T., & Zajonc, R. B. (2000). Subliminal mere exposure: Specific, general, and diffuse effects. *Psychological Science, 11*(6), 462–466.

Montoya, R. M. (2008). I'm hot, so I'd say you're not: The influence of objective physical attractiveness on mate selection. *Personality and Social Psychology Bulletin, 34*(10), 1315–1331.

Montoya, R. M., Horton, R. S., & Kirchner, J. (2008). Is actual similarity necessary for attraction? A meta-analysis of actual and perceived similarity. *Journal of Social and Personal Relationships, 25*(6), 889–922.

Moreland, R. L., & Beach, S. R. (1992). Exposure effects in the classroom: The development of affinity among students. *Journal of Experimental Social Psychology, 28*(3), 255–276.

Morry, M. M. (2005). Relationship satisfaction as a predictor of similarity ratings: A test of the attraction-similarity hypothesis. *Journal of Social and Personal Relationships, 22*(4), 561–584.

Morry, M. M. (2007). The attraction-similarity hypothesis among cross-sex friends: Relationship satisfaction, perceived similarities, and self-serving perceptions. *Journal of Social and Personal Relationships, 24*(1), 117–138.

Moskowitz, D. A., Turrubiates, J., Lozano, H., & Hajek, C. (2013). Physical, behavioral, and psychological traits of gay men identifying as Bears. *Archives of Sexual Behavior, 42*(5), 775–784.

Muehlenhard, C. L., Koralewski, M. A., Andrews, S. L., & Burdick, C. A. (1986). Verbal and nonverbal cues that convey interest in dating: Two studies. *Behavior Therapy, 17*(4), 404–419.

Payne, B. K., Hall, D. L., Cameron, C. D., & Bishara, A. J. (2010). A process model of affect misattribution. *Personality and Social Psychology Bulletin, 36*(10), 1397–1408.

Perper, T. (1989). Theories and observations on sexual selection and female choice in human beings. *Medical Anthropology, 11*(4), 409–454.

Perper, T., & Weis, D. L. (1987). Proceptive and rejective strategies of US and Canadian college women. *Journal of Sex Research, 23*(4), 455–480.

Perrett, D. I., May, K. A., & Yoshikawa, S. (1994). Facial shape and judgements of female attractiveness. *Nature, 368*(6468), 239–242.

Regan, P. C., & Berscheid, E. (1997). Gender differences in characteristics desired in a potential sexual and marriage partner. *Journal of Psychology & Human Sexuality, 9*(1), 25–37.

Reis, H. T., Maniaci, M. R., Caprariello, P. A., Eastwick, P. W., & Finkel, E. J. (2011). Familiarity does indeed promote attraction in live interaction. *Journal of Personality and Social Psychology, 101*(3), 557–570.

Remmers, H. H. (1934). Reliability and halo effect of high school and college students' judgments of their teachers. *Journal of Applied Psychology, 18*(5), 619–630.

Renninger, L. A., Wade, T. J., & Grammer, K. (2004). Getting that female glance: Patterns and consequences of male nonverbal behavior in courtship contexts. *Evolution and Human Behavior, 25*(6), 416–431.

Rhodes, G., Proffitt, F., Grady, J. M., & Sumich, A. (1998). Facial symmetry and the perception of beauty. *Psychonomic Bulletin & Review, 5*(4), 659–669.

Rosen, K. H. (1996). The ties that bind women to vioalent premarital relationships: Processes of seduction and entrapment. In D. D. Cahn & S. A. Lloyd (Eds.), *Family violence from a communication perspective* (pp. 151–176). Thousand Oaks, CA: Sage.

Scull, M. T. (2013). Reinforcing gender roles at the male strip show: A qualitative analysis of men who dance for women (MDW). *Deviant Behavior, 34*(7), 557–578.

Sinclair, H. C., Hood, K. B., & Wright, B. L. (2014). Revisiting the Romeo and Juliet effect (Driscoll, Davis, & Lipetz, 1972). *Social Psychology, 45*, 170–178.

Singh, D. (1993a). Adaptive significance of female physical attractiveness: Role of waist-to-hip ratio. *Journal of Personality and Social Psychology, 65*(2), 293–307.

Singh, D. (1993b). Body shape and women's attractiveness: The critical role of waist-to-hip ratio. *Human Nature, 4*(3), 297–321.

Singh, D., & Randall, P. K. (2007). Beauty is in the eye of the plastic surgeon: Waist-hip ratio (WHR) and women's attractiveness. *Personality and Individual Differences, 43*(2), 329–340.

Sprecher, S. (1988). Investment model, equity, and social support determinants of relationship commitment. *Social Psychology Quarterly, 51*, 318–328.

Taylor, L. S., Fiore, A. T., Mendelsohn, G. A., & Cheshire, C. (2011). "Out of my league": A real-world test of the matching hypothesis. *Personality and Social Psychology Bulletin, 37*, 942–954.

Thornhill, R., & Gangestad, S. W. (1994). Human fluctuating asymmetry and sexual behavior. *Psychological Science, 5*(5), 297–302.

U.S. Census Bureau. (2010). *2010 Census data.* Retrieved from https://www.census.gov/programs-surveys/decennial-census/data/datasets.2010.html

Van Horn, K. R., Arnone, A., Nesbitt, K., Desilets, L., Sears, T., Giffin, M., & Brudi, R. (1997). Physical distance and interpersonal characteristics in college students' romantic relationships. *Personal Relationships, 4*(1), 25–34.

Wade, T. J., & Feldman, A. (2016). Sex and the perceived effectiveness of flirtation techniques. *Human Ethology Bulletin, 31*, 30–44.

Walster, E., Aronson, V., Abrahams, D., & Rottman, L. (1966). Importance of physical attractiveness in dating behavior. *Journal of Personality and Social Psychology, 4*(5), 508–516.

Wang, S. S., Moon, S., Kwon, K. H., Evans, C. A., & Stefanone, M. A. (2010). Face off: Implications of visual cues on initiating friendship on Facebook. *Computers in Human Behavior, 26*(2), 226–234.

Wenzel, A., & Emerson, T. (2009). Mate selection in socially anxious and nonanxious individuals. *Journal of Social and Clinical Psychology, 28*(3), 341–363.

Wignall, A. E., Heiling, A. M., Cheng, K., & Herberstein, M. E. (2006). Flower symmetry preferences in honeybees and their crab spider predators. *Ethology, 112*(5), 510–518.

Williams, S., Ryckman, R. M., Gold, J. A., & Lenney, E. (1982). The effects of sensation seeking and misattribution of arousal on attraction toward similar or dissimilar strangers. *Journal of Research in Personality, 16*(2), 217–226.

Williams, T. (1955/2014). *Cat on a hot tin roof.* London, England: Bloomsbury.

Zaidel, D. W., & Hessamian, M. (2010). Asymmetry and symmetry in the beauty of human faces. *Symmetry, 2*(1), 136–149.

Zajonc, R. B. (1968). Attitudinal effects of mere exposure. *Journal of Personality and Social Psychology, 9*, 1–27.

Zajonc, R. B. (2001). Mere exposure: A gateway to the subliminal. *Current Directions in Psychological Science, 10*(6), 224–228.

Chapter 9

47, XYY Syndrome. (2018). *Genetics Home Reference.* Retrieved September 23, 2018, from https://ghr.nlm.nih.gov/condition/47xyy-syndrome

5-Alpha Reductase Deficiency. (2018). *Genetics Home Reference.* Retrieved September 23, 2018, from https://ghr.nlm.nih.gov/condition/congenital-adrenal-hyperplasia-due-to-11-beta-hydroxylase-deficiency

American College Health Association. (2017, fall). *American College Health Association-National College Health Assessment II: Reference group executive summary.* Hanover, MD: Author.

American Psychiatric Association. (2013). *Diagnostic and statistical manual of mental disorders* (5th ed.). Arlington, VA: Author.

Androgen Insensitivity Syndrome. (2018). *Genetics Home Reference.* Retrieved September 23, 2018, from https://ghr.nlm.nih.gov/condition/androgen-insensitivity-syndrome

Aral, S. O., & Leichliter, J. S. (2010). Non-monogamy: Risk factor for STI transmission and acquisition and determinant of STI spread in populations. *Sexually Transmitted Infections, 83*(3), iii29–iii36.

Atkins, D. C., Baucom, D. H., & Jacobson, N. S. (2001). Understanding infidelity: Correlates in a national random sample. *Journal of Family Psychology, 15*(4), 735–749.

Backstrom, L., Armstrong, E. A., & Puentes, J. (2012). Women's negotiation of cunnilingus in college hookups and relationships. *Journal of Sex Research, 49*(1), 1–12.

Balzarini, R. N., Campbell, L., Kohut, T., Holmes, B. M., Lehmiller, J. J., Harman, J. J., & Atkins, N. (2017). Perceptions of primary and secondary relationships in polyamory. *PLoS One, 12*(5), e0177841.

Balzarini, R. N., Dharma, C., Kohut, T., Holmes, B. M., Campbell, L., Lehmiller, J. J., & Harman, J. J. (2019). Demographic comparison of American individuals in polyamorous and monogamous relationships. *Journal of Sex Research, 56*(6), 681–694.

BBC. (2015). The extraordinary case of the Guevedoces. Retrieved September 23, 2018, from https://www.bbc.com/news/magazine-34290981

Bevan, T., & Chasin, L. (Producers), Hooper, T. (Director). 2015. *The Danish girl* [Motion picture]. United States: Working Title Films.

Blanc, A. K. (2001). The effect of power in sexual relationships on sexual and reproductive health: An examination of the evidence. *Studies in Family Planning, 32*(3), 189–213.

Blow, A. J., & Hartnett, K. (2005). Infidelity in committed relationships II: A substantive review. *Journal of Marital and Family Therapy, 31*(2), 217–233.

Blumstein, P., & Schwartz, P. (1983). *American couples: Money-work-sex.* New York, NY: William Morrow.

Bogaert, A. F. (2004). Asexuality: Prevalence and associated factors in a national probability sample. *Journal of Sex Research, 41*(3), 279–287.

Bostwick, H. (1860). *A treatise on the nature and treatment of seminal diseases, impotency and other kindred affections* (12th ed.). New York, NY: Rogers.

Brabaw, K. (2017, March 31). Everything you need to know about "bathroom bills." *Refinery29.* Retrieved September 23, 2018, from https://www.refinery29.com/2017/03/148085/anti-transgender-bathroom-bills-what-you-need-to-know

Bradshaw, C., Kahn, A. S., & Saville, B. K. (2010). To hook up or date: Which gender benefits? *Sex Roles, 62*(9–10), 661–669.

Brettell, C., & Sargent, C. (2016). *Gender in cross-cultural perspective.* New York, NY: Routledge.

Burley, M. A. (Producer). (2013–Present). *Orange Is the New Black* [Television series]. United States: Tilted Productions.

Chalkley, A. J., & Powell, G. (1983). The clinical description of forty-eight cases of sexual fetishism. *British Journal of Psychiatry, 142*, 292–295.

Charny, I. W., & Parnass, S. (1995). The impact of extramarital relationships on the continuation of marriages. *Journal of Sex & Marital Therapy, 21*(2), 100–115.

Coleman, E. (1996). *What sexual scientists know about compulsive sexual behavior.* Allentown, PA: Society for the Scientific Study of Sexuality.

Congenital Adrenal Hyperplasia Due to 11-Beta-Hydroxylase Deficiency. (2018). *Genetics Home Reference.* Retrieved September 23, 2018, from https://ghr.nlm.nih.gov/condition/congenital-adrenal-hyperplasia-due-to-11-beta-hydroxylase-deficiency

Conley, T. D., Moors, A. C., Matsick, J. L., & Ziegler, A. (2013). The fewer the merrier? Assessing stigma surrounding consensually non-monogamous romantic relationships. *Analyses of Social Issues and Public Policy, 13*(1), 1–30.

Conley, T. D., Moors, A. C., Ziegler, A., & Karathanasis, C. (2012). Unfaithful individuals are less likely to practice safer sex than openly nonmonogamous individuals. *Journal of Sexual Medicine, 9*(6), 1559–1565.

DeGeneres, E., & Lassner, E. (Producers). (2003–Present). *The Ellen DeGeneres Show* [Television series]. United States: A Very Good Production.

Diamond, L. M. (2005). 'I'm straight, but I kissed a girl': The trouble with American media representations of female-female sexuality. *Feminism & Psychology, 15*(1), 104–110.

Dworkin, S. L., & O'Sullivan, L. (2005). Actual versus desired initiation patterns among a sample of college men: Tapping disjunctures within traditional male sexual scripts. *Journal of Sex Research, 42*, 150–158.

Ellis, B. J., & Symons, D. (1990). Sex differences in sexual fantasy: An evolutionary psychological approach. *Journal of Sex Research, 27*(4), 527–555.

Epstein, M., Calzo, J. P., Smiler, A. P., & Ward, L. M. (2009). "Anything from making out to having sex": Men's negotiations of hooking up and friends with benefits scripts. *Journal of Sex Research, 46*(5), 414–424.

Feldman, S. S., & Cauffman, E. (1999a). Sexual betrayal among late adolescents: Perspectives of the perpetrator and the aggrieved. *Journal of Youth and Adolescence*, 28(2), 235–258.

Feldman, S. S., & Cauffman, E. (1999b). Your cheatin' heart: Attitudes, behaviors, and correlates of sexual betrayal in late adolescents. *Journal of Research on Adolescence*, 9(3), 227–252.

Finkel, E. J., Eastwick, P. W., Karney, B. R., Reis, H. T., & Sprecher, S. (2012). Online dating: A critical analysis from the perspective of psychological science. *Psychological Science in the Public Interest*, 13(1), 3–66.

Gagnon, J., & Simon, W. (1973). *Sexual conduct: The social sources of human sexuality*. Chicago, IL: Aldine.

Garcia, J. R., Gesselman, A. N., Siliman, S. A., Perry, B. L., Coe, K., & Fisher, H. E. (2016). Sexting among singles in the USA: Prevalence of sending, receiving, and sharing sexual messages and images. *Sexual Health*, 13(5), 428–435.

Garcia, J. R., Reiber, C., Massey, S. G., & Merriwether, A. M. (2012). Sexual hookup culture: A review. *Review of General Psychology*, 16(2), 161–176.

Geffen, S. (2014, October 18). Remember that Britney Spears and Madonna VMA kiss? It wasn't as spontaneous as it looked. *MTV News*. Retrieved September 24, 2018, from http://www.mtv.com/news//1967925/britney-spears-madonna-vma-kiss/

GLAAD. (2018). *Tips for allies of transgender people*. Retrieved September 23, 2018, from https://www.glaad.org/transgender/allies

Goodfriend, W. (2012). Sexual script or sexual improv? Nontraditional sexual paths. In M. Paludi (Ed.), *The psychology of love* (Vol. 1, pp. 59–71). Santa Barbara, CA: Praeger.

Guadagno, R. E., Okdie, B. M., & Kruse, S. A. (2012). Dating deception: Gender, online dating, and exaggerated self-presentation. *Computers in Human Behavior*, 28(2), 642–647.

Herbenick, D., Bowling, J., Fu, T. C. J., Dodge, B., Guerra-Reyes, L., & Sanders, S. (2017). Sexual diversity in the United States: Results from a nationally representative probability sample of adult women and men. *PLoS One*, 12(7), e0181198.

Herdt, G. H. (1982). *Rituals of manhood: Male initiation in Papua New Guinea*. Berkeley: University of California Press.

Herdt, G., & McClintock, M. (2000). The magical age of 10. *Archives of Sexual Behavior*, 29(6), 587–606.

Hinderliter, A. C. (2009). Methodological issues for studying asexuality. *Archives of Sexual Behavior*, 38(5), 619–621.

Hitsch, G. J., Hortaçsu, A., & Ariely, D. (2010). What makes you click? Mate preferences in online dating. *Quantitative Marketing and Economics*, 8(4), 393–427.

James, E. L. (2012). *Fifty shades of Grey*. New York, NY: Vintage Books.

Joyal, C. C., & Carpentier, J. (2017). The prevalence of paraphilic interests and behaviors in the general population: A provincial survey. *Journal of Sex Research*, 54(2), 161–171.

Joyal, C. C., Cossette, A., & Lapierre, V. (2015). What exactly is an unusual sexual fantasy? *Journal of Sexual Medicine*, 12(2), 328–340.

Kafka, M. P. (2010). The DSM diagnostic criteria for fetishism. *Archives of Sexual Behavior*, 26, 357–362.

Kaplan, M. S., & Krueger, R. B. (2010). Diagnosis, assessment, and treatment of hypersexuality. *Journal of Sex Research*, 47(2–3), 181–198.

Kinsey, A. C., Pomeroy, W. B., & Martin, C. E. (1948). *Sexual behavior in the human male*. Bloomington, IN: Indiana University Press.

Kinsey, A. C., Pomeroy, W. B., Martin, C. E., & Gebhard, P. H. (1953). *Sexual behavior in the human female*. Bloomington, IN: Indiana University Press.

Klaassen, M. J., & Peter, J. (2015). Gender (in)equality in Internet pornography: A content analysis of popular pornographic Internet videos. *Journal of Sex Research*, 52(7), 721–735.

Klinefelter Syndrome. (2018). *Genetics Home Reference*. Retrieved September 23, 2018, from https://ghr.nlm.nih.gov/condition/klinefelter-syndrome

Lane, B. L., Piercy, C. W., & Carr, C. T. (2016). Making it Facebook official: The warranting value of online relationship status disclosures on relational characteristics. *Computers in Human Behavior*, 56, 1–8.

Laumann, E. O., Gagnon, J. H., Michael, R. T., & Michaels, S. (1994). *The social organization of sexuality: Sexual practices in the United States*. Chicago, IL: University of Chicago Press.

Lehmiller, J. (2018a). Sexual violence is a huge problem, but don't blame porn. *Tonic.vice.com*. Retrieved October 13, 2018, from https://tonic.vice.com/en_us/article/9kgjwp/sexual-violence-is-a-huge-problem-but-dont-blame-porn

Lehmiller, J. (2018b). *Tell me what you want: The science of sexual desire and how it can help you improve your sex life*. New York, NY: Da Capo Press.

Lehmiller, J. J. (2015). A comparison of sexual health history and practices among monogamous and consensually nonmonogamous sexual partners. *Journal of Sexual Medicine*, *12*(10), 2022–2028.

Lehne, G. K. (2009). Phenomenology of paraphilia: Lovemap theory. In F. M. Saleh, A. J. Grudzinskas, J. M. Bradford, & D. J. Brodsky (Eds.), *Sex offenders: Identification, risk assessment, treatment, and legal issues*. New York, NY: Oxford University Press.

Lerner, M. (2016, July 14). He, she or ze? Pronouns could pose trouble under University of Minnesota campus policy. *Star Tribune*. Retrieved September 23, 2018, from http://www.startribune.com/he-she-or-ze-pronouns-could-pose-trouble-under-u-campus-policy/488197021/

Lesher, E. C. (2013). Protecting poly: Applying the fourteenth amendment to the nonmonogamous. *Tulane Journal of Law & Sexuality*, *22*, 127–145.

Levine, M. P., & Troiden, R. R. (1988). The myth of sexual compulsivity. *Journal of Sex Research*, *25*(3), 347–363.

Marshall, D. (1971). Sexual behavior on Mangaia. In D. Marshall & R. Suggs (Eds.), *Human sexual behavior*. New York, NY: Basic Books.

Masters, N. T., Casey, E., Wells, E. A., & Morrison, D. M. (2013). Sexual scripts among young heterosexually active men and women: Continuity and change. *Journal of Sex Research*, *50*(5), 409–420.

Paul, B., & Shim, J. W. (2008). Gender, sexual affect, and motivations for Internet pornography use. *International Journal of Sexual Health*, *20*(3), 187–199.

Pells, R. (2016, December 12). Oxford University students 'told to use gender neutral pronoun ze.' *Independent*. Retrieved September 23, 2018, from https://www.independent.co.uk/student/news/oxford-university-students-gender-neutral-pronouns-peter-tatchell-student-union-ze-xe-a7470196.html

Pew Research Internet Project. (2013). *Online dating and relationships*. Retrieved October 9, 2018, from http://www.pewinternet.org/2013/10/21/online-dating-relationships/

Phillips, L. M. (2000). *Flirting with danger*. New York, NY: New York University Press.

Plato. (360 B.C.E.) (translated by Benjamin Jowett, 1939). *Symposium*.

Plutarch. (75 A.D.) (translated by Bernadotte Perrin, 1917). *The life of Pelopidas*. Loeb Classical Library edition.

Preidt, R. (2013, July 23). Is 'sex addiction' for real? Study says maybe not. *HealthDay.com*. Retrieved September 30, 2018, from https://consumer.healthday.com/sexual-health-information-32/sex-disorder-news-606/is-sex-addiction-for-real-study-says-maybe-not-678528.html

Previti, D., & Amato, P. R. (2004). Is infidelity a cause or a consequence of poor marital quality? *Journal of Social and Personal Relationships*, *21*(2), 217–230.

Rowatt, W. C., Cunninghan, M. R., & Druen, P. B. (1998). Deception to get a date. *Personality and Social Psychology Bulletin*, *24*(11), 1228–1242.

Rubin, J. D., Moors, A. C., Matsick, J. L., Ziegler, A., & Conley, T. D. (2014). On the margins: Considering diversity among consensually non-monogamous relationships. *Journal für Psychologie*, *22*(1), 1–23.

Ryan, P. (2017, June 7). Can porn be feminist? These female directors say 'yes.' *USA Today*, 2D.

Sandfort, T. G. M., & Dodge, B. (2009). Homosexual and bisexual labels and behaviors among men: The need for clear conceptualizations, accurate operationalizations, and appropriate methodological designs. In V. Reddy, T. G. M. Sandfort, & R. Rispel (Eds.), *Perspectives on same-sex sexuality, gender and HIV/AIDS in South Africa: From social silence to social science* (pp. 51–57). Pretoria, South Africa: Human Sciences Research Council.

Schoenfeld, E. A., Loving, T. J., Pope, M. T., Huston, T. L., & Štulhofer, A. (2017). Does sex really matter? Examining the connections between spouses' nonsexual behaviors, sexual frequency, sexual satisfaction, and marital satisfaction. *Archives of Sexual Behavior*, *46*(2), 489–501.

Schweingruber, D., Cast, A. D., & Anahita, S. (2008). 'A story and a ring': Audience judgments about engagement proposals. *Sex Roles, 58*(3–4), 165–178.

Seligman, L., & Hardenburg, S. A. (2000). Assessment and treatment of paraphilias. *Journal of Counseling & Development, 78*(1), 107–113.

Sheff, E., & Hammers, C. (2011). The privilege of perversities: Race, class and education among polyamorists and kinksters. *Psychology & Sexuality, 2*(3), 198–223.

Shor, E., & Seida, K. (2019). "Harder and harder"? Is mainstream pornography becoming increasingly violent and do viewers prefer violent content? *Journal of Sex Research, 56*(1), 16–28.

Spanier, G. B., & Margolis, R. L. (1983). Marital separation and extramarital sexual behavior. *Journal of Sex Research, 19*(1), 23–48.

Star Wars Report. (2016, July 28). Star Wars: Aftermath: Life debt – A beyond the films review. Retrieved September 23, 2018, from http://www.starwarsreport.com/2016/07/28/star-wars-aftermath-life-debt-a-beyond-the-films-review/

Steele, V. R., Staley, C., Fong, T., & Prause, N. (2013). Sexual desire, not hypersexuality, is related to neurophysiological responses elicited by sexual images. *Socioaffective Neuroscience & Psychology, 3*(1), 20770.

Stoller, R. J., & Herdt, G. H. (1982). The development of masculinity: A cross-cultural contribution. *Journal of the American Psychoanalytic Association, 30*(1), 29–59.

Storms, M. D. (1978). Sexual orientation and self-perception. In P. Pliner, K. R. Blanstein, I. M. Spigel, T. Alloway, & L. Krames (Eds.), *Advances in the study of communication and affect: Vol. 5, Perception of emotion in self and others* (pp. 165–180). New York, NY: Plenum.

Storms, M. D. (1980). Theories of sexual orientation. *Journal of Personality & Social Psychology, 38*(5), 783–792.

Thaczuk, D. (2007, June 28). MSM in Africa: Highly stigmatised, vulnerable and in need of urgent HIV prevention. *AIDSmap.* Retrieved September 24, 2018, from https://web.archive.org/web/20070701184934/http://www.aidsmap.com:80/en/news/16F65073-E5CE-40B9-B189-50763B6B8E06.asp

Toma, C. L., Hancock, J. T., & Ellison, N. B. (2008). Separating fact from fiction: An examination of deceptive self-presentation in online dating profiles. *Personality and Social Psychology Bulletin, 34*(8), 1023–1036.

Tooke, W., & Camire, L. (1991). Patterns of deception in intersexual and intrasexual mating strategies. *Ethology and Sociobiology, 12*(5), 345–364.

Turner Syndrome. (2018). *Genetics Home Reference.* Retrieved September 23, 2018, from https://ghr.nlm.nih.gov/condition/turner-syndrome

Valkenburg, P. M., & Peter, J. (2007). Who visits online dating sites? Exploring some characteristics of online daters. *CyberPsychology & Behavior, 10*(6), 849–852.

Veaux, F., & Rickert, E. (2014). *More than two: A practical guide to ethical polyamory.* Portland, OR: Thorntontree Press.

Walton, M. T., Lykins, A. D., & Bhullar, N. (2016). Beyond heterosexual, bisexual, and homosexual: A diversity in sexual identity expression. *Archives of Sexual Behavior, 45*(7), 1591–1597.

Warn, S. (2003). VMA's Madonna-Britney-Christina kiss: Progress or publicity stunt? *Afterellen.com.* As quoted in Diamond (2005).

Wendig, C. (2016). *Star Wars: Aftermath.* New York, NY: Del Rey.

Wilkinson, S. (1996, May). Bisexuality "a la mode." *Women's Studies International Forum, 19*(3), 293–301.

Wosick-Correa, K. (2010). Agreements, rules and agentic fidelity in polyamorous relationships. *Psychology & Sexuality, 1*(1), 44–61.

Yarber, W. L., & Sayad, B. (2016). *Human sexuality: Diversity in contemporary America* (9th ed). New York, NY: McGraw-Hill.

Zanna, M. P., & Pack, S. J. (1975). On the self-fulfilling nature of apparent sex differences in behavior. *Journal of Experimental Social Psychology, 11*(6), 583–591.

Zurbriggen, E. L., & Yost, M. R. (2004). Power, desire, and pleasure in sexual fantasies. *Journal of Sex Research, 41*(3), 288–300.

Chapter 10

Ambady, N., Hallahan, M., & Conner, B. (1999). Accuracy of judgments of sexual orientation from thin slices of behavior. *Journal of Personality and Social Psychology, 77*(3), 538–547.

Ambady, N., Krabbenhoft, M. A., & Hogan, D. (2006). The 30-sec sale: Using thin-slice judgments to evaluate sales effectiveness. *Journal of Consumer Psychology, 16*(1), 4–13.

Ambady, N., & Rosenthal, R. (1993). Half a minute: Predicting teacher evaluations from thin slices of nonverbal behavior and physical attractiveness. *Journal of Personality and Social Psychology, 64*(3), 431–441.

Asch, S. E. (1946). Forming impressions of personality. *Journal of Abnormal and Social Psychology, 41*(3), 258–290.

Bar, M., Neta, M., & Linz, H. (2006). Very first impressions. *Emotion, 6*(2), 269–278.

Baumeister, R. F. (1998). The self. In D. Gilbert, S. Fiske, & G. Lindzey (Eds.), *Handbook of social psychology* (4th ed., pp. 680–740). Boston, MA: McGraw-Hill.

Bazzini, D. G., & Shaffer, D. R. (1995). Investigating the social-adjustive and value-expressive functions of well-grounded attitudes: Implications for change and for subsequent behavior. *Motivation and Emotion, 19*(4), 279–305.

Blanck, P. D., Rosenthal, R., Hart, A. J., & Bernieri, F. (1990). The measure of the judge: An empirically-based framework for exploring trial judges' behavior. *Iowa Law Review, 75*, 653–684.

Brockner, J. (1984). Low self-esteem and behavioral plasticity: Some implications for personality and social psychology. *Review of Personality and Social Psychology, 4*, 237–271.

Brookings, J. B., & Serratelli, A. J. (2006). Positive illusions: Positively correlated with subjective well-being, negatively correlated with a measure of personal growth. *Psychological Reports, 98*(2), 407–413.

Camp, P., & Ganong, L. (1997). Locus of control and marital satisfaction in long-term marriages. *Families in Society: The Journal of Contemporary Social Services, 78*(6), 624–631.

Catania, J. A., & White, C. B. (1982). Sexuality in an aged sample: Cognitive determinants of masturbation. *Archives of Sexual Behavior, 11*(3), 237–245.

Cobb, R. A., DeWall, C. N., Lambert, N. M., & Fincham, F. D. (2013). Implicit theories of relationships and close relationship violence: Does believing your relationship can grow relate to lower perpetration of violence? *Personality and Social Psychology Bulletin, 39*(3), 279–290.

Constantine, J. A., & Bahr, S. J. (1980). Locus of control and marital stability: A longitudinal study. *Journal of Divorce, 4*(1), 11–22.

Cox, C. R., & Arndt, J. (2012). How sweet it is to be loved by you: The role of perceived regard in the terror management of close relationships. *Journal of Personality and Social Psychology, 102*(3), 616–632.

Darley, J. M., & Gross, P. H. (1983). A hypothesis-confirming bias in labeling effects. *Journal of Personality and Social Psychology, 44*(1), 20–33.

Dijkstra, P., Barelds, D. P., Groothof, H. A., & Van Bruggen, M. (2014). Empathy in intimate relationships: The role of positive illusions. *Scandinavian Journal of Psychology, 55*(5), 477–482.

Dill, K. E., & Thill, K. P. (2007). Video game characters and the socialization of gender roles: Young people's perceptions mirror sexist media depictions. *Sex Roles, 57*(11–12), 851–864.

Dilmac, B., Hamarta, E., & Arslan, C. (2009). Analysing the trait anxiety and locus of control of undergraduates in terms of attachment styles. *Educational Sciences: Theory and Practice, 9*(1), 143–159.

Doherty, W. J., & Ryder, R. G. (1979). Locus of control, interpersonal trust, and assertive behavior among newlyweds. *Journal of Personality and Social Psychology, 37*(12), 2212–2220.

Drigotas, S. M., Rusbult, C. E., Wieselquist, J., & Whitton, S. W. (1999). Close partner as sculptor of the ideal self: Behavioral affirmation and the Michelangelo phenomenon. *Journal of Personality and Social Psychology, 77*(2), 293–323.

Dweck, C. S. (1996). Implicit theories as organizers of goals and behavior. In P. M. Gollwitzer & J. A. Bargh (Eds.), *The psychology of action: Linking cognition and motivation to behavior* (pp. 69–90). New York, NY: Guilford Press.

Dweck, C. S. (2006). *Mindset.* New York, NY: Ballantine Books.

Dweck, C. S. (2013). Self-theories: Their role in motivation, personality, and development. In R. Dienstbier (Ed.), *Nebraska Symposium of Motivation: Vol. 38. Perspectives on motivation* (pp. 199–235). Lincoln: University of Nebraska Press.

Dweck, C. S., Chiu, C. Y., & Hong, Y. Y. (1995). Implicit theories and their role in judgments and reactions: A word from two perspectives. *Psychological Inquiry, 6*(4), 267–285.

Dweck, C. S., Hong, Y. Y., & Chiu, C. Y. (1993). Implicit theories individual differences in the likelihood and meaning of dispositional inference. *Personality and Social Psychology Bulletin, 19*(5), 644–656.

Eden, D. (1990). *Pygmalion in management: Productivity as a self-fulfilling prophecy.* Lexington, MA: Lexington Books.

Feeney, J. A., Peterson, C., Gallois, C., & Terry, D. J. (2000). Attachment style as a predictor of sexual attitudes and behavior in late adolescence. *Psychology & Health, 14*(6), 1105–1122.

Ferris, A. L., Smith, S. W., Greenberg, B. S., & Smith, S. L. (2007). The content of reality dating shows and viewer perceptions of dating. *Journal of Communication, 57*(3), 490–510.

Finkel, E. J., Burnette, J. L., & Scissors, L. E. (2007). Vengefully ever after: Destiny beliefs, state attachment anxiety, and forgiveness. *Journal of Personality and Social Psychology, 92*(5), 871–886.

Florian, V., Mikulincer, M., & Hirschberger, G. (2002). The anxiety-buffering function of close relationships: Evidence that relationship commitment acts as a terror management mechanism. *Journal of Personality and Social Psychology, 82*(4), 527–542.

Franiuk, R., Cohen, D., & Pomerantz, E. M. (2002). Implicit theories of relationships: Implications for relationship satisfaction and longevity. *Personal Relationships, 9*(4), 345–367.

Franiuk, R., Pomerantz, E. M., & Cohen, D. (2004). The causal role of theories of relationships: Consequences for satisfaction and cognitive strategies. *Personality and Social Psychology Bulletin, 30*(11), 1494–1507.

Freimuth, V. S., Hammond, S. L., Edgar, T., McDonald, D. A., & Fink, E. L. (1992). Factors explaining intent, discussion and use of condoms in first-time sexual encounters. *Health Education Research, 7*(2), 203–215.

Goethals, G. R., Messick, D. M., & Allison, S. T. (1991). The uniqueness bias: Studies of constructive social comparison. In J. Suls & T. A. Wills (Eds.), *Social comparison: Contemporary theory and research* (pp. 149–176). Hillsdale, NJ: Lawrence Erlbaum.

Gombrich, E. H. (1995). *The story of art* (16th ed.). London, England: Phaidon Press.

Goodfriend, W. (2004). *Partner-esteem: Romantic partners in the eyes of biased beholders.* Dissertation, Purdue University.

Goodfriend, W., Agnew, C. R., & Cathey, P. (2017). Understanding commitment and partner-serving biases in close relationships. In J. Fitzgerald (Ed.), *Foundations for couples' therapy: Research for the real world* (pp. 51–60). New York, NY: Routledge.

Greenberg, J., Pyszczynski, T., & Solomon, S. (1986). The causes and consequences of a need for self-esteem: A terror management theory. In *Public self and private self* (pp. 189–212). New York, NY: Springer.

Hay, E. L., & Fingerman, K. L. (2005). Age differences in perceptions of control in social relationships. *International Journal of Aging and Human Development, 60*(1), 53–75.

Hecht, M. A., & LaFrance, M. (1995). How (fast) can I help you? Tone of voice and telephone operator efficiency in interactions. *Journal of Applied Social Psychology, 25*(23), 2086–2098.

Hefner, V., & Wilson, B. J. (2013). From love at first sight to soul mate: The influence of romantic ideals in popular films on young people's beliefs about relationships. *Communication Monographs, 80*(2), 150–175.

Hirschberger, G., Florian, V., & Mikulincer, M. (2002). The anxiety buffering function of close relationships: Mortality salience effects on the readiness to compromise mate selection standards. *European Journal of Social Psychology, 32*(5), 609–625.

Hirschberger, G., Florian, V., & Mikulincer, M. (2003). Strivings for romantic intimacy following partner complaint or partner criticism: A terror management perspective. *Journal of Social and Personal Relationships, 20*(5), 675–687.

Hong, Y. Y., Chiu, C. Y., & Dweck, C. S. (1995). Implicit theories of intelligence. In M. Kernis (Ed.), *Efficacy, agency, and self-esteem* (pp. 197–216). New York, NY: Plenum.

Johnson, K. R., & Holmes, B. M. (2009). Contradictory messages: A content analysis of Hollywood-produced romantic comedy feature films. *Communication Quarterly, 57*(3), 352–373.

Jones, M. (1993). Influence of self-monitoring on dating motivations. *Journal of Research in Personality, 27*(2), 197–206.

Klein, H. A., Tatone, C. L., & Lindsay, N. B. (1989). Correlates of life satisfaction among military wives. *Journal of Psychology, 123*(5), 465–475.

Knee, C. R. (1998). Implicit theories of relationships: Assessment and prediction of romantic relationship initiation, coping, and longevity. *Journal of Personality and Social Psychology, 74*(2), 360–370.

Knee, C. R., Nanayakkara, A., Vietor, N. A., Neighbors, C., & Patrick, H. (2001). Implicit theories of relationships: Who cares if romantic partners are less than ideal? *Personality and Social Psychology Bulletin, 27*(7), 808–819.

Knee, C. R., Patrick, H., Vietor, N. A., & Neighbors, C. (2004). Implicit theories of relationships: Moderators of the link between conflict and commitment. *Personality and Social Psychology Bulletin, 30*(5), 617–628.

Kumashiro, M., Rusbult, C. E., Wolf, S. T., & Estrada, M. J. (2006). The Michelangelo phenomenon: Partner affirmation and self-movement toward one's ideal. In K. Vohs & E. Finkel (Eds.), *Self and relationships: Connecting intrapersonal and interpersonal processes* (pp. 317–341). New York, NY: Guilford Press.

Lantz, H. R., Schmitt, R., Britton, M., & Snyder, E. C. (1968). Pre-industrial patterns in the colonial family in America: A content analysis of colonial magazines. *American Sociological Review*, 413–426.

Learman, L. A., Avorn, J., Everitt, D. E., & Rosenthal, R. (1990). Pygmalion in the nursing home: The effects of caregiver expectations on patient outcomes. *Journal of the American Geriatrics Society, 38*(7), 797– 803.

Lee, S. W., & Schwarz, N. (2014). Framing love: When it hurts to think we were made for each other. *Journal of Experimental Social Psychology, 54*, 61–67.

Leone, C., & Hawkins, L. B. (2006). Self-monitoring and close relationships. *Journal of Personality, 74*(3), 739–778.

Loue, S., Cooper, M., Traore, F., & Fiedler, J. (2004). Locus of control and HIV risk among a sample of Mexican and Puerto Rican women. *Journal of Immigrant Health, 6*(4), 155–165.

Marks, G. (1984). Thinking one's abilities are unique and one's opinions are common. *Personality and Social Psychology Bulletin, 10*, 203–208.

Martz, J. M., Verette, J., Arriaga, X. B., Slovik, L. F., Cox, C. L., & Rusbult, C. E. (1998). Positive illusion in close relationships. *Personal Relationships, 5*, 159–181.

Maxwell, J. A., Muise, A., MacDonald, G., Day, L. C., Rosen, N. O., & Impett, E. A. (2017). How implicit theories of sexuality shape sexual and relationship well-being. *Journal of Personality and Social Psychology, 112*(2), 238–279.

Mercier, J. M., Paulson, L., & Morris, E. W. (1988). Rural and urban elderly: Differences in the quality of the parent-child relationship. *Family Relations, 37*, 68–72.

Mikulincer, M., & Florian, V. (2000). Exploring individual differences in reactions to mortality salience: Does attachment style regulate terror management mechanisms? *Journal of Personality and Social Psychology, 79*(2), 260–273.

Mikulincer, M., Florian, V., Birnbaum, G., & Malishkevich, S. (2002). The death-anxiety buffering function of close relationships: Exploring the effects of separation reminders on death-thought accessibility. *Personality and Social Psychology Bulletin, 28*(3), 287–299.

Mikulincer, M., Florian, V., & Hirschberger, G. (2003). The existential function of close relationships: Introducing death into the science of love. *Personality and Social Psychology Review, 7*(1), 20–40.

Miller, D. T., & Ross, M. (1975). Self-serving biases in the attribution of causality: Fact or fiction? *Psychological Bulletin, 82*, 213–225.

Miller, P. C., Lefcourt, H. M., Holmes, J. G., Ware, E. E., & Saleh, W. E. (1986). Marital locus of control and marital problem solving. *Journal of Personality and Social Psychology, 51*(1), 161–169.

Miller, P. C., Lefcourt, H. M., & Ware, E. E. (1983). The construction and development of the Miller Marital Locus of Control scale. *Canadian Journal of Behavioural Science, 15*(3), 266–279.

Morry, M. M. (2003). Perceived locus of control and satisfaction in same–sex friendships. *Personal Relationships, 10*(4), 495–509.

Morse, K. A., & Neuberg, S. L. (2004). How do holidays influence relationship processes and outcomes? Examining the instigating and catalytic effects of Valentine's Day. *Personal Relationships, 11*(4), 509–527.

Murray, S. L., & Holmes J. G. (1993). Seeing virtues in faults: Negativity and the transformation of interpersonal narratives in close relationships. *Journal of Personality and Social Psychology, 65*, 707–722.

Murray, S. L., & Holmes, J. G. (1994). Storytelling in close relationships: The construction of confidence. *Personality and Social Psychology Bulletin, 20*, 650–663.

Murray, S. L., & Holmes, J. G. (1997). A leap of faith? Positive illusions in romantic relationships. *Personality and Social Psychology Bulletin, 23*, 586–604.

Myers, D. G., & Diener, E. (1995). Who is happy? *Psychological Science, 6*, 10–19.

Norris, S. L., & Zweigenhaft, R. L. (1999). Self-monitoring, trust, and commitment in romantic relationships. *Journal of Social Psychology, 139*(2), 215–220.

Prager, K. J. (1986). Intimacy status: Its relationship to locus of control, self-disclosure, and anxiety in adults. *Personality and Social Psychology Bulletin, 12*(1), 91–109.

Pyszczynski, T., Greenberg, J., & Holt, K. (1985). Maintaining consistency between self-serving beliefs and available data: A bias in information processing. *Personality and Social Psychology Bulletin, 11*, 179–190.

Pyszczynski, T., Greenberg, J., & Solomon, S. (1999). A dual-process model of defense against conscious and unconscious death-related thoughts: An extension of terror management theory. *Psychological Review, 106*(4), 835–845.

Pyszczynski, T., Solomon, S., & Greenberg, J. (2003). *In the wake of 9/11: The psychology of terror.* Washington, DC: American Psychological Association.

Pyszczynski, T., Wicklund, R. A., Floresku, S., Koch, H., Gauch, G., Solomon, S., & Greenberg, J. (1996). Whistling in the dark: Exaggerated consensus estimates in response to incidental reminders of mortality. *Psychological Science, 7*(6), 332–336.

Rivadeneyra, R., & Lebo, M. J. (2008). The association between television-viewing behaviors and adolescent dating role attitudes and behaviors. *Journal of Adolescence, 31*(3), 291–305.

Rosenthal, R., & Jacobsen, L. (1968). *Pygmalion in the classroom: Self-fulfilling prophecies and teacher expectations.* New York, NY: Holt, Rhinehart, and Winston.

Rotter, J. B. (1966). Generalized expectancies for internal versus external control of reinforcement. *Psychological Monographs: General and Applied, 80*(1), 1–28.

Rotter, J. B. (1975). Some problems and misconceptions related to the construct of internal versus external control of reinforcement. *Journal of Consulting and Clinical Psychology, 43*(1), 56–67.

Rudman, L. A., & Heppen, J. B. (2003). Implicit romantic fantasies and women's interest in personal power: A glass slipper effect? *Personality and Social Psychology Bulletin, 29*(11), 1357–1370.

Rusbult, C. E., Coolsen, M., Kirchner, J., Stocker, S., Kumashiro, M., Wolf, S., ... Clarke, J. (2005). *Partner affirmation and target movement toward ideal in newly-committed relationships.* Unpublished manuscript, Vrije Universiteit, Amsterdam, Netherlands.

Rusbult, C. E., Finkel, E. J., & Kumashiro, M. (2009a). The Michelangelo phenomenon. *Current Directions in Psychological Science, 18*(6), 305–309.

Rusbult, C. E., Kumashiro, M., Kubacka, K. E., & Finkel, E. J. (2009b). "The part of me that you bring out": Ideal similarity and the Michelangelo phenomenon. *Journal of Personality and Social Psychology, 96*(1), 61–82.

Rusbult, C. E., Kumashiro, M., Stocker, S. L., Kirchner, J. L., Finkel, E. J., & Coolsen, M. K. (2005). Self processes in interdependent relationships: Partner affirmation and the Michelangelo phenomenon. *Interaction Studies, 6*(3), 375–391.

Schonert-Reichl, K. A., & Muller, J. R. (1996). Correlates of help-seeking in adolescence. *Journal of Youth and Adolescence, 25*(6), 705–731.

Segrin, C., & Nabi, R. L. (2002). Does television viewing cultivate unrealistic expectations about marriage? *Journal of Communication, 52*(2), 247–263.

Snyder, M. (1974). Self-monitoring of expressive behavior. *Journal of Personality and Social Psychology, 30*(4), 526–537.

Snyder, M., & Gangestad, S. (1986). On the nature of self-monitoring: Matters of assessment, matters of validity. *Journal of Personality and Social Psychology, 51*(1), 125–139.

Snyder, M., & Simpson, J. A. (1984). Self-monitoring and dating relationships. *Journal of Personality and Social Psychology, 47*(6), 1281–1291.

Snyder, M., Simpson, J. A., & Gangestad, S. (1986). Personality and sexual relations. *Journal of Personality and Social Psychology, 51*(1), 181–190.

Sprecher, S., & Metts, S. (1989). Development of the 'Romantic Beliefs Scale' and examination of the effects of gender and gender-role orientation. *Journal of Social and Personal Relationships, 6*(4), 387–411.

Sprecher, S., & Metts, S. (1999). Romantic beliefs: Their influence on relationships and patterns of change over time. *Journal of Social and Personal Relationships, 16*(6), 834–851.

Steele, C. M. (1988). The psychology of self-affirmation: Sustaining the integrity of the self. In L. Berkowitz (Ed.), *Advances in experimental social psychology* (Vol. 21, pp. 261–302). New York, NY: Academic Press.

Suls, J., & Wan, C. K. (1987). In search of the false-uniqueness phenomenon: Fear and estimates of social consensus. *Journal of Personality and Social Psychology, 52*, 211–217.

Taylor, S. E. (1989). *Positive illusions: Creative self-deception and the healthy mind.* New York, NY: Basic Books.

Taylor, S. E., & Brown, J. D. (1988). Illusion and well-being: A social psychological perspective on mental health. *Psychological Bulletin, 103*, 193–210.

Tennen, H., & Herzberger, S. (1987). Depression, self-esteem, and the absence of self-protective attributional biases. *Journal of Personality and Social Psychology, 52*, 72–80.

Terry, D. J. (1991). Stress, coping and adaptation to new parenthood. *Journal of Social and Personal Relationships, 8*(4), 527–547.

Whiteley, P., Sy, T., & Johnson, S. K. (2012). Leaders' conceptions of followers: Implications for naturally occurring Pygmalion effects. *Leadership Quarterly, 23*(5), 822–834.

Willis, J., & Todorov, A. (2006). First impressions: Making up your mind after a 100-ms exposure to a face. *Psychological Science, 17*(7), 592–598.

Wisman, A., & Goldenberg, J. L. (2005). From the grave to the cradle: Evidence that mortality salience engenders a desire for offspring. *Journal of Personality and Social Psychology, 89*(1), 46–61.

Wood, E., Senn, C. Y., Desmarais, S., Park, L., & Verberg, N. (2002). Sources of information about dating and their perceived influence on adolescents. *Journal of Adolescent Research, 17*(4), 401–417.

Zurbriggen, E. L., & Morgan, E. M. (2006). Who wants to marry a millionaire? Reality dating television programs, attitudes toward sex, and sexual behaviors. *Sex Roles, 54*(1–2), 1–17.

Chapter 11

Acitelli, L. K., & Young, A. M. (1996). Gender and thought in relationships. Knowledge structures in close relationships. In G. J. O. Fletcher & J. Fitness (Eds.), *Knowledge structures in close relationships: A social psychological approach* (pp. 147–168). Mahwah, NJ: Lawrence Erlbaum.

Ackerman, R. A., Kashy, D. A., Donnellan, M. B., Neppl, T., Lorenz, F. O., & Conger, R. D. (2013). The interpersonal legacy of a positive family climate in adolescence. *Psychological Science, 24*(3), 243–250.

Agnew, C. R., Loving, T. J., & Drigotas, S. M. (2001). Substituting the forest for the trees: Social networks and the prediction of romantic relationship state and fate. *Journal of Personality and Social Psychology, 81*(6), 1042–1057.

Appel, H., Gerlach, A. L., & Crusius, J. (2016). The interplay between Facebook use, social comparison, envy, and depression. *Current Opinion in Psychology, 9*, 44–49.

Aries, E. (1996). *Men and women in interaction: Reconsidering the differences.* New York, NY: Oxford University Press.

Aron, A., Melinat, E., Aron, E. N., Vallone, R. D., & Bator, R. J. (1997). The experimental generation of interpersonal closeness: A procedure and some preliminary findings. *Personality and Social Psychology Bulletin, 23*(4), 363–377.

Barnard, C. (Producer), Jonze, S. (Director). 2013. *Her* [Motion picture]. United States: Annapurna Pictures.

Baxter, L. A., & Montgomery, B. M. (1996). *Relating: Dialogues and dialectics.* New York, NY: Guilford Press.

Bermudez, J. M., Reyes, N. A., & Wampler, K. S. (2006). Conflict resolution styles among Latino couples. *Journal of Couple & Relationship Therapy, 5*(4), 1–21.

Bermúdez, J. M., & Stinson, M. A. (2011). Redefining conflict resolution styles for Latino couples: Examining the role of gender and culture. *Journal of Feminist Family Therapy, 23*(2), 71–87.

Blake, R., & Mouton, J. (1964). *The managerial grid: The key to leadership excellence.* Houston, TX: Gulf.

Bowe, G. (2010). Reading romance: The impact Facebook rituals can have on a romantic relationship. *Journal of Comparative Research in Anthropology & Sociology, 1*(2), 61–77.

Bradbury, T. N., Fincham, F. D., & Beach, S. R. (2000). Research on the nature and determinants of marital satisfaction: A decade in review. *Journal of Marriage and Family, 62*(4), 964–980.

Brundage, L. E., Derlega, V. J., & Cash, T. F. (1976). The effects of physical attractiveness and need for approval on self-disclosure. *Personality and Social Psychology Bulletin, 3*(1), 63–66.

Buckels, E. E., Trapnell, P. D., & Paulhus, D. L. (2014). Trolls just want to have fun. *Personality and Individual Differences, 67*, 97–102.

Busby, D. M., & Holman, T. B. (2009). Perceived match or mismatch on the Gottman conflict styles: Associations with relationship outcome variables. *Family Process, 48*(4), 531–545.

Cai, D., & Fink, E. (2002). Conflict style differences between individualists and collectivists. *Communication Monographs, 69*(1), 67–87.

Chotpitayasunondh, V., & Douglas, K. M. (2016). How "phubbing" becomes the norm: The antecedents and consequences of snubbing via smartphone. *Computers in Human Behavior, 63*, 9–18.

Craker, N., & March, E. (2016). The dark side of Facebook: The Dark Tetrad, negative social potency, and trolling behaviours. *Personality and Individual Differences, 102*, 79–84.

Creasey, G. (2002). Associations between working models of attachment and conflict management behavior in romantic couples. *Journal of Counseling Psychology, 49*(3), 365–375.

Creasey, G., & Hesson-McInnis, M. (2001). Affective responses, cognitive appraisals, and conflict tactics in late adolescent romantic relationships: Associations with attachment orientations. *Journal of Counseling Psychology, 48*(1), 85–96.

Creasey, G., Kershaw, K., & Boston, A. (1999). Conflict management with friends and romantic partners: The role of attachment and negative mood regulation expectancies. *Journal of Youth and Adolescence, 28*(5), 523–543.

Cross, S. E., & Madson, L. (1997). Models of the self: Self-construals and gender. *Psychological Bulletin, 122*(1), 5–37.

Cupach, W. R., & Canary, D. J. (1995). Managing conflict and anger: Investigating the sex stereotype hypothesis. In P. J. Kalbfleisch & M. J. Cody (Eds.), *Gender, power, and communication in human relationships* (pp. 233–252). Hillsdale, NJ: Lawrence Erlbaum.

Cupples, J., & Thompson, L. (2010). Heterotextuality and digital foreplay: Cell phones and the culture of teenage romance. *Feminist Media Studies, 10*(1), 1–17.

Debrot, A., Schoebi, D., Perrez, M., & Horn, A. B. (2013). Touch as an interpersonal emotion regulation process in couples' daily lives: The mediating role of psychological intimacy. *Personality and Social Psychology Bulletin, 39*(10), 1373–1385.

Dolgin, K. G., & Minowa, N. (1997). Gender differences in self-presentation: A comparison of the roles of flatteringness and intimacy in self-disclosure to friends. *Sex Roles, 36*(5–6), 371–380.

Duran, R. L., Kelly, L., & Rotaru, T. (2011). Mobile phones in romantic relationships and the dialectic of autonomy versus connection. *Communication Quarterly, 59*(1), 19–36.

Ekman, P., Friesen, W. V., & Ellsworth, P. (1972). *Emotion in the human face: Guidelines for research and a review of findings.* New York, NY: Permagon.

Elphinston, R. A., & Noller, P. (2011). Time to face it! Facebook intrusion and the implications for romantic jealousy and relationship satisfaction. *Cyberpsychology, Behavior, and Social Networking, 14*(11), 631–635.

Emmen, R. A., Malda, M., Mesman, J., van IJzendoorn, M. H., Prevoo, M. J., & Yeniad, N. (2013). Socioeconomic status and parenting in ethnic minority families: Testing a minority family stress model. *Journal of Family Psychology, 27*(6), 896–904.

Fine, M., & McClelland, S. (2006). Sexuality education and desire: Still missing after all these years. *Harvard Educational Review*, *76*(3), 297–338.

Finkel, E. J., Eastwick, P. W., Karney, B. R., Reis, H. T., & Sprecher, S. (2012). Online dating: A critical analysis from the perspective of psychological science. *Psychological Science in the Public Interest*, *13*(1), 3–66.

Fitzpatrick, M. A. (1987). Marriage and verbal intimacy. In V. J. Derlega & J. H. Berg (Eds.), *Self-disclosure: Theory, research, and therapy* (pp. 131–154). New York, NY: Plenum Press.

Freedman, G., Powell, D. N., Le, B., & Williams, K. D. (2019). Ghosting and destiny: Implicit theories of relationships predict beliefs about ghosting. *Journal of Social and Personal Relationships*, *36*(3), 905–924.

Gibbs, J. L., Ellison, N. B., & Lai, C. H. (2011). First comes love, then comes Google: An investigation of uncertainty reduction strategies and self-disclosure in online dating. *Communication Research*, *38*(1), 70–100.

Gordon-Messer, D., Bauermeister, J. A., Grodzinski, A., & Zimmerman, M. (2013). Sexting among young adults. *Journal of Adolescent Health*, *52*(3), 301–306.

Gottman, J. M. (1979). *Marital interaction: Experimental investigations*. New York, NY: Academic Press.

Gottman, J. M. (1993). The roles of conflict engagement, escalation, and avoidance in marital interaction: A longitudinal view of five types of couples. *Journal of Consulting and Clinical Psychology*, *61*(1), 6–15.

Gottman, J. M. (1999). *The marriage clinic: A scientifically-based marital therapy*. New York, NY: Norton.

Gottman, J. M., & Carrère, S. (1994). Why can't men and women get along? Developmental roots and marital inequities. In D. J. Canary & L. Stafford (Eds.), *Communication and relational maintenance* (pp. 203–229). San Diego, CA: Academic Press.

Greeff, A. P., & De Bruyne, T. (2000). Conflict management style and marital satisfaction. *Journal of Sex & Marital Therapy*, *26*(4), 321–334.

Hand, M. M., Thomas, D., Buboltz, W. C., Deemer, E. D., & Buyanjargal, M. (2013). Facebook and romantic relationships: Intimacy and couple satisfaction associated with online social network use. *Cyberpsychology, Behavior, and Social Networking*, *16*(1), 8–13.

Hardaker, C. (2010). Trolling in asynchronous computer-mediated communication: From user discussions to academic definitions. *Journal of Polymer Research*, *6*, 215–242.

Hartup, W. W. (1992). Conflict and friendship relations. In C. U. Shantz & W. W. Hartup (Eds.), *Conflict in child and adolescent development* (pp. 186–215). New York, NY: Cambridge University Press.

Hasinoff, A. A. (2013). Sexting as media production: Rethinking social media and sexuality. *New Media & Society*, *15*(4), 449–465.

Hertenstein, M. J. (2011). The communicative functions of touch in adulthood. In M. Hertenstein & S. Weiss (Eds.), *The handbook of touch: Neuroscience, behavioral, and health perspectives* (pp. 299–327). New York, NY: Springer.

Hitsch, G. J., Hortaçsu, A., & Ariely, D. (2010). What makes you click? Mate preferences in online dating. *Quantitative Marketing and Economics*, *8*(4), 393–427.

Hobbs, M., Owen, S., & Gerber, L. (2017). Liquid love? Dating apps, sex, relationships and the digital transformation of intimacy. *Journal of Sociology*, *53*(2), 271–284.

Hojjat, M. (2000). Sex differences and perceptions of conflict in romantic relationships. *Journal of Social and Personal Relationships*, *17*(4–5), 598–617.

Holman, T. B., & Jarvis, M. O. (2003). Hostile, volatile, avoiding, and validating couple-conflict types: An investigation of Gottman's couple-conflict types. *Personal Relationships*, *10*(2), 267–282.

Holt, J. L., & DeVore, C. J. (2005). Culture, gender, organizational role, and styles of conflict resolution: A meta-analysis. *International Journal of Intercultural Relations*, *29*(2), 165–196.

Human Performance Resource Center. (2019). How conflict can work for couples. Retrieved February 28, 2019, from https://www.hprc-online.org/articles/how-conflict-can-work-for-couples

Jin, B., & Park, N. (2013). Mobile voice communication and loneliness: Cell phone use and the social skills deficit hypothesis. *New Media & Society*, *15*(7), 1094–1111.

Joinson, A. N. (2008, April). Looking at, looking up or keeping up with people? Motives and use of Facebook. *Proceedings of the SIGCHI Conference on Human Factors in Computing Systems*, 1027–1036.

Jones, W. H., Hobbs, S. A., & Hockenbury, D. (1982). Loneliness and social skill deficits. *Journal of Personality and Social Psychology, 42*(4), 682–689.

Krasnova, H., Abramova, O., Notter, I., & Baumann, A. (2016). *Why phubbing is toxic for your relationship: Understanding the role of smartphone jealousy among "Generation Y" users.* Paper presented at the 24th European Conference on Information Systems, Istanbul, Turkey.

Kurdek, L. A. (1994). Conflict resolution styles in gay, lesbian, heterosexual nonparent, and heterosexual parent couples. *Journal of Marriage and the Family, 56,* 705–722.

Kurdek, L. A. (1995). Lesbian and gay couples. In A. R. D'Augelli & C. J. Patterson (Eds.), *Lesbian, gay, and bisexual identities over the lifespan* (pp. 243–261). New York, NY: Oxford University Press.

Lampe, C., Ellison, N., & Steinfield, C. (2006, November). A Face(book) in the crowd: Social searching vs. social browsing. *Proceedings of the 2006 20th Anniversary Conference on Computer Supported Cooperative Work,* 167–170.

LeFebvre, L. (2017). Ghosting as a relationship dissolution strategy in the technological age. In N. M. Punyanunt-Carter & J. S. Wrench (Eds.), *The impact of social media in modern romantic relationships* (pp. 219–235). New York, NY: Lexington Books.

LeFebvre, L. E. (2018). Swiping me off my feet: Explicating relationship initiation on Tinder. *Journal of Social and Personal Relationships, 35*(9), 1205–1229.

Lehmiller, J. (2018). *Tell me what you want: The science of sexual desire and how it can help you improve your sex life.* New York, NY: Da Capo Press.

Lenhart, A. (2009). Teens and sexting. *Pew Internet & American Life Project, 1,* 1–26.

Leshnoff, J. (2009). Sexting not just for kids. *AARP. org.* Retrieved from https://www.aarp.org/relationships/love-sex/info-11-2009/sexting_not_just_for_kids.html

Livingstone, S. (2008). Taking risky opportunities in youthful content creation: Teenagers' use of social networking sites for intimacy, privacy and self-expression. *New Media & Society, 10*(3), 393–411.

March, E., Grieve, R., Marrington, J., & Jonason, P. K. (2017). Trolling on Tinder (and other dating apps): Examining the role of the Dark Tetrad and impulsivity. *Personality and Individual Differences, 110,* 139–143.

Margolin, G., & Wampold, B. E. (1981). Sequential analysis of conflict and accord in distressed and nondistressed marital partners. *Journal of Consulting and Clinical Psychology, 49*(4), 554–567.

Monsour, M. (1992). Meanings of intimacy in cross- and same-sex friendships. *Journal of Social and Personal Relationships, 9*(2), 277–295.

Morey, J. N., Gentzler, A. L., Creasy, B., Oberhauser, A. M., & Westerman, D. (2013). Young adults' use of communication technology within their romantic relationships and associations with attachment style. *Computers in Human Behavior, 29*(4), 1771–1778.

Muise, A., Christofides, E., & Desmarais, S. (2009). More information than you ever wanted: Does Facebook bring out the green-eyed monster of jealousy? *CyberPsychology & Behavior, 12*(4), 441–444.

Noller, P., & Fitzpatrick, M. A. (1988). *Perspectives on marital interaction* (Vol. 1). Bristol, England: Multilingual Matters.

Papp, L. M., Cummings, E. M., & Goeke-Morey, M. C. (2009). For richer, for poorer: Money as a topic of marital conflict in the home. *Family Relations, 58*(1), 91–103.

Pearson, V. M., & Stephan, W. G. (1998). Preferences for styles of negotiation: A comparison of Brazil and the US. *International Journal of Intercultural Relations, 22*(1), 67–83.

Penney, T. (2014). Bodies under glass: Gay dating apps and the affect-image. *Media International Australia, 153*(1), 107–117.

Pike, G. R., & Sillars, A. L. (1985). Reciprocity of marital communication. *Journal of Social and Personal Relationships, 2*(3), 303–324.

Pistole, M. C. (1989). Attachment in adult romantic relationships: Style of conflict resolution and relationship satisfaction. *Journal of Social and Personal Relationships, 6*(4), 505–510.

Powell, A. (2010). Configuring consent: Emerging technologies, unauthorized sexual images and sexual assault. *Australian & New Zealand Journal of Criminology, 43*(1), 76–90.

Putnam, L. L., & Poole, M. S. (1987). Conflict and negotiation. In F. M. Jablin, L. L. Putnam, K H.

Roberts, & L. W. Porter (Eds), *Handbook of organizational communication*. Thousand Oaks, CA: Sage.

Ramirez, A. Jr., Dimmick, J., Feaster, J., & Lin, S. F. (2008). Revisiting interpersonal media competition: The gratification niches of instant messaging, e-mail, and the telephone. *Communication Research, 35*(4), 529–547.

Rands, M., Levinger, G., & Mellinger, G. D. (1981). Patterns of conflict resolution and marital satisfaction. *Journal of Family Issues, 2*(3), 297–321.

Raush, H. L., Barry, W. A., Hertel, R. K., & Swain, M. A. (1974). *Communication, conflict, and marriage*. San Francisco, CA: Jossey-Bass.

Rawlins, W. (2017). *Friendship matters*. New York, NY: Routledge.

Reid, D. J., & Reid, F. J. (2007). Text or talk? Social anxiety, loneliness, and divergent preferences for cell phone use. *CyberPsychology & Behavior, 10*(3), 424–435.

Reis, H. T., & Patrick, B. C. (1996). Attachment and intimacy: Component processes. In E. T. Higgins & A. W. Kruglanski (Eds.), *Social psychology: Handbook of basic principles* (pp. 523–563). New York, NY: Guilford Press.

Reis, H. T., & Shaver, P. (1988). Intimacy as an interpersonal process. In S. Duck, D. F. Hay, S. E. Hobfoll, W. Ickes, & B. M. Montgomery (Eds.), *Handbook of personal relationships: Theory, research and interventions* (pp. 367–389). Oxford, England: John Wiley & Sons.

Ringrose, J., Gill, R., Livingstone, S., & Harvey, L. (2012). *A qualitative study of children, young people and "sexting": A report prepared for the NSPCC*. London, England: National Society for the Prevention of Cruelty to Children.

Roberts, J. A., & David, M. E. (2016). My life has become a major distraction from my cell phone: Partner phubbing and relationship satisfaction among romantic partners. *Computers in Human Behavior, 54*, 134–141.

Ruble, T. L., & Thomas, K. W. (1976). Support for a two-dimensional model of conflict behavior. *Organizational Behavior and Human Performance, 16*(1), 143–155.

Rusbult, C. E., Johnson, D. J., & Morrow, G. D. (1986). Impact of couple patterns of problem solving on distress and nondistress in dating relationships. *Journal of Personality and Social Psychology, 50*(4), 744–753.

Rusbult, C. E., Zembrodt, I. M., & Gunn, L. K. (1982). Exit, voice, loyalty, and neglect: Responses to dissatisfaction in romantic involvements. *Journal of Personality and Social Psychology, 43*(6), 1230–1242.

Safronova, V. (2015, June 26). Exes explain ghosting, the ultimate silent treatment. *The New York Times*. Retrieved from https://www.nytimes.com/2015/06/26/fashion/exes-explain-ghosting-the-ultimate-silent-treatment.html

Sales, N. J. (2015). Tinder and the dawn of the "Dating Apocalypse." *Vanity Fair*. Retrieved from http://vanityfair.com

Schaap, C., Buunk, B., & Kerkstra, A. (1988). *Marital conflict resolution*. Bristol, England: Multilingual Matters.

Segrin, C. (1996). Interpersonal communication problems associated with depression and loneliness. In P. A. Anderson & L. H. Guerrero (Eds.), *Handbook of communication and emotion* (pp. 215–242). San Diego, CA: Academic Press.

Shulman, S., Tuval-Mashiach, R., Levran, E., & Anbar, S. (2006). Conflict resolution patterns and longevity of adolescent romantic couples: A 2-year follow-up study. *Journal of Adolescence, 29*(4), 575–588.

Sinclair, L., & Fehr, B. (2005). Voice versus loyalty: Self-construals and responses to dissatisfaction in romantic relationships. *Journal of Experimental Social Psychology, 41*(3), 298–304.

Smith, A. (2016). 15% of American adults have used online dating sites or mobile dating apps. *Pew Research Center*. Retrieved from http://www.pewinternet.org

Smith, A., & Duggan, M. (2013, October 21). Online dating and relationships. *Pew Research Center Internet & Technology*. Retrieved October 9, 2018, from http://www.pewinternet.org/2013/10/21/online-dating-relationships/

Stern, L. A., & Taylor, K. (2007). Social networking on Facebook. *Journal of the Communication, Speech & Theatre Association of North Dakota, 20*, 9–20.

Sumter, S. R., Vandenbosch, L., & Ligtenberg, L. (2017). Love me Tinder: Untangling emerging adults' motivations for using the dating application Tinder. *Telematics and Informatics, 34*(1), 67–78.

Thomas, K. W. (1976). Conflict and conflict management. In M. D. Dunnette (Ed.), *Handbook of industrial and organizational psychology* (pp. 889–935). Chicago, IL: Rand McNally.

Thomas, K. W. (1992). Conflict and conflict management: Reflections and update. *Journal of Organizational Behavior, 13*(3), 265–274.

Thurlow, C., & Bell, K. (2009). Against technologization: Young people's new media discourse as creative cultural practice. *Journal of Computer-Mediated Communication, 14*(4), 1038–1049.

Tokunaga, R. S. (2011). Social networking site or social surveillance site? Understanding the use of interpersonal electronic surveillance in romantic relationships. *Computers in Human Behavior, 27*(2), 705–713.

Tolman, D. L. (2009). *Dilemmas of desire: Teenage girls talk about sexuality.* Boston, MA: Harvard University Press.

Tooke, W., & Camire, L. (1991). Patterns of deception in intersexual and intrasexual mating strategies. *Ethology and Sociobiology, 12*(5), 345–364.

Utz, S., & Beukeboom, C. J. (2011). The role of social network sites in romantic relationships: Effects on jealousy and relationship happiness. *Journal of Computer-Mediated Communication, 16*(4), 511–527.

Valenzuela, S., Park, N., & Kee, K. F. (2009). Is there social capital in a social network site? Facebook use and college students' life satisfaction, trust, and participation. *Journal of Computer-Mediated Communication, 14*(4), 875–901.

Valkenburg, P. M., Peter, J., & Schouten, A. P. (2006). Friend networking sites and their relationship to adolescents' well-being and social self-esteem. *CyberPsychology & Behavior, 9*(5), 584–590.

Van de Vliert, E., & Hordijk, J. W. (1986). *The cognitive distance between compromising and other styles of conflict management.* Paper presented at the 21st International Congress of Applied Psychology, Jerusalem, Israel.

Wagner, H. L., MacDonald, C. J., & Manstead, A. S. (1986). Communication of individual emotions by spontaneous facial expressions. *Journal of Personality and Social Psychology, 50*(4), 737–743.

Wang, X., Xie, X., Wang, Y., Wang, P., & Lei, L. (2017). Partner phubbing and depression among married Chinese adults: The roles of relationship satisfaction and relationship length. *Personality and Individual Differences, 110*, 12–17.

Ward, J. (2016). Swiping, matching, chatting: Self-presentation and self-disclosure on mobile dating apps. *Human IT: Journal for Information Technology Studies as a Human Science, 13*(2), 81–95.

Waring, E. M., Tillman, M. P., Frelick, M. D., Russell, L., & Weisz, G. (1980). Concepts of intimacy in the general population. *Journal of Nervous and Mental Disease, 168*, 471–474.

Weisbuch, M., Ambady, N., Clarke, A. L., Achor, S., & Weele, J. V. V. (2010). On being consistent: The role of verbal–nonverbal consistency in first impressions. *Basic and Applied Social Psychology, 32*(3), 261–268.

Weiser, D. A., & Weigel, D. J. (2014). Testing a model of communication responses to relationship infidelity. *Communication Quarterly, 62*(4), 416–435.

Weisskirch, R. S. (2012). Women's adult romantic attachment style and communication by cell phone with romantic partners. *Psychological Reports, 111*(1), 281–288.

Wheeler, L. A., Updegraff, K. A., & Thayer, S. M. (2010). Conflict resolution in Mexican-origin couples: Culture, gender, and marital quality. *Journal of Marriage and Family, 72*(4), 991–1005.

Yeo, T. E. D., & Fung, T. H. (2018). "Mr. Right Now": Temporality of relationship formation on gay mobile dating apps. *Mobile Media & Communication, 6*(1), 3–18.

Chapter 12

Anderson, K. M., Renner, L. M., & Danis, F. S. (2012). Recovery: Resilience and growth in the aftermath of domestic violence. *Violence Against Women, 18*(11), 1279–1299.

Arnocky, S., & Vaillancourt, T. (2014). Sex differences in response to victimization by an intimate partner: More stigmatization and less help-seeking among males. *Journal of Aggression, Maltreatment & Trauma, 23*(7), 705–724.

Arriaga, X. B. (2002). Joking violence among highly committed individuals. *Journal of Interpersonal Violence, 17*(6), 591–610.

Arriaga, X. B., Capezza, N. M., Goodfriend, W., Rayl, E. S., & Sands, K. J. (2013). Individual well-being and relationship maintenance at odds: The unexpected perils of maintaining a relationship with an aggressive partner. *Social Psychological and Personality Science*, *4*(6), 676–684.

Association of American Universities. (2019). Report on the AAU campus climate survey on sexual assault and misconduct. Retrieved October 16, 2019, from https://www.aau.edu/key-issues/campus-climate-and-safety/aau-campus-climate-survey-2019

Banyard, V. L. (2011). Who will help prevent sexual violence: Creating an ecological model of bystander intervention. *Psychology of Violence*, *1*(3), 216–229.

Banyard, V. L., Moynihan, M. M., & Plante, E. G. (2007). Sexual violence prevention through bystander education: An experimental evaluation. *Journal of Community Psychology*, *35*(4), 463–481.

Banyard, V. L., Plante, E. G., & Moynihan, M. M. (2004). Bystander education: Bringing a broader community perspective to sexual violence prevention. *Journal of Community Psychology*, *32*(1), 61–79.

Barnett, O. W., Miller-Perrin, C. L., & Perrin, R. D. (1997). *Family violence across the lifespan: An introduction*. Thousand Oaks, CA: Sage.

Basile, K. C. (2002). Attitudes toward wife rape: Effects of social background and victim status. *Violence and Victims*, *17*(3), 341–354.

Berkowitz, A. D. (2002). Fostering men's responsibility for preventing sexual assault. In P. A. Schewe (Ed.), *Preventing violence in relationships: Interventions across the life span* (pp. 259–179). Washington, DC: American Psychological Association.

Boals, A., & Schuler, K. L. (2017). Reducing reports of illusory posttraumatic growth: A revised version of the Stress-Related Growth Scale (SRGS-R). *Psychological Trauma: Theory, Research, Practice, and Policy*, *10*(2), 19.

Boals, A., & Schuler, K. (2019). Shattered cell phones, but not shattered lives: A comparison of reports of illusory posttraumatic growth on the Posttraumatic Growth Inventory and the Stress-Related Growth Scale—Revised. *Psychological Trauma: Theory, Research, Practice, and Policy*, *11*(2), 239–246.

Breiding, M. J., Smith, S. G., Basile, K. C., Walters, M. L., Chen, J., & Merrick, M. T. (2014). Prevalence and characteristics of sexual violence, stalking, and intimate partner violence victimization—National intimate partner and sexual violence survey, United States, 2011. *Morbidity and Mortality Weekly Report, Surveillance Summaries*, *63*(8), 1–18.

Breitenbecher, K. H. (2000). Sexual assault on college campuses: Is an ounce of prevention enough? *Applied and Preventive Psychology*, *9*(1), 23–52.

Buddie, A. M., & Miller, A. G. (2001). Beyond rape myths: A more complex view of perceptions of rape victims. *Sex Roles*, *45*(3–4), 139–160.

Buehler, R., & McFarland, C. (2001). Intensity bias in affective forecasting: The role of temporal focus. *Personality and Social Psychology Bulletin*, *27*(11), 1480–1493.

Burn, S. M. (2009). A situational model of sexual assault prevention through bystander intervention. *Sex Roles*, *60*(11–12), 779–792.

Burt, M. R. (1980). Cultural myths and supports for rape. *Journal of Personality and Social Psychology*, *38*(2), 217–230.

Campbell, J. C. (2002). Health consequences of intimate partner violence. *The Lancet*, *359*(9314), 1331–1336.

Carmo, R., Grams, A., & Magalhães, T. (2011). Men as victims of intimate partner violence. *Journal of Forensic and Legal Medicine*, *18*(8), 355–359.

Cathey, P., & Goodfriend, W. (2012). *Voices of hope: Breaking the silence of relationship violence*. Storm Lake, IA: Institute for the Prevention of Relationship Violence.

Chapleau, K. M., Oswald, D. L., & Russell, B. L. (2008). Male rape myths: The role of gender, violence, and sexism. *Journal of Interpersonal Violence*, *23*(5), 600–615.

Chester, D. S., & DeWall, C. N. (2018). The roots of intimate partner violence. *Current Opinion in Psychology*, *19*, 55–59.

Christopher, F. S., & Lloyd, S. A. (2000). Physical and sexual aggression in relationships. In C. Hendrick & S. S. Hendrick (Eds.)., *Close relationships: A sourcebook* (pp. 331–343). Thousand Oaks, CA: Sage.

Cobb, A. R., Tedeschi, R. G., Calhoun, L. G., & Cann, A. (2006). Correlates of posttraumatic growth in survivors of intimate partner violence. *Journal of Traumatic Stress*, *19*(6), 895–903.

Coker, A. L., Davis, K. E., Arias, I., Desai, S., Sanderson, M., Brandt, H. M., & Smith, P. H. (2002). Physical and mental health effects of intimate partner violence for men and women. *American Journal of Preventive Medicine, 23*(4), 260–268.

Coker, A. L., Weston, R., Creson, D. L., Justice, B., & Blakeney, P. (2005). PTSD symptoms among men and women survivors of intimate partner violence: The role of risk and protective factors. *Violence and Victims, 20*(6), 625–643.

Cole, A. S., & Lynn, S. J. (2010). Adjustment of sexual assault survivors: Hardiness and acceptance coping in posttraumatic growth. *Imagination, Cognition and Personality, 30*(1), 111–127.

Coxell, A., King, M., Mezey, G., & Gordon, D. (1999). Lifetime prevalence, characteristics, and associated problems of non-consensual sex in men: Cross sectional survey. *British Medical Journal, 318*, 846–850.

Cruz, J. M. (2003). 'Why doesn't he just leave?': Gay male domestic violence and the reasons victims stay. *Journal of Men's Studies, 11*(3), 309–323.

Davies, B. (1992). Women's subjectivity and feminist stories. In C. Ellis & M. Flaherty, *Investigating subjectivity: Research on lived experience* (pp. 53–76). Newbury Park, CA: Sage.

DeMaris, A. (1997). Elevated sexual activity in violent marriages: Hypersexuality or sexual extortion? *Journal of Sex Research, 34*(4), 361–373.

Department of Justice. (2013). *Female victims of sexual violence, 1994–2010.* Washington, DC: Office of Justice Programs, Bureau of Justice Statistics.

Desai, A., Edwards, K., & Gidycz, C. (2008). Testing an integrative model of sexual aggression in college men. In A. C. Aosved (Chair), *Sexual violence perpetration: Individual and contextual factors.* Symposium conducted at the annual meeting of the Association for Behavioral and Cognitive Therapies, Orlando, FL.

Dobash, R. E., & Dobash, R. P. (1992). *Women, violence and social change.* New York, NY: Routledge.

Dunham, K., & Senn, C. Y. (2000). Minimizing negative experiences: Women's disclosure of partner abuse. *Journal of Interpersonal Violence, 15*(3), 251–261.

Dutton, D. G. (1998). *The abusive personality: Violence and control in intimate relationships.* New York, NY: Guilford Press.

Edwards, K. M., Turchik, J. A., Dardis, C. M., Reynolds, N., & Gidycz, C. A. (2011). Rape myths: History, individual and institutional-level presence,

and implications for change. *Sex Roles, 65*(11–12), 761–773.

Ehrlich, S. (2003). *Representing rape: Language and sexual consent.* Abingdon-on-Thames, England: Routledge.

Elderton, A., Berry, A., & Chan, C. (2017). A systematic review of posttraumatic growth in survivors of interpersonal violence in adulthood. *Trauma, Violence, & Abuse, 18*(2), 223–236.

Elliot, P. (1996). Shattering illusions: Same-sex domestic violence. *Journal of Gay & Lesbian Social Services, 4*(1), 1–8.

Elliott, D. M., Mok, D. S., & Briere, J. (2004). Adult sexual assault: Prevalence, symptomatology, and sex differences in the general population. *Journal of Traumatic Stress, 17*(3), 203–211.

Feild, H. S. (1978). Attitudes toward rape: A comparative analysis of police, rapists, crisis counselors, and citizens. *Journal of Personality and Social Psychology, 36*(2), 156–179.

Festinger, L., & Carlsmith, J. M. (1959). Cognitive consequences of forced compliance. *Journal of Abnormal and Social Psychology, 58*(2), 203–210.

Finkel, E. J. (2008). Intimate partner violence perpetration: Insights from the science of self-regulation. In J. P. Forgas & J. Fitness (Eds.), *Social relationships: Cognitive, affective, and motivational processes* (pp. 271–288). New York, NY: Psychology Press.

Finkel, E. J. (2014). The I³ model: Metatheory, theory, and evidence. *Advances in Experimental Social Psychology, 49*, 1–104.

Finkel, E. J., DeWall, C. N., Slotter, E. B., McNulty, J. K., Pond Jr, R. S., & Atkins, D. C. (2012). Using I³ theory to clarify when dispositional aggressiveness predicts intimate partner violence perpetration. *Journal of Personality and Social Psychology, 102*(3), 533–549.

Finkel, E. J., DeWall, C. N., Slotter, E. B., Oaten, M., & Foshee, V. A. (2009). Self-regulatory failure and intimate partner violence perpetration. *Journal of Personality and Social Psychology, 97*(3), 483–499.

Finkel, E. J., & Hall, A. N. (2018). The I³ model: A metatheoretical framework for understanding aggression. *Current Opinion in Psychology, 19*, 125–130.

Fisher, B. S., Daigle, L. E., Cullen, F. T., & Turner, M. G. (2003). Acknowledging sexual victimization as rape: Results from a national-level study. *Justice Quarterly, 20*(3), 535–574.

Foubert, J. D. (2000). The longitudinal effects of a rape-prevention program on fraternity men's attitudes, behavioral intent, and behavior. *Journal of American College Health, 48*(4), 158–163.

Gidycz, C. A., Orchowski, L. M., & Berkowitz, A. D. (2011). Preventing sexual aggression among college men: An evaluation of a social norms and bystander intervention program. *Violence Against Women, 17*(6), 720–742.

Gilbert, D. T., Pinel, E. C., Wilson, T. D., Blumberg, S. J., & Wheatley, T. P. (1998). Immune neglect: A source of durability bias in affective forecasting. *Journal of Personality and Social Psychology, 75*(3), 617–638.

Goetting, A. (1999). *Getting out: Life stories of women who left abusive men.* New York, NY: Columbia University Press.

Goodfriend, W., & Arriaga, X. B. (2018). Cognitive reframing of intimate partner aggression: Social and contextual influences. *International Journal of Environmental Research and Public Health, 15*(11), 2464.

Gylys, J. A., & McNamara, J. R. (1996). Acceptance of rape myths among prosecuting attorneys. *Psychological Reports, 79*(1), 15–18.

Hart, B. (1986). Lesbian battering: An examination. In K. Lobel (Ed.), *Naming the violence: Speaking out about lesbian battering* (pp. 173–189). Seattle, WA: Seal Press.

Haven Project. (2017). *The college power and control wheel.* Retrieved from http://www.iup.edu/haven/news/

HelloFlo.com. (2017). *'Survivor' versus 'victim': Why choosing your words carefully is important.* Retrieved from http://helloflo.com/survivor-vs-victim-why-choosing-your-words-carefully-is-important/

Hinck, S. S., & Thomas, R. W. (1999). Rape myth acceptance in college students: How far have we come? *Sex Roles, 40*(9–10), 815–832.

Hoerger, M., Quirk, S. W., Lucas, R. E., & Carr, T. H. (2010). Cognitive determinants of affective forecasting errors. *Judgment and Decision Making, 5*(5), 365–373.

Holtzworth-Munroe, A., & Meehan, J. C. (2004). Typologies of men who are maritally violent: Scientific and clinical implications. *Journal of Interpersonal Violence, 19*(12), 1369–1389.

Holtzworth-Munroe, A., Meehan, J. C., Herron, K., Rehman, U., & Stuart, G. L. (2000). Testing the Holtzworth-Munroe and Stuart (1994) batterer typology. *Journal of Consulting and Clinical Psychology, 68*(6), 1000–1019.

Holtzworth-Munroe, A., & Stuart, G. L. (1994). Typologies of male batterers: Three subtypes and the differences among them. *Psychological Bulletin, 116*(3), 476–497.

Jackson, S. (1993). Women and the family. In D. Richardson & V. Robinson (Eds.), *Thinking feminist: Key concepts in women's studies* (pp. 177–200). New York, NY: Guilford Press.

Jackson, S. (2001). Happily never after: Young women's stories of abuse in heterosexual love relationships. *Feminism & Psychology, 11*(3), 305–321.

Jacobson, N. S., & Gottman, J. M. (1998). *When men batter women: New insights into ending abusive relationships.* New York, NY: Simon & Schuster.

Johnson, M. P. (1995). Patriarchal terrorism and common couple violence: Two forms of violence against women. *Journal of Marriage and the Family, 57*(2), 283–294.

Johnson, M. P. (2007). The intersection of gender and control. In L. O'Toole, J. R. Schiffman, & M. L. K. Edwards (Eds.), *Gender violence: Interdisciplinary perspectives* (2nd ed., pp. 257–268). New York, NY: New York University Press.

Jones, A. (2000). *Next time, she'll be dead: Battering and how to stop it.* Boston, MA: Beacon Press.

Katz, J. (1994). *Mentors in Violence Prevention (MVP) trainer's guide.* Boston, MA: Northeastern University Center for the Study of Sport in Society.

Kearns, M. C., Edwards, K. M., Calhoun, K. S., & Gidycz, C. A. (2010). Disclosure of sexual victimization: The effects of Pennebaker's emotional disclosure paradigm on physical and psychological distress. *Journal of Trauma & Dissociation, 11*(2), 193–209.

Kilpatrick, D. G. (2004). What is violence against women? Defining and measuring the problem. *Journal of Interpersonal Violence, 19*(11), 1209–1234.

Kirkwood, C. (1993). *Leaving abusive partners: From the scars of survival to the wisdom for change.* Thousand Oaks, CA: Sage.

Kleim, B., & Ehlers, A. (2009). Evidence for a curvilinear relationship between posttraumatic growth and posttrauma depression and PTSD in assault survivors. *Journal of Traumatic Stress, 22*(1), 45–52.

Klein, E., Campbell, J., Soler, E., & Ghez, M. (1997). *Ending domestic violence: Changing public perceptions/halting the epidemic.* Thousand Oaks, CA: Sage.

Koss, M. P., Gidycz, C. A., & Wisniewski, N. (1987). The scope of rape: Incidence and prevalence of sexual aggression and victimization in a national sample of higher education students. *Journal of Consulting and Clinical Psychology, 55*(2), 162–170.

Krahé, B., Temkin, J., Bieneck, S., & Berger, A. (2008). Prospective lawyers' rape stereotypes and schematic decision making about rape cases. *Psychology, Crime & Law, 14*(5), 461–479.

Kunst, M. J. J. (2011). Affective personality type, post-traumatic stress disorder symptom severity and post-traumatic growth in victims of violence. *Stress and Health, 27*(1), 42–51.

Leone, J. M., Johnson, M. P., & Cohan, C. L. (2007). Victim help seeking: Differences between intimate terrorism and situational couple violence. *Family Relations: An Interdisciplinary Journal of Applied Family Studies, 56*(5), 427–439.

Loh, C., Gidycz, C. A., Lobo, T. R., & Luthra, R. (2005). A prospective analysis of sexual assault perpetration: Risk factors related to perpetrator characteristics. *Journal of Interpersonal Violence, 20*(10), 1325–1348.

Lonsway, K. A., & Fitzgerald, L. F. (1994). Rape myths: In review. *Psychology of Women Quarterly, 18*(2), 133–164.

McMahon, S. (2010). Rape myth beliefs and bystander attitudes among incoming college students. *Journal of American College Health, 59*(1), 3–11.

McMahon, S., & Farmer, G. L. (2011). An updated measure for assessing subtle rape myths. *Social Work Research, 35*(2), 71–81.

Muehlenhard, C. L., Friedman, D. E., & Thomas, C. M. (1985). Is date rape justifiable? The effects of dating activity, who initiated, who paid, and men's attitudes toward women. *Psychology of Women Quarterly, 9*(3), 297–310.

Muehlenhard, C. L., Goggins, M. F., Jones, J. M., & Satterfield, A. T. (1991). Sexual violence and coercion in close relationships. In M. McKinney & S. Sprecher (Eds.), *Sexuality in close relationships* (pp. 155–175). Hillsdale, NJ: Lawrence Erlbaum.

Page, A. D. (2008). Judging women and defining crime: Police officers' attitudes toward women and rape. *Sociological Spectrum, 28*(4), 389–411.

Payne, D. L., Lonsway, K. A., & Fitzgerald, L. F. (1999). Rape myth acceptance: Exploration of its structure and its measurement using the Illinois rape myth acceptance scale. *Journal of Research in Personality, 33*(1), 27–68.

Pence, E., & Paymar, M. (1993). *Education groups for men who batter: The Duluth model.* New York, NY: Springer.

Pennebaker, J. W. (1997). Writing about emotional experiences as a therapeutic process. *Psychological Science, 8*(3), 162–166.

Peterman, L. M., & Dixon, C. G. (2003). Domestic violence between same-sex partners: Implications for counseling. *Journal of Counseling & Development, 81*(1), 40–47.

Peterson, Z. D., & Muehlenhard, C. L. (2004). Was it rape? The function of women's rape myth acceptance and definitions of sex in labeling their own experiences. *Sex Roles, 51*(3–4), 129–144.

Rabin N., Heller, J., Modell, J., Rizov, V., Adams, E., Matos, M., Gordon, S., Gilmer, M., Adams, S., Robinson, T., & Koski, G. (2011, June 20). The hits keep coming: 30 songs inspired by domestic violence. *AV Club.* Retrieved April 21, 2019 from https://music.avclub.com/the-hits-keep-coming-30-songs-inspired-by-domestic-vio-1798226415

Rosen, K. H. (1996). The ties that bind women to violent premarital relationships: Processes of seduction and entrapment. In D. D. Cahn & S. A. Lloyd (Eds.), *Family violence from a communication perspective* (pp. 151–176). Thousand Oaks, CA: Sage.

Rosen, K. H., & Stith, S. M. (1997). Surviving abusive dating relationships: Processes of leaving, healing and moving on. In G. Kantor & J. Jasinski (Eds.), *Out of the darkness: Contemporary perspectives on family violence* (pp. 170–182). Thousand Oaks, CA: Sage.

Sanday, P. R. (1996). Rape-prone versus rape-free campus cultures. *Violence Against Women, 2*(2), 191–208.

Schwartz, M. D., & DeKeseredy, W. (1997). *Sexual assault on the college campus: The role of male peer support.* Thousand Oaks, CA: Sage.

Sharma-Patel, K., Brown, E. J., & Chaplin, W. F. (2012). Emotional and cognitive processing in sexual assault survivors' narratives. *Journal of Aggression, Maltreatment & Trauma, 21*(2), 149–170.

Shaw, J., Campbell, R., Cain, D., & Feeney, H. (2017). Beyond surveys and scales: How rape myths manifest in sexual assault police records. *Psychology of Violence, 7*(4), 602–614.

Sinozich, S., & Langton, L. (2014). *Rape and sexual assault victimization among college-age females, 1995-2013*. Washington, DC: U.S. Department of Justice.

Smyth, J. M. (1998). Written emotional expression: Effect sizes, outcome types, and moderating variables. *Journal of Consulting and Clinical Psychology, 66*(1), 174–84.

Song, L. Y. (2012). Service utilization, perceived changes of self, and life satisfaction among women who experienced intimate partner abuse: The mediation effect of empowerment. *Journal of Interpersonal Violence, 27*(6), 1112–1136.

Stephens, K. A., & George, W. H. (2009). Rape prevention with college men: Evaluating risk status. *Journal of Interpersonal Violence, 24*(6), 996–1013.

Stoll, L. C., Lilley, T. G., & Pinter, K. (2017). Gender-blind sexism and rape myth acceptance. *Violence Against Women, 23*(1), 28–45.

Straus, M. A. (1979). Measuring intrafamily conflict and violence: The conflict tactics (CT) scales. *Journal of Marriage and the Family, 41*(1), 75–88.

Street, A. E., & Arias, I. (2001). Psychological abuse and posttraumatic stress disorder in battered women: Examining the roles of shame and guilt. *Violence and Victims, 16*(1), 65–78.

Struckman-Johnson, C., & Struckman-Johnson, D. (1992). Acceptance of male rape myths among college men and women. *Sex Roles, 27*(3–4), 85–100.

Tashiro, T. Y., & Frazier, P. (2003). "I'll never be in a relationship like that again": Personal growth following romantic relationship breakups. *Personal Relationships, 10*(1), 113–128.

Taylor, J. Y. (2004). Moving from surviving to thriving: African American women recovering from intimate male partner abuse. *Research and Theory for Nursing Practice, 18*(1), 35–50.

Tedeschi, R. G., & Calhoun, L. G. (1996). The posttraumatic growth inventory: Measuring the positive legacy of trauma. *Journal of Traumatic Stress, 9*(3), 455–471.

Tedeschi, R. G., & Calhoun, L. G. (2004). Posttraumatic growth: Conceptual foundations and empirical evidence. *Psychological Inquiry, 15*(1), 1–18.

Turchik, J. A., & Edwards, K. M. (2012). Myths about male rape: A literature review. *Psychology of Men & Masculinity, 13*(2), 211–226.

Turchik, J. A., Hebenstreit, C. L., & Judson, S. S. (2016). An examination of the gender inclusiveness of current theories of sexual violence in adulthood: Recognizing male victims, female perpetrators, and same-sex violence. *Trauma, Violence, & Abuse, 17*(2), 133–148.

Valdez, C. E., & Lilly, M. M. (2015). Posttraumatic growth in survivors of intimate partner violence: An assumptive world process. *Journal of Interpersonal Violence, 30*(2), 215–231.

Walby, S., & Allen, J. (2004). *Domestic violence, sexual assault and stalking: Findings from the British Crime Survey*. London, England: Home Office Research, Development and Statistics Directorate.

Walker, L. E. (1979). Behind the closed doors of the middle-class wifebeater's family. *Contemporary Psychology, 24*(5), 404–405.

Walker, L. E. (1980). *The battered woman*. New York, NY: Harper and Row.

Walker, L. E. (1984). Battered women, psychology, and public policy. *American Psychologist, 39*(10), 1178–1182.

Weiss, K. G. (2010). Male sexual victimization: Examining men's experiences of rape and sexual assault. *Men and Masculinities, 12*(3), 275–298.

West, C. M. (1998). Leaving a second closet: Outing partner violence in same-sex couples. In J. L. Jasinski & L. M. Williams (Eds.), *Partner violence: A comprehensive review of 20 years of research* (pp. 163–183). Thousand Oaks, CA: Sage.

Chapter 13

Adams, J. S. (1963). Towards an understanding of inequity. *Journal of Abnormal and Social Psychology, 67*(5), 422–436.

Aron, A., & Aron, E. N. (1986). *Love and the expansion of self: Understanding attraction and satisfaction*. New York, NY: Hemisphere.

Aron, A., Aron, E. N., & Norman, C. C. (2001). Self-expansion model of motivation and cognition in close relationships and beyond. In G. J. O. Fletcher & M. Clark (Eds.), *Blackwell handbook of social psychology: Interpersonal processes* (pp. 478–501). Malden, MA: Blackwell.

Aron, A., Aron, E. N., Tudor, M., & Nelson, G. (1991). Close relationships as including other in the self. *Journal of Personality and Social Psychology, 60*(2), 241–253.

Baucom, D. H., Epstein, N., Sayers, S. L., & Sher, T. G. (1989). The role of cognitions in marital relationships: Definitional, methodological, and conceptual issues. *Journal of Consulting and Clinical Psychology, 57*(1), 31–38.

Baucom, D. H., Epstein, N. B., & Stanton, S. (2006). The treatment of relationship distress: Theoretical perspectives and empirical findings. In A. Vangelisti & D. Perlman (Eds.), *Cambridge handbook of personal relationships* (2nd ed., pp. 745–765). New York, NY: Cambridge University Press.

Baumeister, R. F. (2000). Ego depletion and the self's executive function. In A. Tesser & R. B. Felson (Eds.), *Psychological perspectives on self and identity* (pp. 9–33). Washington, DC: American Psychological Association.

Baumeister, R. F., Vohs, K. D., & Tice, D. M. (2007). The strength model of self-control. *Current Directions in Psychological Science, 16*(6), 351–355.

Baxter, L. A. (1984). Trajectories of relationship disengagement. *Journal of Social and Personal Relationships, 1*(1), 29–48.

Becker, C. S. (1988). *Unbroken ties: Lesbian ex-lovers.* Boston, MA: Alyson Books.

Benson, L. A., McGinn, M. M., & Christensen, A. (2012). Common principles of couple therapy. *Behavior Therapy, 43*(1), 25–35.

Bograd, M. (1984). Family systems approaches to wife battering: A feminist critique. *American Journal of Orthopsychiatry, 54*(4), 558–568.

Bolger, N., Zuckerman, A., & Kessler, R. C. (2000). Invisible support and adjustment to stress. *Journal of Personality and Social Psychology, 79*(6), 953–961.

Canary, D. J., & Stafford, L. (1992). Relational maintenance strategies and equity in marriage. *Communications Monographs, 59*(3), 243–267.

Christensen, A., Atkins, D. C., Baucom, B., & Yi, J. (2010). Marital status and satisfaction five years following a randomized clinical trial comparing traditional versus integrative behavioral couple therapy. *Journal of Consulting and Clinical Psychology, 78*(2), 225–235.

Clark, M. S., & Grote, N. K. (1998). Why aren't indices of relationship costs always negatively related to indices of relationship quality? *Personality and Social Psychology Review, 2*(1), 2–17.

Clark, M. S., & Mills, J. (1979). Interpersonal attraction in exchange and communal relationships. *Journal of Personality and Social Psychology, 37*(1), 12–24.

Clark, M. S., & Mills, J. (1993). The difference between communal and exchange relationships: What it is and is not. *Personality and Social Psychology Bulletin, 19*(6), 684–691.

Cody, M. J. (1982). A typology of disengagement strategies and an examination of the role intimacy, reactions to inequity and relational problems play in strategy selection. *Communication Monographs, 49*(3), 148–170.

Conger, R. D., Rueter, M. A., & Elder, G. H., Jr. (1999). Couple resilience to economic pressure. *Journal of Personality and Social Psychology, 76*(1), 54–71.

Dicks, H. V. (1967). *Marital tensions.* New York, NY: Basic Books.

Doss, B. D., Simpson, L. E., & Christensen, A. (2004). Why do couples seek marital therapy? *Professional Psychology: Research and Practice, 35*(6), 608–614.

Duck, S. W. (1982). A topography of relationship disengagement and dissolution. In S. W. Duck (Ed.), *Personal relationships, Vol. 4: Dissolving personal relationships* (pp. 1–30). London, England: Academic Press.

Eidelson, R. J., & Epstein, N. (1982). Cognition and relationship maladjustment: Development of a measure of dysfunctional relationship beliefs. *Journal of Consulting and Clinical Psychology, 50*(5), 715–720.

Epstein, N., & Eidelson, R. J. (1981). Unrealistic beliefs of clinical couples: Their relationship to expectations, goals and satisfaction. *American Journal of Family Therapy, 9*(4), 13–22.

Finkel, E. J. (2018). *The all-or-nothing marriage: How the best marriages work.* New York, NY: Dutton.

Finkel, E. J., Cheung, E. O., Emery, L. F., Carswell, K. L., & Larson, G. M. (2015). The suffocation model: Why marriage in America is becoming an all-or-nothing institution. *Current Directions in Psychological Science*, *24*(3), 238–244.

Gable, S. L., Gonzaga, G. C., & Strachman, A. (2006). Will you be there for me when things go right? Supportive responses to positive event disclosures. *Journal of Personality and Social Psychology*, *91*(5), 904–917.

Geiss, S. K., & O'Leary, K. D. (1981). Therapist ratings of frequency and severity of marital problems: Implications for research. *Journal of Marital and Family Therapy*, *7*(4), 515–520.

Gottman, J. M. (1993). A theory of marital dissolution and stability. *Journal of Family Psychology*, *7*(1), 57–75.

Gottman, J. M. (1994). *Why marriages succeed or fail*. New York, NY: Fireside.

Gottman, J. M., & Silver, N. (2015). *The seven principles for making marriage work: A practical guide from the country's foremost relationship expert*. New York, NY: Harmony.

Griffith, R. L., Gillath, O., Zhao, X., & Martinez, R. (2017). Staying friends with ex-romantic partners: Predictors, reasons, and outcomes. *Personal Relationships*, *24*(3), 550–584.

Haley, J. (1963). *Strategies of psychotherapy*. New York, NY: Grune & Stratton.

Hatfield, E., & Rapson, R. L. (2012). Equity theory in close relationships. In P. Van Lange, A. W. Kruglanski, & E. T. Higgins (Eds.), *Handbook of theories of social psychology* (Vol. 2, pp. 200–217). Thousand Oaks, CA: Sage.

Higgins, E. T. (1997). Beyond pleasure and pain. *American Psychologist*, *52*(12), 1280–1300.

Hill, C. T., Rubin, Z., & Peplau, L. A. (1976). Breakups before marriage: The end of 103 affairs. *Journal of Social Issues*, *32*(1), 147–168.

House, J. (1981). *Work stress and social support*. Reading, MA: Addison-Wesley.

Jacobson, N. S., & Margolin, G. (1979). *Marital therapy: Strategies based on social learning and behavior exchange principles*. New York, NY: Brunner/Mazel.

James, S., Hunsley, J., & Hemsworth, D. (2002). Factor structure of the relationship belief inventory. *Cognitive Therapy and Research*, *26*(6), 729–744.

Joel, S., & Eastwick, P. W. (2018). Intervening earlier: An upstream approach to improving relationship quality. *Policy Insights From the Behavioral and Brain Sciences*, *5*(1), 25–32.

Johnson, S. M. (2012). *The practice of emotionally focused couple therapy: Creating connection* (2nd ed.). New York, NY: Routledge.

Johnson, S. M., & Denton, W. (2002). Emotionally focused couple therapy: Creating secure connections. In A. S. Gurman & N. S. Jacobson (Eds.), *Clinical handbook of couple therapy* (3rd ed., pp. 221–250). New York, NY: Guilford Press.

Johnson, S. M., & Greenberg, L. S. (1985). Differential effects of experiential and problem-solving interventions in resolving marital conflict. *Journal of Consulting and Clinical Psychology*, *53*(2), 175–184.

Kressel, K. (1985). *The process of divorce: How professionals and couples negotiate settlements*. New York, NY: Basic Books.

Lannutti, P. J., & Cameron, K. A. (2002). Beyond the breakup: Heterosexual and homosexual post-dissolutional relationships. *Communication Quarterly*, *50*(2), 153–170.

Lavner, J. A., Karney, B. R., & Bradbury, T. N. (2012). Do cold feet warn of trouble ahead? Premarital uncertainty and four-year marital outcomes. *Journal of Family Psychology*, *26*(6), 1012–1017.

Lee, L. (1984). Sequences in separation: A framework for investigating endings of the personal (romantic) relationship. *Journal of Social and Personal Relationships*, *1*(1), 49–73.

Lewandowski, G. W., Aron, A., Bassis, S., & Kunak, J. (2006). Losing a self-expanding relationship: Implications for the self-concept. *Personal Relationships*, *13*, 317–331.

Markman, H. J., Floyd, F. J., Stanley, S. M., & Lewis, H. (1986). Prevention. In N. Jacobson & A. Gurman (Eds.), *Clinical handbook of marital therapy* (pp. 174–194). New York, NY: Guilford.

Mason, A. E., Law, R. W., Bryan, A. E. B., Portley, R. M., & Sbarra, D. A. (2012). Facing a breakup: Electromyographic responses moderate self-concept recovery following a romantic separation. *Personal Relationships*, *19*, 551–568.

McNulty, J. K., Olson, M. A., Meltzer, A. L., & Shaffer, M. J. (2013). Though they may be unaware, newlyweds implicitly know whether their marriage will be satisfying. *Science, 342*(6162), 1119–1120.

Minuchin, S. (1974). *Families and family therapy.* Cambridge, MA: Harvard University Press.

Molden, D. C., & Winterheld, H. A. (2013). Motivations for promotion or prevention in close relationships. In J. A. Simpson & L. Campbell (Eds.), *Oxford handbook of close relationships* (pp. 321–347). Oxford, England: Oxford University Press.

Nardi, P. M. (1992). Sex, friendship, and gender roles among gay men. In P. M. Nardi (Ed.), *Men's friendships* (pp. 173–185). Thousand Oaks, CA: Sage.

Orbuch, T. L. (1988). *Reponses to and coping with nonmarital relationship termination.* Doctoral dissertation, University of Wisconsin, Madison.

R29 Editors. (2018, December 14). The best movies for getting over your ex. *Refinery29.com.* Retrieved May 10, 2019, from https://www.refinery29.com/en-us/how-to-move-on

Rafaeli, E., & Gleason, M. E. (2009). Skilled support within intimate relationships. *Journal of Family Theory & Review, 1*(1), 20–37.

Reissman, C., Aron, A., & Bergen, M. R. (1993). Shared activities and marital satisfaction: Causal direction and self-expansion versus boredom. *Journal of Social and Personal Relationships, 10*(2), 243–254.

Rollie, S. S., & Duck, S. (2006). Divorce and dissolution of romantic relationships: Stage models and their limitations. In M. A. Fine & J. H. Harvey (Eds.), *Handbook of divorce and relationship dissolution* (pp. 223–240). East Sussex, England: Psychology Press.

Russell, L. (1990). Sex and couples therapy: A method of treatment to enhance physical and emotional intimacy. *Journal of Sex & Marital Therapy, 16*(2), 111–120.

Scharff, J. S., & Bagnini, C. (2002). Object relations couple therapy. In A. S. Gurman & N. S. Jacobson (Eds.), *Clinical handbook of couple therapy* (3rd ed., pp. 59–85). New York, NY: Guilford Press.

Scharff, J. S., & Scharff, D. E. (1997). Object relations couple therapy. *American Journal of Psychotherapy, 51*(2), 141–173.

Schneider, C. S., & Kenny, D. A. (2000). Cross-sex friends who were once romantic partners: Are they platonic friends now? *Journal of Social and Personal Relationships, 17*(3), 451–466.

Schwarzer, R., & Gutierrez-Dona, B. (2005). More spousal support for men than for women: A comparison of sources and types of support. *Sex Roles, 52*(7–8), 523–532.

Shadish, W. R., & Baldwin, S. A. (2003). Meta-analysis of MFT interventions. *Journal of Marital and Family Therapy, 29*(4), 547–570.

Shah, J. Y., Friedman, R., & Kruglanski, A. W. (2002). Forgetting all else: On the antecedents and consequences of goal shielding. *Journal of Personality and Social Psychology, 83*(6), 1261–1280.

Sprecher, S. (1994). Two sides to the breakup of dating relationships. *Personal Relationships, 1*(3), 199–222.

Sprecher, S. (2001). Equity and social exchange in dating couples: Associations with satisfaction, commitment, and stability. *Journal of Marriage and Family, 63*(3), 599–613.

Stanley, S. M., Markman, H. J., St. Peters, M., & Leber, B. D. (1995). Strengthening marriages and preventing divorce: New directions in prevention research. *Family Relations, 44,* 392–401.

Strong, G., & Aron, A. (2006). The effect of shared participation in novel and challenging activities on experienced relationship quality: Is it mediated by high positive affect? In K. D. Vohs & E. J. Finkel (Eds.), *Self and relationships: Connecting intrapersonal and interpersonal processes* (pp. 342–359). New York, NY: Guilford.

Stuart, R. B. (2003). *Helping couples change: A social learning approach to marital therapy.* New York, NY: Guilford Press.

Todd, T. C. (1986). Structural-strategic marital therapy. In A. S. Gurman & N. S. Jacobson (Eds.), *Clinical handbook of couple therapy* (3rd ed., pp. 71–105). New York, NY: Guilford Press.

Waldman, K., & Rubalcava, L. (2005). Psychotherapy with intercultural couples: A contemporary psychodynamic approach. *American Journal of Psychotherapy, 59*(3), 227–245.

Walster, E., Walster, G. W., & Berscheid, E. (1978). *Equity: Theory and research.* Boston, MA: Allyn & Bacon.

Weinstock, J., & Rothblum, E. D. (2014). *Lesbian ex-lovers: The really long-term relationships.* London, England: Routledge.

Weissman, M. M. (1987). Advances in psychiatric epidemiology: Rates and risks for major depression. *American Journal of Public Health, 77*(4), 445–451.

Weston, K. (1997). *Families we choose: Lesbians, gays, kinship.* New York, NY: Columbia University Press.

Whisman, M. A., Dixon, A. E., & Johnson, B. (1997). Therapists' perspectives of couple problems and treatment issues in couple therapy. *Journal of Family Psychology, 11*(3), 361–366.

Wills, T. A. (1985). Supportive functions of interpersonal relationships. In S. Cohen & S. L. Syme (Eds.), *Social support and health* (pp. 61–82). Orlando, FL: Academic Press.

Wilmot, W. W., Carbaugh, D. A., & Baxter, L. A. (1985). Communicative strategies used to terminate romantic relationships. *Western Journal of Communication, 49*(3), 204–216.

Xue, M., & Silk, J. B. (2012). The role of tracking and tolerance in relationship among friends. *Evolution and Human Behavior, 33*(1), 17–25.

• Glossary •

47, XYY syndrome: When an individual is born with XYY chromosomes.

5-alpha reductase deficiency: When an XY person is unresponsive to prenatal testosterone but becomes responsive in adolescence.

Accommodation: Inhibiting the urge to retaliate when angered by a partner, and instead trying to forgive and forget.

Adult attachment interview: A method of measuring attachment style that asks adults about their childhood relationship experiences.

Affective forecasting: Attempts to predict how we'll feel in the future, under different circumstances.

Analysis of variance (ANOVA): A statistical technique in which three or more groups are compared to each other.

Androgen insensitivity syndrome: When an XY fetus is unresponsive to prenatal testosterone, resulting in a feminized body.

ANOVA: See *analysis of variance*.

Anxious-ambivalent attachment: A type of insecure attachment in which people worry about whether they can trust their partner and whether their partner truly loves them.

Applied research: Research studies aimed toward application and solving real-world problems.

Appraisal support: Offering feedback to someone regarding their progress toward a goal.

Archival data: Data originally gathered for another purpose, such as census data, newspaper announcements, and so forth.

Asexual: Low levels of sexual attraction, regardless of sex or gender labels.

Assortative mating: The tendency for people to date and marry others with the same level of physical attractiveness as themselves.

Attachment style: Someone's pattern of interacting with important others, including feelings of trust, stability, and so on.

Attachment theory: The idea that our first relationship in life will influence the types of relationships we have through adulthood.

Attraction-similarity hypothesis: The prediction that people tend to form relationships with others who have the same attitudes, values, and demographics as themselves.

Autism spectrum disorder: A neurological condition with several symptoms, often including a seeming lack of social communication and connection to others.

Averaged faces: See *composite faces*.

Avoidant attachment: A type of insecure attachment in which people decide not to actively pursue social interaction, due to past negative experiences.

Badges: Visual icons that can mark if a study used open science practices.

Basic research: Research studies aimed toward advancing theory or expanding our base of knowledge.

Beauty and the Beast fantasy: The idea that self-sacrificing women can turn violent men into loving, sensitive men.

Behavioral therapy: A form of counseling that emphasizes observable behaviors by replacing negative ones with positive ones.

Bereavement: The psychological process of dealing with the death of a loved one.

Bilateral symmetry: When the left half of someone's face and body matches the right half.

Bisexual: Sexual attraction to both men and women.

Bystander intervention programming: Workshops that educate people about sexual assault and hope to empower witnesses to intervene, to prevent it from happening.

Categorical approach: A system based on groups or types, such as friendships versus romantic partners.

Child attachment interview: A method of measuring attachment style that asks children specific questions about their feelings and behaviors with other people.

Cinderella effect: The increased risk of harm/abuse from stepparents to stepchildren (compared to biological children).

Cinderella fantasy: The idea that strangers can "rescue" women from their problems by removing them from their past and/or family.

Cisgender: People who feel comfortable with the sex assigned to them at birth and don't wish to change it.

CL: See *comparison level*.

CL$_{alt}$: See *comparison level for alternatives*.

Cobras: Abusers who become physiologically relaxed and calm during conflicts.

Coercive paraphilia: When sexual arousal is obtained by victimizing someone else.

Cognitive dissonance: The anxiety we feel when our thoughts or actions don't match our values or self-concept.

Cognitive interdependence: Mental representations of the self as tied to your relationship partner; a mental "we."

Cognitive-behavioral therapy: A form of counseling that emphasizes the unhealthy thoughts behind negative behaviors.

Cohabitation: Living with an intimate partner without being legally married.

Collectivistic cultures: Cultures in which values and norms focus on the needs of the larger group.

Commitment: In Sternberg's triangular theory of love, this is the cognitive component. In other theories, commitment also refers to the conscious decision to be dedicated to a person or relationship, usually exclusively.

Communal orientation: A mindset in which we engage in generosity or altruism with a partner, without the need to be "paid back."

Comparison level (CL): Your abstract standard of what an "average" relationship is like.

Comparison level for alternatives (CL$_{alt}$): The most attractive option you'd have if you ended your current relationship.

Composite faces: Digitally created faces that are morphs of several individual faces.

Conceptual replication: An attempt to redo a study in concept, but using new measures or procedures.

Conflict: Any disagreement or difference of opinion between two people.

Conflict intentions: The strategic goals or motivations someone has in a disagreement with someone else.

Conflictive: A conflict management style that escalates disagreement and results in negative feelings.

Congenital adrenal hyperplasia: When an XX fetus is exposed to an unusually high amount of prenatal testosterone, resulting in a masculinized body.

Conscientiousness: A personality trait involving one's level of discipline, motivation, and focus on long-term goals.

Consensual nonmonogamy: An "open" relationship in which neither person is expected to be sexually exclusive.

Construct: A theoretical, abstract, or invisible concept or idea (such as "love").

Contact comfort: A sense of psychological or emotional security and comfort, resulting from physical touch.

Contempt: Feeling that your partner is inferior to you or is disgusting.

Continuous approach: A system based on ranges or continuums, such as degrees of liking or loving.

Control group: The participants in a study who serve as a neutral or baseline group, used as a comparison to the experimental group.

Correlation: A statistical technique measuring the degree two continuous variables are associated with each other.

Correlation coefficient: A number indicating the strength of association between two variables, ranging from zero to one (absolute value).

Couple disclosure: When a couple member reveals private information about the relationship to a friend or third party.

Criticism: Verbally attacking someone's overall character or personality in a global way.

Cross-cultural psychology: A subfield that studies the influence of regional social norms on one's thoughts and behaviors.

Cross-sectional study: A study completed in a single, one-time-only session.

Current outcomes: The ratio of positive to negative outcomes in your current relationship.

Cycle of violence: The prediction that abuse will have three phases: (1) tension-building, (2) explosion, and (3) contrition.

Debriefing: A session at the end of a research study in which full information (such as the hypothesis) is provided to the participants.

Deception: Misleading participants about the true nature of a study because full knowledge might change their responses.

Defensiveness: The sense that all problems in a relationship are the other person's fault.

Dependence: How much you rely on your current relationship for happiness (determined by your current alternatives).

Dependent variable: An experimental outcome or effect of being in one experimental group versus another.

Derogation of alternatives: The motivation to downgrade other possible partners because we're already in a commitment relationship.

Destiny beliefs: A set of beliefs that potential partners are either "meant to be" or not, like "soul mates."

Detachment: The process of mourning the loss of someone attached to you, such as a parent or romantic partner.

Dialectical perspective: An approach in communication research that assumes all relationships consist of opposing forces, pulling us in different directions.

Direct replication: An attempt to redo a study following the exact same procedures.

Dismissing attachment: A type of insecure attachment in which people have a positive view of the self, but a negative view of others.

Disorders of sex development (DSD): Conditions in which either chromosomes or hormones are neither traditionally "male" nor "female."

Dispositional attributions: Determining that an outcome was caused by something internal to a person, such as skill or effort.

Downplaying: Attempts to minimize conflict by avoiding the disagreement.

Dunbar's number: The idea that primate species (including humans) can only maintain a certain number of people in our social network at any given time.

Dyadic analysis: Statistical tests that analyze results on a couples level instead of on an individuals level.

Dyadic stage: Step 2 of breaking up, when partners discuss whether to end things or stay together.

Dyadic withdrawal: The trend for young adults to spend less time with friends in exchange for more time with a romantic partner.

Emotional infidelity: Having strong feelings for someone who is not your current partner.

Emotionally focused therapy: A form of counseling that helps clients understand and control their moods and reactions.

Enhanced fitness: Increased chances of survival, access to food and reproductive resources, and so on due to certain genes or traits.

Equity theory: Proposes that people are happiest in relationships when their rewards and costs are fair.

Erotophilia: A personality trait involving one's level of sexual interest and obscenity.

Esteem support: Help in the form of providing validation of one's self-esteem or worth.

Ethological approach: The study of human social behavior from a biological perspective, comparing humans to other species.

EVLN model of conflict: A theory that conflict management is based on destructive versus constructive and active versus passive approaches to disagreement. EVLN stands for exit, voice, loyalty, and neglect.

Evolutionary psychology: A subfield that studies the influence of biological instincts on one's thoughts and behaviors.

Exchange orientation: A mindset in which we seek balance, fairness, or reciprocity in the exchange of resources, favors, or effort.

Excitation transfer: See *misattribution of arousal*.

Experiment: A study in which participants are randomly assigned to be in one of the groups of interest.

Experimental group: The participants in a study who are exposed to a treatment, intervention, or manipulation of interest.

External locus of control: The belief that our outcomes or future is determined by forces outside of us, such as luck, fate, or a powerful other.

External validity: Whether a given study's results can be applied to other people and settings.

False dichotomy: A dilemma presented as if there are only two possible answers or outcomes, when the solution might be a third option or a combination of outcomes (a compromise).

Fearful attachment: A type of insecure attachment in which people have both a negative view of self and a negative view of others.

Femme porn: Pornography designed to highlight feminist values and strong female characters.

Fetish: Sexual arousal from an object (shoes, underwear, etc.) or nongenital body part (feet, etc.).

Fixation: When a specific genetic advantage occurs in 100% of a given population.

Four horsemen: Four patterns of bad communication that predict the end of a relationship.

Gender expression: The degree to which someone presents themselves as masculine and/or feminine.

Ghosting: Cutting off all forms of contact from a previous romantic partner.

Glass slipper effect: When endorsement of traditional romantic beliefs leads women to be less interested in personal empowerment.

Gottman model of conflict: A theory of conflict management that separates tactics into volatile, validator, avoider, and hostile approaches.

Grave-dressing stage: Step 4 of breaking up, when ex-partners mentally move on from the relationship and maintain their self-esteem.

Growth beliefs: A set of beliefs that all relationships will encounter conflict and challenge, but these problems can be worked out.

Halo effect: When a single trait about someone affects our entire impression of them.

Happiness: A high ratio of pleasure to pain, or mostly positive emotional experiences.

Hedonic adaptation: The idea that happiness goes temporarily up or down due to major events, but then returns to baseline levels.

Heteroflexibility: The idea that people can be heterosexual but experiment with same-sex attraction or behaviors.

Heterosexual: Sexual attraction to only people of the "opposite" sex.

High-K strategy: When a parent produces fewer children, but each has access to more attention and resources.

High-r strategy: When a parent produces many children, but must distribute attention and resources among them.

Homophily: The degree to which two people are similar to each other; greater homophily is tied to greater likelihood of friendship.

Homosexual: Sexual attraction to only people of the same sex.

Hookups: Brief sexual encounters outside of a relationship that range from kissing to intercourse.

Hypersexuality: Intense or excessive desire for frequent sexual activity.

Hypothesis: A specific statement of what a researcher believes will be the outcome of a given study.

I3 model: An attempt to predict the likelihood of relationship violence based on aspects of the situation and couple members.

Ideal self: Our aspirations or the self-concept we hope to achieve.

Implicit beliefs: Foundational ideas about the nature of relationships that affect our perceptions and decisions.

Imprinting: The tendency for some species (such as ducks) to attach themselves to the first living organism they see after hatching.

Inclusion of Other in the Self Scale (IOS scale): A series of overlapping circles that represent "self" and "other" in terms of mental closeness or interdependence.

Independent self-construals: A view of the self emphasizing uniqueness and autonomy.

Independent variable: What makes groups in an experiment different from each other at the beginning of the study; the cause of any changes or differences in an experimental outcome.

Individualistic cultures: Cultures in which values and norms focus on the needs of each, single person.

Informational support: Help in the form of providing facts or details that help someone make decisions or feel more knowledgeable.

Informed consent: A research participant's right to know the basics of any given study before it begins.

Insecure attachment: Feelings of mistrust and instability when interacting with others.

Institutional review board (IRB): A committee of people who weigh the ethical implications of any proposed research study.

Instrumental support: Help in the form of providing physical aid, financial resources, or other pragmatic resources.

Integrative: Attempts to understand the other person's view during conflict and negotiate a mutual solution.

Interdependence theory: Proposes behaviors in relationships are based on getting the best possible outcome, and two partners' outcomes affect each other.

Interdependent self-construals: A view of the self emphasizing one's relationships and concerns for others' needs.

Interdisciplinary approach: Scientific study of a topic (such as relationships) that combines theories, methods, and results from a variety of academic fields.

Internal locus of control: The belief that we are generally in control of what happens to us.

Internal validity: How well a study is constructed and whether results can be interpreted correctly.

Interpretive filter: The lens through which we interpret someone else based on our own fears, goals, and motives.

Intersex: See *disorders of sex development (DSD).*

Intersexual selection: When an individual chooses a mate from the other sex (e.g., a man chooses a woman).

Intimacy: An interpersonal, dynamic, emotional process that can go up or down over time as two people learn about each other. In Sternberg's triangular theory of love, this is the emotional component.

Intimacy process model: A framework for how intimacy can change when two people communicate with each other.

Intimate terrorism: A form of relationship violence in which one partner uses physical, sexual, emotional, and psychological abuse and manipulation.

Intrapsychic stage: Step 1 of breaking up, when one partner starts to consider ending the relationship.

Intrasexual competition: When individuals within a given sex compete with each other (e.g., men compete with other men) for access to the other sex.

Inverted parenting: When a parent demands support and attention from a child, instead of the other way around.

Investment model: Proposes that relationship commitment is predicted by satisfaction, alternatives, and investments.

Investments: Resources put into a relationship that would be lost if the relationship ended (time, effort, etc.).

IOS scale: See *Inclusion of Other in the Self Scale*

IRB: See *institutional review board.*

Jigsaw classroom: A setup in which each student's grades are dependent upon others in the class, requiring teamwork.

Klinefelter syndrome: When an individual is born with XXY chromosomes.

Locus of control: A worldview regarding the extent to which you believe you can bring about desired outcomes.

Loneliness: The feeling of isolation and dissatisfaction about a perceived lack of intimate relationships.

Longitudinal: A study done over time, with multiple data collection sessions.

Machiavellianism: A personality trait regarding how much someone likes to manipulate and control others.

Marginalized relationships: Those less accepted by some parts of society (e.g., interracial or same-sex).

Matching hypothesis: The idea that we tend to date people who are similar to us in important qualities, because we are more compatible with them.

Mate guarding: A form of mate retention that involves keeping potential rivals away from your current partner.

Mate poaching: Attempts to lure away someone who is already in a relationship with someone else.

Mate retention: Attempts to keep a current partner committed and monogamous.

Maternal deprivation: When a child experiences temporary separation from a mother (or other primary caregiver).

Maternal sensitivity: How responsive and perceptive a mother is to her child's needs.

Maximizing: A problem-solving strategy in which every possible solution is considered until the "best" is found.

Meaning: A mental state of growth and self-expression.

Mere exposure: The tendency to like things and people more, the more we're around them.

Meta-analysis: A research study that combines the results of several smaller, individual studies.

Michelangelo phenomenon: When one partner helps the other achieve their goals or ideal self.

Minimization: When abuse victims downplay the significance or severity of what occurred.

Misattribution of arousal: When we misinterpret physiological reactions in our bodies that are really caused by the situation, but we think they are caused by attraction to someone who happens to be nearby.

Monogamous: A relationship in which both people agree to have sex only with each other.

Moral commitment: A sense of obligation to your current relationship; you "should" stay.

Mortality salience: Conditions in research studies in which participants are reminded of their own eventual death.

Narrative therapy: A counseling technique in which trauma survivors write their autobiographies as a way to heal.

Natural selection: An evolutionary process in which traits that help survival are more likely to be passed on to the next generation.

Naturalistic observation: A method of gathering data through scientific surveillance of people in their natural environments (such as at work, on a playground, etc.).

Negative correlation: When two variables move in opposite directions together (as one goes up, the other goes down).

Neotenous features: "Youthful" features in adult faces, such as large eyes and full lips.

Nonverbal communication: Signals we send to others through our body motions, posture, tone of voice, and facial expressions.

Nonvoluntary dependence: Feeling trapped in an unsatisfying relationship due to lack of alternatives.

Nymphomania: A nonpsychological and disapproving term for people with excessive interest in sex.

Open science: A movement to make science more transparent, cooperative, reproducible, and honest.

Operationalize: Defining constructs in specific, measurable ways.

Ostracism: Being socially rejected by one's peers.

Outcome matrices: Tables showing outcome patterns in a given situation.

Overbenefitted: The experience of feeling guilt due to receiving too many rewards in a relationship.

Pansexual: Sexual attraction that is not based on categorical labels of "male" or "female."

Paraphilia: A persistent and intense sexual arousal pattern, such as a fetish.

Paraphilic disorder: When a persistent arousal pattern causes distress, harm, or impairment.

Parental investment: The effort and resources a parent gives to successfully reproduce and to help children survive.

Participant observation: A technique for naturalistic observation in which scientists pretend to be a natural part of the environment, to avoid reactivity.

Partner behavioral affirmations: When one partner behaves in ways that elicit ideal-congruent reactions from the other partner.

Partner perceptual affirmations: When one partner perceives the other as compatible with their ideal self.

Partner-serving cognitive biases: Patterns of belief or perception that enhance our impression of our current romantic partner.

Passion: In Sternberg's triangular theory of love, this is the physical or sexual component.

Paternity uncertainty: The fact that a man can't be sure that when a woman becomes pregnant, he is the father of the child.

Pederasty: An ancient Greek practice in which older men train younger boys in a variety of topics, including sexual behavior.

Pennebaker paradigm: A research method in which some participants write about a trauma while control participants write about a neutral topic.

Personal commitment: The desire to stay due to attraction; you "want" to stay.

Phubbing: Ignoring people around you by focusing on your cell phone instead.

Pit bulls: Abusers who become physiologically aroused during conflicts.

Polyamory: When partners in a relationship agree that either can have additional sexual or romantic partners.

Positive correlation: When two variables move in the same direction together (as one goes up, the other goes up, or vice versa).

Positive illusions: Unrealistically generous beliefs or perceptions of someone.

Post-traumatic growth: Feelings of positive psychological change and resilience after experiencing adversity.

Preoccupied attachment: A type of insecure attachment in which people have a negative view of the self, but a positive view of others.

PREP: See *Prevention and Relationship Enhancement Program.*

Preregistration: Specifying your hypothesis, procedure, and statistical plan for a study before collecting data.

Prevention and Relationship Enhancement Program (PREP): A 12-hour series of workshops helping engaged couples learn to handle conflict and promote intimacy.

Prevention-focused goal: A goal framed as something we're trying to avoid.

Primacy effect: What we perceive about someone first affects how we interpret later information.

Primary prevention: Stopping violence before it begins on an individual level.

Procedural artifact: A research study finding that results from how the experiment was conducted, not from a real or valid psychological phenomenon.

Proceptive behaviors: Actions signaling interest or attraction, such as smiling and nodding.

Projective test: A method of measuring a variable in which someone interprets ambiguous images or objects (such as inkblots or photographs).

Promotion-focused goal: A goal framed as something we're trying to achieve or accomplish.

Propinquity: The sharing of a physical environment, or proximity.

Psychodynamic therapy: A form of counseling that emphasizes unconscious thoughts and fears, usually from childhood.

PsycINFO: An electronic database of published books and journal articles in psychology.

Qualitative study: A study that gathers open-ended, non-numerical data (such as essays or interviews).

Quantitative study: A study that gathers empirical, quantitative data (such as numerical scores on personality scales).

Quasi-experiment: A study comparing two or more naturally occurring groups (such as Republicans vs. Democrats).

r/K theory: The idea that individuals choose between producing more children (with fewer resources each) versus fewer children (with more resources each).

Random assignment: A technique for experiments in which each participant has an equal chance of being placed in any of the study's groups.

Random sampling: When a study's participants are chosen at random from the larger population.

Rape myths: False beliefs about sexual assault, based on sexism, that justify sexual aggression.

Reactance: When our desire for something or someone goes up after we're told we cannot have it.

Reactivity: People's change in behavior because they are aware of being observed.

Reciprocal self-disclosure: Two people who reveal personal information to each other at a matching level of intimacy.

Reciprocity principle: The idea that we're more attracted to people if we think they are attracted to us.

Rejective behaviors: Actions signaling lack of interest or attraction, such as frowning and leaning away.

Replication: This occurs when the results of a study are found again, by other researchers and with other participants.

Representative sample: When a study's participants have the same general characteristics as the larger population of interest and thus "represent" all parties involved.

Results-blind peer review: Practice of asking experts to judge a potential study's value and quality before the data have been collected and analyzed.

Resurrection stage: Step 5 of breaking up, when ex-partners learn from experience and date someone new.

Robbers Cave Study: A famous experiment in which prejudice within young boys in a summer-camp environment was both created and eliminated.

Romantic attachment: Our psychological bonds with intimate romantic partners in adolescence and adulthood.

Romantic myths: Cultural messages regarding traditional gendered ideas of romance.

Romeo and Juliet effect: When attraction to people is increased when we think our friends or family disapprove of them.

Rubin's liking and loving scales: Self-report surveys based on the theory that liking and loving are two types of intimate relationship with varying levels or degrees.

Rusbult model of conflict: See *EVLN model of conflict*.

Satisfaction: Perceiving that current relationship outcomes are positive and better than the "average" relationship.

Satisficing: A problem-solving strategy in which the first acceptable solution is used, even if it's not necessarily the "best."

Scatterplot: A graph displaying patterns of two continuous variables, used to calculate correlations.

Schema: A cognitive structure that organizes and categorizes social people and events.

Scientific method: A systematic, evidence-based approach to the study of any topic.

Script: A specific type of schema that provides a specified order of behaviors for a given event or situation.

Secondary prevention: Intervening after violence has begun and trying to prevent it from continuing.

Secure attachment: Feelings of trust and stability when interacting with others; healthy relationship behaviors.

Secure base: When an attachment figure (such as a mother or romantic partner) provides security and trust, allowing the other person to be confident in exploring the world.

Self-disclosure: Sharing personal, intimate information about yourself to others.

Self-expansion theory: The idea that we are all motivated to grow our self-concept, and one way to do this is through our relationships.

Self-fulfilling prophecies: When an expectation or prediction about someone else makes that expectation come true.

Self-monitoring: A personality trait regarding how much someone purposely adjusts their behavior across situations.

Self-regulation theory: The idea that we manage our thoughts, emotions, and behaviors to reach specific goals we've set for ourselves.

Self-report survey: Questionnaires in which people are asked to honestly respond to questions about their thoughts, emotions, or behaviors.

Self-serving cognitive biases: Patterns of belief or perception that enhance our self-concept.

Sex stereotype hypothesis: The prediction that women will approach conflict from a positive and passive stance, while men will approach from a negative and competitive stance.

Sex therapy: A form of counseling that focuses on positive sexual communication and mutual enjoyment through intimacy.

Sexting: Sending sexually explicit words, images, or photos through a phone or online.

Sexual infidelity: Having sexual encounters with someone who is not your current partner.

Sexual scripts: Assumptions or expectations about the particular order of events in sexual contexts.

Sexual selection: The idea that some behaviors lead to better mating opportunities, and those traits are more likely to be passed on to the next generation.

Sexual spectrum: The diversity and range found in sex, gender, and sexual orientation; the idea that these variables should be defined as continuous instead of categorical.

Sexy sons hypothesis: The idea that women are particularly interested in bearing physically attractive sons (compared to daughters).

Shyness: Enduring anxiety about social situations that leads to introverted behavior.

Singlism: Prejudice and negative stereotypes about adult, single people.

Situational attributions: Determining that an outcome was caused by something external to a person, such as the environment or circumstances.

Situational couple violence: A form of relationship violence in which either partner or both partners can lose control during conflicts.

Social allergens: Traits in someone else that are minor, but eventually lead to disgust, boredom, or dissatisfaction over time.

Social cognition: The study of how perceptions, beliefs, judgments, and memories about people form.

Social desirability: A potential problem for self-report surveys in which participants respond dishonestly so that they look better.

Social exchange: Occurs when people work together to gain the best possible outcome for everyone.

Social penetration theory: A model that predicts intimacy increases over time as self-disclosures grow in breadth and depth.

Social skills deficit hypothesis: The idea that some people are lonely because they lack communication skills that would help establish or maintain relationships.

Social stage: Step 3 of breaking up, when ex-partners share their decision with friends, family, and co-workers.

Social support: The number and quality of relationships people have, on which they can rely in times of need.

Socioemotional selectivity theory: The idea that as we age and become increasingly aware of death, we choose to spend time on things that really matter to us.

Stalking: Patterns or acts of pursuit that are unwanted, harassing, and illegal.

Sternberg triangular theory of love: A theory suggesting that love relationships are made up of three components: intimacy, passion, and commitment.

Stigma: An invisible mark of disgrace or embarrassment for certain social groups.

Stonewalling: Mentally tuning out and avoiding your partner, or emotionally distancing yourself.

Strange situation: An experimental setting in which attachment in infants is measured by observing them as their mothers leave the room and then return.

Structural commitment: A feeling of constraint or barriers to leaving; you "have to" stay.

Subjective norms: Our perception of whether other people in our social lives approve of our choices and behaviors.

Supermale syndrome: See *47, XYY syndrome.*

Swinging: When couples have sex with another couple.

Systems therapy: A form of counseling that sees problems within their larger context, such as a family, institution, or culture.

Terror management theory: The idea that awareness of our own mortality causes anxiety, which we decrease by clinging to either comforting beliefs or our relationships.

Tertiary prevention: Trying to decrease violence through education and empathy in the larger community.

Thin slices of behavior: Brief (under 5 minutes) exposure to someone else.

Thomas model of conflict: A theory that conflict management is based on balancing one's own concerns with the concerns of the other person.

Transformation of motivation: Occurs when one's approach to partner interactions shifts due to changing long-term needs.

Transgender: People with a mismatch between their assigned biological sex and how they feel, psychologically.

Trauma advocacy: A field of work in which people help trauma survivors find the resources they need to escape and heal.

Trolling: Online harassment or insults designed to provoke someone else into a response.

_t_-test: A statistical technique in which two groups are compared to each other.

Turner syndrome: When an individual is born with only 45 chromosomes, usually noted as XO.

Underbenefitted: The experience of feeling anger or resentment due to not receiving enough rewards in a relationship.

Unrequited love: Attraction or emotional attachment to someone who does not return those feelings.

Victim blaming: When the responsibility for bad circumstances is put on the target instead of the person who caused it.

Waist-to-hips ratio: The circumference of someone's waist compared to the circumference of their hips.

Waist-to-shoulders ratio: The circumference of someone's waist compared to the circumference of their shoulders.

Well-being: An overall summary of someone's happiness, mental health, and ability to cope with stress.

Westgate Housing Study: A study that found that propinquity (physical proximity) often leads to interpersonal liking.

What-is-beautiful-is-good effect: The trend that people tend to believe good-looking others also have other positive qualities, such as intelligence or kindness.

Willingness to sacrifice: The motivation to give up personal preferences for the sake of making your partner happy.

Worldviews: Perceptions and beliefs about the world that provide structure, meaning, and comfort.

• Index •